D0189364

> "USUALLY I'M OKAY.
> BUT THERE'S ANOTHER SIDE
> THAT TAKES OVER AND
> CONTROLS ME.
> I'M A GOOD MOTHER.
> BUT MY OTHER SIDE
> MAKES ME ACT CRAZY!"

Anorexia . . . Alcoholism . . . Depression . . . Drug addiction . . . Often these and other serious psychological ailments mask an even greater problem: Borderline Personality Disorder. Though remarkably widespread, for years this syndrome went undetected and misdiagnosed. But now the psychiatric community has established BPD as a fundamental disorder—one whose root causes can be uncovered . . . and successfully treated.

I HATE YOU —
don't leave me

**UNDERSTANDING
THE BORDERLINE
PERSONALITY**

JEROLD J. KREISMAN, M.D., & HAL STRAUS

AVON BOOKS ❖ NEW YORK

AVON BOOKS, INC.
1350 Avenue of the Americas
New York, New York 10019

Copyright © 1989 by Jerold Jay Kreisman, M.D., and Hal Straus
Front cover design by Brenda Leach
Published by arrangement with The Body Press, Price Stern Sloan, Inc.
Library of Congress Catalog Card Number: 89-605
ISBN: 0-380-71305-5
www.avonbooks.com

The Body Press edition contains the following Library of Congress Cataloging in Publication Data:

Kreisman, Jerold Jay.
    I hate you, don't leave me : understanding the borderline personality / Jerold Jay Kreisman, Hal Straus.
       p.   cm.
       Bibliography: p.
       Includes index.
   1. Borderline personality disorders. I. Straus, Hal. II. Title.
   RC569.5.B6K74   1989
   616.89—dc19   89-605

First Avon Books Printing: February 1991

AVON TRADEMARK REG. U.S. PAT. OFF. AND IN OTHER COUNTRIES, MARCA REGISTRADA, HECHO EN U.S.A.

Printed in the U.S.A.

WCD   30   29   28   27   26   25   24   23   22   21

As all things,
for Doody

Acknowledgments

So many people contributed to this book that to mention them all by name would make us sound uncomfortably like entertainers whose acceptance speeches drone on and on through television awards ceremonies. There are, however, a few people who must be named.

The hospital administration of St. John's Mercy Medical Center, St. Louis, and its CEO, John T. Farrell, and the Department of Psychiatry and its chairman, Duane Q. Hagen, M.D., provided unflagging support for this book, and more importantly, great understanding when the project seemed overwhelming and threatened to deter me from other obligations.

The staff of the medical center's Comprehensive Treatment Unit—the nurses, social workers, pastoral care workers, psychiatric counselors, and activities therapists—provided the supportive working milieu from which many of the ideas of this book emerged. Without this staff of dedicated professionals, who shared their experience and expertise so unselfishly, this book could not have been written.

My office staff, medical colleagues, and friends tolerated with good humor the frenzy necessary for me to complete this book and remained unconditionally accepting of my intemperance and irascibility throughout the project.

Nadia Ramzy, Ph.D., a talented anthropologist and psychoanalyst, provided considerable insight into the links between culture and the borderline personality. Barbara Linder, M.Ed., a psychiatric counselor on the CTU, and her patients, generously donated audio tapes of group sessions, which allowed us to capture a more visceral feeling for the healing process.

Craig Cuddeback of Cracom Corporation and the editors

at HP Books/Price Stern Sloan expressed enthusiasm in our initial proposals and offered insight and guidance throughout the writing process. Jean Hohl helped type the manuscript and provided some valuable editorial suggestions.

Finally, we wish to thank our wives and children who supported us with their encouraging presence and spurred us on to tackle this project. They had to endure more than they bargained for in our writing of this book. We hope our efforts justify their forbearance.

Though all of these people were important contributors, it is our patients who ultimately teach us everything we know. They courageously share their lives and offer their trust, which we can only hope to justify. They are the people, most of all, who make this book possible and are the final arbiters of its worth.

Grateful acknowledgment is made for permission to reprint excerpts from:

Your Inner Child of the Past by W. Hugh Missildine, © 1963 by W. Hugh Missildine, reprinted by permission of Simon & Schuster, Inc.

Marilyn, A Biography by Norman Mailer, © 1973 by Alskog, Inc., and Norman Mailer, reprinted by permission of the author and the author's agent, Scott Meredith Literary Agency, Inc., 845 Third Avenue, New York, NY 10022.

Marilyn by Gloria Steinem, © by East Toledo Productions, reprinted by permission of Henry Holt & Company, Inc.

The Culture of Narcissism by Christopher Lasch, © 1978 by W.W. Norton & Company, Inc., reprinted by permission of W.W. Norton & Company, Inc.

Thomas Wolfe, A Biography by E. Nowell, © 1960, reprinted by permission of Doubleday, a division of Bantam, Doubleday, Dell Publishing Group.

Diagnostic and Statistical Manual of Mental Disorders, Third Edition, © 1987 by the American Psychiatric Association, reprinted by permission of the American Psychiatric Association.

Contents

Preface

For decades, physicians treated diseases and illnesses as the symptoms occurred, with little attention to prevention. The idea of preventing heart attacks and strokes, for example, by implementing certain lifestyle changes—diet, exercise, nicotine/drug abstinence—was almost completely unheard of. Aside from a few basic home remedies, self-care was viewed only as a poor second choice to prescribed medications and treatments.

In general, patients relied on the medical profession to correct their condition rather than prevent it. They did not expect thorough explanations of diseases, nor did doctors provide them as part of their professional services. Basically, the public viewed illnesses as numbers on a roulette wheel—one was lucky and stayed healthy or one became sick or injured and went to a doctor for treatment.

This approach has changed radically over the past thirty years. Self-care and preventive medicine have become central components of quality health care programs. Medical research, consumer awareness, and dramatically rising health care costs have led to a recognition that many diseases can be prevented with proper preventive measures. More than ever, people are concerned about their health; they want to understand and take control of it.

This trend has also been apparent in the area of mental health. Clinicians are making concerted efforts to educate patients on the origins and treatment of specific disorders. The American Psychiatric Association (APA) and other professional groups are much more active in promoting legislation and increasing general awareness of mental illness. Consumer organizations, such as the National Alliance for the Mentally Ill (NAMI), are disseminating educational pamphlets and offering hot line services to help patients and their families cope with various forms of mental illness.

Yet, despite this general trend, people are rarely given the opportunity to read about mental illness in easily understandable language. Countless times in my practice I have been asked by patients and their families for reading material on Borderline Personality Disorder (BPD)—the focus of this book. Each time, I have had to mutter apologies about the lack of published material for the layperson.

Perhaps the most exacting price we've had to pay for an uninformed populace is the continued and unfair social stigma attached to mental illness. Physical illnesses are rarely blamed on the victim. In the popular vernacular, one typically "comes down with," "is afflicted by," or "contracts" a certain physical disease; blame is typically attributed to some form of environmental condition or microorganism.

Not so in the case of many mental disorders. The general perception is that one "is" or "becomes" manic-depressive, neurotic, schizophrenic, or borderline; the implication is subtle, but inescapable—the victim shoulders much of the blame. While this may be true in some cases, in many cases it is not. Regardless, this perception has, in general, fostered misunderstanding, antagonism, and uneasiness about the mentally ill. People who would not think twice about visiting a friend in a hospital, for example, may dread—or feel extremely embarrassed about—visiting the same friend in a psychiatric hospital. People who seem to understand complex explanations of physical diseases cannot fathom the origins or behaviors associated with mental disorders. In many ways, our understanding of mental illness has not caught up to our understanding of physical illness; our empathy for the victims is certainly light years behind. Though this situation is certainly unfortunate, it is also quite predictable: Psychology wasn't really deemed a science until around the turn of the century, and still today the physiological complexity of the human mind remains one of life's greatest mysteries.

Our lack of understanding has also resulted in a high societal price tag: lack of adequate public funding for mental health facilities, frequent abuses of the mentally ill, and the myriad of violent acts associated with mental illness—wife and child abuse, incest, alcohol- and drug-related crimes, to name only a few. The number of the severely mentally ill keep increasing, yet the facilities for treating these people are actually decreasing. Ultimately, the financial and moral costs for cleaning up the "toxic waste" that spill from the inadequate treatment of the mentally ill are enormous.

Due to an information lag, a gap has formed between the myths concerning BPD and accurate, widely disseminated information on its causes and treatment. Though BPD afflicts an estimated 10 million Americans, very few people in the general population could even vaguely describe the disorder. There are many reasons for this—the relative newness of the diagnosis, its controversial standing among some members of the mental health profession, and, perhaps most importantly, the elusive, inconsistent, contradictory nature of the disorder itself.

Yet despite these factors BPD involves some of our most vital social issues—child abuse, poor quality day care, destruction of the nuclear family, divorce, geographical mobility, the changing roles of women. In addition, borderline personality offers a new context in which to view some of our most baffling, yet increasingly widespread, psychological maladies—bulimia, anorexia nervosa, alcohol and drug abuse, depression, and suicide.

In fact, many in the mental health profession believe that we are living in a "borderline era." Just as the hysterical neurotic of Freud's time represented the repressive European culture of the early twentieth century, the borderline's fragmented sense of identity and difficulty in maintaining stable relationships may reflect the fragmentation of stable units in contemporary society.

This book seeks to fill the present information gap on Borderline Personality Disorder; as such, it is intended for general audiences who simply want to know more about this widespread and disturbing syndrome. But we have tried to do more than merely inform: We have tried to explore the syndrome in such a way that the reader can understand intellectually—and feel emotionally—what it is like to be a borderline personality. From the identification with this kind of subjective experience, we believe, springs true understanding.

Loneliness, fear of abandonment, impulsive self-destructiveness, storminess in relationships, inability to achieve intimacy—these are feelings that we all experience at one time or another. The borderline personality, however, lives with these feelings almost constantly and experiences them to a much higher degree. Many people are in great mental and emotional pain—pain that can be just as searing and perhaps even more frightening than physical pain—and do not know why or what to do about it or how to seek help. Those readers who have been diagnosed with the syndrome, or are considering therapy, will find explanatory material unburdened (when at all possible) by complex psychiatric jargon. Hopefully, this book will lead to self-knowledge, provide comfort, reassurance, and coping strategies, and offer some practical options for therapy not heretofore available.

We have also identified certain aspects of contemporary society that increasingly foster borderline characteristics and we suggest some directions for change.

Though the book is geared for a general lay audience, professionals should also find it a great help. It may be used not only as a reference but also as recommended reading for patients and clients who are hungry for knowledge about BPD. The wide-ranging symptomology of BPD given in this book should apply to the work of psychiatrists, clinical and research psychologists (particularly those focusing on child development), psychotherapists and family therapists, substance abuse counselors, pastoral counselors, eating disorder specialists, stress consultants, and others. The Appendices—covering DSM-III-R classifications and medications used for treatment of borderline personality disorders, the evolution of borderline personality disorder in psychoanalytic thought and other theories of borderline personality—should be particularly appealing to the professional.

We hope this book provides families and friends of borderlines with workable strategies for coping with this most distressing illness. Borderline Personality Disorder is generally recognized as one of the most frustrating psychiatric conditions to live with and to treat. Yet, diagnostically and practically, the borderline is defined by the nature of his past and present relationships with others. We believe this essential human interdependency, when properly directed, can be used as a tool that can help the borderline and those closest to him or her. We hope this book will make the trip easier.

The World of the Borderline

"Everything looked and sounded unreal.
Nothing was what it is. That's what I wanted—
to be alone with myself in another world
where truth is untrue and life can hide from
itself."
—From *A Long Day's Journey Into Night*
 by Eugene O'Neill

Dr. White thought it would all be relatively straightforward. Over the five years he had been treating Jennifer, she had few medical problems. Her stomach complaints were probably due to gastritis, he thought, so he treated her with antacids. But when her stomach pains became more intense despite treatment and routine testing proved normal, Dr. White admitted Jennifer to the hospital.

After a thorough medical work-up, Dr. White inquired about stresses Jennifer might be experiencing at work and home. She readily acknowledged that her job as a personnel manager for a major corporation was very pressured, but as she put it, "Many people have pressure jobs." She also revealed that her home life was more hectic recently: She was trying to cope with her husband's busy legal practice while tending to the responsibilities of being a mother. But she doubted the connection of these factors to her stomach pains.

When Dr. White recommended that Jennifer seek psychiatric consultation, initially she resisted. It was only after her discomfort turned into stabs of pain that she reluctantly agreed to see the psychiatrist, Dr. Gray.

They met a few days later. Jennifer was an attractive

blonde woman who appeared younger than her twenty-eight years. She lay in bed in a hospital room that had been transformed from an anonymous cubicle into a personalized lair. A stuffed animal sat next to her in bed and another lay on the night stand beside several pictures of her husband and son. Get-well cards were meticulously displayed in a line along the window sill, flanked by flower arrangements.

At first, Jennifer was very formal, answering all of Dr. Gray's questions with great seriousness. Then she joked about how her job was "driving me to see a shrink." The longer she talked, the sadder she looked. Her voice became less authoritative and more childlike.

She told him how a job promotion was exacting more demands—duties about which she felt unsure. Her five-year-old son was starting school, which was proving to be a difficult separation for both of them. Conflicts with Allan, her husband, were increasing. She described rapid mood swings and trouble sleeping. Her appetite had steadily decreased and she was losing weight. Her concentration, energy, and sex drive had all diminished.

Dr. Gray recommended a trial of antidepressant medications, which improved her gastric symptoms and seemed to normalize her sleeping patterns. In a few days she was ready for discharge and agreed to continue outpatient therapy.

Over the following weeks, Jennifer talked more about her upbringing. Reared in a small town, she was the daughter of a prominent businessman and his socialite wife. Her father, an elder in the local church, demanded perfection from his daughter and her two older brothers, constantly reminding the children that the community scrutinized their behavior. Jennifer's grades, her behavior, even her thoughts were never quite good enough. She feared her father, yet constantly—and unsuccessfully—sought his approval. Her mother remained passive and detached. Her parents evaluated her friends, often deeming them unacceptable. As a result, she had few friends and even fewer dates.

Jennifer described her roller-coaster emotions, which seemed to have worsened when she started college. She began drinking for the first time, sometimes to excess.

Without warning, she would feel lonely and depressed and then high with happiness and love. On occasion, she would burst out in rage against her friends—fits of anger that she had somehow managed to suppress as a child.

It was about this time that she also began to appreciate the attention of men, something she had previously always avoided. Though she enjoyed being desired, she always felt she was "fooling" or tricking them somehow. After she began dating a man, she would sabotage the relationship by stirring up conflict.

She met Allan as he was completing his law studies. He pursued her relentlessly and refused to be driven away when she tried to back off. He liked to choose her clothes and advise her on how to walk, how to talk, and how to eat nutritiously. He insisted she accompany him to the gym where he frequently worked out.

"Allan gave me an identity," she explained. He advised her on how to interact with other lawyers, when to be aggressive, when to be demure. She developed a cast of "repertoire players" whom she could call on stage on cue.

They married, at Allan's insistence, before the end of her junior year. She quit school and began working as a receptionist, but her employer recognized her intelligence and promoted her to more responsible jobs.

At home, however, things began to sour. Allan's career and his interest in body-building caused him to spend more time away from home, which Jennifer hated. Sometimes she would start fights just to keep him home a little longer. Occasionally she provoked him into hitting her. Afterward she would invite him to make love to her.

Jennifer had few friends. She devalued women as gossipy and uninteresting. She hoped that Scott's birth, coming two years after her marriage, would provide the comfort she lacked. She felt her son would always love her and always be there for her. But the demands of an infant were overwhelming, and after a while, Jennifer decided to return to work.

Despite frequent praise and successes at work, Jennifer continued to feel insecure, that she was "faking it." She became sexually involved with a co-worker, who was almost forty years her senior.

"Usually I'm okay," she told Dr. Gray. "But there's another side that takes over and controls me. I'm a good mother. But my other side makes me a whore; it makes me act crazy!"

Jennifer continued to deride herself, particularly when alone; during times of solitude, she would feel abandoned, which she attributed to her own unworthiness. Anxiety would threaten to overwhelm her unless she found some kind of release. Sometimes she'd indulge in eating binges, once consuming an entire bowl of cookie batter. She would spend long hours gazing at pictures of her son and husband, trying to "keep them alive in my brain."

Jennifer's physical appearance at her therapy sessions fluctuated dramatically. When coming directly from work, she would dress in a business suit that exuded maturity and sophistication. But on days off she showed up in short pants and knee socks, with her hair in braids; at these appointments she acted like a little girl with a high-pitched voice and a limited vocabulary.

Sometimes she would transform right before Dr. Gray's eyes. She could be insightful and intelligent, working collaboratively toward greater self-understanding, and then become a child, coquettish and seductive, pronouncing herself incapable of functioning in the adult world. She could be charming and ingratiating or manipulative and hostile. She could storm out of one session, vowing never to return, and at the next session cower with the fear that Dr. Gray would refuse to see her again.

Jennifer felt like a child clad in the armor of an adult. She was perplexed at the respect she received from other adults; she expected them to see through her disguise at any moment, revealing her as an emperor with no clothes. She needed someone to love and protect her from the world. She desperately sought closeness, but when someone came too close, she ran.

Jennifer is afflicted with Borderline Personality Disorder (BPD). She is not alone. Recent studies estimate that 10 million or more Americans may be affected by BPD.[1,2] Between 15 and 25 percent of all patients seeking psychiatric care are diagnosed with the disorder, and it is by far the most common of all personality disorders.[3]

Yet despite its prevalence, BPD remains virtually unknown to the general public. Ask the man-on-the-street about anxiety, depression, or alcoholism, and he would probably be able to provide a sketchy, if not technically accurate, description of the illness. Ask him to define Borderline Personality Disorder, and he would probably give you a blank stare. For more than a decade, BPD has been lurking as a kind of "Third World" of mental illness—indistinct, massive, vaguely threatening.

BPD has been underpublicized partly because the diagnosis is so new. For years, "borderline" was used as a catch-all category for patients who did not fit more established diagnoses. People described as "borderline" seemed more ill than neurotics (who experience severe anxiety secondary to emotional conflict), yet less ill than psychotics (whose detachment from reality makes normal functioning impossible.)

The disorder also appeared to coexist with, and border on, other mental illnesses: hysteria, manic-depressive disorder, schizophrenia, hypochondriasis, multiple personality disorder, sociopathy, alcoholism, eating disorders, phobias, and obsessive compulsive disorders.

Psychiatrists could not seem to agree on the separate existence of the syndrome, much less on the specific symptoms necessary for diagnosis. Even today, studies corroborate that about 90 percent of patients with the BPD diagnosis also share at least one other psychiatric diagnosis.[4]

In many ways, the borderline syndrome has been to psychiatry what the virus is to general medicine: an inexact term for a vague but pernicious illness that is frustrating to treat, difficult to define, and impossible for the doctor to explain adequately to his patient.

Though the term *borderline* was first coined in the 1930s, the condition was not clearly defined until the 1970s. As more and more people began to seek therapy for a unique set of life problems, the parameters of the disorder crystallized. In 1980, Borderline Personality Disorder was included in the American Psychiatric Association's third edition of *The Diagnostic and Statistical Manual* (DSM III), the diagnostic "bible" of the psychiatric profession. (The revised DSM-III-R, published in 1987, further refines the diagnosis.) Though various schools within psychiatry still quarrel over the exact nature, causes, and treatment of BPD, the disorder is officially recognized as a major mental health problem in America today.

DEMOGRAPHIC BORDERS

Who are the borderline people one meets in everyday life? She is Carol, a friend since grade school. Over a minor slight, she accuses you of stabbing her in the back and tells you that you were really never her friend at all. Weeks or months later, Carol calls back, congenial and blasé, as if nothing had happened between you.

He is Bob, a boss in your office. One day, Bob bestows glowing praise on your efforts in a routine assignment; another day he berates you for an insignificant error. At times he is reserved and distant; other times he is suddenly and uproariously "one of the boys."

She is Arlene, you son's girlfriend. One week, she is the picture of preppy; the next, she is the epitome of punk. She breaks up with your son one night, only to return hours later, pledging endless devotion.

He is Brett, your next door neighbor. Unable to come to grips with his collapsing marriage, he denies his wife's obvious unfaithfulness in one breath, and then takes complete blame for it in the next. He clings desperately to his family, caroming from guilt and self-loathing to raging attacks on his wife and children who have so "unfairly" accused him.

If the people in these short profiles seem inconsistent, it should not be surprising—inconsistency is the hallmark of BPD. Unable to tolerate paradox, borderlines are walking paradoxes, human Catch-22s. Their inconstancy is a major reason why the mental health profession has had such difficulty defining a uniform set of criteria for the illness.

If these people seem all too familiar, this also should not be surprising. The chances are good that you have a spouse, relative, close friend, or coworker who is borderline. Perhaps you know a little bit about BPD or recognize borderline characteristics within yourself.

Though it is difficult to get a firm grasp on the figures, mental health professionals generally agree that the number of borderlines in the general population is growing—and at a rapid pace—though some observers claim that it is the therapists' awareness of the disorder that is growing rather than the number of borderlines.

Is borderline personality really a modern-day "plague," or is merely the diagnostic label *borderline* new? In any event, the disorder has provided new insight into the psychological framework of several related conditions. Numerous studies have linked BPD with anorexia, bulimia, drug addiction, and teenage suicide—all of which have increased alarmingly over the last decade. Some studies have uncovered BPD in approximately 50 percent of all patients who have eating disorders.[5] Other studies have found that over 50 percent of substance abusers also fulfill criteria for BPD.[6,7]

Self-destructive tendencies or suicidal gestures are very common among borderlines—indeed, they are one of the syndrome's defining criteria. The incidence of documented death by suicide is about 8 to 10 percent among borderlines and even higher for borderline adolescents. A history of previous suicide attempts, a chaotic family life, and a lack of support systems increase the likelihood. The risk multiplies even more among borderline patients who also suffer from depressive or manic-depressive disorders, or from alcoholism or drug abuse.[8]

EMOTIONAL HEMOPHILIA

DSM-III-R lists eight criteria for BPD, five of which must be present for diagnosis.[9] At first glance, these criteria may seem unconnected or only peripherally related. When explored in-depth, however, the eight symptoms are seen to be intricately connected, interacting with each other so that one symptom sparks the rise of another like the pistons of a combustion engine.

The eight criteria may be summarized as follows (each is described in-depth in Chapter 2):

(1) Unstable and intense interpersonal relationships.
(2) Impulsiveness in potentially self-damaging behaviors, such as substance abuse, sex, shoplifting, reckless driving, binge eating.
(3) Severe mood shifts.
(4) Frequent and inappropriate displays of anger.
(5) Recurrent suicidal threats or gestures, or self-mutilating behaviors.
(6) Lack of clear sense of identity.
(7) Chronic feelings of emptiness or boredom.
(8) Frantic efforts to avoid real or imagined abandonment.

Beneath the clinical nomenclature lies the anguish experienced by borderlines and their families and friends. For the borderline, much of life is a relentless emotional roller coaster with no apparent destination. For those living with, loving, or treating the borderline, the trip can seem just as hopeless and frustrating.

Jennifer and millions of other borderlines are provoked to rage uncontrollably against the people they love most. They feel helpless and empty, dissipating their identity.

Mood changes come swiftly, explosively, carrying the borderline from the heights of joy to the depths of depression. Filled with anger one hour, calm the next, he often has little inkling about why he was driven to such wrath. Afterward, the inability to understand the origins of the episode brings on more self-hate and depression.

A borderline suffers a kind of emotional hemophilia; he lacks the clotting mechanism needed to moderate his spurts of feeling. Stimulate a passion, and the borderline emotionally bleeds to death.

Sustained periods of contentment are foreign to the borderline. Chronic emptiness eats at him until he is forced to do anything in order to escape. In the grip of these lows, the borderline is prone to a myriad of impulsive, self-destructive acts—drug and alcohol binges, eating marathons, anorexic fasts, bulimic purges, gambling forays, shopping sprees, sexual promiscuity, and self-mutilation. He may attempt suicide, often not with the intent to die but to feel *something*, to confirm he is alive.

"I hate the way I feel," confesses one borderline.

"When I think about suicide, it seems so tempting, so inviting. Sometimes, it's the only thing I relate to. It is difficult not to want to hurt myself. It's like, if I hurt myself, the fear and pain will go away."

Central to the borderline syndrome is the lack of a core sense of identity. When describing themselves, borderlines typically paint a confused or contradictory self-portrait, in contrast to neurotic patients who had a much clearer sense of who they are. To overcome their indistinct and mostly negative self-image, borderlines, like actors, are constantly searching for "good roles," complete "characters" they can use to fill the identity void. So they often adapt like chameleons to the environment, situation, or companions of the moment, much like the title character in Woody Allen's film, *Zelig*, who literally assumes the personality, identity, and appearance of anyone around him.

The lure of ecstatic experiences, whether attained through sex, drugs, or other means, is sometimes overwhelming for the borderline personality. In ecstasy, he can return to a primal world where the self and the external world merge— a form of second infancy. During periods of intense loneliness and emptiness, the borderline will go on drug binges, bouts with alcohol, sexual escapades (with one or several partners), sometimes lasting days at a time. It is as if when the struggle to find identity becomes intolerable, the answer is either to lose identity altogether or to achieve a semblance of self through pain or numbness.

The family background of a borderline is often marked by alcoholism, depression, and emotional disturbances. A borderline childhood is often a desolate battlefield, scarred with the debris of indifferent, rejecting, or absent parents, emotional deprivation, and chronic abuse. One study reported that a history of verbal, physical, and/or sexual abuse, or of prolonged separation or neglect by primary caregivers was the most important factor in distinguishing borderline patients from those with other disorders.[10] Other studies have found a history of severe psychological, physical, or sexual abuse in 20 to 75 percent of borderline patients.[10, 11]

These unstable relationships carry over into adolescence

and adulthood, where romantic attachments are highly charged and usually short-lived. The borderline will frantically pursue a man (or woman) one day and send him packing the next. Longer romances—usually measured in weeks or months rather than years—are usually filled with turbulence and rage, wonder, and excitement.

SPLITTING:
THE BLACK-AND-WHITE WORLD
OF THE BORDERLINE

The world of a borderline, like that of a child, is split into heroes and villains. A child emotionally, the borderline cannot tolerate human inconsistencies and ambiguities; he cannot reconcile another's good and bad qualities into a constant coherent understanding of that person. At any particular moment, one is either "good" or "evil"; there is no in-between, no gray area. Nuances and shadings are grasped with great difficulty, if at all. Lovers and mates, mothers and fathers, siblings, friends, and psychotherapists may be idolized one day, totally devalued and dismissed the next.

When the idealized person finally disappoints (as we all do, sooner or later), the borderline must drastically restructure his one-dimensional conceptualization. Either the idol is banished to the dungeon, or the borderline banishes himself in order to preserve the "all-good" image of the other person.

This type of behavior, called "splitting," is the primary defense mechanism employed by the borderline. Technically defined, splitting is the rigid separation of positive and negative thoughts and feelings about oneself and others, that is, the inability to synthesize these feelings. Normal persons are ambivalent and can experience two contradictory feeling states at one time; borderlines characteristically shift back and forth, entirely unaware of one feeling state while in another.

Splitting creates an escape hatch from anxiety: The borderline typically experiences a close friend or relation (call him "Joe") as two separate people at different times. One day, she can admire "Good Joe" without reservation, perceiving him as completely good; his negative qualities do not exist; they have been purged and attributed to "Bad Joe." Other days, she can guiltlessly and totally despise "Bad Joe" and rage at his badness without self-reproach—for now his positive traits do not exist; he fully deserves the rage.

Intended to shield the borderline from a barrage of contradictory feelings and images—and from the anxiety of trying to reconcile those images—the splitting mechanism often achieves quite the opposite effect: The frays in the personality fabric become full-fledged rips; the sense of his own identity and the identities of others shifts even more dramatically and frequently.

STORMY RELATIONSHIPS

Though feeling continually victimized by others, a borderline ironically and desperately seeks out new relationships, for solitude, even temporary aloneness, is more intolerable than mistreatment. To escape the loneliness, the borderline will flee to singles bars, the arms of recent pick-ups, somewhere—anywhere—to meet someone who might save her from the torment of her own thoughts, much like Theresa Dunn in Judith Rossner's *Looking for Mr. Goodbar*.

In the relentless search for a structured role in life, the borderline is typically attracted to—and attracts to her—others with complementary personality disorders. The domineering, narcissistic personality of Jennifer's husband, for example, cast her in a role with little effort. He was able to give her an identity even if the identity involved submissiveness and mistreatment.

Yet, for a borderline, relationships often disintegrate quickly. Maintaining closeness with a borderline requires an understanding of the syndrome and a willingness to endure a long walk on a perilous tightrope. Too much closeness threatens the borderline with suffocation. Keeping one's distance or leaving a borderline alone—even for brief periods—recalls the sense of abandonment he felt as a child. In either case, the borderline reacts intensely.

In a sense, the borderline carries only a sketchy map of interpersonal relations; he finds it extremely difficult to gauge the optimal psychic distance from others, particularly significant others. To compensate, he caroms back and forth from clinging dependency to angry manipulation, from outpourings of gratitude to irrational hate. He fears abandonment, so he clings; he fears engulfment, so he pushes away. He craves intimacy and is terrified of it at the same time. He winds up repelling those with whom he most wants to connect.

JOB PROBLEMS

Though borderlines have extreme difficulties managing their personal lives, many are able to function productively in a work situation—particularly if the job is well-structured, clearly defined, and supportive. Many perform well for long periods, but then suddenly—because of a change in the job structure, or a drastic shift in personal life, or just plain boredom and a craving for change—they abruptly leave or sabotage their position and go on to the next opportunity.

The work world can provide sanctuary from the anarchic setting of social relationships. For this reason, borderlines frequently function best in highly structured work environments. The helping professions—medicine, nursing, clergy, counseling—also attract many borderlines who strive to achieve the power or control that elude them in social relationships. In these roles borderlines provide the care for others that they yearn for in their own lives.

Borderlines are often very intelligent and display striking artistic abilities; fueled by easy access to powerful emotions, they can be creative and successful.

But a highly competitive or unstructured job, or a highly critical supervisor, can trigger the intense, uncontrolled anger and the hypersensitivity to rejection to which the borderline is susceptible. The rage can permeate the work place and literally destroy a career.

A "WOMAN'S ILLNESS"?

Recent estimates indicate that women borderlines out-number men by two to one among outpatients and perhaps by as much as four to one among hospitalized patients.[3] Why do women seem so much more vulnerable to BPD than men? Some researchers propose that the same constitutional-hereditary factors that predispose women to affective (mood) disorders are responsible for their vulnerability to BPD. Since some doctors feel BPD is closely associated with affective disorders, and affective disorders are more common in women, then BPD would be more frequently observed in females.[12]

Another theory is that the separation-individuation phase between mother and infant is more difficult for girls, resulting in more identity problems later in life.[13] Many theoreticians point to the influence of social factors on women, particularly women's shifting role patterns over the past twenty-five years (see Chapter 4).[14]

Though the statistics are quite straightforward, some critics dispute their reliability, pointing out that women are more likely to enter therapy than men, so are more likely to be diagnosed as borderline.[14] Other critics feel that a kind of clinician bias operates with borderline diagnoses: Psychotherapists perceive problems with identity as more "normal" in men; as a result, they may underdiagnose BPD among men.[15]

Still other researchers believe that just as many men fulfill borderline criteria as women, but whereas women tend to become depressed, attempt suicide, or seek psychiatric care, men tend to act out violently against the world. The effect of not being able to regulate emotion in females leads to internalized, self-directed violence; the same problem in males results in aggressive and antisocial behavior. Eventually, the males are diagnosed as sociopathic and are channeled through the criminal justice system, where they may elude correct diagnosis forever.

BPD IN DIFFERENT AGE GROUPS

Many of the features of the borderline syndrome—impulsivity, tumultuous relationships, identity confusion, mood instability—are major developmental problems for the adolescent. Indeed, establishing a core identity is the primary quest for both the teenager and the borderline. It follows, then, that BPD is diagnosed more commonly among adolescents and young adults than other age groups.[16]

Early investigations of BPD among the elderly led to the impression that the syndrome was rare in this age group. Some researchers hypothesized that older borderline adults were able to achieve stabilization over time; or, at least, they reached a point where they were no longer distressed enough to seek out further medical care.

More recently, however, BPD has been increasingly recognized among the elderly, challenging the presumption that borderlines "mature out" over time. On the other hand, this observation may also be a function of the increased interest in older populations who have often been neglected in research studies in the past.[16, 17, 18]

Older adults must contend with a progressive decline in physical and mental functioning, which can be a perilous adaptive process for the aging borderline. For the fragile identity, the task of altering expectations and adjusting self-image can exacerbate symptoms. The aging borderline may deny deteriorating functions, project the blame for deficiencies onto others, and become increasingly paranoid; at other times, he may exaggerate handicaps and become more dependent.

SOCIOECONOMIC FACTORS

Borderline pathology has been identified in about equal proportions in all cultures and economic classes in the United States. However, the consequences of poverty on infants and children—higher stress levels and lack of good child care, psychiatric care, and pregnancy care (perhaps resulting in brain insults or malnutrition)—might lead to higher incidence of BPD among the poor. Perhaps the poor have not been diagnosed borderline more often because they have less access to medical care or are less interested in obtaining psychiatric help.

GEOGRAPHIC BORDERS

Although most of the theoretical formulations and empirical studies of the borderline syndrome have been conducted in the United States, other countries—Canada, Mexico, Israel, Sweden, Denmark, other Western European nations and the USSR—have recognized borderline pathologies within their populations.

Comparative studies are scant at this point but could provide great insight into the child-rearing, cultural, and social threads that compose the causal fabric of the syndrome.

BORDERLINE BEHAVIOR
IN WELL-KNOWN PEOPLE
AND FICTIONAL CHARACTERS

Whether the borderline personality is a new phenomenon, or simply a new label for an interrelated cluster of internal feelings and external behaviors, is a topic of considerable debate in the mental health community. Most psychiatrists believe that the borderline syndrome has been around for quite some time; that its increasing prominence results not so much from the mind of the patient but from the mind of the clinician. Indeed, many psychiatrists believe that some of Freud's most interesting cases of "neurosis" at the turn of the century would today be clearly diagnosed as borderline.[19]

Perceived in this way, the borderline syndrome becomes an interesting new perspective from which to understand some of our most complex personalities—both past and present, real and fictional. Conversely, well-known figures and characters can be used to illustrate different aspects of the syndrome. Along these lines, biographers and others have speculated that the term might apply to such wide ranging figures as Marilyn Monroe, Zelda Fitzgerald, Thomas Wolfe, T.E. Lawrence, Adolf Hitler, and Moamar Kadafi. Cultural critics can observe borderline features in Blanche Dubois in *A Streetcar Named Desire;* Martha in *Who's Afraid of Virginia Woolf?;* Sally Bowles in *Cabaret;* Travis Bickle in *Taxi Driver;* Howard Beale in *Network;* Carmen in Bizet's opera; and Terry Dunn in *Looking for Mr. Goodbar.*

THE QUESTION OF BORDERLINE "PATHOLOGY"

To one degree or another, we all struggle with the same issues as the borderline—the threat of separation, fear of rejection, confusion about identity, feelings of emptiness and boredom. How many of us have not had a few intense, unstable relationships? Or flew into a rage now and then? Or felt the allure of ecstatic states? Or dreaded being alone, or gone through mood changes, or been self-destructive in some way?

If nothing else, BPD serves to remind us that the line between "normal" and "pathological" may sometimes be a very thin one. Do we all display, to one degree or another, some symptoms of borderline personality? The answer is probably "Yes," but not all of us are controlled by the syndrome to the degree that it disrupts—or rules—our lives. With its extremes of emotion, thought, and behavior, BPD represents some of the best and worst of human character—and of our society in the waning years of the twentieth century. By exploring its depths and boundaries, we may be facing up to our ugliest instincts and our highest potentials—and the hard road we must travel to get from one point to the other.

2

Chaos and Emptiness

"All is caprice. They love without measure
those whom they will soon hate without reason."
—Thomas Sydenham, 17th-century English
   physician on "hystericks," the equivalent of
   today's borderline personality.

"I sometimes wonder if I'm possessed by the devil," says
Carrie, a social worker in the psychiatric unit of a large
hospital. "I don't understand myself. All I know is, this
borderline personality of mine has forced me into a life
where I've cut everyone out. So it's very, very lonely."

Carrie was diagnosed with the borderline syndrome in
1983, after twenty-two years of therapy, medications, and
hospitalizations for a variety of mental and physical illnesses. By then, her medical file resembled a well-worn
passport, the pages stamped with the numerous psychiatric
"territories" through which she had traveled.

"For years I was in and out of hospitals, but I never
found a therapist who understood me and knew what I
was going through."

Carrie's parents were divorced when she was an infant,
and she was raised by her alcoholic mother until she was
nine. A boarding school took care of her for four years
after that.

When she was twenty-one, overwhelming depression
forced her to seek therapy; she was diagnosed and treated
for depression at that time. A few years later, her moods
began to fluctuate wildly and she was treated for bipolar
disorder (manic-depression). Throughout this period she

repeatedly overdosed on medications and cut her wrists many times.

"I was cutting myself and overdosing on tranquilizers, antidepressants, or whatever drug I happened to be on," she recalls. "It had become almost a way of life."

In her mid-twenties, she began to have auditory hallucinations and became severely paranoid. At this time she was hospitalized for the first time and diagnosed schizophrenic.

And still later in life, Carrie was hospitalized in a cardiac-care unit numerous times for severe chest pains, subsequently recognized to be anxiety-related. She went through periods of binge-eating and starvation-fasting; over a period of several weeks, her weight would vary by as much as seventy pounds.

When she was thirty-two, she was brutally raped by a physician on the staff of the hospital in which she worked. Soon after, she returned to school and was drawn into a sexual relationship with one of her female professors. By the age of forty-two, her collection of medical files was filled with almost every diagnosis imaginable, including schizophrenia, depression, bipolar disorder, hypochondriasis, anxiety, anorexia nervosa, sexual dysfunction, and post-traumatic stress disorder (following the rape).

Despite her mental and physical problems, Carrie was able to perform her work fairly well. Though she changed jobs frequently, she managed to complete a doctorate in social work. She was even able to teach for a while at a small women's college.

Her personal relationships, however, were severely limited. "The only relationships I've had with men were ones in which I was sexually abused. A few men have wanted to marry me, but I have a big problem with getting close or being touched. I can't tolerate it. It makes me want to run. I was engaged a couple of times, but had to break them off. It's unrealistic of me to think I could be anybody's wife."

As for friends, she says, "I'm very self-absorbed. I say everything I think, feel, know, or don't know. It's so hard for me to get interested in other people."

After more than twenty years of treatment, Carrie's

symptoms were finally recognized and diagnosed in 1983 as BPD. Her dysfunction evolved from ingrained, enduring personality traits, more indicative of a personality or "trait" disorder than her previously diagnosed, transient "state" illnesses.

"The most difficult part of being a borderline personality has been the emptiness, the loneliness, and the intensity of feelings," she says today. "The extreme behaviors keep me so confused. At times I don't know what I'm feeling or who I am."

A better understanding of Carrie's illness has led to more consistent treatment. Medications have been useful for treating acute symptoms and providing the glue for maintaining a more coherent sense of self; at the same time, she has acknowledged the limitations of the medications.

Her psychiatrist, working with her other physicians, has helped her to understand the connection between her physical complaints and her anxiety and to avoid unnecessary medical test, drugs, and surgeries. Psychotherapy has been geared for the "long haul," focusing on her dependency and stabilization of her identity and relationships, rather than on an endless succession of acute emergencies.

Carrie, at forty-six, has had to learn that an entire set of previous behaviors are no longer acceptable. "I don't have the option of cutting myself, or overdosing, or being hospitalized anymore. I vowed I would live in and deal with the real world, but I'll tell you, it's a frightening place. I'm not sure yet whether I can do it or whether I *want* to do it."

BORDERLINE: A PERSONALITY DISORDER

Carrie's journey through this maze of psychiatric and medical symptoms and diagnoses exemplifies the confusion and desperation experienced by individuals afflicted with mental illness and by those who minister to them. Though the specifics of Carrie's case might be considered extreme by some, thousands of women—and men—suffer similar problems with relationships, intimacy, depression, and drug abuse. Perhaps if she had been diagnosed earlier and more accurately, she could have been spared some of the pain and loneliness.

Though borderline personalities suffer a tangle of painful symptoms that severely disrupt their lives, only recently have psychiatrists begun to understand the disorder and treat it effectively. What is a "personality disorder"? What exactly does borderline border? How is borderline personality similar to and different from other disorders? How does the borderline syndrome fit into the overall schema of psychiatric medicine? These are difficult questions even for the professional, particularly in light of the elusive, paradoxical nature of the illness and its curious evolution in psychiatry.

As a personality disorder, BPD is distinguished by a cluster of longstanding, ingrained traits that are prominent in an individual's character. These traits are relatively inflexible and result in maladaptive patterns of perceiving, behaving, and relating to others.

BPD is one of eleven personality disorders noted in DSM-III-R. In DSM-III terminology, personality disorders are categorized on Axis II. (See Appendix A for a more detailed discussion of categorization in DSM-III-R.)

In contrast, state disorders (Axis I in DSM-III-R) are usually not as enduring as trait disorders. State disorders, such as depression, schizophrenia, anorexia nervosa, chemical dependency, are more often time- or episode-limited. Symptoms may emerge suddenly and then be resolved, as the patient returns to "normal." Many times these illnesses are directly correlated with imbalances in the body's physiology and can often be treated with medications, which virtually eliminate the symptoms.

Symptoms of a personality disorder, on the other hand, tend to be more durable traits and change only gradually; medications are, in general, less effective. Psychotherapy is primarily indicated, though other treatments, including medication, may alleviate some of the more acute symptoms, such as severe agitation or depression (see Chapter 7). Borderline and other personality disorders may be a secondary diagnosis, describing the underlying characterological functioning of a patient who exhibits more acute and prominent symptoms of a state disorder

Comparisons to Other Disorders

Because the borderline syndrome often masquerades as a different illness and is often associated with other illnesses, clinicians often fail to recognize that BPD may be an important component in evaluating a patient. As a result, the borderline often becomes, like Carrie, a well-traveled patient, evaluated by multiple hospitals and doctors and accompanied throughout life by an assortment of diagnostic labels.

BPD can interface with other disorders in several ways. First, BPD can coexist with state (Axis I) disorders in such a way that borderline pathology is camouflaged. For example, BPD may be submerged in the wake of a more prominent and severe depression. After resolution of the depression with antidepressant medications, borderline characteristics may surface and only then be recognized as the underlying character structure requiring further treatment.

Second, BPD may be closely linked and perhaps even contribute to the development of another disorder. For example, the impulsivity, self-destructiveness, interpersonal difficulties, deflated self-image, and moodiness often exhibited by patients with substance abuse or eating disorders may be more reflective of BPD than the primary Axis I disorder. Although it could be argued that chronic abuse of alcohol could eventually alter personality characteristics in such a way that a borderline pattern could evolve secondarily, it seems more likely that underlying character pathology would develop first and lead to alcoholism.

The question of which is the chicken and which is the egg may be impossible to resolve, but the development of illnesses associated with BPD may represent a kind of psychological vulnerability to stress. Just as certain individuals may have genetic and biological vulnerabilities to physical diseases—heart attacks, cancers, gastrointestinal disorders, etc.—many may also have biologically determined propensities to psychiatric illnesses, particularly when stress is added to an underlying vulnerability to BPD. Thus, under stress, one borderline turns to drugs, another develops an eating disorder, still another becomes severely depressed.

Third, BPD may so completely mimic another disorder that the patient may be erroneously diagnosed with schizophrenia, hypochondriasis, bipolar disease, or other illnesses.

Comparison to Schizophrenia

Schizophrenic patients are usually much more severely impaired than borderlines and less capable of manipulating and relating to others. Both kinds of patients may experience agitated, psychotic episodes, but these are usually less consistent and less pervasive over time for borderlines. Schizophrenics are much more likely to grow accustomed to their hallucinations and delusions and are often less disturbed by them. Additionally, both may be destructive and self-mutilating. But where the borderline usually can function appropriately the schizophrenic is much more severely impaired socially.

Comparison to Affective Disorders
(Bipolar and Depressive Disorders)

Episodes of depression or mania represent radical departures in functioning. Between mood swings, these individuals maintain relatively normal lives and can usually be treated effectively with medications. Borderlines, however, typically have difficulties in functioning (at least internally) even when not experiencing mood swings. When self-destructive, threatening suicide, hyperactive, or experiencing wide and rapid mood swings, the borderline may appear bipolar (manic-depressive), but these mood variations are much more transient and less predictable in the borderline.

BPD and Hypochondriasis

The borderline may focus on his physical ills, complaining loudly and dramatically to medical personnel and acquaintances, in order to maintain dependency relationships with them. He may be considered merely a hypochondriac, while the underlying understanding of his problems go completely ignored.

BPD and Multiple Personality Disorder

Some psychiatrists consider multiple personality—a state disorder—a special type of BPD.[1,2,3] Both disorders share common symptoms—impulsivity, angry outbursts, disturbed relationships, marked mood changes, and a propensity for self-mutilation. Splitting is a primary defense mechanism in both illnesses. Several studies have shown a high prevalence of BPD in patients with multiple personality disorder—as high as 82 percent in one report.[4,5]

BPD and Post-Traumatic Stress Disorder

Post-traumatic stress disorder (PTSD) is a complex of symptoms that follow an extraordinarily severe traumatic event, such as a natural disaster or combat. It is characterized by intense fear, emotional re-experiencing of the event, nightmares, irritability, exaggerated startle response, and so on. One study found BPD pathology in half of the patients diagnosed with PTSD.[6]

BPD and Associated Personality Disorders

Many characteristics of BPD overlap with those of other personality disorders. For example, the dependent personality shares with the borderline the features of dependency, avoidance of being alone, and strained relationships. But the dependent personality lacks the self-destructiveness, anger, and mood swings of a borderline. Similarly, the schizotypal personality exhibits poor relations with others and difficulty in trusting, but is more eccentric and less self-destructive. Often a patient exhibits enough characteristics of two or more personality disorders to warrant diagnoses for each. For example, a patient may demonstrate characteristics that lead to diagnoses of both borderline personality disorder and obsessive compulsive personality disorder.

In DSM-III-R, BPD is grouped in a cluster of personality disorders that generally reflect dramatic, emotional, or erratic features. The others in this group are narcissistic, antisocial, and histrionic personality disorders, to which BPD is often compared.

Both borderlines and narcissists display hypersensitivity to criticism; failures or rejections can precipitate severe depression. Both exploit others; both demand almost constant attention. The narcissistic personality, however, usually functions at a higher level. He has an inflated sense of self-importance, displays disdain for others, and lacks even a semblance of empathy. In contrast, the borderline has a lower self-esteem and is highly dependent on others' reassurance. The borderline desperately clings to others and is usually more sensitive to their reactions.

Like the borderline, the antisocial personality exhibits impulsivity, poor tolerance of frustration, and manipulative relationships. The antisocial personality, however, lacks a sense of guilt or conscience; he is more detached and is not purposefully self-destructive.

The histrionic personality shares with the borderline tendencies of attention-seeking, manipulativeness, and shifting emotions. The histrionic, however, usually develops more stable roles and relationships. He is usually more flamboyant in speech and manner, and emotional reactions are exaggerated. Physical attractiveness is the histrionic's primary concern.

BPD and Substance Abuse

BPD and chemical abuse are frequently associated. Two studies found that between 13 and 56 percent of hospitalized chemical abusers were also diagnosed with BPD.[7,8] Alcohol or drugs might reflect self-punishing, angry, or impulsive behaviors, a craving for excitement, or a mechanism of coping with loneliness. Drug dependency may be a substitute for nurturing social relationships, a familiar, comforting way to stabilize or self-medicate fluctuating moods, or a way to establish some sense of belonging or self-identification. These possible explanations for the appeal of chemical abuse are also some of the defining criteria for BPD.

*The Anorexic Borderline
or the Borderline Anorexic?*

Anorexia nervosa and bulimia have become major health problems in this country, especially among young women.[9] Eating disorders are fueled by a fundamental distaste for one's own body and a general disapproval of one's identity. The anorexic sees herself in absolute, black or white extremes—as either obese (which she always feels) or thin (which she feels she never completely achieves). Since she constantly feels out of control, she impulsively utilizes starvation or binging and purging to maintain an illusion of self-control. The similarity of this pattern to the borderline pattern has led many mental health professionals to infer a connection between the two. Some studies have uncovered BPD in almost 50 percent of patients who have eating disorders.[10] Many experts in the field feel the percentage is actually much higher.

BPD and Compulsive Behaviors

Certain compulsive or destructive behaviors may reflect borderline patterns. For example, a compulsive gambler may continue betting despite a shortage of funds. He may be seeking a thrill from a world that habitually leaves him bored, restless, and numb. Or the gambling may be an expression of impulsive self-punishment.

Shoplifters often steal items they do not need. Fifty percent of bulimics exhibit kleptomania, drug use, or promiscuity.[11] When these behaviors are governed by compulsion, they may represent a need to feel or a need to self-inflict pain.

Promiscuity often expresses a need for constant love and attention from others, in order to hold on to positive feelings about oneself. The borderline typically lacks consistent positive self-regard and requires continuous reassurance. A borderline woman, lacking in self-esteem, may perceive her physical attractiveness as her only asset and may require confirmation of her worth by engaging in frequent sexual encounters. Such involvements avoid the pain of being alone and provide artificial relationships she can totally control. Feeling desired can instill a sense of identity. When self-punishment becomes a prominent part of the psychodynamics, humiliation and masochistic perversions may enter the relationships. From this perspective, it is logical to speculate that many prostitutes and pornographic actors and models may be borderline.

Difficulties with relationships may result in private, ritualistic thinking and behaviors, often expressed as obsessions or compulsions. A borderline may develop specific phobias as he employs magical thinking to deal with fears; sexual perversions may evolve as a mechanism to approach intimacy.

Suicide Among Adolescents

Suicidal threats or behaviors is one of the criteria of BPD. The suicide rate among adolescents has more than doubled over the past twenty years and is now the second leading cause of death among fifteen to twenty-four-year-olds.[12,13] Most youths who commit suicide have a history of psychiatric illness, usually affective disorder, or substance abuse.[14] Although studies on adolescent suicide are limited, BPD may be a primary factor in prompting an alienated youth to "go over the edge" and complete the act of suicide.

Appeal of Cults

Because borderlines yearn for direction and acceptance, they may be attracted to strong leaders of disciplined groups. The cult can be very enticing since it provides instant and unconditional acceptance, automatic intimacy, and a paternalistic leader who will be readily idealized. The borderline can be very vulnerable to such a black and white world view in which "evil" is personified by the outside world and "good" is encompassed within the cult group.

CLINICAL DEFINITION OF BORDERLINE PERSONALITY DISORDER

The current official definition of borderline pathology is contained in the DSM-III-R diagnostic criteria of Borderline Personality Disorder.[15] This description, initially developed by John Gunderson and others, emphasizes descriptive, observable behavior.[16] As such, it is narrower than Otto Kernberg's (see Appendix B), which pays more attention to causes and intrapsychic functioning.

The following criteria have been demonstrated to discriminate BPD from other illnesses 80 percent or more of the time.[17] The diagnosis of BPD is confirmed when at least five of the following eight criteria are present:

The Relentless Search for Mr/Ms. Right
Criterion 1. Unstable and intense interpersonal relationships, with marked shifts in attitudes toward others (from idealization to devaluation or from clinging dependency to isolation and avoidance), and prominent patterns of manipulation of others.

The borderline's unstable relationships are directly related to his intolerance of separation and fear of intimacy. The borderline is typically dependent, clinging, and idealizing until the lover, spouse, or friend repels or frustrates these needs; then the borderline caroms to the other extreme—devaluation, resistance to intimacy, and outright avoidance. A continual tug-of-war develops between the wish to merge and be taken care of on the one hand, and the fear of engulfment on the other. For the borderline, engulfment means the obliteration of separate identity, the loss of autonomy, and a sense of feeling nonexistent. The borderline vacillates between wishes for closeness to relieve the emptiness and boredom, and fears of intimacy, which is perceived as the thief of self-confidence and independence.

In relationships, these internal feelings are dramatically translated into intense, shifting, manipulative couplings. The borderline often makes unrealistic demands of others, appearing to observers as spoiled. Manipulativeness is manifested through physical complaints and hypochondriasis, expressions of weakness and helplessness, provocative actions, and masochistic behaviors. Suicidal threats or gestures are often used to obtain attention and rescue (see criterion 5). The borderline may use seduction as a manipulative strategy, even with someone known to be inappropriate and inaccessible, such as a therapist or minister.

Though very sensitive to others, the borderline lacks true empathy. He may be dismayed to encounter an acquaintance, such as teacher, co-worker, or therapist, outside of his usual place of business because it is difficult to conceive of that person as having a separate life. Furthermore, he may not understand or be extremely jealous of his therapist's separate life, or even of other patients he may encounter.

The borderline lacks "object constancy," the ability to understand others as complex human beings who nonetheless can relate in consistent ways. The borderline experiences another on the basis of his most recent encounter, rather than on a broader-based, consistent series of interactions. Therefore, a constant, predictable perception of another person never emerges, as the borderline continues to respond to that person as someone new on each occasion.

Because of the borderline's inability to see the big picture, to learn from previous mistakes and to observe patterns in his own behavior, he often repeats destructive relationships. A female borderline, for example, will typically return to her abusive ex-husband, who proceeds to abuse her again; a male borderline frequently couples with similar, inappropriate women with whom he repeats sadomasochistic affiliations.

The borderline's endless quest is to find a perfect caregiver who will be all-giving and omnipresent. The search often leads to partners with complementary pathology; both lack insight into their mutual destructiveness. For example, Michelle desperately craves protection and comfort from a man. Mark displays a bravura self-assurance; even though the self-assurance covers a deep insecurity, it fits the bill for Michelle. Just as Michelle needs Mark to be her protective white knight, so Mark needs Michelle to remain helpless and dependent on his beneficence. After a while, both fail to live up to their assigned stereotypes. Mark cannot bear the narcissistic wounds of challenge or failure and begins to cover his frustrations with alcohol and by physically abusing Michelle. Michelle bristles under his controlling yoke, yet becomes frightened when she sees his weaknesses. The dissatisfactions lead to more provocation and more conflict.

Afflicted with self-loathing, the borderline distrusts others' expressions of caring. Sam, for example, was a twenty-one-year-old college student whose chief complaint in therapy was "I need a date." An attractive man with serious interpersonal problems, Sam characteristically approached inaccessible women. Whenever his overtures were accepted, he immediately devalued the woman as no longer desirable.

All of these characteristics make it difficult for borderlines to achieve real intimacy. As Carrie relates, "A few men have wanted to marry me, but I have a big problem with getting close or being touched. I can't tolerate it." The borderline cannot seem to gain enough independence to be dependent in healthy, rather than desperate, ways. True sharing is sacrificed to a demanding dependency and a desperate need to join with another person in order to complete one's own identity, as kind of Siamese twins of the soul.

The Impulsive Character
Criterion 2. Impulsiveness in at least two areas that are potentially self-destructive, e.g., chemical abuse, sexual promiscuity, gambling, shoplifting, excessive spending, overeating, anorexia nervosa, or bulimia.

The borderline's behaviors may be sudden and contradictory since they typically result from strong, momentary feelings—perceptions that represent isolated, unconnected snapshots of experience. The immediacy of the present exists in isolation, without the benefit of the experience of the past, or the hopefulness of the future. Because historical patterns, consistency, and predictability are unavailable to the borderline, similar mistakes are repeated again and again.

The borderline is in the ironic yet untenable position of achieving what an entire generation strove for in the 1960s—"living in the now." For the borderline, there is no escape from the "now," if even for brief respite and perspective. Reality is, as Octavio Paz calls it, "an endless instant": "a staircase going neither up or down, we don't move, today is today, always is today."[18]

The borderline's limited patience and need for immediate gratification may be connected to behaviors that define other BPD criteria: Impulsive conflict and rage may emerge from the frustrations of a stormy relationship (criterion 1); precipitous mood changes (criterion 3) may result in impulsive outbursts; inappropriate outbursts of anger (criterion 4) may develop from a failure to control impulses; self-destructive or self-mutilating behaviors (criterion 5) may result from the borderline's frustrations. Often, impulsive actions such as drug and alcohol abuse serve as defenses against feelings of loneliness and abandonment.

Joyce was a thirty-one-year-old divorced woman who increasingly turned to alcohol after her divorce and her husband's subsequent remarriage. Though attractive and talented, she let her work deteriorate and spent more time at bars. "I made a career out of avoiding," she later said. When the pain of being alone and feeling abandoned became too great, she would use alcohol as anesthesia. She would sometimes pick up men and take them home with her. Characteristically, after such alcohol or sexual binges, she would berate herself with guilt and feel deserving of her husband's abandonment. Then the cycle would start again, as she required more punishment for her worthlessness. Thus, self-destructiveness became both a means of avoiding pain and a mechanism for inflicting it as expiation for her sins.

Radical Mood Shifts
Criterion 3. Affective instability: marked shifts from baseline mood to depression, irritability, or anxiety, usually lasting a few hours and only rarely more than a few days.

The borderline undergoes abrupt mood shifts, lasting for short periods—usually hours. His base mood is not usually calm and controlled, but more often either hyperactive and irrepressible or pessimistic, cynical, and depressed.

Thomas Wolfe, one of America's great novelists, often bounced between periods of energetic creativity and boundless enthusiasm to periods of morbid self-pity, unproductivity, and depression, when he would project blame for his failures onto others.

At one point while working prodigiously on his writings, he experienced morbid melancholia. At that time he was traveling in Europe, separated from his wife.

Today has been a horrible one. I was able to sleep only the most diseased and distressed sleep, the worst sort of American in Europe sleep and I got sick with the shakes, the day was the most horrible European sort, something that passes understanding. The wet, heavy air that deadens the soul, puts a lump of indigestible lead in the solar plexus, depresses and fatigues the flesh until one seems to lift himself leadenly through the thick, wet, steaming air. With this terrible kind of fear, an excitement that is without hope, that awaits only the news of some further grief, failure or humiliation and torture. A lassitude that enters the soul and makes one hope for better things and better work tomorrow but hope without belief and conviction.[19]

Raging Bull
Criterion 4. Inappropriate, intense anger, or lack of control of anger, e.g., frequent displays of temper, constant anger, recurrent physical fights.

The borderline's outbursts of rage are as unpredictable as they are frightening. Violent scenes are disproportionate to the frustrations that trigger them. Domestic fracases that may involve chases with butcher knives and thrown dishes are typical of borderline rage. The anger may be sparked by a particular (and often trivial) offense, but underneath the spark lies an arsenal of fear from the threat of disappointment and abandonment.

The rage, so intense and so near the surface, is often directed at the borderline's closest relationships—spouse, children, parents. Borderline anger may represent a cry for help, a testing of devotion, or a fear of intimacy—whatever the underlying factors, it pushes away those whom the borderline needs most. The spouse, friend, lover, or family member who sticks around despite these assaults may be very patient and understanding or, sometimes, very disturbed himself. In the face of these eruptions, empathy is difficult and the relation must draw on every resource at hand in order to cope (see Chapter 8).

The rage often carries over to the therapeutic setting, where psychiatrists and other mental health professionals become the target. Carrie, for example, often raged against her therapist, constantly looking for ways to test his commitment to staying with her in therapy. Treatment becomes precarious in this situation (see Chapter 7) and many therapists have been forced to drop borderline patients for this reason. Most therapists will, whenever possible, try to limit the number of borderline patients they treat.

Pleas for Help
Criterion 5. Recurrent suicidal threats, gestures, or behavior, or self-mutilating behaviors.

Suicidal threats and gestures—reflecting both the borderline's propensity for overwhelming depression and hopelessness, and his knack for manipulating others—are prominent features of BPD. Often, the frequent threats or half-hearted suicide attempts are not a wish to die but rather a way to communicate pain and a plea for others to intervene. Unfortunately, when habitually repeated, these suicidal gestures often lead to just the opposite scenario—others get fed up and stop responding, which may result in progressively more serious attempts. Suicidal behavior is one of the most difficult BPD symptoms for family and therapists to cope with: Addressing it can result in endless unproductive confrontations; ignoring it can result in death (see Chapters 6–8).

Self-mutilation—except when clearly associated with psychosis—is the hallmark of BPD. This behavior, more closely connected to BPD than any other psychiatric malady, may take the form of self-inflicted wounds to the genitals, limbs, or torso. For these borderlines, the body becomes a road map highlighted with self-inflicted scars. Razors, scissors, fingernails, and lit cigarettes are some of the more common instruments used; excessive use of drugs, alcohol, or food can also inflict the damage.

Often, self-mutilation begins as an impulsive, self-punishing action, but over time it may become a studied, ritualistic procedure. In such instances the borderline may carefully scar body areas that are covered by clothing—which illustrates the borderline's intense ambivalence: He feel compelled to flamboyantly self-punish, yet he carefully conceals the evidence of his tribulation.

Jennifer (see Chapter 1) would fulfill her need to self-inflict pain by scratching her wrists, abdomen, and waist, leaving deep fingernail marks that could easily be covered.

Sometimes the self-punishment is more indirect. The borderline may often by the victim of recurrent "quasi-accidents." He may provoke frequent fights. In these incidents, the borderline feels less directly responsible; circumstances or others provide the violence for him.

When Harry, for example, broke up with his girlfriend, he blamed his parents. They had not been supportive enough or friendly enough, he thought, and when she ended the affair after six years, he was forlorn. At twenty-eight he continued to live in an apartment paid for by his parents, and worked sporadically in his father's office. Earlier in his life he had attempted suicide but decided he wouldn't give his parents "the satisfaction" of killing himself. Instead he engaged in increasingly dangerous behaviors. He had numerous automobile accidents, some while intoxicated, and continued to drive despite the revocation of his driver's license. He frequented bars where he sometimes picked fights with men much bigger than he. Harry recognized the destructiveness of his behavior and sometimes wished that "one of these times I would just die."

These dramatic self-destructive behaviors and threats

may be explained in several ways. The self-inflicted pain may reflect the borderline's need to feel, to escape an encapsulating numbness. Borderlines form a kind of insulating bubble that not only protects them from emotional hurt but also serves as a barrier from the sensations of reality. The experience of pain, then, becomes an important link to existence. Often, however, the inflicted pain is not strong enough to transcend this barrier (though the blood and scars may be fascinating for the borderline to observe), in which case the frustration may compel him to accelerate attempts to induce pain.

Self-induced pain can also function as a distraction from other forms of suffering. One patient, when feeling lonely or afraid, would cut different parts of her body as a way ''to take my mind off'' the loneliness. Another would bang her head in the throes of stress-related migraine headaches.

Self-damaging behavior can also serve as an expiation for sin. One man, guilt-ridden after the breakup of his marriage for which he totally blamed himself, would repeatedly drink gin—a taste he abhorred—until reaching the point of retching. Only after enduring this discomfort and humiliation would he feel redeemed and able to return to his usual routine.

Painful, self-destructive behavior may be employed in an attempt to constrict actions that are felt to be dangerously out of control. One adolescent boy cut his hands and penis to dissuade himself from masturbation, an act he considered loathsome. He hoped that the memory of the pain would prevent him from further indulging in this repugnant behavior.

Impulsive, self-destructive acts (or threats) may result from a wish to punish another person, often a close relation. One woman consistently described her promiscuous behavior (often involving masochistic, degrading rituals) to her boyfriend. These affairs invariably occurred when she was angry and wanted to punish him.

Finally, self-destructive behavior can also evolve from a manipulative need for sympathy or rescue. One woman, after arguments with her boyfriend, repeatedly slashed her wrists in his presence, forcing him to secure medical assistance for her.

Many borderlines deny feeling pain during self-mutilation and even report a calm euphoria after it. Before hurting themselves, they may experience great tension, anger, or overwhelming sadness; afterwards there is a sensation of release and relief from anxiety.

This relief may result from psychological or physiological factors, or a combination of both. Physicians have long recognized that following severe physical trauma, such as battle wounds, the patient may experience an unexpected calm and a kind of natural anesthesia despite the lack of medical attention. Some have hypothesized that during such times, the body releases biological substances, such as endorphins, which serve as the organism's self-treatment of pain.

Who Am I?
Criterion 6. Marked and persistent identity disturbance manifested by uncertainty in at least two of the following: self-image, sexual orientation, long-term goals or career choice, type of friends desired, preferred values.

Borderlines lack a constant, core sense of identity, just as they lack a constant core conceptualization of others. The borderline does not accept her own intelligence, attractiveness, or sensitivity as constant traits, but rather as comparative qualities to be continually re-earned and judged against others'. The borderline may view herself as intelligent, for example, based solely on the results of a just-administered IQ test. Tomorrow, when she makes a "dumb mistake," she will revert to seeing herself as "stupid." The borderline considers herself attractive until she spies a woman whom she feels is prettier; then, she feels ugly again.

For the borderline, identity is graded on a curve. Who she is (and what she does) today determines her worth, with little regard to what has come before. The borderline allows herself no laurels on which to rest. Like Sisyphus, she is doomed to roll the boulder repeatedly up the hill, needing to prove herself over and over again. Self-esteem is only attained through impressing others; so pleasing others becomes critical to loving herself.

In *Marilyn,* Norman Mailer describes how Marilyn Monroe's search for identity became Marilyn's driving force, absorbing all aspects of her life:

> What an obsession is identity! We search for it, because the private sensation when we are in our own identity is that we feel sincere as we speak, we feel *real,* and this little phenomenon of good feeling conceals an existential mystery as important to psychology as the *cogito ergo sum*—it is nothing less than that the emotional condition of feeling real is, for whatever reason, so far superior to the feeling of a void in oneself that it can become for protagonists like Marilyn a motivation more powerful than the instinct of sex, or the hunger for position or money. Some will give up love or security before they dare to lose the comfort of identity.[20]

Later, Marilyn found sustenance in acting, particularly in "the Method":

> Actors in the Method will *act out;* their technique is designed, like psychoanalysis itself, to release emotional lava, and thereby enable the actor to become acquainted with his depths, then possess them enough to become possessed by his role. A magical transaction. We can think of Marlon Brando in "A Streetcar Named Desire." To be possessed by a role is *satori* (or intuitive illumination) for an actor because one's identity can feel whole so long as one is living in the role.[21]

The borderline's struggle in establishing a consistent identity is related to a prevailing sense of inauthenticity—a constant sense of "faking it." Most of us experience this sensation at various times in our lives. When one starts a new job, for example, one tries to exude an air of knowledge and confidence. After one has gained experience, the confidence becomes increasingly genuine because one has learned the system and no longer needs to fake it. As Kurt Vonnegut says, "We are what we pretend to be."

The borderline never reaches that point. He continues to feel like he is faking it and is terrified that he will, sooner or later, be "found out." This is particularly true when the borderline achieves some kind of success—it feels misplaced, undeserved.

This chronic sense of nongenuineness probably originates in childhood. As explored in Chapter 3, the preborderline often grows up feeling inauthentic due to various environmental circumstances—suffering physical or sexual abuse, being forced to adopt an adult's role while still a child or to parent his own sick parent. At the other extreme, he may be discouraged from maturing and separating, and be trapped in a dependent child's role well past an appropriate time for separation. In all of these situations, the borderline never develops a separate sense of self, but continues to "fake" a role which is prescribed by someone else. If he fails in the role, he fears he will be punished; if he succeeds, he is sure he will be uncovered as a fraud and be humiliated.

Unrealistic attempts at achieving a state of perfection are often part of the borderline pattern. For example, a borderline anorexic might try to maintain a constant low weight and become horrified if it varies as little as one pound, unaware that this expectation is unrealistic. Perceiving themselves as static, rather than in a dynamic state of change, borderlines may view any variation from this inflexible self-image as shattering.

Conversely, the borderline may search for satisfaction in the opposite direction—by frequently changing jobs, careers, goals, friends, sometimes even gender. By altering external situations and making drastic changes in lifestyle, he hopes to achieve inner contentment. Some instances of so-called "mid-life crisis" or "male menopause" represent an extreme attempt to ward off fears of mortality or deal with disappointments in life choices. An adolescent borderline may constantly change his clique of friends—from "jocks" to "burnouts" to "brains" to "geeks"—hoping to achieve a sense of belonging and acceptance. Even sexual identity can be a source of confusion for the borderline. Some writers have noted an increased incidence of homosexuality, bisexuality, and sexual perversions among borderline personalities.[22]

Cult groups that promise unconditional acceptance, a structured social framework, and a circumscribed identity are powerful attractions for the borderline personality. When the individual's identity and value system merge with the accepting group's, the group's leader assumes extraordinary power—to the point where he can induce followers to emulate his actions, even if fatal, as witnessed by the Jonestown Massacre in 1978.

Aaron, after dropping out of college, attempted to assuage his feelings of aimlessness by joining the Moonies. He left the cult after two years, only to return after two more years of directionless wandering among different cities and jobs. Ten months later, he left the group again, but this time, lacking a stable set of goals or a comfortable sense of who he was or what he wanted, he attempted suicide.

The phenomenon of "cluster suicides," especially among teenagers, may reflect weaknesses in identity formation. The national suicide rate dramatically leaps upward after the suicide of a famous person, such as Marilyn Monroe or Freddie Prinze. The same dynamics may operate among adolescents with fragile identity structures: They are susceptible to the suicidal tendencies of the peer group leader or of another suicidal teenage group in the same region.

Always Half Empty
Criterion 7. Chronic feelings of emptiness or boredom.

Lacking a core sense of identity, borderlines commonly experience a painful loneliness that motivates them to search for ways to fill up the "holes." The reports of many borderlines are akin to the almost physical sensation that Graham Greene describes in *A Sort of Life:* "Boredom seemed to swell like a balloon inside the head; it became a pressure inside the skull; sometimes I feared this balloon would burst and I would lose my reason."[23]

Many writers, of course, have labeled emptiness and boredom as the quintessential problems of the twentieth century and no attempt will be made here to go into the psychological ramifications. Suffice it to say that, for the borderline, the search for a way to relieve the boredom usually results in impulsive ventures into destructive acts and disappointing relationships. In many ways, the borderline seeks out a new relationship or experience not for its positive aspects but to escape the feeling of emptiness, acting out the existential destinies of characters described by Sartre, Camus, and other philosophers.

The borderline frequently experiences a kind of existential angst. This can be a major obstacle in treatment for it saps the motivational energy to get well. From this feeling state radiate many of the other features of BPD. Suicide may appear to be the only rational response to a perpetual state of emptiness. The need to fill the void or relieve the boredom can lead to outbursts of anger, self-damaging impulsiveness, especially drug abuse, and mood swings designed to elicit sensations of feeling.

"Others Act Upon Me, Therefore I Am"
Criterion 8. Frantic efforts to avoid real or imagined abandonment.

Just as an infant cannot distinguish between the temporary absence of her mother and her "extinction," the borderline often experiences temporary aloneness as perpetual isolation. As a result, the borderline becomes severely depressed over the real or perceived abandonment by significant others and then enraged at the world (or whoever is handy) for depriving her of this basic fulfillment.

Particularly when they are alone, borderlines may lose the sensation of existing, of feeling real. Rather than embracing Descartes' "I think, therefore I am" principle of existence, they live by a philosophy closer to "Others act upon me, therefore I am."

The theologian Paul Tillich wrote that "loneliness can be conquered only by those who can bear solitude." Because the borderline finds solitude so difficult to tolerate, she is trapped in a relentless metaphysical loneliness from which the only relief comes in the form of the physical presence of others. So she will often rush to singles bars or other crowded haunts, much like Theresa Dunn in *Looking for Mr. Goodbar,* often with similar disappointing—or even violent—results.

In *Marilyn: An Untold Story,* Norman Rosten recalled Marilyn Monroe's hatred of being alone. Without people constantly around her, she would fall into a void, "endless and terrifying."[24]

Lee Strasberg, also a close friend and noted acting teacher, would spend hours with Marilyn, giving her the nurturing she had missed as a child. Her difficulty sleeping led to frequent bouts with drugs, and Strasberg would try to help her sleep without drugs, according to Gloria Steinem in *Marilyn.* "She wanted to be held. Not to be made love to but just supported, because when she'd taken the pills they'd somehow react on her so that she would want more. We wouldn't give them to her. That's why she got in the habit of coming over and staying over. I'd hold her a little and she'd go to sleep."[25]

Toward the end of her life, Marilyn felt "unimportant and insignificant," according to her last psychiatrist, Dr. Ralph Greenson. "The main mechanism she used to bring some feeling of stability and significance to her life was the attractiveness of her body."

When her body started to go, when another man she looked to as a father figure abandoned her, when she failed to have a child, when she was criticized, rejected, or blamed in her professional life, Marilyn's world caved in. She was "found out." She was only Norma Jean again, vulnerable to the massive depression and hopelessness that persona, or more closely lack of persona, meant to her. By most biographers' count, she attempted suicide at least three times and had numerous other close calls with death before finally succeeding.

For most of us, solitude is longed for, cherished, a rare opportunity to reflect on memories and matters important to our well-being—a chance to get back in touch with ourselves, to rediscover who we are: "The walls of an empty room are mirrors that double and redouble our sense of ourselves," John Updike writes in *The Centaur.*

But the borderline, with only the weakest sense of self,

looks back at only vacant reflections. Aloneness recapitulates the panic that he experienced as a child when faced with the prospect of abandonment by parents: Who will take care of me? The pain of loneliness can only be relieved by the rescue of a fantasized lover, as expressed in the lyrics of countless love songs.

In addition to these eight criteria defining BPD, a ninth criterion—brief psychotic experiences—has been proposed by Gunderson. DSM-III-R, however, does not yet accept this criterion because of controversy over its frequency and its overlap with psychotic illnesses. The borderline may become transiently psychotic when confronted with stressful or very unstructured situations. For example, psychiatrists sometimes observe episodes of psychosis during classical psychoanalysis, which relies heavily on free association and uncovering past trauma in an unstructured setting. Psychosis may also be stimulated by illicit drug use. Unlike patients with psychotic illnesses, such as schizophrenia, mania, psychotic depression, or organic/drug illnesses, borderline psychosis is usually of shorter duration and perceived as more acutely frightening to the patient and extremely different from his ordinary experience. The most common psychotic experiences for the borderline involve feelings of unreality and paranoid delusions.

Just as DMS-III-R modified some of the language and features of BPD standardized in DSM-III, so we can expect future diagnostic refinements to evolve, particularly as more clinical and statistical research is done. Perhaps future formulations will include more psychodynamic features, such as the defense mechanisms that Kernberg emphasizes in his formulations of Borderline Personality Organization (see appendix B).

The borderline personality is clearly becoming acknowledged by mental health professionals as one of the most common psychiatric maladies in this country. The professional must be able to recognize the features of BPD to treat effectively large numbers of patients. The layperson must be able to recognize them to better understand those with whom he shares his life.

Roots of the Borderline Syndrome

"All happy families resemble one another; every unhappy family is unhappy in its own fashion."
—From *Anna Karenina* by Leo Tolstoi

Growing up was not easy for Dixie Anderson. Her father was rarely at home and when he was, he didn't say much. For years, she didn't even know what he did for a living, just that he was gone all the time. Margaret, Dixie's mother, called him a "workaholic." Throughout her childhood, Dixie sensed that her mother was hiding something, though Dixie was never quite sure what it was.

But when Dixie turned eleven, things changed. She was an "early developer," her mother said, but Dixie really wasn't sure what that meant. All she knew was that her father was suddenly home more than he had ever been and he was also more attentive. Dixie enjoyed the new attention and the new feeling of power she had over him when he was finished touching her. After he was done, he would do whatever she asked him.

About this same time, Dixie suddenly became more popular in the family's suburban neighborhood. The kids began to offer her their secret stashes of pot, and a few years later acid, coke, and angel dust.

Junior high school was a drag. Halfway through a school day, she'd wind up fighting with some of the other kids. She didn't care. She was tough; she had friends and drugs; she was cool. Once, she even punched her science teacher, whom she felt was a real jerk. He went to the principal, who expelled her.

At age thirteen she saw her first psychiatrist, who diagnosed her as hyperactive and treated her with several medications. She decided to run away. She packed an overnight bag, took a bus to the interstate, stuck out her thumb, and in a few minutes was on her way to Las Vegas.

The way Margaret saw it, no matter what she did, it always seemed to turn out the same with Dixie: Her older daughter could not be pleased. Dixie was so much like her husband Roger, always criticizing the way Margaret looked and the way she kept the house. She had tried everything to lose weight, amphetamines, booze, even the stomach operation, yet nothing seemed to work. She'd always been fat, always would be.

She often wondered why Roger married her. He was a handsome man; from the beginning she could not understand why he wanted her. After awhile it was obvious he didn't want her. He simply stopped coming home at night.

Dixie was the one bright spot in Margaret's life. Her other daughter, Julie, was already obese at age five and seemed a lost cause. But Margaret would do anything for Dixie. She clung to her daughter like a lifeline. But the more Margaret clung, the more Dixie resented it. She became more demanding, throwing tantrums, and screaming about her mother's weight. The doctors could not nothing to help Margaret; they said she was manic-depressive and addicted to alcohol and amphetamines. The last time she was in the hospital they gave her electroshock treatment. And now with Roger gone and Dixie always running away, the world was closing in.

Los Angeles was the same story as Las Vegas for Dixie: She was promised cars and money and good times. Well, she had ridden in a lot of cars, but the good times were few and far between. Her friends were losers and sometimes she had to sleep with a guy to "borrow" a few bucks. Finally, with nothing but a few dollars in her jeans, she went back home.

Dixie arrived to find Roger gone and her mother in a

thick fog of depression and drug-induced numbness. In all this bleakness at home, it wasn't long before she fell back into her alcohol and drug habits. At fifteen she had been hospitalized twice for chemical abuse and was treated by a number of therapists. At sixteen, she became pregnant by a man she had met only a few weeks before. She married him soon after the pregnancy tests.

Seven months later, when Kim was born, the marriage began to fall apart. Dixie's husband was a weak and passive oaf who could not get his own life together, much less provide a solid home environment for their child.

By the time the baby was six months old, the marriage was over, and Dixie and Kim moved in with Margaret. It was then that Dixie became obsessed with her weight. She would go entire days without eating, and then eat frantically and voluminously only to vomit it all up in the toilet. What she couldn't get rid of by vomiting she eliminated by other ways: She ate squares of Ex-Lax as if they were candy. She exercised until sweat drenched her clothes and she was too exhausted to move. The pounds dropped off—but so did her health and her mood. Her periods stopped; her energy waned; her capacity to concentrate weakened. She became very depressed about her life and for the first time suicide seemed like a real alternative.

Initially she felt safe and comfortable when she was readmitted to the hospital, but soon her old self returned. By the fourth day, she was trying to seduce her doctor; when he didn't respond, she threatened him with all sorts of retaliation. She demanded extra privileges and special attention from the nurses and refused to participate in unit activities.

As abruptly as she had gone into the hospital, she pronounced herself cured and demanded discharge two weeks after admission. Over the next year, she would be readmitted to the hospital several times. She would also see several psychotherapists, none of whom seemed to understand or know how to treat her dramatic mood shifts, her depression, her loneliness, her impulsiveness with men and drugs. She began to doubt that she could ever be happy.

It wasn't long before Margaret and Dixie were again fighting and screaming at each other. For Margaret it was like seeing herself growing up all over again and making the same mistakes. She couldn't bear to watch it any longer.

Margaret's father had been just like Roger, a lonely, unhappy man who had little to do with his family. Her mother ran the family much like Margaret ran hers. And just as Margaret clung to Dixie, so had her mother clung to Margaret, trying desperately to mold her every step of the way. Margaret was fed her mother's ideas and feelings—and enough food for a battalion. By the age of sixteen, she was grossly obese and taking large amounts of amphetamines prescribed by the family doctor to suppress her appetite. By the age of twenty, she was drinking alcohol and taking Fiorinal to bring her down from the amphetamines.

Margaret was never able to please her mother in spite of the constant struggle for control between the two. Neither could Margaret please her own daughter or husband. She had never been able to make anyone happy, she realized, not even herself. Yet she persisted in trying to please people who would not be pleased.

Now, with Roger gone and Dixie so sick, Margaret's life seemed to be falling apart. Dixie finally told her mother how Roger had sexually abused her. And before Roger left, he had bragged all about his women. Despite everything, Margaret still missed him. He was alone, she knew, just like she was.

It was time, Dixie recognized, to do something about the plight of this self-destructive family. Or at least herself anyway. A job would be the first priority, something to combat the relentless boredom. But she was nineteen years old with a two-year-old child and no husband, and she still hadn't graduated from high school.

With characteristic compulsiveness, she flung herself into a high school equivalency program and received her diploma in a matter of months. Within days of obtaining her diploma, she was applying for loans and grants to attend college.

Margaret had begun to take care of Kim and in many ways, the arrangement looked like it might work: Raising Kim gave Margaret some meaning in her life, Kim had built-in child care, and Dixie had time for her new mission in life. But soon, the system showed cracks: Margaret sometimes got too drunk or depressed to be of any help. When this happened, Dixie had a simple solution: She would threaten to take Kim away from Margaret. Both the grandmother and granddaughter obviously needed each other desperately, so Dixie was able to totally control the household.

Through it all, Dixie still managed to find time for men, though her frequent liaisons were usually of short duration. She seemed to follow a pattern: Whenever a man started to care for her, she became bored. Distant, older men—unavailable doctors, married acquaintances, professors—were her usual type, but she would drop them the instant they responded to her flirtations. The young men she did become involved with were all members of a church that was strictly opposed to premarital sex.

Dixie avoided women and had no female friends. She thought women were weak and uninteresting. Men, at least, had some substance. They were fools if they responded to her flirtations and hypocrites if they did not.

As time went on, the more Dixie succeeded in her studies, the more frightened she became. She could pursue a particular interest—school, a certain man—relentlessly, almost obsessively, but with each success her demands on herself escalated into unrealistic proportions. Despite good grades, she would explode in rage and threaten to kill herself when she performed below expectations on an exam.

At times like these, her mother would try to console her, but Margaret was also becoming preoccupied with suicide, and the roles often reversed. Mother and daughter were again shuffling in and out of the hospital trying to overcome depression and chemical abuse.

Like her mother and grandmother, Kim didn't know her father very well either. Sometimes he came to visit, sometimes she went to the house that he shared with his mother. He always seemed awkward around her.

With her mother detached and her grandmother ineffectual or preoccupied with her own problems, Kim took control of the household by the time she was four. She ignored Dixie, who responded by ignoring her. If Kim threw a tantrum, Margaret would cave in to her wishes.

The household was in an almost constant state of chaos. Sometimes both Margaret and Dixie would be in the hospital at the same time, Margaret for her drinking, Dixie for her bulimia. Kim would then go to her father's house, although he was unable to care for her and would have his mother tend to her.

On the surface, Kim seems oddly mature for a six-year-old, despite the chaos around her. To her, other kids are "just kids," without her experience. She doesn't think her particular type of maturity is unusual at all: She has seen old photographs of her mother and grandmother when they were her age, and in the snapshots they have the same look.

ACROSS GENERATIONS

In many respects, the Andersons' saga is typical among borderline cases: The factors contributing to the borderline syndrome often transcend generations. The genealogy of BPD is often rife with deep and long lasting problems, including suicide, incest, drug abuse, violence, losses, and loneliness.

It has been observed that borderlines often have borderline mothers, who, in turn, have borderline mothers.[1] This hereditary predisposition of BPD prompts a number of questions, such as: How do borderline traits develop? How are they passed down through families? Are they, indeed, passed down at all?

In examining the roots of this illness, these questions resurrect the traditional "nature versus nurture" question. The two major theories on the causes of BPD—one emphasizing developmental (psychological) roots, the other constitutional (biological and genetic) origins—reflect the dilemma.

A third theoretical category, which focuses on the grander environmental and sociocultural factors, such as our fast-paced fragmented societal structure, destruction of the nuclear family, increased divorce rates, increased reliance on nonparental daycare, greater geographical mobility, and changing patterns of women's roles, is also important (see Chapter 4). Though empirical research has yet to be conducted on these environmental elements, many professionals speculate that these factors would tend to increase the prevalence of BPD.

The available evidence points to no one definitive cause—or even type of cause—of BPD. Rather, a combination of early developmental, neurobiological, and social factors are probably responsible for the illness.

A WORD ABOUT RESEARCH DATA

Most studies on the development and transmission of psychiatric syndromes employ indirect means of investigation, that is, retrospective reviews, patients' reconstructions of past events, interviews with relatives, and so on. These methods are fraught with inaccuracies and obstacles that make their validity suspect. Longitudinal research—following and objectively evaluating identified subjects and their families prospectively over time—is a much more accurate approach. Unfortunately, such methods have not yet been widely used in BPD research due to the relatively recent congealing of the diagnosis and the tremendous expense, time, and manpower necessary for such work.

DEVELOPMENTAL ROOTS

Developmental theories on the causes of BPD focus on the delicate interactions between child and caregivers, especially during the first few years of life. The ages of eighteen to thirty months, when the child begins the struggle to gain autonomy, are particularly crucial. Some parents actively resist the child's move toward separation and insist instead on a controlled, exclusive, often suffocating symbiosis. At the other extreme, other parents offer only erratic parenting (or are absent) during much of the child-raising period and so fail to provide sufficient attention to, and validation for, the child's feelings and experiences. Either extreme of parental behavior can eventuate in the child's failure to develop a positive, stable sense of self and may lead to a constant, intense need for attachment and chronic fears of abandonment.

In many cases the disturbed parent-child relationship takes the more severe form of early parental loss or prolonged, traumatic separation, or both. As with Dixie, many borderlines have an absent or psychologically disturbed father. Primary mother figures (who may sometimes be the father) tend to be erratic and depressed and have significant psychopathology themselves, usually BPD. The borderline's family background is frequently marked by incest, violence, and/or alcoholism. Many cases show an ongoing hostile or conflictual relationship between mother and preborderline child.

Object Relations Theory and Separation-Individuation in Infancy

Object relations theory, a model of infant development, emphasizes the significance of the child's interactions with his environment, as opposed to internal psychic instincts and biological drives unconnected to sensations outside himself. According to theory, the child's relationships with "objects" (people and things) in his environment determines his later functioning.

The primary object relations model for the early phases of infant development was created by Margaret Mahler and colleagues.[2] They postulated that the infant's first one to two months of life were characterized by an obliviousness to everything except himself (the autistic phase). During the next four or five months, designated the *symbiotic phase*, he begins to recognize others in his universe, not as separate beings, but as extensions of himself.

In the following *separation-individuation period* extending through ages two to three years, the child begins to separate and disengage from the primary caregiver and begins to establish a separate sense of self. Mahler and others consider the child's ability to navigate through this phase of development successfully to be crucial for later mental health.

During the entire separation-individuation period, the developing child begins to sketch out boundaries between self and others, a task complicated by two central conflicts—the desire for autonomy versus closeness and dependency needs, and fear of engulfment versus fear of abandonment.

A further complicating factor during this time is that the developing infant tends to perceive each individual in the environment as two separate personae. For example, when mother is comforting and sensitive, she is seen as "all good." When she is unavailable or unable to comfort and soothe, she is perceived as a separate, "all bad" mother. When she leaves his sight, the infant perceives her as annihilated, gone forever, and cries for her return to relieve the despair and panic. As the child develops, this normal "splitting" is replaced by a healthier integration of mother's good and bad traits, and separation anxiety is replaced by the knowledge that mother exists even when she is not physically present and will, in time, return—a phenomenon commonly known as *object constancy* (see below).

Mahler divides separation-individuation into four overlapping subphases.

Differentiation Phase (5–8 months). In this phase of development, the infant becomes aware of a world separate from mother. "Social smiling" begins—a reaction to the environment, but directed mostly at mother. Near the end of this phase, the infant displays the opposite side of this same response—"stranger anxiety"—the recognition of unfamiliar people in the environment.

If the relationship with mother is supportive and comforting, reactions to strangers are mainly characterized by curious wonder. If the relationship is unsupportive, anxiety is more prominent; the child begins to separate positive and negative emotions toward other people, relying on splitting to cope with these conflicting emotions.

Practicing Phase (8–16 months). The practicing phase is marked by the infant's increasing ability to move away from mother, first by crawling, then by walking. These short separations are punctuated by frequent reunions to "check in" and "refuel," behavior that demonstrates the child's first ambivalence toward his developing autonomy.

Rapprochement Phase (16–25 months). In the rapprochement phase, the child's expanding world sparks the recognition that he possesses an identity separate from those around him. Reunions with mother and the need for her approval shape the deepening realization that she and others are separate, real people. It is in the rapprochement phase, however, that both child and mother confront conflicts that will determine future vulnerability to the borderline syndrome.

The mother's role during this time is to encourage the child's experiments with individuation, yet simultaneously provide a constant, supportive, refueling reservoir. The normal two year old develops a strong bond with parents, but also learns to separate temporarily from them with sadness rather than with rage or tantrum. When reunited with the parent, the child is likely to feel happy as well as angry over the separation. The nurturing mother empathizes with the child and accepts the anger without retaliation. After many separations and reunions, the child develops an enduring sense of self, love and trust for parents, and a healthy ambivalence about others.

The mother of a preborderline, however, tends to respond to her child in a different way—either by pushing her child away prematurely and discouraging reunion (perhaps due to her own fear of closeness), or by insisting on a clinging symbiosis (perhaps due to her own fear of abandonment and need for intimacy). In either case, the child becomes burdened by intense fears of abandonment and/or engulfment that are mirrored back to him by mother's own fears.

As a result, the child never grows into an emotionally separate human being. Later in life, the borderline's inability to achieve intimacy in personal relationships reflects this infant stage. When an adult borderline confronts closeness, she may resurrect from childhood either the devastating feelings of abandonment that always followed her futile attempts at intimacy or the feeling of suffocation from mother's constant smothering. To defy such controls risks losing mother's love; to satisfy her risks losing oneself.

This fear of engulfment is well illustrated by T.E. Lawrence (*Lawrence of Arabia*) who at age thirty-eight writes about his fear of closeness to his overbearing mother: "I have a terror of her knowing anything about my feelings, or convictions, or way of life. If she knew, they would be damaged; violated; no longer mine.''[3]

Object Constancy Phase (25–36 months). By the end of the second year of life, assuming the previous levels of development have progressed satisfactorily, the child enters the object constancy phase, wherein the child recognizes that the absence of mother (and other primary caregivers) does not automatically mean her annihilation. The child learns to tolerate ambivalence and frustration. The temporary nature of mother's anger is recognized. The child also begins to understand that his own rage will not destroy mother. He begins to appreciate the concept of unconditional love and acceptance and develops the capacity to share and to empathize. The child becomes more responsive to father and others in the environment. Self-image becomes more positive, despite the self-critical aspects of an emerging conscience.

Aiding the child in all these tasks are transitional objects—the familiar comforts (teddy bears, dolls, blankets) that represent mother and are carried everywhere by the child to help ease separations. The object's form, smell and texture are physical representations of the comforting mother. Transitional objects are one of the first compromises made by the developing child in negotiating the conflict between the need to establish autonomy and the need for dependency. Eventually, in normal development, the transitional object is abandoned when the child is able to internalize a permanent image of a soothing, protective mother figure.

Developmental theories propose that the borderline is never able to progress to this object constancy stage. Instead, the borderline is fixated at an earlier developmental phase, in which splitting and other defense mechanisms remain prominent.

Because they are locked into a continual struggle to achieve object constancy, trust, and a separate identity, adult borderlines continue to rely on transitional objects for soothing. One woman, for example, always carried in her purse a newspaper article that contained quotes from her psychiatrist. When she was under stress, she would take it out, calling it her "security blanket." Seeing her doctor's name in print reinforced his existence and his continued interest and concern for her.

Ritualized, superstitious acts, when done in extremes, may represent borderline utilization of transitional objects. Although the ballplayer who wears the same socks or refuses to shave while in the midst of a hitting streak, for example, may be exhibiting borderline tendencies of relying on superstitious symbols to provide soothing and protection, it is only when such behaviors are repeated compulsively and inflexibly, and when they take on unrealistic proportions, that such a person crosses the border into the borderline syndrome.

Childhood Conflicts

The child's evolving sense of object constancy is consistently rechallenged as he progresses through developmental milestones. The toddler entranced by fairy tales filled with all-good and all-bad characters encounters numerous situations in which he uses splitting as a primary coping strategy. Though now trusting mother's permanent presence, the growing child must still contend with the fear of losing her love. The four-year-old who is scolded for being "bad" may feel threatened with the withdrawal of mother's love; he cannot yet conceive of the possibility that mother may be expressing her own frustrations quite apart from his own behavior, nor has he learned that mother can be angry and yet love him just as much at the same time.

Eventually, children are confronted with the separation anxiety of starting school. "School phobia" is neither a real phobia nor related exclusively to school itself, but instead represents the subtle interplay between the child's anxiety and the reactions of parents who may reinforce the child's clinging with their own ambivalence about the separation.

Adolescent Conflicts

Separation-individuation issues are repeated during adolescence, when questions of identity and closeness to others once again become vital concerns. During both the rapprochement phase of infancy and adolescence, the child's primary mode of relating is less acting than *react*-ing to others, especially parents. While the two-year-old tries to elicit approval and admiration from parents by molding his identity to emulate caregivers, the adolescent tries to emulate peers or adopts behaviors that are consciously different—even opposite—from those of parents. In both stages, the child's behavior is based less on independently determined internal needs than on reacting to the significant people in the immediate environment. Behavior becomes a quest to discover identity rather than to reinforce an established one.

An insecure teenager may ruminate endlessly about her boyfriend in a "he loves me, he loves me not" fashion. Failure to integrate these positive and negative emotions and to establish a firm, consistent perception of others leads to continued splitting as a defense mechanism. The adolescent's failure to maintain object constancy results in later problems with sustaining consistent, trusting relationships, establishing a core sense of identity, and tolerating anxiety and frustration.

Often, entire families adopt a borderline system of interaction, with the family members' undifferentiated identities alternately merging with and separating from each other. Melanie, the adolescent daughter in one such family, closely identified with her chronically depressed mother, who felt abandoned by her philandering husband. With her husband often away from home and her other children of much younger age, the mother fastened onto her teenage daughter, relating intimate details of the unhappy marriage and invading the teenager's privacy with intrusive questions about her friends and activities. Melanie's feelings of responsibility for her mother's happiness interfered to the point where she could not attend to her own needs. She even selected a college nearby so she could continue to live at home. Eventually Melanie developed anorexia nervosa, which became her primary mechanism for feeling in control, independent and comforted.

Similarly, Melanie's mother felt responsible and guilty for her daughter's illness. The mother sought relief in extravagant spending sprees (which she concealed from her husband) and then covered the bills by stealing money from her daughter's bank account. Mother, father and daughter were trapped in a dysfunctional family swamp, which they were unwilling to confront and from which they were unable to escape. In such cases, treatment of the borderline may require treatment of the entire family (see Chapter 7).

Traumas

Major traumas—parental loss, neglect, rejection, physical or sexual abuse—during the early years of development can increase the probability of BPD in adolescence and adulthood. Indeed, case histories of borderline patients are typically desolate battlefields, scarred by broken homes, chronic abuse and emotional deprivation.

Norman Mailer describes the effect of an absent parent on Marilyn Monroe, who never knew her father. Though his absence would contribute to her emotional instability in later life, it would also ironically be one of the motivating forces in her career:

> Great actors usually discover they have a talent by first searching in desperation for an identity. It is no ordinary identity that will suit them, and no ordinary desperation can drive them. The force that propels a great actor in his youth is insane ambition. Illegitimacy and insanity are the godparents of the great actor. A child who is missing either parent is a study in the search for identity and quickly becomes a candidate for actor (since the most creative way to discover a new and possible identity is through the close fit of a role).[4]

Raised in an orphanage during many years of her early childhood, Marilyn had to learn to survive with a minimum of love and attention. It was her self-image that suffered the most and led to her manipulative behavior with lovers later in life:

> One housemother for ten orphans—how can an institution afford more?—and yet what competition to get the fragment of good feeling available in a woman who must

divide that small pie of her working heart into ten slices. How little can be there, yet for the children what huge and ruthless elbowing to get up under her nose for reward, often by telling the most skillful lies, all the while knowing the most complete loneliness if one is to the rear. The real horror is that slowly, progressively, the child loses all sense of inhabiting even the fair volume of its own body.[5]

Throughout her life, Marilyn searched for a father to replace the one she had never known. Marilyn's mother had kept a photograph of Clark Gable on her bureau, a memory Marilyn kept her whole life. In many ways, Clark Gable became her "fantasy father."[6] When Gable, Marilyn's costar in *The Misfits,* died shortly after production of the movie, it was an excruciating loss.

Not all children who are traumatized or abused become borderline adults, of course; nor do all borderline adults have a history of trauma or abuse. Further, most studies on the effects of childhood trauma are based on inferences from adult reports and not on longitudinal studies that follow young children through to adulthood. Finally, other studies have demonstrated less extreme forms of abuse in the histories of borderlines, particularly neglect (sometimes from the father), and a rigid, tight marital bond that excludes adequate protection and support for the child.[7,8,9] Nevertheless, the large amount of anecdotal and statistical evidence demonstrates a link between various forms of abuse, neglect, and BPD.

CONSTITUTIONAL FACTORS

Some psychiatrists believe that biological and genetic factors play a crucial role in the development of borderline personality. This viewpoint is supported by the fact that individuals vary widely in their responses to poor childraising. Even many professionals who accept the importance of developmental influences also feel that some kind of biological predisposition is probable. Though no specific biological or genetic markers, such as a blood test or an identifiable gene, have as yet been found, some research has yielded interesting results.

Biochemical Imbalances

Some theorists believe that BPD may result at least partly from biochemical imbalances, similar to those implicated in other psychiatric illnesses. These theories are supported by the fact that certain medications, including antidepressants, major tranquilizers and antiseizure medicines, have relieved disabling symptoms in some borderline patients (see appendix C). In most of these cases, however, it appears that despite improvements in the targeted symptoms, the underlying character pathology persists.

Recent studies have proposed a link between impulsive acts and abnormalities in the metabolism of serotonin, a chemical neurotransmitter implicated in mood disorders.[10] Researchers have suggested that the same impulsivity observed among borderlines (and perhaps bulimics and substance abusers) may be related to similar metabolic defects.[11]

The borderline's frequent abuse of food, alcohol and other drugs—typically interpreted as self-destructive behavior—may also be seen as an attempt to self-medicate inner emotional turmoil. Borderlines frequently report the calming effects of self-mutilation; rather than feeling pain, they experience soothing relief or distraction from internal psychological pain. Self-mutilation, like any other physical trauma or stress, may result in the release of endorphins—the body's natural narcotic-like substances that provides relief during childbirth, physical traumas, long-distance running, and other physically stressful activities.

Neurological Factors

BPD has been associated with certain neurological disorders, some of which may be inherited: learning disabilities, attention deficit disorder (hyperactivity), epilepsy, head trauma, and encephalitis. This link has been observed mostly among borderline adolescents.[12]

Some studies have revealed abnormal brainwave activity over the temporal lobe of borderline patients, suggesting possible dysfunction in this part of the brain. These researchers also found abnormally high levels of a pituitary hormone during tests.[13]

Studies have demonstrated that during sleep borderlines exhibit a distinctive brainwave activity known as short REM latency—an abbreviated time span preceding the onset of dreaming—a characteristic pattern documented in depressed patients. These patterns were present in most borderlines whether they were depressed or not.[14,15,16]

A Genetic Connection?

Psychiatrists frequently find that one or both parents of borderlines also display borderline characteristics. The fact that many borderline mothers have borderline children has long been known, but the inference has been that borderline personality has been transmitted through parent-child interaction rather than through genes.

Some genetic studies have confirmed that borderline patients have a higher than expected percentage of mood disorders, alcoholism and other personality disorders among blood relatives.[17,18,19] Debate continues on the genetic transmission of both schizophrenia and BPD.[20,21,22] Since many of these bordering disorders have themselves been linked to genetic factors, it stands to reason that BPD may also have genetic roots.

NATURE VERSUS NURTURE

The "nature-nurture" question is, of course, a longstanding and controversial one that applies to many aspects of human behavior. Is one afflicted with BPD because of a biological destiny inherited from parents—or because of the way parents handled—or mishandled—upbringing? Do the biochemical and neurological signs of the disorder cause the illness—or are they caused *by* the illness? Why do some people develop BPD in spite of an apparently healthy upbringing? Why do others, burdened with a background filled with trauma and abuse, not develop it?

These "chicken-or-egg" dilemmas can lead to false assumptions. For example, one might conclude, based on developmental theories, that the causal direction is strictly downward, that is, an aloof, detached mother would produce an insecure borderline child. But the relationship might be more complex, more interactive than that: A colicky, unresponsive, unattractive infant may generate disappointment and detachment in the mother. Regardless of which comes first, both continue to interact and perpetuate interpersonal patterns, which may endure over many years and extend to other relationships. The mitigating effects of other factors—a supportive father, accepting family and friends, superior education, physical and mental abilities—will help determine the ultimate emotional health of the individual.

Though no evidence supports a specific BPD gene, humans may inherit chromosomal vulnerabilities that are later expressed as a particular illness, depending on a variety of contributing factors—childhood frustrations and traumas, specific stress events in life, healthy nutrition, access to health care and so on. Just as some have postulated that inheritable biological defects in the body's metabolism of alcohol may be associated with an individual's propensity to alcoholism, so there may exist a genetic predisposition for BPD involving a biological weakness in stabilizing mood and impulses.

As many borderlines learn that they must reject the either-or, black-or-white ways of thinking, researchers are beginning to appreciate that the most likely model for BPD (and for most medical and psychiatric illnesses) recognizes multiple contributing factors—nature and nurture—working and interacting simultaneously. Borderline personality is a complex tapestry, richly embroidered with innumerable, intersecting threads.

4

The Borderline Society

"Where there is no vision, the people perish."
—Proverbs. 29:18.

"States are as the men are; they grow out of
human characters."
—From Plato's *Republic*

From the beginning Lisa couldn't do anything right. Her older brother was the golden boy; good grades, respectful, athletic, perfect. Her younger sister, who had asthma, was also lavished with constant attention. Lisa was never good enough, especially in the eyes of her father. She remembered how he constantly reminded all of the children that he had started with nothing, that his parents had no money, didn't care about him, and drank too much. But he had prevailed. He had worked his way through high school, college, and even medical school. Now he was a well-respected surgeon, chairman of the department.

Lisa's earliest memories of her mother were of her lying on the couch either sick or in pain, ordering her about to clean house. Lisa tried hard to care for her mother and to convince her to stop taking the pain pills that seemed to make her so foggy.

Lisa felt that if she was just good enough, she could not only make her mother better but also please her father. Though her grades were always very good (even better than her brother's), her father always maligned her achievements: the course was too easy or she could have done better. At one point, she thought she might want to become a doctor, but her father said she would never make it.

When her father drank too much, he became violent, sometimes hitting the kids harder than he intended. The most frightening time of all was when he was drunk and their mother was spaced out on pain pills; then there was no one to take care of them—except Lisa, and she hated it.

During those times she felt lost and isolated. It was similar to the way she felt in biology class when she'd look around the room and observe the other kids looking in the microscopes, taking notes, apparently knowing exactly what to do, while she experienced a queasy sensation in her stomach of not quite understanding what was expected of her, and feeling too frightened to ask for help.

After awhile she just stopped trying. In high school she began to hang out with the "wrong kids." She made sure her parents saw them and how freaky they dressed; she made sure they saw her kiss the Hispanic boy, whom they despised.

Because her father insisted she couldn't make it as a doctor, Lisa went into nursing. At her first hospital job, she met a "free spirit" who wanted to bring his nursing expertise to underprivileged areas. Lisa was enthralled by him and they married soon after meeting. His habitual, "social" drinking became more prominent as the months went by, and he began hitting her. Bruised and battered, Lisa still felt it was her fault—she just wasn't good enough, couldn't make him happy. She had no friends, she said, because he wouldn't let her have any, but deep down she knew it was due more to her own fears of closeness.

She was relieved when he finally left her. She had wanted the split but couldn't cut the cord herself. But after the relief came fear: "Now what do I do?"

Between the divorce settlement and her salary Lisa had enough money to return to school. This time she was determined to be a doctor and, much to her father's surprise, she was accepted into medical school. She was starting to feel good again, valued and respected. But then in medical school the self-doubts returned. Her supervisors said she was too slow, clumsy with simple procedures, disorganized. They criticized her for not ordering the right tests or getting lab results back in time. Only with the patients did she feel comfortable because with them she could be whomever she needed to be: kind and compassionate when that was needed; confrontive and demanding when that was called for.

Lisa also experienced a great deal of prejudice in medical school. She was older than most of the other students; she had a much different background; and she was a woman. Many of the patients called her "nurse" and some of the male patients didn't want "no lady doctor." She was hurt and angry because, like her parents, society and its institutions had also robbed her of her dignity.

THE DISINTEGRATING CULTURE

Psychological theories take on a different dimension when looked upon in light of the culture and time period from which they emanate. At the turn of the century, for instance, when Freud was formulating the system that would become the foundation of modern psychiatric thought, the cultural context was a formally structured, Victorian society. His theory that the primary origins of neuroses were the repression of unacceptable thoughts and feelings—aggressive and especially sexual—was entirely logical in this strict social context.

Now, nearly a century later, aggressive and sexual instincts are expressed more openly, and the social milieu is much more confused. What it means to be a man or a woman is much more ambiguous in modern western civilization than in turn-of-the-century Europe. Social, economic, and political structures are less fixed. The family unit and cultural roles are less defined and the very concept of "traditional" is unclear.

Though social factors may not be direct causes of BPD (or other forms of mental illness), they are, at the least, important indirect influences. Social factors interact with BPD in several ways and cannot be overlooked. First, if borderline pathology originates early in life—and much of the evidence points in this direction—an increase in the pathology is likely tied to the changing social patterns of family structure and parent-child interaction. In this regard, it is worthwhile to examine social changes in the area of childraising patterns, stability of home life, and child abuse and neglect.

Second, social changes of a more general nature have an exacerbative effect on people already suffering from the borderline syndrome. The lack of structure in American society, for example, is especially difficult for borderlines to handle, since they typically have immense problems creating structure for themselves. Women's shifting role patterns (career versus homemaker, for example) tend to aggravate identity problems. Indeed, some researchers attribute the prevalence of BPD among women to this social role conflict, now so widespread in our society. The increased severity of BPD in these cases may, in turn, be transmitted to future generations through parent-child interactions, multiplying the effects over time.

Third, the growing prominence of character disorders in general, and borderline personality more specifically, may be seen as a natural and inevitable response to—or an expression of—our contemporary culture. As Christopher Lasch notes in *The Culture of Narcissism:*

> Every society reproduces its culture—its norms, its underlying assumptions, its modes of organizing experience—in the individual, in the form of personality. As Durkheim said, personality is the individual socialized.[1]

For many, American culture has lost contact with the past and remains unconnected to the future. Our flooding of technical advancement and information requires greater individual commitment to solitary study and practice, thus sacrificing opportunities for socialization. Increasing divorce rates, expanding use of day care, and greater mobility have all contributed to a society that lacks constancy and reliability. Personal, intimate relationships become difficult or even impossible to achieve, and deep-seated loneliness, self-absorption, emptiness, anxiety, depression, and loss of self-esteem ensue.

The borderline syndrome represents a pathological response to these stresses. Without outside sources of stability and validation of worthiness, borderline symptoms of black-and-white thinking, self-destructiveness, extreme mood changes, impulsivity, poor relationships, impaired sense of identity, and anger become understandable reactions to our culture's tensions. Borderline traits, which may be present to some extent in most people, are being elicited—perhaps even bred—on a wide scale by the prevailing social conditions. *New York Times* writer Louis Sass put it this way:

> Each culture probably needs its own scapegoats as expressions of society's ills. Just as the hysterics of Freud's day exemplified the sexual repression of that era, the borderline, whose identity is split into many pieces, represents the fracturing of stable units in our society.[2]

Though the conventional wisdom is that borderline pathology has increased over the last few decades, some psychiatrists believe that the symptoms were just as common early in the twentieth century. They claim that the change is not in the prevalence of the disorder, but in the fact that it is now officially identified and defined, and so merely diagnosed more frequently. Even some of Freud's early cases, scrutinized in the light of current criteria, might be diagnosed today as borderline personalities.

This possibility, however, by no means diminishes the importance of the growing number of borderline patients who are ending up in psychiatrists' offices and of the growing recognition of borderline characteristics in the general population. In fact, the major reason why it has been identified and covered so widely in the clinical literature is its prevalence in both therapeutic settings and the general culture.

THE BREAKDOWN OF STRUCTURE: A FRAGMENTED SOCIETY

Few would dispute the proposition that society has become more fragmented since the end of World War II. Family structures in place for decades—the nuclear family, extended family, one wage-earner households, geographical stability—have been replaced by a wide assortment of patterns, movements, and trends. Divorce rates have soared. Drug and alcohol abuse and child abuse have sky-rocketed. Crime, terrorism, and political assassination have become widespread, at times almost commonplace.

Some of these changes may be related to society's failure to achieve a kind of "social rapprochement." As noted in Chapter 3, during the separation-individuation phase, the infant ventures cautiously away from mother but returns to her reassuring warmth, familiarity, and acceptance. Disruption of this rapprochement cycle often results in a lack of trust, disturbed relationships, emptiness, anxiety, and an uncertain self-image—characteristics that make up the borderline syndrome. Similarly, it may be seen that contemporary culture interferes with a healthy "social rapprochement" by obstructing access to comforting anchors. In most areas of the country, the need for two incomes to maintain a decent standard of living forces many parents to relinquish parenting duties to others; precious few employers offer support in the way of paid parental leave or on-site day care for new parents. Jobs, as well as economic and social pressures, encourage frequent moves, and this geographical mobility, in turn, removes us from our stabilizing roots. We are losing (or have already lost) the comforts of neighborhood, nearby family, and consistent social roles.

When the accoutrements of custom disappear, they may be replaced by a sense of abandonment, of being adrift in unchartered waters. Our children lack a sense of history and belonging—of an anchored presence in the world. To establish a sense of control and comforting familiarity in an alienating society, the individual may resort to a wide range of pathological behavior—substance addiction, eating disorders, criminal behaviors, and so on.

Society's failure to provide rapprochement with reassuring, stabilizing bonds is reflected in the relentless series of sweeping societal movements over the past three decades. We have roller coastered from the explosive "We Decade" of the sixties, to the narcissistic "Me Decade" of the seventies, to the materialistic, fast-paced, "Whee Decade" of the eighties. Accompanying these external changes have been internal shifts in values: from the other-directed "peace, love, and brotherhood" of the sixties, to the "self-awareness" of the seventies, to the "self-seeking materialism" of the eighties.

One of the big losers in this shift to individualism and self-absorption has been group loyalties—devotion to family, neighborhood, church, occupation, and country. As society continues to foster detachment from people and institutions that provide reassuring rapprochement, individuals are responding in ways that virtually define the borderline syndrome: decreased sense of validated identity, worsening interpersonal relationships, isolation and loneliness, boredom, and (without the stabilizing force of group pressures) impulsivity.

Like the world of the borderline, ours in many ways is a world of massive contradictions. We presume to believe in peace, yet our streets, movies, television, and sports are filled with aggression and violence. We are a nation virtually founded on the principle of "Help thy neighbor," yet we have become one of the most politically conservative, self-absorbed, and materialistic societies in the history of mankind. Assertiveness and action are encouraged; reflection and introspection are equated with weakness and incompetency.

Contemporary social forces implore us to embrace a mythical polarity—black or white, right or wrong, good or bad—relying on our nostalgia for simpler times, for our own childhoods. The political system presents candidates who adopt polar stances: "I'm right, the other guy is wrong"; America is good, the Soviet Union is "the Evil Empire." Religious factions exhort us to believe that theirs is the only route to salvation. The legal system, built on the premise that one is either guilty or not guilty with little or no room for gray areas, perpetuates the myth that life is intrinsically fair and justice can be attained—that is, when something bad does happen, it is necessarily someone's fault and that person should pay.

The flood of information and leisure alternatives in our increasingly affluent and highly technical society makes it difficult to establish priorities in living. Ideally, we—as individuals and as a society—attempt to achieve a balance between nurturing the body and the mind, between work and leisure, between altruism and self-interest. But in an increasingly materialistic society it is a small step from assertiveness to aggressiveness, from individualism to alienation, from self-preservation to self-absorption.

The ever-growing reverence for science and technology has led to an obsessive pursuit of precision. Calculators and computers replace memorized multiplication tables and slide rules. Velcro deprives children of learning how to tie shoelaces. Creativity and intellectual diligence are sacrificed to convenience and precision.

All these attempts to impose order and fairness on a naturally random and unfair universe endorse the borderline's futile struggle to choose only black or white, right or wrong, good or bad. But the world is neither intrinsically fair nor exact; it is composed of subtleties that require less simplistic approaches. A healthy civilization can accept the uncomfortable ambiguities. Attempts to eradicate or ignore uncertainty tend only to encourage a borderline society.

We would be naive to believe that the cumulative effect of all this change—the excruciating pull of opposing forces—has had no effect on our psyches. In a sense, we all live in a kind of "borderland"—between the prosperous, healthy, high-technology America on the one hand, and the underbelly of poverty, homelessness, drug abuse, and mental illness on the other; between the dream of a sane, safe, secure world and the insane nightmare of nuclear holocaust.

The price tag of social change has come in the form of stress and stress-related physical disorders, such as heart attacks, strokes, and hypertension. We must now confront the possibility that mental illness has become part of the psychological price.

DREAD OF THE FUTURE

Over the past two decades, therapeutic settings have seen a basic change in psychopathology from symptom neuroses to character disorders. As far back as 1975, psychiatrist Peter L. Giovachinni wrote, "Clinicians are constantly faced with the seemingly increasing number of patients who do not fit current diagnostic categories. [They suffer not from] defini-

tive symptoms but from vague ill-defined complaints . . .
When I refer to this type of patient, practically everyone
knows to whom I am referring.''[3]

In the eighties, of course, such reports have become
commonplace, as personality disorders have replaced classical neurosis as the prominent pathology. Which social
and cultural factors have influenced this change in pathology? Many social observers, including Lasch, believe that
one factor is our devaluation of the past:

> To live for the moment is the prevailing passion—to live
> for yourself, not for your predecessors or posterity. We
> are fast losing the sense of historical continuity, the
> sense of belonging to a succession of generations orig-
> inating in the past and stretching into the future.[4]

This loss of historical continuity works both ways in
terms of time. Devaluation of the past breaks the perceptual link to the future, which becomes a vast unknown, a
source of dread as much as hope. Time is perceived as
isolated points instead of as a logical, continuous string of
events influenced by past achievement and present action.

The threat of nuclear annihilation is one contributor to
our lack of faith in the past and our dread of the future.
Empirical studies with adolescents and children consistently show "awareness of the danger, hopelessness about
surviving, a shortened time perspective, and pessimism
about being able to reach life goals. Suicide is mentioned
again and again as a strategy for dealing with the threat.''[5]
Other studies have found that the threat of nuclear war
rushes children to a kind of "early adulthood," similar to
the type witnessed in those preborderline children who are
forced to take control of families that are out of control
due to BPD, alcoholism, and other mental disorders.[6] According to Berkeley child psychologist Edward Levin, a
common response from adolescents when asked, "What
do you picture yourself doing ten years from now?" is,
"We'll all be dead.''[7]

The borderline, as we have seen, personifies this orientation to the "now." With little interest in the past, the
borderline is almost a cultural amnesiac; his cupboard of

warm memories (which sustain most of us in troubled times) is bare. As a result, he is doomed to suffer torment with no breathers, no concrete memories of happier times to get him through the tough periods. Unable to learn from his mistakes, he is doomed to repeat them.

Parents who fear the future are not likely to be engrossed by the needs of the next generation. A modern parent, emotionally detached and alienated—yet at the same time pampering and overindulgent—becomes a likely candidate to mold future borderline personalities.

THE JUNGLE OF INTERPERSONAL RELATIONSHIPS

Perhaps the hallmark changes over the last two decades have come in the area of sexual mores, roles, and practices—from the suppressed sexuality of the fifties to the "free-love" and "open marriage" ethics of the sixties' sexual revolution to the massive sexual reevaluation in the eighties, resulting in large part from the fear of AIDS.

Societal forces have been making deep and lasting friendships, love affairs, and marriages increasingly difficult to achieve and maintain. Half of the couples who married in the seventies will divorce in the eighties.[8] Lasch has noted that, "As social life becomes more and more warlike and barbaric, personal relations, which ostensibly provide relief from those conditions, take on the character of combat."[9]

Borderlines may be well suited for this kind of combat. The narcissistic man's need to dominate and be idolized fits well with the borderline woman's ambivalent need to be controlled and punished. Borderline women often marry at a young age to escape the chaos of family life. They cling to dominating husbands with whom they re-create the miasma of home life. Both may enter a kind of "Slap! . . . 'Thanks, I needed that' " sadomasochistic dyad. Less typical, but still common, is a reversal of these roles, with a borderline male linked with a narcissistic female partner.

Masochism is a prominent characteristic of borderline relationships. Dependency coupled with pain elicits the familiar refrain "love hurts." As a child, the borderline experiences pain and confusion in trying to establish a maturing relationship with his mother or primary caregiver. Later in life, other partners—spouse, friends, minister, doctor—renew this early confusion. Criticism or abuse particularly reinforces the borderline's self-image of worthlessness. Lisa's later relationships with her husband and supervisors, for example, recapitulated the profound feelings of worthlessness that were ingrained by the constant criticisms of her father.

Sometimes the borderline's masochistic suffering transforms into sadism. For example, Ann would sometimes encourage her husband Larry to drink, knowing about his drinking problem. Then she'd instigate a fight, fully aware of Larry's violent propensities when drunk. Following a beating, Ann would wear her bruises like battle scars, reminding Larry of his violence, and insisting they go out in public, where Ann would explain away her marks as such "accidents" as "running into doors."

After each episode, Larry would feel profoundly regretful and humiliated, while Ann would present herself as a long-suffering martyr. In this way Ann used her beatings to exact punishment from Larry. The question of the real victim in this relationship became increasingly vague.

Even when a relationship is apparently ruptured, the borderline comes crawling back for more punishment, feeling he deserves the denigration. The punishment is comfortably familiar, easier to cope with than the frightening prospect of change and solitude.

A typical scenario for modern social relationships is the "overlapping lover" pattern—the need to establish a new romance before severing a current one. The borderline exemplifies this constant need for partnership: As the borderline climbs the jungle gym of relationships, he cannot let go of the last bar until he has firmly grasped the next. Typically, the borderline will not leave his current, abusive spouse until a new "white knight" is at least visible on the horizon.

Periods of relaxed social-sexual mores and less structured romantic relationships (such as in the late-sixties and seventies) are more difficult for borderlines to handle; increased freedom and lack of structure paradoxically imprison the borderline, who is greatly handicapped in devising his own individual system of values. Conversely, the sexual withdrawal period of the late-eighties (due in part to the AIDS epidemic) can be ironically helpful for borderline personalities. Social fears enforce strict boundaries that can be crossed only at the risk of great physical harm; impulsivity and promiscuity now have severe penalties. This external structure can help protect the borderline from his self-destructiveness.

SHIFTING GENDER ROLE PATTERNS

Earlier in the century, social roles were fewer, well-defined and much more easily combined. Mother was domestic, working in the home, in charge of children. Outside interests, such as school involvement, hobbies, and charity work, flowed naturally from these duties. Father's work and community visibility also combined smoothly. And, together, their roles worked harmoniously for the most part.

The complexities of modern society, however, dictate that the individual develop a plethora of social roles—many of which do not come together so easily. The working mother, for example, has two distinct roles and must struggle to perform both well. The policies of most employers demand that the working mom keep the home and workplace separate; as a result, many mothers feel guilty or embarrassed when problems from one impact the other.

A working father also finds work and home roles compartmentalized. He is no longer the owner of the local grocery who lives above the store. More likely, he works miles from home and has much less time to be with his family. Furthermore, the modern dad plays an increasingly participatory role with familial responsibility.

Shifting role patterns over the last twenty-five years are central to theories on why BPD is so prevalent among women. The latest studies report that approximately two-thirds of people afflicted with BPD are women (see Chapter 1). In the past, a woman had essentially one life course—getting married (usually in her late teens or early twenties), having children, staying in the home to raise those children, and repressing any career ambitions. Today, in contrast, a young woman is faced with a bewildering array of role models and expectations—from the single career woman, to the married career woman, to the traditional nurturing mother, to the "supermom," who strives to combine marriage, career, and children successfully.

Men have also experienced new roles and expectations, of course, but not nearly so wide-ranging—nor conflicting—as women. Today, men are expected to be more sensitive and open and to take a larger part in childraising than in previous eras, yet these qualities and responsibilities usually fit within the overall role of "provider" or "coprovider." It is the rare man who, for example, abandons, or even seriously considers abandoning, career ambitions for the role of "househusband"—nor is this expected of him.

Men have fewer adjustments to make during the evolution of relationships and marriages. For example, relocations are usually dictated by the man's career needs, since he is most often the primary wage earner. Throughout pregnancy, birth, and child rearing, few changes occur in the man's day-to-day reality. The woman not only endures the physical demands of pregnancy and childbirth and must leave her job to give birth, but it is also she who must make the transition back to work or give up her career. And yet in many dual-earner households, although it may not be openly stated, the woman simply assumes the primary responsibility for the maintenance of the home. She is the one who usually adjusts her plans to stay home with a sick child or waits for the repairman to come.

Though women have struggled successfully to achieve increased social and career options, they may have had to pay an exacting price in the process: excruciating life decisions about career, families, and children; strains on their relationships with their children and husband; the stress resulting from making and living with these decisions; and confusion about who they are and who they want to be. From this perspective, it is understandable that women should be more vulnerable to BPD, a disorder in which identity and role confusion are such central components.

Yet despite the statistical evidence pointing to BPD as a "woman's illness," some clinicians claim that there are not more women borderlines today; rather, their symptoms are just more evident. The borderline symptom of angry outbursts, for example, socially unacceptable for women in previous eras, is now allowed to surface. For today's woman, living in an era that accepts—even encourages—open and honest expression of emotion and communication, releasing anger and other deep emotions has come to be recognized as a healthy antidote to repression. Career women particularly are expected to be assertive in their jobs and many "assertiveness training" seminars are directed at working women. Suddenly, after centuries of trying to mold "shy, demure creatures," and many girls are still brought up this way, our male-dominated society encourages women to express aggressive behavior and deep emotion—and simultaneously expects them to shut it off at will.

To illustrate another type of cultural bias, one study found that BPD is diagnosed with almost equal frequency among both Hispanic men and women, as opposed to most studies, which find a higher prevalence of borderline women than borderline men. The researchers speculate that the reason may be a combination of sociocultural differences and a kind of clinician bias:

> It is possible that borderline personality disorder was overdiagnosed among the Hispanic men in our study because most of the clinicians were white and did not speak Spanish . . . Behavior within the normal limits of the Puerto Rican culture may be regarded as deviant when judged outside its original social context; for example, the display of exuberant mannerisms and dramatic behavior by a Hispanic man may lead a clinician unfamiliar with such demeanor to perceive impulsivity, inappropriate anger, and affective instability, all of which are DSM-III criteria for borderline personality disorder.[10]

Similarly, predominantly white and English-speaking therapists may dismiss traits, such as histrionic behavior, poor control of anger and impulsiveness, as mannerisms typical of the Hispanic woman—or, more closely, the *ste-*

reotype of the Hispanic woman—when they should be more objective in evaluating these as symptoms.

Whether BPD is a "woman's illness" is a controversial issue, and the argument cannot be settled here. Suffice it to say that, just as the price for women's increased freedom may be the jarring turmoil of role confusion, the price for increased responsibility may be a whole set of undesirable (and traditionally male) behaviors. The combination of all these factors can at least exacerbate the severity of borderline personality among women.

Sexual Orientation and Borderlines

Sexual orientation is also a part of the borderline's role confusion. In line with this theory, some researchers estimate a significantly increased rate of homosexuality, bisexuality and sexual perversions among borderlines.[11,12] Homosexuality in the borderline may originate early in childhood, resulting from a number of possible factors: lack of role models, sexual assaults, an insatiable need for affection and attention, discomfort with one's own body, and inconsistent sexual information.

FAMILY AND CHILD-REARING PATTERNS

Since the end of World War II, our society has experienced striking changes in family and child-rearing patterns:

- The institution of the nuclear family has been in steady decline. Largely due to divorce, it is estimated that 58 percent of American children spend a significant part of their lives in a single-parent home.[13]
- Alternative family structures (such as "blended families," in which a single parent with children combines with another one-parent household to form a new family unit) have led to situations in which many children are raised by persons other than their birth parents.
- Due to increased geographical mobility, the traditional extended family, with grandparents, siblings, cousins,

and other family relations living in close proximity, is almost extinct, leaving the nuclear family virtually unsupported.

- The number of women working outside the home has increased dramatically. In 1980, more than half the mothers in the U.S. were employed outside the home, and current estimates indicate that by 1990, 75 percent of all American mothers will work. Ten times as many mothers of preschool-age children work now as did in 1945.[14]
- As a result of women working outside the home, more children than ever before are being placed in various forms of day care—and at a much earlier age. The number of infants in day care has increased 45 percent since 1980.[15]
- The evidence clearly suggests that the incidence of child physical and sexual abuse has increased significantly over the past decade.[16]

What are the psychological effects of these child-rearing changes—on both children and parents? Though many of these changes (such as blended families) are too new to be the subject of intensive studies, psychiatrists and developmental experts generally agree that children growing up in settings marked by turmoil, instability, or abuse are at much greater risk for emotional and mental problems in adolescence and adulthood. Moreover, parents in such environments are much more likely to develop stress, guilt, depression, lower self-esteem—all characteristics associated with BPD.

James Masterson notes that governments with extensive social welfare systems—such as the Scandinavian countries and increasingly the United States—promote a social dependency that discourages autonomy and increases borderline and sociopathic behaviors among the citizenry. In Israel the primary mode of child rearing is often the kibbutz nursery, where the central caregivers are not the birth parents but rather a collection of parental figures. This type of family structure may develop soldiers and other cogs in a cooperative society but tends to diffuse the task of separation and individuation and to mute the growth of an autonomous self and a sense of individuality. In Japan the mother characteristically initially indulges the grandiosity of the child and later controls him through use of guilt. Masterson feels that this results in a nation prominent in smooth social functioning but severely lacking in personal qualities of creativity, autonomy, and intimacy.[17]

Infant Day Care: The Unknown Quantity

During the first months of life, the infant begins developing emotional and cognitive awareness of self and the nurturing "other" (see Chapter 3). The baby is learning about herself, developing an ego base. Simultaneously, the parents are also learning about themselves as nurturers. A two-way communication-feedback system develops—the baby's first exposure to social communication. The infant experiences emotion and at the same time learns to elicit and respond to the emotions of nurturant adults.[18]

According to T. Berry Brazelton and other noted developmental experts, these early months are a crucial precursor for future emotional development, response patterns, and self-esteem: "The experience of completing an anticipated act of social communication closes a feedback cycle, creating a sense of mastery that confirms children's sense of self and fuels them toward further development."[19]

The weight of the evidence suggests that an infant who is deprived of this chance to learn about herself will be more likely to experience impaired emotional and cognitive development. Later in life, the child is much more likely to have problems with identity, self-esteem, security, separations, and social relationships—all issues, as we have seen, in the borderline syndrome.

The effects of day care on parents are also significant. Study after study has shown day care to be a primary source of stress for working parents.[20] Parents deprived of the chance to stay at home during their baby's early months are more apt to feel depressed, cheated, guilty, and inadequate as parents. Mothers particularly are susceptible to feelings of powerlessness and guilt and frequently form defenses to cope with the feelings: (1) denial that the feelings are real; (2) projecting the role of "good mother" onto the day-care provider and adopting the role of "bad mother" herself, or vice-versa; and (3) detaching emotionally from the child because of the pain of separation.[21]

Some recent studies on infant day care indicate that extensive day care initiated in the first year of life may lead to insecure mother-infant attachments and noncompliance, aggression, and insecurity later in childhood.[22] The conclusions of these studies are disputed by some mental health professionals who point out the positive aspects of day care for both the cognitive and social development of the child. Because the phenomenon of infant day care is simply so new, the long-term consequences may not be fully understood for many years. "Almost an entire generation of children is being raised in a way that has never been done before," writes noted child expert and Yale psychologist Edward Zigler. "We won't know the ultimate effects until these infants have grown into adults."[23]

Child Abuse and Neglect: Destroyer of Trust

Child abuse and neglect are becoming increasingly recognizable health problems. Even conservative estimates report that one million children per year in the United States are mistreated by parents. More than 200,000 children per year are sexually abused and 200,000 to 300,000 are psychologically abused.[24] Some studies estimate that 25 percent of girls experience some form of sexual abuse (from parents or others) by the time they reach adulthood.[25]

Characteristics of physically abused preschool-age children include: inhibition, depression, attachment difficulties, behavior problems (such as hyperactivity and severe tantrums), poor impulse control, aggressiveness, and peer-relation problems.[26]

"Violence begets violence," said John Lennon, and this is particularly true in the case of battered children. Because those who are abused often become abusers themselves, this problem can self-perpetuate over many decades and generations.

The incidence of abuse or neglect among borderlines is high enough to be a factor that separates BPD from other personality disorders. Verbal or psychological abuse is the most common form, followed by physical and then sexual abuse. Physical and sexual abuse may be more dramatic in nature, but the emotionally abused children can suffer total loss of self-esteem.

Emotional child abuse can take several forms:

- **Degradation**—constantly devaluing the child's achievements and magnifying misbehavior. After awhile, the child becomes convinced that he really is bad or worthless.
- **Unavailability**—psychologically absent parents show little interest in the child's development, and provide no affection in times of need.
- **Domination**—use of extreme threats to control the child's behavior. Some child development experts have compared this form of abuse to the techniques used by terrorists to brainwash captives.[27]

The pattern of the neglected child, as described by psychologist Hugh Missildine, mirrors the dilemmas of borderlines in later life:

> If you suffered from neglect in childhood, it may cause you to go from one person to another, hoping that someone will supply whatever is missing. You may not be able to care much about yourself, and think marriage will end this, and then find yourself in the alarming situation of being married but emotionally unattached . . . Moreover, the person who [has] neglect in his background is always restless and anxious because he cannot obtain emotional satisfaction . . . These restless, impulsive moves help to create the illusion of living emotionally . . . Such a person may, for example, be engaged to be married to one person and simultaneously be maintaining sexual relationships with two or three others. Anyone who offers admiration and respect has appeal to them—and because their need for affection is so great, their ability to discriminate is severely impaired.[28]

From what we understand of the roots of BPD (see Chapter 3), abuse, neglect, or prolonged separations early in childhood can greatly disrupt the developing infant's establishment of trust. Self-esteem and autonomy are crippled. The abilities to cope with separation and to form identity do not proceed normally. As they become adults, abused children may recapitulate frustrating relationships with others. Pain and punishment may become associated with closeness—they come to believe that "love hurts." As the borderline matures, self-mutilation may become the proxy for the abusive parent.

Children of Divorce: The Disappearing Father

Due primarily to divorce, more children than ever before are being raised without the physical and/or emotional presence of their father. Because most courts award children to the mother in custody cases, the large majority of single-parent homes are headed by mothers. Even in cases of joint custody or liberal visitation rights, the father, who is likely to remarry soon after divorce and start a new family, often fades from the child's upbringing.

The recent trend in child raising, toward a more equal sharing of parental responsibilities between mother and father, makes divorce even more upsetting for the child. Children clearly benefit from dual parenting, but they also lose more when the marriage dissolves, especially if the breakup occurs during the formative years when the child still has many crucial developmental stages to hurdle.

Studies on the effects of divorce typically report profound upset, neediness, regression, and acute separation anxiety related to fears of abandonment in children of pre school age.[29] A significant number are found to be depressed[30] or antisocial in later stages of childhood.[31]

During separation and divorce, the child's need for physical intimacy increases. For example, it is typical for a child at the time of separation to ask a parent to sleep with him. If the practice continues, becoming the parent's need as well, the child's own sense of autonomy and bodily integrity may be threatened. This, combined with the loneliness and severe narcissistic injury caused by the divorce, places some children at high risk for developmental arrest or, if the need for affection and reassurance becomes desperate, for sexual abuse. A father separated from the home may demand more time with the child in order to relieve his own feelings of loneliness and deprivation. If the child becomes a lightning rod for his father's resentment and bitterness, he may again be at higher risk for abuse.

In many situations of parental separation, the child becomes the pawn in a destructive battle between his parents. One father, who usually ignored his visitation privileges, suddenly demanded that his daughter stay with him whenever he was angry at her mother. These visits were usually unpleasant for the child as well as for her father and his new family, yet were used as punishment for his ex-wife, who would feel guilty and powerless at his demands. Another child became embroiled in conflicts between his divorced parents when his mother periodically took his father back to court to extract more child support monies. Bribes of material gifts or threats to cut off support for school or home maintenance are common weapons used between continuously skirmishing parents; the bribes and threats are usually more harmful to the children than they are to the parents.

Children may even be drawn into court battles and forced to testify about their parents. In these situations neither the parents, nor the courts, nor social welfare organizations can protect the child, who is often left with a sense of overwhelming helplessness (conflicts continue despite his input), or of intoxicating power (his testimony controls the battle between his parents). He may feel enraged at his predicament and yet fearful that he could be abandoned by everyone. All of this becomes fertile ground for the development of borderline pathology.

In addition to divorce, the past two decades have witnessed the maturing of children of thousands of World War II, Korean War, and Viet Nam War veterans and of many prison-camp and concentration-camp survivors. Not only were many of these fathers absent during significant portions of their children's development, but many were found to develop post-traumatic stress disorders and delayed mourning ("impacted grief") related to combat that also influenced child development.[32] By 1970, 40 percent of World War II and Korean War POWs had met violent death by suicide, homicide, or auto-accident (mostly one-car single-occupant accidents).[33] Children of holocaust survivors often have severe emotional difficulties, rooted in their parents' massive psychic trauma.[34]

The "absent father syndrome" can lead to pathological consequences. Often in families torn by divorce or death, the mother tries to compensate by becoming the ideal parent, arranging every aspect of her child's life; naturally, the child has limited opportunity to develop his own identity. Without the buffering of another parent, the mother-child link can be too close to allow for healthy separating.

Though the mother often seeks to replace the missing father, in many cases it is actually the child who tries to replace the absent father. In the absence of father, the symbiotic intensity of the bond with mother is greatly magnified. The child grows up with an idealized view of the mother and fantasies of forever trying to please her. And a parent's dependence on the child may persist, interfering with growth and individuation, planting the seeds of BPD.

Permissive Child-Rearing Practices

Modern permissive child-rearing practices, involving the transfer of traditional parental functions to outside agencies—the school, mass media, industry—have significantly altered the quality of parent-child relationships. Parental "instinct" has been supplanted by a reliance on books and child-rearing experts. Child rearing, in many households, takes a back seat to the demands of dual careers. "Quality time" becomes a guilt-induced euphemism for "not enough time."

Many parents overcompensate by lavishing attention on the child's practical and recreational needs, yet providing little real warmth. Narcissistic parents perceive their children as extensions of themselves or as objects/possessions, rather than as separate human beings. As a result, the child suffocates in emotionally distant attention, leading to an exaggerated sense of his own importance, regressive defenses, and loss of a sense of self.

Geographical Mobility: Where Is Home?

We are moving more than ever before. Greater geographical mobility can bring rich educational benefits and cultural exchange for a child, but numerous relocations are often also accompanied by a feeling of rootlessness. Some investigators have found that children who move frequently and stay in one place for only short periods of time often have confused responses, or no response at all, to the simple question, ''Where is your home?''[35]

Because hypermobility is typically correlated with career-oriented lifestyles and job demands, one or both parents in mobile families tend to work long hours and so are less available to their children. Having few enough constants in their environment to provide ballast for development, mobility adds another disruptive force—the world turns into a menagerie of changing places and faces. Such children may grow up bored and lonely, looking for constant stimulation. Continually forced to adapt to new situations and people, they may lose the stable sense of self encouraged by firm community anchors. Though socially graceful, they typically feel they are gracefully faking it.

With increasing geographical mobility, the stability of the neighborhood, community school systems, church and civic institutions, and friendships are weakened. Generations are becoming separated by long distances, and the extended family is lost for emotional support and child care. Children are raised without knowing their grandparents, aunts, uncles, and cousins, losing a strong connection to the past and a source of love and warmth to nurture healthy emotional growth.

5

Understanding and Healing

"Now here, you see, it takes all the running you can do to keep in the same place. If you want to get somewhere else, you must run at least twice as fast as that."
—Lewis Carroll, *Through the Looking Glass*

"I feel like I have a void in me that I can never quite fill." Elizabeth, an attractive, witty twenty-eight-year-old woman, was originally referred for therapy by her family doctor. She had been married for six years to a man who was ten years older than she and had been her boss at one time. Five months before, she had given birth to her first child, a daughter, and was now severely depressed.

She yearned for something she could call her own, something that would show "the rest of the world knew I was here." Inside, she felt her "real self" was a swamp of childish emotions, and that she was always hiding her feelings, which were "ugly and bad." These realizations turned into self-hate; she wanted to give up.

By her count, Elizabeth had had nine extramarital affairs over the previous six years—all with men she met through work. They began soon after the death of her father. Most were relationships that she totally controlled, first by initiating them and later by ending them. She had found it exciting that these men seemed so puzzled by her advances and then by her sudden rejections. She enjoyed the physical closeness, but acknowledged she dreaded being too emotionally involved. Although she controlled these relationships, she never found them sexually satisfying; nor was she sexually responsive to her husband. She said she felt safer using sex to "equalize" relationships, to stay in control. Her intellect and personality, she felt, were not enough to hold a man.

Reared in a working-class Catholic family, Elizabeth had three older brothers and a younger sister, who had drowned in a swimming accident at age five. Elizabeth was only eight at the time and had little understanding of the event except to observe her mother becoming more withdrawn.

For as long as Elizabeth could remember, her mother had been hypercritical, constantly accusing Elizabeth of being "bad." When she was a young girl, her mother insisted that she attend church with her, and forced her father to construct an altar in Elizabeth's bedroom. Elizabeth felt closer to her father, a passive and quiet man, who was dominated by his wife. As she entered puberty, he became more distant and less affectionate.

Growing up, Elizabeth was quiet and shy. Her mother disapproved of her involvement with boys and closely watched her friendships with girls; she was expected to have "acceptable" friends. Her brothers were always favored; she would kid with them, trying to be "one of the guys." Elizabeth achieved good grades in high school but was discouraged from going to college. After graduation, she began working full time as a secretary.

As time went on, the conflicts with her mother escalated. Even in high school, Elizabeth's mother had denounced her as a "tramp" and constantly accused her of promiscuity, although she had had no sexual experience. After a while, having endured the shouting contests with her mother, she saved enough money to move out on her own.

During this turmoil, Elizabeth's boss separated from his wife, and was in the midst of a painful divorce. Elizabeth offered solace and sympathy. He reciprocated with encouragement and support. They began dating, and married soon after his divorce was finalized. Naturally, her mother berated her for marrying a divorced man, particularly one who was ten years older and a lapsed Catholic.

Her father remained detached. One year after Elizabeth married, he died.

Five years later, her marriage was disintegrating, and Elizabeth was blaming her husband. She saw him as a "thief" who had stolen her youth. She was only nineteen when she met him, and needed to be taken care of so badly that she traded in her youth for security—the years when she could have been "experimenting with what I wanted to be, could be, should have been."

In the early stages of treatment, Elizabeth began to talk of her most recent and most important affair: David was twelve years older, a longtime family friend, and the parish priest. He was someone known and loved by her whole family, especially by her mother. He was the only man to whom Elizabeth felt attached. This was the only relationship that she did not control. On and off, over a period of two years, he would abruptly terminate the affair and then restore it. Later, she confessed to her psychiatrist that David was the father of her child. Her husband was apparently unaware.

Elizabeth became more withdrawn. Her relationship with her husband, who was frequently away traveling, deteriorated. She became more alienated from her mother and brothers and allowed her few friendships to flounder. She resisted attempts to include her husband in therapy, feeling he and her doctor colluded and favored "his side." So, even therapy reinforced her belief that she couldn't trust or place faith in anyone because she would only be disappointed. All her thoughts and feelings seemed to be laden with contradictions, as if she were in a maze of dead end paths. Her sexuality seemed the only way out of the maze.

Her therapist was often the target of her complaints because he was the one "in control." She would yell at him, accuse him of being incompetent, threaten to stop therapy. She hoped he would get mad, yell back, and stop seeing her, or become defensive and plead with her to stay. But he did neither, and she railed against his unflappability as evidence that he had no feelings.

Even though she was accustomed to her husband's frequent business trips, she started to become more frightened when left alone. During these trips, for reasons not yet clear to her, she slept on the floor. When he returned, she raged constantly at him. She became more depressed. Suicide became less an option than a destiny, as if everything were leading to that end.

Elizabeth's vision of reality became more frail: She yearned to be psychotic, to live in a fantasy world where she could "go anywhere" in her mind. The world would be so far removed from reality, no one—not even the best psychiatrist—could get to her and "see what's underneath."

In her daydreams she envisioned herself protected by a powerful, handsome man who actively appreciated all of her admirable qualities and was endlessly attentive. She fantasized him to be a previous teacher, her doctor, the family veterinarian, and, eventually her psychiatrist. Although all of these men were perceived as powerful, they were also recognized as unavailable. But in her fantasies they were overwhelmed by her charm and drawn irresistibly to her. When reality did not follow her script—when an attractive man did not aggressively flirt with her—she became despondent and self-loathing, feeling she was not attractive enough.

Everywhere she looked she saw women who were prettier, smarter, better. She wished her hair was prettier, her eyes a different color, her skin clearer. When she looked in a mirror, she saw distortions—not a beautiful young woman, but an old hag with sagging breasts, a wide waist, plump calves. She despised herself for being a woman, whose only value was her beauty. She longed to be a man, "so my mind would count."

In her second year of outpatient therapy, Elizabeth experienced several losses, including the death of a favorite uncle to whom she had grown close. She was haunted by recurring dreams and nightmares that she could not remember when she awoke. She became more depressed and suicidal and was finally hospitalized.

With the aid of hypnosis she began recalling traumatic childhood events, opening up a Pandora's box of flooding memories. She recalled severe physical beatings by her mother and then began to remember her mother's sexual abuses—episodes in which her mother had inflicted vaginal douches and enemas and fondled her in order to "clean" her vagina. These rituals began when Elizabeth was about eight, shortly after her sister's death, and persisted until puberty. She recalled looked into her mother's face and noting a benign, peaceful expression; these were the only times Elizabeth could remember when it appeared her mother was not disapproving.

Elizabeth recalled sitting alone in the closet for many hours and often sleeping on the floor for fear of being molested in her bed. Sometimes she would sleep with a ribbon or award she had won in school. She found these actions to be comforting and continued them as an adult, often favoring the floor for the bed and spending time alone in a quiet room or dark closet.

In the hospital Elizabeth spoke of the different sides to her personality. She described fantasies of being different people and even gave these personality fragments separate names. These persona were independent women, had unique talents, and were either admired by others or snobbishly avoided social contacts. Elizabeth felt that whenever she accomplished something or was successful, it was due to the talents of one of these separate personality segments. She had great difficulty integrating these components into a stable self-concept.

Nonetheless, she did recognize these as personality fragments and they never took over her functioning. She suffered no clear periods of amnesia or dissociation, nor were her symptoms considered aspects of multiple personality disorder—although this syndrome is frequently associated with BPD.

Elizabeth used these "other women" to express the desires and feelings that she herself was forced to repress. Believing she was worthless, she felt these other partial identities were separate, stronger entities. Gradually, in the hospital, she learned that this simply was not so, that they were always a part of her. Recognizing this gave her relief and hope. She began to believe that Elizabeth was stronger and less crazy than she had imagined and this marked a turning point in her life.

But she could not claim victory yet. Like a field officer, she marshaled the separate sides of her personality to stand before her and found that they could not go into battle without a unifying resolve. Elizabeth—the core of her being—was still afraid of change, love, and success, still searched in vain for safety, still fled from relationships.

Coming to accept herself was going to be more difficult than she had ever imagined.

After six weeks Elizabeth left the hospital and continued in outpatient care. As she improved, her relationship with her husband deteriorated. But instead of blaming herself, as she typically did, she attempted to resolve the differences and to stay with him. She distanced herself from unhealthy contacts with family members. She developed more positive self-esteem. She began taking college courses and did remarkably well, achieving academic awards. She slept with her first award under her pillow, as she did when she was a child. Later she entered law school and received merit awards for being the top student in her class. She developed new relationships, with men and women, and found she was comfortable in these, without having to be in control. She became more content with her own femaleness.

Little by little, Elizabeth started to heal. She felt "the curtains raising." She compared the feeling to looking for a valuable antique in a dark attic filled with junk—she knew that it was in there somewhere but couldn't see it because of all the clutter. When she finally did spot it, she couldn't get to it because it was "buried under a pile of useless garbage." But now and then she could see a clear path to the object, as if a flash of lightning had illuminated the room for a brief instant.

The flashes were all too brief. Old doubts reared up like ugly faces in an amusement-park fun house. Many times she felt as if she were going up a down escalator, struggling up one step only to fall down two. She kept wanting to sell herself short and give credit to others for her accomplishments. But her first real challenge—becoming an attorney—was almost a reality. Five years before, she wouldn't have been able to talk about school, much less have had the courage to enroll. The timbre of her depressions began to change: Her depression over failing was now evolving, she recognized, into a fear of success.

GROWING AND CHANGING

"Change is real hard work!" Elizabeth often noted. It requires conscious retreat from unhealthy situations and the will to build healthier foundations. It entails coping with drastic interruption of a long-established equilibrium.

Like Darwinian evolution, individual change happens almost imperceptibly, with much trial and error. The individual instinctively resists mutation. He may live in a kind of swamp, but it is *his* swamp; he knows where everything is, what's in all the bogs and marshes. To leave his swamp means venturing into the unknown and perhaps falling into an even worse swamp.

For the borderline, whose world is so clearly demarcated by black and white parameters, the uncertainty of change is even more threatening. She may clutch at one extreme for fear of falling uncontrollably into the abyss of another. The borderline anorexic, for example, starves herself out of the terror that eating—even a tiny morsel—will lead to total loss of control and irrevocable obesity.

The borderline's fear of change involves a basic distrust of her "brakes." In healthier people these psychic brakes allow a gradual descent from the pinnacle of a mood or behavior to a gentle stop in the "gray zone" of the incline. Afraid that his set of brakes won't hold, the borderline believes that he won't be able to stop, that he will slide out of control to the bottom of the hill.

Change, however gradual, requires the alteration of automatic reflexes. The borderline is in a situation much like a child playing a game of "Make me blink" or "Make me laugh," struggling valiantly to stifle a blink or a laugh while another child waves her hand or makes funny faces. Such reflexes, established over many years, can be adjusted only with conscious, motivated effort.

Adults sometimes engage in similar contests of will. A man who encounters an angry barking dog in a strange neighborhood resists the automatic reflex to run away from the danger. He recognizes that if he runs, the dog would likely catch up with him and present an even greater threat.

Instead, he does the opposite—he stands perfectly still, allows the dog to sniff him, and then walks slowly on.

Psychological change requires resisting unproductive automatic reflexes and consciously and willfully choosing other alternatives—choices that are different, even opposite, from the automatic reflex—sometimes these new ways of behaving are frightening, but they hopefully are more efficient ways of coping.

The Beginnings of Change: Self-Assessment

Change for the borderline involves more of a fine-tuning than a total reconstruction. It is best initiated gradually, with only slight alterations at first, and must begin with self-assessment: One must first recognize his current position and understand in which direction modification must progress.

Imagine personality as a series of intersecting lines, each representing a specific character trait (see figure 5–1). The extremes of each trait are located at the ends of the line, with the middle ground in the center. For example, on the "conscientiousness at work" line, one end might symbolize obsessive over concern or "workaholicism" and the other end "irresponsibility"; the middle would be an attitude somewhere between these two extremes, such as "calm professionalism." On the "concern about appearance" line, one end might exemplify "narcissistic attention to surface looks," and the other end, "total disinterest." Ideally, one's personality make-up would look like the spokes of a perfectly round wheel, with all these lines intersecting near their midpoints in the wheel "hub."

Of course, no one is completely centered all the time. It is important to identify each line in which change is desired and locate one's position on that line in relation to the middle. Change then becomes a process of knowing where you are and how far you want to go towards the middle. Except at the extreme ends, no particular locus is intrinsically "better" or "worse" than another. It is a matter of knowing oneself (locating oneself on the line) and moving in the adaptive direction.

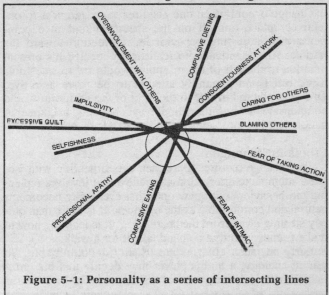

Figure 5–1: Personality as a series of intersecting lines

For example, if we isolate the "caring for others" line (see figure 5–2), one end ("self-sacrificing over concern") represents the point where concern for others interferes with taking care of oneself; such a person may need to dedicate himself totally to others in order to feel worthwhile. This position may be perceived as a kind of "selfish unselfishness," because such a person's "caring" is based on subconscious self-interest. At the other end ("don't give a damn") is a person who has little regard for others, who only "looks out for number one." In the middle is a kind of balance—a combination of concern for others and the obligation to take care of one's own needs as well. A person whose compassion trait resides in this middle zone recognizes that only by taking care of his own important needs first can he hope to help others, a kind of "unselfish selfishness."

"self-sacrificing | "don't give
overconcern"   a damn"

Figure 5–2: The "caring for others" personality trait line

Change occurs when one acquires the awareness to objectively place oneself on the spectrum and then compensate by adjusting behavior in a direction toward the middle. An individual who realistically located his present position to the left of the midpoint would try to say "no" more often and generally attempt to be more assertive. One who places himself to the right of the midpoint would compensate toward the middle by choosing a course of action that is more sensitive to the needs of others.

Practicing Change

True change requires more than experimenting with isolated attempts to alter automatic reflexes; it involves replacing old behaviors with new ones that eventually become as natural and comfortable as the old ones. It is more than quietly stealing away from the hostile dog; it is learning how to make friends with that dog and take it for a walk.

Early on, such changes are usually uncomfortable. To use an analogy, a tennis player may decide that his unreliable backhand is in need of refinement. So he embarks on a series of tennis lessons. The new techniques that he learns to improve his game initially yield poor results. The new style is not as comfortable as his old stroke. He is tempted to revert to his previous technique. Only after continuous practice is he able to eradicate his prior bad habits and adopt the more effective and eventually more comfortable new reflexes. Likewise, psychological change requires the adoption of new reflexes to replace old ones. Only after persistent practice can such a substitution effectively, comfortably, and, therefore, permanently occur.

Learning How to Limp

Change is a monumental struggle for the borderline, much more difficult than for others because of the unique features of the disorder. Splitting and the lack of object constancy (see Chapter 2) combine to form a menacing barricade against trusting oneself and others and developing comfortable relationships.

In order to initiate change, the borderline must break out of an impossible Catch-22 position: To accept himself and others, he must learn to trust; but to trust others means to accept their consistency and dependability—quite a task for someone who, like a small child, believes others "disappear" when they leave the room. "When I can't see you," said Elizabeth to her psychiatrist early in her treatment, "it's like you don't exist."

Like someone with an injured leg, the borderline must learn to limp. If he remains bedridden, his leg muscles will atrophy and contract; if he tries to exercise too vigorously, he will reinjure the leg even more severely. Instead, he must learn to limp on it—putting just enough weight on the leg to build strength gradually, but not so much as to strain it and prevent healing. Likewise, healing in the borderline requires placing just enough pressure by challenging himself to move forward.

Leaving the Past Behind

The borderline's view of the world, like that of most people, is shaped by his childhood experiences in which the family served as a microcosm of the universe. Unlike healthier individuals, however, the borderline cannot easily separate himself from other family members, nor can he separate his family from the rest of the world.

Unable to see his world through adult eyes, the borderline continues to experience life as a child—with a child's intense emotions and perspective. When a young child is punished or reprimanded, he sees himself as unquestionably bad; he cannot conceive of the possibility that mother might be having a bad day. As the healthy child matures, he sees his expanding world as more complex and less dogmatic. But the borderline remains stuck—a child in an adult's body.

"There is always one moment in childhood when the door opens and lets in the future," wrote Graham Greene in *The Power and the Glory*. In most borderlines' childhoods, the responsibilities of adulthood arrive too early; the door opens ever more widely but he cannot face the light. Or perhaps it is the unrelenting opening that makes facing it so difficult.

Change for the borderline comes when he learns to see current experiences—and review past memories—through adult "lenses." The new "vision" is akin to watching an old horror film on TV that you haven't seen in years: The movie, once so frightening on the big screen, seems tame—even silly—on a small screen with the lights on; you can't fathom why you were so scared when you saw it the first time.

When Elizabeth was well into her journey in psychotherapy, she began to look at her early childhood feelings in a different light. She began to accept them, to recognize the value of her own experience; if not for those early feelings and experiences, she realized, she would not have been able to bring the same fervor and motivation she was bringing to her new career in law. "Feelings born in my childhood," she said, "still continue to haunt me. But I'm even seeing that in a different light. The very ways I have hated I now accept as part of me."

Playing the Dealt Hand

The borderline's greatest obstacle to change is her tendency to evaluate in absolute extremes. The borderline must either be totally perfect or a complete failure; she grades herself either an "A+" or, more commonly, an "F." Rather than learning from the "F," she wears it like a scarlet letter and so makes the same mistakes again and again, oblivious to the patterns of her own behavior, patterns from which she could learn and grow.

Unwilling to play the hand that is dealt her, the borderline keeps folding every time, losing the ante, waiting to be dealt four aces. If she cannot be assured of winning, she won't play out the hand. Improvement comes when she learns to accept the hand for what it is, and recognize that, skillfully played, she can still win.

The borderline is sometimes paralyzed by indecisiveness. Various alternatives seem overwhelming and the borderline feels incapable of making any decisions. But as she matures, choices appear less frightening and may even become a source of pride and growing independence. At that point the borderline recognizes that she faces decisions which only she is capable of making. "I'm finding," Elizabeth noted, "that the roots of my indecisiveness are the beginning of success. I mean, the agony of choosing is that I suddenly see choices."

BOUNDARY SETTING:
ESTABLISHING AN IDENTITY

One of the borderline's primary goals is to establish a separate sense of identity and to overcome the proclivity to merge with others. In biological terms, it is like advancing from a parasitic life form to a state of symbiosis and even independence. Either symbiosis or independence can be terrifying, and most borderlines find that relying on themselves is like walking for the first time.

In biology the parasite's existence is entirely dependent on the host organism. If the parasitic tick sucks too much blood from the dog, the dog dies and, thus, so does the tick. Human relationships function best when they are less parasitic and more symbiotic. In symbiosis two organisms thrive better together, but may subsist independently. For example, moss growing on a tree may help the tree by shading it from direct sunlight, and help itself by having access to the tree's large supply of underground water. But if either the moss or the tree dies, the other may continue to survive, though less well. The borderline sometimes functions as a parasite whose demanding dependence may eventually destroy the person to whom he so strongly clings; when this person leaves, the borderline may be destroyed. If he can learn to establish more collaborative relationships with others, all may learn to live more contentedly.

Elizabeth's increasing comfort with others started with her relationship with her psychiatrist. After months of testing his loyalty by berating and criticizing him and threatening to terminate therapy, Elizabeth began to trust his commitment to her. She began to accept his flaws and mistakes, rather than see them as proof of the inevitability of his failing her. After a while, Elizabeth began to extend the developing trust between her therapist and herself to others in her life. And she began to accept herself, imperfections and all, just as she was accepting others the same way.

As Elizabeth continued to improve, she became more confident that she would not lose her "inner core." Where once she would squirm in a group of people, feeling self-conscious and out of place, she could now feel comfortable with others, letting them take responsibility for themselves and she for herself. Where once she felt compelled to adopt a role in order to fit into the group, she could now hold on to her more constant, immutable sense of self; now, she could "stay the same color" more easily.

Establishment of a constant identity means the ability to stand alone without relying on someone else to lean upon. It means trusting one's own judgment and instincts and then acting rather than waiting for the feedback of others and then reacting.

BUILDING RELATIONSHIPS

As the borderline forges a distinct core sense of identity, he also differentiates himself from others. Change requires an appreciation of others as independent persons and an empathy to understand their struggles. Their flaws and imperfections must not only be acknowledged but also understood as separate from the borderline himself.

The borderline must learn to integrate the positive and negative aspects of other individuals. When the borderline wants to get close to another person, he must learn to be independent enough to be dependent in comfortable, not desperate, ways. He learns to function symbiotically, not parasitically. The healing borderline develops a constancy about himself and about others; trust—of others and of his own perceptions—develops. The world becomes more balanced, more in-between.

Just as in climbing a mountain, the fullest experience comes when the climber can appreciate all the vistas: to look up and keep his goal firmly in view; to look down and recognize his progress as he proceeds. And finally, to rest, look around, and admire the view from right where he is at the moment. Part of the experience is recognizing that no one ever reaches the pinnacle; life is a continuous climb up the mountain. A good deal of mental health is being able to appreciate the journey—to be able to accept the reality of the Serenity Prayer of Saint Francis of Assisi: "God grant me the serenity to accept the things I cannot change, the courage to change the things I can, and the wisdom to know the difference."

Recognizing the Effect of Change on Others

When an individual first enters therapy, he often does not understand that it is "he," not others, who must make changes. However, when he does make changes, important people in his life must also adjust. Stable relationships are dynamic, fluctuating systems that have attained a state of equilibrium. When one person in that system makes significant changes in his ways of relating, others must adjust in order to recapture homeostasis, or the state of balance. If these readjustments do not occur, the system may collapse and the relationships may shatter.

For example, a woman consults a psychotherapist for severe depression and anxiety. In therapy, she rails against her alcoholic husband, whom she blames for her feelings of worthlessness. Eventually she recognizes her own role in the crumbling marriage—her own need to have others become dependent upon her, and her fears of reaching for independence. She begins to blame her husband less. She develops new, independent interests and relationships. She stops her crying episodes; she stops initiating fights over his drinking; the equilibrium of the marriage is altered.

The husband may now find that the situation is much more uncomfortable than it was before. He escalates his drinking in an unconscious attempt to reestablish the old equilibrium and have his wife return to her martyred, care-taking role. He accuses her of seeing other men and tries to disrupt their relationship, now intolerable to him.

Or, he too can begin to see the necessity for change and his own responsibility in maintaining this pathological equilibrium. He may take the opportunity to see his own actions more clearly, and reevaluate his own life, just as he has seen his wife do. Participation in therapy may be a valuable experience for everyone affected.

The more interesting and knowledgeable Elizabeth became, the more ignorant her husband seemed to her. The more open-minded she became—the more gray she was able to perceive in a situation—the more black and white he became in order to reestablish equilibrium.

She felt that she was "leaving someone behind." That person was her—or, more closely, a part of her she no longer needed or wanted. She was, in her words, "growing up."

As Elizabeth's treatment wound down, she met less regularly with her doctor, yet still had to contend with other important people in her life. She fought with her brother, who refused to own up to his drug problem. He accused her of being "uppity," of "using her new psychological crap as ammunition." They argued bitterly over the lack of communication within the family. He told her that even after all the "shrinks," she was still "screwed up." She fought with her mother, who remained demanding, complaining, and incapable of showing her any love. She contended with her husband, who professed his love but continued to drink heavily and criticize her desire to pursue her education. He refused to help with their son and after a while she suspected his frequent absences were related to an affair with another woman.

Finally, Elizabeth began to recognize that she did not have the power to change others. She began to accept them for who they were, love them as best she could, and go on with her own life. She recognized the need for new friends and new activities in her life. Elizabeth called this "going home."

Communicating with the Borderline

"All right . . . what do you want me to say?
Do you want me to say it's funny, so you can
contradict me and say it's sad? Or do you want
me to say it's sad so you can turn around and
say no, it's funny. You can play that damn little game any way you want to, you know!"
—From *Who's Afraid of Virginia Woolf?*
by Edward Albee

Confronting borderline behavior is problematic for everyone
in regular contact with the borderline personality because,
as we have seen, their explosions of anger, rapid mood
swings, suspiciousness, impulsive actions, unpredictable
outbursts, self-destructive actions and inconsistent communications are upsetting to everyone around them.

In this chapter we will describe a consistent, structured
method of communicating with borderlines—the SET system that can be easily understood and adopted by family,
friends, and therapists for use on a daily basis, and which
may even help in convincing a borderline to consider treatment (see Chapter 7).

Developed by the staff of the Comprehensive Treatment
Unit of Saint John's Mercy Medical Center in St. Louis, the
SET system evolved as a structured framework of communication with the borderline in crisis. During such times,
communication with the borderline is hindered by his im-
penetrable, chaotic internal force field, characterized by three

major feeling states: terrifying aloneness, feelings of being misunderstood, and overwhelming helplessness.

As a result, concerned individuals are often unable to reason calmly with the borderline and instead are forced to confront outbursts of rage, impulsive destructiveness, self-harming threats or gestures, and unreasonable demands for caretaking. SET responses can serve to address the underlying fears, dilute the borderline conflagration, and prevent a "meltdown" into greater conflict.

Although SET was developed for the borderline in crisis, it can also be useful for others who require concise, consistent communication, even when not in crisis.

SET COMMUNICATION

"SET"—Support Empathy Truth—is a three-part system of communication. During confrontations of destructive behavior, important decision-making sessions, or other crises, interactions with the borderline should invoke all three of these elements.

The "S" stage of this system, "Support," invokes a personal statement of concern. "I am sincerely worried about how you are feeling" is an example of a Support statement. The emphasis is on the speaker's own feelings and is essentially a personal pledge to try to be of help.

With the "Empathy" segment, one attempts to acknowledge the borderline's chaotic feelings: "How awful you must be feeling. . . ." It is important not to confuse Empathy with sympathy ("I feel so sorry for you. . . ."), which may elicit rage over perceived condescension. Also, Empathy should be expressed in a neutral way with minimal personal reference to the speaker's own feelings. The emphasis here is on the borderline's painful experience, not the speaker's. A statement like "I know just how bad you are feeling" invites a mocking rejoinder that, indeed, you do not know, and only aggravates conflict.

The "T" statement, representing "Truth" or reality, emphasizes that the borderline is ultimately responsible for his life and that others' attempts to help cannot preempt this primary responsibility. While Support and Empathy are subjective statements acknowledging how the principals feel, Truth statements show recognition that a problem exists and address the practical issue of what can be done to solve it. "Well, what are you going to do about it?" is one essential Truth response. Other characteristic Truth expressions refer to actions that the speaker feels compelled to take in response to the borderline's behaviors, which should be expressed in a matter-of-fact, neutral fashion ("Here's what happened. . . . These are the consequences. . . . This is what I can do. . . . What are you going to do?"). But they should be stated in a way that avoids blaming and sadistic punishing ("This is a fine mess you've gotten us into!" "You made your bed; now lie in it!"). The Truth part of the "SET" system is the most important and the most difficult for the borderline to accept since so much of his world excludes or rejects realistic consequences.

Communication with the borderline should attempt to include all three messages. However, even if all three parts are stated, the borderline may not integrate all of them. Predictable responses result when one of these levels is either not clearly stated or is not "heard."

For example, when the Support stage of this system is bypassed, the borderline characteristically accuses the other of not caring or not wanting to be involved with him. The borderline then tends to tune out further exchanges on the basis that the other person does not care, or may even wish him harm. The accusation from a borderline that, "You don't care!" usually suggests that the Support statement is not being integrated.

The inability to communicate the Empathy part of the message leads to feelings that the other person does not understand what the borderline is going through. ("You don't know how I feel.") Here, the borderline will justify his rejection of the communication by saying he is misunderstood. Since the other person cannot appreciate the pain, his responses can be devalued. When either the Support or the Empathy overtures are not accepted by the borderline, further communications are not heard.

When the Truth element is not clearly expressed, a more dangerous situation emerges. The borderline interprets others' acquiescence in ways he finds most comfortable for his needs, usually as confirmation that others really can be responsible for him, or that his own perceptions are universally shared and supported. The borderline's fragile merger with these other people eventually disintegrates when the relationship is unable to sustain the weight of his unrealistic expectations. Without clearly stated Truth and confrontation, the borderline continues to be overly entangled with others. His needs gratified, the borderline will insist that all is well or, at least, that things will get better. Indeed, the evidence for this enmeshment is often a striking, temporary absence of conflict: the borderline will exhibit less hostility and anger. However, when his unrealistic expectations are eventually frustrated, the relationship collapses in a fiery maelstrom of anger and disappointment.

BORDERLINE DILEMMAS

The SET principles can be used in a variety of settings in attempts to defuse unstable situations. Following are some typical borderline predicaments in which the SET strategy may be used.

Damned If You Do, and Damned If You Don't

Borderline confusion often results in contradictory messages to others. Frequently, the borderline will communicate one position with words, but express a contradictory message with behavior. Although the borderline may not be consciously aware of this dilemma, he frequently places a friend or relation in a no-win situation in which the other person is condemned no matter which way he goes.

Case 1: Gloria and Alex. Gloria tells her husband Alex that she is forlorn and depressed. She says she plans to kill herself but forbids him from seeking help for her.

In this situation, Alex is confronted with two contradictory messages: 1. Gloria's overt message, which essentially states, "If you care about me, you will respect my wishes and not challenge my autonomy to control my own destiny and even die, if I choose," and 2. the opposite message, conveyed in the very act of announcing her intentions, which says, "For God's sake, if you care about me, help me, and don't let me die."

If Alex ignores Gloria's statements, she will accuse him of being cold and uncaring. If he attempts to list reasons why she should not kill herself, she will frustrate him with relentless counter-arguments and will ultimately condemn him for not truly understanding her pain. If he calls the police or her doctor, he will be rejecting her requests and proving that she cannot trust him.

Because Gloria doesn't feel strong enough to take responsibility for her own life, she looks to Alex to take on this burden. She feels overwhelmed and helpless in the wake of her depression. By drawing Alex into this drama, she is making him a character in her own scripted play, with an uncertain ending to be resolved not by herself, but by Alex. She faces her ambivalence about suicide by turning over to him the responsibility for what will happen to her.

Further, Gloria splits off the negative portions of her available choices and projects them onto Alex, preserving for herself the positive side of the ambivalence. No matter how Alex responds, he will be criticized. If he does not actively intercede, he is uncaring and heartless and she is "tragically misunderstood." If he tries to stop her suicide attempts, he is controlling and insensitive, while she is bereft of her self-respect.

Either way, Gloria envisions herself a helpless and self-righteous martyr—a victim who has been deprived by Alex of achieving her full potential. As for Alex, he is damned if he does and damned if he doesn't!

SET principles may be helpful in confronting a difficult situation like this. Ideally, Alex's responses should embrace all three sides of the SET triangle.

Alex's "S" statement should be a declaration of his commitment to Gloria and his wish to help her. If they can identify the specific areas of concern that are adding to her anguish, he could suggest solutions or proclaim his willingness to help: "I am very concerned about how bad you are feeling and want to help because I love you. I think some of this might be related to the problems you've been having with your boss. Let's discuss some of the alternatives. Maybe you could ask for a transfer. Or if the job is causing you this much difficulty, I want you to know that it's okay with me if you want to quit and look for another job.''

The ''E'' statement should attempt to convey Alex's awareness of Gloria's current pain and his understanding of how such extreme circumstances might lead her to contemplate ending her life: ''The pressure you've been under these past several months must be getting unbearable. All of this agony must be bringing you to the edge, to a point where you feel like you just can't go on any more.''

The most important part of Alex's ''T'' statement should identify his untenable ''damned-if-he-does and damned-if-he-doesn't'' dilemma. He should also attempt to clarify Gloria's ambivalence about dying by acknowledging that in addition to that part of her that wants to end her life, another part of her wishes to be saved and helped. Alex's ''T'' responses might be something like: ''I recognize how bad you are feeling and your wish to die. I know you said that if I cared at all for you, I should just leave you alone. But if I cared, how could I possibly sit back and watch you destroy yourself? Your telling me about your suicidal plans tells me that, as much as you wish to die, there is at least some part of you that doesn't want to die. And it is to that part that I feel I must respond. I want you to come with me to see a doctor to help us with these problems.''

Depending on the immediacy of the circumstances, Alex should insist that Gloria be psychiatrically evaluated soon or, if she is in imminent danger, he should take her to an emergency room or seek help from police or paramedics.

At this juncture Gloria's fury may be exacerbated as she blames Alex for forcing her into the hospital. But Truth statements should remind Gloria that she is there not so much because of what Alex did, but because of what Gloria did—threatening suicide. The borderline may frequently need to be reminded that others' reactions to him are based primarily on what *he* does, and that *he* must take responsibility for the consequences, rather than blaming others for realistic responses to his behavior.

When the immediate danger has passed, subsequent ''T'' statements should refer to Gloria's unproductive patterns of handling stress and the need to develop more effective ways of dealing with her life. Truth considerations should also include how Gloria's and Alex's behaviors affect each other and their marriage. Over time they may be able to work out a system of responding to each other, either on their own or within therapy, that will fulfill the needs of both.

This kind of problem is especially common within families of borderlines who display prominent self-destructive behaviors. Delinquent or suicidal adolescents, alcoholics, and anorexics may present similar no-win dilemmas to their families. They actively resist help, while behaving in obviously self-destructive ways. Usually, direct confrontation that precipitates a crisis is the only way to help. Some groups, such as Alcoholics Anonymous, recommend standardized confrontational situations in which family, friends, or coworkers, together with a counselor, confront the patient with his addictive behavior and demand treatment.

"Tough Love" groups believe that true caring is forcing the individual to face the consequences of his behaviors rather than protecting him from them. Tough Love groups for parents of teenagers, for example, may insist that an adolescent drug abuser either be hospitalized or barred from the home. This type of approach emphasizes the Truth element of the SET triangle but may ignore the Support and Empathy segments. Therefore, these systems may be only partially successful for the borderline, who may go through the motions of change that Truth confrontations force on him; underneath, however, the lack of nurturing and trust provided by Support and Empathy hinder his motivation for dedicated and lasting change.

Feeling Bad About Feeling Bad

Borderlines typically respond to depression, anxiety, frustration, or anger with more layers of these same feelings. Because of the borderline's perfectionism and tendency to perceive things in black-and-white extremes, he attempts to obliterate unpleasant feelings rather than understand or cope with them. When he finds that he cannot simply erase these bad feelings, he becomes even more frustrated or guilty. Since feeling bad is unacceptable, he feels bad about feeling bad. When this makes him feel worse, he becomes caught in a seemingly bottomless downward spiral.

One of the goals for the borderline's therapists and other close relations is to crack through these successive layers to locate the original feeling and help the borderline accept it as part of himself. The borderline must learn to allow himself the luxury of "bad" feelings without rebuke, guilt, or denial.

Case 2: Neil and Friends. Neil, a fifty-three-year-old bank officer, has had episodes of depression for more than half his life. Neil's parents died when he was young, and he was reared mostly by his much older and unmarried sister, who was cold and hypercritical. She was a religious zealot who insisted he attend church services daily, and frequently accused him of sinful transgressions.

Neil grew up to become a passive man, dominated by his wife. He was reared to believe that anger was unacceptable and denied ever feeling angry at others. He was hard-working and respected at his job, but received little affection from his wife. She rejected his sexual advances, which frustrated and depressed him. Neil would initially get angry at his wife for her rejections, then feel guilty and get angry at himself for being angry, and then lapse into depression. This process permeated other areas of Neil's life. Whenever he experienced negative feelings, he would pressure himself to end them. Since he could not control his inner feelings, he became increasingly disappointed and frustrated with himself. His depression worsened.

Neil's friends tried to comfort him. They told him they were behind him and were available whenever he wanted to talk. They empathized with his discomfort at work and his problems in dealing with his wife. They pointed out that "he was feeling bad over feeling bad," and that he should straighten up. This advice, however, didn't help; in fact, Neil felt worse because he now felt he was letting his friends down on top of everything else. The harder he tried to stop his negative feelings, the more he felt like a failure, and the more depressed he became.

SET statements could help Neil confront this dilemma.

Neil received much Support and Empathy from his friends, but their Truth messages were not helpful. Rather than trying to erase his unpleasant emotions (an all-or-none proposition), Neil must understand the necessity of accepting them as real and appropriate.

Further Truth statements would acknowledge the reasons for Neil's passive behavior and the behaviors of his wife and others in his life. He must recognize that, to some degree, he places himself in a position of being abused by others. Although he can work to change this situation in the future, he must now deal with the way things are currently. This means recognizing his anger, that he has reasons to be angry, and that he has no choice but to accept his anger, for he cannot make it disappear, at least not right away. Though he may regret the presence of unacceptable feelings, he is powerless to change them (a ditum similar to those used by Alcoholics Anonymous). Accepting these uncomfortable feelings means accepting himself as an imperfect human being and relinquishing the illusion that he can control uncontrollable factors. If Neil can accept his anger, or his sadness, or any unpleasant feeling, the "feeling bad about feeling bad" phenomenon will be short-circuited. He can move on to change other aspects of his life.

The borderline trapped in this dilemma will often break free when he least expects it—when he relaxes, becomes less obsessive and self-demanding, and learns to accept himself. It is no coincidence that the borderline who seeks a healthy love relationship more often finds it when he is least desperate for one and more engaged in self fulfilling activities. For it is at this point that he is more attractive to others and less pressured to grasp at immediate and unrealistic solutions to loneliness.

The Perennial Victim

The borderline frequently involves himself in predicaments in which he becomes a victim. Neil, for example, perceived himself as a helpless character upon whom others act. The borderline frequently is unaware that his behavior is provocative or dangerous, or that it may in some way invite persecution. The woman who continually chooses men who abuse her is typically unaware of the patterns she is repeating. The borderline's split view of himself includes a special, entitled part and an angry, unworthy part that masochistically deserves punishment, although he may not be consciously aware of one side or the other. In fact, a pattern of this type of "invited" victimization is often a solid indication of BPD pathology.

Although being a victim is most unpleasant, it can also be a very appealing role. A helpless waif, buffeted by the turbulent seas of an unfair world, is very attractive to some people. A match between the helpless waif and one who feels a strong need to rescue and take care of others satisfies needs for both parties. The borderline finds a "kind stranger" who promises complete and total protection. And the partner fulfills his own desire to feel strong, protective, important, and needed—to be the one to "take him away from all this."

Case 3: Annette. Born to a poor black family, Annette lost her father at a very young age when he abandoned the family. A succession of other men briefly occupied the "father" chair in the home. Eventually her mother remarried, but her second husband was also a drinker and carouser. When Annette was about eight, her stepfather began sexually abusing her and her sister. Annette was afraid to tell her mother, who gloried in the family's finally achieving some financial security. So Annette allowed it to continue—for her mother's sake.

At seventeen, Annette became pregnant and married the baby's father. She managed to graduate from high school, where her grades were generally good, but other aspects of her life were in turmoil: Her husband drank and ran with other women. After awhile, he began beating her. She continued to bear more of his children, complaining and enduring—for the children's sake.

After six years and three children, Annette's husband left her. His departure prompted a kind of anxious relief—the wild ride was finally over, but concerns over what to do next loomed ominously.

Annette and the kids tried to make things work, but she felt constantly overwhelmed. Then she met John, who was about twenty-five years older (he refused to tell her his exact age) and seemed to have a genuine desire to take care of her. He became the good father Annette never had. He encouraged and protected her. He advised her on how to dress and how to talk. After awhile, Annette became more self-confident, got a good job, and began enjoying her life. A few months later, John moved in—sort of. He lived with her on weekends but slept away during the week because of work assignments that made it "more convenient to sleep at the office."

Deep inside, Annette knew John was married, but she never asked. When John became less dependable, stayed away more and generally became more detached, she held in her anger. On the job, however, this anger surfaced, and she was passed over for many promotions. Her supervisors said that she lacked the academic qualifications of others and that she was abrasive sometimes, but Annette wouldn't accept those explanations. Incensed, she attributed the rejections to racial discrimination. She became more and more depressed and eventually entered the hospital.

In the hospital, Annette's racial sensitivities exploded. Most of the doctors were white, as were most of the nurses and most of the other patients. The hospital decor was "white" and the meals were "white." All of the anger built up over the years was now focused on society's discrimination against blacks. By concentrating exclusively on this global issue, Annette avoided her own personal demons.

Her most challenging target was Harry, a music therapist on staff at the hospital. Annette felt that Harry (who was white) insisted on playing only "white" music, and that his looks and whole demeanor embodied "whiteness." Annette vented her fury on this therapist, and she would stalk away angrily from the music therapy sessions.

Although Harry was frightened by the outbursts, he sought out Annette. His Support statement reflected his personal concern about Annette's progress in the hospital program. Harry expressed his Empathy for Annette by voicing his recognition of how frustrating it feels to be discriminated against, and cited his own experiences as one of the only Jews in his educational program. Then Harry attempted to confront the Truth, or reality, issues in Annette's life, pointing out that railing against racial discrimination was useless without a commitment to work toward changing it. Annette's need to remain a victim, Harry said, shielded her from assuming any responsibility for what happened in her life. She could feel justified in cursing the fates rather than bravely investigating her own role in continuing to be used by others. By wrapping herself in a veil of righteous anger, Annette was avoiding any kind of frightening self-examination or confrontation that might induce change, and thereby was perpetuating her impotency and helplessness.

At the next music therapy session, Annette did not stalk out of the room. Instead, she berated Harry and the other patients. She suggested different songs to play. At the following meeting the group agreed to play some civil-rights protest songs of Annette's choosing.

Harry's response exemplified SET principles and would have been useful for Annette's boss, her friends—anyone who faced her angry outbursts on a regular basis.

SET communication can free a borderline or anyone who is locked into a victim role by pointing out the advantages of being a victim (being cared for, appearing blameless for bad results, disavowing responsibility) and the disadvantages (abdicating autonomy, maintaining obsequious dependency, remaining fixated and immobile amidst life's dilemmas). The borderline "victim" must, however, hear all three parts of the message; otherwise the impact of the message will be lost. If "the Truth will set you free," then Support and Empathy must accompany it to insure it will be heard.

Quest for Meaning

Much of the borderline's dramatic behavior is related to his interminable search for something to fill the emptiness that continually haunts him. Relationships and drugs are two of the mechanisms the borderline uses to beat the loneliness and to capture a sense of existing in a world that feels real.

Case 4: Rich. "I guess I just love too much!" said Rich in describing his problems with his girlfriend. He was a thirty-year-old divorced man who experienced a succession of disastrous affairs with women. He would cling obsessively to these women, showering them with gifts and attention. Through them he felt whole, alive, and fulfilled. But he demanded from them—and from other friends—total obedience. In this way he felt in control, not only of them but more importantly of his own existence.

He became distraught when these women acted independently. He cajoled, insisted, and threatened. To stave off the omnipresent sense of emptiness, he attempted to control others; if they refused to comply with his wishes, Rich became seriously depressed and out of control. He would turn to alcohol or drugs to recapture his sense of being or authenticity. Sometimes he would pick fights or cut himself when he feared he was losing touch with his sensory or emotional feelings. When the anger and pain no longer brought changes, he would take up with another woman who perceived him as "misunderstood" and merely needing "the love of a good woman." Then the process would start all over again.

Rich lacked insight into his dilemma, insisting that it was always "the bitches' fault." He dismissed his friends as not caring or not understanding—they were not able to convey Support or Empathy. The women he became involved with were initially sympathetic, but lacked the Truth component. Rich needed to be confronted with all three aspects.

In this situation, the "S" message would convey caring about Rich. The "E" part would accept without challenge Rich's feeling of "loving too much" but would also help him understand his sense of emptiness and his need to fill it.

The Truth message would attempt to point out the patterns in Rich's life that seem to repeat endlessly. Truth should also help Rich see that he uses women as he does drugs and self-mutilation—as objects or maneuvers to relieve numbness and feel whole. As long as Rich continues to search outside himself for inner contentment, he will remain frustrated and disappointed, because he cannot control outside forces and especially others, as he can control himself. For instance, despite his most frenzied efforts to regulate her, a new girlfriend will retain some independence outside the realm of Rich's control. Or, he could lose a new job due to economic factors that may eliminate the position. But Rich *can* control his own creative powers, intellectual curiosity, and so on. Independent personal interests—books, hobbies, arts, sports—can serve as reliable and enduring sources of satisfaction, which cannot easily be taken away.

Search for Constancy

Adjusting to a world that is continually inconsistent and untrustworthy is a major problem for the borderline. The borderline's universe lacks pattern and predictability. Friends, jobs, and skills can never be relied upon. The borderline must keep testing and retesting all of these aspects of his life; he is in constant fear that a trusted person or situation will change into its total opposite—absolute betrayal. A hero becomes a devil; the perfect job becomes the bane of his existence.

Case 5: Pat and Jake. Pat was an attractive twenty-nine-year-old woman in the process of divorcing her second husband. As with her first husband, she accused him of being an alcoholic and of abusing her. Her lawyer, Jake, saw her as an unfortunate victim in need of protection. He called her frequently to be sure she was all right. They began to have lunch together. As the case proceeded, they became lovers. Jake moved out of his house and away from his wife and two sons. Though not yet divorced, Pat moved in with him.

At first, Pat admired Jake's intelligence and expertise. Where she felt weak and defenseless, he seemed "big and strong." But over time she became increasingly demanding. As long as Jake was protective, Pat cooed. But when he began to make demands, she became hostile. She resented his going to work and particularly his involvement in other divorce cases. She resisted his visits to his children and accused him of choosing them over her. She would initiate brutal fights, which often culminated in her rushing out of the house to spend the night with a male "platonic friend."

Pat lacked object constancy (see Chapter 2 and Appendix B). Friendships and love relationships had to be constantly tested because she never felt secure with any human contact. Her need for reassurance was insatiable. She had been through countless other relationships in which she first appeared ingenuous and in need of caretaking and then tested them with outrageous demands. The relationships all ended with precisely the abandonment she feared; then she would repeat the process in her next romance.

At first, when Pat perceived Jake as supportive and reassuring, she idealized their relationship. But when he exhibited signs of functioning separately, she became enraged, cursing and denigrating him. When he was at the office, she would call him incessantly because, as she said, she was "forgetting him." To her friends, Jake sounded like two completely different people—for Pat, he was.

SET confrontations of object inconstancy require recognition of this borderline dilemma. Support statements must convey that caring is constant, unconditional. Unfortunately, the borderline personality, or Pat in this case, has difficulty grasping that she does not need to earn acceptance continuously. She is in constant fear that Support could be withdrawn if at any point she displeases.

The Empathy message should confirm an understanding that Pat has not yet learned to trust Jake's attempts at reassurance. Jake tries to communicate his awareness of the horrific anxieties Pat is experiencing and how frightening it is for her to be alone.

Truth declarations must include attempts to reconcile the split parts. Jake has to explain that he cares for Pat all the time, even when he is frustrated by her. He must also declare his intention not to allow himself to be abused. Capitulation to Pat's demands will only result in more demands. Trying to please and satisfy Pat is an impossible task, for it is never finished—new insecurities will always arise. Truth will probably mandate ongoing therapy for both of them, if their relationship is to continue.

The Rage of Innocence

Borderline rage is often terrifying in its unpredictability and intensity. It may be sparked by relatively insignificant events and appear without warning. It may be directed at previously valued people. The threat of violence frequently accompanies this anger. All of these features make borderline rage much different from typical anger.

In an instant, Pat could transform from a docile, dependent, childlike woman into a demanding, screaming harpy. On one occasion she suggested that she and Jake have a quiet lunch together. But when Jake told her he had to go to the office, she suddenly began screaming at him, inches from his face, accusing him of being inconsiderate of her needs. She viciously attacked his manhood, his failures as a husband and father, and his profession. She threatened to report him to the Bar Association for misconduct. When Jake's attempts to placate her failed, he would silently leave the scene, which infuriated Pat even more. But when he returned, both would act as if nothing had ever happened.

SET principles must first of all address safety issues. Volatility must be contained. In the scenario above, Jake's Support and Empathy messages should come first, though Pat will probably reject them as insincere. In such cases it is imprudent for Jake to continue to argue that he cares and understands that she is upset. He must move immediately to Truth statements, which must first declare that no one will be hurt. He must firmly tell her to back off, to allow some physical distance. He can inform her of his wish to communicate calmly with her. If she will not allow this, he can state his intention of leaving until the situation quiets down, at which point they can resume discussions. He must try to avoid physical conflict, despite Pat's provocations. Although unconsciously Pat may actually want Jake to physically overpower her, this need is based on unhealthy experiences from her past, and will likely later be used to criticize him more.

Truth statements made during angry confrontations are often better directed toward the underlying dynamics than toward the specifics of the clash. Further debate about whether taking Pat to lunch is more important than going to the office will probably be unproductive. However, Jake might address Pat's apparent need to fight and her possible wish to be overpowered and hurt. He might also confront Pat's behavior as a need to be rejected. Is she so fearful of anticipating rejection that she is precipitating it in order to "hurry up and get it over with"? The primary Truth message is that this behavior is driving Jake away. He may ask if this is really what Pat wants.

Fatal Attraction

In the movie *Fatal Attraction*, Dan Gallager is a happily married man who engages in a tempestuous affair with Alex Forrest, an attractive, apparently successful career woman. Though the film does not explore Alex's character in depth, it is obvious that the filmmakers had several borderline traits in mind when creating the role. Alex has few (if any) friends and a history of several job changes. When Dan attempts to terminate the relationship, Alex becomes enraged at being abandoned and panicked at the thought of being alone. From a sophisticated, carefree seductress she changes into a clinging, dependent, suicidal child. In desperation, she impulsively cuts her wrists and manipulates Dan into staying with her.

From this point, the film moves through a series of dramatic and sometimes violent confrontations between Alex, Dan, and Dan's wife, Beth. The film's story of an apparent borderline personality's descent into madness—and how others dealt with it—must have touched some kind of chord of recognition in the American public for the movie was one of the biggest box office successes of 1987 and the most popular video rental of 1988.

In a sense, the film itself was a borderline creation in its Hollywood portrayal of black-and-white "good guys" and "bad guys": Alex was portrayed as a stereotype "evil villainess," rather than a complex, anguished, mentally ill woman; Dan was the "good husband who happened to stray" rather than a weak-willed adulterer who had at least an indirect role in the ensuing violence. It was no accident that, like old-time white-hat, black-hat westerns, the movie typically elicited cheers and boos in movie theatres.

Dan's reactions to Alex ignored basic SET principles, which inevitably led all three main characters to the film's bloody ending. The following script would not have been nearly so sensational (nor probably as successful) as the original, but might have saved everyone a great deal of anguish:

When confronted by Alex's bleeding wrists, Dan should have first expressed his Support and concern for Alex—"I am extremely shocked and upset at what you have done, and want to help you.'' Further Support would have included aiding in cleansing and bandaging her wounds.

His Empathy message would have reflected understanding of her anguish. "You are obviously very upset, more than I realized, and must be hurting very badly inside." Encouraging her to talk about her loneliness—what she was feeling and why—would have been helpful "E" input.

In the film, Dan—due to his own character flaws—was unable to confront the Truth side of either Alex's or his own actions, and thus became hopelessly ensnared. Truth messages would have included reminders that, even though both had had the fling as equal partners, Alex knew he was married and would return to his family. More importantly, it was Alex, not he, who was behaving self-destructively. Depending on the seriousness of Alex's cuts, he might have insisted that she seek medical attention. He would have strongly encouraged her to seek psychiatric care (while acknowledging that he could not force her to do so). He would also have admitted his role in what is clearly a destructive relationship, and the obvious need to terminate it. In all of these Truth messages, Dan would have tried to delineate the borders—between what he can do and what Alex can do.

THE NEED FOR CONSISTENCY

All Truth statements must, indeed, be true. For the borderline, already living in a world of inconsistencies, it is much worse to make idle threats about the consequences of an action than to passively allow inappropriate behaviors to continue. In *Fatal Attraction,* Alex was used to resisting rejection by manipulating others. For Dan to say he was going to end the relationship without unequivocally doing so was destructive. Of course, he didn't know that following the termination of an intense relationship, the borderline is unable to "be just friends"—an "in-between" relationship that the borderline finds intolerable.

Because the borderline has such difficulty with equivocation, intentions must be backed up with clear, predictable actions. A parent who threatens his adolescent with revocation of privileges for certain behaviors, for example, and then does not carry out his promises, exacerbates the problem. A therapist who purports to set limits for therapy—establishing fees, limiting phone calls, etc.—but then does not follow through, invites increased borderline testing.

Borderlines are often reared in situations in which threats and dramatic actions are the only ways to achieve what is wanted. Just as the borderline perceives acceptance as conditional, so rejection can also be seen this way. The borderline feels that if only he is attractive enough, or smart enough, or rich enough, or demanding enough, he will ultimately get what he wants. The more outrageous behavior is rewarded, the more the borderline will employ such maneuvers.

Although the SET principles were developed for working with borderline patients, they can be useful for dealing with others. When communications between people are stalled, SET can help focus on messages that are not being successfully transmitted. If an individual feels that he is not supported or respected, or that he is misunderstood, or if he refuses to address realistic problems, specific SET steps can be taken to reinforce these flagging areas. In today's complex world, a clear set of communication principles that includes both love and reason are necessary to overcome the tribulations of borderline chaos.

Seeking Therapy

"I'm gonna give him one more year, and then I'm going to Lourdes."
—Woody Allen, talking about his psychiatrist in *Annie Hall*

Dr. Smith, a nationally-known psychiatrist, had called me about his niece. She was depressed and in need of a good psychotherapist. He was calling to say that he had recommended me.

Arranging an appointment was difficult. She could not rearrange her schedule to fit my openings. So, I juggled and rearranged by schedule to fit hers. I felt pressure to be accommodating and brilliant, so that Dr. Smith's faith in me would be justified. I had just opened my practice and desperately needed some validation of my professional skills. Yet, I knew that these feelings were a bad sign: I was nervous.

Julie was strikingly attractive. Tall and blonde, she easily could have been a model. A law student, she was twenty-five, bright, and articulate. She arrived ten minutes late and neither apologized for nor acknowledged this slight on her part. When I looked closely, I could see that her eye makeup was a little too heavy, as if she were trying to conceal a sadness and exhaustion inside.

Julie was an only child, very dependent on her successful parents, who were always travelling. Because she couldn't stand being alone, she cruised through a series of affairs. When a man would break off the relationship, she'd become extremely depressed until embarking on the next affair. She was now "between relationships." Her most recent man had left her and "there was no one to replace him."

It wasn't long before her treatment established a routine. As a session would near its end, she'd always bring up something important, so our appointments would end a little late. The phone calls between sessions became more frequent and lasted longer.

Over the next six weeks we met once a week, but then mutually agreed to increase the frequency to twice a week. She talked about her loneliness and her difficulties with separations, but continued to feel hopeless and alone. She told me that she often burst out in rage against her friends, though these outbursts were hard to imagine because she was so demure in my office. She had problems sleeping, her appetite decreased, and she was losing weight. She began to talk about suicide. I prescribed antidepressant medications for her, but she felt even more depressed and was unable to concentrate at school. Finally, after three months of treatment, I recommended hospitalization, which she reluctantly accepted. Clearly, more intense work was needed to deal with this unremitting depression.

The first time I saw the anger was the day of her admission, when Julie was describing her decision to come to the hospital. Crying softly, she spoke of the fear she had experienced when explaining her hospitalization to her father.

Then suddenly her face hardened, and she said, "Do you know what that bitch did?" A few moments passed before I realized that Julie was now referring to Irene, the nurse who had admitted her to the unit. Furiously, Julie described the nurse's lack of attention, her awkwardness with the blood pressure cuff, and a mix-up with a lunch tray. Her ethereal beauty mutated into a face of rage and terror. I jumped when she pounded the table.

After a few days, Julie was galvanizing the unit with her demands and tirades. Some of the nurses and patients tried to calm and placate her; others bristled when she threw tantrums (and objects) and walked out of group sessions.

"Do you know what *your* patient did this morning, doctor?" asked one nurse as I stepped onto the floor. The accent was clearly on "your," as if I were responsible for

Julie's behavior and deserved the staff's reprimands for not controlling her. "You're overprotective. She's manipulating you. She needs to be confronted."

I immediately came to my own—and Julie's—defense. "She needs support and caring," I replied. "She needs to be reparented. She needs to learn trust." How dare they question my judgment! Do I dare question it?

Throughout the first week, Julie had complained about the nurses, the other patients, the other doctors. She said I was understanding and caring and I had much greater insight and knowledge than the other therapists she had seen.

Julie needed a weekend pass to run errands. The nurses were skeptical; they didn't know her well enough. She hadn't talked much about herself either to them or in group therapy. She was talking only to her doctor; but she needed the pass, so I authorized it.

She returned drunk and with scratches on her wrist. Though the nurses never actually said, "I told you so," their haughty looks were unmistakable and insufferable. I began to avoid them even more than I had until that point. I resumed Julie's therapy on an individual basis, and dropped her from group sessions.

On the following weekend she needed another pass. When I turned down the request, she exploded. "I thought you trusted me," she said. "I thought you understood me. All you care about is power. You just love to control people."

Maybe she's right, I thought. Perhaps I am too controlling, too insecure. Or was she just attacking my vulnerable areas, my need to be perceived as caring and trusting? Was she just stoking my guilt and masochism? Was she the victim here, or was I?

"I thought you were different," she said. "I thought you were special. I thought you really cared." The problem was, I thought so too.

A few weeks later, I gave her another pass. She returned, intoxicated and tearful, after a sleazy liaison with a stranger in a bar. The situation was becoming clearer to me. She was begging for limits and controls and structure, but couldn't acknowledge this dependency. So she acted outrageously to make controls necessary, and then got angry and denied her wish for them.

I could see this, but she couldn't. Gradually I stopped looking forward to seeing her. Whenever I visited her, I was reminded of my failure, and I found myself wishing that she would either get well or disappear. When she voiced the opinion that maybe her roommate's doctor would be better for her, I interpreted this as a means of running away from herself and the real issues at stake. A change would be counterproductive for her, I knew, but silently I hoped that she would change doctors for my sake. She still talked of killing herself, and I guiltily fantasized that it would be almost a relief for me if she did. Her changes had changed me from a masochist to a sadist.

During her third week in the hospital, another patient hanged himself while home on a pass. Frightened, Julie flew into a rage: "Why didn't you and the staff know he was going to kill himself?" she screamed. "How could you let him do it? Why didn't you protect him?"

Julie was devastated. Who was going to protect *her?* Who would make the pain go away? I finally realized that it would have to be Julie. No one else lived inside her skin. No one else could totally understand and protect her. It was starting to make some sense, both to me and to Julie.

She could see that no matter how hard she tried to run away from her feelings, she could not escape being herself. Even though she wanted to run away from the bad person she thought she was, she had to learn to accept herself, flaws and all. Ultimately, she would see that just being herself was okay.

Julie's anger at the staff gradually moved to the suicide victim, who "didn't give himself a chance." When she saw his responsibility, she began to see hers. She discovered that people who really cared about her did not let her do whatever she wanted, as her parents had done; sometimes caring meant setting limits. Sometimes it meant telling her what she didn't want to hear. And sometimes it meant reminding her of her accountability to herself.

It wasn't long before all of us—Julie, the staff, and I—began working together. I stopped trying so hard to be likeable, wise, and unerring; it was more important to be consistent and reliable—to *be there*.

After seven weeks, Julie left the hospital; she was still

lonely and afraid, but she didn't need to hurt herself any more. Even more important, she was accepting the fact that she could survive loneliness and fear but could still care about herself.

After a while, Julie found a new man who really seemed to care about her. As for me, I learned some of the same things as Julie did—that distasteful emotions determine who I am to a great extent and that accepting these unpleasant parts of myself helps me to better understand my patients.

Therapists who treat borderline personality often find that the rigors of treatment place a great strain on their professional abilities, as well as on their patience. Treatment sessions are stormy, frustrating, and unpredictable. The treatment period proceeds at a snail-like pace; most psychotherapists agree that effective treatment requires at least several years. More than 90 percent of borderline patients who seek therapy eventually drop out prematurely.[1]

Treatment is so difficult because the borderline responds to it in much the same way as to other personal relationships. The borderline will see the therapist as caring, capable, and honest one moment, deceitful, devious, and uncaring the next.

In therapy, the borderline can be extremely demanding, dependent, and manipulative. It's not uncommon for a borderline patient to telephone incessantly between sessions and then appear unexpectedly in the therapist's office, threatening bodily harm to himself unless the therapist meets with him immediately.

Angry tirades against the therapist and the process of therapy are common. Often, the borderline can be very perceptive about the sensitivity of the therapist and eventually goad him into anger, frustration, self-doubt, and hopelessness.

Given the wide range of possible causes of BPD, and the extremes of behavior involved, there is a predictably wide range of treatment methods: (1.) psychoanalytically-oriented psychotherapy; (2.) so-called ''supportive'' psychotherapy; (3.) special forms of psychotherapy, such as group, family, and expressive (art, music, dance) psychotherapy; (4.) psychopharmacological (drug) therapy; and (5.) hospital-based therapy. These methods can overlap (for example, group therapy can be exploratory or supportive). Because they have met with variable levels of success, there is wide debate within the mental health profession on the most appropriate methods of treatment.

Other forms of therapy, such as behavior modification and hypnosis, are not usually employed in treating the borderline, except in special circumstances. For carefully selected patients, hypnotherapy, for example, can be useful to help recall past traumas. However, because a trance state may induce an unstructured or unfamiliar state of consciousness, severe panic or psychosis may be precipitated in the borderline patient who is inappropriately selected for this treatment.

THE BORDERLINE ON THE COUCH

During the forties and fifties, individual psychoanalysis was considered the premier treatment for all mental illnesses. However, as the concept of the borderline personality disorder became more defined over the ensuing decades, it became increasingly clear that traditional psychoanalysis was not effective for those patients diagnosed as borderline.

In classical psychoanalysis patients are asked to engage in "free association"—speaking freely on whatever comes to mind, without censoring thoughts, and without specific guidance from the analyst. Patients typically explore early childhood memories and associate to dreams and random thoughts.

For the borderline patient, however, such unstructured therapy can be devastating. In classical psychoanalysis, the borderline's defenses are attacked, but he lacks the resources to replace them; transference feelings toward the therapist and for others can be so intense that they take on psychotic proportions.

Analysts soon discovered that borderlines became worse "on the couch." The stimulation of analysis, which could be therapeutic for the healthier patient, produced panic in the borderline. Anxieties emerged that could not be controlled or solved. Borderline patients sometimes lost contact with reality.

Over the past thirty years the borderline syndrome has increasingly displaced other psychiatric illnesses as one of the most common maladies encountered by clinical psychiatrists. Formerly masquerading as traditional neurotics, borderline patients were initially engaged in classical psychoanalysis, which led to disastrous results. But as the shift in the psychiatric population became more widely recognized, modifications of traditional psychoanalytic techniques were developed. Such therapy adjustments may be termed "psychoanalytically-oriented" or "psychodynamic." In essence they retain the theoretical base of psychoanalysis but without the trappings. The couch, the "silent" analyst, and free association are replaced by face-to-face communications with a more interactive therapist.

During the fifties, other treatment approaches also became more accepted. Nonanalytic individual therapies acquired their own scientific bases. Family and group techniques were recognized to have value in the treatment of a variety of mental illnesses.

The advent of the "pharmacotherapy era" brought promise of cure through drug treatments. Hospital care was evolving, providing a controlled, structured, and intensive treatment milieu that obliterated the notion of the hospital as warehousing asylum.

GOALS OF THERAPY

All treatment approaches strive for a common goal: more effective functioning in a world that is experienced as less mystifying, less harmful, and more pleasurable. The process usually involved developing insight into the unproductiveness of current behavior. This is the easy part. More difficult is the process of reworking old reflexes and developing new ways of dealing with life's stresses.

The most important part of any therapy is the relationship between the patient and therapist. This interaction forms the foundation for trust, object constancy, and emotional intimacy. The therapist must become a trusted figure, a mirror to reflect a developing, consistent identity.

Starting with this relationship, the borderline learns to extend to others appropriate expectations and trust.

The primary goal of the therapist is to work toward losing (not keeping) his patient. This is accomplished by directing the patient's attention to certain areas for examination, not by controlling him. Though the therapist serves as the navigator, pointing out landscapes of interest and helping to re-route the itinerary around storm conditions, it is the patient who must remain firmly in the pilot's seat. Family and loved ones are also usually included on this journey. A major objective is for the patient to return home and improve relationships, not to abandon them.

Some people are fearful of psychiatry and psychotherapy, perceiving the process as a form of "mind control" or behavior modification perpetrated on helpless, dependent patients who are molded into robots by bearded, Svengali-like mesmerists. The aim of psychotherapy is to help a patient individuate and achieve more freedom and personal dignity. Unfortunately, just as some people erroneously believe that you can be hypnotized against your will, so some believe you can be therapized against your will. Such irrational fears may deprive people of opportunities to escape self-imposed captivity and achieve self-acceptance.

LENGTH OF THERAPY

Because of the prominence of psychoanalysis, which characteristically requires several years of treatment, most people view any form of psychotherapy as being extended and drawn out, and, therefore, very expensive. The addition of medications and specialized treatments (such as so-called "time-limited" therapy) to the therapeutic armamentarium are responses to the need for practical and affordable treatment methods. Broken bones heal and infections clear up, but scars on the psyche may require much longer treatment.

If therapy terminates quickly, one may question if it was too superficial. If it extends for many years, one may wonder if it is merely intellectual game playing that enriches psychotherapists while financially enslaving their dependent and helpless patients.

How long should therapy last? The answer depends on the specific goals. Resolution of specific, targeted symptoms—such as depression, severe anxiety, or temper outbursts—may be accomplished in relatively brief time spans, such as weeks or months. If the goal is more profound restructuring, much more time will be required.

Therapy may be interrupted. It is not unusual for borderlines to engage in several separate rounds of therapy, with different therapists and different techniques. Breaks in therapy may be useful to solidify ideas, or to try out new insights, or merely to catch up with life and allow time to grow and mature. Financial limitations, significant life changes, or just a need for a respite from the intensity of treatment may mandate a time out.

Usually, the borderline requires years of therapy, in order to achieve substantive changes in functioning. When the changes come slowly, it can be difficult to determine whether more work should proceed, or if "this is as good as it gets." The therapist must consider both the borderline's propensity to run from confrontations with his unhealthy behaviors, and his tendency to cling dependently to the therapist (and others).

For some borderlines therapy may never formally end. They may derive great benefit from continuing intermittent contacts with a trusted therapist. Such arrangements would be considered "refueling stops" on the road to greater independence, provided the patient does not rely on these contacts to drive his life.

HOW PSYCHOTHERAPY WORKS

Therapy is the process of discussing the past and present in order to discover patterns that can affect the future. Whether in an individual, group, or family setting, the therapist tries to guide clients to examine their experience and serves as a touchstone for experimenting with new behaviors. Ultimately, the patient begins to accept his own choices in life and to change his self-image as a helpless pawn moved by forces beyond his control. Much of this process emerges from the primary relationship between therapist and patient.

During therapy, both develop intense feelings, called "transference" and "countertransference."

Transference

Transference refers to the patient's unrealistic projections onto the therapist of feelings and attitudes previously experienced from other important persons in the patient's life. For example, a patient may get very angry with the doctor, based not on the doctor's communications, but on feelings that the doctor is much like his mother, who in the past elicited much anger from him. By itself, transference is neither negative or positive; but it is always a distortion, a projection of past emotions onto current objects.

Borderline transference is likely to be extremely inconsistent, just like other aspects of the patient's life. The borderline will see the therapist as caring, capable, and honest one moment, deceitful, devious, and unfeeling the next. These distortions make the establishment of an alliance with the therapist most difficult. Yet establishing and sustaining this alliance is the most important part of any treatment.

In the beginning stages of therapy, the borderline both craves and fears closeness to the therapist. He wants to be taken care of but fears being overwhelmed and controlled. He attempts to seduce the doctor into taking care of him and rebels against his attempts "to control his life." As the therapist remains steadfast and consistent in withstanding his tirades, object constancy develops—the borderline begins to trust that the therapist will not abandon him. From this beachhead of trust, the borderline can venture out with new relationships and establish more trusting contacts. Initially, however, such new friendships can be difficult to sustain for the borderline who, in the past, may have learned that the formation of new alliances was disloyal. He may even fear that his mate, friend, or therapist may become jealous and enraged if he broadens his social contacts.

As the borderline progresses, he settles into a more comfortable, trusting dependency. As he prepares for termination, however, there may again be a resurgence of turmoil in the relationship. He may pine for his previous ways of functioning and resent needing to proceed onward; he may feel like a tiring swimmer who realizes he has already swum more than halfway across the lake but must now continue on to the other side before resting.

At this point the borderline must also deal with his separateness and recognize that he, not the therapist, has effected change. Like Dumbo, who first attributes his flying ability to his "magic feather" but then realizes it is due to his own talents, the borderline must begin to recognize and accept his own abilities to function independently. And he must develop new coping mechanisms to replace the ones that no longer work.

As the borderline improves, the intensity of the transference diminishes. The anger, impulsive behaviors, and mood changes—often directed at, or for the benefit of, the therapist—become less severe. Panicky dependency may gradually wither and be replaced by a growing self-confidence; anger erupts less often, replaced by greater determination to be in charge of one's own life. Impatience and caprice diminish, because the borderline begins to develop a separate sense of identity that can evolve without the need for attachment.

Countertransference

Countertransference refers to the therapist's own emotional reactions to the patient, which are based less on realistic considerations than on the therapist's past experiences and needs. An example is the doctor who perceives the patient as more needy and helpless than is truly the case because of the doctor's need to be a caretaker, to perceive himself as compassionate, and to avoid confrontation.

The borderline is often very perceptive about others, including the therapist. This sensitivity often provokes the therapist's own unresolved feelings. The doctor's needs for appreciation, affection, and control can sometimes prompt him into inappropriate behavior. He may be overly protective of the patient and encourage dependency. He may be overly controlling, demanding that the patient carry out his directions. He may complain of his own problems and induce the patient to take care of him. He may even enter into a sexual relationship with the patient "to teach intimacy." The therapist may rationalize all these as necessary for a "very sick" patient, but in reality they are satisfying his own needs.

The borderline can provoke feelings of anger, frustration, self-doubt, and a hopelessness in the therapist that mirrors his own. Goaded into emotions that challenge his professional self-worth, the therapist may experience genuine countertransference hate for the patient and view him as untreatable. Treatment of the borderline personality can be so infuriating that the term "borderline" has been inaccurately used sometimes by professionals as a derogatory label for any patient who is extremely irritating or who does not respond well to therapy. In these cases "borderline" more accurately reflects the countertransference frustration of a therapist than a scientific diagnosis of his patient.

THE PATIENT-THERAPIST "FIT"

All of the treatments described in this chapter can be productive approaches to the borderline patient. None have proved to be superior to the others. No therapeutic techniques have been shown to be uniformly curative in all cases. The only factor that seems to correlate consistently with improvement is a positive, mutually respectful relationship between patient and therapist.

Even when a doctor is successful in treating one or many borderline patients, this does not guarantee automatic success in treating others. The primary determining factor of success is usually a positive, optimistic feeling shared between the participants—a kind of patient-therapist "fit."

A good fit is difficult to define precisely, but refers to the abilities of both the patient and therapist to tolerate the predictable turbulence of therapy, while maintaining a sturdy alliance while therapy takes place.

The Therapist's Role

Because treatment of BPD may entail a combination of several therapies—individual, group and family psychotherapies, medications, and hospitalization—the therapist's role in treatment may be as varied as the different therapies available. The doctor may be confrontational or nondirective; he may either spontaneously exhort and suggest, or initiate fewer interactions and expect the patient to assume a heavier burden for the progress of psychotherapy. More important than the particular doctor or treatment method is the feeling of comfort and trust enjoyed by both patient and therapist. Both must sense commitment, reliability, and true partnership from the other.

To achieve this feeling of mutual comfort, both patient and doctor must understand and share common objectives. They should agree upon methods and have compatible styles. Most importantly, the therapist must recognize when he is treating a borderline patient.

The therapist should suspect that he is dealing with BPD when he takes on a patient whose past psychiatric history includes contradictory diagnoses, multiple past hospitalizations, or trials of many medications. The patient may report being "kicked out" of previous therapies and becoming persona non grata in the local emergency room, having frequented the E.R. enough times to have earned a nickname (such as "Overdose Eddie") from the medical staff.

The experienced doctor will also be able to trust his countertransference reactions to the patient. Borderlines usually elicit very strong emotional reactions from others, including therapists. If early on in the evaluation, the therapist experiences strong feelings of wanting to protect or rescue the patient, of responsibility for the patient, or of extreme anger toward the patient, he should recognize that his intense responses may signal reactions to a borderline personality.

Choosing a Therapist

Therapists with differing styles may perform equally well with borderlines. Conversely, doctors who possess special expertise or interest in BPD and who generally do well with borderline patients cannot guarantee success with every patient.

A patient can choose from a variety of mental health professionals. Though psychiatrists have years of training in psychotherapy techniques (and, as physicians, are the only professionals capable of dealing with concurrent medical illnesses, prescribing medications, and arranging hospitalization), other skilled professionals—psychologists, social workers, counselors, psychiatric nurse-clinicians—may also attain expertise in psychotherapy with borderline patients.

In general, a therapist who works well with BPD possesses certain qualities that a prospective patient can usually recognize. He should be experienced in the treatment of BPD and remain tolerant and accepting in order to help the patient develop object constancy (see Chapter 2). He should be flexible and innovative, in order to adapt to the contortions through which therapy with a borderline may twist him. He should possess a sense of humor or at least a clear sense of proportion to present an appropriate model for the patient and to protect himself from the relentless intensity that such therapy requires.

Just as the doctor evaluates the patient during the initial assessment interviews, so should the patient evaluate the doctor to determine if they can work together profitably.

First, the patient should consider whether he is comfortable with the therapist's personality and style. Will he be able to talk with him openly and candidly? Is he too intimidating, too pushy, too wimpy, too seductive?

Secondly, do his assessment and goals coincide with the patient's? Treatment should be a collaboration in which both parties share the same view and use the same language. What should therapy hope to achieve? How will you know when you get there? About how long should it take?

Finally, are the recommended methods acceptable to the patient? There should be agreement on the type of psychotherapy advocated and the suggested frequency of meetings. Will the doctor and patient meet individually or together with others? Will there be a combination of approaches, which might include, say, individual therapy on a weekly basis, along with intermittent conjoint meetings with the spouse? Will therapy be more exploratory or more supportive? Will medications or hospitalization likely be employed? What kind of medicines and which hospitals?

This initial assessment period usually requires at least one interview, often more. Both the patient and the doctor should be evaluating their ability and willingness to work with the other. Such an evaluation should be recognized as a kind of "no-fault" interchange: It is irrelevant and probably impossible to blame the therapist or the patient for the inability to establish rapport. It is necessary only to determine whether a therapeutic alliance is possible. However, if a patient continues to find every psychotherapist he sees unacceptable, his commitment to treatment should be questioned. He should consider the possibility that he is merely avoiding therapy, and should perhaps choose an admittedly imperfect doctor and get on with the task of getting better.

Obtaining a Second Opinion

Once therapy is underway, it is not unusual for treatment to stop and start, or for the form of therapy to change over time. Adjustments may be necessary because the borderline may require changes in his treatment as he progresses.

Sometimes, however, it is difficult to distinguish when therapy is stuck from when it is working through painful issues; it is sometimes difficult to separate dependency and fear of moving on from the agonizing realization of unfinished business. At such times there will arise a question of whether to proceed along the same lines or to take a step back and regroup. At this point a consultation with another doctor may be indicated. Often the treating therapist will suggest this, but sometimes the patient must consider this option on his own.

Although the patient may fear that a doctor is offended by a request for consultation, a competent and secure therapist would not object or be defensive about such a request. It is, however, an area for exploration in the therapy, in order to assess whether the patient's wish for a second evaluation might constitute a running away from difficult issues or represent an unconscious angry rebuke. A second opinion may be helpful for both the patient and the doctor in providing a fresh outlook on the process of treatment.

Getting the Most from Therapy

Appreciating treatment as a collaborative alliance is the most important step in maximizing therapy. The borderline frequently loses sight of this primary principle. Instead, he sometimes approaches treatment as if the purpose were to please the doctor or to fight with him, to be taken care of or to pretend to have no problems.

The borderline may need to be frequently reminded of the parameters of therapy. He should understand the ground rules, including the doctor's availability and limitations, the time and resource constraints, and the agreed upon mutual goals.

The patient must not lose sight of the fact that he is bravely committing himself, his time, and his resources to the frightening task of trying to understand himself better and to effect alterations in his life patterns. Honesty in therapy is therefore of paramount importance for the *patient's* sake. He must not conceal painful areas or play games with the therapist to whom he has entrusted his care. He should abandon his need to control, or wish to be liked by, the therapist. In the borderline's quest to satisfy a presumed role, he may lose sight of the fact that it is not his obligation to please the therapist but to work with him as an equal.

Most important, the patient should always feel that he is actively collaborating in his treatment. He should avoid either the extreme of assuming a totally passive role, completely controlled by the doctor, or that of becoming a competitive, contentious rival, unwilling to listen to contributions from the therapist. Molding a viable relationship with the therapist becomes the borderline's first and, initially, most important task in embarking on a journey toward mental health.

INDIVIDUAL THERAPIES

Most clinicians divide individual therapy approaches into exploratory and supportive techniques. Though both styles overlap, they are distinguished by the intensity of therapy and the strategies utilized.

Exploratory Therapy

Exploratory psychotherapy, as recommended by Otto Kernberg, James Masterson and others for treatment of borderlines, is a modification of classical analysis. Sessions are usually conducted three or more times per week. This form of individual therapy is more intensive than supportive therapy, and has a more ambitious goal—to alter personality structure. The therapist provides little direct guidance to the patient, utilizing confrontation instead to point out the destructiveness of specific behaviors and to interpret unconscious behaviors in the hopes of eradicating them.

As in less intensive forms of therapy, a primary focus is on here-and-now issues. Genetic reconstruction, with its concentration on childhood and developmental issues, is important, but emphasized less than in classical psychoanalysis. The major goals in the early stages of treatment are to diminish behaviors that are self-destructive and disruptive to the treatment process (including prematurely terminating therapy), to solidify the patient's commitment to change, and to establish a trusting, reliable relationship between patient and doctor. Later stages emphasize the processes of formulating a separate, self-accepting sense of identity, establishing constant and trusting relationships, and tolerating aloneness and separation (including those from the therapist) adaptively.[2, 3] Of course, these stages overlap.

Transference in exploratory therapy is more intense than in supportive therapy. Dependency on the therapist, together with idealization and devaluation, are experienced more passionately, as in classical psychoanalysis. Most therapists estimate the duration of treatment to be a minimum of four years, but often six to ten years.

Supportive Therapy

Supportive individual therapy, the most common form of therapy used for borderline personality, is usually conducted on a once weekly basis. Direct advice, education, and reassurance replace the confrontation and interpretation of unconscious material typically used in exploratory therapy.

This approach is meant to be less intense and to bolster more adaptive defenses. In supportive psychotherapy the doctor may reinforce suppression, discouraging discussion of painful memories that cannot be resolved. Rather than question the roots of minor obsessive concerns, the therapist may encourage them as "hobbies" or minor eccentricities. For example, a patient's need to keep his apartment spotless may not be dissected as to causes, but be acknowledged as a useful means to retain a sense of mastery and control when feeling overwhelmed. This contrasts with psychoanalysis, in which the aim is to analyze defenses and then eradicate them.

Focusing on current, more practical issues, supportive therapy tries to quash suicidal and other self-destructive behaviors rather than to explore them fully. Impulsive action and chaotic interpersonal relationships are identified and confronted, without necessarily acquiring insight into the underlying factors that cause them.

Supportive therapy most often continues on a once weekly frequency for four to five years before proceeding on an as-needed basis. Intermittent contacts may continue indefinitely and the therapist's continued availability may be very important. Therapy gradually terminates when other lasting relationships form, and when outside, gratifying activities become more important in the patient's life.

In supportive therapy the patient tends to be less dependent on the therapist and to form a less intense transference. Though some clinicians argue that this form of therapy is less likely to institute lasting change in borderline patients, others have induced significant behavioral modifications in borderline patients with this kind of treatment.[4]

Dr. Ralph Greenson used a combination of supportive and exploratory therapies in his treatment of Marilyn Monroe. Though supportive therapy had only recently come into vogue in the late fifties (and the borderline diagnosis was more than twenty years from being formally adopted), he sensed Marilyn's need for something more consoling and structured than classical psychoanalysis.

He allowed Marilyn to become friendly with his family, even to the extent of having her as a guest in his home. He told Norman Rosten that she needed both supportive and analytical psychotherapy because "the treatment has to suit the patient." In her case, he felt she needed actual experiences in her present life to compensate for the emotional deprivation of her childhood.[5]

Interestingly, Freud's examination office was in his home and he often allowed contacts between his patients and his

family. But Greenson realized that allowing Marilyn to
form attachments to his family was considered profession-
ally inappropriate, though he felt it necessary for effective
treatment.

> It may seem to you that I have broken rules, but I feel
> that if I am fortunate enough, perhaps some years from
> now, Marilyn may become a psychoanalytic patient. She
> is not ready for it now. I feel I can tell you these things
> because she considers you and Hedda her closest friends
> and there must be somebody with whom I can share my
> responsibilities. By the way, I have spoken to Marilyn
> and she had given me permission to talk to you in gen-
> eral terms about herself.[6]

GROUP THERAPIES

Treating the borderline in a group makes perfect sense. A
group allows the borderline patient to dilute the intensity of
feelings directed toward one individual (such as the therapist)
by recognizing emotions stimulated by others. In a group the
borderline can more easily control the constant struggle between emotional closeness and distance; unlike individual
therapy, in which the spotlight is always on him, the borderline can attract or avoid attention in a group. Confrontations
by other group members may sometimes be more readily
accepted than those from the idealized or devalued therapist,
because a peer may be perceived as someone "who really
knows what I'm going through."

The borderline's demandingness, egocentrism, isolating
withdrawal, abrasiveness and social deviance can all be
more effectively challenged by group peers. In addition,
the borderline may accept more readily the group's expressions of hope, caring and altruism.[7,8,9]

The progress of other group members serves as a model
for growth. When a group patient attains a goal, he serves
as an inspiration to others in the group who have observed
his growth and have vicariously shared his successes. The
rivalry and competition so characteristic of borderline relationships are vividly demonstrated within the group setting and can be identified and addressed in ways that would

be inaccessible in individual therapy. Finally, a group provides a living, breathing experimental laboratory in which the borderline can attempt different patterns of behavior with other people, without the risk of penalties from the "outside world."

Because of the demands on the borderline patient in group therapy, most therapists recommend combining group with individual treatment, so as to maintain individualized support for the patient. Therapists disagree, however, on the ideal composition of the groups. Some feel that groups composed exclusively of borderlines are most effective because they allow maximum identification with others experiencing similar struggles. But most believe that borderlines fare better in a mixed group consisting of other borderline patients and healthier patients who serve as models for more adaptive ways of functioning. Nonborderline patients also benefit from this mix, for they may have difficulty accessing their own emotions. The borderline can stimulate feelings and serve as a model for expressing emotions.[10]

Yet, research on group therapy as a treatment for BPD is surprisingly spare. The very features that make group therapy a potentially attractive treatment for borderlines are the very reasons many such patients resist group settings. The demand for individual attention, envy and distrust of others, the contradictory wish for, and fear of, intense closeness, all contribute to the reluctance of many borderline patients to enter group treatment. Higher functioning borderlines can tolerate these frustrations of group therapy and use the "in vivo" experiences to address defects in interrelating. Lower-functioning borderlines, however, often won't join and, if they do, won't stay.

The borderline patient may experience significant obstacles in group therapy. His self-absorption and lack of empathy often prevent involvement with others' problems. If the borderline's concerns are too deviant or the material too intense, he may feel isolated and disconnected. For example, a patient who discusses childhood incest, or deviant sexual practices, or severe chemical abuse may fear that he may shock the other group members. And, indeed, some members may have difficulty relating to upsetting material. When several borderlines are in a group, they may share the feeling that their needs are not being met by the therapist. In such situations they may attempt to take care of each other in ways they wished they were being cared for. This may lead to contacts between patients outside of the group setting and perpetuation of dependency needs as they try to "treat" each other. Romances or even business dealings between group members usually end disastrously, because these patients will not be able to use the group objectively to explore the relationship, which is often a continuation of unproductive searches to be cared for.

Elaine, a twenty-nine-year-old woman, was referred for group therapy after two years of individual psychotherapy. The oldest of four daughters, Elaine was sexually abused by her father, staring around age five and continuing over ten years. She perceived her mother as weak and ineffectual and her father as demanding and unable to be pleased. In adolescence, she became the caretaker for the whole family. As her sisters married and had children, Elaine remained single, entering college and then graduate school. She had few girlfriends and dated infrequently. Her only romantic relationships involved two married men, much older than she, who supervised her work. Most of her off-work time was devoted to organizing family functions, caring for ill family members, and generally taking care of family problems.

Isolated and depressed, Elaine sought individual therapy. Recognizing the limitations in her social functioning, she later requested a referral for group therapy. There, she quickly established a position as the helper for the others, denying any problems of her own. She often became angry with the therapist, whom she perceived as not helpful enough to the group members.

The group members encouraged Elaine to examine issues she had previously been unable to confront—her constant scowling and intimidating facial expressions and her subtly angry verbal exchanges. Although this process took many frustrating months, she was eventually able to acknowledge her disdain for women, which became obvious in the group setting. Elaine realized that her anger at the male therapist was actually transferred anger from her father and recognized her compulsive attempts to repeat this father-daughter relationship with other men. Elaine began to experiment in the group with new ways of interacting with men and women. Simultaneously, she was able to pull back from the suffocating immersion in her family's problems.

FAMILY THERAPIES

Family therapy is a very logical approach to the treatment of the borderline patient, who often emerges from disturbed relationships with parents engaged in persistent conflicts that may eventually entangle the borderline's own spouse and children.

Though family therapy is sometimes implemented with outpatients, it is most often invoked as part of in-hospital treatment, where individual and other supportive therapies can be simultaneously administered. In addition, the family's resistance to participating in treatment can be more easily overcome following a crisis situation that necessitated the hospitalization.

The families of borderlines often balk at treatment for several reasons. They may feel guilt over the patient's problems and fear being blamed for them. Also the bonds in borderline family systems are often very strong; family members are often suspicious of outsiders and fearful of change. Though family members may be colluding in the perpetuation of the patient's behaviors (consciously or unconsciously), the attitude of the family is often, "Make him better, but don't blame us and, most of all, don't change us."[11]

Yet it is imperative to gain some support from the family, for without it therapy may be sabotaged. For adolescents and young adults, family therapy involves the patient and his parents, and sometimes his siblings. For the adult borderline who is married or involved seriously in a romantic relationship, family therapy will often include the spouse or lover and sometimes the couple's children.

The dynamics of borderline family interaction usually adopt one of two extremes—either very strongly entangled or very detached. In the former case, it is important to build an alliance with all family members, for without their support, the patient may not be able to maintain treatment independently. When the family is estranged, the therapist must carefully assess the potential impact of family involvement: If reconciliation is possible and healthy, it may be an important goal; if, however, it appears that reconciliation may be detrimental or hopelessly unrealistic, the patient may need to relinquish fantasies of reunion. In fact, mourning the loss of an idealized family interrelationship may become a major milestone in therapy.

Debbie, a twenty-six-year-old woman, entered the hospital with a history of depression, self-mutilation, alcoholism, and bulimia. Family assessment meetings revealed an ambivalent, but basically supportive relationship with her husband. The course of therapy began to focus on previously undisclosed episodes of sexual abuse by an older neighbor boy, starting when the patient was about eight years old. In addition to sexually abusing her, this boy had also forced her to share liquor with him and then would make her drink his urine from the bottle, which she would later vomit. He had also cut her when she tried to refuse his advances.

These past incidents were re-enacted in her current pathology. As these memories unfolded, Debbie became more conscious of longstanding rage at her alcoholic, passive father and at her weak, disinterested mother, whom she perceived as unable to protect her. Although she had previously maintained a distant, superficial relationship with her parents, she now requested an opportunity to meet with them in family therapy to reveal her past hurts and disappointment in them.

As she predicted, her parents were very uncomfortable with these revelations. But for the first time Debbie was able to confront her father's alcoholism and her disappointment in him and in her mother's detachment. At the same time all could confirm their love for each other and acknowledge the difficulties in expressing it. Although she recognized there would be no significant changes in their relationship, Debbie felt she had accomplished much and was more comfortable in accepting the distance and failures in the family interactions.

Therapeutic approaches to family therapy are similar to those for individual treatment. A thorough history is important and may include the construction of a family tree. Such a diagram may stimulate exploration of how grandparents, godparents, namesakes, or other important relatives may influence family interactions across generations.

As in individual therapy, family therapy approaches may be primarily supportive-educational or exploratory-reconstructive. In the former, the therapist's primary goals are to ally with the family; minimize conflicts, guilt, and defensiveness; and unite them in working toward mutually supportive objectives. Exploratory-reconstructive family therapy is more ambitious, directed more toward recognizing the members' complementary roles within the family system and attempting actively to change these roles.

At one point in therapy, Elaine focused on her relationship with her parents. After confronting them with the revelation of her father's sexual abuse, she continued to feel frustrated with them. Both parents refused further discussion about the abuse and discouraged her from continuing in therapy. Elaine was puzzled by their behavior—sometimes they were very dependent and clinging; other times she felt infantilized, especially when they insistently continued to refer to her by her childhood nickname. Elaine requested family meetings, to which they reluctantly agreed.

During these meetings Elaine's father gradually admitted that her accusations were true, though he continued to deny any recollection of his assaults. Her mother realized that in many ways she had been emotionally unavailable to her husband and children and recognized her own indirect responsibility for the abuse. Elaine learned for the first time that her father had also been sexually abused during his childhood. The therapy succeeded in releasing skeletons from the closet and establishing better communication in the family. Elaine and her parents began for the first time speaking to each other as adults.

EXPRESSIVE THERAPIES

Individual, group, and family therapies require patients to express their thoughts and feelings with words, but the borderline patient is often somewhat handicapped in this area, more likely to exhibit inner concerns through actions rather than words. Expressive therapies utilize art, music, literature, physical movement, and drama to encourage communication in nonverbal ways.

In art therapy, patients are encouraged to create drawings, paintings, collages, self-portraits, clay sculpture, dolls and so on that express inner feelings. In our Comprehensive Treatment Unit (CTU) at Saint John's Mercy Medical Center in St. Louis, patients are presented with a book of blank pages, in which they are invited to draw representations of a variety of experiences, such as inner secrets, closeness, or hidden fears.

Music therapy uses melodies and lyrics to stimulate feelings that may otherwise be inaccessible. Music often unlocks emotions and promotes meditation in a calm environment.

Body movement and dance use physical exertion to express emotions. In another type of expressive therapy called psychodrama, patients and the "therapist-director" act out specific problems of the patient. Bibliotherapy is another therapy technique in which patients read and discuss literature, short stories, plays, poetry, movies, and videos. Edward Albee's *Who's Afraid of Virginia Woolf?* is a popular play to read, and, especially perform, because its emotional scenes provide a catharsis as patients recite lines of rage and disappointment that reflect problems in their own lives.

Irene's chronic depression was related to sexual abuses that she had endured at an early age from her older brother and that she had only recently begun to remember. At 25 and living alone, she was flooded with recollections of these early encounters and eventually required hospitalization as her depression worsened. Because she felt overwhelmed by guilt and self-blame, she was unable to verbalize her memories to others, or allow herself to experience the underlying anger.

During an expressive-therapy program that combined art and music, the therapists worked with Irene to help her become more aware of the fury that she was avoiding. She was encouraged to draw what her anger felt like while loud, pulsating rock music played in the background. Astonishing herself, she drew penises, to which she then added mutilated disfigurements. Initially fearful and embarrassed about these drawings, she soon became more aware and more accepting of her rage and obvious wish for retaliation.

As she discussed her emotional reactions to the drawings, she began to describe her past abuse and the accompanying feelings. Eventually, she began to talk more openly, individually with doctors, and in groups, which afforded her the opportunity to develop mastery over these frightening experiences, and to place them in proper perspective.

PHARMACOTHERAPY

The efficacy of medications for treating borderline patients remains unclear. Because the borderline syndrome borders so closely on other illnesses— such as schizophrenia and depression—drugs useful for these other conditions have been tried with borderline patients. Most authorities agree that medications are more likely to be effective when specific symptoms, such as psychosis or classical depression, are overt rather than masked, and when there is a clear family history of these maladies or response to these drugs among blood relatives.

Although drugs may relieve some significantly debilitating symptoms, they are not expected to alter longstanding personality characteristics or behavior patterns. Further, pharmacotherapy must be used judiciously since borderline patients easily develop physiological or psychological drug dependencies. Of the classes of medications outlined in Appendix C, only the minor tranquilizers present a significant potential hazard of physical addiction.

One significant complication in treating borderline patients is their tendency to "split"—not only people but also treatment approaches (see Chapter 2). Some border-lines idealize psychotherapeutic approaches as the only legitimate way to improve, and denigrate pharmacotherapy as a kind of mind control designed to chemically strait-jacket them into submission. Other borderlines accept medication as the only scientific approach to curing their "chemical imbalance," and devalue psychotherapy, used by the therapist to promote dependency as a process for financial gain. When combined treatment is indicated (as is often necessary), the psychiatrist must carefully present to the patient the rationales for each approach.[12,13,14,15]

For detailed discussion of medications used in treating BPD, see Appendix C.

HOSPITALIZATION

Borderline patients constitute a significant proportion of all hospitalized psychiatric patients, and BPD is far and away the most common personality disorder encountered in the hospital setting.[16] The borderline's propensities for impulsivity, self-destructive behaviors (suicide, drug over-doses), and brief psychotic episodes are the usual acute precipitants of hospitalization.

The hospital provides a structured milieu to help contain and organize the borderline's chaotic world. The support and involvement of other patients and staff present the borderline with important feedback that challenges some of his perceptions and validates others.

The hospital minimizes the borderline's conflicts in the external world and provides greater opportunity for intensive self-examination. It also allows a respite from the intense relationships between the borderline and his outpatient therapist and permits diffusion of this intensity onto other staff members within the hospital setting. In this more neutral milieu, the patient can reevaluate his personal goals and program of therapy.

At first, the inpatient borderline typically protests admission, but by the time of discharge he is fully ensconced in the hospital setting, often fearful of discharge. He has an urgent need to be cared for, yet at the same time may become a leader of the ward, trying to control and "help" other patients. At times he appears overwhelmed by his catastrophic problems; on other occasions he displays great creativity and initiative.

Characteristically, the hospitalized borderline creates a fascinating pas de deux of splitting and projective identification (see Chapter 2) with staff members. Some staff perceive the borderline as a pathetic, but appealing gamin; others see him as a calculating, sadistic manipulator. These disparate views emerge when the patient splits staff members into all good (supportive, understanding) and all bad (confrontive, demanding) projections, much like he does with other people in his life. When staff members accept the assigned projections—both "good" ("You're the only one who understands me") and "bad" ("You don't really care; you're only in it for the paycheck")—the projective identification circle is completed: Conflict erupts between the "good" staff and the "bad" staff.

Amidst this struggle the hospitalized borderline recapitulates his external world interpersonal patterns: a seductive wish for protection, which ultimately leads to disappointment, then to feelings of abandonment, finally to self-destructive behaviors and emotional retreat.

Therapeutic approaches to the hospitalized borderline patient are distinguished primarily by the time period proposed for confinement. Although there are no clear-cut demarcations, short-term hospitalization generally extends for several weeks, but usually less than three months. Long-term hospitalization is usually at least six months but may extend as long as two to three years, and sometimes longer. All of the therapies discussed above may be integral parts of hospital care.[17]

Short-Term Hospitalization

Due to increasing hospital costs and declining insurance coverage, short-term hospitalization is more common for most psychiatric patients. However, some psychiatrists feel that brief hospitalization is preferable for all borderline patients regardless of expense or inconvenience because it minimizes opportunities for regression and avoids the development of extreme dependency, both of which occur during longer confinements.

Inpatient care usually follows crises, such as suicide attempts, violent outbursts, psychotic breaks, self-destructive episodes (chemical abuse, anorexia/bulimia, or gambling). Hospitalization is also indicated for diagnostic evaluation and consultation for the outpatient therapist when progress in therapy is stalled.[18] Short-term hospitalization may also be necessary as a preventative measure, in anticipation of impending crises. For example, a borderline patient who is overly dependent on her dying mother may benefit from a short hospital confinement in order to prepare for working through her grief and to short-circuit an anticipated suicide gesture. Fragile patients who have been maintained outside the hospital may benefit from a short hospitalization when predictable external events (especially separations), such as the finalization of a divorce, or an extended therapist's vacation, loom threateningly and anticipate disruption of an uneasy calm.

The hospital milieu focuses on structure and limit-setting. Support and positive rapport are emphasized. Treatment centers around practical, adaptive responses to turmoil. Vocational and daily living skills are evaluated. Conjoint meetings with family, when appropriate, are initiated. A formalized contract between patient and staff may help solidify mutual expectations and limits. Such a contract may outline the daily therapy program, which the patient is obligated to attend, and the patient's specific goals for the hospitalization, which the staff agrees to address with him.

The primary goals of short-term hospitalization include resolving the precipitating crises, terminating destructive behaviors, and relieving severe depression and anxiety. Personal and environmental strengths are identified and bolstered. Important therapy issues are uncovered or re-evaluated and modifications for outpatient therapy may be recommended. Deeper exploration of these issues is limited on a short-term, inpatient unit, and is more thoroughly pursued on an outpatient basis or during long-term hospitalization. Since the overriding concern is to return the patient to the outside world as quickly as possible, plans for discharge and after care commence immediately upon admission.[19]

Long-Term Hospitalization

Today, extensive hospitalization is reserved for the very wealthy or for those with exceptional insurance coverage for psychiatric illness. Proponents of long-term hospitalization recognize the dangers of regression but argue that true personality change requires extensive and intensive treatment. Indications for long-term confinement include chronically low motivation, inadequate or harmful social supports (such as enmeshment in a pathological family system), severe impairments in functioning which preclude holding a job or being self-sufficient, and repeated failures at outpatient therapy and short hospitalizations. Such features make early return to the outside environment unlikely.

During longer hospitalizations, the milieu may be less highly structured. The patient is encouraged to assume more shared responsibility for treatment. In addition to current, practical concerns, the staff and patient explore past, archetypal patterns of behavior and transference issues. The hospital can function like a laboratory, in which the borderline identifies specific problems and experiments with solutions in his interactions with staff and other patients.

Eventually, Jennifer (see Chapter 1) entered a long-term hospital. She spent the first six months in the closet—literally and figuratively. She would often sit in her bedroom closet, hiding from the staff. After a while she became more involved with her therapist, getting angry at him and attempting to provoke his rage. She alternately demanded and begged to leave. As the staff held firm, she talked more about her father, how he was like her husband, how he was like all men. Jennifer began to share her feelings with the female staff, something that had always been difficult because of her distrust of and disrespect for women. Later during the hospitalization, she decided to divorce her husband and give up custody of her son. Although these actions hurt her, she considered them "unselfish selfishness"—trying to take care of herself was the most self-sacrificing and caring thing she could do for those she loved. She eventually returned to school and sought a professional degree.

The goals of longer hospitalization extend those of short-term care—not only to identify dysfunctional areas, but also to modify these characteristics. Increased control of impulses, greater ability to trust and relate to others, a more defined sense of identity, and better tolerance of frustration are the clearest signs of a successful hospital treatment. Educational and vocational objectives may be achieved during an extensive hospitalization. Changes in unhealthy living arrangements—moving out of the home, divorce, etc.—may be completed.

The greatest potential hazard of long-term hospitalization is regression. If staff do not actively confront and motivate the patient, the borderline can become mired in an even more helpless position, in which he is even more dependent on others to direct his life.[20]

Partial Hospitalization

Partial (or day) hospital care is a form of therapy in which the patient attends hospital activities during the day and then returns home in the evening. Other partial hospital programs may be held in the evenings, following work or school, and may allow sleeping accommodations when alternatives are not available.

This innovative approach allows the borderline to benefit from the intensity and structure of hospital care, while maintaining an independent living situation. Hospital dependency occurs less frequently. Because partial hospitalization is usually much less expensive than traditional inpatient care, it may be favored for cost considerations.

Borderlines who require more intensive care, but not twenty-four-hour supervision, who are in danger of severe regression if hospitalized, who are making a transition out of the hospital to the outside world, who must maintain vocational or academic pursuits while requiring hospital care, who experience severe financial limitations on care, may all benefit from this treatment. The hospital milieu and therapy objectives are similar to those of the associated inpatient program.[21, 22]

Most of the studies on the effectiveness of hospitalization for borderline patients focus on long-term facilities. These findings primarily demonstrate significant improvement in patients after discharge. One study found that the most significant predictor of positive outcome to hospitalization was a valued patient-therapist relationship.[23] More studies are needed to monitor the effects of short-term care. Comparative studies are also required to evaluate the effectiveness of various types of hospital programs, including the advantages and disadvantages of inpatient units composed exclusively of borderline patients.

CAN BORDERLINES BE CURED?

Since no specific therapy seems superior to the others, the choice of treatment is most often dictated by nontherapeutic considerations, such as time and financial resources, therapist availability, and so on. Even more important is the question of whether therapy helps at all. Some studies estimate that as many as 50 percent of borderline patients drop out of treatment within six months; only approximately one out of ten patients complete the course of therapy, which usually extends for several years.[24] Some have argued that borderlines eventually "mature out" of their pathology spontaneously and that therapy does not substantially affect this natural process. "Fortunately, psychoanalysis is not the only way to resolve inner conflicts," wrote Karen Horney in *Our Inner Conflicts*. "Life itself remains a very effective therapist." However, recent studies imply a significant suicide rate among borderlines (8 to 10 percent).[25] So first, they have to stay alive long enough to get better.

Studies attempting to track the progress of borderline patients, with and without treatment, generally agree that treatment is significantly beneficial. Most of these studies have examined individual therapy, both in and out of the hospital. Appropriate drug treatment successfully relieves many serious symptoms. Psychotherapy also clearly produces improvement. Although most patients continue to have some difficulty with routine functioning and may continue to exhibit remnants of ingrained characterological patterns, and therefore may not be considered com-

pletely "cured," they often no longer satisfy the criteria
that define the diagnosis of BPD.[1, 25]

Such patients also display a greater capacity to trust and
establish satisfactory (even if not very close) relationships.
They have a clearer sense of direction and a more stable
sense of themselves. In a sense, then, they have become
better borderlines.

"You always spoke of unconditional acceptance," said
one borderline patient to her therapist, "and somewhere
in the recent past I finally began to feel it. It's wonderful. . . . You gave me a safe place to unravel—to unfold.
I was lost somewhere inside my mind. You gave me
enough acceptance and freedom to finally let my true self
out."

8

Coping with the Borderline

> "But he's a human being, and a terrible thing is happening to him. So attention must be paid. He is not to be allowed to fall into his grave like an old dog. Attention must be finally paid to such a person."
> —From *Death of a Salesman* by Arthur Miller

No one knew quite what to do with Ray. He had been in and out of hospitals and had seen many doctors over the years, but he could never remain long in treatment. Nor could he stay with a job. His wife, Denise, worked in a dentist's office and spent most of her leisure time with her friends, generally ignoring Ray's complaints of chest pains, headaches, backaches, and depression.

Ray was the only child of wealthy, protective parents. When he was nine, his father's brother committed suicide. Although he never knew his uncle very well, he understood that his parents were greatly affected by the suicide. After this event, his parents became even more protective and would insist he stay home from school whenever he felt ill. At the age of twelve, Ray announced he was depressed and began seeing what became a parade of therapists.

An indifferent student, he went on to college where he met Denise. She was the only woman who had ever shown any interest in him, and after a short courtship they were married. Both quit college and dutifully went to work, but relied on Ray's parents to subsidize their household and Ray's continuing therapy.

The couple moved frequently; whenever Denise got

bored with a job or a location, they would move to a different part of the country. She would quickly acquire a new job and new friends, but Ray had great difficulty and would remain out of work for many months.

As they both began drinking more, their fighting worsened. When they battled, Ray would sometimes leave and return to live with his parents; there he would stay until the family began to quarrel and then he'd return to Denise.

Frequently Ray's wife and parents would get fed up with his moodiness and multiple medical complaints, but then he'd threaten to kill himself and his parents would become panic-stricken. They insisted he see new doctors and flew him around the country to consult with various experts. They arranged hospitalizations in several prestigious institutions, but after a short time Ray always signed himself out against medical advice, and his parents would send him plane fare home. They continuously vowed to withhold further financial support but never stuck to their word.

Friends and jobs became an indistinguishable blur of unsatisfying encounters. Whenever new acquaintance or occupation disappointed in any way, Ray quit. His parents wrung their hands; Denise basically ignored him. Ray continued spinning out of control with no one to limit him, including himself.

RECOGNIZING BPD IN FRIENDS AND RELATIONS

On the surface a borderline personality can be very difficult to identify, despite the underlying volcanic turbulence. Unlike many people afflicted with other mental disorders—such as schizophrenia, bipolar (manic-depressive) disease, alcoholism, or eating disorders—the borderline can usually function extremely well in work and social situations without appearing overtly pathological. Indeed, some of the hallmarks of borderline behavior are the sudden, unpredictable eruptions of anger, extreme suspiciousness, or suicidal depression from someone who has appeared so "normal."

The borderline's sudden outbursts are usually very

frightening and mystifying—both to the borderline himself and to those closest to him. Because of the sudden and extreme nature of certain prominent symptoms, the concerned party can be easily misled and not recognize that it is a manifestation of BPD rather than a separate primary illness. For example, a person who attempts to kill himself by overdosing or cutting his wrists may be diagnosed with depression, and prescribed antidepressant medications and brief, supportive psychotherapy. If the patient is suffering from a chemical depression, this regimen should improve his condition and he should recover relatively quickly and completely. If, however, the destructive behaviors have been triggered by BPD, his self-harming will continue, unabated by the treatment. Even if he is both depressed and borderline (a common combination), this approach will only partially treat the illness and further problems will ensue. If the borderline features are not recognized, the continuation of suicidal or other destructive behaviors, despite treatment, becomes puzzling and frustrating for the patient, the doctor, and everyone concerned.

Abby, a twenty-three-year-old fashion model, was treated in a chemical dependency unit for alcoholism. She responded very well to this program, but as she continued to abstain from alcohol, she became increasingly, compulsively bulimic. She then entered an eating-disorders unit in which she was again successfully treated.

A few weeks later, she began experiencing severe panic episodes in stores, offices, even while driving in her car, and eventually became afraid to leave her house. In addition to these phobias, she was becoming more depressed. As she considered entrance to a phobia clinic, a psychiatric consultant recognized all of her symptoms to be representative of BPD and recommended instead admission to a psychiatric unit specializing in borderline conditions. Where her previous treatments had focused exclusively on alcoholism or bulimia, this hospitalization took a more holistic view of her life.

Eventually, Abby was able to connect her problems to her continued ambivalent relationship with her parents, who had interfered with her attempts to separate, mature, and be more independent. She realized that her various illnesses were really means to escape her parents' demands without guilt. Her bulimia, drinking, and anxieties occupied all her energy, distracting her from addressing the conflicts with her parents. Further, her ''sick'' role excused her from even feeling obligated to work on this relationship. The illnesses also kept her attached to them: Because her parents had serious marital problems (her mother was an alcoholic and her father was chronically depressed), she could stay close to them by replicating their roles.

After a brief hospitalization she continued individual outpatient psychotherapy. Her mood improved and her anxieties and phobias dissolved to a great degree. She also continued to abstain from alcohol and purging.

Abby's case illustrates how a prominent behavior may actually represent an underlying BPD in which one or more of its features—unstable relationships, impulsivity, mood shifts, intense anger, suicidal threats, identity disturbances, feelings of emptiness, or frantic efforts to avoid abandonment—result in psychiatric symptoms that might mistakenly lead to incomplete diagnosis or even misdiagnosis.

COPING AND HELPING

It is important to remember that BPD is an illness, not a willful attempt to get attention. The borderline lacks the boots, much less the bootstraps, with which to pull himself up. It is useless to get angry or to cajole and plead with the borderline to change; without help he is bereft of the tools to alter his behavior.

However, this does not imply that the borderline is helpless and should not be held responsible for his behavior. Actually, the opposite is true. He must accept, without being excused or protected, the real consequences of his actions, even though initially he may be powerless to alter them.

The borderline's extremes of behavior typically lead to either a hard-nosed ''You lazy good-for-nothing SOB, pull yourself together and fly right'' response, or a cajoling ''You poor baby, you can't do it; I'll take care of you'' pat on the head. All must be aware of how their interactions may encourage or inhibit borderline behaviors.

Those who interact with a borderline must attempt to walk a very thin line between, on the one hand, providing reassurance of the borderline's worthiness and, on the other, confirming the necessary expectations. They must try to respond supportively, but without overreacting. Affection and physical touching, such as hugging and holding a hand, can communicate to the borderline that he is a valued person, but if it is exploitative, it will hinder trust. If caring results in overprotectiveness, the borderline stops feeling responsible for his behavior.

In most settings, concentrating on the Truth segments of SET principles (see Chapter 6) can allow for reasonable guidelines. But when suicide is threatened, it is usually time to contact a mental health professional or suicide-prevention facility. Suicide threats should not be allowed to become "emotional blackmail," whereby the friend or relation is manipulated to behave as the borderline demands. Threats should be taken seriously and met with prompt, predictable, realistic reactions, such as demanding that the borderline obtain professional help (a Truth response).

Jack, a forty-one-year-old single man, worked part time while attempting to return to school. His widowed mother continued to support him financially, and whenever he failed at work, school, or with a relationship, she would reinforce his helplessness, by insisting he could not succeed in achieving his goals and suggesting he return "home" to live with her. Therapy involved not only helping Jack understand his wish to remain helpless and reap the inherent benefits of helplessness, but also confronted his mother's role in perpetuating his dependency.

It takes only one actor in the drama to initiate change. Jack's mother can respond to his dependency with SET responses that express her caring (Support), understanding (Empathy), and acknowledgment of reality (Truth)—the need for Jack to take responsibility for his own actions. If his mother is unwilling to alter her behavior, Jack must recognize her role in his problems and distance himself from her.

Contending with Borderline Rage

After awhile, for someone close to a borderline, unpredictable behaviors may become commonplace and therefore "predictably unpredictable." One of the most common, the angry outburst, usually comes with no warning and appears way out of proportion.

The close friend, relation, or coworker should resist the temptation to "fight fire with fire." The louder and angrier the borderline gets, the quieter and more composed the other person should become, thereby refusing to collaborate in aggravating the emotional atmosphere, and demonstrating the comparative outlandish intensity of the borderline's rage. If the concerned individual senses the potential for physical violence, he should leave the scene immediately. Borderline rage often cannot be reasoned with, so discussion and debate are unnecessary and may only worsen the situation. Instead, one should try to cool off the conflict by acknowledging the difference in opinion and agreeing to disagree. Further discussion can come later when the atmosphere is more settled.

Living with Borderline Mood Swings

Rapid mood changes can be equally perplexing to the borderline and to those around him. From an early age, Meredith had always been aware of her moodiness. Without reason she could soar to great heights of excitement and joy, only to plummet, without warning, to the lower reaches of despair. Her parents indulged her moodiness by tiptoeing softly around her, never challenging her irritability. In school, friends would come and go, put off by her unpredictability. Some called her "the manic-depressive" and tried to kid her out of her surliness.

Her husband, Ben, said he was attracted to her "kindness" and "sense of fun." But Meredith could change dramatically from playful to suicidal. Similarly, her interactions with Ben would change from joyful sharing to gloomy isolation. Her moods were totally unpredictable and Ben was never sure how he would find her upon his return at the end of the day. At times he felt that he should enter their home by putting his hat on a stick and poking it into the doorway to see if it would be embraced, ignored, or shot at.

Ben was locked into a typical borderline "Damned if you do and damned if you don't" scenario. Confronting her depression would prompt more withdrawal and anger, but ignoring it would seem to demonstrate lack of concern. The SET principles would address this conflict and insist on Meredith's input into how he (and others) should react to her moods.

For Meredith, these shifts in mood, unresponsive to a variety of medications, were equally distressing. Her task was to recognize such swings, take responsibility for having them, and learn to adapt by compensating for their presence. When in a state of depression, she could subsequently identify it and learn to explain to others around her that she was in a down phase and would try to function as well as she could. If she was with people to whom she could not comfortably explain her situation, Meredith could maintain a low profile and actively try to avoid dealing with some of the demands on her. A major goal would involve establishing constancy—consistent, reliable attitudes and behaviors—toward herself and others.

Handling Impulsivity

Impulsive acts can be extremely frustrating for the borderline's friends and relations, particularly if the acts are self-destructive. This trait is especially unnerving when it emerges (as it often does) at a relatively stable point in the borderline's life. Indeed, impulsive behaviors may emanate precisely because life is settling and the borderline feels uncomfortable in a crisis-free state.

Larry, for example, was in a marriage that was comfortably boring. Married for over twenty years, he and Phyllis rarely interacted. She reared their sons while Larry toiled for a large company. His life was a self-imposed prison of daily routine and compulsive behaviors. He took hours to dress, in order to arrange his clothing just so. At night before bed, he engaged in rituals to maintain a sense of control—the closet doors had to be opened in a special way, the bathroom sink had to be carefully cleaned, and the soap and toilet articles arranged in a certain pattern.

But within this tightly regimented routine, Larry would impulsively get drunk, pick fights, or abruptly leave town for an entire day without warning. On two occasions he impulsively overdosed on his heart medicine "to see what it felt like." Usually he would absorb Phyllis' anger by turning somber and quiet; but every so often he would strike out at her, often over trivial matters.

He would remain dry for several months and then, just as he was receiving praise for abstaining, he would get abusively and loudly drunk. His wife, friends, and counselors pleaded and threatened, but to no avail.

SET techniques might have helped Phyllis to deal with Larry's impulsivity. Rather than beg and threaten, she might have emphasized her caring for Larry and her growing realization that he was becoming more and more dissatisfied with his life. Truth statements would communicate her own unhappiness with their current situation and the crucial need to do something about it, such as enter therapy.

It is also often helpful to be able to predict impulsive behaviors from past experiences. For example, after a period of sobriety, Phyllis might remind Larry that in the past, when things have gone well, he has built up pressures that have exploded into drinking binges. By pointing out previous patterns, one can help the borderline become more aware of feelings that preview the onset of impulsivity. In addition, the borderline learns that behaviors that he has perceived as chaotic and unpredictable can actually be anticipated, understood, and thereby controlled.

Finally, in therapy, Larry began to see that his seemingly unpredictable behaviors represented anger at himself and others. He realized how he would become abusive to his wife or begin drinking when frustrated with himself. This impulsive behavior would result in guilt and self-chastisement, which, in turn, served to expiate his sins. As Larry began to value himself more highly and respect his own ideals and beliefs, his destructive activities diminished.

UNDERSTANDING YOUR OWN EMOTIONS

When you join the borderline on his roller-coaster ride, you also must expect to experience a variety of emotions, especially guilt, fear, and anger. When self-destructive, the borderline may appear helpless and project responsibility for his behavior onto others, who may all too readily accept it. Guilt is a strong inhibitor of honest confrontation. Similarly, fear of physical harm—to the borderline, others or yourself—may also be a powerful deterrent to open interactions. Anger is a common reaction when, as frequently occurs, you feel manipulated or simply don't like or understand a certain behavior.

Lois' mother called Lois frequently, complaining of severe headaches, loneliness, and an overall disgust with life. With her father long dead and her siblings estranged from the family, Lois was the "good daughter," the only child who cared.

Lois felt guilty when her mother was alone and in pain. Despite Lois' love for her mother and the feelings of guilt her mother triggered, Lois began feeling angry when she saw her mother becoming progressively more helpless and unwilling to take care of herself. Lois began to recognize that she was being taken advantage of by her mother's increasing dependency. But when Lois expressed her anger, her mother just became more tearful and helpless, and Lois felt more guilty, and the cycle repeated again. Only when Lois untangled herself from this interlocked system was her mother forced to achieve a healthier self-sufficiency.

SPECIAL PARENTING PROBLEMS

Most borderlines describe childhoods with characteristic features. Often, one parent was missing or frequently absent, had major commitments to outside affairs, hobby or career interests, or abused alcohol or drugs.

If both parents did live in the home, their relationship was usually not harmonious. There was often a lack of consensus about child rearing and, subsequently, one parent, usually the mother, assumed the primary parenting role. Such parents are rarely capable of presenting a united, collaborative front to their children. For such children, the world abounds with inconsistencies. When the child requires structure, he receives contradictions; when he needs firmness, he gets ambivalence. Thus, the future borderline is deprived of the opportunity to develop a consistent, core identity.

The mother of a borderline may be blatantly ill, but more often her pathology is quite subtle. She may even be perceived by others as the "perfect mother" because of her total "dedication" to her children. Further observation, however, reveals her overinvolvement in her children's lives, her encouragement of mutual dependencies, and her unwillingness to allow her children to mature and separate naturally.

Separations

Separations from parents, particularly during the first few years of life, are common in the borderline biography. On the surface, these separations may appear insignificant, yet they have profound effects. For example, the birth of a sibling takes the mother away from her normal activities for a few weeks, but when she returns, she is no longer as responsive to the older child—mother has disappeared and has been replaced by someone who will always be different, one who now has mothering duties with a younger sibling. For the healthy child in a healthy environment, this trauma is easily overcome, but for the borderline in a borderline setting it may be one of a series of losses and perceived abandonments. Extended illnesses, frequent travels, divorce, or the death of a parent also deprive the developing infant of consistent mothering at crucial times, which may interfere with his abilities to develop trust and constancy in his unstable and unreliable world.

The Trauma of Child Abuse

Severe physical and/or sexual abuse is a common trauma in the history of the borderline personality. When a child is abused, he invariably blames himself because (consciously or subconsciously) it is the best of the available alternatives. If he blames the adult, he will be terrified by his dependency on incompetents who are unable to take care of him. If he blames no one, pain becomes random and unpredictable and therefore even more frightening because he has no hope of controlling it. Blaming himself makes the abuse easier to understand and therefore possible to control—he can feel that he somehow causes the abuse and therefore will be able to find a way to end it; or he will give up and accept that he is "bad."

The borderline learns early in life that he is bad, that he causes bad things to happen. He begins to expect punishment and may only feel secure when being punished. Later, self-mutilation may sometimes be the borderline's way of perpetuating this familiar, secure feeling of being chastised. He may see abuse as a kind of love and repeat the abuse with his own children. As an adult he remains locked in the child's confusing world, in which love and hate co-mingle, only good and bad exist with no in-between, and only inconsistency is consistent.

Abuse can take subtler forms than physical violence or deviant sexuality. Emotional abuse—expressed as verbal harassment, sarcasm, humiliation, or frigid silence—can be equally devastating. Stephanie, for example, could never please her father. When she was young, he called her "Chubby," and laughed at her clumsy tomboy attempts to please him by playing sports. She was "stupid" when her grades were less than perfect and when she broke dishes while trying to clear the kitchen. He ridiculed her strapless gown on prom night, and on graduation day, insisted that she would amount to nothing.

As an adult, Stephanie was always unsure of herself, never trusting flattering comments and hopelessly trying to please people who were impossible to please. After a long string of destructive relationships, Stephanie finally met Ted, who seemed caring and supportive. At every turn, however, Stephanie tried to sabotage the relationship, constantly testing his loyalty and questioning his commitment.

Ted needed to understand Stephanie's background and recognize that trust could not realistically be established except over long periods of time. Not everyone is willing to wait. Ted was.

Recognizing BPD in Adolescence

By definition, the struggles of adolescence and BPD are extremely similar: Both the normal adolescent and the borderline struggle for individuality and separation from parents, seek bonds with friends and identification with groups, try to avoid being alone, tend to go through dramatic mood changes, and are generally prone to impulsivity. The teenager's easy distractibility is analogous to the borderline's difficulty to commit himself to a goal and follow through. Adolescents' eccentric dress styles, prehistoric eating habits, and piercing music are usually attempts to carve out a distinctive identity and relate to specific groups of peers, efforts similar to those of borderlines.

A normal adolescent may listen to gloomy music, write pessimistic poetry, glorify suicidal celebrities, dramatically scream, cry, and threaten. However, the normal adolescent does not cut his wrists, binge and purge several times a day, become addicted to drugs, or attack his mother; and it is these extremes that herald BPD.

Some parents will deny the seriousness of an adolescent's problems (a drug overdose, for example) by dismissing them as a typical teenager's bid for attention. Though it is true that children often seek attention in dramatic ways, neither suicide attempts nor any destructive behaviors are "normal." They instead suggest the possibility of incipient borderline personality or another disorder and should be evaluated by a professional.

Usually others—parents, teachers, employers, friends—will recognize when the normal teenager crosses the border into borderline behavior, even before the adolescent himself. Continuous drug abuse, serial tumultuous relationships, or anorexic fasting are good indicators that deeper problems may be involved. The teen's whole style of functioning should be the focus of examination, rather than individual symptoms. This is especially crucial when considering the potential for suicide.

Suicide is the second leading cause of death among teenagers, after accidents, and is particularly prevalent in children who are depressed, abuse drugs, act impulsively, and have few support systems—all prominent features of BPD.[1] Threats of self-harm should always be taken seriously. Attempts to self-mutilate or harm oneself "only for attention" can go tragically awry. Parents who try to distinguish "real suicide" from "attention-seeking" miss the point—both are seriously pathological behaviors and require treatment, often hospitalization.

WORKING WITH THE BORDERLINE

In the work environment, borderlines are often perceived as "strange" or "eccentric": They may tend to isolate themselves, avoid personal contacts, and keep others away with an aura of surliness, suspicion, or eccentricity. Others habitually complain of physical ailments or personal problems, and occasionally have fits of paranoia and rage. Still others may act perfectly normal in the work situation, but appear awkward or uncomfortable around coworkers outside the workplace.

Over the last decade, many employers started Employee Assistant Programs (EAPs), in-house counselors and referral departments initially designed to help employees deal with alcohol and drug abuse problems. Today many EAPs are also available to help workers confront other emotional problem, as well as legal and financial difficulties. Although many EAP counselors are well-equipped to identify features of alcohol or drug abuse, or of prominent psychiatric illnesses such as depression or psychosis, they may be less familiar with the more intricate symptoms of BPD. Though the employee's supervisor, coworkers, counselor, even the employee himself may be aware of some dysfunctional or disruptive behaviors, the borderline might not be referred for treatment because his behaviors cannot be clearly associated with more familiar disorders.

The prospective employer may suspect borderline characteristics in an applicant who has a history of frequent job changes. These terminations will often be explained by "personality conflicts" (which, indeed, is often accurate). Other job separations may be sparked by a significant change—a new supervisor, new computer system, or an adjustment in job description—that disrupted a very structured (perhaps, even monotonous) routine.

Because the borderline may be very creative and dedicated, he may make a most valuable employee. When functioning on a higher level, he can be colorful, stimulating, and inspiring to others. Most borderlines function optimally in a well-defined, structured environment in which expectations are clearly delineated.

Coworkers will be most comfortable with the borderline when they recognize his tendency to see the world as black or white and accept his need for well-defined structure. They should avoid "kidding around" with him and stay away from "good natured" mocking, which the borderline may often misconstrue. It may be helpful to intercede if the borderline becomes the target of others' jokes. Frequent compliments for good work, and matter-of-fact, noncondemning recognition of mistakes with suggestions for improvement can aid the borderline's functioning in the workplace.

Similarly, when the borderline is in an executive position, it is important for employees to recognize and learn to deal with his black-or-white thinking. Employees should learn to expect and accept his changeability with a minimum of hurt feelings. They should avoid entanglement in logical arguments, because consistency may not always be possible for the borderline. They should look for allies elsewhere in the organization to provide reliable feedback and evaluations.

Playing with the Borderline

At play the borderline is typically unpredictable and sometimes very disconcerting. He may have great difficulty with recreation and play with a seriousness that is out of proportion to the relaxed nature of the activity. He may be your newly assigned tennis doubles partner who at first seems nice enough, but as the game goes on becomes increasingly frustrated and angry. Though you continually remind him that "it's just a game," he may stomp around, curse himself, throw the racket, and swear to give up the sport. He may be your son's Little League coach who works well with the kids, but suddenly becomes wildly abusive to the teenage umpire or angrily humiliating to his own son—seen as an extension of himself—who strikes out with the bases loaded. Although these examples may describe borderline-like traits in some people who in fact are not borderline, when these behaviors are extreme or represent a consistent pattern, they may be indications of a true borderline personality.

The borderline's intensity interferes with his ability to relax and have fun. Others' attempts at humor may frustrate him and make him angry. It is virtually impossible "to kid him out of it." If you elect to continue playing tennis with your borderline partner, judicious use of SET principles may make the experience more tolerable.

The Maturing Borderline

Higher-functioning adult borderlines may have successful careers, assume traditional family roles, and have a cadre of friends and support systems. They may generally live satisfactory lives within their own separate corner of existence, despite recurrent frustrations with themselves and others who inhabit that niche.

Lower-functioning borderlines, however, have difficulty maintaining a job and friends and may lack family and support systems; they may inhabit lonelier and more desperate "black holes" within their own personal universe.

Common to all borderlines is an element of unpredictability and erratic behavior. It may be more obvious in the lonely isolate, but those who know the contented family man well can also detect inconsistencies in his behavior which belie the superficial rationality. At work even the borderline who is a successful businessman or professional may be known by those working closely with him to be a bit strange, if not mad, even if they can't quite localize what it is that projects that aura of imbalance.

As many borderlines grow older, they may "mellow out" to some degree. Impulsivity, mood swings, and self-destructive behaviors seem to diminish in dramatic intensity. This pattern might be an objective reflection of change or a subjective evaluation of those living and working with the borderline; the borderline's friends and lovers may have adjusted to his erratic actions over time and no longer notice or respond to the outrageousness.

Maybe it is because he has settled into a more routine lifestyle that no longer requires periodic outbursts—drinking binges, suicide threats, or other dramatic gestures—to achieve his needs. Perhaps with age the borderline loses the energy to maintain the frenetic pace of borderline living. Or perhaps there is simply a natural healing process that takes place for some borderlines as they mature. In any event, those sharing life with the borderline can expect his behaviors over time—maybe a very long time, and sometimes without treatment—to become more tolerable. At this point the unpredictable reactions become more predictable and therefore easier to manage, and it becomes possible for the borderline to learn how to love and be loved in a more healthy fashion.

Appendix A

DSM-III-R Axis Classifications

This appendix lists diagnostic categories for psychiatric illnesses, as officially recognized by the *Diagnostic and Statistical Manual of Mental Disorders,* Third Edition-Revised (Washington, D.C.: American Psychiatric Association, 1987).

AXIS I DIAGNOSES

The following, a partial list of Axis I diagnoses, are primarily ''state'' disorders (see Chapter 2).

Disorders Usually First Evident in Infancy, Childhood, or Adolescence:
    disruptive behavior disorders
        attention-deficit hyperactivity disorder
        conduct disorder
    anxiety disorders
    eating disorders
        anorexia nervosa
        bulimia nervosa
    tic disorders
        Tourette's

Organic Mental Disorders:
    dementias
        Alzheimer's

Psychoactive Substance Use Disorders:
    alcohol
    amphetamine
    cannabis
    cocaine
    hallucinogen
    opioid

Schizophrenia:
  catatonic
  disorganized
  paranoid
  undifferentiated

Psychotic Disorders Not Elsewhere Classified:
  brief reactive psychosis
  schizophreniform disorder
  schizoaffective disorder

Mood Disorders:
  bipolar disorder
  depressive disorder
    major depression
    dysthymia

Anxiety Disorders:
  panic disorder
  agoraphobia
  social phobia
  simple phobia
  obsessive compulsive disorder
  post-traumatic stress disorder
  generalized anxiety disorder

Somatoform Disorders:
  hypochondriasis
  conversion disorder
  somatization disorder
  somatoform pain disorder

Dissociative Disorders:
  multiple personality disorder
  psychogenic amnesia

Sexual Disorders:
  exhibitionism
  fetishism
  voyeurism
  pedophilia

erectile (impotence) disorder
inhibited orgasm
premature ejaculation
sexual masochism
sexual sadism

Sleep Disorders:
insomnia disorder
hypersomnia disorder

Factitious Disorders:
with physical symptoms
with psychological symptoms

Impulse Control Disorders:
intermittent explosive disorder
kleptomania
pathological gambling
pyromania

Adjustment Disorders:
with anxiety
with depression
with disturbance of conduct
with physical complaints

AXIS II DISORDERS (COMPLETE LISTING)

These Axis II disorders are personality ("trait") disorders.

Cluster A—People appear odd or eccentric.
paranoid
schizoid
schizotypal

Cluster B—People appear dramatic, emotional, or erratic.
antisocial
borderline
histrionic
narcissistic

Cluster C—People appear anxious or fearful.
  avoidant
  dependent
  obsessive compulsive
  passive aggressive

Appendix B

Evolution of the Borderline Syndrome

The concept of the borderline personality has evolved primarily through the theoretical formulations of psychoanalytic writers. Current DSM-III-R criteria—observable, objective, and statistically reliable principles for defining this disorder—are derived from the more abstract, speculative writings of psychoanalytic theorists over the past eighty years.

FREUD

During Freud's era at the turn of the century, psychiatry was a branch of medicine closely aligned with neurology. Psychiatric syndromes were defined by directly observable behaviors, as opposed to unobservable, mental, or "unconscious" mechanisms, and most forms of mental illness were attributed to neurophysiological aberrations.

Though Freud himself was an experienced neurophysiologist, he explored the mind through different portals. He developed the concept of the unconscious and initiated a legacy of psychological—rather than physiological—exploration of human behavior. Yet he remained convinced that physiological mechanisms would eventually be uncovered to coincide with his psychological theories.

Ninety years after Freud's landmark work, we have come almost full circle: Today, diagnostic classifications are once again defined by observable phenomena, and new frontiers of research into borderline and other types of mental illness are again exploring neurophysiological factors (see

Chapter 3), while not lessening the impact of psychological and environmental factors.

Freud's explication of the unconscious mind is the underpinning of psychoanalysis. He believed that psychopathology resulted from the conflict between primitive, unconscious impulses and the conscious mind's need to prevent these abhorrent, unacceptable thoughts from entering awareness. He first used hypnosis, and later "free association" and other classical psychoanalytical techniques, to explore his theories.

Ironically, Freud intended classical psychoanalysis to be primarily an investigative tool rather than a form of treatment. His colorful case histories—"The Rat Man," "The Wolf Man," "Little Hans," "Anna O," etc.—were published to support his evolving theories, not only to promote psychoanalysis as a treatment method. Many current psychiatrists believe that these patients, whom Freud felt exhibited hysteria and other types of neuroses, would today clearly be identified as borderline.

POST-FREUD PSYCHOANALYTIC WRITERS

Psychoanalysts who followed Freud were the main contributors to the modern concept of the borderline syndrome. In 1925, Wilhelm Reich's *The Impulsive Character* described attempts to apply psychoanalysis to certain unusual characterologic disorders that he encountered in his clinic. He found that the "impulsive character" was often immersed in two sharply contradictory feeling states at the same time but was able to maintain the states without apparent discomfort via the splitting mechanism—a concept that has become central to all subsequent theories on the borderline syndrome, particularly Kernberg's (see below).[1]

In the late twenties and early thirties, the followers of the British psychoanalyst Melanie Klein investigated the cases of many patients who seemed just beyond the reach of psychoanalysis. The Kleinians focused on psychological factors as opposed to biological-constitutional factors.

The term *borderline* was first coined by Adolph Stern in 1938 to describe a group of patients who did not seem to fit into the primary diagnostic classifications of "neuroses" and "psychoses."[2] These patients were obviously more ill than neurotic patients—in fact, "too ill for classical psychoanalysis,"—yet they did not, like psychotic patients, continually misinterpret the real world. Though, like neurotics, they displayed a wide range of anxiety symptoms, neurotic patients usually had a more solid, consistent sense of identity and used more mature coping mechanisms.

Throughout the forties and fifties, other psychoanalysts began to recognize a population of patients who did not fit existing pathological descriptions. Some patients appeared to be neurotic or mildly symptomatic, but when they engaged in traditional psychotherapy, especially psychoanalysis, they "unraveled." Similarly, hospitalization would also exacerbate symptoms and increase the patient's infantile behavior and dependency on the therapist and hospital.

Other patients would appear to be severely psychotic, often diagnosed schizophrenic, only to make a sudden and unexpected recovery within a very short time. (Such dramatic improvement is inconsistent with the usual course of schizophrenia.) Still other patients exhibited symptoms suggestive of depression, but their radical swings in mood did not fit the usual profile of depressive disorders.

Psychological testing also confirmed the presence of a new, unique classification. Certain patients performed normally on structured psychological tests (such as IQ tests), but on unstructured, projective tests requiring narrative personalized responses (such as the Rorschach [inkblot] test), their responses were much more akin to those of psychotic patients, who displayed thinking and fantasizing on a more regressed, more childlike level.

During this postwar period, psychoanalysts fastened onto different aspects of the syndrome, seeking to develop a succinct delineation. In many ways the situation was like the old tale of the blind men who stood around an elephant and touched its various anatomical parts, trying to identify it. Each man described a different animal, of course, depending on which part he touched. Similarly, researchers were able to touch and identify different aspects of the borderline syndrome but could not quite see the whole animal. Many researchers (Zilboorg, Hoch and Polatin, Bychowski, and others)[3,4,5] and DSM-II (1968)[6] rallied around the schizophrenia-like aspects of the disorder, using such terms as "ambulatory schizophrenia," "pre-schizophrenic," "pseudoneurotic schizophrenia," and "latent schizophrenia" to describe these patients. Others concentrated on these patients' lack of a consistent, core sense of identity. In 1942, Helen Deutsch described a group of patients who overcame an intrinsic sense of emptiness by a chameleon-like altering of their internal and external emotional experiences to fit the people and situations they were involved with at the moment. She termed this tendency of adopting the qualities of others as a means of gaining or retaining their love the "as-if personality."[7]

In 1953, Robert Knight revitalized the term borderline in his consideration of "borderline states."[8] He recognized that, even though certain patients presented markedly different symptoms and were categorized with different diagnoses, they were expressing a common pathology.

After Knight's work was published, the term borderline became more popular, and the possibility of using Stern's general borderline concept as a diagnosis became more acceptable. In 1968, Roy Grinker and his colleagues defined four subtypes of the borderline patient: 1. a severely afflicted group who bordered on the psychotic; 2. a "core borderline" group with turbulent interpersonal relationships, intense feeling states, and loneliness; 3. an "as-if" group easily influenced by others and lacking in stable identity; and 4. a mildly impaired group with poor self-confidence and bordering on the neurotic end of the spectrum.[9]

Yet, even with all this extensive pioneering research, the diagnosis of borderline personality, among working clinicians, was still drenched in ambiguity. It was considered a "wastebasket diagnosis" by many, a place to "dump" those patients who were not well understood, who resisted therapy, or who simply did not get better; the situation remained that way well into the seventies.

As the borderline personality became more rigorously defined and distinguishable from other syndromes, attempts were made to change the ambiguous name. At one point, "unstable personality" was briefly considered during the development of DSM-III. However, borderline character pathology is relatively fixed and invariable despite its chaos—it is predictably stable in its instability. No other names have been prominently proposed as a replacement.

In the seventies, two major schools of thought evolved to delineate a consistent set of criteria for defining the borderline syndrome. Like some other disciplines in the natural and social sciences, psychiatry was split ideologically into two primary camps—one more concept-oriented; the other more influenced by descriptive, observable behavior that could be more easily retested and studied under laboratory conditions.

The empirical school, led by John Gunderson of Harvard and favored by many researchers, developed a structured, more behavioral definition, one that is based on observable criteria and thus more accessible to research and study. This definition is the most widely accepted and in 1980 was adopted by DSM-III (see Chapter 2).

The other more concept-oriented school, led by Otto Kernberg of Cornell and favored by many psychoanalysts, proposes a more psychostructural approach that describes the syndrome based on intrapsychic functioning and defense mechanisms rather than overt behaviors.

KERNBERG'S "BORDERLINE PERSONALITY ORGANIZATION" (BPO)

In 1967, Otto Kernberg introduced his concept of Borderline Personality Organization (BPO), a broader concept than DSM-III's Borderline Personality Disorder (BPD). Kernberg's conceptualization places BPO midway between neurotic and psychotic personality organization.[10,11] A patient with BPO, as defined by Kernberg, is less impaired than a psychotic, whose perceptions of reality are severely contorted, making normal functioning impossible. On the other hand, the borderline is more disabled than a person with neurotic personality organization, who experiences intolerable anxiety as a result of emotional conflicts. The neurotic's perception of identity and system of defense mechanisms are usually more adaptive than those of the borderline.

BPO encompasses other Axis II, or characterologica., disorders, such as paranoid, schizoid, antisocial, histrionic, and narcissistic personality disorders. In addition, it includes obsessive-compulsive and chronic anxiety disorders, hypochondriasis, phobias, sexual perversions, and dissociative reactions (such as multiple personality disorder).

In Kernberg's system, patients currently diagnosed with BPD would constitute only about 10 to 25 percent of patients classified BPO. A patient diagnosed with BPD is conceived as occupying a low-functioning, high-severity level within the overall BPO diagnosis.

Though Kernberg's system was not officially adopted by the APA, his work has had (and continues to have) enormous influence as a theoretical model for both clinicians and researchers. In general, Kernberg's schema emphasizes the inferred internal mechanisms discussed below:

Variable Sense of Reality

Like neurotics, borderlines retain contact with reality most of the time; however, under stress the borderline can regress to a brief psychotic state. (This trait is not recognized as an official criterion of BPD in DSM-III-R, but it is included in Gunderson's concept of BPD and was proposed, though not adopted, as a ninth criteria.)

Marjorie, a twenty-nine-year-old married woman, sought therapy for increasing depression and marital disharmony. An intelligent, attractive woman, Marjorie related calmly throughout her eight sessions. She eagerly assented to a joint interview with her husband, but during the session she turned uncharacteristically loud and belligerent. Dropping her facade of self-control, she began tc berate her husband for alleged infidelities. She accused her therapist of taking her husband's side ("You men always stick together!") and accused both of engaging in a conspiracy against her. The sudden transformation from a relaxed, mildly depressed woman to a raging, paranoid one is quite characteristic of the kind of rapidly shifting borders of reality observed in the borderline.

Nonspecific Weaknesses in Functioning

Borderlines have great difficulty tolerating frustration and coping with anxiety. In Kernberg's framework, impulsive behavior is an attempt to diffuse this tension. Borderlines also have defective sublimation tools; that is, they are unable to channel frustrations and discomforts in socially adaptive ways. Though borderlines may display extreme empathy, warmth, and guilt, these exhibitions are often rote, more manipulative gestures for display purposes only rather than true expressions of feeling.

Indeed, the borderline may act as if he has totally forgotten a dramatic effusion that occurred only moments before, much like a child who suddenly emerges from a temper tantrum all smiles and laughter.

Primitive Thinking

Borderlines are capable of performing well in a structured work or professional environment, but below the surface linger grave self-doubts, suspiciousness, and fears. The internal thought processes of borderlines may be surprisingly unsophisticated and primal, camouflaged by a stable facade of learned and rehearsed platitudes. Any circumstance that pierces the protective structure shielding the borderline may unleash a flood of chaotic passions concealed within. The example of Marjorie (above) illustrates the point.

Projective psychological tests also reveal the borderline's primitive thought processes. These tests—such as the Rorschach and Thematic Apperception Test (TAT)—elicit associations to ambiguous stimuli, such as inkblots or pictures, around which the patient creates a story. Borderline responses typically resemble those of schizophrenics and other psychotic patients. Unlike the coherent, organized responses usually observed among neurotic patients, those from borderlines often describe bizarre, primitive images—the borderline might see vicious animals cannibalizing one another, where the neurotic sees a butterfly.

Primitive Defense Mechanisms

The coping mechanism of splitting (see Chapters 2 and 3) preserves the borderline's perception of a world of extremes—a view in which people and objects are either good or bad, friendly or hostile, loved or hated—in order to escape anxiety.

In Kernberg's conceptualization, splitting often leads to "magical thinking": Superstitions, phobias, obsessions, and compulsions are used as talismans to ward off unconscious fears. Splitting also results in derivative defense mechanisms:

- Primitive idealization—insistently placing a person or object in the "all good" category so as to avoid the anxiety accompanying the recognition of faults in that person.
- Devaluation—an unrelenting negative view of a person or object; the opposite of idealization. Using this mechanism, the borderline avoids the guilt of his rage—the "all-bad" person fully deserves it.
- Omnipotence—a feeling of unlimited power in which one feels incapable of failure or sometimes even of death. (Omnipotence is also a common feature in the narcissistic personality.)
- Projection—disavowing features unacceptable to the self and attributing them to others.
- Projective identification—a more complex form of projection in which the projector continues an ongoing manipulative involvement with another person, who is the object of the projection. The other person "wears" these unacceptable characteristics for the projector, who works to insure their continued expression.

For example, Mark, a young, married man who is diagnosed as borderline finds his own sadistic and angry impulses unacceptable and projects them onto his wife, Sally. Sally is then perceived by Mark (in his black-and-white fashion) to be a "totally angry woman." All of her actions are interpreted as sadistic. He unconsciously "pushes her buttons" to extract angry responses, thus confirming his projections. In this way Sally is feared yet simultaneously controlled by Mark.

Pathological Concept of Self

"Identity diffusion" describes Kernberg's conception of the borderline's lack of a stable, core sense of identity. The borderline's identity is the consistency of jello: It can be molded into any configuration that contains it but slips through the hands when you try to pick it up. This lack of substance leads directly to the identity disturbances outlined in criterion 6 of DSM-III's description of BPD (see Chapter 2).

Pathological Concept of Others

As "identity diffusion" describes the borderline's lack of a stable concept of self, "object inconstancy" describes the lack of a stable concept of others. Just as his own self-esteem depends on current circumstances, the borderline bases his attitude toward another person on the most recent encounter rather than on a more stable and enduring perception grounded in a consistent, connected series of experiences.

Often, the borderline is unable to hold onto the memory of a person or object when he, she, or it is not present. Like a child who becomes attached to a transitional object that represents a soothing mother figure (such as Linus to his blanket), the borderline uses objects, such as pictures and clothing, to simulate the presence of another person. When a borderline is separated from home, for example, for even a brief period, he typically takes many personal objects as soothing reminders of home. Teddy bears and other stuffed animals accompany him to bed and snapshots of family are carefully placed around the room. If he is left home while his wife is away, he often stares longingly at her picture and her closet, smells her pillow, and so on. For many borderlines, "out of sight, out of mind" is an excruciatingly real truism. Panic sets in when the borderline is separated from a loved one because the separation feels permanent. Because memory cannot be adequately utilized to retain an image, the borderline forgets what the object of his concern looks like, sounds like, feels like. To escape the panicky sensation of abandonment and loneliness, the borderline tries to cling desperately—calling, writing, using any means to maintain contact.

Appendix C

Medications Used to Treat BPD

MAJOR TRANQUILIZERS (NEUROLEPTICS, ANTIPSYCHOTICS)

This class of medicines is used primarily to alleviate psychosis and to control destructive or paranoid behaviors and feelings of unreality. But these drugs may also help the nonpsychotic patient by quelling impulsive behaviors, angry and hostile outbursts, and severe agitation—all of which could be destructive to the patient or others. They also relieve throbbing anxiety states and sometimes reduce pain symptoms. The most common drugs in this class are: Thorazine (chlorpromazine), Stelazine (trifluoperazine), Trilafon (perphenazine), Mellaril (thioridazine), Serentil (mesoridazine), Haldol (haloperidol), Navane (thiothixene), Prolixin (fluphenazine), Loxitane (loxapine), Moban and Lidone (molindone).

Several recent studies have compared these drugs with placebos and antidepressants in treating borderline patients. In all of these studies neuroleptics provided greater improvement in all measured symptoms, including depression.[1]

Antidepressants

Depressive disorder is probably the most common diagnosis associated with BPD. When depression includes distinctive physical symptoms—such as changes in sleeping, eating, concentration, and energy—and when there is a strong family history of depression, antidepressant medicines often improve symptoms dramatically. Complicating the picture, however, are reports that some borderlines actually get worse with antidepressants.[2]

181

There are several classes of antidepressants:

Cyclic antidepressants. These are some of the oldest and most commonly employed antidepressants. (Cyclic refers to the rings in the molecular structure of the drug prototype.) These include Elavil (amitriptylene), Pamelor and Aventyl (nortriptylene), Vivactil (protriptylene), Tofranil (imipramine), Sinequan and Adapin (doxepin), Norpramin and Pertofrane (desipramine), Desyrel (trazodone), Ludiomil (maprotilene), Asendin (amoxapine), Surmontil (trimipramine), and Prozac (fluoxetine).

Monoamine oxidase (MAO) inhibitors. This group of antidepressants is utilized less frequently partly because these drugs may precipitate dangerous episodes of high blood pressure when mixed with certain medications (such as decongestants, diet pills, or some analgesics, such as Demerol) or with certain foods (such as aged cheeses, some wines and other alcoholic drinks, chicken livers, etc.). Patients on MAO inhibitors, therefore, must reliably follow a certain diet. The most common MAO inhibitors are Nardil (phenelzine) and Parnate (tranylcypromine).

MAO inhibitors seem to be more beneficial for patients with atypical features of depression, such as difficulty falling asleep, increased appetite, marked sensitivity to rejection, and mood changes associated with changes in situation. In contrast, typical depression is more usually characterized by middle-of-the-night insomnia (after easily falling asleep initially), decreased appetite, and less vulnerability to situational changes. Many borderlines experience atypical signs.

Both cyclic antidepressants and MAO inhibitors are sometimes used to treat other symptoms, such as primary anxiety, phobias, obsessive-compulsive disorders, and some pain syndromes.

Lithium. Lithium, most commonly associated with manic-depressive illness, provides benefit for borderline patients who exhibit depression or precipitous swings in mood. Lithium has also been proven useful in treating impulsive and aggressive behaviors. Some studies have suggested that lithium is an effective medication for alcoholism.

Psychostimulants. This class of drugs, used less frequently in treating depression, includes Ritalin (methylphenidate), Dexedrine (dextroamphetamine), and Cylert (pemoline). These medicines have also proven effective in treating attention-deficit disorder (hyperactivity), which is usually diagnosed in children but sometimes persists into adulthood. In this syndrome patients are often physically clumsy and have difficulty concentrating, sitting still, and attending to one task and seeing it through to completion.

Electroconvulsive treatment (ECT). Despite continued controversy regarding its use, ECT remains one of the most effective therapies for depression, with a higher response rate than even antidepressant medicines. It remains a relatively safe procedure, despite the necessity for accompanying anesthesia. In contrast to some anecdotal claims, none of the many scientific studies have ever demonstrated any anatomical evidence of brain damage resulting from ECT. There is, however, frequent temporary or permanent short-term memory loss that occurs at the time of ECT administration. This usually clears over time, but the acute memory dysfunction interferes with psychotherapy and is the major drawback to using ECT in treating depression in a patient who also requires concomitant psychotherapy.

Anti-Anxiety Agents

Minor Tranquilizers. This group of drugs is designed to treat the omnipresent anxiety that often relentlessly pursues the borderline. The earliest progenitors in this group were the barbiturates (Seconal, Nembutal, Pentothal, Amytal). Later entries included Equanil and Miltown (meprobamate), Placidyl (ethchlorvynol), Doriden (glutethimide), Quaalude and Sopor (methaqualone), Noludar (methyprylon), Noctec (chloral hydrate). All of these drugs are highly addictive, can precipitate dangerous withdrawal when stopped, are lethal in higher doses, and are not optimally effective in treating anxiety. Benadryl (diphenhydramine), Paral (paraldehyde), Phenergan (promethazine), Vistaril and Atarax (hydroxyzine) are somewhat less toxic, but also less effective.

Benzodiazepines. This group of drugs, first synthesized thirty years ago, has proved to be more valuable in relieving anxiety symptoms. Although these medicines may induce dependency and subsequent withdrawal phenomena, they are less toxic with overdosage. Librium (chlordiazepoxide), Valium (diazepam), Xanax (alprazolam), Tranxene (chlorazepate), Serax (oxazepam), Klonopin (clonazepam), Paxipam (halazepam), Centrax (prazepam) are in this category.

Although many studies have cited the usefulness of benzodiazepines in treating BPD, a few have noted that some borderline patients react to these drugs with greater impulsivity, aggression, and loss of control.[3,4]

Buspar (buspirone) is a recently developed drug for anxiety that appears to have fewer side effects, including less sedation and less propensity for addiction. Its efficacy with borderlines is not as clearly established.

Beta-Blockers. Some of the body's automatic responses to anxiety—palpitations, rapid heartbeat, tremors, sweating, and muscle twitching—are caused by the secretion of hormones, such as adrenaline. Medicines called beta-blockers interfere with the release of these substances and relieve some of these components of anxiety. Inderal (propranolol) is the most commonly used beta-blocker. This group of drugs is used less frequently for BPD.

Anticonvulsants

Because the borderline's impulsivity, mood swings, rageful outbursts, and uncontrollable behavior sometimes resemble epilepsy or other neurological disorders, some psychiatrists recommend anti-seizure medicine for treating BPD. In addition, some studies have documented abnormal EEGs (brain-wave tests) in a significant group of borderline patients.[5,6] Tegretol (carbamazepine) is the anticonvulsant that has been most extensively investigated, thus far. Some studies indicate that this drug improves the borderline's ability to control impulsive outbursts.[7,8] Other anticonvulsants, such as Dilantin (diphenylhydantoin) and Depakene (valproate), have been suggested but not yet adequately studied.

For Further Exploration

The following organizations provide materials, services, or information for consumers on BPD and mental health in general.

National Alliance for the Mentally Ill
1901 North Fort Myer Drive
Suite 500
Arlington, Virginia 22209

National Mental Health Consumers' Association
311 South Juniper Street
Room 902
Philadelphia, PA 19107

Notes

CHAPTER 1: THE WORLD OF THE BORDERLINE

1. A. Loranger, J. Oldham, and E. Tulis, "Familial Transmission of DSM-III Borderline Personality Disorder," *Archives of General Psychiatry* 39 (1982): 795–799.
2. Miron Baron et al., "Familial Transmission of Schizotypal and Borderline Personality Disorders," *American Journal of Psychiatry* 142 (1985): 927–934.
3. John G. Gunderson, *Borderline Personality Disorder* (Washington, D.C.: American Psychiatric Press, 1984).
4. Minna R. Fyer et al., "Comorbidity of Borderline Personality Disorder," *Archives of General Psychiatry* 45 (1988): 348–352.
5. Craig Johnson, David Tobin, and Amy Enright, "Prevalence and Clinical Characteristics of Borderline Patients in an Eating-Disordered Population," *Journal of Clincal Psychiatry* 50 (1989): 9–15.
6. Edgar P. Nace, J. Saxon, and N. Shore, "A Comparison of Borderline and Non-Borderline Alcoholic Patients," *Archives of General Psychiatry* 40 (1983): 54–56.
7. David J. Inman, Loy O. Bascue, and Thomas Skoloda, "Identification of Borderline Personality Disorders Among Substance Abuse Inpatients," *Journal of Substance Abuse Treatment* 2 (1985): 229–232.
8. Michael H. Stone, David K. Stone, and Stephen W. Hurt, "Natural History of Borderline Patients Treated by Intensive Hospitalization," *Psychiatric Clinics of North America* 10 (1987): 185–206.
9. American Psychiatric Association: *Diagnostic and Statistical Manual of Mental Disorders*, 3rd-revised ed. (Washington, D.C.: American Psychiatric Association, 1987), 346–347.

10. Craig Johnson, David Tobin and Amy Enright, "Prevalence and Clinical Characteristics of Borderline Patients in an Eating-Disordered Population," *Journal of Clinical Psychiatry* 50 (1989): 9–15.

11. Jeffrey B. Bryer et al., "Childhood Sexual and Physical Abuse as Factors in Adult Psychiatric Illness," *American Journal of Psychiatry* 144 (1987): 426–430.

12. Hagop S. Akiskal, "Subaffective Disorders: Dysthymic, Cyclothymic, and Bioplar II Disorders in the Borderline Realm," *Psychiatric Clinics of North America* 4 (1981): 25–46.

13. Margaret Mahler, F. Pine, and A. Bergman, *The Psychological Birth of the Human Infant* (New York: Basic Books, 1975).

14. Katherine A. Henry and Carl I. Cohen, "The Role of Labeling Processes in Diagnosing Borderline Personality Disorder," *American Journal of Psychiatry* 140 (1983): 1527–1529.

15. Ricardo Castaneda and Hugo Franco, "Sex and Ethnic Distribution of Borderline Personality Disorders in an Inpatient Sample," *American Journal of Psychiatry* 142 (1985): 1202–1203.

16. Thomas H. McGlashan, "The Chestnut Lodge Follow-Up Study III, Long-term Outcome of Borderline Personalities," *Archives of General Psychiatry* 43 (1986): 20–30.

17. Joel Sadavoy and Barbara Dorian, "Treatment of the Elderly Characterologically Disturbed Patient in the Chronic Care Instituion," *Journal of Geriatric Psychiatry* 16 (1983): 223–240.

18. Daniel J. Siegel and Gary W. Small, "Borderline Personality Disorder in the Elderly: A Case Study," *Canadian Journal of Psychiatry* 31 (1986): 859–860.

19. Louis Sass, "The Borderline Personality," *New York Times Magazine*, Aug. 22, 1982.

CHAPTER 2: CHAOS AND EMPTINESS

1. Owen D. Buck, "Multiple Personality as a Borderline State," *The Journal of Nervous and Mental Disease* 171 (1983): 62–65.

2. David G. Benner and Brenda Joscelyne, "Multiple

Personality as a Borderline Disorder,'' *The Journal of Nervous and Mental Disease* 172 (1984): 98–104.
3. William F. Clary, Kenneth J. Burstin, and John S. Carpenter, ''Multiple Personality and Borderline Personality Disorder,'' *Psychiatric Clinics of North America* 7 (1984): 89–99.
4. E. L. Bliss, ''Multiple Personality: A Report of 14 Cases with Implications for Schizophrenia and Hysteria,'' *Archives of General Psychiatry* 36 (1980): 1388–1397.
5. Richard P. Horevitz and Bennett G. Braun, ''Are Multiple Personalities Borderline?'' *Psychiatric Clinics of North America* 7 (1984): 69–87.
6. Vicki Westherford, paper presented at the Annual Meeting of the American Psychiatric Association, May, 1988.
7. Edgar P. Nace (1983), 54–56.
8. David J. Inman (1985): 229–232.
9. Hilda Bruch, ''Four Decades of Eating Disorders,'' in *Handbook of Psychotherapy for Anorexia and Bulimia,* eds. David M. Garner and Paul E. Garfinkle (New York: Guilford Press, 1985), 7–18.
10. Craig Johnson, David Towbin and Amy Enright, ''Prevalence and Clinical Characteristics of Borderline Patients in an Eating-Disordered Population,'' *Journal of Clinical Psychiatry* 50 (1989): 9–15.
11. Regina C. Casper et al., ''Bulimia: Its Incidence and Clinical Importance in Patients with Anorexia Nevrosa,'' *Archives of General Psychiatry* 37 (1980): 1030–1035.
12. Centers for Disease Control, *Suicide Surveillance, 1970–1980* (Atlanta: U.S. Dept. of Health and Human Services, 1985).
13. D. Shaffer and P. Fisher, ''The Epidemiology of Suicide in Children and Young Adolescents,'' *Journal of the American Academy of Child Psychiatry* 20 (1981): 545–565.
14. Gerald L. Klerman, ''Clinical Epidemiology of Suicide,'' *Journal of Clinical Psychiatry* 48 supp. (1987): 33–53.

15. American Psychiatric Association, DSM-III-R (1987), 346–347.
16. John G. Gunderson and Margaret T. Singer, "Defining Borderline Patients: An Overview," *American Journal of Psychiatry* 132 (1975): 1–10.
17. John G. Gunderson and Jonathan E. Kolb, "Discriminating Features of Borderline Patients," *American Journal of Psychiatry* 135 (1978): 792–796.
18. Octavio Paz, *The Endless Instant* (1966).
19. E. Nowell, *Thomas Wolfe, A Bibliography* (New York: Doubleday, 1960), 167.
20. Norman Mailer, *Marilyn* (New York: Grosset & Dunlap, 1973), 86.
21. Ibid, 108.
22. George S. Zubenko et al., "Sexual Practices Among Patients with Borderline Personality Disorder," *American Journal of Psychiatry* 144 (1987): 748–752.
23. Graham Greene, *A Sort of Life* (New York: Simon and Schuster, 1971).
24. Norman Rosten, *Marilyn: An Untold Story* (New York: New American Library, 1967), 112.
25. Gloria Steinem, *Marilyn* (New York: New American Library, 1986), 154.

CHAPTER 3:
ROOTS OF THE BORDERLINE SYNDROME

1. James F. Masterson, *The Narcissistic and Borderline Disorders: an Integrated Developmental Approach* (New York: Brunner/Mazel, 1981), 131–133.
2. Margaret S. Mahler (1975).
3. A Letter from T. E. Lawrence to Charlotte Shaw, August 18, 1927, as quoted by John E. Mack, *A Prince of Our Disorder: The Life of T. E. Lawrence* (Boston: Little, Brown and Co., 1976), 31.
4. Norman Mailer (1973).
5. Ibid, 36.
6. Norman Rosten (1967), 89.
7. John G. Gunderson, John Kerr, and Diane Woods Englund, "The Families of Borderlines: A Comparative Study," *Archives of General Psychiatry* 37 (1980): 27–33.
8. Hallie Frank and Joel Paris, "Recollections of Family

Experience in Borderline Patients,'' *Archives of General Psychiatry* 38 (1981): 1031–1034.

9. Ronald B. Feldman and Herta A. Guttman, "Families of Borderline Patients: Literal Minded Parents, Borderline Parents, and Parental Protectiveness,'' *American Journal of Psychiatry* 141 (1984): 1392–1396.

10. Stewart A. Montgomery, "The Psychopharmacology of Borderline Disorders,'' *ACTA of Psychiatry of Belgium* 87 supp. (1987): 260–266.

11. Paul H. Soloff, *Journal of Clinical Psychiatry* 48 supp. (1987): 13.

12. Paul A. Andrulois et al., "Organic Brain Dysfunction and the Borderline Syndrome,'' *Psychiatric Clinics of North America* 4 (1980): 47–66.

13. Scott Snyder and W. N. Pitts, Jr., "Electroencephalography of DSM III Borderline Personality Disorder,'' *ACTA of Psychiatry of Scandinavia* 69 (1984): 129 ff.

14. J. Bell et al., "Effect of Pre-Existing Borderline Personality Disorder on Clinical and EEG Sleep Correlates of Depression,'' *Psychiatry Resources* 9 (1983).

15. C. F. Reynolds III et al., "Depression in Borderline Cases: A Prospective EEG Study,'' *Psychiatry Resources* 14 (1985): 1–15.

16. Hagop Akiskal et al., "The Nosologic Status of Borderline Personality: Clinical and Polysomnographic Study,'' *American Journal of Psychiatry* 142 (1985): 192–198.

17. Harrison G. Pope, Jr, et al., "The Validity of DSM III Borderline Personality Disorder: A Phenomenologic, Family History, Treatment Response and Long Term Follow-Up Study,'' *Archives of General Psychiatry* 40 (1983): 23–30.

18. Paul H. Soloff and James Millward, "Psychiatric Disorders in the Families of Borderline Patients,'' *Archives of General Psychiatry* 40 (1983): 37–44.

19. Miron Baron (1985): 927–934.

20. Seymour S. Kety et al., "The Types and Problems of Mental Illness in the Biological and Adoptive Families of Adopted Schizophrenics,'' in *The Transmission of Schizophrenia,* eds. David Rosenthal and

Seymour S. Kety (Oxford: Pergamon Press, 1968): 345–362.

21. Michael H. Stone, "The Borderline Syndrome: Evolution of the Term, Genetic Aspects and Prognosis," *American Journal of Psychotherapy* 31 (1977): 345–365.

22. Thomas A. Aronson, "Historical Perspectives on the Borderline Concept: A Review and Critique," *Psychiatry* 48 (1985): 209–222.

CHAPTER 4: THE BORDERLINE SOCIETY

1. Christopher Lasch, *The Culture of Narcissism* (New York: W. W. Norton, 1978), 34.
2. Louis Sass (1982), 13.
3. Peter L. Giovachinni, *Psychoanalysis of Character Disorders* (New York: Jason Aronson, 1975).
4. Christopher Lasch (1978), 5.
5. David S. Greenwald, *No Reason to Talk About It* (New York: Norton, 1987).
6. Paul A. Andrulonis, personal communication, 1987.
7. Nancy Traub, "Supertots: The Collapse of Childhood," *Diablo,* June, 1987.
8. T. Berry Brazelton, "Issues of Working Parents," *American Journal of Orthopsychiatry* 56 (1986): 15.
9. Christopher Lasch (1978), 30.
10. Ricardo Castaneda (1985), 1202–1203.
11. George S. Zubenko (1987), 748–752.
12. Otto Kernberg, "Borderline Personality Organization," *Journal of the American Psychoanalytic Association* 15 (1967): 642–685.
13. Brazelton (1986), 15.
14. Thomas J. Gamble & Edward Zigler, "Effects of Infant Day Care: Another Look at the Evidence," *American Journal of Orthopsychiatry* 56 (1986): 26–42.
15. Edward F. Zigler, "A Solution to the Nation's Child Care Crisis," paper presented at the National Health Policy Forum, Washington, D.C. (1987), 1.
16. Cecilia M. Lilliston, "Child Sexual Abuse: An Advocacy-Outreach Treatment Model," American

Orthopsychiatric Association paper, Annual Conference, 1987.

17. James F. Masterson, *The Real Self: A Developmental, Self, and Object Relations Approach* (New York: Brunner/Mazel, 1985).

18. Brazelton (1986), 26–42.

19. Brazelton (1986), 20.

20. Brazelton (1986), 14.

21. Brazelton (1986), 22–23.

22. Betty Holcomb, "Where's Mommy? The Great Debate over the Effects of Day Care," *New York,* April 13, 1987, p. 75.

23. Hal Straus, "The Day Care Dilemma," *American Health,* Sept. 1988, p. 61.

24. Vincent J. Fontana, "Child Maltreatment and Battered Child Syndromes," in *Comprehensive Textbook of Psychiatry,* 4th ed., ed. Harold I. Kaplan and Benjamin J. Sadock (Baltimore: Williams & Wilkins, 1985), 1816.

25. Judith L. Herman, *Father-Daughter Incest* (Cambridge, Mass.: Harvard University Press, 1981).

26. Lawrence Claman and J.J. Stephens, "Improving Intervention Services for Preschool-Age Child Victims of Physical Abuse and Neglect," paper presented at American Orthopsychiatric Association meeting, 1988.

27. Susan Jacoby, "Emotional Child Abuse: The Invisible Plague," *Glamour,* October 1984; Edna J. Hunter, quoted in *USA Today,* August 1985, 11.

28. W. Hugh Missildine, *Your Inner Child of the Past* (New York: Simon and Schuster, 1963).

29. Judith Wallerstein and J. B. Kelly, "The Effect of Parental Divorce: Experiences of the Preschool Child," *Journal of the American Academy of Child Psychiatry* 14 (1975): 600–616.

30. Ibid.

31. M. Hetherington, "Children and Divorce," in *Parent-Child Interaction: Theory, Research, and Prospect,* ed. R. Henderson (New York: Academic Press, 1981).

32. Chaim F. Shatan, "Through the Membrane of Reality: 'Impacted Grief' and Perceptual Dissonance in

Vietnam Combat Veterans," *Psychiatric Opinion* 11 (1982): 6–15.

33. Chaim F. Shatan, "The Tattered Ego of Survivors," *Psychiatric Annals* 12 (1982): 1031–1038.
34. Chaim F. Shatan, "War Babies," *American Journal of Orthopsychiatry* 45 (1975): 289.
35. Paul Andrulonis (1987).

CHAPTER 7: SEEKING THERAPY

1. John G. Gunderson, *Borderline Personality Disorder* (Washington D.C.: American Psychiatric Press, 1984), 77.
2. Otto Kernberg, *Borderline Conditions and Pathological Narcissism* (New York: Jason Aronson, 1975).
3. James F. Masterson, *Psychotherapy of the Borderline Adult* (New York: Brunner/Mazel, 1976).
4. William Goldstein, *An Introduction to the Borderline Conditions* (New York: Jason Aronson, 1985), 201–203. Also, Gunderson (1984), 51–52.
5. Norman Rosten (1972), 100.
6. Ibid, 100–101.
7. Norman D. Macaskill, "Therapeutic Factors in Group Therapy with Borderline Patients," *International Journal of Group Psychotherapy* 32 (1) (1982): 61–73.
8. Wendy Froberg and Brent D. Slife, "Overcoming Obstacles to the Implementation of Yalom's Model of Inpatient Group Psychotherapy," *International Journal of Group Psychotherapy* 37 (3) (1987): 371–388.
9. Leonard Horwitz, "Indications for Group Therapy with Borderline and Narcissistic Patients," *Bulletin of the Menninger Clinic* 1 (3) (1987): 248–260.
10. Gunderson (1984), 170–172.
11. Stephen A. Jones, "Family Therapy with Borderline and Narcissistic Patients," *Bulletin of the Menninger Clinic* 51 (3) (1987): 285–295.
12. Gunderson (1984), 162–169.
13. Paul H. Soloff, "A Pharmacologic Approach to the Borderline Patient," *Psychiatric Annals* 17 (3) (1987): 201–205.
14. Phillip A. Berger, "Pharmacological Treatment for

Borderline Personality Disorder," *Bulletin of the Menninger Clinic* 51 (3) (1987): 277–284.

15. Rex W. Cowdry and David L. Gardner, "Pharmacotherapy of Borderline Personality Disorder," *Archives of General Psychiatry* 45 (1988): 111–119.

16. Gunderson (1984).

17. Michael Rosenbluth, "The Inpatient Treatment of the Borderline Personality Disorder: A Critical Review and Discussion of Aftercare Implications," *Canadian Journal of Psychiatry* 32 (1987): 228–237.

18. Daniel H. Jacobs et al., "The Neglected Alliance: The Inpatient Unit as a Consultant to Referring Therapists," *Hospital and Community Psychiatry* 33 (5) (1982): 377–381.

19. Jerold J. Kreisman, "CTU: The Systematic Inpatient Treatment of the Borderline Patient," *Res Medica* 3 (2) (1986): 19–26.

20. Daniel Silver, Robert J. Cardish, and Edward J. Glassman, "Intensive Treatment of Characterologically Difficult Patients: A General Hospital Perspective," *Psychiatric Clinics of North America* 10 (2) (1987): 219–245.

21. Maetin Pildis et al., "Day Hospital Treatment of Borderline Patients: A Clinical Perspective," *American Journal of Psychiatry* 135 (5) (1978): 594–596.

22. Alan B. Eppel and Mary Thomas Dart, "Day Hospital Treatment of the Borderline," paper presented at the Annual Meeting of the American Psychiatric Association, May 1985.

23. Han Soo Lee, "Patients' Comments on Psychiatric Inpatient Treatment Experiences: Patient-Therapist Relationships and Their Implications for Treatment Outcome," *Psychiatric Quarterly* 51 (1) (1979): 39–54.

24. Robet J. Waldinger and John G. Gunderson, "Completed Psychotherapies with Borderline Patients," *American Journal of Psychotherapy* 38 (1984): 190–202.

25. Michael H. Stone, David K. Stone, and Stephen W. Hurt, "Natural History of Borderline Patients Treated

by Intensive Hospitalization," *Psychiatric Clinics of North America* 10 (2) (1987): 185–206.

26. Robert J. Waldinger and John G. Gunderson, *Effective Psychotherapy with Borderline Patients: Case Studies* (New York: Macmillan Publishing Company, 1987).

CHAPTER 8: COPING WITH THE BORDERLINE

1. David A. Brent et al., "Risk Factors for Adolescent Suicide," *Archives of General Psychiatry* 45 (June, 1988): 581–588.

APPENDIX B:
EVOLUTION OF THE BORDERLINE SYNDROME

1. Michael H. Stone, "The Borderline Syndrome: Evolution of the Term, Genetic Aspects and Prognosis," *American Journal of Psychotherapy* 31 (1977): 345–365.

2. Adolph Stern, "Psychoanalytic Investigation of and Therapy in the Border Line Group of Neuroses," *The Psychonalytic Quarterly* 7 (1938): 467–489.

3. G. Zilboorg, "Ambulatory Schizophrenia," *Psychiatry* 4 (1941): 149–155.

4. Paul Hoch and Philip Polatin, "Pseudoneurotic Forms of Schizophrenia," *Psychiatric Quarterly* 23 (1949): 248–276.

5. G. Bychowski, "The Problem of Latent Psychosis," *Journal of the American Psychoanalytic Association* 4 (1953): 484–503.

6. *Diagnostic & Statistical Manual of Mental Disorders,* 2nd edition (Washington, D.C.: American Psychiatric Association, 1968).

7. Helen Deutsch, "Some Forms of Emotional Disturbance and the Relationship to Schizophrenia," *The Psychoanalytic Quarterly* 11 (1942): 301–321.

8. Robert P. Knight, "Borderline States," *Bulletin of the Menninger Clinic* 17 (1953): 1–12.

9. Roy R. Grinker, B. Werble, and R. C. Drye, *The Borderline Syndrome* (New York: Basic Books, 1968).

10. Otto Kernberg, "Borderline Personality Organization," *Journal of the Psychoanalytic Association* 15 (1967): 641–685.

11. Otto Kernberg, *Borderline Conditions and Pathologi-*

cal Narcissism (New York: Jason Aronson, 1975). Psychiatric Quarterly 23 (1949): 248–276.

APPENDIX C:
MEDICATIONS USED TO TREAT BPD

1. Paul H. Soloff, Anselm George, and R. Swami Nathan, "Progress in Pharmacotherapy in Borderline Disorders," *Archives of General Psychiatry* (43) (1986): 691–697.

2. Paul H. Soloff, Anselm George, and R. Swami Nathan, "Paradoxical Effects of Amitriptyline on Borderline Patients," *American Journal of Psychiatry* 143 (1986): 1603–1605.

3. Frank J. Faltus, "The Positive Effect of Alprazolam in the Treatment of Three Patients with Borderline Personality Disorder," *American Journal of Psychiatry* 141 (6) (1984): 802–803.

4. R. Gaind and R. Jacoby, "Benzodiazepines Causing Aggression," in Vol. 1 *Current Themes in Psychiatry,* eds. R. Gaind and B. L. Hudson (London: Macmillan Publishing Company, 1978), 371–379.

5. Scott Snyder and Wesley M. Pitts, Jr., "Electroencephalography of DSM-III Borderline Personality Disorder," *Acta Psychiatry, Scandinavia* 69 (1984): 129–134.

6. Jack R. Cornelius et al., "EEG Abnormalities in Borderline Personality Disorder: Specific or Non-Specific," *Biological Psychiatry* 21 (1986): 977–980.

7. David L. Gardner and Rex W. Cowdry, "Positive Effects of Carbamazepine on Behavioral Dyscontrol in Borderline Personality Disorder," *American Journal of Psychiatry* 143 (4) (1986): 519–522.

8. David L. Gardner and Rex W. Cowdry, "Anticonvulsants in Personality Disorders," in *Use of Anticonvulsants in Psychiatry: Recent Advances,* eds. Susan L. McElroy and Harrison G. Pope (Clifton, N.J.: Oxford Health Care, 1988), 127–140.

Index

DAWN ON A DISTANT SHORE

"The likable protagonists, a multitude of amusing secondary characters and exciting escapades make this a compelling read." —*Publishers Weekly*

"Donati's skillfully told and captivating romantic historical saga brings a tumultuous era and dashing characters to life in what promises to be a very popular and rewarding series." —*Booklist*

"Donati masterfully weaves the evocative history of the founding of America with the powerful challenges faced by those, like the Bonners, who settled this new world. The strengths they find in themselves provide a timely reminder that this melting pot nation is a rich fabric, woven by the lives of ordinary people who rise to extraordinary challenges." —*BookPage*

"Like *Into the Wilderness, Dawn on a Distant Shore* will keep readers up into the wee hours. We can only hope Donati has her own supply of midnight oil that she is using to write the third installment of this worthy and satisfying series." —*The Orlando Sentinel*

"Set in the wilderness of 1794 New-York . . . [*Dawn on a Distant Shore*] features an imaginative plot that interconnects characters without straining credibility or leaving loose ends. It's a balanced blend of bravery, treachery, romance, suffering and hope." —*The Tampa Tribune Times*

"This novel is a sequel to the earlier epic, *Into the Wilderness,* but although there's a strong sense of the

characters' past, it's perfectly enjoyable on its own terms. If you haven't read the earlier book, however, you're likely to make immediate tracks in your own quest to aquire it." —*The Seattle Times*

"Sara Donati has created a worthy historical epic here, enriched by solid intrigues and a compelling cast of characters." —*The Bellingham Herald*

"Remarkably written. Outstanding." —*Rendezvous*

"The story line is impressive as the plot fully entertains the audience. Sara Donati creates an Americana epic that will receive much acclaim from fans and critics." —*The Midwest Book Review*

INTO THE WILDERNESS

"My favorite kind of book is the sort you live in, rather than read. *Into the Wilderness* is one of those rare stories that let you breathe the air of another time, and leave your footprints on the snow of a wild, strange place. I can think of no better adventure than to explore the wilderness in the company of such engaging and independent lovers as Elizabeth and her Nathaniel." –Diana Gabaldon

"The author builds a powerful adventure story, animating everyone— German villagers, slaves, and Scottish trappers alike—in a gorgeous, vividly described American landscape. The erotic passages aren't bad either." —*People*

"Donati's captivating saga is much like the books in Diana Gabaldon's bestselling *Outlander* series, and it is definitely the romance of the year when it comes to transcending genre boundaries and appealing to readers who love lush historical epics or thrilling backwoods adventures." —*Booklist*

Bantam Books
by Sara Donati

INTO THE WILDERNESS

DAWN ON A DISTANT SHORE

———

DAWN ON A DISTANT SHORE

Sara Donati

BANTAM BOOKS

New York Toronto London Sydney Auckland

This edition contains the complete text
of the original hardcover edition.

DAWN ON A DISTANT SHORE
A Bantam Book

PUBLISHING HISTORY
Bantam hardcover edition published March 2000
Bantam mass market edition / June 2001

Library of Congress Catalog Card Number: 99-40438.

ISBN 0-553-57855-3

Published simultaneously in the United States and Canada

Bantam Books are published by Bantam Books, a division of Random
House, Inc. Its trademark, consisting of the words "Bantam Books"
and the portrayal of a rooster, is Registered in U.S. Patent and
Trademark Office and in other countries. Marca Registrada. Bantam
Books, 1540 Broadway, New York, New York 10036.

PRINTED IN THE UNITED STATES OF AMERICA
OPM   10 9 8 7 6 5 4 3 2 1

For my daughter, Elisabeth

She discovered with great delight that
one does not love one's children
just because they are one's children
but because of the friendship formed
while raising them.

—*Gabriel García Márquez*

Acknowledgments

Just after I began writing this novel, we moved across the country. My sincere thanks to old friends who didn't lose sight of me or my characters, and to new friends—in particular, Suzanne Paola, Bruce Beasley, and Robin Hemley—for spending so much of their time with me on the high seas of historical fiction. I am especially grateful to Suzanne, Bruce, and Jin Woo for their support and friendship in interesting times. I truly don't know what we would do without them, and I hope we never have to find out.

I owe a special debt of gratitude to He-Who-Must-Remain-Anonymous, the editor of the Baronage website (www.baronage.co.uk), whose expertise and generosity made many things possible. The blueprints of Carryckcastle came from him; he discovered the earl's genealogy and unearthed his coat of arms. Without the help of Anonymous and his staff (most particularly, Brother Septimus and his nose for scandal), my Alasdair Scott, fourth Earl of Carryck, would be a mere shadow of himself.

At most I am an armchair sailor, and so in the writing of this story I depended greatly on the help of those who love the sea: Ric Day, James Doody, Steven L. Lopata, John Woram, and Ray Briscoe shared their expertise and experience, and I am thankful to them. I married into a sailing family, and I thank my husband, Bill, and my parents-in-law, Ken and Mary, for background information and, most of all, encouragement.

Another anonymous friend was of great help in my attempts to render eighteenth-century Scots into an accessible form. Accuracy must be the first casualty in such an endeavor, for which I take full responsibility.

I am indebted to Michelle LaFrance for close readings, supportive words, Gaelic translations, and perspective; George Bray III for extensive help on eighteenth-century military history, dress, and customs; Hakim Ibrahim Chishti for invaluable detail on Islamic medical practices, naming conventions, history, and theology; Dr. Jim Gilsdorf for background on specific illnesses and their surgical treatment; Dr. Ellen Mandell for medical history, convincing detail, and photocopies; and Mac Beckett, Jo Bourne, Rob Carr, Leigh Cooper, Lisa Dillon, Walter Hawn, Nurmi Husa, Susan Leigh, Rosina Lippi, Susan Martin, Sandra Parshall, Susan Lynn Peterson, Stephen Ratterman, Beth Shope, Elise Skidmore, Jack Turley, Arnold Wagner, Karen Watson, and Michael Lee West. Thanks to another obsessive (obsessed?) writer of historical fiction, Mr. Calwaugh, for dessert, garden tours, and rounding up half of Portland for readings.

The Women of the Wilderness at AOL have been consistently supportive. Many times when I was having trouble putting one word after the next they kept me going. Maria, Pokey, Tracey, Lynn, Nancy, Jeanette, Melinda, Liz, Justine, Kit, Sue, Tara, Julie, Sharon, Theresa, Rose Mary, Barb, Christy, Chris, Lee, Mary Rose, Kim Elaine, Susan, Jenni, Michelle, Judy, Ann, Kathleen, and the Kathies—these generous and supportive women have been a great source of energy and inspiration for me, and I hope they find this novel worth the wait.

About four chapters into this undertaking I asked Diana Gabaldon if the second volume in a series is the hardest, to which she immediately shot back, "No, the fifth one is." My thanks to Diana for perspective, for worry-stones and phone calls, and for her friendship and support in an endeavor that never gets easier.

My continued thanks to Jill Grinberg, my friend and agent and ever the voice of calm in the storm; and to Wendy McCurdy, Nita Taublib, and Irwyn Applebaum at Bantam for their continued enthusiasm and for invigorating phone calls.

Tamar Groffman has gotten me and mine through many a rough spot with sound good words and dahlias, for which I will always be thankful. Now if she would only adopt me.

I am ever thankful for my daughter, Elisabeth, who is learning to cope with a Mother Who Writes without losing her sense of humor, and to Bill, who refuses to be surprised by any of this. Without them, the whole business would be no fun at all.

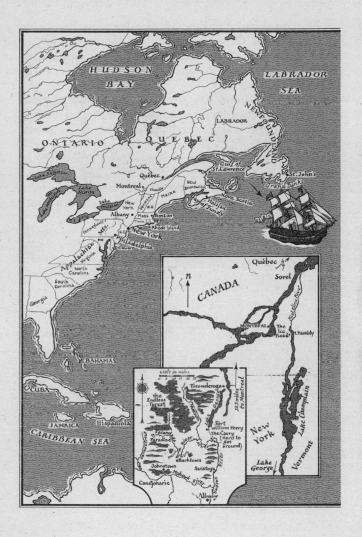

Chief Characters

Where they are first encountered

PARADISE, ON THE EDGE OF THE NEW-YORK WILDERNESS

Judge Alfred Middleton, landowner

Curiosity Freeman, a freed slave, his house-keeper

Galileo Freeman, a freed slave, the manager of his farm and holdings, and Curiosity's husband

Axel Metzler, owner of the tavern

LAKE IN THE CLOUDS

Nathaniel Bonner (also known as Wolf-Running-Fast or Between-Two-Lives), a hunter and trapper

Elizabeth Middleton Bonner (also known as Bone-in-Her-Back), a schoolteacher and Nathaniel's wife

Hannah (also known as Squirrel), Nathaniel's daughter by his first wife

Mathilde (Lily) and Daniel Bonner, Elizabeth and Nathaniel's children

Liam Kirby, an orphan living with the Bonners

Falling-Day, of the Kahnyen'kehàka (Mohawk) Wolf clan, Nathaniel's former mother-in-law

Many-Doves, Falling-Day's daughter and the wife of Runs-from-Bears

Runs-from-Bears, of the Kahnyen'kehàka Turtle clan

Blue-Jay, infant son of Many-Doves and Runs-from-Bears

ALBANY

General Major Phillip Schuyler and his wife, Catherine; some of their children and grandchildren

Augusta Merriweather, Lady Crofton, Elizabeth Bonner's aunt, visiting from England along with her daughter,

Amanda Spencer, Lady Durbeyfield, with her husband, William Spencer, Viscount Durbeyfield

Grievous Mudge, ship's captain

CANADA

Dan'l Bonner (known also as Hawkeye), Nathaniel's father

Robbie MacLachlan, Scot, hunter and trapper

Iona Fraser, a Scottish immigrant to Canada and

Luke, her grandson

Otter, son of Falling-Day

Pépin, a pig farmer

Denier, a butcher

Ron Jones, a sergeant of the dragoons

Angus Moncrieff, secretary and factor to the Earl of Carryck

George Somerville, Lord Bainbridge, lieutenant governor of Lower Canada, also called Pink George

Giselle Somerville, daughter of Lord Bainbridge

Sir Guy Carleton, Lord Dorchester, governor of Lower Canada

Maria Carleton, Lady Dorchester, the governor's wife

Mac Stoker, Irish by birth, captain and owner of the *Jackdaw*

Horace Pickering, captain of the *Isis*, a merchantman

AT SEA

Aboard the Jackdaw

Anne Bonney Stoker (Granny), Mac Stoker's grandmother

Connor, his first mate

Captain Christian Fane of the *Leopard*

Aboard the Isis
(The Lass in Green)

Hakim Ibrahim Dehlavi ibn Abdul Rahman Balkhi, ship's surgeon

Charlie, the Hakim's cabin boy and servant

Mungo, another cabin boy and Charlie's brother

Margreit MacKay, wife of the first officer

Adam MacKay and Jonathan Smythe, first and second officers

SCOTLAND
Solway Firth and Dumfries

Robert Burns, exciseman

Dandie Mump, innkeeper at Mump's Hall

At Carryck and Carryckcastle

Alasdair Scott, 9th Lord Scott of Carryckcastle, 4th Earl of Carryck

Jean Hope, housekeeper; Jennet, her daughter

MacQuiddy, house steward

Monsieur Dupuis, a permanent houseguest

Some of the earl's men: Richard Odlyn; Dugald and Ewen Huntar; Thomas, Lucas, and Ronald Ballentyne; Jamie Dalgleish; Ebenezer Lun

Monsieur Contrecoeur, a visiting French wine merchant

Madame Marie Vigée and Mademoiselle Julie LeBrun, cousins and traveling companions to Contrecoeur

Leezie Laidlaw, a widow

Gelleys Smaill, a retired washerwoman

Minister Willie Fisher

At Moffat

Flora, Countess of Loudoun, an orphan

John Campbell, 4th Earl of Breadalbane, chief of the Glenorchy line, and Flora's guardian

Walter Campbell, illegitimate son of Breadalbane by an unknown lady, appointed by his father as the curator of the Loudoun holdings

Isabel Campbell, née Scott, his wife

The Family Tree for the Carryck Line

* indicates nonfictional character

ROBERT, 5TH LORD SCOTT, WAS KILLED IN THE SERVICE OF CHARLES II;
by Beatrix Scott of Pykeston had an only child, Robert,
6th Lord Scott, who was created Earl of Carryck and
Viscount Moffat by his grateful sovereign in 1660

|

ROBERT SCOTT, 6TH LORD SCOTT OF CARRYCKCASTLE,
1ST EARL OF CARRYK;

married Frances, illegitimate daughter of *Francis Scott,
2nd Earl of Buccleuch (a prominent Royalist)

|

ROBERT, 7TH LORD SCOTT OF CARRYCKCASTLE,
2ND EARL OF CARRYCK;

married Margaret, illegitimate daughter of *James Morton,
11th Earl of Morton; died 1755

|

RODERICK SCOTT, 8TH LORD SCOTT OF CARRYCKCASTLE,
3rd Earl of Carryck, born 1690 (elder twin);

married Appalina Forbes, heiress daughter of William Forbes of
Agardston, a retired merchant of Danzig who restored Agardston
Tower, extended its lands, and established a shipping fleet at the port
of Aberdeen, and heiress sister to her two unmarried half
brothers, who created a huge fortune trading in the American
colonies in sugar, tobacco, and slaves; died 1775

|

ALASDAIR SCOTT,
9th Lord Scott of Carryckcastle, 4th Earl of Carryck, born 1721;

married Marietta, daughter by an unknown French lady of *Arthur
Elphinstone, 6th Lord Balmerinoch (executed 1746 as a Jacobite);
Marietta is a cousin to Flora, Countess of Loudoun

|

ISABEL,
born 1764;

eloped in 1790 to marry Walter Campbell, the illegitimate son
of *John Campbell, 4th Earl of Breadalbane; Walter serves Flora,
Countess of Loudoun, as her curator

JAMES SCOTT,
born 1690 (younger twin); disappeared 1718;

married Margaret Montgomerie of Edinburgh
in Albany, NY, 1722; died 1728

|

DAN'L [BONNER] AKA HAWKEYE,
born 1725 on the NY frontier;

married Cora Munro, daughter of a Munro cadet of Foulis, an officer
of His Majesty's Forces in the North American Colonies, in 1756

|

NATHANIEL BONNER,
born 1757;

first wife: Sings-from-Books, granddaughter of the clan mother of the
Wolf Longhouse of the Kahnyen'kehàka people;

second wife: Elizabeth Middleton, originally of Oakmere, Devon, in 1793

DAUGHTER HANNAH
(Squirrel) by his first wife

SON DANIEL AND DAUGHTER MATHILDE
(twins) by his second wife

Prologue

To the Earl of Carryck
Carryckcastle
Annandale
Scotland

My Lord,

Allow me to report success: at long last I have located the man I believe to be your cousin. He is known as Dan'l Bonner, called Hawkeye by his associates, Indian and White. Even if there were not plentiful documentary evidence that he is your uncle Jamie Scott's son by Margaret Montgomerie, the sight of him alone would convince anyone that he is indeed a Scott of Carryck.

Bonner resides on the northernmost frontier of the State of New-York, where he was raised—as you always believed—by Natives. I trust you will be pleased to learn that he took as guidwife a Scotswoman (now deceased), whose father was, by fortunate circumstance, a Munro cadet of Foulis. She bore a son, called Nathaniel, now some thirty-six years of age, in robust health and with a new guidwife in hopeful expectation. Both father and son have made their living as hunters and trappers in the wilderness that the Natives call the endless forests, between this place and the Mohawk Valley. That is where I found Nathaniel,

who then directed me here to Montréal. He is a likely young man, and I believe you will be well pleased with him.

Before I can carry out the task entrusted to me and convey Bonner and his son home to Carryck, Dan'l must first be disengaged from the military garrison where he is currently being held for questioning, in the matter of a large shipment of the King's gold, missing for some forty years.

You see that the family resemblance is more than simple physiognomy.

I have had word from Pickering, who has docked the *Isis* at Halifax, but first getting to Bonner is a very complicated undertaking, and one which may require some drastic steps. The whole venture is made even more complex by the interference of the Lieutenant Governor, Lord Bainbridge. My Lord will remember Pink George from the unfortunate incident with the pig, I trust. He, at any rate, has not forgot it.

Yours at command, My Lord
Angus Moncrieff
Montréal, this third day of January, 1794

To Mr. Nathaniel Bonner
Paradise, on the West Branch of the Sacandaga
State of New-York

Sir—

With the prodigious help of Rab MacLachlan and your excellent directions, I have found your father. Unfortunately, the Lieutenant Governor had found him first and he paces a cell in the garrison gaol while being questioned on a matter referred to only as the "Tory gold," details of which MacLachlan scruples to share with me. While I

have seen your father for only a moment I can report that he seems to be in good health. A message in two parts:

First, a young man called Otter, of the Mohawk (or Kahnyen'kehàka as I understand they call themselves), was arrested with him, but is unharmed. Second, your father believes that a "visit to the pomkin patch" is the only way to resolve his current difficulties.

If, as I suspect, this means that you will be coming to Montréal, I beg you to call on me in my rooms in the rue St. Gabriel. You will find me to be an experienced and willing assistant in the garden. I ask only for your father's ear for an hour to present my lordship's case.

I believe your lady's time must be close at hand. Please allow me to send my very best wishes for her safe delivery, and for the continuing health of your entire family.

Your Willing Servant
Angus Moncrieff
Secretary and Factor to the Earl of Carryck
Montréal, this third day of January, 1794

PART I

North to Canada

I

1 February, 1794

On the edge of the New-York wilderness

In the middle of a blizzard in the second half of the hardest, snowiest winter anyone in Paradise could remember, Elizabeth Middleton Bonner, sweat soaked, naked, and adrift in burning pain, wondered if she might just die of the heat.

Once again she grabbed the leather straps tied to the bed frame to haul herself forward, and bore down with all her considerable strength.

"Come, little one," sang the girl who crouched, waiting, at the foot of the bed. Her ten-year-old face was alight with excitement and fierce concentration, her bloodied hands outstretched, beckoning.

From a basket before the warmth of the hearth came the high, keen wail of Elizabeth's firstborn: a daughter, just twenty minutes old.

"Come, child," crooned Hannah. "We are waiting for you."

We are all waiting for you.

In the grip of a contraction that threatened to set her on fire, Elizabeth bore down again and was rewarded with the blessed sight of a crowning head. With shaking fingers she touched the slick, wet curls and her own flesh, stretched drumtight: her body on the brink of splitting itself in two.

One last time, one last time, one last time. She
strained, feeling the child flex and turn, feeling its will,
as strong as her own. Elizabeth blinked the sweat from
her eyes and looked up to find Hannah's gaze fixed on
her.

"Let him come," the girl said in Kahnyen'kehàka. "It
is his time."

Elizabeth pushed. In a rush of fluid her son, blue-
white and already howling, slid out into her stepdaughter's waiting hands. With a groan of relief and
thanksgiving, Elizabeth collapsed backward.

For one sweet moment, the wailing of the newborns
was louder than the scream of the blizzard rampag-
ing through the endless forests. Their father was out
there, trying to make his way home to them. With
her arms crossed over the warm, squirming bundles
Hannah laid against her skin, Elizabeth muttered a
prayer for Nathaniel Bonner's safe delivery from the
storm.

As Elizabeth labored, the small handful of farmers and
trappers with the good sense to be stranded by the blizzard in Paradise's only tavern sat huddled over cards
and ale, waiting out the weather. While the winds
worked the rafters like starving wolves at a carcass,
they told stories in easy, slurred voices, but they
watched their cards and tankards and the long,
straight back of the man who stood, motionless, at the
window.

"Strung as tight as my fiddle," muttered one of the
card players. "Say something to him, Axel."

Axel Metzler shrugged a shoulder in frustration, but
he turned toward the window. "Set down, Nathaniel,
and have a drink. I broke out my best ale, here. And the
storm won't be letting up for you staring at it."

"Women will have babies at the worst times," announced the youngest of the men solemnly.

"Now, what would you know about it, Charlie? You got a wife hid away somewhere?"

"A man don't need a wife of his own to see that it's damn hard luck to have run into this weather."

The storm raised its voice as if to argue. The roof groaned in response, and a fine sifting of dust settled over the room and the uncovered tankards.

Axel plucked the pipe from his mouth in disgust and pointed his tattered white beard toward the heavens, exposing a long neck much like that of a plucked turkey. "Shut up, you old *Teufel*! Quiet!"

The winds howled once more, let out a longish whine, and fell silent. For a moment the men stared at each other and then Axel tucked his pipe back in the corner of his mouth with a satisfied grunt.

A woman appeared at the door from the living quarters just as the man at the window turned. The light of the fire threw his face into relief: half shadow, all worry, his high brow furrowed and his mouth pressed hard. In his hand was a crumpled sheet of paper, which he tucked into his shirt with one hand while he reached for his mantle with the other.

"Curiosity?" he asked, his voice hoarse with disuse.

"I'm right here, Nathaniel." Long and wiry, straight backed in spite of her near sixty years, Curiosity Freeman moved briskly through the room, her skirts snapping and swirling. The hands adjusting the turban that towered above her head were deep brown against the sprigged fabric. She turned to a boy who sat near the fire, big boned, ginger haired, and pale with sleeplessness. "You there, Liam Kirby. Look lively, now. You fetch me my snowshoes, will you?"

He sprang up, rubbing his eyes. "Yes'm."

Axel stood and stretched. "Good luck, Nathaniel! Give Miz Elizabeth our best!"

Nathaniel raised a hand in acknowledgment. "Thank you, Axel. Jed, I was supposed to send Martha Southern word, would you take care of that for me?"

"I will. Tomorrow we'll wet the child's head, proper like."

"We'll do that, God willing."

Liam had gone out onto the porch, but the older woman hung back to put a hand on Nathaniel's arm. "Elizabeth's strong, and Hannah's with her. That girl of yours has got the touch, you know that."

She's only ten years old.

Nathaniel could see that thought sitting there in the troubled lines that bracketed Curiosity's mouth. "Elizabeth asked for you. She wanted you." *And me. I should be there.*

Curiosity squinted at him. Never the kind to offer false comfort, she nodded, and followed him outside.

Strung out in single file with Nathaniel leading and Liam bringing up the rear, they left the village on snowshoes. They carried tin lanterns that cast dancing pinpricks of light over the new snow: a scattering of golden stars to match the fiery ones overhead. The night sky had been scrubbed clean; the moon was knife edged and cold, as cold as the air that stung the throat and nose.

Nathaniel glanced over his shoulder now and then to gauge Curiosity's pace. Thus far she showed no signs of tiring, in spite of the late hour and interrupted sleep. *Frontier women,* his father often said. *When one of their own is in need, they can set creation on its ear.*

He had set out to fetch her almost twenty-four hours ago. She was his father-in-law's housekeeper, but Curiosity Freeman was more than that: Elizabeth's friend, and his own, the clearest head in the village and the closest thing Paradise had to a doctor since Richard Todd had decided to spend the winter in Johnstown; she had always been a better midwife, anyway. With a midwife's sense of timing, she had been ready for him, her basket packed. She wiped the flour from her hands

and arms and passed the kneading over to her daughter, calling out to her husband, Galileo, that she was on her way. Judge Middleton was still abed, and they left without disturbing him.

"Let him sleep," she had said, strapping on her snowshoes. "Ain't nothing a man can do to ease a daughter in labor anyways, and my Polly will see to his breakfast. Did you send Anna word? I'd be glad of her help, with the rest of your womenfolk away."

"Liam's gone to fetch her."

"Let's get moving, then. First children ain't usually in a hurry, but you never know."

But the whiteout had come down on them just outside the village, turning the world he knew tree by tree into a flickering mirror of silver and white, impossible to navigate. That they had found the trading post was a miracle in itself; that he had been able to wait there hour after hour without losing his mind was another. Nathaniel could not put the picture out of his head: Elizabeth in labor with only Hannah beside her. He had lost his first wife—Hannah's mother—in childbirth on a warm summer night that felt nothing and everything like this one.

He wiped the freezing sweat from his brow, and increased his pace.

The mountain was called Hidden Wolf, and the high vale where his father had built a homestead forty years ago, Lake in the Clouds. This was a translation of the Kahnyen'kehàka name, but the whites had never found anything better to call the place where the mountain folded inward on itself. Triangular in shape, the valley was big enough for two L-shaped cabins, a barn, kitchen gardens, and a sizable cornfield on its outer edge, where the shoulder gave way to the precipice. At the opposite end, a waterfall dropped into a shallow gorge in a series of glittering, frozen arches. Below it a small lake was ringed with concentric collars of ice.

When he was within earshot of the falls, Nathaniel broke away and left the others to struggle on without him. Past the first cabin where he had been raised, dark now with his father gone to Montréal and the rest of the family at Good Pasture. On through the small grove of beech, pine, and blue spruce to the far cabin, built less than a year ago for his new bride, Elizabeth Middleton. She had come from England to join her father. Well educated, able to speak her mind and willing to listen, with money and land of her own, and plans to teach. She had called herself a spinster without flinching, showing him sharp edges and soft ones, bone-deep curiosity and a well of raw strength and courage. From Chingachgook, his Mahican grandfather, Elizabeth had earned the name Bone-in-Her-Back.

On the porch Nathaniel kicked off his snowshoes and threw open the door to fading firelight and warmth. The cabin smelled as it always did: of woodsmoke, pine sap, lye soap and tallow, curing meat, corn bread baking, dried apples and herbs, of the dogs and of pelts newly stretched and scraped, and of her smells, for which he had no names but a hundred images. And there was the smell of blood recently shed: copper and hot salt.

Nathaniel put down his weapons and dropped his overcoat and mitts as he strode across the room, scattering ice and clots of snow. He paused before the open door of the small bedroom to breathe in. To force himself to breathe. His own blood hammered in his ears so that he could hear nothing else.

They were there, asleep. The banked fire showed him his Hannah, curled at the foot of the bed, one arm across the long line of Elizabeth's legs. Her face was hidden in the shadows.

He crossed the room without a sound and went down on his knees. Elizabeth was breathing, her mouth slightly open, her lips cracked and beaded with blood. There was no fever flush—she was pale, her skin cool to

the touch. The fist in his gut began to loosen, finger by finger, to be replaced by a warm wash of relief.

Nathaniel pulled his gaze away from Elizabeth's face to the bundle at her side. And blinked.

Two infants, swaddled in the Kahnyen'kehàka way. Dark hair, rounded cheeks, white and pink faces smaller than the palm of his hand. One pair of eyes flickered open, unfocused. A tiny red mouth contorted, the cheeks working, and then relaxed.

Twins. Nathaniel put his forehead on the bed, drew in a long breath, and felt his heart take up an extra beat.

2

The winter morning came with a pure, cold light, setting
the ice and snow aflame with color and casting a rainbow
across Hannah's face to wake her. She lay for a moment,
listening to the morning sounds: Liam was feeding the fire,
humming to himself. The dogs whined at the door, and
then a woman's voice: familiar and welcome, but unusual
here, so early in the day.

The events of the previous night came to her in a
rush and she stumbled out of her loft bed and down the
ladder, pulling her quilt with her.

Liam held out a bowl. "Porridge," he said, without
the least bit of enthusiasm. Since he had come to live
with them Hannah had learned that Liam's first allegiance was always to his stomach, but she could not
keep her gaze from moving toward the bedroom door.
It stood slightly ajar.

Curiosity appeared as if Hannah had called for her.

"Miz Hannah," she said formally. "Let me shake your
hand, child. Are we proud of you? I should say so."

Hannah found her voice. "She's all right?"

"She is. And those babies, too." Curiosity laughed
out loud. "If the Lord had made anything prettier he
would have kept it for hisself."

There was a feeble cry from the next room. Hannah stepped in that direction, only to be caught up by Curiosity, who took her by the elbow and steered her back toward the table.

"Just set and eat, first. Pass some of that porridge over here, Liam, and stop pulling faces. It's honest food, after all."

"They are awful small," Hannah said, accepting the bowl and spoon automatically. "I was worried."

"Twins tend to be small," said Curiosity. "You were, when you come along. Nathaniel could just about hold you in one hand, and he did, too. Carried you around tucked into his shirt for the longest time."

"He carried you up to bed last night, too. Guess you didn't even notice," said Liam.

"Well, he's feeling perky, is Nathaniel." Curiosity put a cup of cider on the table in front of Hannah.

"A boy," said Liam. "Chingachgook was right. Nathaniel's got a son."

"So he does. And two fine daughters," added Curiosity. "Never can have enough daughters, is how I look at it."

Hannah's smile faded. "My grandfather should be here. He should know. I wish we had some word of him."

Curiosity sat down with a bowl of her own, and leaned toward the girl to pat her hand. "It looks like the good Lord is smiling on you today, missy. Jan Kaes brought a letter in from Johnstown just before the storm broke. Came all the way from Montréal."

"From my grandfather?" Hannah sat up straighter.

Curiosity pursed her mouth thoughtfully. "Don't think so. It was writ with a fancy hand, so I'd guess it was from that Scot—Moncrieff was his name, wasn't it? The one that come through here at Christmas. I'll wager he had some word of Hawkeye, though."

Outside, the dogs began barking and Liam got up to see to them.

"That'll be the judge," said Curiosity. "And half the village with him, by the sound of it. Ain't good news louder than Joshua's horn?"

"It is," said Nathaniel from the doorway. He looked tired, but there was an easiness to the line of his back that Hannah hadn't seen in a long time. She launched herself at her father; he caught her neatly, and bent over to whisper in her ear.

"Squirrel," he said in Kahnyen'kehàka, hugging her so hard that her ribs creaked. "I am mighty proud of you. Thank you."

"Is there word of Grandfather?" she whispered back.

A sudden wave of cold air and an eruption of voices at the door pulled Nathaniel's attention away. He patted her back as she let him go, but not before she saw the flash of worry move across his face, only to be carefully masked as he turned to greet his father-in-law.

Elizabeth Bonner believed herself to be a rational being, capable of logical thought and reasonable behavior, even in extreme circumstances. In the past year she had had opportunity enough to prove this to herself and to the world. But next to her, soundly asleep in the cradle beside the bed, were two tiny human beings: her children. She could not quite grasp it, in spite of all the evidence to hand.

Look, Curiosity had called, holding up first one and then the other to examine by the light of the rising sun. *Look what you made!*

The day had been filled with visitors and good wishes, the demands of her own body, the simple needs of the infants. She was tired to the bone, but still Elizabeth looked. She lay on her side, watching the babies sleep. Her children, and Nathaniel's.

"Boots," Nathaniel said from the chair before the fire. "You think too hard."

"I can't help it," she said, stretching carefully. "Look at them."

He put down the knife he had been sharpening and came to her. She had seldom seen him look more weary, or more content. Crouched by the side of the cradle with his hands dangling over his knees, he studied the small forms.

"You did good, Boots, but you need your sleep. They'll be looking for you again before you know it."

She nodded, sliding down into the covers. "Yes, all right. But you're tired, too. Come to bed."

Now Elizabeth's attention shifted to Nathaniel. She watched as he shed his buckskins, thinking what she must always think, and always keep to herself: that he was as beautiful to her as these perfect children. The line of his back, the way his hair swung low over the wide span of his shoulders, the long tensed muscles in his thighs, even his scars, because they told his stories. When he lay down beside her she moved closer to his warmth instinctively. But instead of drifting to sleep, she was caught up in his wakefulness.

In the year they had been together she had at first been amazed and then slightly resentful of Nathaniel's ability to fall instantly to sleep—it was a hunter's trick, a warrior's skill as important as the ability to handle a gun. But not tonight.

"Now you are thinking too hard," she said to him finally. "I can almost hear you."

He sought out her hand. "You knew about the twins. Why didn't you tell me?"

She hesitated. "Falling-Day thought you would worry overmuch. So did I. After what happened to Sarah—" Elizabeth looked into the cradle. Hannah's twin brother had died in Nathaniel's hands. Sarah had borne him one more son, and he had buried that child, too, in his mother's arms. It was inevitable that he would think of those losses, even on this joyful day.

He said, "I should have been here."

"Nathaniel—"

"You must have been scared, when the storm came down."

He was determined to hear it, and so she told him.

"Yes," she said, "But soon after the pain started in earnest and I had little energy for anything else. And no choice, as you had no choice. But we managed, did we not?"

He made a sound in his throat that was less than total agreement. Elizabeth brought his hand up to rub against her cheek.

"Shall we name them for your father, and my grandmother? Daniel and Mathilde. Would that please you?"

"Aye, it would. And it will please Hawkeye." He turned to her, but his thoughts were far away. Gently, he fit his face to the curve of her neck and shoulder. He smelled of himself: honest sweat, leather and gunpowder, woodsmoke and the dried mint he liked to chew.

"You've been thinking of Hawkeye a lot today."

She felt the tension rise in him, coming to the surface of his skin like sweat.

"What is it? Tell me."

"There was a letter down at the tavern for me," he said, his voice muffled. "From Moncrieff. He's in Montréal."

She waited, slightly tensed now. "Moncrieff found your father?"

"Aye. In the garrison, under arrest."

Suddenly very much awake, Elizabeth sat up and winced as her sore muscles protested.

"Somerville's men took him for questioning," Nathaniel continued. "There's rumors about the Tory gold."

"Oh, Lord." With a glance toward the cradle, Elizabeth folded her hands before her. "Tell me all of it."

Nathaniel recited the letter; he had had nothing to

do in the long hours of the whiteout but to read it again and again, and the words came to him easily.

When he had finished, she lay back down. "You'll have to go."

"You believe Moncrieff, then?"

She raised a brow. "I doubt he would make up such a thing. To what end, after all. It is true that we do not know him well, Nathaniel, but in this much I think he can be trusted." She paused. "We both know that you cannot leave Hawkeye locked up."

Nathaniel let out a hoarse laugh, but his look was troubled. "I can't leave him in gaol, and I can't leave you here alone. And you can't travel."

Elizabeth shifted to a more comfortable position. "It's true that I don't like the idea of your going so far, right now. But I don't see you have any choice."

In spite of the seriousness of their situation, Nathaniel grinned. He caught the plait that fell over her shoulder to her waist and gave it a good tug. "You're the one with the talent for breaking men out of gaol."

She flicked her fingers at him, but color rose on her cheeks. "Do you have any idea how we could possibly get Hawkeye out of a military garrison?"

"I'm sure something would come up," he said. "There's money enough, and money opens more locks than keys ever will. But I'm not about to leave you here alone with two new babies."

"Of course you must go. Moncrieff and Robbie cannot do it without you. Your father needs you."

"Boots," Nathaniel said wearily. "My ma always told me never to cross a woman in childbed, but—"

"A wise woman," interrupted Elizabeth. "Most excellent advice."

Deep in the night, Nathaniel brought first the girl child and then the boy to her for nursing as she could not yet manage them both at once. Curiosity had come to the

door at the first hungry cries, but seeing that Nathaniel was attending to Elizabeth's needs, she nodded and slipped back to the bed she was sharing with Hannah in the sleeping loft.

Yawning widely, Elizabeth sat up against the bolsters and watched her son's small face. He tugged so enthusiastically that she had to bite back a small cry. Nathaniel sat beside her, his gaze fixed on the boy. Mathilde was on his lap, newly wound and already asleep.

Elizabeth said, "I wish that you did not have to go, Nathaniel. But I cannot be so selfish. You will never rest easy here, knowing that your father needs your help. Someday you may call Daniel to you the same way, and I expect that he will do what he must to come. I trust that he will."

The candlelight lay like gold on the baby's cheek. Nathaniel touched the tender skin with one finger. "You need me, too," he said hoarsely. "It ain't right to leave you, Boots."

"You will come back to me, will you not? To us?"

"Aye," he said, his breath warm on her skin. "Never doubt it."

News traveled fast in Paradise. The next morning Judge Middleton stood at the foot of his daughter's bed and demanded the whole story while he kneaded his tricorn between his hands; he reminded her of nothing so much as one of her students with a guilty conscience. Looking at him now, she could not help marking the likeness to her brother. Julian had had the same high coloring and handsome features, and the same propensity for self-indulgence.

The judge cleared his throat repeatedly. "I am sorry to hear of Hawkeye's troubles, but I can see no reason for you to be alone on this mountain in the middle of winter. Come home with me. There's room for all of you." But he could not quite meet Elizabeth's eye.

She concentrated on the child in her lap, and at length her silence forced him to the heart of the matter.

"Curiosity can look after you there as well as here," he said gruffly. "Better."

The simple truth was, the judge feared that Nathaniel's journey would cost him his housekeeper. Elizabeth was disappointed, but she knew that to argue this with her father would not be worth the effort. She said, "I will not leave Lake in the Clouds, but I will talk to Curiosity."

Greatly relieved to have this conversation over, the judge spent a few minutes admiring his grandchildren.

"I think both of them will have your mother's coloring." Carefully the judge picked up Mathilde and examined her face. "She has your mother's chin, too, but then, so do you. You do resemble your mother so, Elizabeth." He narrowed his eyes at her, as if he were seeing her for the first time. "Both of you so independent. It is your curse, and your blessing. I fear this little girl will carry on in the same vein."

"I hope that she will," Elizabeth said, somewhat taken aback by this uncharacteristic thoughtful turn in her father.

He passed the baby over. "Life might be easier, if you would allow it."

"Life would have been easier for you, too, if you had stayed in Norfolk."

He smiled at that, and suddenly they were easier together than they had been in some time. Then Curiosity's voice came to them from the other room, and the judge grew flustered. In no time at all, he had rushed out with the excuse of a meeting in the village.

"That man," Curiosity muttered when Elizabeth recounted her conversation with the judge. "Botherin' a woman in childbed with his little man-pains. It's a good thirty years me and my Galileo been free, and I ain't about to start jumpin' when he snap his fingers. Ain't my girls as good at housekeepin' as me?"

Elizabeth agreed that they were.

"Polly right there with nothing to do but feed the man, and Daisy not far off, either. I'll tell you plain: he can just eat their cooking a while longer. Askin' me to walk away from his only daughter new delivered 'cause he bored. No wonder he run off before I could have a word with him."

Elizabeth buried her smile in Mathilde's fragrant neck, but Curiosity's fury was not yet spent. She had brought in a bucket of hot water for the hip bath, and she tapped an impatient melody on the tin as she muttered to herself. Then her head snapped up and she grinned at Elizabeth. "We'll send Martha up to the house to look after him. That'll do the trick."

Martha Southern was a widow with three young children, and Curiosity had recently had the idea that the judge watched her with an oversolicitous eye.

"You make me laugh, Curiosity. You will find an opportunity to matchmake even in this."

"You begrudge the judge a young wife?"

"Of course not." And then in response to Curiosity's raised eyebrow: "If I were to worry about this at all, it would be that Martha might deserve a better sort of husband, after Moses."

Curiosity put her fists on her hips. "The judge might be a good enough husband, with the right kind of wife. And Martha alone, with three little ones. If it ain't the judge, it may well be Charlie LeBlanc, and he ain't got a hiccup to call his own."

She poured the second bucket of hot water into the tub and then produced a cake of soap from her apron pocket. "Come on now, let's set you to soaking some of them sore spots away. Got some of the soap that Merriweather woman left behind. You'll smell like a tavern maid lookin' for a cosy man, but I suppose that don't matter none. Quick, now, afore the men come back and let the cold air in."

"Where's Nathaniel?" Elizabeth asked, climbing carefully out of bed.

"Out in the barn with Liam," Curiosity said. "Talking man talk."

Once, Nathaniel could have been ready for this trip north in an hour. With the buckskins on his back, a supply of no-cake and dried venison, all the powder and ammunition he could carry, he would have simply started walking. But these days he and Liam were the only men at Lake in the Clouds, and that made leaving even harder.

"Firewood alone will keep you busy," Nathaniel said, repeating something he had said before and that Liam knew anyway. But the boy didn't seem to mind hearing it all again: Liam was a good worker: dogged, and thorough. Book learning was a chore for him, but he could track a buck all day and never lose the trail, and Nathaniel had never heard him complain, or seen him walk away from a task, no matter how dirty. They had taken Liam in last fall when his brother Billy died, and the boy worked hard to earn his place at Lake in the Clouds.

"You call on Galileo or Jed to help out if things get too much for you," Nathaniel said. "I already had a word with them about it."

"I can manage," Liam said. He squinted out into the snowdrifts beyond the barn door. "How long do you think you'll be?"

There was the question that gnawed. Nathaniel pushed out his breath in a cloud.

"If the rivers don't break up before time, four weeks. If they do, and the rains come early, six. I'll stop at Kayenti'ho on my way north, let Falling-Day and Many-Doves know what's happened. They may send Runs-from-Bears this way, once they hear."

A small flickering in Liam's pale eyes. "I can manage the work," he said, his voice cracking.

"I know you can," Nathaniel said, remembering what it was like to be fourteen: raw and untried and

dead curious about the world, resentful of being led; afraid to move on alone. "Listen to me now, Liam. If Bears comes this way, that don't mean I don't trust you. I do. I wouldn't leave Elizabeth now if I didn't."

The boy looked down at his oversized boots. When he raised his head again, there was a shimmer in his eyes.

"Don't know why you should."

Nathaniel put a hand on the bony shoulder. "You look in the mirror and you see your brother. But I'm here to tell you that I knew him better than you did, and you ain't nothing like Billy." For a moment Nathaniel struggled with a set of memories he could not share: the brother that Liam had only suspected, but would never know, if it could be helped.

He said, "Would I leave my wife and children in your care otherwise?"

Then he walked away, letting the boy sit with that for a while. Nathaniel busied himself hanging the deer he had shot and cleaned this morning; when he looked up, Liam's face was splotched, but dry.

"I'll do my best by them."

"I know you will." Nathaniel wiped his hands on a piece of sacking. "I'll be leaving at sunrise, but there's something to do this afternoon first, and I'll need your help."

In winter, Hidden Wolf was mean-spirited: quick to punish any misstep, and unforgiving. Nathaniel focused on the wind, feeling the mountain talking to him through the web of his snowshoes. Liam followed closely. They had things to discuss but it wasn't wise in such a wet cold, the kind that would settle in the chest if you gave it the chance.

They walked uphill through stands of beech and maple and birch. All around them pine and hemlock were heavy armed and dragging with snow. Grouse startled and fussed as they passed; overhead the squirrels whirred and screeched at them, flinging beechnut

shells. There was plentiful evidence of the wolf pack that roamed the mountain. They didn't hide the remains of their prey: small game, mostly, but they had feasted recently on a young buck, leaving nothing behind but gnawed bone, a sprouting two-point rack, and a tattered hide.

Nathaniel made a wide berth around a hump that another man might have climbed right over, an elevation that looked like nothing more than a downed tree covered with snow. He pointed out the vent hole and the faint mist of rising breath to Liam.

"It's there for the taking if things get lean."

Liam looked around himself, taking his bearings. Later in the season he would almost certainly come back here to brush away the snow and put a bullet through the bear's eye. The hard part would be getting the carcass back to the cabin.

On the backbone of the mountain they were met by a merciless wind that wanted nothing more than to send them flying out over the forests. Moving carefully on the exposed ridge, they made their way to a small plateau where a few boulders provided a windbreak. There they stopped to take off snowshoes and strap them to their backs, and then they started down a cliff face. Liam grabbed at stunted juniper to steady himself on the way down, catching himself easily when he began to slide. Nathaniel saw him taking his bearings again; the boy wasn't lost, and could find his way back to Lake in the Clouds alone if need be.

When he had Liam's attention, Nathaniel pointed out a spalt in the cliff face that might have been nothing more than shadow. Without any explanation, he reached up and pulled himself into the mountainside.

The rushing wall of water that formed the outer boundary of the cave sent a wave of cold right to the bone. From a store of wood stacked against the far wall they lit a fire, and then a torch.

"I didn't imagine it like this," Liam said as he

warmed his hands. "I thought it would be bigger." His eyes kept moving to the long line of wolf skulls wedged into a crack in the far wall.

Nathaniel disappeared into the shadows at the back of the cave. There was a dragging sound, and a thump, and he appeared again, wiping his hands on his leggings.

"It is bigger," he said. "Come have a look."

He had rolled away a good-sized boulder to reveal the next cavern. The torchlight danced on barrels and baskets and neatly bundled pelts. Hung from pegs driven into fissures were long ropes of dried corn and squash: provisions enough to take seven or more people through the winter. It was dry and quieter here, but cold.

"This is how you managed, last winter," Liam said, mostly to himself. Some of the men in the village had been set on driving the Bonners and their Kahnyen'kehàka family members off the mountain, resorting to thievery when intimidation got them nowhere. They had raided the cabin in the fall, finding less than they expected in the way of winter stores. Billy had been at the heart of that trouble, and where Billy went, Liam had gone, too.

Nathaniel saw all this moving on the boy's face, anger and shame and the regret for his part of what had happened. But it was Liam's battle and he could not fight it for him, so Nathaniel went to work.

"Lend me a hand with this." He gestured with his chin to the largest of three old chests, squat and battered. Nathaniel kept his voice easy, but he watched Liam from the corner of his eye, saw the flicker of interest and surprise.

The chest was heavy, and they put it down with a grunt near the fire in the front cavern.

"The Tory gold?" Liam asked. His tone had a studied evenness, his voice cracking slightly.

Nathaniel snorted. "You've been listening to Axel's tall tales again," he said, hunkering down. He gave the lock a twist and the lid opened smoothly.

On the top was a bundle of papers rolled in oilskin and tied: the Deed of Gift that had transferred the land patent to Elizabeth, their marriage lines, a sales agreement for the schoolhouse Nathaniel had built and then sold to her at her insistence, other papers that would argue louder and longer in a court of law if they had to fight again to keep Hidden Wolf. There was a wooden box of his mother's things, which he put to the side. Underneath, a faint shimmering, and Liam drew in his breath.

"Silver," he breathed. "Pure?"

"Not exactly." Nathaniel reached for the empty pack he had brought with him. "It's hard to work it here, but we do the best we can."

Liam's blue eyes blinked. "There is a mine on Hidden Wolf, after all."

"Aye," said Nathaniel. "There is."

"The north face?"

Nathaniel nodded.

"Does the judge know?"

"No. Guess he never went looking for it."

Liam was silent. At his sides his hands clenched and unclenched convulsively.

Nathaniel said, "I'm only bothering with this now because I may need it in Montréal. The silver ain't mine, though."

The boy's head snapped up. "It ain't? Whose is it, Elizabeth's?"

"The mine belongs to the Kahnyen'kehàka," said Nathaniel. "So does the silver. But they won't mind me using what I need to get Otter and Hawkeye out of trouble."

Liam crouched down, his eyes fixed on Nathaniel. "But the mountain sits on land that used to belong to the judge. He bought the patent at auction."

"True." Nathaniel continued working, but he watched Liam's face from the corner of his eye.

"And he passed it on to Elizabeth, and then you married her."

"That's true, too," Nathaniel agreed. "Although it didn't seem nearly so simple as that at the time. What's your point?"

Liam stopped and studied his hands. It was a habit he had that made him seem older than his years: thinking through what he had to say before he let it go. Another thing that distinguished him from his brother Billy.

"Hidden Wolf belongs to you, and so does the mine. You have legal claim and the silver is yours—" Liam faltered, seeing the expression on Nathaniel's face.

"There's more than one kind of law," Nathaniel said. "The way I see it is, if anybody has a claim to the mine, it's the Kahnyen'kehàka."

Liam stared through the waterfall toward the place where the cabins stood. "Does Elizabeth see it that way, too?"

"She does. We'd sign the mountain over tomorrow, if the court would allow it."

The boy swallowed so that the muscles in his throat rose and fell in a wave. "My brother would get out of his grave to stop you from giving Hidden Wolf back to the Mohawk."

Nathaniel shifted his weight back on his heels. He could almost see Billy in Liam's face. He had the same low, broad forehead, high cheekbones, and narrow-bridged nose. On his upper lip and the backs of his hands was the red-gold down that marked all the Kirbys. One day soon Liam would be as big as Billy had been, and as strong. But there was something in Liam's eyes that his older brother had been lacking. Nathaniel said, "And you? What would you do?"

"It ain't none of my business," Liam said.

"Ah, but it is," Nathaniel said. "If you're one of us, it's your business. This—" He looked at the chest, and then out through the falling wall of water, his gaze taking it all in: Lake in the Clouds, Hidden Wolf. "This is

Hannah's birthright, and Many-Doves, and their children's. It's my business to keep it safe for them, and it's your business, too. If you're one of us."

The boy flushed, color moving up his throat. He stared at Nathaniel, and then at the silver.

"I'm one of you," he said hoarsely.

"Then let's get to work," Nathaniel said, handing him a pack. "It's too damn cold to talk."

Not quite sunrise, and Elizabeth was wide awake. The babies had nursed just an hour earlier and were resting easily, but she lay unwilling to sleep. She had lit a candle, willfully putting away the small voice that chided her for this extravagance, and she lay on her side watching the first colors of the dawn through the ice-crusted panes of the single small window. The window was another luxury, and at the moment it was one she regretted. Soon the sun would come over the crest and Nathaniel would wake, and then he would get up and be gone.

She had encouraged him to go; she had insisted on it. And still the idea of his going was suddenly overwhelming. Elizabeth was filled with dread, with vague worries about Montréal and the troubles there, with more detailed imaginings of the things that might come to pass—that often came to pass—in the endless forests, and with irritation at herself. She would not make this leave-taking harder on him.

But she must study his face now. This face she knew so well. He would be thirty-six years old in the spring and already there was a single strand of white at his hairline. Straight brows, a scar beneath his left eye. The strong lines of nose and jaw. His mouth, the curve of it. The groove in his chin where the shadow of his beard was darkest.

The sun had not yet risen, but she sensed a change in the rhythm of his breathing. There was a small tremor

in the muscle of his cheek. She held her breath, hoping that he would settle again, hoping he would sleep until noon if it would keep him here one more day.

His arm came up and around her, and pulled her down to him.

"You're so edgy, Boots," he said softly. "Come, rest with me."

Elizabeth put her face against his neck and said what she had been determined not to say. "I wish you did not need to go."

His arm tightened around her shoulders.

They were quiet together for a moment like that, the only movement between them his fingers on her temple, gently stroking. Under her hands his chest was as hard as oak. She drew in his smells and felt her pores opening, her nerves waking.

"I wish—" she said finally. And stopped. She felt him waiting. When she turned up her face to his, Elizabeth found his eyes open and calm with knowing. He knew, he always knew. Nathaniel kissed her, and then she did cry. Just a little, enough to flavor the kiss with salt and regret and longing. He made a comforting sound against her mouth, his hands cradling her face.

She held him to her, and kissed him back. It was all they could have now, in this little bit of time left, and with her body still so raw. But it was good to hold him, to feel that he wanted her, and to know that she could still want him back. In spite of the astonishing range of aches her body presented to her, still Nathaniel's kiss made her breasts pulse and tingle, and in the pit of her belly there was the blossoming of nerves she had discovered on that winter morning when she had first learned the feel of him.

There was a tightening and then a trickle of milk. She broke away with a sob of surprise.

"Shhh." He caught her up again, pulled her back to him. "Never mind, never mind. That happens. Never mind." With one hand he raised her chin. He was smil-

ing, a small smile. "I'm just sorry I can't take you up on the offer."

She pushed against his shoulder with the palm of her hand, but he wouldn't let go. With his mouth against her temple, he whispered to her.

"I'll come back to you, Boots, and you'll be healed and we'll be together. It'll be warm enough then in the cave. We'll get to know each other again where we started, you and me. How does that sound?"

Elizabeth brushed the hair away from his face. "It sounds as if you should be up and away, so that you can come home again. 'Journeys end in lovers meeting,' after all."

"That's one quote I'll remember." Nathaniel laughed. "It'll serve me well on the long road home."

3

The March winds came off the St. Lawrence in a rush, nosing up Montréal's narrow lanes to seek out Nathaniel where he stood in the shadows of the Auberge St. Gabriel. Most of the city's residents had retreated over slick cobblestones to their dinners by the time the seminary clock chimed four, but Nathaniel stood motionless and attentive, oblivious to the icy snow that rattled on roofs of tin and slate.

The door of the tavern opened and a servant clattered out, bent to one side by the weight of her basket. Behind her followed two redcoats, shoulders hunched. Nathaniel pressed himself harder against the wall, relaxing even as they went past. Their eyes were fixed on their boots, and their minds on the duty that had drawn them away from hearth and ale. He was invisible to them.

Nathaniel continued scanning the darkening street. Between the houses opposite there was a small flash of movement. A child, underdressed, searching the gutter as he slipped along in the shadows. For a moment Nathaniel watched, and then he stepped into the lantern light and held up a coin. The boy's gaze snapped toward the faint shimmer and he angled across the lane in three bounds, to follow Nathaniel into the shadows.

Perhaps ten years old, Nathaniel guessed, and small for his age. Eyes wary, one crusted red; his skin covered with filth and bruises. But he grinned. "Monsieur?"

Nathaniel held out the shilling and it disappeared between quick fingers.

"What's your name?"

"They call me Claude," said the boy. "For another coin I will tell you my family name."

Nathaniel exhaled sharply through his nose. "There's another coin if you get a message to the big Scot inside." It was a long time since Nathaniel had used his French, but the boy's nod was encouraging. "Tell him to meet Wolf-Running-Fast at Iona's, and make sure nobody hears you," he finished.

"The *auberge* is full of Scots," the boy said. "All Montréal is full of them. Will any Scot serve, Monsieur Wolf-Running-Fast?"

"The tallest one in the room," said Nathaniel. "White haired, answers to Rab MacLachlan. With a red dog, almost as big as you."

There was a flicker of interest in the boy's eyes. "A coin for each of them, the man and dog?"

"If they show up alone, you'll get a coin for each of them."

"And one for showing them the way."

Nathaniel laughed softly at the idea; Robbie could find his way to Iona's purblind. "You'll get your coins if you do your job. And a plate of mutton stew, too, I'll wager."

"Wolf-Running-Fast," repeated the boy. "Iona." And at Nathaniel's nod, he disappeared into the darkened alleyway.

Nathaniel had been trained too well to take anything for granted, and so he waited patiently in the shadows opposite Iona's cottage, in spite of the wind and the rumbling in his gut. Now that he was here, finally, he

remembered why he had stayed away all these years. At seventeen he had given up both his innocence and his virginity in Montréal. The first had been lost watching merchants and priests angle for the peltry and the souls of the Huron and Cree, Abenaki and Hodenosaunee. The second he had surrendered with less of a struggle to the lieutenant governor's daughter. The thought of Giselle Somerville left a strange taste in his mouth, as if he had bit into an apple that looked sound but was inwardly foul. He had thought she could not touch him anymore, but it was her at the bottom of this trouble: twenty years, and she had still managed to reach out and put a cold finger on his cheek.

The snow picked up, whipping into his eyes. He pulled his hood down farther and sought the warm center of himself, as he had been trained to do as a boy. At home both hearths would be blazing. There might be venison and corn bread and dried cranberry grunt. Finished with her work, Hannah would be bent over sewing, or a book if she had her way. Nathaniel imagined Elizabeth close by with a child at her breast. He could see her quite clearly; the heart-shaped face, the first worry lines at the corners of her eyes, her mouth the deep red of wild strawberries. By evening time her hair had worked itself free to curl damp against her temple, falling over the angle of her neck and shoulders bent protectively around the child in her arms.

He had no clear pictures of the babies to call on. It had been too short a time.

Nathaniel shook himself slightly. If he could concentrate, if he could get the job done here, he could be on his way home to them in no time at all, traveling with his father and Otter and Rab. The ice roads were frozen solid; they could make good time. At night they would sleep in snow caves and cook whatever they could shoot over a fire of their own making while Otter told his story: how he had landed here in Montréal

when he was supposedly headed west, and how he had got mixed up with the Somervilles. The last word they had had of Otter was in December, when Rab MacLachlan came to Lake in the Clouds and brought the news that the boy was wound up with Giselle. Worse still was Rab's report that Hawkeye was on his way to Montréal to untangle Otter from the mess.

Moncrieff's letter and the news that they were both in gaol hadn't really come as too much of a shock: Canada wasn't a good place for the Bonner men; never had been. Especially not when Giselle Somerville was involved. In the deep cold of the night shadows two things were clear to Nathaniel: they had to get his father and Otter out of the gaol as quickly as it could be managed, and they had to avoid the Somervilles. Once they were safe at home again there would be time enough to deal with Otter. He might be Hannah's favorite uncle, but he was also a seventeen-year-old who had dragged four grown men into a dangerous situation.

A muffled *whoof!* and the red dog appeared in the lane. At the side of Iona's cottage there was a glimmer of white hair and a raised hand, and a door opened and closed. Nathaniel waited five more minutes. When there was no movement, he followed Robbie MacLachlan inside.

It was a small room, lit only by the fire in the hearth and a betty lamp. The house smelled of woodsmoke, roast mutton, tallow, the wet dog who lay like a twitching log in front of the hearth and the unwashed boy who crouched next to her, shoveling stew into his mouth with his fingers. Claude shrugged a hello in Nathaniel's direction, but Robbie had him by the shoulders before he could get out one word in greeting to either of them.

"Nathaniel," said the big man, bent over so as not to knock his head on the low-beamed ceiling, his broad, high-colored face creased in both pleasure and concern. "What are ye doin' here? Shouldna ye be at hame wi' Elizabeth? Is she well? Is the bairn come?"

"She's well, she's very well," Nathaniel reassured him. "And she's given me healthy twins, a boy and a girl."

Robbie's open expression clouded. "But then, why are ye here? What's taken ye fra' yer guidwife's side?"

"I came because I was sent for," Nathaniel said. "Moncrieff wrote to say my father wanted me here. Isn't he with Otter in the garrison gaol?"

Robbie ran a hand over the white bristle on his jowls. "Aye, that's true. But Hawkeye nivver asked that we send for ye. In fact, lad, he was glad tae ken ye safe at hame. I canna think why Moncrieff wad write and tell ye sic a thing."

"But I can," said a calm voice at the low threshold to the other room. A woman appeared there: of small size and uncertain age, the kind who didn't draw attention to herself, unless you took note of the animated expression of her eyes.

"Miss Iona," said Nathaniel. "It's been a long time."

"Yes, it has," she said. When she smiled, it was easier to see the young woman she had once been, and to give the stories credence. Almost twenty years ago Nathaniel had first made her acquaintance: Wee Iona, men in the bush called her, or Sister Iona, for she had once worn the veil and that was a fact few could overlook, or forget. How she had left the convent, and why, was the stuff of legend and rumor.

Now she moved around her small home, offering him her hospitality. "Time has treated you well, Nathaniel Bonner. Take those wet things off now, come along. There's stew, if young Claude here hasn't yet eaten his way to the bottom of the pot." The Gaelic

hovered there just beneath the surface, all her *s* sounds soft and slurred. But her mind was as sharp as her voice was soft, and he felt her taking his measure.

Nathaniel accepted a piece of sacking from her to towel his head. "Do you have reason not to trust Moncrieff?"

She crouched down before the cooking hearth as nimbly as a girl of twenty. "He's a Scot, is he not?"

Claude shot a broken-toothed grin toward Robbie, who blushed and sputtered with indignation.

Nathaniel pulled a few coins from his pocket, and held them out to the boy. He sprang up, wiping his mouth with the back of one grimy hand. At Iona's suggestion of a warm sleeping place in the barn, he shot out the door, pausing only to glance back at Nathaniel.

"If you should have need of me again, you can find me near the *auberge* at sunset."

"I'll remember that," Nathaniel said.

When Claude was well away, Robbie returned immediately to the topic at hand. "Iona, I'm surprised at ye. A Hieland lass born and raised and still ye stan' there and curse every Scot on the continent tae the de'il. It isna fair, lass."

"Perhaps not," she conceded with a raised shoulder. "But you Lowlanders are a troublesome lot, and Moncrieff is worse than most. He wants what he wants."

"And that is?" asked Nathaniel, flexing his fingers in the warmth.

"Is it not clear? He wants you and your father on a ship for Scotland. Which is why you sit here in front of my fire, Nathaniel, instead of with your wife and children at home. Of course, you must first get Hawkeye out of the garrison to bring about that end; Moncrieff is counting on that." There was no anger in her voice, nothing of resentment in her tone: she laid out what she knew for his appreciation, or rejection. Nathaniel's first impulse was to believe her.

"How do you know him so well?"

Robbie cleared his throat. "Moncrieff and I spend a fair amount o' time here, talkin'."

"Did you happen to tell him the story of how Elizabeth broke my father out of Anna's pantry?"

"Aye," said Robbie sheepishly. "That I did. It's too guid a tale tae keep tae masel', laddie. And in aa the time I've spent wi' Moncrieff and aa the tales tolt, I've no' heard him say a solitary word o' ships tae Scotland."

Iona pursed her lips. "Then you were not listening carefully, Robbie MacLachlan. But I suppose that is not a surprise. I recall Isaac Putnam telling you more than once to clean out your ears."

The beginnings of an old argument flashed across Robbie's normally agreeable expression. It might be a score of years since he had last been in Montréal, but there was still a spark between him and Iona.

Nathaniel said, "Maybe my father was hoping to get out of gaol without getting me involved, but here I am and I can't leave him sitting there. If Moncrieff's got more than setting him free in mind, we'll find out soon enough." He paused to peel off a wet winter moccasin. "Once my father is free we'll be headed home, and the whole of Scotland couldn't stop us."

Iona pushed a stray hair away from her cheek, and Nathaniel saw that her white hair had gone very thin. "Don't underestimate him."

Robbie put down his bowl with a thump. "Ye're a distrustfu' lass, Iona, but it's served ye well these muny years. Perhaps I've been a wee owerfriendly wi' Moncrieff."

"Do you know where he is now?" Nathaniel asked.

"Och, aye," Robbie said, throwing him a sidelong glance. "He's dinin' wi' the bonnie Giselle. As he does muny an evenin'."

"I take it her father is out of town," Nathaniel said.

"Somerville is in Québec," confirmed Robbie. "I dinna ken for how lang."

They looked at Iona, who inclined her head to one side thoughtfully. "Governor Carleton will keep him there for another week, I should imagine."

Iona was, for all her simplicity of self and home, the best source of information in Montréal. As a young woman she had moved among the armies of three nations while they battled each other for possession of the land; she had known the men who decided the fate of Canada, and she knew them still. These days they came to sit before her fire and talk, and she welcomed any friend of a friend who did not wear a Roman collar: the Scots who ran the fur trade; the English who commanded the colony; the French who lived in the shadow of the English and controlled the city's goods and food supply. McTavish, McGill, Guy, Latour, Després, Cruikshank, Gibb, Carleton, Monk: they came singly or together to talk, and she gave them strong ale and good food, and she listened.

"Has Moncrieff met Somerville?"

Robbie let out a soft laugh. "Aye, he has. But our Angus Moncrieff is no' on verra guid terms wi' Pink George."

Nathaniel had to grin at Somerville's old nickname, but he did not want to be distracted by a discussion of the man, his oddities or his faults, and so he turned the topic to more practical matters. In a few minutes he had extracted from Robbie the whole story of what had happened here, and it was as brief as he had expected: Hawkeye had come to take Otter home, and they had both been arrested. The authorities said they wanted Hawkeye for questioning about the Tory gold, but it was clear to Robbie and Iona both that something else was at the bottom of it all.

"What is it that Somerville wants from them, then?" Nathaniel asked. "Do you have any sense of it? Did he find out about Otter and Giselle, is that it?"

Iona was sitting on a small stool near the hearth with knitting in her lap, and she did not look up. "He may suspect, but he only knows of his daughter what he chooses to see. Which is very little."

"Then why are my father and Otter still in gaol?"

Robbie spread out his hands. "It's verra simple. Somerville canna risk Otter leavin' Montréal. The governor wants the boy here, ye ken. Otter's the only road they've got to Stone-Splitter."

Nathaniel sat back and rubbed his burning eyes with one hand, trying to make sense of it.

Stone-Splitter was a Kahnyen'kehàka sachem who had never given in to O'seronni ways, and for that reason alone the English feared him above all others: he had a keen understanding of their weaknesses, no need of their gifts, and no taste for their whisky, and thus they had no way to control him. He was a warrior in the ancient tradition, the kind they still told stories about, the kind whose furiosity on the battlefield kept old soldiers jerking and muttering in their uneasy sleep. And the young men of his village were trained in the same manner.

Of all the Kahnyen'kehàka sachem, Stone-Splitter was the only one who had refused to take sides in the war for independence and as a result his people had survived where others struggled. If the governor wanted Stone-Splitter's attention, it had to be because he was arming himself for another war and hoped to have the sachem's support and his warriors. Stone-Splitter was blood kin to Otter.

Nathaniel turned to Iona, and he saw that she had been watching him, and probably knew exactly what was in his thoughts.

"The smell of war is in the air," she said. "But perhaps not for a few years yet."

Another war. Men had talked of it uneasily ever since the last one, for nobody quite believed they had heard the last of the English king. And now here it was,

within reach. The urge to be away was stronger than ever.

He said, "Once we get Otter out of gaol, will it be hard to get him out of Montréal?" Nathaniel was slow to meet Robbie's gaze, but he found no reproach there.

"If ye're askin' aboot Giselle, ye'd ken the answer better than I, laddie. Ye walked awa' frae her once, wi' your faither pushin' frae behind."

Nathaniel wasn't easily embarrassed, but he didn't especially like being reminded of the hours he had spent with Giselle Somerville. He had been young, and healthy and ready to learn; she had been just as young, anything but innocent, and she had enjoyed teaching him. It was almost twenty years ago, but Nathaniel recalled certain moments with perfect clarity, when he let himself. Hawkeye had shown up and asked him straight-out if he wanted the girl to wife, and if she would come home with them to Lake in the Clouds.

And that had been the end of it. Enough to wake him up to the truth: he could not live in Montréal, and she would have laughed at the idea of a life on the edge of the wilderness. And so he left Montréal with his father, and ended up spending the hunting season with Stone-Splitter's people. That was when he had taken note of the oldest granddaughter of the clan mother of the Wolf, Sings-from-Books, who had become his first wife. *Out of the pan and into the fire.*

He shook his head to clear it of the past. "Giselle will try to hold on to Otter, if she's given the chance," Nathaniel said. "She collects men like other women collect jewels."

Iona's head was lowered over her knitting, but Nathaniel saw a tightening of her mouth, and then she spoke up: "That's not very charitable of you, considering what you once were to each other."

It was a well-deserved rebuke, and Nathaniel accepted it with an inclined head. "You're right. I shouldn't pass judgment. But my worry now is for Otter."

"He's a bonnie lad, and gey canny," Rab said. "But he's young, forbye, and—curious. It's a guid thing he's wi' yer faither."

"We need to get him out of here. And us, too."

"Tomorrow, if possible," Iona agreed.

"Aye," said Robbie. "Ye'll get nae argument frae me."

"Have you got any ideas?" Nathaniel asked.

Robbie grinned. "Have ye got iny money?"

When they had talked for another hour, Robbie returned to the lodgings in the rue St. Gabriel, so as to keep Nathaniel's presence a secret for the time being. In two days' time, if all went well, they would be out of Montréal, and Moncrieff would never know he had been there. For a moment Nathaniel could almost feel sorry for the man, who wanted nothing more than to fulfill an obligation to his employer, an old man with no heir and no hopes. But stronger than that was the need to protect his own, and Nathaniel would turn his back on Montréal and Moncrieff without a moment's hesitation.

He slept deeply, and dreamed of the caves under the falls.

4

In his life Nathaniel had spent time in a few cities, but he would never be truly at ease in a crowd. And still he knew that in Montréal the commotion of the pig market was the best kind of camouflage to be had, and so he and Robbie headed there at sunrise. According to Iona, it was where they were most likely to find the sergeant in charge of the night watch at the garrison gaol, a dragoon called Ronald Jones.

The cold was fierce enough to turn breath to ice, but still the sun managed to find purchase here and there, flashing off a tin roof, a cleaver hung on the side of a stall, an unshuttered window, a young River Indian's silver earbob. A man couldn't walk without being stepped on, pushed, touched: overweight merchants, half-drunk foot soldiers, butchers herding sows, maids pulling loaded sledges, beggars, dogs and oxen and horses and pigs everywhere. Despite the extreme cold the air was dense with the stink of swine slurry and curing meat, and it swirled with ashes and cinders from the bonfires that gave the butchers and their customers a place to warm themselves.

Even in this crowd, Nathaniel felt eyes fix on him. Perhaps because he stood head and shoulders over

most; perhaps because he was with Robbie, who stood even taller. They saw him, and forgot him: he was just another backwoodsman wanting liquor or a woman or a good price on his furs. Nathaniel reminded himself it was only for today, maybe for tomorrow. If they could find this man Jones; if he could be bought. He was aware of the weight of the double-sewn leather bags he wore strapped across his chest, some twenty pounds of near-pure silver.

So focused was he on the idea of the Welshman that Nathaniel missed the first signs of the scuffle. From just to the left among the stalls came a guttural scream— *crisse de tête à faux!*—and a fist swung close enough to make him sidestep. Before Nathaniel could even be sure what was happening, the crowd rushed in, their errands and the cold forgotten with the promise of some entertainment.

A butcher and a farmer sputtered and spat at each other across the carcass of a huge pig. The butcher had a head like a cannonball: heavy jowled, with a skull as pink and bristled as the mountainside of unmoving flesh at his feet. The farmer was black haired, twenty years younger, twenty pounds lighter, angrier. There was a fresh cut on his cheek. It made Nathaniel aware of the familiar weight of his rifle across his back, the comforting heft of the tomahawk tucked into his belt to lie flat next to his spine.

All around the crowd heaved like a wasp-stung mule. Robbie swore, and swore again. He loved crowds even less than Nathaniel did.

A man jumped up on a barrel. *"Moe, j'prends pour Pépin, moe, p'is j'y mets dix shillings, là!"* he shouted, waving a coin over his head.

The farmer grinned at that and lunged, fists flying briefly. He fell back before the bigger man could get a lock on him, and new bets were shouted in English, Scots, French, and other languages Nathaniel didn't recognize.

Next to him Robbie grunted as a young boy tried to climb his back for a better view. A ripple and jostling, muttered complaints, and a redcoat pushed his way to the forefront, stopping just opposite Nathaniel. Slope shouldered and soft bellied, frizzled red hair, a mouth full of tiny teeth the color of cheap tobacco. He had the pinched expression of a little man with less authority than he wanted and more than was good for him.

"Jesus wept," muttered Robbie at Nathaniel's ear. "There he is, that's Jones. Ach, will ye look at him strut, the wee Welsh half-a-cockerl."

"Here, here! What goes on, what's this?" With his chest pumped up, Jones's bellow was astoundingly loud, but the men ignored him, locked in a tussle that sent them rolling over the dead pig to crash into the stall. For a moment they were lost in a landslide of smoked ham hocks.

Next to Nathaniel, an old woman in a mangy blanket coat pulled on Jones's sleeve. "Denier has been fooling with the scales again," she hollered above the noise. "Young Pépin decided to teach him a lesson. And high time, too."

The two had rolled apart. The butcher hauled himself up on the ledge of the half-collapsed stall, his fist closing over a meat cleaver as he began a slow turn.

"*Pépin!*" shouted the man who still perched on the barrel. "*Faites attention! Il a un poignard!*"

Nathaniel saw the first flicker of real rage in the young farmer in the way his shoulders loosened and his face drained of color, all in a split second. Crouched in the chaos of the destroyed stall, he grabbed a long boning knife and snapped to his full height, his arm coming up to meet the butcher as he turned. In one smooth motion an acre of canvas apron fell open from neck to hipbone, the flap gaping to expose a hairy fish-white barrel of belly.

Not even Jones could yell over the shouts of surprise and shocked appreciation.

Barking like an enraged boar, the butcher dropped the cleaver to grab at his clothing, the huge head rearing up just in time to catch the knife, in earnest now. An almost careless flick of the younger man's wrist and the vast pink cheek split open. A rainbow of blood in a shower, and Nathaniel flinched the warm drops out of his eyelashes as Denier threw himself forward, only to go sprawling over the pig and strike his head on the corner of the stall.

The crowd fell silent, in surprise or horror, Nathaniel could not tell. Young Pépin's rage was suddenly gone: he shook himself as if he could not quite believe what he saw.

Jones was prodding the butcher with his toe. When he got a groan in response, he nodded.

"Right," he bellowed, hooking his thumbs in his wide leather belt. "It's the magistrate for you both, in-nit?"

But the young farmer seemed not to hear him at all, or not to care. A bottle was making the rounds, and he took a long swallow, staring fixedly at Denier's heaving form.

Jones cleared his throat loudly and flushed the color of his uniform. A vein began to throb in his forehead.

"High time to be away," Nathaniel said, and heard Robbie's grunt of approval. But it was too late; Jones rounded on them and pointed to Robbie, easily the biggest man in the crowd, twice his own size. "You haul the carcass to my sledge over there."

"The pig?" The old woman grinned, her gums showing dull red. "Or Denier?"

Jones's eyes moved over the massive back of the dead animal, and Nathaniel could see him calculating. "Both. The pig comes along as evidence."

"And dinner, forbye," muttered Robbie.

The young farmer's attention shifted from the pig to

Jones, and his brow creased in understanding and the first glimmerings of new rebellion.

"What are you staring at, boyo?" Jones stepped toward him. "It's the magistrate for all of youse, a pig and two frogs—"

"And a Welsh horse's ass," added Robbie in French. There was a single loud guffaw followed by a wave of uneasy laughter.

"What was that?" Jones roared. "What was that?"

Robbie raised a brow. "I said, the lad's got nae English."

"Then bloody tell him in French," snapped Jones. His gaze fixed on Nathaniel. "You there, Jacques. You look a right enough frog to me. You tell him."

Nathaniel considered. He could do what this little man was commanding him to do, or he could do what he wanted to do, and show him his back and his contempt. There was no chance now that Jones would be of any use to them in getting Hawkeye and Otter out of gaol; the question was, how badly could he get in their way.

"Permit me," said a familiar voice. Nathaniel sighed inwardly, not especially surprised to see Angus Moncrieff pushing through the crowd. Well dressed, straight of back, he nodded to Jones and in swift, Scots-accented French he explained to the farmer what he needed to know. When he was finished, he turned to Nathaniel and Robbie.

"Moncrieff," said Nathaniel.

A brief smile in response. "Nathaniel. I'm pleased to see ye here at last."

Moncrieff suggested a place near the docks that would be close to empty early on a workday morning. Because it was cold and there was no way to avoid the conversation, Nathaniel and Robbie went with him to the small tavern in the shadows of Notre Dame de Bonsecours.

It was a clean tavern, warm, and the smells of fresh bread and mutton roasting over a slow fire were inviting. There were only two other customers: a middle-aged man crouched over his ale, and a young sailor with a heavily bandaged leg. The first seemed to have no interest in anything but what he found at the bottom of his tankard; the second snored loudly, his tar-stained hands crossed over his chest and his head thrown back against the wall.

The serving woman greeted Moncrieff by name, and showed them to the best place near the hearth.

Before they were settled, Moncrieff said, "So tell me, man. Have ye guid tidings from Paradise?"

A broad smile broke out on his face when he had heard Nathaniel's news. He was all curiosity and good wishes, asking for details that would interest few men.

"We must drink to your guid fortune, and your lady's health," he announced finally.

The serving woman brought them tankards, kicking up her skirts to flaunt her ankles as she crossed the room. Moncrieff watched her go, tucking his pipe into the corner of his mouth with a thoughtful expression.

"A friend of yours?" Nathaniel asked.

Moncrieff lifted one shoulder in a gesture that spoke more of France than Scotland. But there was no mistaking him for anything but a Lowland Scot: he had the face, long and lean, large eared and strong of nose and chin. Nathaniel had seen faces much like his in his mother's drawings of the family she had left behind: uncles and cousins he had never met, would never know except by the set of their eyes and the angle of jaw. Moncrieff must be in his mid-fifties at least; there were deep wrinkles around his eyes and the beginning of dewlaps at his jawline. But he still had a full head of lank dark hair tied in a neat queue, and an energy that many younger men lacked. The truth was, Nathaniel was inclined to like the man, wanted to believe him, but there was something just below the surface that he

could not be sure of. Trust was a luxury he could not afford, not right now.

"That's Adele," said Robbie, one corner of his mouth twitching upward as they watched the woman move about the room, hips swinging. "A widow woman, is she no'? One o' Angus's muny special friends."

Moncrieff smiled over the edge of his tankard. "Aye, I've a few friends in Montréal. Until today I counted Jones among the useful if less pleasant o' them."

Nathaniel said, "We weren't there to start a fight with the man."

"That I can weel believe. But it's uncommon easy to quarrel wi' Jones. 'Big heid and wee wit, never gaed tegither yet.' Or so it's said."

Robbie snorted in appreciation.

Moncrieff chewed on the stem of his pipe and stared at Nathaniel for a moment. "You were planning to pay Jones to slip Hawkeye and Otter out o' the garrison gaol."

Nathaniel shifted, trying to find a more comfortable spot on the settle. "And if we were?"

Another Gallic shrug. "It isna an especially guid plan to put faith or your money on a man like Jones. He'd sell his mither to the de'il, and were there profit in it." Moncrieff met Nathaniel's eye. "And o' course, he's heard tell o' this Tory gold. He'd be thinking you've got it wi' ye, and wondering how to get his hands on it."

Carefully, Nathaniel put down his tankard as he looked Moncrieff in the eye. "He ain't the first, nor the last, I imagine. But I've got no gold on me, since you seem to be wondering."

It was almost a relief to see the man flush. He put his pipe aside, laid both hands flat on the table, and rocked forward, as if to push it to the floor with his weight.

"I care naething for gold, and had ye a pure ton o' it. It's your faither's fate that concerns me, and getting him out o' gaol. Had I thought it could be done wi' coin

alone, I should ha' seen it done lang syne. My purse isna empty, man."

After a long moment, Nathaniel nodded. "Fair enough."

Robbie cleared his throat. "I suppose ye've got a better plan, Angus?"

"Aye, Rab, perhaps I do. If you care to hear it told."

The serving woman came to refill their tankards, and they were quiet while they waited for her to finish. She took her time, leaning over the table to display her ample bosom to Moncrieff. He patted her hand and murmured something Nathaniel did not quite hear, but understood anyway. Adele left them with a smile.

Nathaniel held up a hand to keep Robbie from answering the question that still hung in the air. "Before this goes any further—"

Moncrieff sighed. "You want an explanation for my letter. Aye, and I've earned some harsh words. Go on, then."

"You admit it?"

"Admit that I lied in my letter, and that it wasna your faither's idea to send for ye? Aye, I admit it. And tell me this: wad ye rather be hame the noo, and him in gaol? I havena kennt ye verra lang, Nathaniel Bonner, but I didna think *that* wad sit weel wi' ye."

With every swallow of ale Moncrieff's English was giving way to Scots. Whether it meant the man was telling the truth or moving farther afield of it, of that much Nathaniel could not be sure. He said, "I would rather have had the whole story, and made up my own mind."

With one fingertip, Moncrieff traced the gouges on the table as if they were an alphabet he alone could read. He had the hands of a man who earned his living with books and paper and ink: fine fingered and unscarred. Nathaniel wished for five minutes of his father's counsel, for he truly did not know what to make of Angus Moncrieff.

On the other side of the room, the sailor roused and hobbled out, tossing a coin to Adele. The man in the corner called for more ale and began to sing softly to himself: a German lullaby or maybe a love song, slow and melancholy. Outside, a girl scolded a herd of goats as she hurried them along, the sound of the bells clear and true in the cold air.

When Moncrieff looked up again, his color had settled and his tone was calmer. "Aye," he said. "You're right. I overstepped my bounds, and I apologize. But now ye're here. You can ha' my help, or leave it. Which will it be?"

Nathaniel sat back to consider.

Robbie had taken to Moncrieff, and after thirty years in the bush Robbie was wary of strangers and slow to give his friendship. He could make a mistake, certainly. But maybe he had not. Elizabeth, who had a keen ear for things left unstated and no patience with half-truths, had not been terribly worried by Moncrieff. She had put the case before Nathaniel with her usual simplicity and clarity: *If Hawkeye decides he needs to go to Scotland, then he will go. However unlikely it seems to us that he might want to do such a thing, he has the right to decide for himself.* And it was the truth; Nathaniel could admit it to her and to himself, but he could not allow Moncrieff to see it in his face.

There were other truths that couldn't be overlooked: they had made an enemy of the man who was their only link to the gaol, whereas Moncrieff had connections, and an idea.

"First things first," Nathaniel said. "Tell me what it is you want with my father once he's free."

"It's verra simple," Moncrieff said softly. "The Earl o' Carryck would like to find his heir before he dies. The laird's wish is that the land and holdings . . ." He paused, and then went on. "And the title stay in the family. Nae mair, nae less than that. What I want from

your faither is an hour o' his time, to tell him o' his kin, and his birthright."

Nathaniel nodded. "You'll have your hour. But listen first, and I'll tell you now what I know in my gut to be true. Maybe my father was born a Scott of Carryck—you seem to be sure of that, and I can't say you're wrong—but he was raised in the wilderness and in his heart he's more Mahican than white."

"And yet he married a Scotswoman," Moncrieff said.

"Who turned her back on Scotland." Nathaniel leaned closer. "Listen to me. Even if that earldom is rightfully his, he'll want nothing to do with it. He'll never get on a ship for Scotland of his own free will. If he tells you that to your face, will you leave here, and go home?"

A flicker in the deep brown eyes: anger or disbelief or perhaps just stubbornness. But Moncrieff inclined his head. "Aye, if your faither tells me sae, I'll be awa' hame to Scotland."

"I'm not coming, either," added Nathaniel. "I'll have no part of it. Are we clear on that?"

"Aye," said Moncrieff. "Verra clear."

Robbie clapped Nathaniel on the back, laughing. "By God, laddie, ye should o' been a lawyer. Angus, tell us wha' ye've got in mind."

Moncrieff took a long swallow and then pulled a kerchief from his sleeve to wipe his brow. "The cook," he said finally, and in response to the blank look he got from both of them, he produced a slanted grin. "Martin Fink, the Somervilles' cook. He has a weakness for cards and whisky, a verra bad combination for a man o' limited resources."

Nathaniel frowned. "Can a cook get us into the gaol, or our people out of it?"

"Ach, nothing so simple as that," said Moncrieff. "But he can let ye bide in Pink George's kitchen, and that's where ye need to be, this evening. Giselle's invited

me tae one o' her parties, and she intends to have Otter and Hawkeye there."

Nathaniel remembered Giselle's parties very well. She gathered men around her for the evening when her father was away, more concerned with amusement than reputation. He had never enjoyed them, and liked the idea even less now. "You're thinking we'll just walk them out of the lieutenant governor's mansion?"

"At the right moment, aye. And why not?"

Why not. Nathaniel hid his grin in his tankard. It was a beautifully simple plan. At the most it would require that they waylay the redcoats assigned to guard the prisoners. With the right management, they would be drunk, too.

But Robbie was blinking at Moncrieff in disbelief, his color rising fast.

"Are ye saying that Giselle has summoned Otter and Hawkeye tae entertain the lairds and officers, like trained monkeys? Hawkeye will ha' nane o' that, and should she stand him at the end of a musket."

"That may be true," Moncrieff said, lowering his voice. "But think on it, Rab. They'll aa be fu' o' drink by midnight. By morning they'll be sober, and we'll be lang awa'."

"My father will see the beauty of that, if we can get word to him." Nathaniel put a hand on Robbie's shoulder. "He'd go a far sight further to get out of gaol than sit next to Giselle Somerville at a dinner table."

Robbie frowned. "Pink George will be in a puir temper when he comes hame and hears o' it. It wadna be the first time he's raised a hand tae his dauchter."

"She'll have to handle that on her own," said Nathaniel, more loudly than he intended. "She's had to deal with him angry, she knows what she's about."

"Ye're an unco' hard man betimes, Nathaniel Bonner." Robbie sighed, rubbing the bridge of his nose with one broad thumb. "Wha's first then in this plan o' yours, Angus?"

"The gaol. We've got to get word to Hawkeye. Wee Iona would be willing to pay a call, perhaps."

"No' Iona," Robbie said in a tone that brooked no discussion.

Nathaniel nodded in agreement. "She's too well known to get involved in this."

Moncrieff studied the tabletop. After a moment, he turned to look over his shoulder at Adele, who was sitting on a stool by the hearth and tending a kettle of beans. She was up before he could even wink at her, soft curves and a warm smile.

"Perhaps a friend, then, wi' a bit o' beef, and a message tucked away in a safe place." He rose with his tankard in hand, tipping back his head to get the last swallow. "I need a private word wi' Adele. Tell me, man. How are ye at cards?"

"I'm better with a rifle," said Nathaniel.

"He's better wi' a bluidy sewin' needle." Robbie grinned.

Nathaniel shrugged. "I expect that's true," he said. "There ain't much I like less than cards."

"You won't have to pretend to lose, then." Angus nodded, satisfied. "Perhaps you and Robbie would care to see if there's any interest in a game." He raised one brow in the direction of the man singing into his ale, and then headed toward the back room where Adele had disappeared.

Robbie straightened, his face creased in confusion. "Why wad we want tae play cards wi' a whey-faced sot like that?" he asked, sending a fierce look toward the corner.

"Because that's Martin Fink," Nathaniel said. "Did you think Moncrieff steered us here by accident?"

Robbie started. "The Somervilles' cook, d'ye mean? Mary bless me, and sae it must be." He rubbed a hand over his face. "I wadna ha' guessed Angus tae be sae verra sly."

Nathaniel picked up his tankard to swallow the last

of his ale, and along with it the worst of his doubts about Angus Moncrieff. They were started down this road now and they would see where it took them, but he would be on guard. He clapped Robbie on the back and leaned over to whisper in the great shell-like ear. "You watch my back, Rab, and I'll watch yours."

A forest away, Elizabeth was half asleep in front of the hearth with both infants at her breast, when faint laughter startled her into full wakefulness.

"What was that?"

Hannah looked up from grinding corn, and wiped a strand of hair away from her face with the back of her hand. "What was what?"

Confused, Elizabeth settled back into the rocker. "I heard something. Perhaps I was dreaming."

"About my father," Hannah concluded.

With a yawn she could barely hold back, Elizabeth pulled the pillows that supported the twins closer to her. There were longer pauses now between gulps, and soon they would be asleep. Elizabeth thought of the cradle and her own bed in the other room, but she was simply too weary to move, and she let herself drift back toward sleep just where she was. For three weeks now she had never had as much as three hours of continuous rest; it was no surprise if she was beginning to confuse waking and sleeping dreams.

Hannah looked worn down, too. All day long she worked, she and Liam with Curiosity's help, to keep the household running, food on the table, the firewood stacked, the hearth cleaned. Seldom did Elizabeth miss her girlhood home, but she found herself thinking more and more these days of Aunt Merriweather's legions of servants. At Oakmere, little girls had been free to be little girls.

As long as they weren't overly interested in the contents of the library, she reminded herself.

Voices outside, coming closer. Liam and Curiosity, and perhaps one of Curiosity's daughters or Martha Southern, up from the village to bring a covered dish or a pound of butter, for they kept no cow here on the mountain. She had good neighbors; they did what they could to help. Elizabeth knew that she should rouse herself, put the babies in their cradle, her clothing to rights, comb out her hair, wash her face, make tea, help with the corn bread, the endless laundering of swaddling clothes, the mending. The ash barrel, the candle box, the spindle, the mortar and pestle—they all called out to her. But the fire crackled peaceably and the babies were so heavy, pinning her down to her chair, to the earth itself: it felt as if she would never be able to stand on her own two feet, to move unencumbered, ever again.

And still, and still. She could not look at them without having her throat close with tears that were equal parts exhaustion and joy: Mathilde's round cheeks working rhythmically even in her sleep; Daniel's small hand spread out on the white skin of her breast.

Voices closer still; Hannah listening now, too, her head cocked to one side, plaits swinging free to her waist. Curiosity must be in the middle of a story. She had so many of them, but the children were always asking for more. They were all storytellers, these people who carved out lives for themselves on the edge of the frontier. It would be years before she had heard all of Nathaniel's.

With her husband's image foremost in her mind, Elizabeth finally let sleep claim her, thinking of the stories he might bring back with him from Montréal, and wondering how much longer it would be before she would hear his voice again.

Deeply asleep, she did not see the flush of excitement and pleasure on Hannah's face at the sound of steps on the porch. Her chores forgotten, Elizabeth and the babies forgotten, Hannah flew across the room as the

door opened for the travelers: her aunt Many-Doves with a wide smile and a cradleboard peeking over her shoulder; Doves' husband, Runs-from-Bears, grinning at her as he swung a willow carry-frame to the floor; and Falling-Day, wrapped in a mantle of fisher pelts the same deep color as her eyes and hair, so much like Hannah's own. With small sounds of welcome, of relief, of joy beyond bearing, Hannah flung herself into her grandmother's open arms.

5

The Somervilles' basement kitchen was as deep and dim as a cave, but there was nothing cool about it: the combined heat of hearth and ovens had set even the walls to sweating. From a remote corner where they were supposed to be waiting to resume their day-long card game with Martin Fink, Nathaniel and Robbie watched the man scramble to send course after course up to Giselle and her guests.

She hadn't lost her appetite for the unusual. In addition to platters of fancy meat pastries, tureens of soup and ragout, a suckling pig, roast mutton, a haunch of venison, three kinds of fish, every manner of pickled or potted vegetable, and breads and rolls stacked in elaborate patterns, there had been a roast swan shouldered by not two but four serving men. Dressed again in its own white feathers after being stuffed, the long neck held up by hidden skewers, the bird went up the stairs, surrounded by doves baked in nests of puff pastry.

Now Fink was laboring over a huge meringue, decorating it with candied fruit. It reminded Nathaniel of the powdered wigs that had gone out of fashion not so long ago. The cook circled the platter with one eye

squeezed shut and a finger pressed to his mouth. Finally he stood back, looked over at the men in the corner, winked conspiratorially, and burst into noisy song. Dish by dish, his mood improved and his songs became louder.

"Aye, sing awa', ye daft bugger," muttered Robbie. "The man canna wait tae take the rest o' the silver frae ye, laddie." He might rarely play cards, but Robbie was having a hard time purposely losing to a half-drunk Alsatian cook with the habit of singing publicly, and off-key. In a burst of winner's generosity, Fink had offered them the finest his kitchen had to offer, but Robbie had accepted only bread and some cold venison. Now he tore off great chunks, never taking his eyes from the cook.

Nathaniel swallowed down a yawn. There would be at least another hour of this: the servants were fussing over blue-veined cheeses, fruit compotes, liquors and coffees and drinking chocolate. Things he had never heard of before he came to Montréal, or thought of much since leaving it. Suddenly the wish to be home was strong enough to make him get to his feet. He pulled on his mantle and picked up his rifle by its sling and slipped it over his shoulder. "I think I'll have a look around upstairs until Fink's ready to deal the next hand."

Robbie gaped up at him. "And how d'ye plan tae do that, wi' a hoose fu' o' redcoats? I suppose Giselle has a secret stair hidden awa'?"

"Not so secret," said Nathaniel. "I wouldn't want to guess how many men know about it, but it's likely that a few of them are at the dinner table right now."

"Gin that's the case," said Robbie, tucking the remainder of his bread and cheese into his sack and lumbering to his feet, "I micht as weel come wi' ye. Yon glaikit lump"—he pointed at Fink with his chin— "will ha' nae use for us afore the eatin's done. Tell him we're goin' tae empty our bladders."

· · ·

It was good to be out of the kitchens, away from the accumulated smells of a thousand meals. Nathaniel drew in cold air and paused in the courtyard, listening. There was no sign of the guard; they were probably warming themselves inside, sloppy with Somerville away.

With Robbie close behind, Nathaniel made his way to a stand of evergreen bushes, and pushing them apart, revealed a small wooden door without a handle. He pressed on two spots simultaneously and it swung silently inward to disclose a narrow stone stair. It smelled of damp and tobacco smoke and of Giselle, too—slightly musky, the scent of her hair when it was uncoiled and free. It was strange and still immediately familiar, and it made his own hair rise on the back of his neck, as if he were being stalked by an enemy just out of sight.

Nathaniel made his way up the short flight with Robbie following silently. They paused on a landing, although the stairs went on into the dark. By touch he found the two stools he remembered, and directed Robbie to one of them in a low voice.

On the other side of the wall were the muffled sounds of laughter and tinkling glassware. Nathaniel felt for the panel, and with a moment's hesitation, slid it back to reveal two sets of peepholes. Candlelight came to them in four perfectly round streams, and the interwoven voices separated themselves into five or six distinct conversations.

His father and Otter were there, to either side of Giselle. Before Hawkeye was a plate of sweets and a full wine glass. Moncrieff was farther down the table, involved in a conversation with a well-dressed man Nathaniel didn't recognize.

"Panthers among peacocks," whispered Robbie. Hawkeye and Otter stood out in their worn buckskin hunting shirts and leggings, flanked by army and cav-

alry officers in scarlets and blues, green plaids, flowing ribbons, brass buttons, gold braid, silk sashes, swords with ornate baskets.

"Hawkeye looks aye crabbit."

"Testy, but in good health," Nathaniel agreed, relieved just to see his father looking himself. He was sixty-nine years old, a man who had spent most of his lifetime out-of-doors, but he sat there as he would sit at his own table, or at a Kahnyen'kehàka council fire, as lean and straight as a man in his prime, his eyes alert and watchful.

There was only a partial view of Otter's face, but the tension in the boy's shoulders was easy enough to read. He was wound up tight and ready to spring. Adele's visit had primed them well.

And there was Giselle. Looking down over the room and not ten feet away from her, they were close enough to count the pearl buttons at the nape of her gown. She sat with her back to them; a good thing, for she had sharp eyes. Nathaniel let himself study her, the dark blond hair pinned up to reveal the long neck, the white skin of her shoulders against deep green silk, the curve of her cheekbone when she turned her head to speak to the servant.

Now that he had got this far Nathaniel couldn't remember why he had dreaded the sight of her so much. She was still beautiful—he could see that even from here—but she wasn't Elizabeth, and she had no power over him. To his surprise, the most he could feel for her was a vague gratitude and reluctant admiration. Giselle did as she pleased. She could be ruthless; she cared nothing at all for the good opinion of others; and there was an air of casual danger about her. Because it suited her to do so, she surrounded herself with men who were eager to amuse, taking from them what she wanted and leaving the rest. Tonight she had placed a seventeen-year-old Kahnyen'kehàka at her right hand over rich and powerful men, and none of them dared challenge her. She had

been having parties like these behind her father's back since she was sixteen.

A cavalry officer was holding up his glass toward Giselle, the wine picking up the candlelight and flashing it back again. His own complexion was equally flushed.

"This Paxareti," he announced in a voice slurred with drink, but just loud enough to claim everyone's attention, "is proof that the Portuguese are not total barbarians. It comes from a monastery a few hours' ride from Jerez, but it is well worth the cost. Well worth it, by God."

"And how very thoughtful of you to bring it to me, Captain Quinn," said Giselle. Her tone was easy, encouraging but not engaging, and her voice was just as Nathaniel had remembered it, deep and slightly rough, as if she had strained it the day—or the night—before. "And how sad that our American friends resist so great a pleasure." She was looking at Hawkeye, but she leaned slightly toward Otter as she spoke.

"It is said that two glasses of strong sherry will render a reticent man more communicative without . . . impairing him," commented an officer of the dragoons who was staring at Hawkeye. He was well grown and broad of shoulder, but when he grinned he revealed a set of ivory teeth too large for his mouth.

Hawkeye raised a brow. "When I've got something to say worth saying, I'll speak up, with or without spirits. So far I ain't heard anything worth the trouble."

Robbie's grunt of approval was lost in the mixture of laughter and protest from below.

"What of your young friend, then?" The dragoon's gaze wandered toward Otter. "Or has he no civilized languages?"

"Major Johnson," Giselle said evenly, before Hawkeye could reply. The toothy smile shifted in her direction; the tilt of his head said he expected her approval.

"At your service, Miss Somerville."

"You are boring me."

He drained of color. "I only meant—"

Giselle turned her attention to the opposite side of the table, ignoring Johnson's apologies.

"Captain Pickering, it has been a very long time indeed since you have come to our cold corner of the world. The navy abandons me at this time of year, but I can always count on you."

The man Giselle was addressing had been turned toward Moncrieff and deep in conversation, but he looked up gladly at her request, and Robbie and Nathaniel both drew up in surprise at this first clear sight of his face.

The bush was a hard place; Nathaniel had grown up in the company of men and women who bore terrible scars with a combination of forbearance and dignity. But Pickering's face was not the result of a tomahawk blow or a battle with the pox or fire. Nathaniel suspected it was much harder to bear. It looked as if his maker had finished with him, disliked what he had produced, and attempted to rub out the errors, mashing an overlarge nose into a face like a soggy oat cake. Everything on him was lopsided, from the small, upward-slanted eyes to the low-hung shelf of brow.

"Maria save us, look at the man's snout," muttered Robbie. "He's mair pickerel than Pickering. Nae wonder he went tae sea."

"Mademoiselle." Pickering inclined his head. "I have brought you more than seafaring tales. If you'll permit—" he half rose, and gestured to someone out of sight in the next room.

Giselle laughed. "Horace. I knew I could count on you. A surprise. I do love surprises. Shall I try to guess?"

"Ha!" called Quinn. "It's anyone's guess what Pickering's got tucked away in that merchantman of his. Could have an elephant or two crashing about in the hold."

A servant appeared at the door, carrying a small lidded basket. There was a great scramble of serving men as plates and platters were cleared to make room for it just in front of Giselle.

"You brought me such a lovely set of ivory carvings from India when last you were here," she said, eyeing the basket. She had turned so that Nathaniel could see her face. Time had not left her untouched, but there was the same spark in her eye and high color in her cheeks, and he didn't wonder that Otter had got caught up, despite the difference in their ages. Stronger and more experienced men had floundered in the good fortune of attracting this woman's favor. There were some prime examples around the table.

Pickering was drawing out the suspense. "We were on our way to Halifax from Martinique . . ."

Quinn put down his glass with a rattle. "Pickering, you sly dog, were you there when Jervis and Grey took Martinique?" They were no sailors, but the promise of direct news of a victory over France would have been very welcome to the army officers.

Pickering smiled politely but did nothing to satisfy their curiosity. Instead he put one hand on the basket, as if to quiet whatever was inside.

"I took these on board not knowing if they would survive the journey, but I had some luck. And my most excellent surgeon, of course, nursed them all the way." With a graceful flourish he flipped back the wooden lid of the basket and reached inside.

"You will note by the sweet smell that they are quite perfectly ripe." And he drew from the basket a pair of swollen and discolored human hands, no larger than those of a child of ten, with lightly curled fingers.

There was a moment of shocked silence as he held them up. Even Giselle's voice seemed to fail her.

A sandy-haired major of the Royal Highlanders leaped to his feet. "By God, man, have you been consortin' with cannibals?"

The room was suddenly in chaotic movement as all the men surged forward. Nathaniel's view was blocked by Otter, who stood with the rest of them. Robbie stood, too, and then, having lost his peepholes, sat again.

"Let me put your mind at rest, MacDermott. These grow on the islands," came Pickering's calming voice from the center of the crowd. "They are called ti-nains by the natives."

"That's a bluidy *fruit*?" demanded one of the merchants.

"Ah," said another, more composed voice. "Bananas. But not of the sort I et in India. These are much smaller. Damned difficult to transport, in any case."

"Ha!" cried Captain Quinn, heading back toward his wine glass. "Fruit! A good joke, that, Pickering! Fruit!"

Johnson was still at the head of the table, peering inside the basket suspiciously. "What civilized person would put such a thing in his mouth?"

"I understand the king is verra partial to bananas, when he can get them," said Moncrieff, leaning in closer to peer at them.

Johnson grunted suspiciously as Pickering held up a single example. "Looks like that dev'lish surgeon of yours lopped 'em off some poor bugger when he wasn't paying attention."

Quinn raised his glass. "If that's all a man has to lose, perhaps he's better off on t'other side of the fence!"

There was a moment of frozen silence, but Giselle's smile set the room at ease. "Please, gentlemen, sit down. James, I believe Captain Quinn would do well with some coffee, but do serve Major Johnson more of the candied quince, that seems more to his liking. Horace, tell me, where does one begin with your lovely ti-nains?"

Johnson looked on in sour disapproval, as if he ex-

pected to hear the snap of bone as Pickering peeled away the dark brown outer shell. The flesh inside was a pinkish tan, and the sweet smell was clear to them even behind the carved wooden panel.

"They are best eaten directly from the tree," Pickering said, putting the fruit on a small plate and presenting it to Giselle. "But I believe you will still find them very tasty."

As she leaned over to draw in the scent, the serving men quickly peeled and distributed the fruits to the rest of the table.

Giselle said, "We will all sample something so rare, will we not, gentlemen? And perhaps a glass of Madeira or champagne, and then it's time we roused ourselves a bit. Shall we have music, or games? What do you think, Mr. Bonner?"

"Suit yourselves," said Hawkeye, his arms crossed across his chest and the plate of banana untouched before him. "I'll watch."

She brought up her gaze slowly. "Really? In my experience, the men of your family are all very *energetic* sorts."

"Oh, I don't doubt they can be distracted from the work at hand, on occasion," Hawkeye said easily. "It's something a man grows out of, though. For the most part."

Giselle let out a small laugh of surprise at this challenge, but a young lieutenant broke in before she could respond.

"This cannot surprise you, Miss Somerville," he said, waving a hand. "Surely you know that Americans are not good sportsmen."

"Not by English rules we ain't, that's true enough," Hawkeye agreed.

Giselle interrupted the young man's sputtering reply. "Lieutenant Lytton, what I have in mind is not an English game, but a Scottish one, directly from Carryckcastle— Mr. Moncrieff tells me it used to be played there regularly, when the earl had guests."

"Hmmpf." Robbie sat up straighter, looking interested.

As Giselle explained the fine points, grins began to appear around the table.

"Ah," said MacDermott. "Razzored Harries is what we called it when I was young. In the end you're all packed together like herrings in a dish of cream."

Johnson pushed away his untouched banana. "It's just the reverse of hide-and-seek. It's played in Shropshire, as well. We called it pickle packing."

"Do I understand correctly?" interrupted Quinn, trying to make sense of the game through a fog brought on by Portuguese sherry. "Should I find the hiding place instead of announcing that fact, I simply . . . join the group already there."

"Yes, and try to keep quiet," Giselle confirmed.

"Quite good sport." Pickering rubbed his hands in anticipation.

"Miss Somerville, may I assume you will be the first to hide?" asked a young merchant.

"But of course, Mr. Gray," said Giselle. "What fun would it be otherwise?"

"Grown men, runnin' aboot and playin' at children's games," muttered Robbie as they made their way back down to the kitchen. "There's nae dignity in it."

Above them there was a shout of laughter and the sound of breaking glass.

"It's not dignity that brings them here," Nathaniel noted dryly.

Robbie pulled up short. "Ye dinna mean—she couldna, no' wi' aa those men—"

"No," Nathaniel said. "I ain't supposing she would. But one of them won't be going straight home. As long as it ain't Otter, that's all that concerns us."

They paused at the door into the kitchen, where two young girls were coping, bleary eyed and short tem-

pered, with great piles of dirty china and crystal. For the moment there was no sign of Fink.

"I wasna cut oot for this kind o' warfare," Robbie announced with a sigh. "A musket wad suit me far better than parlor games wi' a crowd o' nut-hooks."

"Then we'd best get gone," said Hawkeye from the stairs behind them. Nathaniel pivoted. His father was there, with Moncrieff just behind. Hawkeye's grip on his shoulder was still like iron, and the hazel eyes blazed at him with a furious joy.

"Da," he said, hearing the break in his own voice. "High time."

"I cain't say I ain't glad to see you, son. Rab, it's been too long."

Nathaniel said, "Fink will be looking for us."

"Nivver mind about him," said Moncrieff. "He's too drunk tae remember where he put his own nose, and he willna be thinking o' us while he's got a card game with the guards in the upstairs pantry. I'll go fetch Otter." And he ran back up the stairs.

They were itching to be gone, but they could only hope Moncrieff would be fast in cutting Otter loose from the game. Hawkeye was as tense as Nathaniel had ever seen him, but he didn't wonder at that after a few weeks in the garrison gaol. He caught Nathaniel's gaze, and produced a weary grin. "I want the news from home, but first we're best shut of this place, and Moncrieff. I don't trust the man."

Robbie bent in closer. "Wi'oot Moncrieff ye wad still be in gaol, Dan'l."

"I'm not free and clear yet," Hawkeye pointed out. From overhead there was the sound of running feet, a door opening and slamming. A lot of swearing followed, and the footsteps ran off again.

"Moncrieff went to some trouble," Nathaniel said, meeting his father's eye. "He got us in here. I promised in return that you'd listen to what he has to say."

"I ain't hanging around, son. Not for anybody. What is it that he wants?"

Nathaniel glanced up the stairs, and lowered his voice. "You won't believe it when he tells you, Da. But I'd rather he do it himself. We can let him come along as far as Chambly, that will give him opportunity enough."

Hawkeye grunted. "If he can keep up, aye. But first there's the matter of pulling the boy out of her damn game—ah." He nodded, clearly relieved, as Otter appeared at the head of the stairs and started down, with Moncrieff at his heels. Otter came directly to Nathaniel to grasp him by both lower arms.

"Raktsi'a," he murmured. *Older brother.* This was the traditional greeting for the husband of his oldest sister, but it struck Nathaniel that Otter had outgrown it. He was a man now, broad of shoulder and almost tall enough to look Nathaniel in the eye. There was an earnestness in his expression that was new since they had last seen each other.

"How did you get away?" Hawkeye asked.

Otter shrugged. "Maybe I ain't so good at finding her as she wants me to be." He looked away, his expression guarded.

Robbie picked up his pack and his weapons. "We're awa', then, lads."

It had clouded over; there was a spattering of snow, and the wind was bitter. When Nathaniel was sure they wouldn't run into any guards he signaled and the others came out into the open.

Against the far corner of the house nearest the stables, Treenie came to her feet silently, tail wagging.

Otter hissed, "A light!"

The five of them slid deeper into the shadow of the house. Nathaniel forced his breathing to slow, throwing his senses outward into the dark.

It was Captain Quinn, stumbling over the path and laughing to himself. He carried a pierced tin lantern

that seesawed an arc of jagged light over his face. He stopped, peered at the house owlishly, and then tried to fight his way through the bushes one-handed. At first Nathaniel could not make sense of it, and then he realized that Quinn was drunk enough to be searching for the hidden door on the wrong wall of the house.

"Come on, Giselle," he called. "You can't hide from me. I've got your drag, I do. Pickle packing, eh? All tied up in a knot with your savage, but I'll put an end to that."

He drew his short sword and thrashed at the bushes, grunting with the effort. Nathaniel edged backward, just out of his reach. They continued like this for ten yards, until Quinn took a holly branch across the face and pulled up short.

"Moved your little door, have you? Won't do you a bit of good, lovey, I'll find you out in the end. Ask any man jack in the Sixtieth if Jonathan Quinn don't have a way with a woman's doors." He snickered at his own wit, threw back his head and bellowed in earnest. "Giselle!"

Nathaniel swore to himself. The idiot would have the guards here.

A window opened above their heads. "She's not outside, you bloody great booby, Quinn. Come in from the cold." The window shut again.

"Have to piss first," Quinn called back. "Then I shall find her. You shan't have 'er, do you mind me, Johnson?" Muttering, he turned, and shuffled off a few steps, pulling at his breeks as he went.

The five of them started in the opposite direction, crouched low and moving fast. Once around the corner, they bent their heads together.

Hawkeye said, "We'll have to split up and meet at the start of the ice road."

"If I may—" began Moncrieff, and Hawkeye cut him off with a hand on the shoulder.

"If you want to talk to me, you'll have to do it on the run. If you're up to that."

"Giselle!" shouted Quinn, closer now. "Giselle!" Overhead the cloud cover was breaking up so that Nathaniel could see his father's face.

"Giselle!"

The sound of boots in the snow, from the opposite direction. The guards came trotting, finally roused from the warm house and their card game. The hidden staircase was risky, but anything was better than standing exposed in the garden. Otter sprinted for the bushes, with the other men close behind.

Once inside they waited, completely still, for the voices in the garden to fade away, but instead they grew louder. Nathaniel felt the blood thrumming in his hands, his leg muscles twitching with the need to be away. Otter's chest was heaving as if he had run a hot mile, and Moncrieff stood tensed and ready to bolt. *More than he bargained for,* Nathaniel thought. Robbie and Hawkeye kept their calm: old soldiers, they had lived through far worse.

Treenie shifted uneasily in the total dark.

"Wheest," Robbie breathed, and she settled down.

Nathaniel focused on the regular ebb and flow of his father's breathing, ordered his thoughts, and lined up their few options. There was no help for it, so he took the stairs three at a time to listen at Giselle's door. Nothing.

From the courtyard came the sound of horses' hooves on the cobblestones.

At Nathaniel's signal they came up the stairs and into the bedchamber. The smells hung in the air like smoke from a wet-wood fire: beeswax, lavender, crushed roses, musk. Otter stood paralyzed at the door and had to be pushed forward. Nathaniel knew what he was feeling. *I didn't have any intention of ever setting foot in this room again, either.*

More bad news at the window: the courtyard was full of redcoats, horses, servants, a sea of bobbing lanterns and torches. Guards milled below the window, poking in the bushes. Nathaniel caught a glimpse of Pickering and a few of the others, walking away as if they had nothing to do with any of it.

"They're looking for you," he said, turning. Some part of his mind registered the strange sight they made, rough backwoodsmen in the gilt and velvet and silk of Giselle's chamber. Moncrieff had collapsed into a spindle-backed chair; Robbie peered over the top of the canopied bed. The red dog rested her mucky rear quarters on an embroidered footstool, sniffed at the perfumed draperies and sneezed.

Hawkeye came to look through lace panels for himself. "I'd call this a tangle, all right."

Robbie was prowling, opening wardrobes and closing them again in disgust. "Nae place tae hide."

Otter still stood in the middle of the room, frowning into the banked fire in the hearth. Then he turned and walked to a full-length mirror on the wall opposite the bed, and punched at the belly of a gilded angel on the upper right corner. The mirror levered away from the wall with a sigh.

"That's a new one on me," Nathaniel said.

Hawkeye rubbed a hand over his mouth, peering into the cubbyhole. "She's fond of hiding games, ain't she? Does Pink George know about it?"

Otter made a negative sound in his throat.

"There's room enough for one," said Moncrieff.

"We still got a chance to get out of here," said Hawkeye. "Although I'll admit it don't look good." He studied Otter for a long moment. "I have the feeling she'll let you get away, if she can keep her father out of it. Ain't that so?"

Otter nodded. "Hen'en." *Yes.*

Hawkeye cast a glance out the window. In Kahnyen' kehàka he said, "Listen to me. If it comes to that, you slip

away as soon as it's safe, and hightail it for Hidden Wolf." He lowered his voice. "Send Runs-from-Bears back here with gold."

Otter blinked his understanding.

In a rush, Hawkeye's voice lowered to a harsh whisper. "Tell Bears to stay clear of this Scotsman. He don't need to know all our business. You understand why I'm talking to you this way?"

The boy's face stilled, and he nodded. Behind him, Robbie's expression was just as thoughtful. Moncrieff started to speak, and thought better of it.

At the door to the hidden stairs there was a light scratching and they all turned together.

"Giselle?" came a hoarse whisper. "I hear you in there. Let me in, sweetings. It's Jonathan." Quinn had found the hidden door at last, and lost his bluster in the process.

"Giselle," he pleaded.

As if she had heard him call, Giselle's voice rose up from the front hall. Her playful tone was gone. She was agitated, out of breath, and coming this way.

Nathaniel flung the door to the hidden staircase open and grabbed an astounded Quinn by the epaulets to drag him into the room.

"Wha—" was all he could get out before Rab tapped him neatly over the ear with his rifle butt. Otter caught him up as he collapsed onto Giselle's Turkish carpet and tossed him onto the bed.

"There," he said. "That's what he wanted anyway."

Giselle was very close, shouting orders down the stairs. Outside, there were new voices in the garden.

Otter caught Nathaniel's eye. Wordlessly, Nathaniel held out his rifle and his powder horn, and Otter took them and climbed into the cubbyhole behind the mirror.

Hawkeye reached in and pressed Otter's shoulder. "We're putting our trust in you, son. Don't leave us sitting in that gaol any longer than you can manage."

They were away, closing the door behind them and down stone steps, Treenie bringing up the rear. As they reached the bottom, candlelight flooded the stairwell from above just as the door below began to swing inward.

"Damnation," whispered Moncrieff.

"Oh, we ain't that far, yet," said Hawkeye. "We'll live to fight another day."

Colonel George Somerville, Viscount Bainbridge, lieutenant governor of Lower Canada, stood in the doorway before them in a circle of lantern light. Pink George, as he was known to his men and most of Montréal. He was in a muddy traveling cloak, his thin face blotched with the cold, his eyes sparkling some deep satisfaction. At his back was a whole unit of redcoats, bayonets at the ready.

A soft sound of surprise from Giselle, above them. *Caught out at last,* Nathaniel thought. *And us with her.* If it weren't for Elizabeth waiting for him, he might have found some humor in that.

"Gentlemen." The lieutenant governor peered at them over the top of his spectacles, his chin bedded on his chest.

Treenie growled, her hackles rising.

Somerville raised a brow. "Sergeant Jones," he said, one corner of his mouth jerking downward. "Take the dog outside and shoot it. As for the rest of you, I hope you enjoyed my daughter's little dinner party. There won't be another."

6

"Well, now," said Curiosity, bending over Daniel to peer into his face. "I'd say this boy's eyes'll settle down to green any day." The baby waved his fist at her nose, and she laughed.

"Not hazel?" Elizabeth asked, regarding Many-Doves' son in the nest on her lap. Almost four months old and a solid brick of a child, Blue-Jay smiled up at her. He had his parents' black eyes, the same deep color as the halo of hair that stood out all over his head.

"No, ma'am," said Curiosity, flipping Daniel neatly as she wrapped him in flannel. "Green, like new leaves on the sugar maple. And just as sweet, ain't that so, baby?"

From the other room came his sister's wail, as if this news did not suit her in the least. Elizabeth started up from the rocking chair, but Curiosity stopped her with a look, and dropped Daniel in her lap.

"You stay put," she said. "You got a cabin full of women here to help out, after all. I expect between us we'll see to Miss Lily."

"You needn't coddle me, you know," Elizabeth called. But Curiosity simply flapped her hand behind her as she left the bedroom.

Daniel blinked up at her and cooed, all earnest concentration. Elizabeth answered in kind, and he waved his arms enthusiastically, settling in for a good long talk. Of course Curiosity was right: his eyes would be green, just as Mathilde's would be blue. "Blue as the flaglily in May," Curiosity had declared, and thus she had become Lily to one and all. Elizabeth's own solemn gray and Nathaniel's hazel had somehow gotten lost between the two children, but their father was stamped on each of them nonetheless, from the curve of their earlobes to the shape of their toenails. Of herself Elizabeth saw very little in the babies, with the exception of the curls that framed their faces.

Elizabeth yelped as Blue-Jay tugged hard at her plait. Daniel was examining his own hands, as if to ask them how such a task might be undertaken. In the other room Lily had settled down, probably strapped into a cradleboard on Falling Day's back, where all of the babies seemed most content. Elizabeth studied the faces before her and blew softly to ruffle their hair, earning crows of delight from both of them.

Nathaniel had not yet seen the twins smile. He had not seen them since they were three days old.

It was against the rule she had set for herself, but Elizabeth could not help counting the days since he had started north. Soon it would be eight weeks—far too long, much longer than he had anticipated. There was no way to know if he was on the road home, or had ever arrived in Montréal, but her faith in his ability to do what must be done was firm, just as he trusted her to see to their children's welfare. And still, with every passing day she grew more unsettled, and recently she had begun to dream.

The babies slept now for longer periods in the night, and Elizabeth slept, too. She dreamt of snow. The Windigo of the endless forests visited her dreams, their pelts crackling white, stone men with eyes like wet rasp-

berries. In her dreams there was always a winding ice road that gleamed silver and black, but no trace of Nathaniel. And that terrified her most of all.

Blue-Jay began to squirm, and she shook herself out of the daydream. He was working his face into the thoughtful expression that meant he wanted feeding. Elizabeth would have put him to her own breast—just as Many-Doves sometimes nursed Lily or Daniel so that Elizabeth could sleep for another hour—but the first real squawk brought his mother to the door.

He squeaked and chirped with impatience while she put aside the mending she had in her hands and settled on the edge of the bed with him.

"You are well named, my son." Many-Doves spoke Kahnyen'kehàka, as she always did when English could be avoided. She gathered the boy closer to her and loosened her overblouse.

The two women sat in companionable silence for some time, listening to Blue-Jay's contented gulping. There was the sound of new snow scouring the roof, and outside the thud of an axe. It reminded Elizabeth that there were still men on Hidden Wolf, although Falling-Day had banished Liam and Runs-from-Bears to the other cabin so that the women had complete reign in this one.

Daniel was looking decidedly sleepy, and Elizabeth shifted him to a more comfortable position, stifling a yawn of her own.

Doves stroked her son's cheek thoughtfully. "Runs-from-Bears wants to start north," she said, seeking out Elizabeth's eye.

"Ah," Elizabeth said, relief and fear fluttering together under her blouse. "What does Falling-Day think?"

"My mother dreams of the ice road, but there is no sign of our men on it."

In another time, in the life she once lived, Elizabeth

would have been unnerved by this news that she and
Falling-Day were having such similar dreams. But in the
past year she had learned that reason and logic had
boundaries.

Many-Doves was watching her closely.

"When does Bears want to leave?"

"Soon," Doves said. "Perhaps tomorrow."

Just after dawn Elizabeth woke to the sound of a
step on the porch and Falling-Day rising hastily from
her sleeping platform under Hannah's loft. Elizabeth's
heart gave a tremendous leap, and she ran, barefoot,
her nightdress streaming behind her, into the other
room.

In the open door stood Otter, healthy and whole, although his face was drawn and thin. Alone. Elizabeth
pushed past him into the gray early morning, unable
and unwilling to believe what her eyes told her. There
was nothing but the March winter waiting for her, the
snow burning cold under her bare feet.

Nathaniel's rifle was slung across Otter's back. She
reached out to take the sling from his shoulder and he
let it go without a word.

She would know it anywhere, even without the name
carved in the stock. Deerkiller. How many times had
she seen it in his hands? She herself had fired it once,
and that simple act had sent her alone into the wilderness on a desperate race. Nathaniel would no more
leave this rifle behind than he would give up his sight or
hearing.

Otter was talking to her, but she could make no
sense of it. Her blood was thundering in her ears.
Elizabeth shook her head, forcing herself to focus. She
needed to hear him; she wanted to run away.

He took her by the arm and drew her into the cabin.
"I bring you word from your husband, my brother," he
said. "Listen to me. He is alive, he is well."

"Grandfather?" asked Hannah, pulling on Otter's arm. "What of my grandfather?"

"He is well, too, and sends his greetings."

From the cradle in the other room came the howling of the twins, and with that Elizabeth found her voice. "Why are they not here with you? Why do you have Nathaniel's rifle?" But even without the expression on his face, she could see for herself what must have happened. "He went to get you out of gaol, you and Hawkeye. It went wrong, didn't it?"

Otter nodded.

"How long?"

"Somerville arrested them on the first night of the full moon."

Three weeks. Elizabeth swallowed hard. Nathaniel had been sitting in the garrison gaol for three weeks; Hawkeye for much longer. *They are alive,* she reminded herself, rubbing her cheek on the cold metal of the rifle barrel. *Nathaniel is alive.*

Otter began to speak, but his mother interrupted him.

"First you will eat," said Falling-Day. "And then you will talk."

While Elizabeth and Many-Doves went about the business of seeing to the children's needs, Otter submitted to his mother's care. Falling-Day put a bowl of red corn soup in his hands and watched him eat until it was empty. Then she stood Otter before the hearth and stripped him down to the breechclout as if he were a boy of six rather than a well-grown man of seventeen. Her examination was thorough, less than gentle, and accompanied by detailed commentary on his behavior. Otter bore it all without protest, perhaps because he was in pain, or perhaps simply because he was glad to be home, at any price.

"Perhaps Giselle Somerville taught him more about

women than he was ready to learn," Elizabeth whispered to Lily as she nursed. The baby wrinkled her forehead in agreement, her small hand patting Elizabeth's breast as if to comfort her.

Three of Otter's fingers were badly frostbitten, and Hannah was set to rubbing them with a piece of flannel until they came howling back to life. But it was his feet that gave Falling-Day real pause. Liam was sent to fetch Curiosity, and after a long consultation, Runs-from-Bears sharpened a boning knife and they took off two small toes that were festering badly, and beyond their combined skills. Through all of this Otter made no sound at all, although there were beads of perspiration on his upper lip, and his hand shook when he pulled at Hannah's plaits in an attempt to get her to smile.

Elizabeth knew without being told how fortunate Otter was. A late blizzard had kept him trapped in a snow cave for three full days; he was lucky to have survived at all. That he needed food, and medical care, and sleep after hard days on the trail—these things she understood completely, and still she struggled with the urge to shake the story out of him.

Finally, Curiosity withdrew to the other room with all three babies, firm in her belief that the discussion that was about to take place should not include her. Liam too was ready to slip away, when Elizabeth took his arm and directed him to the group around the hearth. He hunkered down, his hands dangling over knees that threatened to poke through homespun breeches, his gaze on the floor. He would not understand very much of what was said, but still she wanted him there.

Elizabeth had heard Otter tell stories many times; he had a strong voice and a way with his audience. But this tale he began in fits and starts, speaking directly to his mother, focusing on her face alone. He spoke of following Richard Todd to Montréal in the late summer, of Hawkeye's arrival at the O'seronni New Year, their preparation to leave Montréal, and the first arrest by

Somerville. He told it all without ever mentioning Giselle Somerville. But when all was said and done, none of the details mattered. The trouble at hand was more than enough: Hawkeye, Nathaniel, and Robbie sat in the garrison gaol in Montréal, and with them Angus Moncrieff.

By the time Otter finished, Elizabeth had broken out in a fine sweat.

"Somebody sent for Somerville," Bears said, finally. "Some traitor."

Otter raised one shoulder. "It looks that way."

Elizabeth pressed her hands together in her lap. "They were charged with helping you escape?"

Otter's gaze flickered away from her, as jumpy as the fire in the hearth. "And with spying."

"Spying!" Hannah jumped up. Many-Doves pulled her back down. Liam shifted uneasily, his gaze roving from face to face.

"In peacetime?" Elizabeth asked, her voice crackling dry and unfamiliar in her throat.

Runs-from-Bears said, "The English are at war with France."

"Then we are fortunate not to be French," proposed Many-Doves, frowning at her husband as if he personally were responsible for the wars Europeans waged upon one another.

Otter said, "It is because the Americans stay out of the war with France that the English are suspicious."

"We are not *Americans*, either," Hannah said defiantly.

Falling-Day said, "The O'seronni look at Wolf-Running-Fast and Hawkeye and they see what they want to see. They do not know how to look deeper than the color of their skin."

"Rab fought under Schuyler in the last war, and so did Nathaniel," Runs-from-Bears pointed out.

"Nathaniel fought with our Kahnyen'kehàka warriors," Falling-Day corrected him.

Elizabeth said, "In any case, the idea of Nathaniel as a spy for France is absurd, and I'm sure they are aware of that. It is only an excuse to hold them there."

Hannah's face crumpled. "They hang spies."

"No," Otter said quickly. "At least, not straight off. Iona says that Carleton himself is supposed to question them, but he won't be in Montréal before May. So there's enough time for Bears to get up there with the gold." He cast an uneasy glance in Liam's direction, but the boy was watching Hannah, and clearly had not understood.

Elizabeth held out an arm and Hannah came to her, her face a misery. "Squirrel," Elizabeth said, using her Kahnyen'kehàka name. "Do you hear? There is time." *Pray God,* she added to herself, her mind racing madly over the few facts she had, and a hundred questions that could not be answered.

Falling-Day turned to Bears. "You will start north tomorrow. Surely the gold will help."

"The gold will do no earthly good at all," said Elizabeth softly, smoothing Hannah's hair. "Bears has no way to know whom to approach. Is that not true?"

Reluctantly, Runs-from-Bears nodded.

Hannah pulled on Elizabeth's sleeve. "There must be a way."

"There is a way," said Elizabeth firmly. "But there is no time to waste. There is somebody in Albany who can help."

Bears raised a brow. "Phillip Schuyler won't be any use in Montréal. He and Somerville are old enemies."

"Perhaps General Schuyler could not sway Somerville," Elizabeth conceded. "But I doubt even Somerville would ignore the son and heir of the chief justice of the King's Bench."

At this switch to English, Liam sat up with a quizzical look. "By God," he said. "Who would that be?"

"Cousin Amanda's husband, Will Spencer, Viscount

Durbeyfield," said Hannah. "You remember, Liam. They came to visit with Elizabeth's aunt in the summer. They haven't gone back to England yet."

"Spencer is in Albany?" Otter asked.

"Yes," said Elizabeth. "I had a letter from them recently."

"Well, then," said Liam with a great sigh of relief. "Send Will Spencer to Montréal. He's a lawyer, ain't he? He'll get them out of gaol."

Falling-Day was watching Elizabeth closely, her head cocked to one side. "Bone-in-Her-Back," she said quietly, using Elizabeth's Kahnyen'kehàka name. "Would you send a man to do work that needs a woman's understanding?"

Elizabeth swallowed hard. This was the question: would she have her cousin go to Montréal to try to achieve a political end to this situation, or would she take it in her own hands? The part of her that was still an English lady of good family could barely conceive of the idea that she might travel so far in the middle of winter on men's business, but there was another part, a stronger voice in her now. And Falling-Day heard it, too, and understood that Elizabeth could not chance Nathaniel's life, could not stand by while others fought for him.

It was unthinkable, and she would do it anyway.

"I would not," Elizabeth said. "I cannot."

"Thayeri," said Falling-Day. *It is proper so.*

For the first time that day, Elizabeth felt she could breathe.

At the open bedroom door, Curiosity said, "You goin' to take those babies into the wilderness?"

Elizabeth started, and came to her feet.

"How could you even think of such a thing? You always talkin' about bein' *rational.*"

"Curiosity," Elizabeth said. "Let me tell you—"

"I heard enough. Don't need to hear no more." And

Curiosity turned on her heel and disappeared back into the bedroom.

"She is the one you must convince," said Falling-Day, reaching for her sewing. "She is the first step in this journey."

In the bedroom, Curiosity was elbow deep in soapy water and dirty swaddling clothes.

"You don't have to do that," Elizabeth said.

Curiosity hummed her disagreement and never looked up.

Elizabeth said, "The way from Albany to Montréal is hardly the wilderness. It is almost as well traveled as the London Road."

The steady rub and rush on the washboard did not falter. "Don't talk to me about no London Road. You got a winter to contend with, here."

"You just told me yesterday that the worst was over, didn't you?"

Curiosity sat back on her heels and wiped her cheek with the back of a hand. "Well, I didn't know you was getting set to go runnin' off with them babies on your back, or I wouldn't have."

Elizabeth managed a smile at that. "They brought Blue-Jay through much rougher country six weeks ago, when the weather was worse. And I won't be on foot."

A long wheeze of impatience. "What, you intendin' to spread your wings and fly? Oh, I see. You think the judge just goin' to hand over his sleigh and team to get you as far as Albany, do you? He'll try to tie you down, and you know it."

"Oh, Curiosity. He's tried that before, has he not?" With a sigh, Elizabeth sat on the edge of the bed where the twins lay, kicking and burbling to each other.

With a voice much steadier than she thought it ought to be, Elizabeth said, "If I do not go, they will try Nathaniel and Hawkeye and Robbie as spies, with no one there to speak for them. Would you expect me to sit here and wait for news that they have been hanged?"

A slight tremor moved Curiosity's shoulders, but she said nothing.

"You would go, if it were one of your own."

"You are like one of my own," Curiosity said, calm now.

"Then help me," Elizabeth said. "I need your help."

A long silence was broken only by the gurgling of the babies. Elizabeth sat on the bed she had shared with her husband and wondered if he would ever walk through the door again, if she would ever hear his voice. There was a curious numbness in her, a burning in her eyes that felt like somebody else's tears. She could have no part of that, not now. With or without Curiosity's help she would do this. Perhaps the older woman saw all this on her face, for her own expression softened.

"I'll talk the judge into it and get the sleigh, on one condition."

"I will not leave my children behind."

"No, missy, you won't." Curiosity tilted up her chin, the dark eyes snapping. "You won't leave me behind, either."

Elizabeth suddenly found herself trembling. She folded her hands in her lap. "You would come with us?"

Curiosity wiped her arms with her apron. "Somebody got to keep you out of trouble," she said. "Let's go see the judge about that sleigh, 'cause I ain't about to walk."

Hannah's hands would not work properly. She dropped a bowl, the sewing basket, her horn tablet, everything she picked up. No one seemed to notice her sudden clumsi-

ness. Her grandmother and aunt were sorting through clothing, wrapping dried venison in corn husks, mending snowshoes, getting ready to send Elizabeth and Runs-from-Bears on a long journey. Bears had gone off to the north face of the mountain to get the gold; Otter had been given willow-bark tea and sent to bed. Elizabeth and Curiosity were in the village.

From across the room Liam caught her gaze, and gestured with his eyes outside.

The stable was their place to talk. In warmer weather Hannah often shelled beans or ground corn here while Liam saw to his chores. Now it was empty, the horses boarded at the blacksmith's for the winter; snow had drifted into every corner.

"Your father and grandfather will be home safe in another month," Liam said. He sat on an upturned bucket, his face hatcheted with shadow.

"Yes," Hannah said. She swallowed hard to banish the tears that swelled without warning.

"You're going with her." Liam pulled his hat from his head to examine the inside of it, as if the worn crown might tell him what he wanted to hear.

She nodded. "If she'll let me."

He laughed a little. "You'll talk her into it. You've been wanting to go off ever since the summer."

Last summer. She had been desperate with worry through those long weeks when her father and Elizabeth had been gone, on the run through the endless forests. Liam had still been living with his brother then, but he had always seemed to show up when she needed to talk. Now she barely knew what to say to him. If it was in her power she would leave him behind and go north with Elizabeth and Runs-from-Bears and Curiosity. He would stay here and split kindling and carry wood and water, clean possum and skin deer, lay traps. He would be more alone than she had been in the summer. She had had her grandmother and aunt and uncles.

"You will like Otter when you get to know him," Hannah said. "He knows all the secret places on the mountain. He'll show them to you."

"Will he?" Liam's voice was hoarse.

"You are one of us now. He will show you."

"I've been thinking." He never raised his eyes to her. "Maybe I should go stay with the McGarritys until you get back. The two women can manage with your uncle here."

"No," Hannah said, more forcefully than she meant to. "Don't do that. You belong here."

"So do you."

She blinked. "She'll need help with my sister and brother—"

His shoulders slumped in defeat. He nodded.

"You'll stay?"

Liam would not meet her eye. "I'll be the only white on Hidden Wolf when you go."

It was like snow on the back of her neck; the chill ran down her spine to settle in her gut. She must have made some sound. His head came up and he studied her with eyes the blue of winter ice.

"I am not white."

"To me you are," he said.

The world blurred, the red-gold of Liam's hair and the bright metal of the traps hung on the wall colliding in a rusty rainbow. Hannah pressed her hands to her eyes to stop it, to take away the look on his face. He thought he had paid her a compliment. *I am the daughter of Sings-from-Books of the Kahnyen'kehàka people*, she thought to say. *I am the granddaughter of Falling-Day, great-granddaughter of Made-of-Bones, great-great-granddaughter of Hawk-Woman, who killed an O'seronni chief with her own hands and fed his heart to her sons.* These names ran like a river through her veins, but they meant nothing to Liam. They were not the names of white women. She opened her mouth to say it again—*I am not white*—but at her shoulder was another grand-

mother. Cora Bonner, who had come here to the edge of the endless forests from across an ocean Hannah had never even seen. Granny Cora, with her fair skin and eyes of indigo blue and her gentle smile that hid a will as hard as flint. From her Scots grandmother Hannah had gifts she could not deny: a love of song, an appetite for words on the page, a talent for languages, the desire to roam. *I am not white:* it was only one part of the truth.

He was looking at her as he did sometimes, as Bears looked at Many-Doves or her father at Elizabeth. It was something she did not understand completely, and so she put it away, a kind of magic to be kept for later when she was older, woman enough to understand what it meant and strong enough to know what to do with it.

"Hannah!"

She paused at the door with her back to him.

"I'll stay if you want me to."

All her words had deserted her, and so she left him there in a pool of cold winter sunshine.

In the night, Runs-from-Bears came to Many-Doves. The sound of his step on the floorboards brought Elizabeth out of a light sleep. On the other side of the wall she heard Doves murmur in welcome. There were small creakings and sighs and a low laugh, suddenly hushed.

She would have gone outside, despite the cold and the late hour, but it would mean walking past them. Elizabeth rolled onto her side and buried her head in the covers, trying to banish the images that came to mind. She called up a different picture, one she had been pushing aside all day: Nathaniel in a gaol cell. It would not be the first time she had visited such a place. Her brother Julian had spent three months in the London debtors' prison be-

fore Aunt Merriweather had paid his bills and seen him clear to get on the boat to New-York. He had left England only reluctantly. So much effort put into giving him a new start, and it had come to nothing. Julian was dead.

But Nathaniel was alive. Elizabeth wondered if they had blankets and a fire and decent food, if they were chained. Her breath caught hard at this thought. Nathaniel teased her about breaking Hawkeye out of gaol, but it was ridiculous to compare a pantry in the trading post secured with nothing more than a rusty lock to the military garrison in Montréal. She must trust that Will could speak persuasively for them, and if he could not, that he would know better than she how to effectively use the gold to bribe the right men. Together with Falling-Day she had sewed two hundred gold coins into sacks that could be worn next to the skin. She and Bears would carry it, but once in Montréal she would hand it over to Will Spencer if he had need of it.

But if Will should fail . . . It was a phrase that ran through her mind like a dirge. If Will should fail; if Somerville were intent on hanging these men he must see as nothing more than backwoodsmen, troublemakers, wayward colonists. Americans.

She would burn their garrison to the ground with her own hands before she let them take Nathaniel to the gallows. She had done worse for his sake, in the heat of summer. She remembered the weight of a strange rifle in her hands. *Vous et nul autre.* Shuddering, she pushed the memory away.

Many-Doves was murmuring, a soft sound. Leave-taking had its own rhythm, a song sung too often in this place on the edge of the endless forests. Bears would be gone from her and Blue-Jay for a month, at least.

Elizabeth was suddenly overwhelmed by sadness, and

fear of what lay ahead, and a great loneliness. *Journeys end in lovers meeting.* How Nathaniel had smiled at that. She wanted him, and he could not come to her. "Very well, then," she whispered to herself, alone in the dark. "I will come to you."

7

The Schuylers' Albany estate was awash in children. A group of boys played snow-snake in the pasture next to the house, in the garden little girls made snow angels, and at the gate where Galileo brought the sleigh to a stop sat two toddlers with fire-red cheeks, wrapped in such a collection of coats and shawls that they resembled apple dumplings. Elizabeth paused at the door, trying to gather both her courage and her energies. General Schuyler and his wife were the kind of friends who would welcome her in time of need, bound as they were to the Bonners over the last thirty years, and to Nathaniel in particular. Their kindnesses were many, but she worried that this unannounced visit might be too much for even them.

Curiosity read her mind. "They put up with your aunt Merriweather visitin' for weeks at a time," she said. "This little call ain't goin' to put them out of joint. It's cold, Elizabeth. Hurry up."

A maid with a baby on her hip answered her knock.

"May I help you?" She had a Dutch accent and a weary air about her. She seemed not at all surprised to find more guests at the door with infants in cradleboards on their backs. Elizabeth asked for the general, which

brought a flicker of interest and surprise to the young woman's face.

"The general is in the city," she said, peering at Elizabeth more closely. "I'll get the missus."

"Another house full of women and children," grumbled Curiosity, pulling her mittens off in the warmth of the hall.

"Not quite," said Will Spencer from the sitting room, closing a book with a snap. "I believe I counted two of the grown sons and a son-in-law among the masses at table today. And there's myself, of course."

Elizabeth turned quickly, finding herself able to smile sincerely for the first time in a day. Will was little changed from the summer—the same slender form, dressed as elegantly as ever. "Cousin. It is very good to see you. Where is Amanda?"

"I fear my lady wife has been caught yet again between Mrs. Schuyler and my mother-in-law. They will be here in no time at all, rest assured. Come, Lizzy, let me help you. And Hannah, how good to see you again. Mrs. Freeman, there's a fire in the hearth here. I see that Mr. Freeman is busy with the team—is that Runs-from-Bears with him?"

Curiosity sniffed, but a grin escaped her as they followed Will into the sitting room.

"You've picked a difficult time to travel, cousin," said Will. "Soon the roads will be very bad with the thaw. Unless you were planning on a longer stay? You realize your aunt will try to keep you here. Lady Crofton takes a very dim view of traveling in such weather, and with infants."

Elizabeth grimaced. "I remember. But this visit will be a very short one." She disengaged Daniel from the second cradleboard and handed him to Hannah. "In fact, it's quite a relief to have you alone for a moment before the others come in—"

"Elizabeth!" Aunt Merriweather's voice echoed through the hall.

"—if you bear me any love, cousin, you will pack your bags and be ready to set off for Montréal with us first thing in the morning."

The smile faded from Will's face. "As important as all that?"

"More important," said Elizabeth, and turned to greet her aunt Augusta Merriweather, Lady Crofton.

She swept into the sitting room on a breeze of her own making, her widow's bombazine and crepe crackling with every step, the fringe on a black silk shawl fluttering behind. Aunt Merriweather was followed by her daughter Amanda, who colored prettily at this unexpected visit. Mrs. Schuyler and two of her married daughters made up the rest of the party. Other daughters and servants came and went in waves with trays of tea, sandwiches, and slabs of butter cake. Elizabeth was very glad of the tea and the chaos; the first was bracing, and the second saved the necessity of answering the most difficult questions immediately. And after two days' journey, she was very willing to sit quietly on Mrs. Schuyler's sofa before the hearth while the ladies conducted their examination of her children.

"Very pretty," Aunt declared at length. "Good constitutions and strong characters, but how could it be otherwise? Elizabeth, mark my words. This little girl will lead you on a fine chase, as you led me—and I shall laugh to see it! I fear she will have your hair, so excessively curly. You needn't scowl at me, Amanda, your cousin knows her hair is too curly, see how it insists on rioting about her face. Most intractable hair. Mathilde—you call her Lily? How curious. Lily has something of your mother in her, which can only be to her benefit. And what a fine strong little man, the image of his father. How alert he is! I fancy he will tell me to mind my manners soon. Look at this boy's eyes, as green as China tea. Not from our side of the family, cer-

tainly. Whatever are you swaddling them in? Oh, I see. How clever." The babies were passed one by one around the circle of ladies, admired soundly by each in turn, and then handed over to nursery maids who were dispatched with firm instructions for warm bathing.

Out on the lawn Bears had been drawn into a game of snow snake; a boy appeared at the door to invite Hannah to join them. Elizabeth waved her on with some relief; at least the child wouldn't be subjected to what was about to come.

"You go, child. Work out some of the kinks," agreed Curiosity. "I myself am going to see where our menfolk have got to." Elizabeth did not protest Curiosity's abandoning her, although she would have preferred to have her nearby. She was a valuable ally in any duel of wills. But tomorrow Galileo would start home for Paradise and Curiosity would not see him for some weeks; it was no wonder that she had little patience for this gathering of ladies.

Suddenly the room was again in motion; there was talk of children's tea, baggage, rooms to be gotten ready, and the afternoon departure of various parties. When Mrs. Schuyler's daughters had left them, Aunt Merriweather folded her hands in her lap, and turned her sharpest gaze on her only niece. "I am glad to see that you have fared so well, Elizabeth. Motherhood agrees with you, although you are grown quite angular. If you would allow me to locate a suitable wet nurse—I see that idea does not please you. Well, I expected as much. Ah, look, here is Aphrodite. Come greet Cousin Elizabeth, my lovely. It has been too long since you last saw her."

Her hands spread in welcome and the cat jumped into her lap. The diamonds on the long fingers and Aphrodite's eyes blinked in exactly the same shade of old yellow.

"You see, she is none the worse for having traveled the seas," Aunt Merriweather observed. "But then I see

to her diet myself. Elizabeth, my special tea will put some color back in your complexion—"

"Mother," Amanda began gently. "Perhaps Elizabeth has other matters to talk to us about. She cannot have come so far for tea."

"I expect that your daughter is right, Lady Crofton," said Mrs. Schuyler. She was as round and soft as Aunt Merriweather was slender and angular, in figure and in voice. "Not that we aren't delighted to have you, Elizabeth. Most especially glad. The last time I had the pleasure was in Saratoga, on your wedding day—almost exactly a year ago . . ." And her voice trailed away, just shy of an actual question.

"It will be a year in two weeks' time," Elizabeth confirmed. In all the worry and rush, she had not lost sight of this fact.

Looking about the company, Mrs. Schuyler said, "Then you must pardon my curiosity and impatience, Elizabeth. But where is Nathaniel, and why are you here without him?"

"Indeed," agreed Aunt Merriweather, stroking Aphrodite thoughtfully. "There must be some extraordinary reason for a lady to travel so far with infants in this abominable weather—a snowstorm on the first of April! I'm quite sure we do very well with less snow in England." She shook herself slightly. "Please enlighten us, Elizabeth, as to your motives."

Will was leaning against the mantel, his arms crossed. Elizabeth caught his eye, and his encouraging nod.

"Nathaniel is in Montréal, with his father and two friends. We are on our way there," said Elizabeth. "It is a matter of great urgency, and we must leave at first light."

There was an astounded silence that lasted until Aunt Merriweather put her cat off her lap with uncharacteristic abruptness. "This is most irregular. You cannot be in earnest."

"But I am indeed in earnest," Elizabeth agreed, meeting her aunt's eye with studied calm.

Mrs. Schuyler leaned over and squeezed Elizabeth's folded hands. "Let's have the whole story," she said in an encouraging tone. "And then you will tell us how we may be of help."

The whole story could not be told. Elizabeth was not so undone by worry that she would reveal what must not be known: she carried with her a part of a lost treasure claimed by both the British and the American governments. Her aunt might be trusted, but to risk any hint of the Tory gold in a household where she had just been introduced to the wife of the secretary of the treasury—the Schuylers' eldest daughter, Betsy—would be foolhardy. Certainly there was no need to mention Moncrieff, or the Earl of Carryck. She told them no more than they needed to know: that Nathaniel had gone to Montréal to see to his father's and Otter's release from gaol, and that he had been arrested in the attempt. She anticipated her aunt's disapproval, but Elizabeth counted also on Lady Crofton's strong instinct to protect the family name. Such situations were not unfamiliar to her, for she had had a husband with more money than good sense or judgment, and she had a son who was made in his father's image.

At the news that Nathaniel, Hawkeye, and Robbie had been charged with spying, Mrs. Schuyler flushed deeply. "This is an outrage."

"A most unfortunate business," agreed Aunt Merriweather, one finger tapping on an elaborately carved armrest. "Clearly something must be done, but it is a matter best left to the men. William must go, of course." She barely glanced his way, and took no note at all of Amanda's stunned expression.

"I would be very thankful to Will if he should agree to come with us," Elizabeth agreed, trying to catch her

cousin's eye. "If Amanda can spare him. I would think that his experience before the bench would be very useful. But I will not stay behind, Aunt. I cannot."

"I see." But it was clear that she saw not at all, and that she was far from being convinced.

"Pardon me, Elizabeth," said Mrs. Schuyler. "But while you and Lady Crofton talk, I will find General Schuyler and inform him of the situation. He will make suitable arrangements. I believe Captain Mudge is docked here, and there is no better man to see you to Montréal."

"Really," breathed Aunt Merriweather before Elizabeth could respond with surprise or thanks. "Pardon me, Mrs. Schuyler, but your kindness is premature. The matter is not settled. You must agree that there is no need for my niece to make this journey herself, if my son-in-law is willing to go. Runs-from-Bears will accompany him; he could not want a better guide."

"I am afraid it is not so simple," said Catherine Schuyler firmly. "If there is any chance that Elizabeth's presence will be of use in bringing about a happy conclusion to this situation, then she should indeed go to Montréal with the viscount."

One thin white eyebrow arched in disbelief. "But my dear Mrs. Schuyler, what possible use could Elizabeth be?"

Mrs. Schuyler's placid expression and matronly demeanor were suddenly transformed, gone with a flash of her mild eyes. "Nathaniel is married to an Englishwoman with good connections, and they have two new infants. This cannot hurt his cause with Carleton—the governor is very family-minded. Beyond that, Lady Crofton, may I point out that there is more at stake than the freedom and lives of these good men. Perhaps you do not realize the potential repercussions."

"Repercussions? Does she mean political repercussions? William, please explain."

He cleared his throat. "Do you really want to concern yourself with the local politics, Lady Crofton?"

Aunt Merriweather tapped sharply with her cane. "I am not an idiot, young man. Politics, indeed. Simply explain."

"Very well," Will said, with a brief bow. "The lieutenant governor of Lower Canada—Somerville, you remember, is also an officer in His Majesty's army—has arrested American citizens and charged them with spying in peacetime. It might be construed as an act of war."

"Exactly," said Mrs. Schuyler. "There are men in our government who would not hesitate to use it as an excuse to take up arms against Canada again—an event I do not like to contemplate. If the worst should happen, and if Somerville, idiotic man that he is, should actually hang one of them—I am sorry, Elizabeth, but we must consider—it would be a catastrophe of larger proportions than you imagine. General Schuyler must be informed at once. He may want to write to President Washington."

Aunt Merriweather let out a small and awkward laugh. "Nathaniel Bonner a spy! He has not the slightest interest in politics!"

"Aunt," said Elizabeth, overcome by a new kind of dread. "The point is that politics may have taken an interest in Nathaniel."

Her first thought at the sound of howling infants was one of relief: better two hungry and angry babies than another half hour of gentle arguing with Aunt Merriweather. Elizabeth claimed the twins from a harried nursery maid and escaped upstairs to the room she was to share with Hannah. They settled down to nursing quite quickly, and Elizabeth was alone with her thoughts.

She was at least two weeks away from Montréal,

two endless weeks of travel by water and land. The thaw was upon them; she could feel its touch in the air, in spite of the late snow. The world would turn to mud, a sea of mud between her and Nathaniel that she must navigate with three children. It might mean a longer route. The thought of leaving Nathaniel and Hawkeye in gaol for even one more day was unbearable. "What canna be changed maun be tholed," Robbie would tell her if he were here.

Robbie had seen her through the hardest times in the summer, when Nathaniel's life had hung in the balance and she feared she would lose her mind with worry. And now Robbie sat in the garrison gaol too.

A wave of exhaustion swept over Elizabeth, and her self-control burst like a seed pod. With both arms supporting the babies, she had not a free hand to wipe her face, and so she lay among the pillows and wept, furious with herself for tears that could serve no good purpose.

Some time later Curiosity came in to stand at the foot of the bed, her hands on her hips and a soft expression in her eyes. "My mama used to say that milk and tears flow from the same well. You showerin' these children with both, looks like."

She leaned over Lily, already asleep and dribbling milk, and dabbed at her with a handkerchief. Then she did the same for Daniel, and finally she took Elizabeth's chin between her cool fingers and turned her face up to dry it. A frown twitched at the corner of the wide mouth, but her tone was as gentle as a lullaby as she wiped the wet cheeks.

"Don' need to tell me, I heard all about it. They still at it down there. Spencer is trying to talk sense to her. The man don't look like much, but he's got a way about him."

"He is perhaps the only person who can convince her," Elizabeth agreed.

"What is that name that Chingachgook gave you?"

"Bone-in-Her-Back." Elizabeth let out a wobbly laugh. "That seems very long ago."

Curiosity turned her face from side to side and, satisfied with her handiwork, let her go with a small shake. "Look like backbone run in the family, all right."

"Were you listening at the door?"

The damp handkerchief fluttered dismissively. "You know me better. That housekeeper, now, ain't much she don't know 'bout what goes on."

"Ah, Mrs. Gerlach. She told stories about Nathaniel at our wedding party."

"I don't doubt it. Mighty fond of a tale, is Sally." Curiosity eased the pillow that supported the sleeping babies off to the side and settled them comfortably.

Elizabeth said, "In case you are wondering, I intend to leave for Montréal in the morning, with or without Will Spencer. General Schuyler is arranging passage with a Captain Mudge."

Curiosity nodded. "I expected as much. I don't suppose Merriweather will throw herself in the road to stop us, but she won't let you go easy, either."

"Yes, well," Elizabeth said wearily. "You forget that I grew up arguing with her."

"She didn't much hold with you leaving England, I reckon."

"No, she didn't."

"And here you are anyway."

"Yes," whispered Elizabeth. "Here I am. She warned me that I would regret it, although at the time I did not realize she meant to come and see to it personally." She managed a small smile. "I see your line of reasoning, Curiosity. You needn't worry, her disapproval won't stop me."

"Didn't think it would. Don't see how an army could stop you now." Curiosity wrung her handkerchief out in fresh water from the washstand, and then put it in Elizabeth's hand.

The cool was welcome on her flushed cheeks. "You

could turn back to Paradise with Galileo, if you wanted to. It isn't too late."

"No, child. I got my mind set on seeing this through, and that's what I'll do."

"Good," said Elizabeth. "It is very selfish of me, but I find that I cannot do without you."

There was a soft scratching at the door.

"Looks like there's folk here feel the same way about you." Curiosity's heels tapped briskly on her way to the door.

"That will be an emissary of my aunt's," said Elizabeth, putting her clothing to rights. "Sent to speak common sense to me."

Amanda's apologies for her mother began before she was in the room. On her way to Elizabeth she paused to embrace Curiosity, which took the older woman by surprise but left a pleased expression on her face.

Elizabeth held out her hands toward her cousin. "I am very glad to see you, Amanda, even if you come bearing disagreeable messages."

Amanda was one of the few people she truly missed since leaving England; she had been closer to Elizabeth than to her sisters. The youngest of Aunt Merriweather's three girls and the prettiest, she also suffered under what her mother called a nervous disposition—a vivid imagination and a demonstratively affectionate manner, both of which put her at a disadvantage in a household of strong-minded, pragmatic women. Now she came to stand by Elizabeth's bedside, but her gaze was fixed on the sleeping infants.

"Come," said Elizabeth, and patted the bed. When Amanda had settled, she put Lily in her arms and together they watched the baby stretch, her mouth working even in her sleep.

Amanda's shoulders bent into a protective bow around the baby. "You know how very fortunate you are."

"Oh, yes. I am very aware of my good fortune."

A soft flush crept up Amanda's neck. When she looked at Elizabeth, there was a nerve fluttering gently in her cheek. "Will is all I have. You will send him back to me as soon as possible?"

"Yes," whispered Elizabeth. "Of course I will."

While Elizabeth visited with Amanda and Aunt Merriweather continued negotiations with Will, Mrs. Schuyler performed a miracle and reduced the population of her sitting room drastically, seeing her visiting children, their families and servants off to their own homes. Even the Hamiltons departed for the first leg of their journey down the Hudson to their estate in New-York City. Elizabeth watched them take leave from her window, vaguely curious about Betsy's husband, the famous Alexander Hamilton. She mentioned his Federalist Papers to Curiosity and found that she had read them, as she read everything that came into the judge's possession, and was little impressed by them or their author.

"Look at him," she snorted. "Fought in the Revolution all right, but there's a man in love with the old ways. Making up to your aunt as if she was wearin' a crown. Don't he put you in mind of one of them yappy ginger-haired dogs, always worrying at a woman's heels?" At Elizabeth's shocked expression, Curiosity sniffed. "The man famous for more than his writing. Cain't resist a lady with a title, and always lookin' to get his belly scratched. And I'll wager it's freckled, too."

Elizabeth might have choked, if not for Curiosity's vigorous thumping between her shoulder blades. "Look at him hard, now, and tell me you don't feel sorry for Betsy."

"I shan't argue with your superior knowledge of his reputation," Elizabeth said when she had regained her composure. She picked up her brushes in a last attempt to tame her hair. "But right now General Schuyler is downstairs waiting to discuss details of the journey

with us, and I think it is not very wise to be criticizing his son-in-law behind his back."

Curiosity laughed loudly at that. "Elizabeth, you wait and see the look on Nathaniel's face the day that Lily bring home a husband. Ain't nobody more critical of a woman's choice than her daddy."

She picked up the gray watered silk, the only formal gown Elizabeth had packed, and smoothed the lace. "You go on and have your set-down with the general. He won't need me there."

Elizabeth looked up in surprise from the unfastening of her traveling gown. "But I need you. I depend upon your judgment. Runs-from-Bears will be there, too."

"Bears is something special, they've known him since he was a boy. But they ain't going to set a place for your daddy's housekeeper at their table, Elizabeth, and don't you get no ideas about teaching them different. You just go see to getting us to Montréal as quick as possible and I'll see to the children."

"I can hardly believe it is almost a year ago since I saw them last," said Elizabeth. "To think that I might have forgot my own first wedding anniversary—" And her voice cracked as she stopped herself.

Curiosity's eyes narrowed. "Don't you lose hope, now. No reason to believe that you won't see Nathaniel before your anniversary come around. And this time there won't be Richard Todd interfering."

"True enough. But there is the small matter of George Somerville."

With a flick of her fingers, Curiosity dismissed the lieutenant governor. Elizabeth hoped it would be so simple.

General Schuyler's study smelled of old paper and strong ink, tobacco and ashes in the cold hearth. Hannah's breath hung milky in the air, but it was quiet

here and there was a deep chair by a window that looked toward the river. She stood there a moment to watch the last of the afternoon sunshine spark rainbows from fingers of ice that hung from the eaves. One crackled suddenly and fell to the softening snow.

A man rode up on a bay gelding and stopped at the gate. Another visitor, this one dressed in a greatcoat, striped breeches, and a slouch hat with a drooping turkey feather. So many callers. At Lake in the Clouds they could go a month without a visitor.

Voices on the stairs; the general was coming this way. Hannah cast a regretful glance over the worn leather volumes that lined the bookshelves, and slipped out into the hall.

Wherever she might go there would be grown-ups talking about their journey. The children she had played with in the afternoon were gone now, away home with their parents. She wondered if they all lived in houses like this, filled with crystal and silver and wood polished until you could see your face in it. Every window was glass, every dish was porcelain, and beeswax candles burned in sconces of silver and brass. No one here wore buckskin and the only linsey-woolsey to be seen was on the backs of the stableboys. The grown-ups were kind enough and more than generous with what they had, but this was a strange silken world and it made Hannah uncomfortable in her skin.

Redskin, one of the older boys had called her during the game of snow-snake; pimple-faced, he bared his buck teeth when he smiled. He had waited until Runs-from-Bears was out of earshot to do it. *Dirty redskin,* and then he yanked hard on her plaits.

He was big and clumsy and she tripped him without a moment's hesitation and left him bloody-nosed in the snow. Then Hannah ran back to the game, showing them all what a red-skinned girl could do, sending the wooden snake slithering so far on the ice track that they

lost sight of it and the boys gave up, muttering among themselves.

There was an unlit stairway at the back of the hall for the servants' use. Hannah found her way there and sat, her knees up under her chin, listening to the house. In the kitchen, maids argued in Dutch until the housekeeper sent them off to set the table. Upstairs a baby wailed and then was quieted. In the front hall the overseer, a huge barrel of a man with an old wig that kept slipping off his head, was talking to the visitor. From behind the closed door of the sitting room came the regular rise and fall of women's voices: Aunt Merriweather, as steady as the tide; Elizabeth's gentle voice in counterpoint. Hannah wished suddenly to be with Elizabeth, who understood this strange place. She had given up a life like this to come to them on Hidden Wolf.

"May I join you?"

Hannah was startled out of her daydream. Will Spencer stood before her at the foot of the stairs. Everything about him shone in the dimness: brass buttons and silver buckles, gleaming white linen at his neck, even the thinning pale hair. He was middle sized, slight of build. Hannah had the urge to take one of his hands and examine it, to see if it was as soft as it looked. His only calluses came from holding a quill, his only scars were drawn in ink.

She pressed over to one side to make room for him.

"Very clever of you to find a peaceful spot. They are few and hard to come by in this household."

"Is this your private hiding place?" Hannah asked.

"Certainly not. There's room enough for both of us." He flipped up his coattails neatly before sitting, took off his spectacles and pulled a handkerchief from his pocket.

In Hannah's experience, white men had three ways of dealing with her: most would ignore her, a few might feel an obligation to question her on the fine points of her ed-

ucation or parentage, and some would ask her silly or insulting questions about the Kahnyen'kehàka way of life. He seemed to lean toward none of these, which was a great relief.

"Are you coming with us?" she asked finally.

"Of course." He tucked his handkerchief into his sleeve. "Elizabeth needs my help. Perhaps I can be of some assistance to your father and grandfather."

It was hard to imagine how this quiet man in his silk hose and striped waistcoat could be of help, but Hannah nodded politely.

"You are very worried," he said.

"Shouldn't I be?"

He thought while he adjusted his spectacles over his ears. "Your stepmother is a very determined and resourceful person. She has one of the finest minds I have ever encountered and she certainly does not lack for courage. If I were sitting in a garrison gaol I would breathe much easier knowing that she was working for my release."

"That's not what I asked you."

Will Spencer inclined his head. "There is cause for concern. But I think that together we may well manage to see a happy end to all of this. We have the law on our side."

And the Tory gold, thought Hannah. "The gaol key would be enough," she said aloud.

He smiled then, the first broad smile she had ever seen from him. "The Canadians will be sorry that they ever took on the Bonners."

"I think the Schuylers already are."

He laughed softly. "General and Mrs. Schuyler seem to thrive on such adventures, and I am sure that their interest and concern for your father and stepmother are sincere. Nathaniel once did them a good turn that they have never forgot. You must know the story of how he saved their eldest son."

"Oh, yes," said Hannah. "But I was thinking more of one of the grandsons. I gave him a bloody nose this afternoon."

"I see," said Will. "The one with the unfortunate teeth, and manners to match?"

She glanced at him from the corner of her eye. "He called me a name."

"That seems in character."

"You aren't going to tell me I should not have tripped him?"

One corner of the pale mouth turned downward. "I suppose I should tell you just that. But I should have done exactly the same thing, and it would be hypocritical to pretend otherwise." He looked her directly in the eye. "I expect that it is not the last time you shall have to deal with such ignorance."

Hannah nodded. "That is just what my grandmother said before I left Hidden Wolf. She said that I would have to use my head rather than my fists."

"A wise woman."

"It is harder to do than to say."

"How true. I would suggest that you begin by observing your stepmother; she has learned the way of it. For the moment, however, I believe we are expected at the table."

The man in the striped breeches turned out to be a Captain Grievous Mudge. He had the biggest hands that Hannah had ever seen, a great waterfall of gray chin whiskers, and a mustache that twitched when he talked, which he did so forcefully and so fast that even Elizabeth's aunt had no opportunity to interrupt. The old lady seemed both fascinated and repelled as she watched the captain inhale peppery white soup, pheasant stuffed with prunes and raisins, ham, creamed potatoes, corn preserves and pickled snap beans—and exhale the story of his life on the waterways.

"I been transporting all manner of goods from Albany to Montréal for thirty year or more now," he concluded. He poked his silver fork toward the travelers. "I can transport you, too."

"Are you originally from New-York, Captain?" asked Amanda.

"I'm a Yorker born and raised," said Mudge, sawing at a hunk of ham with obvious pleasure. "But my mama was a Connecticut Allen, and I'm blood kin to Ethan and the Green Mountain Boys. Nobody knows the big water better." He glanced at Runs-from-Bears, who had been having a quiet conversation with Will Spencer at the far end of the table. "Well, almost nobody. There's the Mohawk, of course. Glad to have you along, Bears. Be like the old days when you tagged along with your daddy."

"I did not realize that you were acquainted," said Elizabeth, looking as surprised as Hannah felt. "Where did you meet?"

Runs-from-Bears looked up from his plate. "Ticonderoga."

The name was enough to set off nods of acknowledgment around the table. In New-York State, there was barely a body breathing who did not know the story of the battle for the fort in every detail. Hannah would have liked to hear it again, but the old aunt thumped the floor with her cane.

"Not another war story! What a bellicose young nation you are. No dinner party seems complete without a discussion of one revolution or another." Her hand made a long corkscrew in the air. "A most untidy business."

"It is the age we live in, Lady Crofton," said General Schuyler. "The world is changing all around us, and for the better, on the whole."

She clucked her tongue at him. "Poppycock. Now and then ladies are taken with the urge to rearrange their sitting rooms. Men do the same with their govern-

ments. Thus it has always been, and thus it will always be."

Hannah hid her smile in her serviette, not so much at Aunt Merriweather, but at these white people who did not know how to cope with a strong-minded woman whose tongue had been loosened by age. Amanda was almost humming her embarrassment, Mrs. Schuyler was examining her wine glasses, and the men made gruff or conciliatory noises. Even Will Spencer, who seemed to Hannah a reasonable man, was staring at his plate, his brow creased hard. Only Elizabeth and Bears were smiling openly.

"Captain Mudge will deliver you safely," General Schuyler said, moving the conversation back toward safer topics. "He's the man to deal with smugglers and ice floes."

"Smugglers!" Amanda flushed, and put a small hand on her husband's arm.

"Fur runners from Lower Canada," explained Runs-from-Bears. "Coming down with the winter's takings. They don't bother folks who stay out of their way."

Will Spencer leaned toward Hannah. "It sounds like high adventure. Are you ready for it?"

"Of course she is not," said Aunt Merriweather, turning a watery eye on Hannah. "Such a sensible girl. She will stay behind with me, will you not, child?"

"No, ma'am," Hannah answered politely.

The captain laughed heartily at Aunt Merriweather's pinched expression. "She's Nathaniel's girl, right enough, missus. Can't hold her back." He turned to Elizabeth. "Folks say you had some adventures of your own last summer, Mrs. Bonner. I'd like to hear the story. I knew Lingo, the old polecat."

Elizabeth's expression went suddenly very still. Hannah felt her own face coloring in apprehension; the subject of Jack Lingo was one best avoided, but all around the table heads were turning. Mrs. Schuyler's curious expression, wondering how Elizabeth would meet this challenge;

Amanda's slightly confused one. The old aunt, looking annoyed at having less information than she believed was her due. Hannah doubted that she would credit it even if she were told the story of what had passed between Jack Lingo and her niece.

"What's this?" the old lady sputtered. "Who is this Lingo? A friend of yours, Elizabeth?"

"No, Aunt," Elizabeth said hoarsely. She touched the base of her throat where a silver chain disappeared into her bodice. "No friend of mine."

General Schuyler coughed softly. "He was just an old *courier du bois,* Lady Crofton."

"A Frenchman?" asked Aunt Merriweather, in the same tone she might have said *heathen.*

The general inclined his head. "I believe he was French born, yes. But more important, he was a thief, and a scoundrel of the highest order. It is not a tale for polite company."

"Hmmpf!" commented the captain around a forkful of ham. His eyes flashed in Elizabeth's direction, but he swallowed down his curiosity.

"I think the travelers are more concerned about the condition of the portages," said Mrs. Schuyler, neatly cutting off the aunt's response.

"Yes," said Elizabeth, more calmly. "I had been wondering about the portages."

The captain swallowed, the mustache twitching with a life of its own. "There's only one thing to do when you've got to cross those carries in April," he said, reaching for the potatoes.

Aunt Merriweather put down her glass with a thump. "Well, man, what is to be done then? Speak up!"

"Pray for a frost, missus," said the captain, meeting her glare with perfect Yorker calm. "Pray mighty hard."

· · ·

Late in the evening, much later than she would have wished, Elizabeth found her way to her room. Hannah was already deeply asleep on a camp bed near the banked hearth, the twins in their cot within her reach. Elizabeth knew that Hannah would wake at the twins' first stirring, and that they might even settle at the sound of her voice. She had a sure and loving touch far beyond her years.

Elizabeth reached down to smooth a strand of hair away from the little girl's brow. Such a serious child, and so dear. She should have left her behind at Lake in the Clouds where she would be safe, but she had given in. As a girl, her own curiosity about the world had been thwarted so often; she could not do the same to Hannah, not with so much at stake. She was young, and still there was so much of Nathaniel in her.

With a last check on the twins, Elizabeth went to the window to look beyond the winter-barren trees to the river. A rustling below her window, and a woman's shape moved away from the house, a long cape sweeping out behind her in a dark arc against the moonlit snow. Her hood fell away and Elizabeth saw blond hair. One of the daughters, then. And slipping away in the night, perhaps to meet a lover.

Elizabeth rubbed her eyes, and tried to focus. What she knew was very simple: Nathaniel and Hawkeye and Robbie slept in a cold gaol far to the north; without intervention they might well hang. There was no time to waste and no energy to spare, and certainly she could let this young woman go on her way. She was forsaking a warm bed and risking the favor of friends and family to go to her lover; Elizabeth could not chide her for that. It seemed not so very long ago that she had gone to Nathaniel in the dead of night. Of her own free will she had gone to him, a back-woodsman in buckskin with an eagle feather in his hair, a man with nothing to recommend him to the world but his honesty, his skill with a rifle, and an affinity for the wilder-

ness. A widower with a dark-skinned daughter. Anything but a gentleman. She had married him on the run, turning her back on her family, their view of the proper order of things, and their expectations, and she regretted none of it.

8

Elizabeth woke on a spring morning to find herself alone in the small cabin of Grievous Mudge's schooner, the *Washington*. Beside her was an empty makeshift cradle and a pile of neatly folded blankets. Blinking in the shifting sunlight, Elizabeth lay for a moment and listened to the steady beat of waves on the hull, the familiar rhythm of men's voices as they called to each other, a hiccup of a cry, and Curiosity's comforting hush in response. With a yawn, Elizabeth walked the two steps to push back the shutters that opened onto the main deck.

Pale blue sky, cloudless and mild. One of the crew whistled by, his shirtsleeves rolled high. How strange, to dread warm weather. But she managed a smile for Curiosity, who sat on a coil of rope rocking the babies in the cradle of her skirt.

"We was just about to come callin'," said Curiosity, catching sight of her. With a practiced dip, she passed a wriggling Daniel down and through the window. Lily followed in short order, and Elizabeth settled back down on the narrow bunk to see to their needs. She longed to get out of the cabin, which smelled of tobacco and sweat and wet winding cloths; she might have nursed the babies in the sunshine with a shawl draped

over herself and no one would have been the wiser, but she feared offending the sailors. The dozen who manned this schooner seemed to be good sorts, but like all seamen they were full of superstitions about women, and she would do nothing to jeopardize their progress toward Montréal.

In short order Curiosity was at the door with a plate of corn bread and venison stew. Somewhat better fare than they might have expected on a schooner stripped down to the bone for the short-run, fast transport of high-value goods, but then the captain was fond of his food.

"Mighty pretty morning," she announced, holding out a tin cup of weak tea. "Nothing like a clear day on the water with the mountains all around."

"Yes," Elizabeth agreed, reaching for the cup over the pillow that supported the babies. "It is pretty here. Where is Hannah?"

"Talking to Mudge."

From the corner of her eye, Elizabeth observed Curiosity's pinched expression. "Captain Mudge has a few stories to tell."

"Some seem to think so."

Elizabeth smiled to herself. More than a week of muddy portages, cold rain, cramped living quarters, and poor food seemed of less concern to Curiosity than the fact that Grievous Mudge was a good storyteller. Elizabeth shifted a bit, and considered.

"You must miss Galileo a good deal."

Curiosity looked up, her dark eyes narrowed. "Of course I miss Galileo. Ain't I been wakin' up next to the man for some thirty year now? We been apart now and then, but it ain't ever easy. Miss my babies, too."

Elizabeth had to laugh, thinking of the size and width of Curiosity's son and of her grown daughters, the most competent of women. Then she shook her head apologetically.

"I am sorry. Please forgive me. I do appreciate you

leaving your family behind to come with us, you know."

"I ain't looking for no apologies," Curiosity said briskly, running a hand along the swaddling clothes that had been hung to dry on a string across the cabin. "Came along of my own free will."

"Yes," said Elizabeth. "So you did. I will always be in your debt."

With a grunt Curiosity sat down on the edge of the bunk and, untangling Lily from Elizabeth's lap, began to change her.

"Seem to me there ain't any call for such talk between us. I know you don't like to be reminded, but you made my Polly a happy woman and I won't ever forget it."

"What did Elizabeth do for Polly?" asked Hannah, leaning in the open shutters on her elbows.

"Nothing," said Elizabeth. "At least, nothing to discuss right now. Is that fresh water you've got there?"

Curiosity raised a brow in Elizabeth's direction but addressed Hannah, who passed a bucket through the window.

"Your stepmama bought Benjamin and his brother free from the Gloves, is what she done, so as my Polly could marry a freed man. Got that Quaker cousin of hers from Baltimore to handle the money, but it come from her and Nathaniel. And look at her, blushing to hear the truth told plain."

"Not at all," said Elizabeth, somewhat less than truthfully. "It's just that Hannah's sleeve is covered with blood."

"It isn't mine," Hannah said. "Mr. Little took some salmon this morning, and I helped with the cleaning. We'll have a good dinner today."

"Is that so?" snorted Curiosity softly, tickling Lily under the chin until she got a smile. She traded her for Daniel, who yawned in her face. "Know as much about cookin' as they do about storytellin'. No tellin' what injury that Little might do to a good salmon."

"Oh, Curiosity," said Hannah brightly. "Mr. Little asked if you'd come along and have a look at Elijah's foot. It isn't healing the way he thought it would. I think it might need to be opened up."

"You see?" asked Curiosity, as if an infected foot told all that needed to be told about Mr. Little's merits as cook, doctor, and human being. "I'll be along as soon as I've wiped your little brother's hindside. And don't you start tending that foot without me, child. You hear?"

Hannah grinned, and disappeared into the sunshine.

"It's good to see her in high spirits," said Elizabeth. "We should reach Chambly tomorrow, and things will not be so cheery once we do."

Curiosity pressed her lips together firmly. "I expect Canada mud wash off just like any other," she said. "You want to come along, have a look at this foot?"

"I think not." Elizabeth pulled her clothing to rights. "You go ahead, and I'll take these two for some sun while it lasts."

She strapped the babies to her chest to go up on deck, where they mouthed their fists and stared wide-eyed at the great expanses of snapping white sail. There was a sailor at the helm, two mending rope near the aft mast, and another swabbing the main deck; she supposed the rest of the crew was below, crowded together around Curiosity and her patient. On the quarterdeck she saw that Will and Runs-from-Bears were in deep conversation, their backs to her. Elizabeth made no attempt to get their attention, glad of a few minutes of rare near-solitude in the open air.

The wind was high, whipping the water into cats'-paws. In the distance the mountains of the endless forests were still dusted with snow, dappled with shadow and early light. Elizabeth studied the east coast, trying to catch sight of some familiar landmark—she had traveled down that very shore in the previous summer by canoe—but it was a blur of cottonwood and maple, willow and

black ash, showing only the vaguest tinge of new green
here and there.

Overhead a crowd of ring-billed gulls screeched, pin-
wheeling with the wind. The babies blinked up at them
thoughtfully, their round cheeks sharp pink in the fresh
air.

A spit of land off a small bay capped by a tumble of
boulders sparked some vague memory that she could
not quite grasp. Nathaniel could put English, Mahican,
and Kahnyen'kehàka names to every corner of the lake;
perhaps he had told her a story about this place.

A sailor swung by, long arms roped with muscle. He
had a face like a pickled walnut and a thin mouth
bracketed by crusty corners; a carved pipe swayed there
with every step he took. Elizabeth beckoned to him and
he paused and touched his cap.

"Pardon me, but could you please tell me what that
bay is called?" She pointed with her chin.

The bristled jaw worked. He spoke around the pipe
in clipped Yankee rhythms. "That there's Button Bay, or
so we calls it," he said.

"Button Bay?"

"Ayuh, it's a strange thing, missus. Walk along the
shore there and you'll find that all the stones have got
holes in 'em, you see, like buttons. Young'uns like to
string 'em together." Eyes like polished pebbles fixed on
the babies. "It'll be a while afore these two get up to
such games. A lad and a maid, ain't that so?"

Elizabeth nodded, and he leaned in to peer into
Daniel's face.

"Look at 'em eyes," said the sailor, his grin showing
off teeth like oak pegs. "Green as the sea when she's
feeling feisty. Make a sailor one day, he will."

Daniel suddenly let out a great chuckle, the small nose
crinkling and bare gums showing pink. Elizabeth started,
for while the babies smiled often, neither of them had yet
produced real laughter. Lily looked at her brother with
some puzzlement.

"You see!" said the sailor. "He knows the truth when he hears it, don' he now? There's no stoppin' a lad born to the sea."

"Did you go to sea as a boy?" asked Elizabeth, charmed by his grin and his admiration of her children.

"Ayuh, so I did." He pulled the pipe from his mouth and cocked his head over the side to spit, never taking his eyes from her. "The Cards of Port Ann was all born for the sea, every last one of us. Why, I saw China when I was no more than fourteen. Believe it or not, missus, when I were seventeen we took a merchant bound home for Bristol. Crippled in a storm north of Cuba, near broke in half. We took her neat and simple before she went down and my good captain sent me home with forty pound of fancy spice, a whole ton of sugar, fifty gallons o' rum, and near a thousand dollar—me! Tim Card as you sees before you, not a respectable whisker on my face that day I walked into me mam's kitchen and thumped down the coin. Gave it all to her, too, every bit of it. Except the rum, of course. She was a bible-reader, was my mam. Had no use for rum." Another flash of the teeth.

"You've always sailed on privateers, then?" asked Elizabeth, a bit unnerved. She had first come to New-York on a British packet, and during that long journey she had heard many stories from the captain, a former Royal Navy officer who detested privateers as much as he feared them. But Tim Card carried on, eager to tell his story.

"Oh, ayuh. Lobster pots left me cold, you see. And I ne'er was what you'd call the military type. The merchants, now—what's in it for a lad, I ask you? Two brothers before me went out on a merchantman and wound up pressed into a Tory frigate. And that's the last we saw of Harry and Jim. Not for me, says I to my mam and off I went to find my fortune. Sailed ten year with Captain Parker on the *Nancy* and longer still with Captain Haraden. P'rhaps you heard tell of him, how we took the *Golden Eagle* in the Bay of Biscay. Not

long after that I come up here to crew on the spider catchers."

"This must be very tame, after your earlier adventures."

The sharp gaze moved over the water. "Don' let the looks of her deceive you, missus. She's got her tricks, and you'd best not forget it." He rubbed his cheek with horny nails so that the stubble rasped.

"Yes," Elizabeth said. "You may not believe it to see me as I am dressed now, Mr. Card, but I am not unfamiliar with these waterways. Last summer I traveled the full length of this lake with my husband, by canoe."

That brought the old sailor up short. He narrowed one eye at her, his head cocked, sparrowlike.

"Is that so?" he said thoughtfully. His gaze took in her good gray traveling gown, the lace at her neck and wrists, the heavy shawl, and then he shrugged. "If you traveled these waters with Nathaniel Bonner you were in good hands, then."

"Do you know my husband?" Elizabeth asked, surprised and pleased and eager for any word of him.

"Ain't many in this part of the world who don't know of Hawkeye and his boy Nathaniel," grinned the old sailor. "I've laid eyes on him once or twice. He would've made a fine sailor." The bright gaze was drawn back to the lake. "Ayuh, I never felt the need to go back to the sea after I been on this water. And privateering is a younger man's game, truth be told." He peered at her. "You've heard tales of the privateers, I suppose. Little better than pirates."

"I've heard a few stories," Elizabeth admitted.

He grunted, clamping down anew on the stem of his pipe so that it bobbed up and down. "Sailin' this part of the world I heard a few tales of the Mohawk," he said thoughtfully. "Torturin' women, eatin' white babies, all that. But I expect you know different, livin' together with them the way you do. Got that girl of Nathaniel's, don' you. Likely maid, that one. Keen eyed, sharp."

Elizabeth observed him closely but she could see nothing untoward in his expression. "I suppose you mean to tell me I shouldn't believe the tales I've heard of American privateers?"

He shrugged, shifting the coil of rope on his shoulder. "Wouldn't go that far, missus. There's some vicious sorts runnin' the seas and not all of 'em fly the Jolly Roger open like. I knowed a few who would as soon toss these young'uns overboard as look at 'em—"

Elizabeth's arms tightened around the twins, who squirmed in protest.

"—but I ain't one o' them," he finished. "And I ne'er sailed with any such. Most is just merchants, missus. Interested in the profit, is all. What ain't profitable goes over the side, you see."

"I'll remember that," Elizabeth said, her voice cracking a bit as she tried to smile.

"Button Bay, we calls her," said Tim Card, his eyes moving over the shore. He touched his cap as he turned away.

If good fortune had been with them, they might have left the *Washington* at Fort Chambly and reached Montréal by sleigh in less than a day's time on the ice road. But all Elizabeth's prayers for a late freeze went unheard: they managed to portage around the Richelieu rapids to find a world made of mud and water. On the marshes the ice was porous and would no longer support the weight of a sleigh of any size. This left the summer route, difficult even in the driest weather but impossible in the spring thaw. Captain Mudge summarized the problem with his usual directness.

"Enough mud for a world of pigs," he said. There was a long and involved story that Elizabeth only half heard, of an ox mired to the shoulders and left to bellow itself to death after a day of fruitless efforts to shift it. The story seemed to distract Hannah, which was a useful thing.

There was no help for it: they must take the longer route, which meant more portages, a transfer to whaleboats that would take them over whitewater to Sorel, and finally the seeking out of another schooner to take them on the last leg from Sorel upriver to Montréal. It had sounded to Elizabeth like a dirge as the captain intoned each step of the journey. To hide her frustration took all of her self-control; for the first time she found herself consciously wishing that she could have left all three of the children safely in Paradise. Without them she would have taken on the more direct route to Montréal, mud and all.

It was Curiosity and Runs-from-Bears who put their heads together and came up with a plan that seemed ideal on its surface, and then occasioned the first disagreement Elizabeth had had with Will Spencer since they were children. To the suggestion that Will travel ahead on the shorter route, he responded first with a thoughtful silence and then with the acknowledgment that he did not like to leave Elizabeth alone for the rest of the journey.

"But I am not alone," she said to him, quite confused at his hesitation. They were on the quarterdeck, wrapped in cloaks and shawls against an unpleasantly cold but not quite freezing drizzle. They had left the fine weather behind them on the great lake; ahead of them Fort Chambly's great hulk shone in the dense fog like a castle in a fairy tale.

"Mrs. Freeman is an excellent traveling companion," Will agreed. "Her good common sense has served us well already. But to travel without sufficient male protection is something I cannot countenance, cousin."

Elizabeth bit back a laugh. "Runs-from-Bears is more than sufficient protection," she pointed out. "He guided you and my aunt from Albany to Paradise last fall, and me through the endless forests in much more difficult circumstances. And for that matter, I have traveled the wilderness here alone for days at a time. Under

the circumstances, cousin, your concern is a luxury that I cannot afford. My first thought is for Nathaniel and his father. I hope you will make them your first concern, as well."

His pale, good-natured face shone with the rain, or perhaps with perspiration; she could see how uneasy it made him to think of leaving her to travel ahead. But for all his quiet ways, Will was no coward. He met her eye directly.

"If you are certain, Elizabeth. I will trust your judgment."

Now she did smile. "I am certain. You serve me best by leaving me now." She glanced around them, and certain that they were unobserved, Elizabeth pressed a small but very heavy sack into his hand. "You may well have need of this."

He tested the weight with a surprised expression, but before he could ask any of the logical and reasonable questions that must immediately come to him, she grasped his sleeve. And in a whispered rush: "Please don't ask, not right now. Sometime I will tell you the whole story, but for the moment I must ask you to think of this gold as your own, and having nothing to do with me or with Nathaniel. You can use it, Will, but I cannot, not without occasioning questions that will bring us into greater difficulties. Spend it all, if it will help in Nathaniel's cause."

One pale brow rose in a surprised arch. "It seems you have been up to some high adventure, Lizzy. I will want that story in every detail once we are reunited in Montréal."

"You shall have it," Elizabeth said, full of gratitude and relief.

And still Elizabeth found it very hard to watch her cousin set off from the fort in the company of a guide Runs-from-Bears had found for him. She must content herself with the idea that he might be in Montréal in two

days' time. Perhaps Nathaniel and the others would be free when she finally arrived with the children. If Will Spencer could manage that feat, Elizabeth would tell him anything he wanted to know, although she feared he would not take the story well. He might be her trusted friend, but he was also an Englishmen of a certain class.

Hannah's warm hand on her arm brought her out of her thoughts.

"Your cousin is not much like other Englishmen," she said, offering her highest compliment. She spoke Kahnyen'kehàka, as they usually did when they were alone.

Elizabeth laughed. "I was just thinking the very opposite. What strikes you as less than English about Will?"

Hannah's expression was earnest. "There is no greed in him," she said finally. "He makes no fist."

Struck silent by the truth of this, Elizabeth turned again to catch some sight of her cousin, but he had disappeared into fog.

9

The butcher was snoring again in deep, wet roars that hauled Nathaniel out of an uneasy doze. There was a scuttle and a dull thud as the young pig farmer's clog connected with flesh. Denier's snoring hitched and trailed away with a mutter.

Nathaniel's stomach gave a loud rumble, and he rolled onto one hip on the wooden cot that he shared with his father, the sparse layer of straw crackling. Hunger focused the mind, he reminded himself. And on a Tuesday morning near dawn, with Thompson alone on guard duty, there was good reason to be focused. They were all awake, and waiting. All except Denier, whose snoring was rising again like a tide.

One by one the men got up to use the overflowing bucket in the corner: Moncrieff shuffling and yawning, Robbie with a groan, Hawkeye tense and silent. Pépin's hobnailed clogs struck blue sparks on the cobblestones. Nathaniel took his turn last, closing his mind to the stench.

The door swung open with a scrape, bringing a wave of fresher air and the tang of burning tallow. Thompson filled the narrow frame, candlelight outlining a huge jaw. Slack-jawed, yellow of complexion, he sought out Hawkeye's gaze.

"Fifteen minutes," he mouthed. He stuck the candle on the shelf next to the door and turned away as if the women waiting behind him were invisible, which Nathaniel supposed was true. A coin of large enough denomination could make a man like Thompson blind to almost anything. Luckily Nathaniel had left most of his silver with Iona, who knew how to put it to good use.

The women slipped in quietly, their arms straining at the weight of the split-oak baskets. Pépin's mother, her face hidden by a deep hood, and the serving woman from the inn. Nathaniel saw Adele's eyes flitting through the dark cell to fix on Moncrieff and flit away again.

Pépin embraced his mother, and she pulled his head down into the curve of her cloak where she could talk to him, a hushed whisper in a country French that only Denier would have understood, had he been awake. Adele busied herself with unpacking the food onto the old board that served as a table. There were meat pies, bacon, sausage, cheese wrapped in brine-soaked cloth, two massive loaves of dark bread and a smaller corn cake still warm from the oven, a crock of beans, and a small keg of ale. To men living on gruel and dry bread, it looked a feast, but it would be a week at least before there would be any more. If other plans did not come to fruition first.

Adele had come to the bottom of the baskets: a bit of soap, some tobacco, and a half-dozen fat tallow candles. She straightened and caught Nathaniel's eye.

"The king of spades," she whispered, and pushed a small packet toward him. Without a backward glance she disappeared toward the shadowy corner where Moncrieff waited for her.

Nathaniel unwound the packet from its paper casing quickly, Robbie and Hawkeye leaning in close to watch. A deck of cards. The round, bland face of the king of spades was circled with neat, careful handwriting. The dark ink seemed to shiver and jump in the guttering candlelight.

Robbie squinted hard. "Iona's hand," he whispered. There was enough sunlight from the small, high window now to see him clearly. He was filthy, tangle-haired, his lower face lost in a snarl of beard.

Nathaniel's heart gave a leap. If Iona would risk sending such a note things must be coming to a head.

Hawkeye made a sound in his throat and Nathaniel tucked the card into his shirt just as Thompson appeared at the door again, chewing on bread so that the crumbs fell in a wet shower over his jacket. He jerked his head over his shoulder. With last murmured words, the women pulled down their hoods and slipped out as quietly as they had come. The guard thumped out after them, his key rasping as it turned in the lock.

Denier woke and came sniffing around the pile of food. The knife cut on his cheek had finally closed, but it still wept an angry yellow-red. His appetite was intact; he retired to his cot with a meat pie and his share of the sausage.

They ate silently, concentrating at first on the meat and on slick white cheese they washed down with Adele's ale in a tin cup that circled once and then again. Nathaniel wished, as he did every day, for water. For all of his life he had begun every day spent at home by diving into the cold pool under the falls at Lake in the Clouds; now he daydreamed of drinking until he had his fill, and more.

"Well?" Moncrieff's voice was thick. He had been sick with a fever for almost a week, and he was still prone to coughing fits.

They waited another five minutes until they could hear Thompson talking out in the courtyard above the normal noise of the garrison. Nathaniel read Iona's note in the light from the little window, and then he pressed his forehead against the cold, damp stone for a moment. When he came back to them, he could see the cautious hope on his father's face.

"Tonight," he said, his voice cracking with the effort

and with relief. "When the seminary clock strikes ten. There'll be a diversion in the barracks and we should be ready to run." The little he knew of the plan worked out between Pépin's brothers and Iona didn't take long to relate.

There was a tense silence when Nathaniel finished, each of them alone with their own thoughts. Denier had stopped eating, and was tugging at one huge ear in a thoughtful way. He muttered a question in Pépin's direction and got a brief word in reply. The escape plans seemed to have brought about an uneasy truce between them, but Nathaniel intended to keep a sharp eye on the butcher.

"Any sign of Runs-from-Bears?" asked Robbie, putting voice to the question that kept Nathaniel awake night after night. They could not even know for sure if Otter had made it out of Montréal.

"Not yet," said Nathaniel, passing the card to his father.

Hawkeye took the king of spades and held it to the guttering candle flame until it was nothing but ash. Then he reached for the corn bread. "Eat up, boys," he said, new energy in his voice. "No sense letting good food go to waste."

Moncrieff was looking between Nathaniel and Pépin. "But what of weapons?"

Although the young farmer's English was spotty, he had followed most of the conversation. Still gnawing on a bit of sausage, he picked up a candle from the pile and handed it to Moncrieff. "From *ma mère*," he said.

Moncrieff raised an eyebrow at the weight of the candle. Then he tested the narrow end with his thumb and jerked in surprise. A bead of blood appeared, bright on his grimy skin.

"It's a wise woman wha' kens the worth o' a guid strong candle," said Robbie grimly as he tore off another chunk of bread. "An' should we meet wi' Pink George on the way oot o' his filthy gaol, I'll demon-

strate the truth o' that tae him wi' great pleasure." He narrowed an eye at Moncrieff. "Did Adele ha' any news o' Somerville?"

Nathaniel caught his father's eye. Robbie was determined to pay Pink George back for the shooting of his dog. If all went well he would never have the chance, but there was no good reason to point that out.

"Aye," said Moncrieff, filling the tin cup again. "Giselle is to be married."

There was a moment of surprised silence.

Hawkeye grunted, his gaze fixed on the food before him. "He'll have a struggle on his hands, whoever he is."

"Perhaps," said Moncrieff. "But Horace Pickering is no man's fool."

Robbie sputtered a mist of ale. "The fish-faced seadog is tae marry Giselle?"

Moncrieff inclined his head. "She might ha' done far worse. Now she'll be free o' her faither, and awa' fra' here. I think it will serve her weel."

"Aye," said Hawkeye lightly. "A husband gone to sea nine months out of twelve may suit her just fine." He stared for a moment at Nathaniel, and then grinned as if he knew full well what his son must be feeling: surprise, some curiosity he would not indulge with questions, and relief. He need think on Giselle Somerville no more.

"Perhaps he'll take her home," Moncrieff said thoughtfully. "He has a house outside o' Edinburgh. Have I told ye about the countryside around Edinburgh?"

The others snorted. Angus Moncrieff had asked the Bonners for a single hour to present his case for Scotland and Carryck and had had their attention, day and night, for a good month. He had paid a high price for the opportunity—for a day at least, Nathaniel had wondered if the cold in his chest might kill him—but he made good use of it. And his easy way with a story was welcome in the long dark days of March when boredom and desperation vied for the upper hand.

Moncrieff's histories were told in a long, comfortable ramble. He spoke of kidnapped kings, land grants and treaties, treacheries and lost opportunities, brave men with weak allies, traitorous Norman nobles. There were complicated tales of English perfidy, clan rivalries and border wars, banking disasters, famines and clearings. Moncrieff gave them such a vivid picture of his homeland and its people that Nathaniel sometimes daydreamed of places he knew only by name and would never see: Stirling and Bannockburn, Falkirk, Holyrood.

Nathaniel had heard many of the same stories from his mother, but Moncrieff told them with the voice and vision of the men who had fought the battles. He was so skilled at spinning tales that it was some good time before Nathaniel noticed those subjects he avoided. He never told his own story in any detail, said almost nothing of his own family or his unshakable allegiance to the Carryck line; and in all his recounting of tangled politics and divided loyalties, he spoke of religion in only the most passing way. Stranger still, while they heard of every battle fought with England for independence since Robert the Bruce, Moncrieff never spoke of the most recent and disastrous, the Rising of '45, although he sang of it now and then. When the mood was on him, Moncrieff would throw back his head and sing in a profound, clear baritone so that even the guards playing dice in the courtyard quieted to listen.

The folks with plaids, the folks with plaids,
The folks with plaids of scarlet,
And folks with checkered plaids of green
Are going off with Charlie.
Were I m'self sixteen years old,
Were I as I would fain be,
Were I m'self sixteen years old
I'd go m'self with Charlie.

Nathaniel thought Moncrieff might be unwilling to talk of the Rising out of sensitivity to Robbie, who had fought for the exiled Catholic king and escaped to the Colonies in a complicated set of circumstances. For his part, Robbie seemed content to let Moncrieff's stories lead where they would go without comment. More than once Nathaniel had wished for privacy in which he could ask some very pointed questions out of Moncrieff's hearing.

Most of all, Moncrieff talked about Carryck. Sometimes Nathaniel fell asleep at night listening to the stories, only to escape in his dreams in the opposite direction, to Elizabeth and Lake in the Clouds, to their children, and to the Kahnyen'kehàka, who were truer family to him than any earl in a stone castle could ever be. They had had no word of Otter and no way of knowing if he had made it home, but deep in his bones Nathaniel was certain that he had. He could almost see Runs-from-Bears on the path. He was on his way here, or he was dead.

Nathaniel knew Moncrieff was probably right, that he was a Scot through and through; but it made no difference. None of it—not the farms or fields or mines or titles—had any claim on his heart or mind. He would go home to Lake in the Clouds and never leave the mountain again. Nathaniel could see the same thought on his father's face now.

"You'll be off home to Scotland," Hawkeye said to Moncrieff. "Glad to see the last of Canada, I'll wager. You came a long way and stayed a long time to be goin' home empty-handed. I'm sorry for it, man, but I can't help you."

The narrow shoulders lifted in a shrug. "It was worth the chance," he said. "I would ha' gone twice the distance to save Carryck. It will ne'er be the same again."

"Nothing ever is," said Hawkeye, but his tone was kind. He understood what it meant to lose home-

lands to an invading army that never seemed to lessen, or tire.

"I saw Carryck when I was no' but a lad," said Robbie, almost to himself. "I was on the road tae Glasgow. A summer nicht, and the midges were nippin' aye fierce, but the sicht o' the castle lit up wi' torches was a gey wonder tae behold. It seemed tae me tae be filled wi' a thousand fine folk."

"The hospitality o' the auld earl was well kennt," agreed Moncrieff. "Men came from as far as Paris and London to hunt wi' him—and he welcomed them all. Even Pink George came to Carryck, back in forty-four. I remember it weel."

"You must have been a boy yourself," said Nathaniel, truly surprised. "That's fifty years ago."

"I was thirteen," said Moncrieff. "And in training under my faither, who was the earl's factor before me. Pink George was no more than twenty himself. I recall that hunting party weel, for the banquet was my first and my faither's last. He died the following year." Moncrieff cleared his throat again, rubbing a hand over his face. "It was that very banquet where our fine host, George Somerville, Lord Bainbridge, earned the name Pink George."

Robbie's head snapped up. "Ye've been sittin' here wi' us in this stinkin' hole for weeks, Angus, and no' tolt the tale? I've lang wondered aboot that name."

"I was saving it for a rainy day."

"The sun is shining," said Hawkeye. "But tomorrow will be too late if luck is with us."

But Nathaniel could not sit still, not even for a well-told story. He got up to pace the room. The warmth of the spring morning touched his face with a tenderness that would have made him despair, if it weren't for his faith that tomorrow they would be away. He would never turn back, of that much he was certain, should the whole city burn to the ground.

". . . more than fifty rode out wi' the hounds that

day, Bainbridge among them. He came back empty-handed, lopsided wi' drink, and in an amorous frame o' mind. Kitchen lassie or duchess, he wasna particular. Bainbridge's appetite for women was the talk o' the land."

"Much like yer own," noted Robbie with a wink, but Moncrieff only raised a dignified brow in his direction, and refused to be drawn into a discussion of his own habits.

"The trouble began when he caught sight o' wee Barbara Cameron, a servin' maid. Just fifteen, with eyes o' lavender, and hair like the moonlight itself. A bonnie lass was Barbara, virtuous, but canty. She was serving drink that evening, and had the poor fortune to come across Bainbridge, who thought he would dispense wi' the niceties and get right to lifting her skirts. But whisky made him slow, and she was quick. She left him wi' nothing but her scent in his nose and a ribbon he snatched from her hair as she slipped awa'."

Moncrieff paused to take another deep swallow. The telling of a story seemed to give him a thirst.

"Now, he was no' so bad to look at himself as a young man, was our Bainbridge. There were other bonnie faces in the hall that night who might've made him forget wee Barbara, if it werena for the fact that she had shunned him in front o' all the other men at his table. 'Oho,' says one o' the stupider Drummonds—just a month later his horse did us all the favor o' throwing him on his heid—'have ye lost your touch, Bainbridge, or is the wild rose of Scotland too thorny for a soft English hand?'"

There was a guffaw from Robbie, who was bent over in a bow, his hands folded between his knees and head cocked.

"From the little ye've seen o' the man, you know verra well that Pink George is the kind that canna thole laughter at his own expense. And so he made a wager wi' softheided Geordie Drummond. He would have

Barbara Cameron in his bed before the dawn, plow the field, and leave a bit more of England putting down roots in Scottish soil when he gaed awa' hame."

Moncrieff shrugged as if to disavow responsibility for what had happened so long ago.

"That was his mistake. Ye see, he drew the auld earl's attention on himself, chasing after a serving maid all evening, for he decided in his drunken state that once she kennt him weel, she couldna withstan' his charms. In the end, his lairdship sent my faither off to get to the bottom o' the matter. And when he came back wi' the whole tale, the earl got a particular light in his eye.

"He was a wily one, the auld earl, sharp as they come and wi' a wicked sense o' humor. Young Bainbridge was an opportunity he couldna let pass. So he goes after the lad—no' to tell him to leave the lass alone, for what game is there in that? No, he asks if there's anything the viscount desires to make his stay more comfortable!"

Pépin had inched a bit closer and was listening hard, although Nathaniel thought he was probably not getting more than half of the story. Denier had gone back to sleep.

"Bainbridge is too deep in his cups to see the strangeness of it, that the Earl o' Carryck should be asking after his wishes personally, and him no' but a lad. But his blood is up now—watching Barbara move through the room, her skirts swinging and her cheeks aa bright wi' color—and he doesna see what is plain to every other man. And the ladies, too, Scotch and English alike, laughing behind their hands.

"Aye, the lass is on his mind and he's blind to all o' it, is George. He winks and nods, and winks again, and presses wee Barbara's hair ribbon into the earl's broad palm. 'What a lovely pink it is,' says he, winking in Barbara's direction. 'I am quite taken with it.'"

In the shadows of the gaol cell they all smiled

broadly, for Moncrieff was a mean mimic and had got Pink George down exactly.

"Now, the earl can barely keep a sober expression, but he nods. 'Aye,' says he. And 'Certainly.' As if it were a weighty matter between men o' the world. He sends Bainbridge off to his room 'Guid things come tae him wha' waits,' says the earl."

Robbie sat up straighter. "Tell me that Carryck didna send the lass in tae Somerville, or I'll lose ma mind."

Moncrieff raised a finger. "If there's anything to ken about the auld earl it is this: he could turn almost any quirk o' fate to his own advantage or amusement, and he never gave awa' what was his.

"So. Off Bainbridge stumbles to his bed, and awa' marches the earl in the other direction wi' most of the party behind him. My faither and I gaed along, too, carrying torches. So lang I live I willna forget the sight o' it—the ladies and gentlemen in their fine clothes, high-stepping through the muck and mud, slipping an' sliding in shite and laughing like boobies on their way tae the barn. More than a few o' them gaed astray in the hayricks, for the moon was full and Bainbridge wasna the only man wi' an eye for the lassies."

Moncrieff stopped to scratch his thinly sprouted beard, extracting a louse that he examined closely before crushing it. Then he looked around the circle of faces, meeting each man's eye.

"And while the laird was seeing to things in the barn, the drink got the better o' Bainbridge and he fell to sleep waiting. But he woke in the morning to find the earl was so guid as his word, for he wasna alone under the kivvers."

"No' wee Barbara in bed wi' him!" whispered Robbie.

"No' Barbara," agreed Moncrieff. "The viscount woke wi' his arms about a fine Scotch sow—twenty stone o' pig—tranked wi' grog to keep her sleepy. A lovely pink she was, wi' a hair ribbon to match tied in a

bow around her neck. Bainbridge's cursing could be heard throughout the castle, and all the way to the Solway Firth, forbye. And from that day to this, he's been known as Pink George. No' to his face, o' course."

When they had stopped laughing, Robbie wiped his eyes. "And what o' Barbara?" he asked. "What became o' her?"

Moncrieff turned away to help himself to more of the sausage. "That winter she sailed off to France in the service of a rich merchant's wife. I believe she married there, and raised a family."

"I for one ain't surprised," said Hawkeye. "Men don't change much in their lifetimes, after all. Unless it's for the worse."

"Pink George," said Robbie, almost singing it to himself. "I wad verra much enjoy oinkin' and snortin' in his face."

From the hall there was a shuffling and Thompson appeared at the grid in the door. "Jones!" he hissed. In a rush what was left of the food was hidden away under the cot in the farthest corner; by the time Ronald Jones had come through the door, they were gathered around a game of cards.

The sergeant stood for a moment watching them, his arms crossed over his paunch. He sucked noisily on the stem of his pipe so that smoke circled the greasy red head. One blue eye narrowed, he took in the cell from corner to corner with a practiced sweep, finally settling on the snoring Denier.

A look of pure disgust passed over his face as he leaned down to bellow in the butcher's ear. "Wake up, you great sack of Frog lard! The sun's long up, innit? Wake up!" A single shove landed Denier on the floor, where he sputtered his way awake while Jones aimed kicks at his legs. He glanced over his shoulder at Pépin, who was watching with a wary expression over his fan of cards.

"If it was up to me I'd let you rot in gaol, the both of

youse Frogs. But he says to let you go, and that's what I'll have to do." He spat, barely missing Denier.

Pépin leaped to his feet. "Go?" He shot an astonished glance at Nathaniel and Hawkeye. "Go?"

"Are youse deaf as well as stupid?" bellowed Jones, his color flushing to a deeper shade of red. He made a great sweeping gesture toward the door with one arm. "Released! Free! You've served your time! Go on now, before I find a reason to keep you here!" He gave the young farmer a push.

Denier scrambled out, but Pépin paused in the doorway, tolerating Jones's shoves and kicks without flinching.

"We will meet again," he said. And he was gone, hurried off by Thompson.

Jones lounged in the doorway, suddenly at ease. He grinned, his teeth showing greenish-yellow in the dim light. "He'll see youse again, all right. On the gallows, and in short order."

Hawkeye stood. Jones took a step backward, one pasty hand moving to the hilt of his short sword, stubby fingers fluttering.

"Go on, then," he said. "I'd be glad to save the hangman some work. What, is that a surprise? Don't tell me you didn't hear them out there, hammering away?"

There was something going on in the courtyard, a persistent sawing and hammering that Nathaniel had not paid much mind to. Now he wanted to go hoist himself up to the window and have a better look, but he would not give Jones the satisfaction.

It was Moncrieff who spoke first. "Even Pink George wouldna dare hang us without a trial." His voice had gone hoarse again and he coughed once.

Jones grinned, but his hand stayed on his weapon and his gaze fixed on Hawkeye. "He won't have to. The governor comes in tomorrow. I expect you'll swing the day after."

"I dinna believe it," muttered Moncrieff.

"Oh, not for you. There's something else on for you, Moncrieff. Word come in with the post this morning, you're wanted in Québec. A Crown matter, no less. Luck is with you, innit?"

Moncrieff rose to his feet with some uncertainty, glancing first at Nathaniel and then at Hawkeye, whose impassive expression did not shift in the slightest. Nathaniel had the urge to say something, but before he could Moncrieff had already been herded out the door.

"I wonder what that's all about," Nathaniel said, after a long silence.

Hawkeye shrugged, his uneasiness sitting clear on his face. "I expect Carleton finally figured out the connection between Moncrieff and the Earl of Carryck."

Robbie moved to the window, pulling himself up on the bars with ease, in spite of his size. There he stayed for three long heartbeats. "Holy Mary," he whispered, and dropped back down to the floor with a thud.

The cell seemed overlarge with three of their number gone so suddenly. They might each have had a cot to themselves, but instead they paced, winding around each other, from the window to the table to the door, and back again. They could not safely discuss the night to come, with Thompson never far away; they had no patience for cards; and the workmen out in the courtyard did not bear watching for very long. Nathaniel reminded himself that Iona was a resourceful woman a hundred times, and a hundred more. With or without Pépin, she would see the plan through tonight.

Robbie was sleeping when a new guard brought them watery soup and stale bread. He was all long arms and hands, not in his full growth yet, with a dusting of dark blond hair on his upper lip. Generally the guards were a talkative lot, but this one just watched them for

a few minutes, sharp eyed and curious for all his silence, and then slipped away without a word.

They roused Robbie and ate without talking, stomachs roiling and clenching in protest. When the sun set, Hawkeye lay down, put an arm over his face, and went to sleep. Robbie tried to follow his example, but Nathaniel could tell by his breathing that he was awake, and uneasy. Outside the small window the sky blazed red and gold with the last of the sun.

Vaguely he was aware of the seminary clock striking the hour. At seven the courtyard was mostly quiet; the men who passed through spoke of their suppers and the weather. At eight it was full dark and a light rain had begun to fall. At nine Hawkeye was awake again, his expression as calm and resolute as Nathaniel had ever seen it. They sat in the dark and damp cold of the spring night, testing the weight of Pépin's candles in their palms, getting a sense of the thin blades inside the wax.

Nathaniel sat on the edge of the cot, facing the door; Robbie stood below the window. Hawkeye took up pacing again, all his consciousness thrown outward into the night. Listening.

The seminary clock struck ten. Nathaniel could hear the rhythm of his own heart, the pulse beating in each fingertip.

The sentry raised his voice in a sleepy challenge at the courtyard gate. A carter with a load of hay. The horse had a loose shoe, clattering over the cobblestones with a hitch.

A minute passed; another. Ten minutes. The carter was telling a story to the guard in a combination of English and country French. In one part of his mind, Nathaniel heard the rise and fall of his voice, but he might have been speaking Latin, for all the sense it made. He was watching his father, as he had watched his father for all his life; just now Hawkeye had the look that came over him when they were on the trail of

a deer, when a single false movement would mean going home empty-handed.

Just a few minutes ago there had been total dark, but now Nathaniel realized that Hawkeye's face was bathed in a flickering light. On the other side of the courtyard, the garrison was on fire.

"Jesus wept," whispered Robbie, rising to his feet.

The garrison erupted like an anthill as the sentry sounded the alarm. The seminary bells began to ring almost immediately, and across the city others joined in. There was nothing like a blaze to wake up a town built of wood. Soon half of Montréal would come pouring in.

Over the noise they could just hear running footsteps in the hall, buttons and weapons and keys jangling. A new guard appeared at the door, his face as white as his shirtfront as he worked at the lock, a musket in one hand. No more than eighteen, but tall and well built. His gaze flitted again and again to the glow of fire in the small window.

"It would be easier if you put down the gun, son," said Hawkeye in an easy way. "We won't rush you."

With a soft curse the boy dropped the musket and used both hands to turn the key. The door swung open. His Adam's apple rode the length of his neck as he met their eyes, one by one.

"Iona sends word. You're to follow me."

"Luke," said Robbie, squinting at the boy. "I should ha' reconized ye." He made a feeble gesture with his hand, as if to present the boy to Nathaniel and Hawkeye.

"Who is this, Rab?" Nathaniel had never heard of this boy, and there was something strange in Robbie's expression.

The boy spoke up. "Iona is my grandmother," he said, and Nathaniel saw Robbie's mouth twitch. But there was no time to be surprised and less to ask questions.

"We are damned glad to see you, lad," Hawkeye said. "But where's the other guard?"

The boy shrugged, calmer now as he picked up the dropped musket. "He felt the sudden need to take a nap. We've got to make tracks, there's no more than ten minutes."

"Until what?" asked Nathaniel.

"Until they put the fire out or it reaches the gunpowder stores," said Luke. "If anybody asks, I'm taking you to the lieutenant governor." He pointed down the dim hall with his musket, and they set off.

They ran with the boy at the rear, his musket pointed at their backs, down stairs that echoed with a hundred shouting voices. In the doorway they hesitated at the sight of the fire, creeping along the north wing of the garrison like a blind animal looking for food. The courtyard was full of smoke and rushing men, dodging the gallows in a ragged bucket line. The hangman's noose twirled in the wind. Thompson and Jones were on the other side of the courtyard, in the line with most of the guards, some of them in nightshirts.

High time to be away.

In the chaos of so many rushing bodies it took a full minute to get to the side gate and push through. Luke led now. He ran into the city, ducking into a maze of narrow back alleys. Without breaking his stride, the boy stripped off his uniform jacket and the white shirt underneath it to reveal homespun and a leather jerkin. Finally he dodged into a barnyard and pressed himself into the shadows behind a shed.

The place smelled of burning charcoal and roast meat, new manure and earth recently turned for planting. Opposite them the little farmhouse was dark. There was a slight movement at the only unshuttered window: a hand raised in greeting and then nothing. Pépin. The men stood pressed close together, listening.

Five more minutes, and no explosion.

"They managed it, then," said the boy, with considerable relief. He wiped the sweat from his face.

Hawkeye put a hand on his shoulder. "You took a chance, Luke. Thank you."

"I wasn't alone," he said, barely able to meet his eye. "But you're welcome."

Nathaniel said, "Tell Iona thank you, too. We're in her debt."

"Most are, one way or the other," he said. "But you can tell her yourself."

Iona had appeared at the open door of the barn. She was wrapped in a cloak and carried a small lantern. She gestured to them silently and they slipped inside.

"Iona," said Hawkeye, when they stood in a circle around her.

"Hawkeye." Her tone was as cool and easy as always. "Nathaniel, Robbie. I am so very glad to see you well."

Robbie drew in a sharp breath. "What a daft thing tae do, woman. Ye should ha' stayed awa'." In the meager light of the lantern his expression was haggard with outrage and fear.

She looked at him as she might have looked at a raging child, half affection and half impatience. "I have news that couldn't wait."

They followed her farther into the barn where the air was damp with the heavy, sweet smells of fresh milk and hay. Two cows shifted in their standing sleep. On the far wall there was a rustling from the pigpen. Nathaniel thought of Pink George, who probably already knew they were gone. He said, "We know about Carleton."

The brown eyes met his own. "Of course. But do you know about William Spencer?"

Nathaniel thought he must have misunderstood. Prayed that he had misunderstood. "Will Spencer? Here?"

"Who the hell is Will Spencer?" asked Hawkeye, looking between them.

"Viscount Durbeyfield," supplied Iona. "A man of some importance in England, as I understand it."

Nathaniel said, "He's the one married to Elizabeth's cousin Amanda. A lawyer." He spoke to his father, but his gaze was fixed on Iona. "Otter was supposed to send Runs-from-Bears, not Will Spencer. What is he doing here?"

"I don't know exactly," said Iona. "He didn't come to me. He went to Somerville and the magistrates to plead your case."

"Sassenach gentry wi' their heids tegither," muttered Robbie. "Lord ha' mercy."

"If we're gone there ain't any case to plead," said Hawkeye.

"Listen to me." Iona's voice dropped to a hoarse whisper, her gaze drawing them all in. "The scout who brought this Will Spencer to Montréal from Chambly says that he got off a schooner that came up Champlain. There were other passengers. A white woman traveling with a black woman and children, and a Mohawk."

Nathaniel's heart leaped into an erratic rhythm. "Christ above. Elizabeth."

"And Runs-from-Bears," whispered Robbie.

Hawkeye grinned. "By God, she's come up here with Curiosity to break us out of gaol. I don't doubt they would've done it, too, if Iona hadn't beat them to it."

"I should have known," said Nathaniel. "I should have known she wouldn't stay behind." And realized suddenly that he had been expecting this news for weeks now. She had crossed the endless forests for him once before.

"They aren't in Montréal yet," said Iona. "I'm sure of that much."

"They'll be traveling up the Richelieu to Sorel," said Nathaniel. He glanced into the barnyard, where Luke was keeping watch. He could not see the boy, but he could sense him there in the shadows. "If Will just got in today, they won't be on the big river yet, not at this time of year. We'll have to head them off."

Iona nodded. "There's a boat waiting for you. Luke

will show you the way. No doubt Somerville realizes you're gone already, so you'd best be off."

"We're in your debt," said Hawkeye, touching her shoulder.

She smiled in the lantern light. "So you are, Dan'l Bonner. I will call that debt home someday."

"I'm worried that Somerville will come after you," Nathaniel said, and saw how at the door Luke's back stiffened. Robbie had a strange look about him, too. But Iona only pressed Nathaniel's arm.

"Somerville is no threat to me," she said calmly. "Rest assured. Now you had best change and be on your way."

"Aye," said Robbie. "But north instead o' south. I fear we may nivver see the end o' Canada."

To Nathaniel's surprise, Iona stepped up to Robbie, and although she was half his size he started. She reached up to take his face between her hands. "Don't talk such rubbish, Rab MacLachlan." Her voice gentled suddenly, touched now with soft Gaelic rhythms. "Keep your eyes and ears open, *mo charaid,* or Canada will see the end of you."

It was good to run again. Luke set a steady pace, weaving through the shadows. They slipped out of the city, circling north to the river, away from the docks where the watch would be alert and edgy after the fire. By now there would be patrols out looking for them. Time and time again Nathaniel put his hands on the weapons Iona had provided, testing the weight of a borrowed rifle, the worn grip of a well-sharpened knife.

With every indrawn breath of the cool night air he felt himself come more alive, his senses waking from a long, unwilling sleep. He would run all night and all day without complaint, run anywhere that took him toward Elizabeth and away from Montréal.

The spring moon was waning, its light further

checked by cloud cover, but Luke never hesitated in his course, not until the smell of river water brought them up short. He signaled for them to wait, and then slipped away through a stand of trees toward the shore. Nathaniel calculated the time by the beat of his own heart. If Iona had managed to find them a decent canoe instead of the clumsy bateaux that filled the river, and if the tides were with them, they could be in Sorel tomorrow. He peered into the darkness for some sign of Luke.

A low whistle and they moved, one by one, down to the riverside.

Luke stood on the bank next to a small boat. Behind him was the shadowy outline of a schooner at anchor in the middle of the river.

"Holy God," breathed Robbie.

"And I thought the best she could do would be a canoe," said Nathaniel.

Hawkeye gave a rough laugh. "I'd like to know how she managed it."

Luke pushed his hair out of his face. "It's the *Nancy*. She's waiting for you."

"Who does she belong to?" Nathaniel asked, wanting to be away but wary of such unexpected good fortune.

"Horace Pickering is her captain."

All three of them pulled up short. Robbie snorted. "Horace Pickering? The Englishman set tae marry Giselle?"

"That's the one," agreed Luke. "I don't think Somerville's search parties will bother you on the *Nancy*."

The three men exchanged glances, and then Hawkeye stepped into the skiff and picked up an oar. "We ain't got much choice," he said. "But I wish she had told us what she had in mind."

Their combined weight pushed the little skiff deep into the icy water of the St. Lawrence. Luke sat in the stern, listening to the river with his face turned away,

every muscle in him tensed. For all his youth there was a calm about him now, a quiet competence and the sense of a good man in the making. In these few moments of waiting, Nathaniel had time to wonder at it: Iona with a grandson, when there had never been any talk he had heard about her children.

When they had reached the *Nancy*, Nathaniel shook his hand. "You know where to come looking for us if we can ever be of help."

"You're welcome anytime," added Hawkeye.

The boy looked between them, his expression blank. "I'll remember that."

Robbie's hand closed on his shoulder. "Take care on the road hame, laddie." He had more to say, but two figures had appeared above them on deck, and from up-river came the sound of oars at work, and men's voices. With a nod to Luke they slipped onto the *Nancy*.

10

The village that the French called Sorel and the British called William Henry turned out to be nothing more than a weary spot at the mouth of the Richelieu, a maze of busy wharves and busier taverns, all stinking of rotting fish, mildewed sails, hot tar, and brewing ale. But the sight of the St. Lawrence was so welcome and such a great relief that Elizabeth could forgive the little town almost anything.

The good news was that Captain Mudge's party had arrived just two days after the ice had broken up and there was a great amount of traffic on the river in both directions, but there was little else to be thankful for. To the captain's displeasure and Elizabeth's despair, the schooner that should have been waiting for them, ready to sail, had instead been hauled out of the river for repairs to her hull. Elizabeth listened with only half an ear to the captain's agent, who told a complicated story of a collision with a whaleboat full of drunken voyageurs; she had already turned her mind to finding another way to Montréal, and that without delay.

In a small place so crowded with sailors and every kind of vessel, she reasoned out loud to Curiosity, this should not be an impossible task. Most certainly they

could have found safe passage with one of the Royal
Navy vessels—she saw two sloops and a brig—but she
could not chance the questions any British officer
would ask. Instead she fixed her attention on the *Nell,*
which was unloading a shipment of pitch and turpen-
tine. Elizabeth rejected out of hand the possibility that
the *Nell* might be set to sail in the opposite direction, to
Québec: they had had enough bad fortune, and could
afford no more. Tomorrow they would be in Montréal,
if she had to take up oars herself.

Captain Mudge traced the owner of the *Nell* to a
public house near the docks, only to find that he would
not deal with women or Indians, but was willing to
spare Grievous Mudge a few minutes. Runs-from-Bears
shrugged off this slight and went off in search of whatever news was to be had of their party in Montréal,
leaving Elizabeth and Curiosity to wait with the children in a crowded common room that smelled strongly
of fermenting yeast and spruce beer. Somewhere in another part of the house the captains were in negotiations, no doubt over generous portions of whisky.

A silver coin got them a table near the hearth. The
innkeeper's wife, harried and immune to the miseries
that travelers brought to her door, had at least provided
a table large enough for them to accommodate the
cradleboards. The twins were content to stay strapped
and swaddled, as long as they were propped up and
could survey the room. There were bowls of steaming
beef broth, a loaf of new bread, a dish of baked leeks
and onions, and a leg of spring lamb that even
Curiosity pronounced well turned. Thus they sat in relative comfort, waiting for word.

A young sailor in the bright blue coat of the Royal
Navy caught Elizabeth's eye. He had ginger hair much
like Liam's and he inched by their table, sending them a
sliding, sideways glance that hesitated on Hannah, and
finally jerked away. Elizabeth realized now that while
she had seen many Indians on the docks and in the

streets, Hannah was the only one in this public house. Suddenly the high cost of the table took on new meaning, which made her distinctly uneasy and vaguely angry.

"I don't like Sorel," said Hannah, calmly dismembering an onion layer by layer. She said it once in English, for Curiosity, and then again in Kahnyen'kehàka, for herself.

"There's a bright child," said Curiosity, stabbing at her meat.

"Further evidence of her good sense," agreed Elizabeth. "But we shall make the best of Sorel, nevertheless. I believe there are rooms for rent here, perhaps even a tub and hot water."

Curiosity eyed the innkeeper's wife and snorted softly. "For the right price, maybe."

Hannah finished her onion and leaned over to wipe a line of dribble from Lily's chin. "I'd like to clean up," she conceded. "If there's time."

"There may well be," said Elizabeth. "Here comes Captain Mudge and I'm afraid it doesn't look like good news."

In fact the news was not good. The captain and owner of the *Nell* was uneasy transporting women and children under normal circumstances, and no amount of coin could move him to do so on his first run of the season. Elizabeth sat, digesting this latest setback, in silence. With one finger she touched the spot between her breasts where she wore a single five-guinea gold piece on a long chain, along with her other treasures. *No amount of coin,* she thought. *I wonder.*

Relieved of his bad news, the captain lit his pipe and leaned back on the settle.

"There's another boat," he said in a gruff but apologetic tone. "I know the captain, and he'd take you, for the right price. But it ain't exactly ladylike on board, Mrs. Bonner."

"It is not a very long journey," Elizabeth said, cast-

ing a glance at the twins, who blinked back at her. "When does he sail?"

Captain Mudge gnawed thoughtfully on his pipe. "Sooner rather than later."

Elizabeth caught Curiosity's eye.

"Seem like there ain't much choice," said the older woman.

"Hannah?"

She nodded. "We might as well move on."

"Well, then," said Elizabeth. "Perhaps we should go talk to this captain—"

"Stoker. An Irishman," said Grievous Mudge. With a creak and a groan he pushed himself up from the table, reaching for his tricorn. "You'd best wait here," he said. "If he don't want to be found I could be a while putting my hands on him." He cast a look over his shoulder at the innkeeper's wife, leaned forward and whispered. "You'll need a room. There's one upstairs, she'd give it to you until the morning for a reasonable price. It has a door and a stairway of its own, you see."

"This Irishman ain't exactly made hisself popular, I take it," said Curiosity, with little regard for whispering.

The captain raised one grizzled eyebrow in salute of her quick understanding. "It would be a sight easier," he agreed.

"What about Runs-from-Bears?" asked Elizabeth.

The broad mouth turned down at one corner. "No need to hand over a list of visitors." Another quick peek over his shoulder and then back again to Elizabeth. "No need at all."

She might have rested, for the feather beds were freshly made with clean linen, and there had been hot water enough for all of them. The babies, bathed and fed, were sleeping deeply, and so was Hannah, twitching slightly in her dreams. After some urging, Curiosity had

even put up her feet and gone to sleep, a worry line etched firmly between her brows.

But she could not rest, and so Elizabeth sat in a chair by the window, drowsing now and then but mostly staring out at the town and river. There were still some ice floes in the St. Lawrence, poking up here and there like rotting teeth. She counted sails and pennants for a while, stark white and dirty gray, blues and yellows and reds against a fitful sky. A bateau headed upriver with a hump of barrels lashed to its deck, courting a reluctant wind with a single sail. Finally oars went into the water to help it along.

On the street below, a carter cursed at his ox, his whip flashing. A boy darted out of a shop with a basket of fish, his bare feet kicking up a mist of muddy water that spattered two Royal Navy officers from heel to the brim of their great boatlike hats. They shook their fists at him, but he never looked back. Elizabeth thought of her schoolchildren in Paradise, many of the boys much like the ones on the street below. For a long moment she fought with tears of frustration and doubt and a simple and overwhelming homesickness for familiar things.

The sight of Runs-from-Bears on the street was welcome. He came around a corner with Captain Mudge, who whirled one arm vigorously in the telling of a story. With the other hand he plucked his pipe from his mouth to point it up the street toward the docks. Then he raised his head and pointed to the window, and catching sight of Elizabeth, bowed, clearly flustered. But it was the expression on Bears' face that got her attention. *More trouble.* Elizabeth thought of waking Curiosity, but then she simply picked up her damp cloak and let herself quietly out of the room. At least one of them should be rested. Whatever new trouble there was, she would handle it on her own.

.   .   .

"Gallows?" she repeated, as if she had never heard the word before and could put no meaning to it.

Runs-from-Bears nodded. "Built yesterday morning."

"It don't mean much," said Captain Mudge. "The Tories like to hang a thief now and then." But he would not meet her eye.

"Bears," Elizabeth said evenly. "This Kahnyen'kehàka you spoke to, did he see the gallows himself?"

"Hen'en." *Yes*.

She searched for her handkerchief, and touched it to her forehead. For a long moment she studied the toes of her boots: her sturdiest pair, mud stained, worn now across the toes in a way she would have never tolerated when she was still Miss Middleton of Oakmere. It seemed very long ago.

"Well, then," she said, struggling for a confident tone. "We'd best be on our way. Captain Mudge, have you located Mr. Stoker?"

"I have." He contemplated the public house for a moment, rocking back on his heels. "I tried to talk him into coming here but he's a difficult man, is Mac Stoker. He's waiting for you aboard the *Jackdaw*. Wants to talk about money."

"By all means," Elizabeth said. "But might I have a word with Runs-from-Bears first?"

When the captain had stepped away to examine a bay mare tied up outside the blacksmithy, Elizabeth said, "Curiosity will worry. Will you go sit with them? But avoid the innkeeper if you can."

He nodded. "And you watch yourself with the Irishman. In Stone-Splitter's village he is called Grabs-Fast."

"I'm afraid that comes as no surprise at all," Elizabeth muttered. She wished for some quiet place to talk to Bears out of public view, but there was no time. "I will be careful," she agreed. "But deal with him I must. We have to get to Montréal today."

"We will get there," said Bears. "But not at any cost."

Of course not, she thought, but again she found herself touching the gold coin hidden beneath her bodice. She had sent a hundred similar coins to Montréal with Will—perhaps he was spending it today, to good end. Curiosity had a hundred more in a leather bag she wore next to her skin. It was a tremendous amount of money for any common sailor; it would even buy a small boat and man it. But for the moment the coins were worthless to her. There was no way to melt them down, and they could not spend a single one of them. Not here with half of the king's navy on the docks and the river, and a good many redcoat officers in the streets and public houses. They might never get out of Canada if a five-guinea gold piece with the profile of George II came to the attention of the Crown's agents.

Bears was watching her face, reading her line of thought as if she had spoken out loud. "Bone-in-Her-Back," he said, and put a hand on her wrist. "To put the smell of gold in the Irishman's nose would not make things easier. Use the silver, there is enough of it."

Elizabeth blinked hard, embarrassed by her own desperation. "Yes, of course you're right."

"Pardon me." A young man had stopped to stare openly at Runs-from-Bears. Elizabeth forgot at times how fierce Bears must look to others: the keen dark eyes, a face pitted with pox scars, a tattoo that stretched from temple to temple like the tracks of the bear whose teeth he wore on a leather thong around his neck. An egret feather dangled from his side braid, and from his belt hung a collection of weapons with well-worn handles.

"Do you require assistance, madam?" Arched brows, and a knowing expression in the gray eyes. She was a lady in intimate conversation with a red-skinned man on a public street; he was an Englishman, sure of his view of the world and his right to intercede. She stared back at him until he began to fluster.

"Not your assistance, sir," she said coolly.

He flushed, bowed stiffly from the shoulders, and walked off.

"Why are you grinning?" she asked Bears, suddenly very cross with him, but not quite sure why she should be.

"It's good to hear you sounding more like yourself."

"It is the only way to deal with such presumption and insolence," Elizabeth said primly.

"Thayeri," said Runs-from-Bears. *It is proper so.*

Mac Stoker was a big man in his prime, barrel chested and black haired, with blue-gray eyes and a chipped front tooth that glimmered when he smiled. A wide scar circled his neck, twisting white and pink like a lady's ribbon against the tanned skin. He was the kind of man that women felt compelled to look at when he came their way, the kind who crooked a finger in return and expected to be obliged. He was known from Halifax to the Huron as Sweet Mac Stoker, and once he would have made Elizabeth uneasy to the bone. But no longer.

She stood with Captain Mudge, watching as Stoker worked alongside his crew, unloading bales of raw wool from the *Jackdaw*. He liked an audience, that was clear, for while the others wore work shirts of homespun or coarse linen, he worked stripped to a pair of overtight breeches, the muscles in the broad back and arms shining with sweat. Elizabeth was not outraged, as her aunt Merriweather would have expected her to be, and neither was she intrigued; she simply appreciated the opportunity to observe him from a distance and get some sense of him. By the time Stoker came rambling down the gangplank, wiping his neck with a discarded shirt, she had taken his measure and felt composed enough. If he really was the only way to get to Montréal quickly—and in this she had no choice but to trust Captain Mudge's judgment—she must deal with

this Mr. Stoker, regardless of what she thought of him, or how he presented himself to the world.

Captain Mudge began the introductions, and launched from there into a rambling story of the journey from Albany. Elizabeth kept her eyes fixed on the ragged eelskin that secured Mac Stoker's queue. He too seemed content to let the older man talk, engaged as he was in close scrutiny of Elizabeth's person.

Captain Mudge had worked himself into high voice about the final portage and the capsizing of one of the cargo barges, when he was interrupted by a shouting and waving of arms from the other end of the dock.

"That's Mr. Little," said Elizabeth. She had not seen the captain's first mate since they had left the bateaux on the Richelieu. Now he stood between a tower of boxes and two taller men; Elizabeth could hear his voice crackling with indignation.

"A-yuh. And excisemen," agreed the captain, yanking on his chin whiskers with a scowl.

Stoker grunted. "That's Wiggins and Montague, the greedy bastards. They'll be after havin' your man Little for breakfast."

As if to prove Stoker right, Mr. Little let out a yelp of distress, and they lost all sight of him.

"Perhaps you had better see what he needs," said Elizabeth. "Mr. Stoker and I can carry on."

"Ain't got much choice." Captain Mudge started off with a thump, and then seemed to remember what he was about.

"Stoker," he said, one eye narrowed down to a slit. "Take unfair advantage of this lady and I'll see to it you never run goods down Albany way again."

Mac Stoker nodded, touching his forehead with one blunt and grimy finger. When Captain Mudge was gone, he winked at her, the chipped tooth flashing. "You're lookin' for passage to Montréal."

"I am," said Elizabeth. "If the cost is right, and the accommodations will serve."

He barked out a surprised laugh. "English, all right. Yous're all the same."

The thought of the gallows at the Montréal garrison made it possible for her to keep her composure and her temper. "I don't see that my country of birth is relevant to our negotiations, Mr. Stoker."

With one thumbnail he raked the bristle on his cheek. "All business, eh? I'm told you tried your luck with the *Nell* first. Don't take it to heart that Smythe turned you down. He's the sort what prefers pretty boys."

Elizabeth met the blue gaze with a single raised brow. "We were discussing the price of passage to Montréal."

He found her amusing. "You're not easily shocked, I'll say that for you. The frontier takes that out of a woman. You've been far, so I hear told."

One of the crew swung by with a barrel on his shoulder: stale tobacco, sweaty clothes, fish oil, rum. The stuff of sailors everywhere. Elizabeth reminded herself that Mr. Stoker was just a man with a ship, and nothing more. Whatever rumors he had heard of her did not matter in the least.

"The fare, Mr. Stoker?"

The chipped tooth again in a grin calculated to irritate her. "You're in a damn hurry to get where you're goin', and I'd wager that *Jackdaw* will suit just fine, rough as she is. Sure, and I'm willing to bet you've got the fare, too. Shall we step on board to discuss it?" The grin, daring her. He scratched the pelt of dark hair on his chest lazily.

"I believe we can conclude our discussions right here," said Elizabeth.

His gaze wandered down the front of her cloak and up again. "I'm goin' on board," he said. "Stay here or come along. Suit yourself."

Not at any cost, Bears had said, and this is what he meant.

"I will pay you fifty dollars, silver," Elizabeth said to his retreating back, taking note of the scars: a long cut along the left ribs, a bullet wound at the shoulder, and the evidence that he had lived through more than one flogging.

When it was clear he was listening, she said it again. "Fifty dollars silver for three adults and three children. And we must have the use of your cabin for the trip."

He glanced at her over his shoulder. "Fifty guineas," said Stoker. "Gold."

She managed a smile, even while her heart tripped into a quicker beat. "Gold guineas? But you've been listening to pirate tales, Mr. Stoker. I am willing to give you sixty dollars in silver if you're enough of a sailor to get us to Montréal safely by morning."

The expression in his eyes was all blue steel and bile.

"I'm enough of a sailor to take youse and the brats to China and beyond, darlin'. But Granny Stoker raised no fools, and I won't take on the Royal Navy for a pretty smile alone."

"Of course not," agreed Elizabeth evenly. "I've offered you sixty dollars in silver for your trouble."

He peered down at her, a muscle fluttering in his cheek. "So you're telling me that you've got no gold. Next you'll be claimin' that you're not the Englishwoman who gave Jack Lingo what he's been askin' for all these years."

Elizabeth was aware of an ox bellowing nearby, gulls overhead, incessant hammering, men singing. She raised her chin and met his eye.

"Seventy-five dollars in silver, Mr. Stoker," she said calmly. "Take it or leave it."

"Jack owed me money," he continued thoughtfully. "It seems only fair that you should take on his obligations, havin' sent the whoreson to the hell he so richly deserved."

Anger crept up her neck. She put a hand there, as if

to stop it. "This is not the only ship in Sorel, Mr. Stoker."

"Sure, and that's true," he said. He glanced over his shoulder at the *Jackdaw* with her much-mended sails. "But she's damn fast, and maybe she's the only one that'll get you to Montréal in time to see some American spies swing for their troubles."

Elizabeth took a single step backward. Perhaps Stoker saw that he had pushed her too far, because his own expression slipped suddenly from a knowing grin to a scowl.

"Mrs. Bonner?"

A stranger at her elbow, bent almost in half in a low bow. She spun around to him in her anger.

"Yes?" More sharply than she intended, but he did not flinch.

"Please pardon my intrusion, madam, but I understand you are in need of passage to Montréal."

A gentleman, deferential of manner, with a kind smile and a face to make anyone gasp in horror. Elizabeth had never seen any person quite so ill-favored by nature, without a single normal or well-turned feature. But his accent marked him for a man of breeding and education, his etched silver buttons and Holland linen for a wealthy merchant with excellent taste, and there was a sharp intelligence in his mild eyes.

"Shove off!" barked Mac Stoker from the gangplank. "By what right d'you come stickin' that ugly gob of yours in me business?"

Captain Stoker might have been invisible for all the attention the stranger paid. His respectful expression remained, his head bobbing deferentially to his sunken chest, hands wound together before him. Elizabeth followed his example, and inclined her head. "You have me at a disadvantage, sir."

"I beg your indulgence for a moment, madam, and pray you will pardon the necessity of such an informal

introduction. Horace Pickering at your service. I bring word from your cousin, Viscount Durbeyfield."

Elizabeth felt herself flush with excitement. "From Will! Sir, this is good news indeed. What report does my cousin send?"

He lifted one shoulder in an apology. "He asked me to keep an eye out for you, and if I should see you here, to take you and your charges to meet him—in Montréal. Time is of the essence, as he put it to me. If I may point out the *Nancy*? You see we docked not a half hour ago."

A great calm moved through Elizabeth: their luck had finally turned. "The *Nancy* is your vessel?"

Stoker snorted, but Pickering only bowed again. "I am her captain for the moment." And at Elizabeth's brow, raised in tacit request for more detail, he inclined his head. "The *Nancy* is available for my use while I conclude some business for my employer in Canada. The ship I command is at dock in Québec."

If Stoker were not breathing down her back, Elizabeth might have been able to formulate the many questions that needed to be asked—foremost and most important, how this man knew Will, and why someone of such obvious position would take on this task. Will could not have told him of their business in Montréal, and so neither could she mention it to him. As it was, she did not have the luxury of a longer interview. "Your timing is excellent, sir. I am delighted to accept your kind offer of assistance."

"We came to an agreement!" Stoker roared.

"Mr. Stoker," Elizabeth said. "The cost of passage on the *Jackdaw* is too high."

Stoker went suddenly silent, his face as icy cold as his tone. "You think passage on the *Nancy* will come any cheaper? There's more than one kind of pirate on the St. Lawrence, me darlin'."

Captain Pickering cleared his throat roughly, but

Elizabeth held up her hand, wanting to settle her business with Mac Stoker on her own terms.

"Pirates are the least of my problems, Mr. Stoker." She managed a polite nod. "Captain Pickering, I must return to my children momentarily—"

The captain produced a broad smile that showed off a row of tiny white teeth. "May I be of assistance?"

Elizabeth saw Stoker's gaze on her. She wanted to ignore him but his expression, all knowing condescension, made it very difficult.

"Thank you, sir. But we will come to the *Nancy* as soon as we are able."

He bowed, and over his back Mac Stoker winked at her.

Elizabeth ran up the stairs of the public house with her skirts held high, pulled forward by the angry howling of two hungry infants.

"Thank the Lord," said Curiosity, thrusting Daniel toward her. "These children just about turnin' themselves inside out."

Hannah was at her elbow, tugging gently on her sleeve. "Is everything all right?"

"We have reliable passage to Montréal," Elizabeth said. "On a fine ship called the *Nancy*. I believe you can see her colors from here. Ouch!" She shifted Daniel to a more comfortable position, and accepted Lily from Curiosity. When the twins had settled to their task, she looked up. Curiosity was studying her with a combination of worry and doubt.

"Thought you went to talk to that Stoker."

"We could not come to terms," Elizabeth said. "We are much better off on the *Nancy*, even so. It was my cousin Will who sent Captain Pickering to fetch us."

"Hmmpf." Curiosity picked up a clean but damp

winding cloth and shook it out with a snap. "How did he manage that, I wonder?"

Elizabeth would have told Curiosity more, if it were not for Hannah. But she could not speak of the gallows in Montréal in front of the child, as much as it would ease her own burden to share the news. "Will would not have engaged Captain Pickering's services if he were not sure of his reputation. He is wellborn, and a gentleman."

"Richard Todd's a gentleman, too," Curiosity reminded her. "And he caused you enough grief."

Hannah had been following the whole exchange with a sober expression. "Runs-from-Bears will be with us," she said. "We will be safe."

"Yes," said Elizabeth. "Bears is waiting downstairs. As soon as we're ready he'll go down with you to the *Nancy*."

"And where will you be, missy, while we're doin' that?" Curiosity was staring at her as if she were sixteen and bent on illicit escapades.

"I have some inquiries to make," said Elizabeth. "There is still the matter of getting out of Montréal again when our business is done there. I will not be an hour, I promise. We sail at sunset."

Hannah's cool hand on her shoulder, all her worry flowing clear as a cold spring down Elizabeth's spine. She turned her head and kissed the smooth copper skin. "All is well, Squirrel," she said in Kahnyen'kehàka. "I promise you."

Gallows at the garrison gaol, whispered another voice inside her. Elizabeth rubbed her cheek against Hannah's hand, and willed the voice away.

She was only a hundred feet away from the *Jackdaw* when Runs-from-Bears caught her up; Elizabeth sensed him even before she turned around.

"I thought you were going to see the others to the *Nancy*," she said, trying to strike a normal tone of voice and cursing the color that rose on her cheeks.

"An officer came from the ship for them," he said. "I was more worried about you, Bone-in-Her-Back."

Elizabeth straightened her shoulders. "You of all people know very well that I am able to take care of myself, Bears."

He blinked at her, his face immobile, and Elizabeth knew that he would wait for her to tell him what he wanted to hear until the sunset. His patience was without end, she knew this from experience. Elizabeth let her shoulders roll forward. "This is something I must do on my own, Bears."

"The Irishman is trouble," he said. "We do not need him."

Elizabeth glanced around herself, and lowered her voice. "But we do. How are we going to get away from Montréal, once the men are free? He has a ship, he knows the waters, and for the right money he will not ask difficult questions, as Pickering would most certainly do."

Bears pursed his mouth. After a moment he said, "I do not like it."

"Nor do I. I like none of this."

He narrowed his eyes at her. "Let us go talk to him, then. There is not much time."

She pushed out a heavy sigh. "Very well," she said, wondering that she could be both relieved and ill at ease. Elizabeth smoothed her hair and then she met his gaze, full on. "Mr. Stoker knows about Jack Lingo."

Runs-from-Bears grunted softly. "That is just why I am coming with you. Look, he is waiting."

Sweet Mac Stoker stood on the deck of his ship, hands on hips, watching them. Elizabeth pulled herself up to her full height, and went to meet him.

"Mr. Stoker," she began. "We were wondering if we might engage your services in another matter."

He grinned. "For the right price, darlin'. For the right price. Come along, and we'll talk."

Elizabeth and Runs-from-Bears came to the *Nancy* just as the sun was about to set. Above their heads the first star showed itself in a sky that melted from blue to rose; on the horizon a group of willows and crab apples showed tender green sprinkled with white blossoms. Overhead, gulls turned and spun, calling to one another. Captain Pickering was at the rail to offer Elizabeth his arm as she stepped onto the shining oak deck, his poor face as bad as she had remembered it. But both the captain and his ship were in impeccable condition, so that for the first time in days Elizabeth was acutely aware of the shocking state of her traveling clothes. And still Pickering bent to her hand as if she were dressed for presentation at court; if he noticed that she was trembling he gave no sign of it.

"You honor us, madam. I trust your business has been favorably concluded?"

How strange and vaguely comforting to deal with Englishmen again, who needed so many words for so little purpose. But she was thankful to this man with his unfortunate face and his kind eyes, and so she nodded politely. "As well as can be expected, thank you."

Elizabeth introduced Runs-from-Bears to the captain, the whole time observing how Hannah bounced impatiently on the balls of her feet as if she would fling herself into the heavens. Even Curiosity's doubts had been laid to rest, if the expression on her face was any indication.

The captain was all condescension and good manners. "I will leave you to your family," he said, bowing. "There is time enough to meet my officers and the . . . other passengers. I hope my cabin will be satisfactory, but if there is anything you desire . . ." And with a

funny little smile he bowed and withdrew, leaving the question of Elizabeth's desires unresolved.

"Well, I hope this will serve," Elizabeth said grimly to a beaming Curiosity. "For otherwise we shall have to steal a dinghy and row to Montréal ourselves. Hannah, you are flushed. Have you had a look at the cabin?"

"Yes, we have," answered Curiosity for them both. "And we like it fine. Don't we, child?"

"Oh, yes," said Hannah, almost laughing out loud. "We put the babies down, but maybe you should go check on them."

Elizabeth looked between them. "What has got into you both?"

"Gettin' closer to home, is all," said Curiosity, putting a hand on Elizabeth's arm and pivoting her toward the steps that would take her to Pickering's cabin.

Elizabeth went, with a glance over her shoulder to Hannah, who was still grinning absurdly as she tugged on Bears' arm, chattering at him in Kahnyen'kehàka. It had been a very long day, too long to pursue whatever was at the bottom of this strange behavior. Passage on the *Nancy* was certainly a piece of the best good luck, but it did not change what was to come: they had built gallows in Montréal. It was a sentence that jangled in her head like loose coin, there at every turn with no escape.

She passed through the narrow and dimly lit corridor to Pickering's quarters, blinded now by the last of the sunlight that sifted through the shutters in flickering bars. Elizabeth made out the narrow bed, the table set with silver and linen for supper, a desk of gleaming mahogany, its cubbyholes spilling paper. And on the far side of the room, a man in a rough white linen shirt and dark breeches bent over the basket where the babies slept. A sharp shiver of fear slid up Elizabeth's spine. She looked around herself for some kind of weapon, but he had already heard her.

His head came up as he turned, the long line of his back straightening.

Nathaniel. Elizabeth stepped backward, feeling the door at her shoulder, so solid and real. She blinked, and still he was there: Nathaniel. He touched the basket as if to steady himself and she recognized his hand as she would her own: the turn of his wrist, the long, strong fingers. The muscles worked along the column of his neck as he swallowed convulsively and swallowed again.

"Aren't you going to talk to me?" he whispered from the other side of the cabin, ten feet and an eternity away.

Her hands were shaking so badly that she had to clasp them together, hard enough to make her wince. "Are you real?"

His smile was so familiar and full of joy that it burned her to look at him.

"Never doubt it, Boots." Suddenly he was in front of her, his hands closing around her upper arms as her knees began to give way. He smelled of strong soap and of his sweet self, Nathaniel. He leaned down to her, his hair swinging forward to touch her cheek.

"I am real," he said. "And by God, wife, so are you."

She might have answered him but he cut her off. He was all a blur to her, for she would not close her eyes even as her mouth went soft and open and slack with want and need to meet him. Then Nathaniel broke away and wiped her wet cheeks with his fingers, crooning small comforting sounds. And he kissed her again, the taste of him sending small shocks into every corner of her being.

"Nathaniel!" she said finally, gasping for breath. "You are supposed to be in gaol! What are you doing here?"

He pulled her to sit beside him on the cot. "Rescuing you."

"Rescuing me?"

"Didn't they tell you on deck?"

"No," Elizabeth said. "They most certainly did not,

the rotters. I thought you were a pirate. Does Captain Pickering know you are on board?"

He laughed out loud at that. "Of course. Did you think we stowed away?"

"But how—"

He kissed her again, her grinning pirate of a husband. "We broke out night before last and headed straight here to keep you from going upriver. By God, Elizabeth, you had me scared out of my wits."

"*You* were scared!" Indignant, she grasped his forearms as hard as she could. "Runs-from-Bears came to me this afternoon with the news that gallows have been built at the garrison gaol. I have never been so frightened."

"It was close, that's true. But we got away before they could try us—"

On the heels of relief a new kind of dread. Elizabeth tightened her grip on him. "The entire army must be looking for you. And what's become of Will?"

"He's on his way to Québec—probably there already."

"This is a fine mess," Elizabeth said. "Why is Will going to Québec? It makes no sense."

"It does if you think about the way things look for him. He shows up to negotiate us out of gaol and the next thing you know, we escaped. Somerville asked Will to chaperone his daughter to Québec—testing him, is the way Pickering looks at it. So Will's in the clear, Boots, and you'll see him soon enough."

"But how shall I see him if he is in Québec?" Elizabeth felt suddenly dizzy. "We are going to Québec? But I want to go home!" She was mortified by her own childish tone, and still more by the tear that spilled down her cheek. But he simply wiped it away and held her.

"God knows we all do, Boots, but Somerville's got troops looking for us all over."

"Nathaniel, Québec is in the wrong direction!"

He kissed the palm of her hand. "We can't go overland with the babies, not with Somerville set on tracking us down. We've got no choice but to go north and look for a ship there that will take us home down the coast from Halifax. If it weren't for Moncrieff and Pickering, we'd be in a worse scrape than we are already."

Elizabeth struggled to order the hundreds of questions that came to mind. "I don't understand why Pickering should go to such trouble for us."

"He's a friend of Moncrieff's."

"Moncrieff." Elizabeth had all but forgotten the Scot and his mission to find her father-in-law. It seemed very unreal right now, and utterly unimportant. "This is very confusing, Nathaniel."

He nodded, smoothing her hair. "I can't tell you exactly how it came to pass, except that Iona got to Pickering through Moncrieff. And more than that, I can't pretend I ain't worried. We'd rather set off overland on our own, but it just ain't safe."

He met her eye but something flickered there, unsaid. It was absurd, the idea that the three of them should somehow be unable to get away—Hawkeye and Robbie and Nathaniel could slip into the forests and Somerville would never be able to put his hands on them. Because she could not deny the truth to him or herself, Elizabeth said what he would not. "I should not have come."

Nathaniel caught her face between his palms. "Listen to me, Boots. I was never so glad to see anybody in my life as I was to see you on that dock."

She laughed then, covering his hands with her own and touching her forehead to his. "But I've made things so much more difficult—"

"We've been in worse spots," he said against her temple.

"Not by much," she muttered.

"I knew you'd come."

She frowned at him. "Did you now?"

"Boots," said Nathaniel softly. "I never doubted you for a moment."

She sighed then, and let herself collapse forward, her head finding the hollow of his shoulder. His arms came around her and she felt the knot of anxiety that had fueled her forward movement for all these weeks begin to unravel.

"We'll manage," Nathaniel whispered. "We can manage anything, you and me. Look at those babies, after all."

As if she had heard her name called, Lily's curly head rose over the edge of the basket. She blinked at them, and then the small button of a face began to collapse in on itself, tears springing into the blue eyes.

Nathaniel was across the room before Elizabeth could move, lifting Lily into the crook of his arm and crooning in the same tone she had had from him just moments ago. Elizabeth could not quite put a name to his expression, half worry and half relief. Her throat tightened with tears and she swallowed them down, determined not to weep.

An indignant squawk pulled her out of her trance. Nathaniel passed Lily to Elizabeth and scooped Daniel up, all flailing arms and legs and a furious expression that settled suddenly at the sight of this strange man. The two of them regarded each other for a long moment and then Daniel sputtered a hello in his father's face.

There was a knock on the door, and a murmuring of familiar voices: Hannah, breathless and happy, Runs-from-Bears, Robbie and Hawkeye. She had last seen Hawkeye on a hot August night, walking away from Lake in the Clouds. Leaving his home and kin because he had come up against laws that made no sense to him, white laws that did not fit the world as he understood it, a world that for him would forever be red. She had feared that she would never see him again, but here he was. He seemed unchanged by his long months in

Montréal's gaol, standing tall in the open door, as lean as leather. Under the mane of hair his gaze was as keen as it had ever been. He had one arm around Hannah, and with the other he pulled Elizabeth to him and looked hard at her.

"I see you've brought me my grandchildren, daughter." He kissed her cheek and bent down to look at Lily.

"Hello, little girl," he said.

Then Nathaniel crossed the room and put Daniel in his grandfather's arms, and Elizabeth watched Hawkeye change before her eyes.

II

It was full dark, the night tempered only with the vague light of a reluctant moon. Coming up on deck, Elizabeth could just make out the pale shapes of the mainsails, and the outlines of human forms at the rail: Hawkeye, Runs-from-Bears, and Robbie, deep in hushed conversation. But before she could join them, Captain Pickering had appeared at her side.

"Madam. May I inquire, is all to your satisfaction?"

She nodded. "Yes, very much so, Captain."

"It is a very small vessel for so many, but I hope it will still serve."

Elizabeth assured him that it would serve very well.

Even in the kind light of the moon his face was not easy to look at, but his manner was sincere as he leaned toward her. "I hope you have forgiven me for my little performance on the dock at Sorel. I could not speak of your husband openly, but it did grieve me to deceive you. Your cousin the viscount did send his very best wishes for your safe delivery."

She smiled. "Please, Captain Pickering. There is no need to speak of deception, or forgiveness. I admit that I have never been so surprised in all my life as when I found Nathaniel here, but nothing could have given me

greater happiness. I am not sure what we have done to merit all the trouble you have taken for our sakes—"

He waved her thankfulness away with a gloved hand. "Had you heard that I am shortly to be married?"

Elizabeth did know; she had had the whole story of Giselle Somerville's dinner party, and its repercussions, from Hawkeye and Robbie. It was a strange set of circumstances, but she wished Pickering joy as if there were nothing unusual at all in the way he had come to his bride, or the party games the bride had chosen to play with other men while she was unattached.

"I hope that we do not cause a rift between yourself and your new father-in-law," she finished.

"The lieutenant governor does not concern me," said Pickering. "I offered my assistance not to thwart him, but to serve justice and to please his daughter." His tone was cool, and it reminded Elizabeth that he might be a gentleman of good breeding, but Pickering was also an accomplished merchant commander and highly successful in his business pursuits.

Elizabeth glanced at Hawkeye, but the men were still turned away from them and deep in conversation. "You surprise me, sir. I thought it was Mr. Moncrieff who had interceded to ask for your assistance."

There was a slight hesitation. "It was Miss Somerville who brought Mr. Moncrieff's concerns to me. And a bridegroom can rarely deny his bride when she asks a favor, especially one with such merit. I do not believe that these men are spies, Mrs. Bonner, and I should have been very sorry to see them hang."

The words sent a small shower of gooseflesh up Elizabeth's back. "Was there truly danger of that, sir?"

He glanced up into the riggings. "I fear so. If Somerville had had his way. He is a man of strong passions—" He hesitated again. "And not easily put off his course. He is the kind who might well start a new war simply to ease his own wounded pride."

This was unsettling, and confirmed Elizabeth's worst fears. "Then our debt to you and Miss Somerville can hardly be repaid."

Pickering touched his hand to his hat, and bowed. "Please do not speak of it," he said. "Now, I am sure you have matters to discuss with your family. If I may wish you good evening . . ."

Elizabeth stood for a moment, watching the line of his back until he had disappeared into the dark of the quarterdeck. Her mind was racing in strange directions, toward Montréal and the gallows that would go untested, and then onward to Québec, where Giselle Somerville waited for her bridegroom and Will Spencer waited for them all. She went to join her party at the rail, her mind preoccupied. As she approached, their conversation stopped.

"Am I interrupting?"

Robbie's hand found her shoulder and squeezed lightly. "Yer bonnie face is verra welcome, lassie. But have ye tired o' Nathaniel already?"

"Hannah needed some time alone with her father."

"Aye, faithers and dauchters," said Robbie. "Nathaniel is a verra fortunate man."

Elizabeth felt Hawkeye's gaze on her, and she realized how very much she had missed him, and what a comfort his calm silence could be. She touched his sleeve.

"I have learned something on this journey."

He smiled. "And what's that?"

"What a fortunate woman I am." She wanted to say the rest of it, to tell all three of them how glad she was to have them around her, but she was still too much an Englishwoman for that kind of public sentiment. Instead, she said, "It seems that Giselle Somerville and her father have not parted on good terms. Pickering tells me that it was Giselle who engaged him to bring you away from Montréal."

Runs-from-Bears' head came up. "Ain't she the one who held up Otter for so long?"

"Aye, she's the one," said Hawkeye.

"We are indebted to her," said Elizabeth. "Whatever her history." *With my husband,* she might have added, but even unspoken she thought it had been clearly heard.

"Ye mustna judge her too harshly, lass." Robbie's tone was almost apologetic.

Elizabeth turned to him in surprise. "I do not judge her at all, I assure you. Miss Somerville's marriage and how she came to it is no business of mine. I am thankful for her part in getting the three of you out of Montréal. No more or less than that." But it was not completely true; she was curious now more than ever about Giselle Somerville, and uneasy that they should be in her debt.

There was silence for a long minute. The rigging whistled and clanked with the wind; on the quarterdeck there were low voices, the hiss of flame set to wick, and the sharp smell of tobacco. They had spent a happy few hours crowded around Captain Pickering's table, but now all of the cheerful high spirits of their reunion had been replaced with something more thoughtful. Elizabeth tried to catch Hawkeye's eye, but he was looking out over the water.

"Is there something else wrong?" she asked.

Hawkeye shifted. "Bears wants to set off overland for Lake in the Clouds," he said. "He could be there in two weeks, maybe less."

Elizabeth searched out Runs-from-Bears' face in the dark, but could make nothing of his expression. "You are worried for them."

He nodded. "We've been away a long time."

"Well, then," Elizabeth said calmly. "When will you go?"

"I'll wait until you find passage out of Québec."

She drew up. "Passage? But I thought we had passage—" She gestured around herself feebly.

Robbie coughed into his hand. "We didna like tae talk o' it before the bairns," he said. "But Pickering

canna take us aa the way hame, lass. The *Isis* will be waitin' for him in Québec, and he mun sail wi'oot delay for Scotland."

Elizabeth leaned on the rail. She was thankful for the dark, for she feared she could not keep her anxiety from her face.

"But they'll be looking for us in Québec, too."

"I expect that's true," Hawkeye said. "But there must be seventy or more boats in port there at this time of year. They won't be too fussy about passengers as long as the fare's right. Moncrieff has been there a whole day, he'll be sniffing around already for us."

"Moncrieff again," said Elizabeth, pulling her shawl more tightly around her shoulders. "Is there no getting away from the man?"

Robbie snorted softly. "He's aye hard tae avoid."

Runs-from-Bears said, "It looks like he's done you more than one good turn."

"Oh, that he has." Hawkeye nodded. "And I expect we'll have to put up with a few more before he sails for home."

"That the Earl of Carryck's influence reaches so far surprises me," said Elizabeth thoughtfully.

"Ye dinna trust the man, it's clear."

"I suppose that I do not," Elizabeth admitted. "But I do not know him as you do, having spent so much time with him at close quarters." She hesitated. "You're not reconsidering the earl's proposal?"

Hawkeye grunted. "Got no interest in anything but getting this family home to Lake in the Clouds as quick as we can manage."

Elizabeth pushed out a sigh. "That is good to know," she said. "The next task is to find Will Spencer and send him back to Amanda straightaway."

There was the sound of a new step on deck, and Nathaniel appeared from Pickering's quarters. He crooked a finger in her direction, and then disappeared again.

"Time enough to worry about this Will Spencer tomorrow," said Hawkeye gruffly. "You've got a homecoming of your own to celebrate."

Elizabeth was glad of the dark, for she knew very well that she was flushing, both with anticipation and embarrassment. "But where will you sleep?"

"The hammocks," said Robbie.

"Under the stars." Runs-from-Bears was grinning; she could hear it in his voice.

"But if it rains—"

Hawkeye pushed her gently toward Nathaniel. "Then we'll bed down with Pickering and his crew. Go on now, he's waiting for you."

The first officer's cabin was all they had, just off the captain's quarters where Curiosity slept with the children. It smelled of raw sugar and coffee beans, and there was barely room for them to stand shoulder to shoulder without Nathaniel striking his head on the hanging lamp. But there was a small porthole left open for the breeze, a tiny washstand, and a cot. And a door with a lock on it.

Elizabeth turned her face up to him. He might have taken her expression for displeasure, if it weren't for the trembling of her hand in his.

"You're as nervous as a cat, Boots."

"Or a bride," she said, finally managing a smile, and blushing to the roots of her hair. It made his heart clench to see it.

"We were apart on our first wedding anniversary."

"Aye, so we were," he said gently. "We're together now."

There was a creaking overhead; the trill of the bosun's whistle, men moving. In the other room Hannah was talking in her sleep.

"It ain't exactly Paradise." Nathaniel pulled her down to sit beside him on the cot. "But it will have to do."

"Oh, it will do," she said, not quite able to meet his eye. And then, in a rush: "It has been a very long time, Nathaniel."

"So it has." He slipped an arm around her shoulders. "You'll have to remind me how to start."

She laughed then, a low throaty laugh, the very laugh that he thought of as his alone. Under his fingers the skin of her neck was cool to the touch, and as soft as he remembered. He traced the outline of her ear and then her jaw, and then he lifted her face to his and kissed her. A quiet kiss, a coming home very different from those first frantic kisses of a few hours ago. She tasted sweet and tart all at once, and his head filled with the smell of her. But she wasn't quite with him; he could feel the hum of her thoughts just below the surface, moving her in a different direction.

In one motion Nathaniel lifted her and settled her on his lap. The round weight of her, the touch of her breasts against his chest, was enough to make him forget everything, but he made an effort: put his forehead against hers so that she could not look away.

"Are you shy of the close quarters?"

Elizabeth turned to study the door as if she could look through wood to where the children slept. Then she spread her hand out on Nathaniel's cheek. "No," she said. "I expect we can . . . manage quietly. We've been in close quarters before, after all." He could see her struggling for her composure, and he might have laughed out loud at the pleasure of seeing her flustered. But there was the worry line between her brows that he knew well.

"Then tell me what's on your mind, Boots. What's wrong?"

She narrowed her eyes at him. "You can't be serious."

Nathaniel kissed her, a hard stamp of his mouth. "I know you, Elizabeth. I know you as well as I know anybody pulling breath. There's something else up, and it ain't just getting out of Canada with our hides intact."

Her fingers began to pull at the ties on his shirt. Elizabeth wiggled slightly on his lap, her color rising. "Is it really talking that you want to do right now, Nathaniel Bonner?" And she tilted her head and kissed him, a soft deep kiss that made the blood rush in his ears.

What he wanted was to lay her down on the narrow cot and to cover her, bury himself in her and stay there forever. Above all of that, what he wanted most in the world was to take away the worried look in her eyes.

But she would have her way; she hushed him, twisting out of her clothing piece by piece until she stood before him in her shift and stockings. Her hair had come undone, a tangle of curls around her face. He took the hem of her shift to lift it over her head, untied one garter and then the other to drag the stockings down over the white skin of her calves. She lifted her feet for him in turn and then stood in the vee of his legs covered in nothing but gooseflesh. Childbearing had changed her shape, marked her for a mother; her hands fluttered up as if to hide the tracings on her belly and he caught them, held them away.

"You know me better," he murmured.

Her breasts were heavier now, her nipples darker, berries not quite ripe. She put her face in his hair, her breath harsh at his ear as he leaned forward. The touch of his tongue drew a single drop of milk and a sigh. He might have pulled away but her hand guided him back, offering freely what he hesitated to take. Nathaniel cupped her hips, pressed his fingers into rounded flesh while he suckled, wide mouthed, both of them convulsing with the sweetness of it. She trembled so that he thought she might fall, her knees buckling until she was on his lap again.

"There is a grave inequity here," she muttered, plucking at his shirt. "Will you not undress?"

"There's no hurry." Nathaniel laughed against her

mouth, because it was a lie; he had never been in such a hurry in his life, but still he would not be rushed.

"It is very strange to see you in breeches." Cool fingers at his crotch, tracing him. "Leggings and a breech-clout suit you better."

He drew in a sharp breath and caught her hand up to bite her palm. Then he stood to pull his shirt over his head and stripped down.

There was too little room on the cot: they were all elbows and knees, awkward until he found her mouth again and they lay for a long time on their sides, kissing; the kind of kiss that had no end and doubled back on itself. Struggling to slow the rush of his blood, covered with sweat and the sweet stickiness of her milk, Nathaniel stroked her thighs, felt her quiver and quicken, sought out softly swollen flesh slippery to the touch.

"Are you still tender?" He touched her and she shivered.

"Yes. No. I am healed, but—"

"Do you want me to stop?"

"No!" She caught his hand, pressed it hard. "Don't stop." This against his neck, hardly more than a whisper. "Nathaniel?"

His fingers busier now, coaxing from her those words she found so hard to give. "What?"

She grabbed his face, dragged it to her own. Gentle suckling and then harder, showing him what she wanted, thrusting her tongue against his. He cupped the saddle of warm flesh between her legs. His own flesh leaped in response, barely under his control.

"I missed you." She whispered against his mouth, harsh and gentle all at once. She was crying, dripping milk and tears and salty moisture over him, drawing him in like the sea. "I missed you."

"God knows I missed you too, Boots. The thought of you like this kept me sane all those weeks."

She wound her fingers in his hair, tugged hard. "Come to me now. Come to me. I want you, I want this." Her legs sliding up and around him, living ropes: another kind of bondage, and one that he came to gladly.

Elizabeth drifted up out of a deep sleep, aware first of the weight of Nathaniel's leg over her own, and the cool breeze from the porthole on damp flesh. Up on deck the watch was changing, but it was Curiosity's voice that woke her. She was crooning to the twins. Elizabeth's own body told her that they would soon need more than soft words.

She turned her head, hungry still for the sight of Nathaniel. In the vague light from the porthole she watched him sleep, resisting the strong urge to put her hands on him and convince herself that he was alive and well, that the tingling of her flesh was more than just a dream.

He cracked an eye at her. "I can hear you thinking, Boots."

Caught out again. She felt herself blushing. "So you always claim." And struck his roving hand away, pulling the blanket up around her shoulders.

Nathaniel came up on one arm to catch her wrist: his strong hands, broad and hard and warm and capable of the softest touch, enough to set her blood humming again. His eyes burning gold in the faint moonlight, the power of his wanting enough to turn her purpose and make her forget everything but the heat in her bones.

"Had enough of me already?"

From the other room, a hungry wail. "Never," she said, her voice wavering. "But I'm afraid you'll have to wait your turn. That is your son calling . . . and your younger daughter, too."

He let her go to reach for his breeches, grinning at

her over his shoulder as he pulled them on, her wolfish husband, teeth flashing white. "Wait here."

"Curiosity will bring them," Elizabeth protested, but he was already halfway out the door.

Alone for a moment, she tried to set the cot to rights, smoothing the rumpled covers and damp sheets. There was no telling what trouble this day might bring; she was tired and more than a little sore from the intensity of Nathaniel's attentions; she could not remember being happier. Aunt Merriweather would not approve or even understand, but it was simple enough: she was in love with her husband, and she had him back again.

Nathaniel appeared at the door with two squirming babies firmly in arm. Elizabeth accepted them, murmuring calm words. She leaned back against the paneled wall and let the children settle down to nursing while Nathaniel busied himself lighting the lamp. Then he came to kneel next to the cot and watch, his chin on his hands and his face in shadow.

"You don't get much sleep, I guess."

Elizabeth looked up in surprise. "They have quieted a great deal this sennight past. Lily often sleeps through the night, now. Or at least until the dawn."

Nathaniel touched one curly head and then the other. "I wondered if I'd ever see them again."

"You're not sorry I brought them so far?"

"No," he said, moving in closer to study Daniel's hand, kneading the white skin of her breast. "I ain't in the least sorry."

"Nathaniel," Elizabeth began slowly. "There is something I need to talk to you about."

He sent her a sliding glance. "I thought so. Well, come on out with it, Boots."

Elizabeth pulled the blanket up tighter around the twins, cleared her throat, and then met his eye.

"Before I knew that you were on board the *Nancy,* I made arrangements to have another boat meet us this

evening, just north of Montréal. I thought we should have to have some means of getting away, and I feared that Captain Pickering could not be trusted with the whole truth."

"That makes sense," said Nathaniel. "But how did you think to get us out of gaol to start with?"

She shrugged. "I was hoping that diplomacy might be enough, with Will's help." Daniel was paddling his feet against her abdomen, and she winced as she shifted him. "But Captain Pickering gives me to believe that Somerville would have hung you in any case."

"Aye, well. Pink George is a fool. Carleton might have been more reasonable, but we'll never know." Nathaniel smoothed a curl away from her face. "So you found a boat with a willing captain . . ."

She nodded, her gaze fixed firmly on Lily, who was slipping off to sleep again. "Yes. And I paid him half, as a deposit. To be sure of his cooperation."

"If that's the case, then I don't see that there's much to worry about—we won't show up, but he's got money in his purse, and he's no the worse for wear. Even if he wanted to go to Somerville with his story, he doesn't know where to look for us. What's his name?"

"Stoker."

The focus of his gaze sharpened suddenly. "Stoker! Why Mac Stoker, of all people?"

"Captain Mudge introduced us."

Nathaniel grunted. "I would have thought Grievous Mudge would have more good sense than that."

Now she flushed with irritation, and was glad of this new kind of energy. "Until Pickering sought me out, the *Jackdaw* was the only hope we had to get to Montréal today. Time was of the essence. I did the best I could, Nathaniel."

His expression cleared suddenly. "I know that, Boots. Christ, I know that." And with a sideways glance: "Did he try to put his hands on you?"

"No!" Elizabeth's head snapped up. "He was rude,

but did me no harm. I went to see him just before we sailed. He took the money, and told me where we would find him tonight. And that's all there was to it."

"I'll guess he drove a pretty hard bargain."

Daniel gulped out of rhythm and coughed, sputtering milk. Lily, already asleep, began to twist her face into a knot at the sudden disturbance.

"Let me," Nathaniel murmured, leaning in to gather Lily up close to his chest so that Elizabeth could deal with Daniel. When the babies were quiet, Nathaniel said: "Mac Stoker ain't the kind to think of paying back money he hasn't earned, and he's not about to go calling on the Crown. He'll spend the silver and forget all about it." He turned to examine Lily's sleeping face in the light of the hanging lantern.

Against the dark heart of the night, the porthole was as round as a coin. Silver coin; yes. A handful of silver coins paid for passage, and she had left the *Jackdaw* so proud of herself and how she managed Mac Stoker that she never even realized that the chain she wore around her neck was gone. Someone had cut the chain as neatly as any London pickpocket, and not even Runs-from-Bears had noticed.

But sooner or later Nathaniel would see that it was gone. If only she had listened to Bears and stayed away from Stoker; but she had let her fear get the best of her common sense. Perhaps men were right and women were not capable of rational thought; perhaps she knew herself not at all. *Let Mac Stoker be satisfied with money for work never done and with a single gold coin.* A strange prayer, and one she feared would not be heard. A man like Stoker was rarely satisfied once the smell of gold was in his nose.

"Elizabeth." Curiosity was at the door, the long plaits running over her shoulders like dark rivers shot through with silver. "Let me put those babies down again," she whispered. "So you two can get some

sleep." The keen brown gaze missed nothing, not the state of the bed or the flush that still mottled Elizabeth's breast or the bite marks on Nathaniel's shoulder, but she simply took the sleeping babies and slipped away.

When the door had closed behind Curiosity, Nathaniel put out the light and dropped his breeches. There was enough moonlight to show her the long flat muscles of his thighs and the intensity of his purpose; it was dark enough so that she could burn bright with the knowledge of her own reckless actions and he would take it for modesty, and for passion. At least that much was real; there was a stirring deep in her belly at the sight of him, as sharp and bright as the single silver earring that sparked against the dark column of his neck.

"So, Boots," he said, one finger moving up the slope of her calf so that her toes curled tight. "Now that you've got that confession off your chest, tell me, is it sleep you've got on your mind, or the lack of it?"

It was midmorning before the *Nancy* sailed into the narrowing of the St. Lawrence that would take them into port at Québec. Even belowdecks the bosun's raised voice could be heard as he sent the crew scrambling to shift sails.

Because they could not show their faces on deck in a port crowded with the king's soldiers and excisemen, the Bonner party stood at the transom windows in Pickering's quarters, watching the traffic on the river. More masts and sails than could be counted; barks and schooners, two frigates, sloops and cutters, merchantmen and whaleboats, private packets, bateaux and canoes, some of them big enough to seat twenty men. Many of them were Royal Navy vessels, which made Elizabeth glad of the heavy draperies that could be pulled shut; she did not like to look very long at the

harbor, which had the feel of a carnival just barely in control.

Curiosity juggled Lily to a more suitable spot on her shoulder and shook her head at the sight of it. "I thought sailors was supposed to be tidy-minded."

Hawkeye snorted softly. "You'll see precious little tidy about Québec at the beginning of the season. The North West Company is just gearing up for the trek to Grand Portage—in another week they'll be off for Lachine and this place will seem like a nunnery. Not that we'll see it."

"Look," said Hannah, pointing to the long dock that seemed to be their destination. Boatworks and a storehouse of brick, all belonging to Forbes & Son Enterprises. The dock itself was dominated by a three-masted merchant ship, square-rigged, newly painted, carved and gilded on every surface. A merchantman, as bright and beautiful a ship as Elizabeth had ever seen.

Hannah said, "Isn't that Captain Pickering's ship? Do you see? The figurehead he told us about, the Lass in Green."

"So it is," said Nathaniel. "The *Isis*." Elizabeth saw him send Hawkeye a look over the child's head.

"What are all those little clapboard windows?" Hannah carried on.

"Gunports," said Robbie. "She's armed tae the teeth, is the *Isis*. Ye see, lass, she carries a valuable cargo but she doesna always sail in convoy as do most o' the merchantmen. She's broad bottomed for cargo, and square-rigged, too—that means that she canna run verra fast, and so she mun be able to protect hersel', for there are privateers enough on the seas these days and a new war wi' France, forbye."

Overhead a great shuffling and Pickering's voice raised in a series of quick orders, the groan of chains and a splash as the last anchors were dropped. A calling

of voices from the wharf to the quarterdeck, and back
again.

"Look, Elizabeth, your cousin Will." Hannah tugged
at her sleeve.

"Yes," said Elizabeth, heaving a great sigh. "Thank
heavens." And then she saw that Will was not alone. A
lady waited on the dock beside him. She wore a round
gown of Mantua silk the color of green pippins, with a
long emerald-green sash. A matching cape billowed in
the wind, and with one gloved hand she held down a
straw-colored gipsy hat tilted to expose coiled dark
blond hair. It was tied under her chin with a silk handkerchief the same color as her sash. The cost of the silk
alone would have paid a sailor for two years. Elizabeth
could not make out the lady's face, but the tension in
Nathaniel's hand on her shoulder told her what she already suspected.

Hannah tugged on Elizabeth's sleeve. "Who is that?"

"That is Miss Somerville," Elizabeth said calmly. She
smiled at Nathaniel, wanting him to see that she was not
worried, or even curious. At least the first was true, but
she did not know if she could convince him of that. "Will
accompanied her here to Québec as a favor to her father."

"She looks a very fine sort of lady to be out among
the boats," said Hannah, taking Miss Somerville's
measure. Elizabeth wondered how much she had heard
about Giselle's history.

Curiosity clicked softly with her tongue. "You remember, child. Pickering told us about Miss Somerville.
They're set to marry, and soon." A sliding glance to
Elizabeth and her mouth turned down at one corner;
Curiosity knew, if Hannah didn't, but Curiosity was not
the kind to judge a woman harshly on the strength of
men's stories.

"Will we get to meet her?" asked Hannah.

"I doubt it," said Nathaniel. "She'll have other
things on her mind."

And so will we, added Elizabeth to herself, for she had caught sight of a schooner, moving fast on the water. Not nearly so fine a vessel as the *Isis,* far smaller and in need of paint. On deck stood her captain with a long glass in his hand. The *Jackdaw.*

Runs-from-Bears caught Elizabeth's eye, and raised a shoulder in a question she could not answer.

12

My dearest Husband Galileo Freeman,

Runs-from-Bears leaves for home shortly and he will fetch this letter to you. God grant we follow, and not long after. We hope to sail to-morrow, in what ship we don't know yet, to what port we ain't yet sure, but Hawkeye and Nathaniel are firm in their faith that it can be managed. Bears will tell you the story of how we came to be in this frenchified place, as it is too long and tiresome a tale to put down on paper.

To the Judge word that his grandchildren are in rude good health. His daughter's spirits have come up too since she has Nathaniel with her again. Little Hannah bids me tell you that the leather purse you worked for her does good service. She wishes you well as do all our friends here.

My loving greetings to our children. I trust our daughters have not forgot the lye barrel as it is high time to set soap. This year more pumpkin and yellow onion should be put out, for last we ran short. Husband, remember your long under-wear, for all that it itches. Otherwise the night

damp will be sure to bring on your Miseries and I ask you, which is worse?

Your Loving Wife of these Many Years,
Curiosity Freeman
writ by her own hand this Fifth Day of May,
1794
Bas-Québec, on board the Nancy

Dearest Many-Doves,

Nathaniel and Hawkeye are now restored to us in good health, and so I understand very well your joy as your husband comes home to you after so long an absence. Runs-from-Bears will give you all the news that prudence prevents me from putting to paper, but know that we will be with you as soon as it is in our power.

The children thrive, for which we thank Providence and pray the same is true of young Blue-Jay. Hannah bids me tell you and her grandmother that she has learned to bind a sprained ankle and that she is very sorry to have missed the maple festival, and so are we all. I fear she misses you more than she will admit, although the twins are a comfort to her and she takes great interest in everything she sees.

I write to beg you to visit the schoolchildren, or send them word. Summer session will begin as soon as we are returned. To Liam, my fond regards and gentle reminders that he should not neglect his reading, writing, or ciphering while we are gone. I hope to see evidence of his industry and good progress.

Hawkeye, Robbie, and Nathaniel send their greetings and loving affection to you, your mother and brother, as do Curiosity, Hannah,

and I. You are always in our thoughts. With deepest affection

Elizabeth Middleton Bonner
5th of May in the Year 1794
Québec

Dear Liam,

I have never writ a letter before but Elizabeth helps me write one now to you, to say that we are soon on our way home. Runs-from-Bears will tell you how it is that my Father and Grandfather and Robbie are free. It is a good story.

On the long carry to the big lake we passed a sawmill. There was a man strung up from a dead oak and his hands struck off, we could not ask for what crime. Robbie's red dog Treenie is dead. A soldier shot her. It made Elizabeth gey sad, but this morning her cousin Will Spencer sought us out. That has been a relief to her, I think.

My little brother and sister are in health, and so are all of us, except Curiosity, who has caught a cold in her chest. She says it is Canada at fault, for no reasonable place should have such a cold, damp spring.

I wonder if you took that bear yet and if you hunt with my uncle Otter. If your leg is bothersome you might ask my Grandmother for a poultice. If I was there I would bind it for you.

We have met a man called Hakim, which means Doctor. He wrote his whole name down for me on a scrap of paper, it is Hakim Ibrahim Dehlavi ibn Abdul Rahman Balkhi. He comes from India where I think they must know very much about healing. He is a surgeon on a great ship called the *Isis*, which sails tomorrow for Scotland. His skin is not so brown as Curiosity's

and not so red as mine. I think my Grandmother
would like to meet him. I wish that you could,
too.

Your Friend Hannah Bonner,
also called Squirrel by the Kahnyen'kehàka
of the Wolf Longhouse, her mother's people

13

Across the river from the cliffs that served as a natural palisade for Québec's upper city, the voyageurs and fur traders had established a town of their own, and it had an Indian heart. Even before Nathaniel and Hawkeye and Runs-from-Bears had managed to best the tide and the ice floes and get the canoe to shore, the sound of drums came across the water. For Hannah it was like a homecoming.

They beached the borrowed canoe on a grassy slope where fifty others like it dried in the afternoon sun. Hawkeye hired a Huron boy to watch over it and Hannah followed the men into the confusion, her hand firmly in her father's and Runs-from-Bears walking behind her. Her attention shifted constantly, for there was a great lot to see, and she wanted to remember it all to tell to Elizabeth and Curiosity.

The North West Company was hiring for the Montréal brigade, looking for voyageurs to paddle their cargo canoes inward to the great lakes. There they would meet the trappers who came out of the northern forests with beaver and mink and fisher furs. Hannah wondered if someday she would see the great white north. She would not mind hard paddling, if it took her someplace worth seeing. But

there were no women around the man in dirty nankeen breeches and a rusty leather jerkin who was doing the hiring. He was talking in a big voice to a crowd of Abenaki and Cree in a combination of English and French and *Atirondaks;* it was a language stripped to the bone, just enough to conduct business: money and distances to be covered, rations of pemmican and pea-and-pork soup. Hannah had never seen any Cree before, although she had heard stories. Her father tugged on her hand before she could make out very much about them beyond the earbobs of silver in large circular shapes.

They walked past men and women with wares spread out on blankets: breeches and leggings, shirts of red-checked cotton, dull homespun, butter-yellow deerskin; hard-tack, venison jerky, and cakes of maple sugar; dried sausages as wide around as a man's wrist, but harder; bundled tobacco and stubby clay pipes to smoke it with. A woman of mixed blood with one eye as milky white as a wampum bead crouched before bowls of dried cranberries and blackberries, stringing them onto long threads.

Now and then someone would call out to them, raising an arm in greeting: *long time no see,* or *by the Christ you're far from home!* But they did not stop to talk or even slow down. Hannah could feel her father's urgency in the way he held on to her hand. So far they had seen one redcoat, but he had been arguing over the cost of a ragged bundle of second-grade beaver pelts and hadn't taken any note of them. They were counting on the crowd, and on the voyageurs' dislike of the English, to keep them out of trouble.

They passed an Abenaki camp where some boys not much older than Liam were roasting a dog over a smoky, spitting fire of green wood. One of them looked at her hard; he had a nose ring that shimmered against his upper lip and a panther tattoo on his forehead. She looked away and still felt his gaze like a stick prodding at her ribs.

Then Bears' hand on her shoulder pointed her toward a small camp under an outcropping of cliff. And there they were, her mother's people. Ten or twelve traders, all of them hunters but warriors, too, their scalps shaved clean around topknots shiny with bear grease. They were from Kayen'tiho, the village to the south of Montréal where Stone-Splitter was sachem; many of them were Wolf clan, and blood kin. Hannah felt completely safe for the first time since they had come to Sorel, and she wished that they hadn't left the women and babies behind in the protection of Robbie and Will Spencer. Surely they would be better off here than they were in port. This morning Hannah had counted two redcoats for every five men out of uniform from her perch on the window seat in the transom.

They were given corn soup in hollow gourds. Hannah ate and listened while the men talked first of family, of the hunting season, the season's trapping and how much money the furs were fetching, and whether it was worth the long trek to Albany for better prices. When those formalities were done, heads bent close together and newer stories were told, and nothing held back. All the men made a natural circle around her grandfather as he talked. Somerville, the gaol, the fire, the young man called Luke, butchers and farmers, Wee Iona . . . Hannah followed the flow of the story again and the comforting rhythm of her grandfather's voice wove itself into a cradle that she could not resist. She fell asleep and woke with a start just a few minutes later to find the youngest son of Spotted-Fox standing over her.

He was gnawing on a knucklebone, his face glistening with fat. His belly had the last roundness of a younger child, but there was a quickness to his eyes. His nose wrinkled as if she smelled bad, and his eyes trailed over her dress of spotted calico.

"You look like one of the People, but you dress like an O'seronni," he said in Kahnyen'kehàka, as if to test her.

In the same language she answered him, "My grand-mother is Made-of-Bones who is *Kanistenha* of the Wolf longhouse where you were born. Don't you re-member me, Little-Kettle? I'm Squirrel. I wiped your nose for you more than once a few winters ago."

He flushed. "Aya. You have your grandmother's sharp tongue." And then, after a look over his shoulder to the circle of men around the fire, he said, "Come. There are things to see."

Hannah's hesitation lasted only for a few heartbeats. For as long as it took for him to challenge her with his eyes: was she one of the Real People, or was she O'seronni?

She followed Little-Kettle into the crowds.

No one took note of them, two red-skinned children among so many. Neither of them had a coin to spend and so they skirted the cook fires where pinfeathers filled the hot air and hungry men bought corn bread and squash stew and blackened duck on long skewers, sprinkled with pepper and maple sugar. For a shilling a Cree woman in a curious cape and hood painted with designs in red and black would cut a hissing slice of venison from a spit, to be juggled from hand to hand and eaten hot enough to scorch the mouth.

On a trampled spot under a triangle of wild plum trees in first blossom people crowded around to watch a man with bloody fists take on all comers. Little-Kettle's eyes grew, but the smell of cheap rum was heavy in the air and Hannah pulled him away, ill at ease. They stayed longer to watch the Huron playing *Guskä'eh*, polished peach-stones rolled in a wooden bowl: white, black, white, black. Four of either at once and coins shifted from one dusty pile to another. But here too the smell of liquor could not be ignored, and Hannah began to think of her father, and to look around herself for the quickest way back to the Kahnyen'kehàka camp.

Little-Kettle had wandered off to look at a man who sat on a shabby blanket.

"Moccasins," the man called out to anyone who passed. "Fine buckskin moccasins. Cured 'em myself."

"Look at him," whispered Little-Kettle. "The Huron must have done that to him."

Hannah looked. Clumps of dark hair streaked white and pulled back in an uneven queue, as if to show off his ears, or what remained of them. They had been notched hard, leaving behind nothing more than frayed strips. It was true that before the priests had got the best of the Huron they had been known to take ears and fingers and more from their war prisoners, but this man had a brand on his cheek, a crooked *t* faded to a bright pink against his graying stubble.

"Not the Huron," she said.

He had the look of the wanderers about him, the ones who had never found a place to settle after the war, too much a colonist for England, too American for Canada, and not welcome anymore by Yankee or Yorker. She had heard the stories around the hearth in Anna's trading post, how loyalists had been stripped of their property and turned out to make their way to the Crown's protection in Canada, or starve. Tar and feathers, split noses and jugged ears and white-hot branding irons. Or worse, if you were a woman. They were soldier's tales and never meant for little girls to hear, but Hannah always had a talent for making herself small and listening hard, and she forgot very little.

She looked at his ruined face and at his moccasins: lopsided, the leather poorly cured, uneven in color and pieced so badly that no woman would claim such work. He made her uneasy, but his moccasins made her sad.

"He's a Tory," she told Little-Kettle, already turning away. Hannah used the Kahnyen'kehàka word for Englishmen, *Tyorhenhshàka*.

But the man's head snapped around toward her as if

she had called his name. He squinted in the sunlight
and his eyes were as brittle and shiny as rocks heated
red hot again and again.

"Wahtahkwiyo," he croaked. *Good shoes.* The hair
rose on the nape of Hannah's neck and all along her
spine there was a sparking, but she could not walk
away as she knew she must; he had used her language
and pinned her to the ground with it.

He laughed, his tongue a pale pink snake among
blackened stumps. "Come along, then, missy," he
hissed, in English now. "Don't run away. Buckskin
moccasins. Took the hides myself, down Barktown way.
Your corner of the world, by the sound of you. Two big
Mohawk bucks, oh yes. Maybe your kin, eh? One of
'em had a turtle tattoo on his cheek. He looked something like you, so he did."

Little-Kettle had no English and he opened his
mouth to ask her what it meant, the look on her face.
But Hannah grabbed him by the shirt and dragged him
away. The man's laughter clung to them like smoke
from an unholy fire.

It was late afternoon when they started back to the
Nancy. Hannah slipped into the canoe between her father and Bears, and wrapped herself in the striped blanket they had bought for her, glad of its prickly warmth:
the wind was coming up cold, setting the new leaves on
the oaks that surrounded the Cree lodge to shivering.

The blanket was well woven, but still Hannah could
not quite stop shaking. She wanted to talk to her father,
but he was so far away from her and his worry so close
to the surface. She didn't know if she had the right
words, anyway. *Are men so cruel?* she wanted to ask
him, but she feared his answer. She hugged her knees to
her chin and stared at her moccasins, worn thin now
across the toes. Last fall she had helped her grand-

mother cure the hide, and then she had pieced and sewn them under Many-Doves' careful eye. They were lined with the fell of a rabbit she had snared herself. The beadwork was uneven, but she had been very proud of them when they were done. Hannah tucked her feet harder under herself and took her lip between her teeth to keep them from chattering.

The *Nancy* and the *Isis* were docked side by side like a hen and chick. Hannah stared hard at the *Nancy* but could make out nothing behind the transom windows, where Elizabeth and Curiosity would most certainly be sitting with the babies. She wanted to climb onto a lap where she could be sure of a calm voice and a close ear and no one would remind her of her age or her color. Maybe words would come to her then, and she could let them go in a flood and wash the trouble out of her head.

In mid-river a boat—a *ship,* Hannah corrected herself—crossed their path. It had two masts, and was running slow with only some of the smaller sails up. This close, Hannah had a view of the Royal Navy that surprised her. Captain Pickering's crew had been well dressed in neat jackets and breeches, but here were men in blue coats faced with scarlet and trimmed with gold braid, the late sun sparking off gilt buttons. Even a young sailor up in the rigging wore a gaudy red neckerchief, a blue jacket over a checked shirt, and loose, red-striped trousers. He reminded her of the juggler she had seen once at a fair in Johnstown, tossing balls in a circle in the air. It was almost enough to lift her spirits, if it hadn't been for the officer—she thought he must be an officer, for his uniform was even frillier than the others, and there was a great deal of gold looping and lace on his hat—staring down at them from the quarterdeck.

Her grandfather made a clicking sound with his mouth and all three of the men lifted their paddles while they rode out the wake, the fragile canoe heaving beneath them. And the little officer with the silly hat

still watched, his head craning around as the ship slid past. Behind her Hannah could feel her father's tension spiral up and then fall off when the man finally looked away, blank-faced.

One of Hannah's plaits had come undone, and the wind whipped her hair against her cheek. She glanced at her father over her shoulder and saw his expression, somber with worry. And just a few canoe lengths behind them, a whaleboat full of redcoats, rowing hard.

Hannah's throat closed in fear. She turned farther and half rose from her crouch, one hand coming up to point out to her father what he must see for himself. His face came alive with surprise and he opened his mouth to shout—*sit down!*—but the wake from the ship was still strong and she had already lost her balance. The canoe rocked hard once and then again, water sloshing up. Hannah slipped over the side into the icy river without a cry.

He had her by the collar as soon as she came up, lifted her sputtering into the still-rocking canoe as if she weighed no more than a trout. Bears' face like thunder, and her father angry, oh, he was angry: she knew the look although she had not seen it often. But she could do nothing but cough and cough and then she began to shake; she couldn't remember ever being so cold. With some separate part of her mind she saw that her nails were tinged blue and understood what that meant. Her father was wrapping the blanket around her, his anger softening into more worry. She heard her grandfather's voice but could make no sense of the words.

But she heard the redcoats. They were laughing, round hats bobbing as they rowed by.

"Good fishing, eh?" shouted one of them.

"A tasty morsel, that!" And a roar of laughter.

Hannah put her head down on her knees and willed her tears away.

·   ·   ·

"If I have understood you correctly, cousin," said Will Spencer, closely examining Daniel's sleeping face, "you have two ways of quitting Québec immediately. The first is to travel by canoe with the Mohawk, if that can be arranged. The second is to sail on to Halifax with the *Isis* and look for passage to Boston or New-York from there."

Elizabeth had been pacing up and down with Lily, who was finally settling after a difficult day, but she stopped and considered her cousin. Will was intelligent and rational and completely worthy of her trust. He had come far for their benefit and risked much. His good name and negotiation skills had never been put to the test, but his journey to Montréal had taken a good end anyway: Somerville had proven too politically astute—or too cowardly—to accuse a fellow peer of complicity in a gaol break. And if Will had the misfortune to be distantly related to a backwoods American fugitive, he was also the only son of the chief justice of the King's Bench. Somerville had not only sent him on his way, he had also asked Will to chaperone his daughter on the first leg of her journey to her new life.

The sight of her cousin's husband in good health was the best that the day had afforded thus far; Elizabeth was inclined not to burden him with more of their difficulties, and simply to send him to join Amanda. But she also knew that Will would be satisfied with nothing but candor.

"There is also the possibility that Mr. Moncrieff will arrange passage for us," she said, bringing up a name that they had not yet discussed. "A friend of Pickering's. He was arrested with our three and released the morning of the day that they . . . got out of Montréal. Pickering tells us that he is hard at work at it, although we have not yet seen him."

Will looked up from his examination of Daniel. "But I have. Seen Moncrieff, I should say. He came to Québec on the *Portsmouth* with me." Something flick-

ered across his face, and then it steadied. "And Miss Somerville, of course."

"Oh, Will," said Elizabeth with a little rush of air. "Do not tell me that you too have fallen under Miss Somerville's spell. Perhaps she is fey, and not quite human at all."

He gave a great hiccup of surprise. "Elizabeth!"

"Don't *Elizabeth* me, Will. Every man who comes in contact with her sacrifices some part of his good common sense—and his heart."

"Is that so?" said Will, one eyebrow arched. "Every man?"

Elizabeth narrowed an eye at him. "Are you infatuated with Giselle Somerville?"

"Of course not." Will laughed. "She could never engage my interests, Elizabeth. Surely you know me that well."

With a sigh of relief, Elizabeth began to pace again. "Well, I am glad to hear it. Now, more important than Giselle Somerville—what did you think of Mr. Moncrieff? Did you trust him?"

With a shrug Will said, "He is Carryck's man, and will have considerable connections here."

From the first officer's cabin where Curiosity had gone to rest there was a fit of coughing. Elizabeth turned in that direction and waited until it had passed. When she was sure that Curiosity did not need her help, she resumed her pacing, which seemed now to have some good effect on Lily. The baby yawned so widely that Elizabeth might have laughed, if she were not trying so hard to get her to settle.

"I did not ask about Carryck, Will. I asked if you mistrusted Moncrieff."

He sighed. "You are not changed at all, Elizabeth. Very well, then, I had only a day with the man. He is not a retiring character."

Lily had finally fallen into a real sleep and Elizabeth eased her gently into the basket, so that it was a mo-

ment before she could turn to her cousin. "Ah. I take it then that his talkativeness set you on guard. He told you then about his theories regarding Hawkeye's parentage?"

Will brought Daniel to her so he could be put down next to his sister. "Yes, he did. He was just out of gaol that morning and highly agitated by the report of the fire and the escape—as was I, of course. I expect that otherwise he would not have been so indiscreet." With one finger he rubbed a scar on his chin that dated from a particularly rousing game of archery when they had been no more than twelve. Elizabeth was taken by a sudden and unexpected swell of homesickness for a time when life had been simpler. Now when she looked at Will he glanced away, as if he had more bad news and did not know where to start.

He said, "You seem very unconcerned by the fact that you may have married into one of the richest lines in Scotland. Carryck is a major shareholder in the East India Company. His personal fleet alone brings in a fortune season by season."

In her relief, Elizabeth laughed out loud. "Is that all? I thought you were about to tell me that Moncrieff was an agent of the king's and on his way here to arrest us all."

"Ah. Then you do not think that Hawkeye is Carryck's heir."

"I did not say that. I think he very well may be. But even so, Hawkeye has not the slightest interest in the connection. And Nathaniel feels as his father does."

That calm gaze was designed to uncover the slightest inconsistency in an opponent's story, and he leveled it at her now. "But what of you, Elizabeth? It would be a far easier life than this one, to be the wife of Carryck's heir. And your son's birthright, as well—I should think it hard to overlook that. Do not look so surprised. This must have occurred to you."

Elizabeth sat down. "But you have surprised me, Will. I may yearn for simplicity, but an easy life has never been my goal. You of all people know that. And as far as my son is concerned—" She looked toward the sleeping children. "He has no need of what Carryck can offer. We Bonners do not put a great deal of value on worldly goods, in case you had not noticed."

"Hmm." Will's gaze flickered toward the bag that he had returned to Elizabeth and Nathaniel earlier in the day. It sat in the clutter of Pickering's desk and might have been full of pebbles, for all the concern that had been shown about it. Elizabeth reached over and took it up, weighed it in her hand.

"I promised to tell you about the gold," she said. "It is a long and quite complicated story."

"Your stories often are, since you came to the Americas."

There was a knock at the door, and Robbie's glowing white hair appeared. In front of him, a head shorter and half his width, was Angus Moncrieff. The dark eyes were sharp in the long, angular face; he cocked his head and put Elizabeth in mind of a magpie on the prowl for shiny things to line its nest.

She slipped the bag of gold into the basket at the babies' feet and tucked the blanket over it.

"Madam," said the Scotsman with a deep bow that made her almost regret her uncharitable thoughts. "It is my verra great honor. I am sorry not to find your guidman and his father with you."

There was a great rush of footsteps from the deck.

Elizabeth said, "Your timing is very good, Mr. Moncrieff. I believe that must be them now."

But it was Captain Pickering, who came with news of a mishap with the canoe. He had seen it from the quarterdeck, where he had been in conversation with his first officer. In a sparse few sentences he let them

know what had happened. His tone was calm, but Elizabeth saw considerable alarm in his expression.

"The cabin boy is on his way with more blankets," he said. "Shall I send for my surgeon?"

"Perhaps an apothecary," Will suggested.

"Ginger tea," said Robbie. "Ma mither claimed there was nowt better for a sudden chill."

"A hot toddy," suggested Moncrieff.

Curiosity announced her presence at the door with a rap of her knuckles on the paneled wall.

"Men," she summarized with a throaty croak. "Fallin' all over each other on account of a little cold water. The child'll need dry clothes and a warm bed to start with. Mr. Spencer, you free to show your face—be so kind as to go over to the *Isis* and ask that Hakim fellow for any willow bark he can spare, and chamomile, if he got it." She punctuated these orders with a cough smothered in her handkerchief.

Moncrieff and Pickering hesitated, until Curiosity fixed them with her hardest stare.

"Don' you two got talkin' to do somewhere else?"

Moncrieff colored slightly, but the captain only bowed politely.

"Yes, of course. We'll be down one deck, Mrs. Bonner, if anyone should need us."

"There's some news that will be o' interest to your menfolk," Moncrieff added.

Suddenly Curiosity and Elizabeth were alone with the sleeping babies. With a small sigh of relief Elizabeth said, "You think it cannot be so bad?"

Curiosity raised both hands, palms up. "She young, and strong. It ain't exactly good luck, though. Be so kind as to move them things off the bed, Elizabeth, I hear them now."

There were more hurried steps and then Nathaniel and Hawkeye and Runs-from-Bears were filling the cabin. Hannah was in Nathaniel's arms, looking woeful. Her wet hair left a trail of water on the polished floor.

"She's chilled through." He put her down on the bed where she looked suddenly small and very young.

"I'm sorry . . ." Hannah began, but before Elizabeth could say a word Curiosity had sat on the edge of the bed to put a hand on her forehead.

"Now what you got to be sorry about, child? Did you leap out of that canoe on purpose?"

Hannah shook her head and a single tear rolled down her cheek. "It was clumsy of me."

Elizabeth crouched down beside the cot. "Hannah," she said softly. "If you are clumsy then there is no hope for the rest of us. A more graceful child has never been put on this earth." But the dark brown gaze that met her own was so sorrowful Elizabeth wondered if the girl even heard what she had said.

"I'm tired," said Hannah. "And cold."

"We'll get you warm, child. Never fear." Curiosity's voice had the crooning tone she used with any hurt thing.

Hannah's face began to crumple in relief or embarrassment and she turned away to the wall.

Hawkeye raised an eyebrow at Curiosity, as if to ask what he could do, and she fluttered her hands at them all. "Go," she said softly. "Leave her to us."

"Yes, do go," said Elizabeth. "Moncrieff is here."

All three men's heads came up as if she had announced the outbreak of a war. Robbie was grinning broadly. "Wee Angus, aye. Now things will happen."

Nathaniel hesitated after Hawkeye and Robbie had gone. "You'll come find me right away if she asks for me?"

"Of course we will." And then, a hand on his arm to stay him: "What news from the Kahnyen'kehàka?"

He shook his head. "We can't travel with them, Boots. It's too dangerous."

She glanced over her shoulder at Curiosity and Hannah, and then followed Nathaniel out into the narrow passageway. In a low voice that gave away more of

her fear than she would have liked, Elizabeth said, "It is just as dangerous to spend another night in this port."

"Not according to Spotted-Fox. Things are quieter here than they are upriver."

She forced herself to meet his gaze. "Nathaniel, I had thought . . . perhaps you and Hawkeye should travel south with the Kahnyen'kehàka, and Curiosity and I should take the children home by way of—"

"No."

"But—"

"No. I will not leave you."

She put a hand on his arm, pressed hard. "Nathaniel, they could show up here any moment and take you away!"

"Listen to me, Elizabeth. It won't do us any good to rush into more trouble. Tomorrow we'll be gone one way or the other—Moncrieff's got something up his sleeve or he wouldn't be here."

"I do not like this delay, Nathaniel. It makes me uneasy."

He ran a hand over her hair. "It makes us all uneasy. Can you trust me a little longer?"

Her tension deflated suddenly, and she leaned forward to put her forehead against his shoulder, still damp with river water. "I'll trust you until my dying day, Nathaniel. But I cannot help but feel that this is all my fault."

"Stop," he said firmly, his mouth against her ear. "Stop it now, I won't hear it. You just hold tight for a little longer, and let us see to business."

She nodded against his shoulder, suddenly very sleepy. "I miss home."

His arms tightened around her. "I'll get you there as soon as I can, Boots. Let me go talk to Moncrieff, eh? And later I'll come see if I can figure some way to distract you from your homesickness."

"You are incorrigible." She turned to the door but Nathaniel swung her back to him.

"Nathaniel. Let me go to Hannah."

"First tell me what that means, incorrigible."

That look of his would be the undoing of her, his eyes half-hooded and his wanting so clear; with all the trouble and worry he could still manage to make her blood rush. Elizabeth said, "It means you are the most stubborn man ever put on the face of the earth."

"I'll take that as a compliment."

"And the dearest," Elizabeth amended.

"Tell the truth and shame the devil," said Nathaniel, and he let her go with a kiss.

The insides of the *Nancy* were a maze that Nathaniel had only just started to figure out after a day, but after a few tries he managed to find his way down the right hatch and to the long room where the crew took their meals. There his father and Robbie sat across from Moncrieff, who was hunched over a plate of beef.

"How is the lassie?" asked Robbie.

Nathaniel pulled up a chair. "More scared than hurt. Moncrieff, it's good to see you in one piece."

"Angus has just been telling us of his escapades," Hawkeye said, rubbing his eyes.

"Aye, well, there's no shortage of them. We've had a few of our own," said Nathaniel. "I reckon I missed the story of what deprived us of your company in Montréal, so sudden like."

"No mystery there." Moncrieff put down his tankard with a thump. "The *Pembroke* came into port a few days ago with a letter for the Governor from Carryck. The two are well acquaint', ye see. As soon as he learned that the earl has an interest in my welfare, the governor ordered my release," said Moncrieff. "And no' a minute too early."

"He's got a mighty long reach, your Earl of Carryck," said Nathaniel.

Robbie snorted into his tankard. "No' lang enough.

The laird might ha' put in a word for us while he was at it."

Moncrieff narrowed one eye and leaned across the table. "Aye, Rab. And so he would have, but he didna ken, did he? And it's no' like I left ye there to hang, is it?"

"It was Iona wha got us out," said Rob.

"But it was I wha sent Pickering your way."

Rab's jaw worked thoughtfully. "For that, we're endebted tae ye, Angus."

"So we are," agreed Hawkeye.

"Weel, then." Moncrieff grinned at the Bonners over the edge of his tankard. "Perhaps ye'll change your minds and sail hame wi' me to Carryck."

Hawkeye laughed. "You never give up, I'll grant you that, Moncrieff. But your business is done and so is ours. We'll be going home to Lake in the Clouds as fast as we can."

"Amen!" Robbie slapped the table with the flat of his hand. "Speak up, Angus, do ye ken a ship for us, or no?"

Moncrieff tugged on a long ear. "I do," he said. "Listen and I'll tell ye."

Nathaniel found Elizabeth sitting under the transom windows with Squirrel's head bedded in her lap. His daughter was deeply asleep, looking so much like the infant that she once had been that Nathaniel stopped in surprise. She smelled of herbs unfamiliar to him, but bitter and clean. When he touched her face she drew a hitching breath in her sleep and turned her head away. Nathaniel picked her up and settled her on the captain's bed, pausing to draw the blanket over her.

"She worries me," Elizabeth said softly behind him.

"Fever?" Nathaniel put a hand on his daughter's cheek.

"No," Elizabeth said. "It's not that."

"More adventure than she counted on. High time to get her home." With a sigh Nathaniel sat down next to Elizabeth and put an arm around her. "Where is Curiosity?"

"Sleeping. She worries me, too."

He tugged on the long plait that hung over Elizabeth's shoulder. "Curiosity is strong," he said, but got only a reluctant nod in return.

"Should we send for Pickering's surgeon after all?"

"No," Elizabeth said. And then, more thoughtfully, "Not yet."

"Bears could slip over to the *Isis* and have him here in ten minutes."

"Runs-from-Bears isn't here. He's gone back across the river to the Indian camps."

"What?" Hannah stirred and Nathaniel lowered his voice. "Why would he do that?"

Elizabeth was studying the shape of her own hands; it was a sign he knew well. "I'm not sure."

"But you've got an idea, Boots. I can see that without being told."

She met his gaze. "Hannah asked him to go."

He stared at her hard, and she only stared back.

"I don't know what errand she sent him on, Nathaniel, or I would tell you. Will went with him, that is all I can say."

Nathaniel stood to get a better view of the river. The sun was almost down, sending a cloak of reds and yellows over the water. On the other shore cook fires flickered in the dusk. Runs-from-Bears had gone off without a word. He could feel the shape of some new trouble, but he could not put a name to it.

"Maybe I should go after them."

"He said to tell you not to worry."

There was a stirring from the babies' basket. Nathaniel walked to the other side of the room and watched as the twins woke, Lily quite quickly and Daniel with less urgency. Their smells were a comfort: the

sweetness of their sweat, milky breath, the tang of wet winding clothes. For as long as he lived they would need his care and guidance, and he would do his best to give it. He lifted Lily up to tuck her into the crook of his arm, and she stretched and turned against him. Hannah had once been a child like this, her wants simple and predictable; she had come to him when she needed something.

"The best you can do for Hannah right now is to get us on a boat home."

Surprised, he turned toward Elizabeth. "And you accuse me of reading your mind."

She lifted one shoulder, a reluctant smile flickering. "Perhaps it's a talent that can be learned."

He said, "There's a packet sailing tomorrow for Boston."

The look of pure joy and relief on her face was worth whatever the passage would cost.

"You're pleased." He sat down beside her.

"Oh, yes," Elizabeth said, holding out her arms for Lily. "I am very pleased, indeed. An American ship?"

Nathaniel passed the baby over as he told her the little he knew of the *Providence* and its captain.

"Good," she said, producing the first really broad smile he had seen from her in Canada. "Very good news."

"Boots," Nathaniel said, watching her closely. "The *Jackdaw* is hanging around port, and I'm wondering if you have any idea why that might be."

Her smile was gone as suddenly as it came. She busied herself with Lily for a moment, and then she looked up at him, her expression torn between distress and irritation.

"Has he approached you?"

"Mac Stoker? No. Will he?"

"I fear so, yes."

Nathaniel considered for a moment. "I can't help if you don't tell me what's going on, Boots."

A squawk from Daniel, which went ignored for the moment while he let Elizabeth stare at him, a tremor at the corner of her mouth and her eyes narrowed. Color crept up her neck and cheeks. She said, "Very well, if you must know. Stoker knows about the Tory gold. At least, he thinks he knows—he has one of the five-guinea pieces."

He didn't know what he had been expecting, but she had managed to surprise him. "You paid Stoker with gold coin?"

"I am not an idiot, Nathaniel." She was struggling for her composure, and not quite able to meet his eye. "I paid him silver. But as we were coming off the *Jackdaw* one of his men dropped a barrel, there was a lot of confusion . . . I was pushed. I felt nothing at the time, but later I realized that my chain was gone." She touched her throat as if to convince herself that the long silver chain she usually wore hidden inside her bodice was really no longer there. She had worn three things on it: a silver-and-pearl pendant that had once belonged to Nathaniel's mother, a panther tooth, and a single five-guinea piece.

"You needn't say anything, I know very well that I should not have gone to see him, even with Bears. That was bad enough, but to let that gold piece fall into Mac Stoker's hands—"

In one movement she was away with Lily clutched to her breast; Nathaniel caught her by the skirt and pulled her up short. Daniel began to cry in earnest and Lily joined him; Elizabeth rounded on Nathaniel with a furious look. "Let me go!"

But he pulled Elizabeth down next to him, trusting that she would put Lily's needs and distress above her own. Then he retrieved Daniel and held him until Elizabeth could handle both infants, suffering her thunderous expression without comment.

When the babies were settled she said, "Aren't you ever going to *say* anything?"

"You told me not to."

A twitching at the corner of her mouth. "I have never known you to be so compliant."

"I'm just biding my time," Nathaniel said.

"Until I come to my senses." She was wound so tight that the muscles in her jaw jumped and all her bones seemed to come up close to the skin.

"Until you get the better of your hurt pride."

She shuddered then, her expression turning from anger to grief with such suddenness that for a moment Nathaniel could see what she might look like as an old woman, with a will as contentious and sharp as a new blade, her heart as tender and strong as ever.

"Of course my pride is hurt. It was a damnably stupid thing to do." Her eyes sparked a warning, daring him to contradict her. Elizabeth rocked the nursing children tighter against her and narrowed her eyes up at him, waiting.

And she was right, it had been a mistake. She had not intended it, but she had given Mac Stoker some power over them. He knew they had at least some of the Tory gold, he knew they were on the run, and he knew exactly where they were.

"It was bad luck," he said quietly.

She laughed hoarsely and then caught herself up suddenly, blinking hard, and turned her face away. "You are kinder than I deserve."

"Christ, Boots. I couldn't be any harder on you than you are on yourself."

She drew in a deep breath. "All day I have been expecting some word from Stoker and wondering how to handle him."

"He'll be nosing around soon enough, that's true. But there's nothing he can do if he can't find us."

Elizabeth's head came up, her expression much brighter. "Shall we go to the *Providence* straightaway, then?"

He looked out at the shape of the *Isis* in the growing

dark, the vaguely shimmering face of the Lass in Green, ivory and gold and ebony. Candlelight glowed from the Great Cabin, and he could just make out movement there.

"What did you think of Pickering's surgeon when he came by?"

She creased her brow at him. "He seemed knowledgeable, and a gentleman. He spoke kindly to Hannah, and he had a conversation with Curiosity. But he was only here for a short time, Nathaniel, so I really could not say more. Why is it relevant?"

"There's more than Stoker to worry about, Boots."

She waited, one brow raised.

Nathaniel said, "Don't it strike you as strange that Somerville's got every redcoat he can muster looking for us upriver, while things are so quiet around here?"

She let out a harsh laugh. "You are not looking for more trouble?"

"Not exactly on the lookout, no. But expecting more than we've run into. There was a whaleboat full of soldiers on the river—that's what startled Hannah into falling out of the canoe—and they never even looked hard at us."

A thoughtful look came over her. "Well, you were traveling with a child. And you have changed your clothes since you left Montréal."

"You think a change of clothes could hide Robbie MacLachlan in a crowd? Or my father, or me, either? If they're looking for us, they ain't looking very hard. It just don't feel right."

Elizabeth was more herself now that he had given her something to puzzle through. He could almost see the thoughts flying behind her eyes. "Wouldn't Pickering or Moncrieff have heard if the search had been called off?"

"I don't know. The thing is, we can't walk into the garrison and ask if they're looking for us."

"But Will could inquire," Elizabeth said, glancing out of the windows. "If only he would come back."

"Aye, well. In the meantime I was thinking that it's time Pickering's surgeon took a look at Curiosity," said Nathaniel. "See what he can do for that cough of hers. We'll all go."

"But surely the *Providence* would be safer? Perhaps the captain could be persuaded to sail this evening . . ."

Nathaniel shook his head. "I ain't comfortable taking you to the *Providence* until we've had a close look at her. Seems to me that the *Isis*'s our only choice for tonight."

Elizabeth closed her eyes for a moment, and then she nodded. "I'll talk to Curiosity and get the children ready. You'll arrange it with Pickering?"

He nodded. "There's no time to lose, Boots."

"There never is." She cast him a sidelong glance, her color rising again. "There's an old acquaintance of yours on board the *Isis*. We saw her arrive today, with all her baggage."

Nathaniel raised an eyebrow. "There's nobody on the *Isis* who interests me, Boots. It's just a place to spend the night, is all. With you."

"Good," said Elizabeth, her eyes snapping a silver-gray warning at him in spite of her smile. "I am so very glad to hear it."

14

Hawkeye carried Hannah to the *Isis,* but when Robbie offered the same service to Curiosity, she chased him away from her sickbed with a croaking laugh.

"My legs is working just fine," she told him. "It's my chest that ain't cooperating." And she walked down the gangplank straight backed, her basket over one arm and a handkerchief pressed firmly to her mouth. Moncrieff popped up beside her as if to offer his assistance and she sent him scuttling with a single sharp glance.

On any of Québec's streets they would surely have drawn attention to themselves for they made a strange, straggling procession. But the boatyards of Forbes & Sons Enterprises were private, and they had no audience beyond a great yellow slug of moon and the watchmen whose lanterns bobbed around the perimeter of the warehouse like fairy lights. And still the short journey seemed very long indeed, so that against Elizabeth's shoulder Lily might have suddenly doubled in weight.

The *Isis* herself was almost completely dark. Elizabeth was the last to step on board, just behind Nathaniel. Pickering was there to meet them with a few

hushed words of welcome; before she could make out
much about the ship at all they had been hurried down
a companionway. Elizabeth did take note of this: no
simple ladder for the *Isis,* but a proper staircase in a
graceful curve. Under her hand the banister was as
smooth and cool as marble, dark wood polished to a
high gloss, inlaid with ivory in an intricate geometric
pattern.

It turned out that their destination was not the Great
Cabin, which was in the possession of Miss Somerville.
In a whisper Pickering informed them that she had already retired for the evening; Elizabeth tried not to look
relieved to hear this news as she assured the captain
that she did not mind at all. A servant boy waited for
them in a puddle of candlelight. He wore a flat cap with
Isis embroidered on the rim in scarlet, and he opened a
door with a bob that was meant to be a bow.

At first Elizabeth could not quite believe that this
would be the *Isis*'s second-best living quarters. Even
Nathaniel let out a grunt of surprise and Robbie whistled softly under his breath.

"The stateroom," said Pickering. "It serves as a sitting area. There are cabins at each corner, as you see."

Curiosity pivoted on her heel, taking in silk cushions
on built-in sofas, a rosewood spinet, a dining table and
sideboard of highly polished cherrywood. A dozen candles in silver sconces reflected in the mahogany paneling
and a broad expanse of casement windows that opened
onto a gallery. Curiosity fingered the draperies of
damask and brocade, and ran her hand over the matching bolsters and cushions on the window seat. "A hard
life these sailors lead," she muttered.

But Pickering seemed not at all insulted. "The *Isis* often transports persons of some importance, and for extended periods," he explained. "There is an obligation
to make them feel at home. When we had the honor of
escorting the Duchess Dalyrimple to join the duke in

Bengal she had the Great Cabin, of course—but these were her daughter's rooms."

"Then I guess it's about good enough for my grand-children," Hawkeye said dryly. "I don't suppose those Dalypimple girls slept on the floor, did they?"

Robbie laughed out loud and in response Hannah began to stir on Hawkeye's arm. There were a few moments of hushed activity as they moved the children into one of the corner cabins. Hannah disappeared into a feather bed piled high with counterpanes, and there was even an ornately carved cradle large enough for the twins, made up with linen that smelled faintly of laven-der.

When Elizabeth came into the main sitting area, Curiosity was sitting on an elegant bow-backed chair covered in striped silk, studying the stateroom and the cabin boys who had appeared to lay out platters of breads and cold meats. She had little to say but produced a steady wheezing cough that Elizabeth liked not at all. Moncrieff and Robbie had put their heads together in front of a painting of a pack of hunting dogs, but she managed to catch Captain Pickering's eye and direct his attention toward Curiosity.

He cleared his throat. "Mrs. Freeman," he began. "My surgeon sends his regrets that he could not be here to greet you personally, but he has a difficult case that requires all his attention."

Curiosity narrowed one eye suspiciously. "Does he now." The long dark fingers fluttered, as if to indicate that more information would not be unwelcome.

"One of the midshipmen with a splinter lodged in the flesh of his upper arm. It was some days before he thought to seek out attention and I fear it is come away badly infected. Hakim Ibrahim would be very thankful for your consultation on the wound—if it is not too much of an imposition."

"I believe he was planning to drain it this evening,"

added Moncrieff, studying a point on the wall well above Curiosity's head.

She scanned their faces one by one. "I don' know, I truly don't. Do I look so simpleminded? Everybody so eager to send me off to see the Hakim, makin' up stories for me to swallow whole."

Pickering flustered visibly, but Hawkeye laughed.

"Well, Christ, woman," he said. "We could just tie you down to let the doctor have a look at you. Though I expect you'd give us a tussle."

To Elizabeth's relief, Curiosity produced a reluctant smile. "You hardly one to talk, Dan'l Bonner. I remember Cora threatening you with a rope more than once when you was fevered."

"Och, aye," said Robbie, glancing between the two of them. "Ye're gey stubborn, the baith o' ye. P'rhaps ye could open a school for mules once ye're hame agin safe. But today, Curiosity ma dear, ye're fair wabblin' wi' fever. Will ye no' take aid and solace when it's offered in friendship?"

"I do wish you would," added Elizabeth softly. "I am quite worried about you."

Curiosity pushed out a ragged breath and then raised one shoulder in defeat. "All right, then. If it'll set your mind at ease. I suppose it won't hurt me to drink his fever teas though I ain't ever yet seen a doctor who knew anything worth knowing about herbals. . . . Lord knows I'm willing to be surprised. Captain, you'll have to show me the way to this Hakim fellow of yours. Elizabeth, I expect you'll cope without me."

"I'll do my best," Elizabeth agreed, suddenly aware of Nathaniel at her back and his breath on her hair.

"Have ye any objection tae company along the way?" Robbie asked Pickering. "She's a bonnie ship, and I expect we'll ne'er see the like agin."

To Elizabeth's amazement, both Hawkeye and Nathaniel seemed just as interested in the prospect of ex-

ploring the ship. She caught Nathaniel by the sleeve. "You won't go off to the *Providence,* will you—"

"Not until Bears comes back," he promised. The look in his eyes was as warm as his touch. He whispered, then, "Don't go to bed without me." And they were off, leaving her suddenly alone in the splendid cabin.

For a while she simply sat, overwhelmed by fatigue. In another life she might have examined the violin laid to rest in its case on the top of the spinet, the coat of arms above it, or the portraits that lined one wall. A young man in brown velvet with an elaborately curled wig seemed almost to be scowling at her in the flickering of the candlelight. And why not? What was she doing here?

Elizabeth got up and took a turn around the room, her feet sinking into the deep Turkish carpet. There was a long shelf of books on the wall with the predictable treatises on weather and navigation, but there were other volumes, too. Novels with well-worn spines, *The History of Tom Jones, a Foundling; Pamela, or Virtue Rewarded; The History of the Adventures of Joseph Andrews; The Castle of Otranto.* Equally well thumbed were the Shakespeare tragedies and what seemed to be a full set of Molière in the original French. There was much more: Aristotle, Dante, Cervantes, Machiavelli, Newton, Bacon, and Galileo. Elizabeth was intrigued in spite of herself, and newly curious about the captain.

With a sigh, she turned her mind to more practical matters: she ate some dried fruit from the platter on the sideboard, checked on the twins once and then again, sat for a little while by Hannah's bedside simply watching her sleep, sorted through their baskets, folded clothing, and made ready for a hasty departure should that prove necessary. After a moment's hesitation she rang for the cabin boy and requested hot water. This he produced in very short order, along with a message.

"Ma'am. Hakim Ibrahim sends word that Mrs. Free-

man is sleeping and he wants to know may he call on
you in the morning?" It came out in an earnest tumble.

"Please thank the Hakim," Elizabeth said. "I will
look forward to his call."

She was almost sorry to send the boy on his way, but
there was the hot water and it was growing late.
Elizabeth found that she did not have the energy to take
on laundry; that would have to wait until they were
safely on board the *Providence*. Instead she had a quick
bathe, changed into her nightdress, and brushed out her
hair. By the casement clock she saw that Nathaniel had
been gone forty minutes. It was a mystery to her that
even sensible and rational men seemed to find gun
decks and cannons endlessly interesting.

A deep settee with an abundance of pillows was
inviting, but her nerves were strung tight and she could
not relax: Runs-from-Bears and Will had been gone
three hours.

With her shawl around her shoulders Elizabeth went
to the long wall of draperies that had been pulled closed
before the transom windows. They put her in mind of
Aunt Merriweather's morning room at Oakmere; she
might pull them apart and find a lawn that sloped down
to the rose gardens, and beyond them, a sea churning in
shades of emerald and evergreen. But when she slipped
between the panels Elizabeth found only the river,
caught up in the moonlight. A hundred masts poked
into the night sky, a web of bony fingers out to snare a
moon riding just out of reach. A shimmering of candlelight came through the draperies so that she could make
out her own vague reflection in the glass, too pale and
the unruly mass of her hair crackling around her head.
"Our very own Medusa," Aunt Merriweather had often declared, convinced that Elizabeth's hair was the result of willful extravagance. But it pleased Nathaniel,
and so she left it.

A wide bench ran the length of the windows, piled
with velvet bolsters, faded to ivory and plum and indigo

in the half-light. It was a comfortable spot; she could rest a little, until Nathaniel came. He had plans for her. And she had plans for him, too—they presented themselves in bright, disjointed images. Her own appetites still surprised and unsettled her, although they had been together for more than a year now.

The splash of oars brought her up out of a half-doze, heart pounding. A bateau or a whaleboat, for a canoe would not make so much noise. She heard men's voices, but could not make out the language and so she put her face closer to the glass. The boat had already moved on out of sight. On the other shore cook fires sputtered like random coals in a cold hearth.

Behind her a door opened. There was a murmuring of voices: Moncrieff, and Nathaniel. Elizabeth stilled, tucking her bare feet up under herself; she had no wish to entertain Angus Moncrieff in her nightdress. After a moment the door opened and closed again.

She waited, and heard nothing. Just when she thought it might be safe to slip out, Nathaniel's voice came to her, not five inches away.

"Boots," he said. "You'd make a godawful spy."

Elizabeth yelped in surprise and tried to rise from the cushions, only to find it was suddenly impossible to negotiate her feet out from underneath herself. But it was too late: Nathaniel had already come inside, the draperies falling to a close. They were almost eye to eye, for she was kneeling on the high bench in front of him. The gentle twitching at the corner of his mouth pleased her not at all.

"Why would I make such a terrible spy?" she demanded.

"Because your shawl was hanging out there for all the world to see. That's why Moncrieff took off so quick."

She pulled the end of the offending garment free of the drapery and wrapped it more securely around herself. "It is just as well, Nathaniel. I am not dressed to receive visitors."

"So I see." He lowered his voice and leaned forward as if to tell her a secret. "I dinna think he wad ha' minded, ava. He's got a verra keen e'e for the lasses, does oor Angus. And ye're lookin' aye fine this evenin', Mrs. Bonner, wi' yer hair aa soft an' curled aboot yer bonnie face."

Elizabeth let out a high hoot of laughter. "I had no idea you were such a good mimic."

One brow shot up. "Ah larned guid Scots at ma mither's knee, woman, an' Ah'll thank ye no' tae forgit it."

She choked back a laugh. "Is that so? And what other talents have you been hiding from me, then?"

He blinked at her thoughtfully as one finger began to skate down the front of her nightdress. "Talents?" His own voice now, as strong and purposeful as the flick of a finger that opened first one button, and then another. "I can't think of any, offhand. Except maybe this knack I've got for making you blush." Three more buttons, and the white linen gaped open from neck to waist.

"See?"

He was tugging at her shawl. She tugged back, but without effect. "Nathaniel! Perhaps this demonstration should wait—"

But he cut her off neatly, catching her up against him, his arm like a vise at her waist so that she could feel him from knee to shoulder. A flush started in the pit of her stomach and curled up like smoke. Oh yes, he had that knack. If she let him start, she would not be able to stop him—or herself.

She turned her head so that his mouth caught her cheek. "It grieves me to say this, Nathaniel, but this is not the time nor the place."

"And why not?" His fingers were tangled in her hair where it fell to the small of her back, jerking every nerve into near painful wakefulness.

"Your father and Robbie—"

"Hip-deep in Pickering's gun collection and not about to come back here, Boots. I'll have to fetch them when Bears shows up."

"Yes, exactly. Runs-from-Bears and Will should be back any moment."

"If that's all you're worried about," Nathaniel said hoarsely, "then don't. We'll be the first to see the canoe from here."

She struggled harder. "Yes, and they will see us! The whole river can see us here." With a wiggle she was out of his arms. She turned, putting her hands against the casement to steady herself. "Look!"

The river was empty. Ships rocked gently at docks for as far as they could see, and not a light burned in any of them.

"Aye, Boots. I'm looking."

His hands were everywhere. She tried to turn back to him but he held her still with his body, his mouth at her ear. "Tell me you don't want me."

"I don't want you."

"Liar." His hand slipped inside her nightdress, fingers moving restlessly.

"Yes, yes, yes. I am a liar," she said, struggling against him in vain. "But oh, Nathaniel, the *windows*—"

"Damn the windows," he muttered. In one motion he pulled the open nightdress down over her shoulders, pressing her forward, bare breasts to the cold glass so that she jerked with the shock of it. Then he let her go and stripped before she could gather her thoughts—*did she want this? Dear God, yes, but the windows!*—and then he was there again.

He crowded up behind her and put his mouth to her neck, breathing a slow litany of promises into her ear while his hands moved over her, folding the hem of her nightdress up around her waist. The words held her in a trance, startling, powerful words. He could coax water from stone with this voice of his, but she was not stone, nothing like stone. Against the cleft of her buttocks his

cock was proof enough of that. His hands insistent on her thighs; all was lost.

"The windows," she muttered. To be cursed both with mind and heart. And with eyes: for there they were, faint reflections in the window glass, coupling for themselves and for all the world.

"We mustn't."

He paused, his mouth hovering over her shoulder. "Don't you want me, Elizabeth?"

"I want you, yes," she hissed. Because she could not lie to him, or herself. "But I can't, I can't."

"Oh, but you can, darlin'." And so he showed her, bent her to his will, and to her own. Covered her and filled her, his mouth on her neck, one arm like a pillar, supporting both of them. The other arm was around her waist, pulling her up and back to meet him. And even the world gave in, retreated and left nothing behind but Nathaniel, the long muscles of his thighs tensed behind her, the heat and the heft of him, his body deep in hers and all around her and still he struggled, they struggled together to bring him closer.

And in the window glass she watched it all, saw their faces torn apart with furious need and stitched back together thrust by thrust. His cheek pressed against her temple and his eyes flashing with the beat of her heart, ready to burst for him. She watched it happen. She would remember it as long as she lived.

An hour later Nathaniel woke Elizabeth with the news that the first mate had sighted Runs-from-Bears and Will from the quarterdeck. She had barely enough time to dress and tame her hair into a plait before they were on board. With the exception of Curiosity, all of the party assembled around the cherrywood table with its covered silver platters, porcelain dishes, and crystal goblets, finery never meant for rough hands. To all this

Bears added a bundle wrapped in buckskin and tied with a length of spruce root.

"That's a mighty small parcel to keep you away such a long time." Nathaniel spoke English, because Will and Moncrieff were with them still.

Bears shrugged and reached for the cold beef. "You want the whole story now?"

Hawkeye cast a sidelong glance in Moncrieff's direction. "I expect we're all curious, but it'll have to wait. Lots going on while you were away."

Beside Elizabeth, Will put down his glass. "I should say so. It did give me a start to see the *Nancy* so dark and deserted."

Nathaniel said, "We're better off here for the moment."

Elizabeth was much relieved that he didn't feel it necessary to raise the topic of Mac Stoker. Her pride was still too raw, and Angus Moncrieff was still too much of a stranger to be trusted with such a confession.

Hawkeye explained what there was to know about the *Providence* in a few sentences. Will's expression brightened even before he finished.

"Well, then, you're off now to have a talk with her captain, I take it? Can I be of any assistance?"

"I dinna think it would be wise," Moncrieff said. "The man lost a leg at Lexington, and he's been nane too fond o' Englishmen ever since. He didna care overmuch for me, either, so p'rhaps it'd be best if I stayed clear of Henry Parker."

Robbie's head came up with a snap. "Wad that be Henry Parker o' Boston?"

Moncrieff scratched his chin thoughtfully. "Aye, I believe he is from Boston. A wee mannie, with a fringe o' hair the color of straw and stare like a new-sharpened bayonet."

"That could weel be him," said Robbie with a grin. "I served wi' a Henry Parker for five years under Isaac

Putnam. Hawkeye, d'ye remember him? He was always whittlin' awa' at birds."

Hawkeye stretched and pushed back his chair. "I do remember him. I suppose we better get along and see if it's the same man. Don't forget the coin, Nathaniel—as I remember, Henry Parker drives a Yankee bargain."

In no time at all Nathaniel, Hawkeye, and Robbie had directions to the spot farther downriver where the *Providence* was at dock, collected their weapons and got themselves ready to go. Elizabeth wished for a moment alone with Nathaniel but had to be satisfied with slipping the strap of his carry bag over his shoulder and taking the chance to touch his cheek.

"Don't be long," she said quietly. He caught her hand and pressed a kiss to her palm.

"You'd best be ready to go right quick," said Hawkeye, squeezing her shoulder on his way out. "It may happen all at once."

Moncrieff went up on deck to make sure they reached their destination, and they were gone with just a nod and a smile.

"It's time I was away to my lodgings," Will said.

"Oh, no," said Elizabeth, drawing him down to sit on the chaise longue next to her. "You and Runs-from-Bears have some explaining to do. You had me very worried."

Bears plucked up the bundle from the table and tossed it to Elizabeth without comment. Inside were some large pieces of cured doeskin of very high quality, a smaller piece of heavier buckskin, a bone needle and a paper of three steel needles, a bowl of loose beads with a fitted lid, and a small basket of spooled threads.

Elizabeth ran her palm over the doeskin. "Hannah asked for these things?"

He shook his head. "She wanted Kahnyen'kehàka clothing, but there was none to be had. It was the best I could do."

"But I don't understand. Why would you go off on such an errand?"

He blinked at her. "Squirrel asked me." He spoke English, which took her by surprise. Then she saw Will's expression and she knew two things: whatever had happened on the other side of the river, they had acted together, and were of one mind; and more, neither of them wanted her to know too much about it. More trouble. Elizabeth had a good chance of arguing them into divulging whatever it was, but right now it was all she could do to keep her mind on the night ahead.

Will cleared his throat softly. "I'm sorry we worried you, cousin."

"You are as mysterious as you ever were," Elizabeth said, getting up to put the bundle on the desk. "But it is too late to interrogate you now. Tomorrow you must find passage. My aunt and Amanda will be waiting for you."

A flickering in Will's normally placid expression and then he turned away from her.

Elizabeth said, "Perhaps it would be better not to trouble my aunt with the details. I expect that otherwise she might make things rather difficult for you."

He laughed softly. "You cannot begrudge Amanda and me the bit of drama and adventure Lady Crofton brings into our quiet lives. Leave my mother-in-law to me, can you?"

"I have little choice," Elizabeth agreed. And then, more soberly: "I will miss you, Will."

With an abrupt movement he turned back to her. "You are not the only one with a confession to make, Elizabeth. Since we left Albany I have been at a loss on how to introduce a rather . . . difficult topic, but I see time has run out on me."

Elizabeth let out an awkward laugh. "So dramatic, cousin? You have me worried."

He shook his head. "You needn't worry for me. At least, not so long as I stay out of England, you need not

worry for me. You have heard perhaps of the London Corresponding Society?"

Because she could not trust her voice, Elizabeth merely nodded.

"Your expression is priceless, Lizzy."

"Will," Elizabeth said. "Are you telling me that you are one of the gentlemen charged with advocating revolution on the French model?"

He flushed. "Revolution? But of course not, Elizabeth. The society prefers the term 'reform.'" He rubbed his forehead and allowed himself a small smile, just a glimpse of the old Will she knew so well. "I suppose I should not be surprised that you are familiar with all of this."

"How could I not be? Every newspaper is full of Lord Braxton and his charges." Elizabeth felt slightly dizzy, and she pinched the web of skin between her thumb and first finger until she was more sure of herself.

"I think it would be best if you stayed out of England, after all."

He laughed. "You and your aunt are of one mind, then. Had you not thought it strange that she would come to New-York so suddenly?"

"Is it as bad as all that?"

Will lifted a shoulder. "The worst that has happened thus far is unexpected change of abode. My friend Hardy is worse off—he has just been arrested; I expect they will send him off to Australia."

Elizabeth felt herself growing pale. "Transported!" She thought of Amanda and understood Aunt Merriweather's rush to get Will away from trouble.

"Unfortunately, the situation has gone from bad to worse and I cannot return home. I had hoped to settle here in Canada, but even that seems improbable given recent events. We may well make our home in Albany, or perhaps in New-York City."

"Oh, Will." Elizabeth sat down heavily. "You have

kept this from Amanda." It was not a question, but his expression gave her an answer in any case.

"We did not see the need to alarm her before the situation was fully known," he said.

After a long moment, Elizabeth raised her head. "I think it most cruel of you to keep this from her, Will. And unnecessary. She will not break under the truth, after all. But, now. Where do you go? Back to Albany? Was all this talk of meeting in Halifax pretense?"

"No," said Will quietly. "We do meet in Halifax. But your aunt will sail for home, and Amanda and I will turn back to New-York. I had thought that perhaps I could appeal to the captain of the *Providence* for berth space. Unless you are too disgusted with me to sail on the same ship."

"Will," Elizabeth said, crossly now. "Do not talk such nonsense." She got up and brushed a hand over his shoulder. "I cannot deny that you surprise me—the Corresponding Society! But I admire you for it, truly I do. And I shall not mind having my family nearby. By all means, you must come along with us to the *Providence* and speak to the captain. You do know that I will want all the particulars of this business?"

"If you will tell me the story of the Tory gold, Elizabeth, I will give you the details of the London Corresponding Society. I don't doubt whose story will be more interesting." He gave her a half-smile. "It is a relief to have this out in the open, cousin. But now I must away to bed."

"Will we see you tomorrow at the *Providence*?"

"You may count on it," said Will. "I would not miss it for the world."

As tired as she was—and it was the kind of weariness that ached deep in the bone—Elizabeth knew that she would not rest easy until they were safely on board the *Providence* and out of Canada. She would have been

glad of Runs-from-Bears' company while she waited for
the men to return, but he went off yawning to one of
the side cabins. With some irritation, Elizabeth sat
down on the feather bed to see if it would serve, and
promptly fell asleep without putting up any struggle at
all.

Dreams plagued her. On a forest path a red dog ran
ahead to disappear into a vast marsh of dead trees hung
with moss like ruined bridal veils. Elizabeth called and
called, *Treenie, Treenie!*, but the dog was gone out of
hearing. And then, without any warning, she was paddling a raft as it bumped and careened down the
Richelieu. People crowded in: Tim Card wearing a
necklace of stones, Hannah wrapped in a striped blanket like the one on the bed at home, Miss Thompson
who had taught her to read so long ago in the Oakmere
nursery. The raft rocked wildly and the wood began to
melt like ice under their feet.

Elizabeth struggled up from sleep as the casement
clock struck midnight, and slipped back into an uneasy
rest at the twelfth chime.

Rain, pounding and pounding. She pulled the pillow
across her face but it was still there: rain on the river,
yes. But something else, too. The sound of men moving
in quick march, heavy boots, the jangle of weapons.
Moncrieff's voice at the door, now. It was no dream.

From its spot on the poop deck, the round-house on the
Isis looked out over the boatyard and docks. Elizabeth
followed Moncrieff there, still fastening the buttons on
her bodice, her hair lashing around her in the wet wind.
Runs-from-Bears followed her, his expression closed
and watchful. Pickering and his officers stood aside for
them. There was no time for pleasantries, given the
scene spread out before them.

Redcoats everywhere. Forbes & Sons was sealed off,
and from their vantage point on the *Isis* they could see

it all: the dock around the *Nancy* was surrounded, her decks crawling with soldiers. Some part of Elizabeth's mind insisted on taking count: a chain of twelve men at the gates; thirty-six men on foot on the dock, two officers on horseback, and another pacing so that his cloak flared around him. Foot soldiers carried lanterns on long poles and the light reflected on the muzzles of their guns, brass buttons, silver spurs.

"The King's Own," said Pickering behind her. "And the sixtieth, too, by God."

Elizabeth rounded on him. "You had no warning?"

"Of course not," he said hoarsely. "None at all."

Moncrieff touched her elbow. "Perhaps you should go below, Mrs. Bonner."

A group of the soldiers had broken off and were headed toward them. A tall man led them, the one in the cloak. She saw now that he wore no uniform. "Who is that?"

"Sir Guy," said Pickering, picking up his hat. "The governor himself. I must go and meet him." There was a tremor in his hand that Elizabeth did not like to see.

"He'll want to search this ship," she said more to herself than to him.

"He wouldna dare!" Moncrieff's tone brought Elizabeth around in surprise.

"Let him," said Runs-from-Bears calmly, his gaze locked on the men moving toward them.

"What?" Moncrieff snapped. "Are ye daft, man?"

Elizabeth put her hand on Moncrieff's forearm and felt the tension leaping there.

"Runs-from-Bears is right," she said quickly. "If you refuse the governor, he will know for certain what he only suspects."

"Can ye lie tae the man's face, then? D'ye ha' any idea wha' a bluidy bastard he can be?"

Elizabeth felt all her concentration shifting down to a fine point. *By the pricking of my thumbs,* she thought, and she smiled.

"I've dealt with a bloody bastard or two in my time," she said, and turned to Bears. "You must get word to Nathaniel and Hawkeye."

He shook his head. "They'd have me followed."

"Lord Dorchester requests permission to come aboard!" called a midshipman.

Elizabeth picked up her skirts and ran with Runs-from-Bears close behind.

Hannah stood in the middle of the cabin. In the candle-light her eyes were very large.

"Are they coming for us?"

Elizabeth clutched the girl to her chest, hugged her hard. Then she tilted up her chin to look directly into her eyes. "Listen to me, Squirrel. Your father and grandfather and Robbie are safe on another ship. There are some soldiers come on board the *Isis* to look for them. We mustn't look frightened or guilty. Do you understand?"

The vacant expression in Hannah's eyes shifted away like sand, and she nodded. She went to her uncle Runs-from-Bears, and he put a hand on her head.

"Dress now, quickly," Elizabeth said, even as she went in search of her shoes. But it was too late, there was a sharp rap at the door and it opened without her bidding. The captain, with a crowd of men behind him. Elizabeth drew in a deep breath, folded her shawl across her bodice, and drew Hannah in to her side to put an arm around her shoulders. Now that it had come to this, she was perfectly calm. She put her mouth to Hannah's ear. "They are only men," she whispered. Hannah's head bobbed, but she said nothing.

"Captain Pickering," Elizabeth said firmly. "What is the meaning of this disturbance?"

Pickering cleared his throat, his expression woeful.

"Lord Dorchester, may I present Mrs. Bonner. And Mr. Runs-from-Bears."

He was tall, with a high sloping forehead and a prim mouth, in his sixties or perhaps even older. The cool gaze took in every detail of her person, from her bare feet and wrinkled skirt to the wild flow of her hair. He was waiting for her curtsy; she could see it in the set of his thin mouth.

Elizabeth nodded. "Sir."

"Mrs. Bonner. Good evening." By his voice she knew him: plummy tones polished to a sheen in the company of great men. But not born to the very highest places, not quite; there was Ulster Irish there just beneath the surface. He meant not to let it show. He was a typical third son, dedicated to the army, advancing only as quickly as his talents, good luck, and connections allowed. Elizabeth had the sense that there was more of luck and connections here than talent, but she might be wrong; she would reserve judgment.

She held up her head and met his gaze while he took her measure. It did not last long. All he would see was an Englishwoman of good birth gone to waste. Run away to marry an American backwoodsman. To him she was at best a simpleton, at worst a whore, but Elizabeth had cut her teeth on the disdain of men who were not her equal. She smiled because he expected it of her. It would pacify him, and she would keep her advantage.

"How may I be of service at this late hour, sir?"

A restless shifting behind him. A little man with a face like an underdone pudding cleared his throat.

"You will give Lord Dorchester his rank," he piped.

Elizabeth inclined her head. "Of course. I am too long away. How may I be of service to you, my lord?"

"We will have your menfolk," said Sir Guy. "Tell me where they are."

Elizabeth raised a hand, palm up. "I would ask you

the same question, sir. I came to Canada to plead their case, and found instead that they were already fled."

"They are not on board this ship?"

"They are not, sir. I hope that they are well on their way home."

"Then you will consent to a search of these cabins."

Elizabeth inclined her head. "As you wish. My lord."

His gaze the color of claret, sweeping over the stateroom now. Hannah seemed to be invisible to him, but Runs-from-Bears was not.

"You." He waved a hand. "You are Mohawk?"

Bears nodded.

"A white man was found murdered this evening in the Indian camps. A peddler but a subject of the Crown, after all. His throat was cut. Major Johnson will look at your weapons."

Elizabeth felt a flush of cold all along her spine. With every bit of her willpower she controlled her expression. Runs-from-Bears seemed neither worried nor intimidated, but simply slipped his knife from the beaded sheath on his belt and held it out. The governor flicked a finger in that direction and Johnson hurried forward to examine the knife.

"No blood, my lord."

"Ah." Carleton tapped one prominent tooth thoughtfully. "Well, then. I would speak to you privately in my offices. Tomorrow morning, at ten. See that you are not late."

Runs-from-Bears said, "I won't be late. I won't be there at all."

The governor's mouth narrowed to a blade.

Elizabeth said, "He cannot oblige you, my lord, because he is bound to accompany us. We sail tomorrow for home." She willed her tone cool and her anger in check.

His gaze came back to her with a jerk. "Do you, indeed? For England?"

She met him without flinching. "My home is in New-

York State." And then, weary of the whole game, she asked him a direct question. "Sir, is it your intention to arrest me?"

Hannah tensed, and Elizabeth squeezed her shoulder gently.

"I had not thought of it," said the governor. "But on the other hand you have not proved especially helpful. I have it on good authority, madam, that the escaped prisoners are indeed in Québec."

"Sir," said Elizabeth. "As you can see, they are not here. But if my word does not satisfy you, perhaps we should send for my cousin, Viscount Durbeyfield. Runs-from-Bears could fetch him in just a few moments' time."

"I think not," said Sir Guy. "The Mohawk will stay on board the *Isis*. We have no need of your cousin the *Viscount*, Mrs. Bonner."

The flush of anger was on her; she could feel it and she knew he could see it. "Are your inquiries concluded then, sir?"

The governor shook his head. "We are not even begun, Mrs. Bonner. But I always conduct these . . . discussions at the Château St. Louis. You needn't worry for your reputation. It is not the gaol, but my residence. My lady wife is present."

Behind the governor, Captain Pickering blanched visibly, but that was a luxury that Elizabeth could not afford. To show this man panic or even the simplest shred of fear would be to surrender.

Pickering said, "My lord, surely you do not wish to take two infants and a young girl out into such weather, and in the dead of night."

"Of course I do not," said the governor, never looking at the captain. "You know me better, Pickering. I have no need for wailing babies. They will stay here in the care of the Mohawk. I will not keep her long."

Elizabeth let her expression go as soft and blank as she could make it, but her mind scrambled frantically.

The man thought to shock her into a confession, hoping that she would fumble and send her men to the gallows in the first flush of fear for her children. He could not keep her long away; Will would see to it.

She squared her shoulders and spoke to Bears in Kahnyen'kehàka.

"I will be back by sunrise. See if you can get word to Will."

Hannah made no sound but a single tear, scalding hot, fell on Elizabeth's hand.

Elizabeth met the governor's hooded eyes. "You will permit me to dress, my lord?"

He inclined his head, all generosity now; he thought she would give in.

In the corner cabin where the babies slept peacefully, Elizabeth took Hannah by the shoulders. "I will deal with them and then I will return. Nothing could keep me away."

Hannah nodded, wiping her face with the back of her hand. "I will take good care of the babies until you get back."

Elizabeth ran a hand over the smooth dark head. "I know that you will."

There was a shuffling in the main cabin, men's voices raised and then a run of notes on the spinet. It made her flush with a fine, hot anger. After a moment's hesitation, she went to the twins' carry basket and rummaged under the covers at one end until she came up with the sack of gold coin that Will had returned to them this morning. She would have preferred a musket or a knife, but money was the only weapon available to her.

Québec had disappeared into a fog. Elizabeth could tell nothing of the city except that it was at the top of some cliffs; the coach wound its way up in a corkscrewlike fashion, jolting and shuddering in the winds and the mudholes. Alone in the coach, she kept the heavy leather

curtains closed, for she did not like the mounted escort so close by. By the time they had reached the Château St. Louis she had reduced her handkerchief to a shredded mass, but her face was composed.

The governor had arrived first, on horseback. A great number of soldiers waited in the courtyard, clearly discomfited by the cold rain. Elizabeth was chilled to the bone, too, but she could feel no sympathy for them. If things were to go badly here, these men would be dispatched to arrest Nathaniel, Hawkeye, and Robbie. The thought could not be borne, and so she thrust it away from herself.

Elizabeth waited for the governor in his drafty front hall, low of ceiling and with a stone floor that radiated a chill even through the thick carpet. There was only a banked fire in the hearth, and no sign of a servant. Major Johnson of the King's Own stood off to one side with his hands crossed at the small of his back, rocking to and fro on his heels. He smelled of onions and frying liver, his teeth were ivory or perhaps the bone of some animal, and his distaste for this guard duty was as clear as the dark stubble on his cheeks.

Elizabeth pulled her muddied cloak closer around herself and returned his stare. "You are impertinent, sir."

"And you are a turncoat, Mrs. Bonner."

"Pardon me, Major Johnson. I mistook you for a gentleman."

He had the good grace to flush, but before he could put words to his contempt, the double doors at the far end of the hall opened, and a small silver-haired lady floated through with Sir Guy just behind her. She was perfectly dressed and groomed at four in the morning—for so proclaimed the mantel clock. Elizabeth supposed she must be used to drama at all hours of the night.

"Mrs. Bonner, my dear." Her tone was contained and carefully modulated, with the breathy quality of those women who never quite got over a presentation

at court. She had never been a beauty, her face too round and her complexion too rough for it, but her eyes snapped with curiosity and intelligence that might be very good or very bad news for Elizabeth. If Lady Dorchester were to take over the questioning, she would have a much harder time of it than she would have with the governor.

Her first words put Elizabeth's concerns to rest.

"Mrs. Bonner. Welcome to the Château St. Louis, and please may I beg your pardon for the abominable treatment you've received at my husband's hands. I am Lady Dorchester. What an outrageous affair, there are no words. No words. Most disconcerting. I hardly know what to say."

"My dear—" Sir Guy began, and she turned on him in a cold fury.

"This is Mrs. Elizabeth Middleton Bonner, Lord Dorchester. Do you hear? Of Oakmere. Lady Crofton's niece, the one she spoke to me about last spring when we met in Montréal. And you have dragged her out of her bed, and away from her children—did he not, my dear? And for what purpose?"

"We are looking for her husband and his father," said Sir Guy, struggling for his dignity and not quite succeeding. "You know very well that it is standard procedure to question suspects alone."

Lady Dorchester gave a very unladylike snort. "She is a suspect?"

"Her husband is."

Elizabeth was so relieved at this unexpected ally that she might have laughed out loud to see the governor's plans so neatly turned on ear.

"Exactly!" Lady Dorchester advanced a step toward the governor. "Her husband. *She* has not committed any crime." Her gaze dared him to contradict her.

She took Elizabeth by the arm. "My dear, we must have patience with them, for they are merely men, after

all. Most excellent men, it is true, but men nonetheless. We will send you back to the *Isis,* my dear, but first you must have dry boots, and this cloak—you must be chilled through."

"Lady Dorchester," Elizabeth began. "Please, a little damp does not bother me. I am worried about my children."

The tiny woman drew up in amazement. "Of course you are, my dear. But this damp is not to be trifled with. It would do no good to send you back as you are to the *Isis;* you will surely take a chill and then how shall I explain myself to Lady Crofton? No, you must have dry things. You are of a size with my elder daughter; I am sure it can be managed quickly." The bright eyes moved to her face. "You have twins, I understand? When do you expect they will need your attention? Surely another hour can be spared."

Elizabeth considered Lady Dorchester's resolute expression, and sighed. She did not wonder that she had made so fast a friendship with her aunt Merriweather; they were fashioned of the same strong stuff.

"An hour, Lady Dorchester. But no more."

The governor was making distressed noises, little chirps that came up from his chest.

"Sir Guy, do speak up if you have something to say." Lady Dorchester's tone was more solicitous now that she had secured Elizabeth's promise.

He scowled. "I have not had a chance to question this lady! There is a serious matter at stake here. You have no consideration for my sense of duty, madam!"

Pale fingers fluttered dismissively around her face. "On the contrary, I am well acquainted with your sense of duty, Sir Guy. I have been at truce with it now for these many years. Very well, ask your questions, if you must. I shall return shortly." She disappeared into the back hallway, calling for servants in a staccato French that must have carried through the house.

Elizabeth was left alone with the governor and Major Johnson. She had feared that Sir Guy would be angry at this complete failure of his scheme to frighten her into a confession, but there was a thoughtful look about him, as if he were weighing his options.

"Mrs. Bonner, I should not have brought you here if I had had your cooperation."

It was as close as he would come to an apology. Elizabeth said, "I am happy to tell you what you most need to know, sir. And that is this: these men you are looking for are not spies. They have no interest in politics of any kind."

Major Johnson narrowed his eyes at her. "And what of their activities during the war?"

Elizabeth managed a cool smile. "We are not at war now, sir, and they serve no army of any nation."

"It is true that we are not at war. At the moment," conceded Sir Guy. "But in my experience, madam, ladies do not always know their husbands' business."

"Perhaps that is true in some cases," Elizabeth said. "But not in my own. May I ask you a question, my lord?"

"If I may ask you one first and get a truthful answer."

She had put herself in the trap; she could do nothing more than agree.

Sir Guy said, "You have never heard your husband, father-in-law, or this Robert MacLachlan plotting to take part in a new attempt to invade Canada?"

Elizabeth suppressed her smile and thanked the heavens that his imagination had taken him in the one direction that she could counter with complete honesty. "My lord, I give you my oath that I have never heard them mention such an invasion at all, much less their part in it."

"I have reason to believe that they are encouraging the Mohawk to move back to New-York and support the American government against the Crown."

Elizabeth might have pointed out that this was a second question, but she simply said, "From this it is clear to me that you know very little about the Mohawk and nothing about my husband and his father."

Major Johnson grunted, but the governor maintained his thoughtful expression.

"Are you an expert on the Mohawk, madam?"

She shook her head. "That would be a fine conceit, indeed. No, I am not."

"But you understand them. You speak their language."

She shrugged. "Imperfectly."

The governor said, "You are an English lady of good family. Will you not make your home here in British Canada? If your husband is truly as disinterested in politics as you claim, then he might as well be on this side of the border, and take up the cause of his wife's homeland. I would be glad of his assistance with the Indians."

Elizabeth had been lulled into a sense of relief by Lady Dorchester's intervention in her dilemma, but now she saw that she had let down her guard too far.

"Sir Guy, I cannot enter into any such agreement, just as Lady Dorchester would not make arrangements for your removal from Canada without consulting you."

Something flickered in his eyes. "But you are mistaken, Mrs. Bonner. I would be immensely grateful to anyone who would arrange my removal home. The day I am recalled cannot come soon enough."

There was a tone she could not quite put a name to: certainly disgust and some good measure of disappointment, but also a deep weariness.

Lady Dorchester's quicksilver step sounded close by.

"You promised me a question, my lord."

He put out a hand, palm up.

"How did you know that I came here on the *Nancy*?"

A vague look of discomfort passed over the smooth

features. Then he drew a folded piece of paper from his
breast pocket and, after a moment's hesitation, handed
it to Elizabeth.

The paper was very fine and scented with musk. An
elegant feminine hand but firm, the black ink in strong
lines:

Sir—
It may interest you to know that Mrs.
Elizabeth Bonner is come to Québec aboard the
Nancy. She does not travel alone.

Giselle Somerville

Elizabeth had never fainted in her life, but she
thought now she might. Confusion and fear made her
knees buckle until she found herself sitting on the hall
bench, her whole body covered in a fine sweat. Why
would Giselle Somerville do such a thing?

"Are you unwell, madam?"

She shook her head and closed her eyes to concentrate, the note clasped hard in her hand. Saw in her
mind the closed door of the captain's quarters, and
heard Pickering tell them again that Miss Somerville
had already retired for the night. Giselle Somerville
sent the note to the governor and then she had gone
to bed. She wanted Elizabeth arrested, but why? Out of
simple maliciousness? Had she heard of the plan to
bring Elizabeth on board the *Isis* and decided that such
a thing was not to be borne? Giselle—or someone close
to Giselle—wanted Elizabeth away from the *Isis*.
But why? What was to be gained by Elizabeth's absence?

What had she left behind on the *Isis* that Giselle
wanted?

A great flush of fear began in a trickle at the back of
her neck. Elizabeth shot up from the bench, a hand at

her throat to keep herself from crying out, just as Lady Dorchester appeared with her arms full of clothing.

"I am sorry, Lady Dorchester, but I must go back to the ship. Immediately. Please, please will you lend me a horse?"

The little woman looked with surprise from Elizabeth to Sir Guy. "But your clothing—"

Elizabeth grabbed Lady Dorchester by the shoulders; she was as small and frail as a bird. As a child. "You must see, I cannot delay. My children. She—someone wanted me away from the ship, that's why they sent the note."

Sir Guy was making small sounds of disbelief. "Surely you cannot think—"

"Sir!" Elizabeth cut him off. "My children are in danger, I can feel that in my bones. If you have any mercy you will not keep me here one moment longer."

Lady Dorchester tapped her foot. "Major Johnson, a horse for Mrs. Bonner, and without delay. Do you hear me, man? Without delay. And ride with her."

Elizabeth took a precious moment to send a look of gratitude to the lady, and then she flew out the door.

The *Isis* was gone.

Elizabeth stood on the dock, her hands pressed to her mouth, and stared. Major Johnson was asking questions, but she could make no sense of them. Her children were gone. She let out one keening sob and then bit down hard enough to taste blood.

A nightwatchman slid up behind her. "Pardon, are you Mrs. Bonner?"

She rounded on him, grabbed him by the grubby blanket coat. The horses danced away in alarm, their hooves striking sparks on the cobblestones. The man looked at her as if she might eat him whole.

And well I might, she thought. "The *Isis*." He tried

to jerk away, and she dug in her fingers. "Where is she?"

He jumped, his eyes round with fear. "Sailed, ma'am. Sailed not an hour ago for home."

"For where? Where is home? Tell me, man, where is that ship bound!"

He let out a cry of pain and yanked free of her grip. "Scotland! She's bound for the Solway Firth."

The Solway Firth! On the southern shore of Dumfrieshire. Where Carryck had his seat.

"Tell me," she said hollowly. "Who owns the *Isis*? Would it be the Earl of Carryck, by any chance?"

Major Johnson made a humming noise, his head nodding. "Yes, that's right. These are Carryck's boatyards, too—I thought you would have known that."

The *Isis* belonged to the Earl of Carryck. This was Moncrieff's doing, all of it, perhaps from the very beginning. Elizabeth's hands went suddenly numb, and she thought she might swoon. But the watchman was talking, and she forced herself to concentrate and listen to him.

"There's a man asking for you," he was saying, still rubbing his arm.

"A man? Where, what man?"

He jerked with his chin toward the warehouse. "We carried him over there. A big Indian, with a bump on his head the size of a cabbage."

But Elizabeth was already off at a dead run, falling once on the wet wood of the dock and then up again before anyone could reach her.

They had propped Runs-from-Bears up against the wall. Blood trailed in spider's legs down his temple, but he blinked up at her. Alive. Alive.

She went down on her knees. "Tell me."

He held up his fist. In it, a letter smeared with dirt and his own blood. Elizabeth's hands shook so that she could barely manage to break the seal. In the light of a single lantern the penstrokes leaped crazily.

My dear Mrs. Bonner:

Permit me to reassure you that Mrs. Freeman and your children are in perfect health and will enjoy every comfort and protection that the *Isis* can offer. I had not planned to sail without you, but the governor saw fit to take you away at a most inopportune moment. Fortunately, the first officer's guidwife is on board and will serve as an excellent wet nurse.

All three children will want for nothing but your company, a lack which will be soon remedied: I have arranged passage for yourself, your husband, and father-in-law with Captain Morris of the *Osiris,* who will present himself to you tomorrow. It is his first and most important obligation to deliver you with all haste to the Solway Firth. With good luck the westerlies will have you there in less than thirty days.

I regret the necessity of such a drastic step, but your father-in-law denied me every other more reasonable alternative. In anticipation of the day on which you will be reunited not with one family, but two, I remain

Your willing servant
Angus Moncrieff

Major Johnson walked up close, his curiosity crawling on his face like lice. "What does it say?"

Elizabeth crumpled the letter against her bodice. "He has stolen my children," she said dully. "My children are gone."

Runs-from-Bears put a bloody hand on her wrist. In Kahnyen'kehàka he said, "You must find Wolf-Running-Fast."

"Your husband," said Johnson, not realizing that he echoed Bears. "Where is your husband? You need him

now." He was trying not to grin, but his expression was sharp and eager in the lantern light.

Contempt filled Elizabeth's mouth with bitterness. He thought anger would cripple her, that grief would rob her of purpose. How little men knew of women; how little this one knew of anything at all.

"I'm going to find them now," she said to Bears in Kahnyen'kehàka. "Tell Will what has happened. And then go home. Go home and tell them that we will be there when we have my children back."

He blinked at her. "Bring Moncrieff's scalp with you."

"With pleasure," said Elizabeth. She put both hands on his face and then she did something she had never done before; she leaned forward and kissed Runs-from-Bears on the cheek. His skin was cold to the touch, but the arm that came up around her was strong.

"Farewell, my friend," she said. She got to her feet, raised her chin, and met the major's eager gaze. "Major Johnson."

"Yes, Mrs. Bonner?"

"I find myself somewhat faint . . ." With a vague movement of her hand she indicated a pile of crates against the far wall of the warehouse. "My cousin the viscount is in rooms in the Rue St. Gabriel. Will you fetch him?"

Johnson snapped to action, marching off to bark orders at the soldiers still milling around the *Nancy*. She had pleased him with this sudden transformation into what he wanted and expected of her: a woman in need.

Bears reached out to squeeze her hand. Elizabeth squeezed back with all her strength, and then she slipped into the shadows.

She made her way quietly, feeling with her mind, throwing her senses out into the dark. How many times had Nathaniel spoken to her of this, the skill of moving through the night. *You feel shapes even when you can-*

not see them. In English it sounded strange but in Kahnyen'kehàka it made perfect sense. Now she whittled down all her senses and moved fast, swallowing the sound of her own breathing and the hollow rattle of her heart. As she came around the far end of the warehouse a watchman passed with a lantern swinging on his pole; she pulled back until he was gone. Hoofbeats on the cobblestones; a man's voice raised in question. She held her breath and then she ran.

It was very near morning, the sky lightening. She knew only that the *Providence* was farther downriver, and so she moved north, slipping in and out of the lanes that radiated off the docks. From a window overhead a baby's cry sounded to her like a trumpet blast; her breasts throbbed with it. She dashed away her tears with an impatient hand and concentrated on the river.

More men were in the lanes, many of them carpenters and workmen headed toward a large boatworks, their tools hung about them. Someone must know where the *Providence* docked. Elizabeth pulled her cloak closer around herself and the hood lower over her face. In French she asked once, and then again and again; but there were too many ships in port at this time of year and all she got was curious glances, shrugs, grins. One of them offered her some of his breakfast, another asked a rough question she did not really understand. But what did she care for the laughter of these men, or what they thought of her? Her children were gone and she must get them back.

When the waterfront was crowded with laborers and seamen she moved out in the open. A merchant in a fine linen coat that might well have been cut in Paris or London turned away from her when she tried to speak to him, would not listen to her in French or English.

A young boy was at her heels; he had been there for some time before she realized. She stopped and turned to him. He stared back at her.

"Do you know of a ship called the *Providence*?"

He blinked.

Elizabeth swallowed down her desperation. "An American captain who whittles birds from wood?"

A spark of recognition: did she imagine it? She repeated herself in French.

"*Oui,*" said the boy, and thrust out his hand.

She took a coin from the sack still tied around her waist and pressed it into his palm; gold. But what difference did it make now?

He ran like the river. It took all of the last of her energy to keep up with him as he wound in and out of warehouse yards, through alleys where pigs rooted in filth, past row houses where women were hanging out steaming wash. "Is it far?" she asked him again and again. But he didn't hear her, or didn't care to answer. There was a brand on his cheek. He had limp blond hair and her children would never look anything like him, and still his dirty neck above a frayed blanket coat made her want to scream.

Another alley, closer to the waterfront again and reeking of tarpots and rotting fish. She could just see the masts of a single ship at the dock, and the sight made her heart leap into her throat.

At the last second she saw the man from the corner of her eye, the shape of him darting out of the doorway; she ducked too late. He had her by the cloak, spun her around to him. And she fell, still, tangled in her skirts, aware as she went of the jolt to her arm and hip and of the man himself: Mac Stoker. *Of course,* she thought, as consciousness flickered and threatened to vanish. *What else?*

She said, "If you try to stop me now I will kill you."

One black brow shot up high. "Sure and you're in no position to be making threats, Mrs. Bonner."

She struggled, but he held her where she was with little effort. The truth was, she had no weapons but money and her wits; she would try the latter first.

"Let me go now, Stoker. I have no time for your games."

He ignored her and spoke to the boy, who had pressed himself against the wall to watch, his eyes alight with excitement. "Away wit' ye, boyo, you've done your job."

Elizabeth's gorge rose in her throat in a blazing rush: she had walked into this without thought. *I am most certainly the stupidest creature Providence ever put on this earth.*

Stoker got a better hold on her to haul her to her feet. "I did warn you, did I not, that there's more than one kind of pirate on the St. Lawrence? And now your babbies are gone. Don't worry yerself, I'm not after yer virtue or your coin. There's a better profit in it if I deliver you safe and sound."

Elizabeth jerked around to him. "*Deliver* me? Where? To whom? The governor?"

Stoker's laugh had an edge. "Sure and you must have noted that I'm not overeager to do business wit' the Crown, or I might well have turned you in two days ago for the reward. No, we're off to the *Jackdaw,* me darlin'. My ship turns out to be of some use after all, it seems. Or so think your menfolk."

PART II

The Lass in Green

Love is swift of foot
Love's a man of war
and can shoot,
and can hit from far.

— George Herbert, 1633

15

Just after sunrise Moncrieff came to tell Hannah what she had already figured out for herself. In tones meant to soothe and deceive he spoke of troops searching every ship, confusion on the docks, and a reunion in Scotland. He never used the word *captive*, but he didn't need to. Hannah knew her people: they would shed blood before they saw their children sail off to a strange land alone. Perhaps they had.

And still Moncrieff stood in the middle of the stateroom and met her eye. He had to raise his voice above the twins' shrieking. It unnerved him, and Hannah was glad, although she let him see none of it, not her anger or the many questions that she would not ask without giving him an advantage over her. Moncrieff talked and talked, but Hannah barely heard him, preoccupied as she was with a simple, bone-deep fear. She held it as she would hold any wild, clawed animal: tightly bound and close, lest it tear free and draw her blood.

When Moncrieff had run out of promises Hannah simply picked up her brother and sister, one on each hip, and waited for him to step aside so she could pass through the door.

"You needna go. You're welcome to keep the use o'

these cabins," he said. "I'll send for Mrs. Freeman, as well."

But she only stared at him, her silence marking him for the liar he was.

He flushed then. Gave in and let her leave. There was only so far she could go, anyway.

There was no sign of Hakim Ibrahim, but Hannah found Curiosity just waking in the small sleeping cabin off the surgeon's quarters, where she had spent the night. She was clear-eyed and finally free of fever, but she made Hannah repeat her story three times before it seemed to take root. They were at sea, not headed for home, and alone.

While they pieced together the few bits of information they had, Curiosity simply rocked the babies. They had settled into a new, softer wailing. Hannah looked away, afraid to be drawn into their web of misery and despair.

"Ain't this a woeful mess." Curiosity's voice was still a little hoarse, and she cleared her throat more than once. "Elizabeth will be out of her head with worry. Not to mention the folks at home." And her voice creaked and broke.

Hannah found she must ask, or let the question choke her. "Do you think they're dead?"

"No." Curiosity's dark eyes met her own, full-on. "It's Hawkeye and your daddy that Moncrieff wants. You and these babies, you nothing but a way to get to them. Your folks all alive and well, and not a day behind us—I'd wager my good right hand on it. Do you hear me?"

Hannah nodded. "There's a wet nurse, Moncrieff says."

"I figured. He wouldn't want to deliver these children half dead to his earl, would he. The devil ain't pure dumb, after all."

"Do you think *she* had something to do with it?"

Curiosity turned as if she could look through the length of the ship to the bed where Giselle Somerville was most certainly still fast asleep.

"Wouldn't be surprised," was all she said. And she rocked the twins all the harder.

A scratching at the door began a procession of cabin boys with platters of food, water, and a note from the captain. This Curiosity did not even unfold before she dropped it into the chamber pot. To the startled cabin boy she said only, "Tell him we don' need no apologies and no excuses. What we need is that wet nurse."

The captain brought the woman to the door himself. Curiosity met him with an expression so dark and seething that Hannah felt the hair rising on her own nape. Pickering dropped his gaze, and withdrew backward.

The wet nurse was called Margreit MacKay. She was the wife of the first officer, delivered of a dead child in Québec; she had a face as bitter as arrowroot and dun-brown hair and eyes like a smear of slugs.

Lily and Daniel met the offered breasts with all the fury they could muster. Lily gave in and suckled only when hunger had grown stronger than her anger, falling into an exhausted sleep after a quarter of an hour, and before she had her fill. Daniel held out longer. Finally he nursed in a frenzy, working his fists and feet against the pasty, slack flesh, winding his fingers in a hank of loose hair until tears sprang into the woman's eyes. When he had taken all Margreit MacKay had to offer, Hannah lifted him up against her shoulder and he collapsed into an indignant sleep, shuddering with every breath.

Mrs. MacKay rubbed her scalp and said, "Soor dooks, the baith o' them. Spoilt wi' gettin' their own road."

Curiosity had Lily in her arms, but she moved so quickly that Hannah could hardly follow it: she

grabbed Margreit MacKay by the elbow and pushed her, bare breasts swaying, to the door.

"Three hours," Curiosity said. "And don' be late, or I'll teach you what you don' know about spoiled." And she shut the door before the astonished Mrs. MacKay could protest.

But when Curiosity turned back her anger was already gone, replaced by a trembling in her hands that Hannah didn't like to see.

Curiosity went to bed with the twins, thinking that her familiar smells and nearness might help them rest. Hannah, agitated and ill at ease, wandered into the middle cabin of the surgeon's quarters, where Hakim Ibrahim examined and treated the sick and injured.

There was still no sign of the doctor. Hannah was both disappointed—she had a strong urge to see him, and to know what part he had played in all of this—and relieved to have some time alone in this cabin that was so pleasing to her. There were no carpets or velvet cushions here, just the clutter that she associated with healers. Folded bandages, baskets of roots, a huge medicine cabinet that took up an entire wall. Overhead dried herbs hung in bunches as they did at home, but here they swung with the rhythm of the hull against the waves.

Hannah made herself breathe in and out slowly, taking in smells strange and familiar: cinnamon, coriander, thyme, little-man root, mint and vinegar, cedar and sandalwood, camphor and rose oil. On her first visit here—she could hardly credit that it was only the day before yesterday—the Hakim had opened jars and bottles and named the powders and oils first in English and then in the musical, winding sounds of his own language, throaty and soft all at once. She had feared he would find her curiosity unseemly, but there was nothing of irritation or impatience in his manner.

Yesterday this medicine cabinet had seemed a wondrous thing, with its cubbyholes to keep jars safe from the rocking of the ship, dark glass bottles stoppered with cork, small drawers labeled with a strange, flowing script she could not read. When she had first come here with Runs-from-Bears, Hannah had wanted nothing more than time to explore this little room and all its treasures. She had wished for it. Perhaps she had called all of this down upon their heads with that wish.

There was a whispering of sound and Hakim Ibrahim came through the door, in his arms a wide, flat basket filled with bread and what seemed to be fruit. He was not so tall as the men of her family, but taller than Moncrieff or the captain, and the way he held his head put her in mind of a Kahnyen'kehàka elder. He did not have the age to be a sachem—she thought he was probably not much older than her father—but he had that way of looking, sharp but not cruel; his gaze cut but drew no blood. He was looking at her that way now, and the welcoming smile on his face faded.

"Are you unwell?" he asked.

Hannah knew that she must find out if this man was enemy or friend. If he was an enemy, they would have no one to trust on the ship. Her voice trembled because she could not help it. "Hakim, did you know about this?" She gestured with one hand to the porthole and the sea beyond.

Puzzlement showed on his face in a line that ran down between his eyebrows. "Did I know that we were to sail? Yes."

"Did you know that we were to sail without my parents or grandfather?"

A ripple of surprise and disquiet moved across the even features. "I did not," he said. "Perhaps you would like to tell me what has happened."

While Hannah talked—in halting words at first and then more quickly, pouring out what she knew

and what she only guessed—he stood listening, the high brow under the neatly folded red turban creased.

Hakim Ibrahim said, "Your stepmother was to sail with us to Scotland, as I understood it."

Hannah's head came up with a jerk. "We never agreed to sail to Scotland! We just wanted to go home to New-York."

For a moment the Hakim considered the basket in his arms.

"Perhaps there is some reasonable explanation. I shall make inquiries. But first I should like to talk to you about how best to care for your brother and sister until your mother is restored to them. Perhaps you will share my breakfast with me while we talk."

It might have been the steadiness of his hands, or the calm expression in his eyes, or perhaps it was just that he gave her a problem to work through, but Hannah felt some relief, a loosening of the knot in her belly. She nodded.

There were small dark fruits in the basket that he called dates, smooth-shelled nuts, and shiny, coarse-skinned globes of a deep orange color that Hannah associated with falling leaves. The Hakim held one out to her: a small sun caught in a web of fingers the color of earth mixed with ash. Hannah made a bowl of her hands and took it. It was heavy and dense, smooth to the touch, warm. She sat down with it, and resisted the urge to rub it against her face. But he was waiting for her to speak.

"They sent in a woman to nurse the twins," she said. "Mrs. MacKay." She did not care to speak Moncrieff's name out loud ever again, and was glad to see that it was not necessary.

"Ah." He pushed his thumb into one of the orange fruits, and the scent of it burst through the room in a shower, light and still faintly sharp. "She is not yet healed from her loss, either in mind or body."

"My sister and brother do not like her," said Hannah,

not wanting to hear about the Scotswoman's problems. And then, in a rush: "I think her milk must be as bitter and mean as she is."

Her grandmother would have chided her for her lack of charity, but the Hakim merely blinked. He tore the golden globe apart with a simple twist of his hands, and then he held out half of it to her, dripping with juice that ran in a river over the strong brown wrist. "Then we must find a better way. But first I must check on Mrs. Freeman, and you must eat."

To Hannah's surprise, there was livestock on board, some of the animals now on the open deck in pens and others in the hold. She did not see them, for she refused to leave Curiosity and the babies, but the Hakim sent the cabin boy away and he came back with eggs still warm from the nest and a jug of fresh goat's milk. On the small stove where he made his decoctions and teas and cooked his own food, Hakim Ibrahim boiled two eggs until the whites had set, mixed them with a little coarse salt and some soft cheese, and gave them to Curiosity with his curious flat bread. He made a new tea while she ate, this one of horehound, bayberry, valerian, and little-man root. Hannah was given a cup of the goat's milk and more of the bread.

"Never thought I'd be so glad of a nanny goat," said Curiosity. She had Lily in her lap, simply because the baby would not let her go, just as Daniel clung to Hannah, touching her face with both hands, patting her cheeks as if to hold her there with him. Both of them were agitated, as unsettled as they had been as newborns although Hannah reckoned them to be a full sixteen weeks old.

Hakim Ibrahim worked the goat's milk into the finely mashed rice until it was a smooth gruel. He looked up from the bowl at Lily and she stared back, round eyed.

"She ain't in a flirting kind of mood," observed Curiosity.

"But she is hungry," said the Hakim. He murmured to the baby in his own language and her brow creased, whether in fear or at the novelty of it, they could not tell. On Hannah's lap, Daniel fidgeted and yanked at her plaits.

Curiosity said, "Let's see, then." She dipped her finger in the warm gruel and touched Lily's full lower lip with it. Lily took the finger after a moment, sucked once, and her face crumpled in dismay. She let out a squeak.

"Try again," said Hannah, shifting Daniel. He was watching the whole undertaking closely as he mouthed his fists.

This time Lily took Curiosity's finger with less hesitation, and her expression turned from dismay to cautious interest.

"I have added a very little cooked honey and a bit of weak fennel water," said Hakim Ibrahim. "To quiet them and help them digest."

"My grandmother would give them a little tea of parsnip root, and maybe blueberry." Hannah was watching him out of the corner of her eye.

Hakim Ibrahim smiled. "I hope you will tell me more of your grandmother's medicines."

"Now you in for it," muttered Curiosity, but she hid a smile against the crown of Lily's head.

With a small flattish spoon Curiosity began to feed Lily, and to Hannah's surprise the baby was swallowing most of what she took in. As if to remind them all that he also had an empty stomach, Daniel thumped Hannah's chest, his expression darkening rapidly. She blew air gently into his face and he stopped, looking both hopeful and confused, for this was something Elizabeth did to get his attention when he was out of sorts.

"Try some of this, little brother," Hannah said to him in Kahnyen'kehàka, dipping her finger in the gruel.

He sucked hard enough to make her wince. Then his mouth popped open in invitation for more.

"Look!" Hannah felt herself flush with relief and pleasure.

"Hunger is the best sauce, so they say." Curiosity sniffed a little. "Thank the Lord."

There was a scratching at the door.

"That will be Mrs. MacKay," said Hakim Ibrahim.

"I don't think we'll need her anymore. Not as long as those goats don't decide to go for a swim," said Curiosity.

Hannah did not particularly want to see Mrs. MacKay again and so she kept her attention on Daniel, who clasped her wrist with both hands as if to guide the spoon toward his mouth. But she could still hear the rise and fall of Hakim Ibrahim's voice, and Mrs. MacKay's response: soft, hesitant, and in a tone that wavered between defiance and breaking. Hannah looked at Curiosity, who only raised a brow in surprise.

The Hakim came back into the room but went straight to his medicine cabinet, where he plucked a small bottle out of an intricate carved stand. Hannah watched him take a bit of some soft material from a jar, and then he spoke a word to Mrs. MacKay.

She closed the door behind her but stood looking past them as if they did not exist. Her eyes were red rimmed and her color was very bad, even for a white woman. There were wet spots on her bodice, and for the first time it occurred to Hannah that Elizabeth was in much the same situation. Except Elizabeth would get her children back—Hannah knew in her heart that this was true—and this woman had no hope of such a reunion. She might have said something to Mrs. MacKay, a word of thanks or even apology, but the Scotswoman refused to meet her gaze.

The Hakim said, "Tilt your head to the left, please." With a turn of his wrist he touched the material to

the lip of the small bottle and a new scent flooded the room, sharp but not unpleasant. Then Hakim Ibrahim touched the soaked cloth to the inner shell of Mrs. MacKay's exposed right ear and held it there for a moment, murmuring something under his breath that Hannah could not quite make out. Finally he stepped back and bowed from the shoulders.

Mrs. MacKay said, "I've a few shillings." But she seemed relieved when the Hakim would not take her money, and slipped away without another glance in their direction.

Hannah said, "What did you give her?"

"There is no medicine for grief," said Hakim Ibrahim, taking up his mortar and pestle again. "But sandalwood oil will quiet her womb."

Curiosity pushed out a sigh. "There's women who never get over a stillbirth."

Hannah had heard this before. Listening to birthing stories was a chore a girl couldn't escape: the spinning and the washing and the garden hoe would always be there, and so would the idea that someday she would find herself in childbed and have to struggle to come out of it alive. Once you had started down the road you could no more walk away from your fate than they could walk away from this ship on foot.

Her own mother had failed at it. When Hannah closed her eyes she could see her still. In death one corner of her mouth had turned down a little as it often did when she was irritated. She left the world angry, but at whom? The women who failed to stop her bleeding? Maybe it was the waxen-faced child they had folded so lovingly into the cold cradle of her arms. Or maybe she had been angry with herself, and her failure. Hannah had often wondered at it.

Daniel yanked hard at her plait and she roused herself out of her daydream to scoop more gruel into his mouth. She said, "I wish I had been kinder to her."

With a hushing sound Curiosity said, "There's

enough on your shoulders, child. You cain't take on the woes of the world, too."

But the Hakim said nothing, and only looked at her with a thoughtful expression.

By midday Hannah could hardly contain her need to be up on the quarterdeck, where she could scan the horizon for sails that might mean a quick rescue. But Curiosity would not go where she might see Moncrieff, and Hannah was not so desperate that she would leave her alone with the babies. Work might have distracted her, but there was little to do: every possible need was attended to. The cabin boy had even taken away a basket of dirty swaddling clothes to wash.

"Don' look so surprised," said Curiosity. "I suppose a little poop ain't the worst of what those boys have to put up with." She had found the bundle that Runs-from-Bears brought from the voyageurs' camp, and now she stood over the Hakim's table where she had spread out the deerskin. Sewing would have been a distraction, if Hannah could only make herself concentrate.

The cabin boy preoccupied her. His name was Charlie, and he seemed to her a very ordinary sort of boy, a little younger than Liam but older than she was. She knew nothing about him except that he was from Scotland, had been at sea for three years already, and that his hands—red knuckled and work hardened—were cleaner than her own. When he brought fresh water she asked him about this.

"The Hakim says that the devil hides beneath the fingernails, miss." Hannah could hear him trying to swallow his Scots and sound like the doctor. It made her curious about him, even though she knew that it would not be a good idea to be too friendly; he might be reporting everything to Moncrieff or the captain. And still she was inclined to like him, for his competence and quickness, and perhaps just because they had too few allies on the *Isis* to take him for granted.

"I ain't sure it's the best idea for you to be up on deck anyway," said Curiosity, angling borrowed scissors down the length of the deerskin, her brow creased in concentration. "What you need is sleep."

Hannah nodded, because she could not find the energy to disagree.

In the drowsy confusion of a warm, dim place, Hannah woke disoriented and with an aching head. For a moment she lay listening to the counterpoint of the babies' quiet breathing interwoven with women's voices: Curiosity and Elizabeth together at the hearth, waiting for her to join them and take up her part of the work and the conversation.

Then all around her the timber box that was the ship creaked and shifted, and she knew where she was—but the voices were there still. Hannah sat up with a little cry, rolled out of her hammock, and was at the door in two steps.

But it wasn't Elizabeth who looked around at her. Nor was it Mrs. MacKay, who might have come back in the end for the company of her own kind. Across from Curiosity sat Miss Giselle Somerville.

She seemed to have sprouted up out of the earthy colors of the surgery. Her gown glowed in the pale green of new grass, touched here and there with a pattern of winding roses; in the sunlight her hair was the gold of old cornsilk. This close Hannah could see the softening line of her jaw and the web of soft lines at the corners of her eyes that gave away her age, but she held herself like a much younger woman. For a long moment Hannah stared at Giselle Somerville and she looked back, neither smiling nor frowning. As if it were the most normal thing in the world for her to be here, come to call to pass the long afternoon with old friends. Hannah felt herself flushing with surprise and something else that made her fingers twitch.

"Come and say good day." Curiosity's voice had an unfamiliar tone: guarded, and grating faintly with the effort. Hannah might have turned back to the other cabin, to stay there in the warm dark where her little brother and sister slept. But Curiosity's expression said that she wanted Hannah here, and Hannah could not disobey her; she would not shame her before this woman.

Giselle Somerville said, "I suppose you have heard of me from your father. He and I were once good friends." Her tone was not warm, but there was a hidden kind of eagerness in her eyes.

She wants to win me over, thought Hannah. *I am nothing more than another prize to her.*

Hannah swallowed. "I don't think you could have ever been my father's friend."

Curiosity blinked, but Miss Somerville smiled.

"It was a long time ago. We were both very young."

It was a peace offering of a kind, but Hannah was not in the mood for peace. "You kept my uncle Otter in Montréal so that my grandfather had to come after him," she said. "If it weren't for you, none of this would have happened and we would be at home where we belong." She flushed with the power of speaking the truth to this white woman, and saw from the corner of her eye how Curiosity's back had straightened, whether in pride or alarm she could not tell.

But Giselle Somerville only raised one thin eyebrow in a surprised arch.

"I see little of your father in your face, but you are very much like him."

"She ain't much of a one for games, that's true," said Curiosity. "Maybe you better just tell us what you got on your mind."

"Very well." Giselle inspected an embroidered rose on her sleeve. When she raised her head she was all cool determination again. "I intend to slip away. If you like, you can join me."

In her surprise, Hannah looked to Curiosity, but the older woman's attention was focused on Giselle Somerville.

"Well, now," she said. "If you know Nathaniel Bonner as well as you say you do, then you'll know that he ain't far behind us—and his father and wife with him. No need for us to run off on our own."

A smile slid across the even features and then was gone. "Nathaniel and his father—yes, I suppose they will try to follow. And his wife, of course. What is the name that Otter had for her? Bone-in-Her-Back, I believe. From what I saw of her, a very determined type if not very pretty."

Curiosity put a cool hand on Hannah's wrist, as if to steady her, or quiet her. Hannah bit down hard and willed herself to stay calm.

Giselle smiled. "But there is little chance of it, after all. They have no ship and no prospects of finding one for such a long journey."

Because she could not stop herself, Hannah said, "Moncrieff says they are on their way."

Giselle had a way of blinking that put Hannah in mind of the white owl that sat in the rafters of the barn at Lake in the Clouds, always watching for those small creatures who put hunger or curiosity above caution. "Moncrieff is devious, is he not? Any lie to meet his end. But surely you must realize that his only task is to deliver an heir to Carryck. The child will be less trouble, and the same end will be achieved—the title and the estate will be safe from the Campbells and the Crown. That is all any of them care about—they are Scots, after all, and cannot be trusted to be reasonable. If the Bonners are alive at all, it is certain that they are not on the *Osiris*."

Curiosity's hand on Hannah's arm tightened like a vise. She smiled, quite broadly. "Ain't nobody said a word about the *Osiris*."

There was a slight tensing around Giselle's mouth, and it made Hannah's breath come easier to see this, the

first sign that she could not stand up to Curiosity. Few women could, after all, but for a moment she had been worried that this one with her jewels and silks and a knife blade of a smile might be as dangerous as she wanted to seem.

"It only makes sense that Moncrieff would have promised such a thing," Giselle said, utterly calm now. "What else might he say to keep you in your place, and acquiescent? You are, after all, nothing to him but a way to keep the boy in good health until he can turn him over to the earl. And of course Moncrieff likes to think of himself as irresistible."

"He ain't alone in that, now is he?" said Curiosity.

Giselle rose suddenly, her bracelets tinkling. "I was offering you a way to save these children from being delivered to Carryck. I see my concern is not welcome. I will bid you good day."

Curiosity held out her hand, fingers curling in an easy invitation. "Now hold on. You ain't afraid of a little straight talk, are you?"

Giselle slitted her eyes, but she sat again. Her back was as straight as a rifle, her head cocked at an angle.

They watched each other for a moment, and then Curiosity leaned forward as if she had a secret to tell. "You don' talk much to womenfolk, do you? Don' like dealing with your own kind if you can avoid it. Well, never mind, we won' keep you long. Now, this is what I see. Your daddy marrying you off to the captain to get shut of you. You just as glad to get away from him, and so off you go to Scotland. Ain't nothing unusual in any of it—women been trading one man for another as long as we been putting children in this world. But the captain don' suit you—maybe he ain't pretty enough, or maybe he too tame for you, or maybe you just don' want the vexation. So you set to run off from him before he can tie you down, legal like. Seen that happen before, too, and not so long ago. Sometimes women got to take things in they own hands, after all. Now, I

can see you ain't slow-witted, so I expect you got a plan."

She paused, and because the younger woman did not correct her, she continued.

"I imagine you got some men bribed to look the other way when the time come. A boat, or a horse, or some way to put some distance betwixt yourself and the captain. Got your valuables tied up in a sack, ready to go, and you'll leave the rest behind, travel light and fast. Now, why would you want to drag a contentious old black woman and three little ones along when you on the run, and so much at stake? We cain't travel fast, and if you're interested in layin' low, why, we'll stick out like that old sore thumb folks always talking about. So I'm asking myself here, are you offering something, or are you looking for something?"

"How very clever of you," said Giselle Somerville in a chilly tone. "And what is your conclusion?"

Curiosity shrugged. "Money come to mind first. There's some gold around here someplace, and you'll have heard tell about that. Gold might be useful to you, even if we ain't."

Giselle smiled thinly. "As perceptive as you seem to be, you must have recognized already that money is of little concern to me."

Curiosity shrugged. "You ain't never been hungry, neither. But that day could come, and you don't seem the kind to jump without looking. And then agin maybe you don' care so much about gold as you do about gettin' your way when it comes to men. Showin' them for the fools they can be. Ain' that so?"

There was a glimmer of something in Giselle's eyes: satisfaction, or disdain. Curiosity nodded as though she had spoken out loud.

"I know, truly I do. Now, maybe it's just your daddy you want to get even with—but I'm wondering if there's something else. Maybe you got an eye on Nathaniel, ready to make him pay for what went on all those years

ago. Maybe Otter was a part of that plan, and maybe this a part of it, too. Revenge is right tasty cold, after all.

"So you tell me, Miss Somerville, if I'm just a stupid old woman too scairt to think straight, or if you ain't tolt us the real story yet."

Giselle Somerville's gaze flickered toward Hannah and back again to Curiosity, even as she rose with a graceful swing of her skirt. "I have some things to consider before we continue our conversation," she said. "I bid you good day."

When she had closed the door behind herself, Curiosity turned to Hannah to grasp her hard by both hands. "Was the *Osiris* the ship that Moncrieff told you about?"

Hannah jerked in surprise. "Yes. I'm sure it was."

Curiosity smiled grimly. "And did Elizabeth take the gold with her when she went to see the governor?"

"One of the sacks, yes. She took it from the carry basket at the last minute."

"And the other sack? When did you see that last?"

Curiosity's expression was almost more upsetting to Hannah than Giselle Somerville's claims, but she tried to gather her thoughts.

"My grandfather had it. Why?"

Curiosity rose to pace the cabin, her arms crossed hard under her breasts and her chin tucked down in concentration. Then she stopped, and looked Hannah in the eye. "We ain't got nothing more than a little silver, then. But listen to me, child, we got to let her think that we got the gold here with us. Do you hear me?"

Hannah nodded, confused and distracted. "You don't believe her, do you? You don't think that Moncrieff—" She hesitated, because she could not say out loud what she feared might be true, that they might be alone not just on this wide sea, but that her father and grandfather and Elizabeth were nowhere to be found in the world at all.

Curiosity shook her head hard. "No. I don' believe

her. That old earl wanted Hawkeye, and Moncrieff will deliver him if he can. But she's after something else, and I ain't sure what, yet. She gave away the game, you see, telling us that she's going to bolt."

"Maybe she won't," Hannah said. "Bolt, I mean. Maybe she just wanted to see how we'd react."

"Helping out Moncrieff, you mean? Spying for him?"

Confused, Hannah shook her head. "No, I suppose not. She doesn't like him much, does she?"

Curiosity said, "She ain't easy to read, but there's one thing for sure—what Pickering has to offer ain't what she got in mind."

"Because of his face?"

"No, child. 'Cause of his heart."

From the other room came the humming sounds that meant Lily was struggling up from sleep. In a moment she would realize that the one person in the world she must have was not with her, and in her despair she would wake Daniel and then the process of soothing them would begin all over again.

"She wants Elizabeth," Hannah said, feeling that truth in her own belly.

Curiosity let out a sigh and she pulled Hannah to her, hugged her hard. She smelled as she always did, of lye soap and lavender and of herself, honest Curiosity, strong minded and gentle hearted. Hannah was loath to let her go, and Curiosity seemed to know that. She cupped Hannah's cheek in her palm and wobbled her head gently from side to side. "Don' you lose faith now, you hear me?"

Hannah said, "Do you think Miss Somerville will come back?"

"Before sunset," said Curiosity. "What do you want to wager?"

Through the afternoon they waited. While they ground rice and mixed it with goat's milk and fed the twins,

they waited. The Hakim came and went on his daily business, but by unspoken agreement they said nothing of Giselle Somerville; they did not know how far his loyalties reached, and neither of them cared to test him. He made Curiosity more of his medicine, and then went out once again to take tea with the captain.

Curiosity could not sit without some work in her hands and so they took up the sewing, listening all the while for the sound of a soft step at the door. Hannah pieced together leggings and tried to remember why it seemed so important just a day ago to put aside calico and linsey-woolsey for Kahnyen'kehàka dress. The old Tory with his ragged ears seemed like a dream, or a story she had heard once at the hearth when elders told tales of the days before the O'seronni came.

Charlie brought tea and polite inquiries from the captain. They were feeding the babies goat's milk from a bowl, and he stopped to touch Lily's sticky cheek with one light finger, smiling in pleasure when she grabbed at his work-hardened hand.

"Tell me," Curiosity said to him in a casual tone that made Hannah's ears prick up. "Is this here *Isis* the only boat the earl calls his own?"

Charlie bristled, surprised and offended, and began a long inventory of the ships owned by the Earl of Carryck. He spoke of merchantmen and sloops and cutters as if they belonged to him personally, and Hannah realized that in a way they were his—the company was his family, and this ship might be his home for as long as he lived. It made her sad for him, and vaguely curious, too.

Curiosity seemed less impressed.

"Uh-huh." She interrupted him casually, all her attention on the chore of extracting the feeding spoon from Daniel's fist. "I'm fond of stories myself. But I don' suppose you ever *seen* one of them ships, now, have you?"

He stared at her. "But I have, and no' two days past.

The *Osiris* came intae Québec just as we set sail." As he grew more agitated his careful imitation of the Hakim's English gave way and his own Scots came bubbling to the surface.

"The *Osiris*?" Curiosity snorted softly. "That big East Indiaman you told us about? What would that ship be doing over in Canada?"

Charlie flushed such a deep color that Hannah almost felt sorry for him, a poor confused mouse to Curiosity's cat.

"But it was the *Osiris*! I would ken her anywhere. The earl is always sending ships on errands—did we no' sail oot o' our way tae Martinique for his cursed ti-nain plants, and hasna the Hakim been slaving e'er since tae see that they thrive? He'll ha' sent the *Osiris* tae Québec tae fetch a bird he fancies, or the pelt of some strange beast that canna be bred in Scotland, or some such wastefulness. Is that no' the way o' rich men?"

"I suppose it is." Curiosity had a particular smile that she saved for her menfolk when they had pleased her. Hannah had seen even Judge Middleton duck his head in pleasure at it, just the way Charlie did now, his ears tinged an earnest red.

"It was the *Osiris*, Mrs. Freeman, and she's headed hame for the Firth, too. You'll see her there."

"I expect you must be right," Curiosity said, shifting Daniel to a more convenient spot on her lap. "Cain't claim to know too much about ships, anyway, can I?"

Hannah could barely keep her surprise or her admiration to herself. Curiosity had put so little work into finding out what she wanted to know, and Charlie was none the worse for it, and even pleased to have been of service to her. The *Osiris* was headed this way, and probably not far behind. A great shudder of relief moved down her spine. Hannah put her nose to Lily's neck and took a settling breath.

Charlie was at the door when Curiosity called one

more question after him. "Oh, and child, tell me this. Who are these Campbells I hear tell about now and then? Do you know of them?"

His expression darkened with surprise. "Oh, aye. Who doesna ken the Campbells?"

"Friends of the earl's, are they?"

The question agitated the boy, for he flushed again to the tips of his ears. "The Campbells friends to Carryck? They're naught but treacherous hounds, all widdershins tae honest men."

Curiosity turned to Hannah as the door fell shut behind him. "I figure that ain't exactly a compliment."

Hannah had to smile. "Granny Cora used to tell stories of the clan wars. The sachem called their men 'hounds.'" She closed her eyes and reached for the familiar rhythms of her grandmother's voice. "'Sons o' the hounds, come and eat flesh'—it's how they were called to battle."

"And they call your kind barbarians." Curiosity grunted softly. "Now I wonder what Miss Priss meant about the Campbells being a worry to Carryck." She stood, lifting Daniel onto her hip, and looked out the window to the rolling sea.

Sunset, and the sea tugged the light out of the day. With a sleeping Lily in her arms, Hannah leaned against the wall to watch seabirds wheeling white against a sky of bruised blue and scarlet. Through the wall of the surgery she could hear the Hakim as he sang his prayers: he had a hoarse voice and a tin ear and still his chant wound softly around her like a silk veil. Hannah understood nothing of his language or of his god, except that they were a comfort to him, so far away from home. She leaned harder against the wall, held in place by Lily's sleeping weight, her breath damp and sweet. Behind lids the color of seashells the baby's eyes darted: even in her sleep she looked for her mother.

Curiosity's humming stopped, and Hannah roused herself. Over Daniel's sleeping head she saw Curiosity's face creased in concentration. "Listen," she whispered.

Hannah cocked her head and closed her eyes, but she could hear only the sea and the creaking of the ship around her. Nothing of Giselle Somerville. *Nothing yet,* she corrected herself.

"What is it?"

Curiosity flapped a hand. "Listen!"

Hannah closed her eyes. Overhead, men were moving, as they did so often to change the watch, shift sails, wash down the deck, haul rope, or look to the hundreds of other chores that divided the day into its parts. But the ship had her own voice, too, and it came to Hannah softly, a faint shudder and then a sighing, as a woman sighs at the end of a long day.

"Are we slowing?"

Curiosity spread out a hand, palm up, as if to weigh the question.

From the doorway Hakim Ibrahim said, "We are heaving-to."

"Stopping?" Curiosity drew in her breath on a hiss.

The smooth brow under the Hakim's turban creased. "Not quite, but almost. Perhaps we have lost a sail." And in response to Curiosity's expression of disbelief: "Such a loss is not unknown, Mrs. Freeman."

Hannah touched his sleeve. "Are we near land?"

The Hakim took a rolled parchment from a cubbyhole in his desk and spread it out for her to see. Hannah shifted Lily across her chest and brushed the baby's curls out of her face, leaning forward to look.

"We are not within sight of a port, if that is your question." One strong brown finger made an arc across the map. "This whole area is called the Grand Banks—shoal reefs. Fishermen come from as far away as Portugal." From another cubby in the desk he took stones to anchor the curling parchment, and then he

stood looking at it, one corner of his mouth turned down. "I will go to the captain and see what is to be learned. If you will excuse me."

When he was gone, Curiosity smiled at Hannah over Daniel's head.

"What?" Hannah asked. "What?"

"Sail, my foot," said Curiosity. "We been moving fast since we left Canada behind, and all of a sudden we ain't. Heaving-to, he say. Maybe we're waitin' for somebody to catch up."

Hannah's heart fluttered, and in perfect imitation of its rhythm came a tripping knock at the door. She jumped, and Lily frowned in her sleep.

Curiosity pointed with her chin to the sleeping cabin. "Keep out of sight," she whispered.

"Give me Daniel."

"No," said Curiosity. "I need him here."

"I see you ain't finished with us, after all," said Curiosity. "Come on in and set, then. I cain't get up with this child so sound asleep."

In the darkened sleeping cabin Hannah put Lily down in the cradle and covered her carefully. Then she inched back to stand in the shadows near the door. She had left it standing slightly open, so that from this angle she could see only a bit of Curiosity's back and half of Giselle Somerville.

"I waited until the doctor came up on deck," Giselle said.

"You don' trust him, then."

A surprised laugh. "Do you?"

Hannah wished to see Curiosity's face, but then her long silence told quite a lot on its own.

Giselle's expression was calm, too, as if they were discussing nothing more than the possibility of a summer's outing. When she spoke her voice was very cool.

"You must pardon my confusion," she said. "It was my impression that you were on this voyage against your will."

Curiosity laughed, but there was nothing cheerful in the sound. "Oh, you got it right. I never did think to cross this sea. Never even cared to lay eyes on it. My mama crossed it in chains when she weren't much older than Nathaniel's Hannah. Made a slave of her, and she died a slave."

Hannah hugged her arms closer around herself, afraid to breathe lest she miss even a word. From Giselle Somerville there was no sound at all, but Curiosity seemed not to notice.

"Now, I been free some thirty years," she continued. "My children were born free. I s'pose somewhere deep inside I had 'free' mixed up with 'safe.' For a woman most especially it ain't the same thing, though, is it?"

A flush was rising on Giselle's neck. "No," she said. "It is not." She lowered her gaze and then raised it again, so that Hannah realized suddenly what a strange color her eyes were, violetlike in the very white face. She said, "I am offering you an opportunity to get away."

Curiosity leaned forward without any warning and simply thrust the sleeping Daniel into Giselle's arms. Giselle let out a startled sound, and for the first time real surprise showed on her face.

"Look at that child," said Curiosity. "Pretty, ain't he? But he's made of blood and bone. Look hard and think about this: if harm come to any of these children I will have to answer to Nathaniel and Elizabeth, just as sure as one day I will have to answer to my God."

"Take him back," said Giselle, her voice trembling with outrage. "*Take him back.*"

When Curiosity had done just that, Giselle said, "That was a very silly thing to do." Her eyes blazed now, all her calm indifference gone. Her gaze flitted back to Daniel

and her color rose another notch. "Am I a young girl to lose my wits over an infant? Did you think I would offer up some great secret with a child in my arms?"

"My," said Curiosity softly. "What a fuss over a little baby. As if you ain't never held one before."

Giselle Somerville froze, her face suddenly very still. "What do you mean by that?"

"Why, nothing at all," said Curiosity. "What did you think I meant?"

After a moment Giselle smiled. "I understand that the safety of the children is paramount. Listen now and I'll tell you what opportunity I can offer, and you may take it or leave it as you wish. It might be as much as a day from now, but sooner or later a small ship will anchor nearby flying a particular signal flag. When that ship is in sight, I will create a diversion on board and slip away to meet it. It will all have to happen very quickly, for when this vessel shows itself the *Osiris* will be very close at hand."

Curiosity let out a little laugh. "So, we are stopped to wait for the *Osiris* after all."

"Yes. Of course." Giselle was not in the least embarrassed to have been caught in a lie.

"Well then, missy, tell me this. Why would we want to run off, just when our people about to catch us up?"

Giselle sighed. "You mustn't forget what you know of Moncrieff. He will wait for the *Osiris*, of course, but he is not enough of a fool to let Nathaniel Bonner get within rifle range. No, the minute we see the *Osiris* within reasonable distance, we will sail off again for Scotland."

"Now, wait a minute," Curiosity said. "Seems to me you and Moncrieff been workin' together for some time now. How does he fit into your little plan?"

Giselle's mouth pursed with irritation. "I should say rather that Moncrieff was working for me, although he did not realize it. It suited me to let him think that it

was all his plan, when in fact—well." She pushed out a small breath. "I had business to see to, and it suited me to use him."

Curiosity might have spoken, but Giselle held up a hand to stop her. "If you leave the *Isis* with me we can signal the *Osiris* to stop and take you on board. Given the fact that Carryck wants the child, there is no doubt that they would do so."

"And we'd still be on our way to Scotland," said Curiosity.

Giselle spread out her hands on her lap. "Yes," she said simply. "But with Nathaniel and Hawkeye watching over you, Moncrieff would not dare approach the *Osiris* to get you back, and thus you would all be together. Which seems to be the thing you want most." She said this as if it were a mystery to her, and vaguely amusing. She looked at Daniel.

"He's very dark haired, isn't he?"

Curiosity shrugged. "It ain't a surprise, looking at his folks."

Giselle looked away suddenly. "If you do not care to come away with me, then a word of warning."

"We cain't pay you for your advice, Miz Somerville."

The younger woman looked more annoyed than disappointed at this interruption. A frown line etched its way down the pale brow. "Carryck wants this boy badly," she said. "And there are others who will want him, too."

"Those Campbells, I suppose," said Curiosity.

"I pity the man who underestimates you." Giselle laughed. "Yes, the Campbells. It suits them best that Carryck is without a male heir, and they will do what they must to keep things that way. Do I make myself clear?"

Curiosity said, "You do. And now let me speak plain, miss."

"I don't suppose I could stop you," said Giselle with a half-smile that was meant to disarm.

"I'm wondering about you, how desperate you are. Who this man is you're running off with, and what he's got in mind for these children. After all, they are worth something to Carryck, or to those Campbells."

Giselle rose slowly. She walked to the window and stood for a long minute watching the sky. With her back still to Curiosity she said, "I could tell you any number of stories that might satisfy you. Perhaps I should tell them all, and leave you to sort out the truth. But in the end there is only one thing that matters: you can take these children and get off this ship and away from Moncrieff, if you care to."

"Is that so. And I suppose you ain't ever heard tell about folks jumping out of a frying pan right into the fire." Curiosity was rocking quietly now, one hand stroking Daniel's back in a small circle.

Giselle turned from the window. "You have no reason to trust me. Just the opposite. But let me tell you something about myself, and perhaps it will change your mind." She crossed her arms below her breasts and dropped her gaze to the floor. When she raised her head, there was a glittering in her eye. "My mother was French, of good family but modest resources. My father regretted the union. He speaks of it as unfortunate and untimely, an indiscretion. He divorced my mother under English law and sent her home to France. I have not seen her since. I do not even know her real name, or if she is alive. Perhaps she has not survived the Terror in France. But I do intend to find out, and the man I am meeting will take me there. It was my one condition."

Curiosity made a sound, but Giselle Somerville held her off with a raised hand.

"Please. I would much prefer your silence to your sympathy. Now, you can take that story and make of it what you will. I will send word when the time comes. It may be quite soon, or it may not be until tomorrow night. You will act according to your best judgment."

When she was gone, Curiosity said, "Come on out here, child, and talk to me. What did you think of that little story of hers?"

Hannah said, "She never met your eye. I think she was lying."

Curiosity grunted softly. "Maybe. Even if she weren't, it still don't sit right, none of it."

"I don't think we should go with her," said Hannah. "At least, not unless we get a good look at the ship."

Curiosity got up with a groan, and shifted Daniel to her shoulder. "That's just what we'll do," she said. "But pack the basket, just in case."

At dusk Hannah could stand it no longer, and she went up on deck. She found a spot at the rail where she thought she might not be in the way. The sailors ignored her; after a while she began to relax, to take some pleasure in the fresh air and the wind. There were fishing boats in the distance, and she wondered what kind of life it would be to live on the water and to learn to read it as her people could read the sky and the mountains.

"The Indian," said a man's voice. "Come to worship the settin' sun, are ye?"

The first officer stood, hands folded behind him and his chin pressed to his chest. Mr. MacKay was a big man, heavily built with a seaman's squint, a great shelf of a jaw, a high sloping forehead, and a nose so short and mean it looked like it was trying to burrow back into his skull. But it was his eyes that worried her, alive with a moody curiosity that made her sorry to have come up on deck.

And no one else about, and no way to get past him unless he let her go.

"Sir?"

"Have ye been baptized in Christ?" He spoke so softly that she had to strain to hear him.

It was a simple question, and she did not want to answer it. But by his expression she knew that she had no choice. "I was baptized, sir."

His eyes narrowed. "Is that so? And wha guid man came among the savages to save ye from eternal damnation?"

Hannah pressed her back harder into the rail. "I don't remember him, sir. I was very small. A Jesuit, I think."

The long face flushed such a deep shade of red, and that so quickly, that Hannah's unease was pushed aside with the thought that Mr. MacKay might be suffering a stroke before her eyes.

His mouth twisted with disgust. "Papists among the savages. Aye, and I heard tell o' sic travesties. And the puir wee babbies, have they been damned wi' ye?"

Hannah looked about hoping for a friendly face, but the sailor at the helm was watching the horizon. Mr. MacKay was waiting for her answer, and so she shook her head.

"They are not yet baptized, in any faith."

"Ach. There's hope, then. Now you listen to me," Mr. MacKay began, in a more kindly fashion. "'The angels shall come forth, and take out the wicked from among the righteous, and will cast them into the furnace of fire; there shall be weeping and gnashing of teeth.'" He thrust his face forward, within inches of her own. "It's no' in your nature tae understan' the Holy Scripture— savage and female, ava—but it's my duty tae tell the truth and shame the de'il. Lass, ye're bound for hellfire should ye no' see the error o' yer ways."

"I must go," Hannah said, and her voice cracked. "I must go back to the Hakim now."

"The Hakim. Anither infidel." Mr. MacKay shook his head. "Innocent babes among the heathens. Can a guid Christian stand by and watch?"

Hannah's blood beat heavy in her ears, but she made

herself speak up. She said, "Stay away from us. Stay away from us all, or I'll tell Captain Pickering."

Mr. MacKay sucked in his lower lip and pushed it out again. "And does it matter, wha ye tell? The Almighty kens aa, and sees aa, and ye canna run fra' him tae yer Captain Pickering. 'His wrath is poured out like fire, and in the end ye will burn.'"

He rocked back and forth on his heels, his mouth pursed thoughtfully. "Noo, tell me, lass. Will ye be saved fra' yer infidel ways, ye and the wee ones wi' ye?"

"Mr. MacKay, sir!" the bosun called. "The helmsman needs a word wi' ye, sir!"

"Hear me now," he said, peering closely at her. "It's up tae ye whether the babbies burn in hell. We'll talk agin."

Hannah forced herself to breathe in and out as he walked away. When she could make her legs obey her, she went below. And wondered if she would ever come back on deck again.

16

The *Jackdaw* was seventy-five feet of hard-worn oak and peeling black paint, but as the St. Lawrence widened toward the open sea something became clear to Nathaniel: the schooner might have seen better days, but she still loved the wind and the wind loved her back. It was true that they were twelve hours behind the *Isis,* but there were other truths, too, and he didn't have to reach far for them: they had an able captain who would stop at nothing to earn his prize, and while the *Isis* idled along like a fat cow for home, the *Jackdaw* was a cougar of a ship, fast and lean, carrying no cargo beyond provisions for a skeleton crew of thirty, ammunition, and the monumental force of the Bonners' combined fury.

Nathaniel could see the full strength of it now in Elizabeth's face as she paced the deck, her arms wound around herself. Once before he had seen her this close to broken, but that battle had left the kind of bruises that healed. This time there would be no healing for either of them until they had the children and Curiosity back.

The *Jackdaw* was only eighteen feet at the beam; Nathaniel could almost reach out and touch his wife as

she paced by. But she looked to the horizon for comfort, and seemed not to take note of him at all. Since she had come on board and spilled out the whole story of what had passed she had barely spoken a word.

"It ain't her fault," said Hawkeye when she had passed them once again. "You need to make her understand that."

"If there's anyone tae blame, it must be me," said Robbie hoarsely. "I was a fool tae trust Moncrieff. I tried tae tell her so, but she wouldna listen."

Nathaniel said, "It'll take more than words to set her right."

Hawkeye grunted, for it was the simple truth. But Robbie's troubled expression settled on Nathaniel.

"Aye, but words are a start, lad. Dinna let her grieve alone." He put a hand on Nathaniel's shoulder, but it was the weight of the word, the idea of grieving, that brought him to his feet.

He scanned the length of the ship, from the forecastle where Stoker was deep in conversation with his first mate, to the bow.

"She's gone below," said Hawkeye, his unease showing clear. He had been raised among strong-minded women and had had another one to wife. His daughter-in-law was made in the same mold, and he liked and admired her; it wouldn't occur to him to forbid Elizabeth to go anywhere. But Stoker's crew was a rough lot—Americans and Irishmen, and a handful of the kind who claim no home and want none. Nathaniel saw the worry in his father's face, and thought his own expression probably gave away just as much. He went after her.

At the bottom of the companionway Nathaniel stopped to clear his head of the sound of the sea. What he heard took him by surprise: an old woman's voice, and Elizabeth's quiet tones in reply. Alone for a moment on a ship where there would be precious little privacy, too tall to stand in the cramped space, Nathaniel

crouched down to listen. His head ached, and he was tired, and he wondered if he would ever be able to sleep again. Even in sleep he could not escape the fact that his children had been taken from him without a struggle, and by a man he had given his trust. *I regret the necessity of such a drastic step, but your father-in-law denied me every other more reasonable alternative.* That single sentence echoed in his head, carved deep in the very bones of his skull. If this ship should go down now and kill him outright Nathaniel knew that he would walk the sea floor to get to them. And to Angus Moncrieff, who would be taught the meaning of reason, and regret.

The sound of throaty laughter from the cabin startled him out of his daydream. Elizabeth's voice again, in reply. He thought of joining them, but then he had spent much of his life in the company of women and he knew the sound of a conversation where men were not welcome. And the truth was, he had little comfort to offer.

He went back up on deck to ask again after their speed and to find some work to do. For the moment hard labor was the only thing that would keep him sane.

She was old, so old that time had reversed its path: the hair under the tightly knotted kerchief was baby-fine and only two teeth were left in the wide, thin-lipped mouth. These were on the right side, and served as the anchor for a pipe that wobbled and waved over a sunken breast covered with a mass of chains and baubles. But there was nothing childlike about the woman's mind, and she squinted at Elizabeth from a fog of tobacco smoke with a bright and inquisitive expression, plucking her pipe from her mouth to point at a tea chest.

"Sit!"

Elizabeth hesitated, but the pipe tapped smartly on

the arm of the chair and she seemed to have little choice but to comply.

"I had no intention of disturbing you," she said, resting very uncomfortably on the edge of the chest, and trying not to stare around herself at the crowded cabin, nor to inhale too deeply the mingled smells of stale tobacco, rank clothing, and fish oil. "I was just looking for a quiet spot."

The old woman let out a hoot of laughter. "Cor, a quiet spot on the *Jackdaw*. Now, *there's* a pretty notion."

The reedy, wobbling voice was London with an overlay of Ireland and other places Elizabeth could not quite put a name to. Here was a mystery that would have intrigued at any other time, but Elizabeth was so tired she could not focus on the most obvious things. Nor could she quite bring herself to do what she wanted to do, which was to give in to her low spirits and simply walk away.

"Please permit me to introduce myself—"

"I know who you are," said the old woman. "Saw you when you come with that bloody great Indian to talk to Mac, though I expect you didn't see me. Annie is my name, but most call me Granny Stoker. Mac is the youngest son of me youngest son."

"Ah," said Elizabeth. "I recall that he mentioned you the first time I spoke to him."

"Eh? And what did he say?"

"He did not say that you sail with him. I'm glad not to be the only woman on board, but I am somewhat surprised to find you here."

The old lady's mouth worked around the stem of the pipe. "Don't be. Women been on the water since the first raft was pushed off, even if some don't like to admit it. Now me, I don't go on land unless I'm dragged. First shipped out when I was just fifteen. That was seventy-seven years ago. I'll wager you've heard of me. I went by Anne Bonney back then, when I ran with Calico Jack."

Elizabeth thought it might be bad policy to admit she had not heard either name, but to her relief, the old woman's attention had already shifted. She fumbled for a cane at her knee and with it she poked at Elizabeth's skirts.

"You need breeches," she said, in the unapologetic tones of the very old when they had made a personal decision for someone younger. "Skirts tie you down on board. In breeks you'd move freer, and fight better when the time comes. But I expect you'll tell me it isn't your way. You're that type."

Elizabeth found herself bristling. "I'm not sure what type you mean, but the fact is, I have worn leggings. All of last summer I wore them, when I was—" She hesitated. "On the New-York frontier."

The brown eyes snapped at her under a creased brow. "So I hear tell. Jack Lingo was a tough one, weren't he?"

Elizabeth rubbed her forehead. "I suppose your grandson told you."

"I keep my ears open," said Annie Stoker. "And my eyes."

Wearily, Elizabeth said, "And what do you see?"

The knotty hands gripped the arms of the chair as the old woman leaned forward, her beads and chains making a soft clinking sound. "I see a woman et up with anger, and no place to go with it. You won't weep, not in front of me. Maybe not in front of anybody. That Scot don't know what kind of trouble he's called down on his head with you. Took your babbies, and left you with more than one kind of pain. I expect if I put a finger to your breast it might feel ready to burst about now."

Elizabeth composed her expression. "It's not so bad."

The old lady had a whoop of a laugh with very little of amusement in it. "Maybe you can make your menfolk believe that, but you look at me again, girl, and see what you're looking at. Ten children I've brought into

this world, the first one when I was sixteen years old. The last one was Mac's da, when I was forty-five. But when I look at you I'm put in mind of my second. My only girl, and they took her away from me before I could give her a name." She picked up the cane again and pointed it at Elizabeth's bodice with two quick jabbing motions. "They ache like two bad teeth. Ain't that so?"

Elizabeth folded her arms across herself and tried not to flinch as her breasts, rock-hard, pulsed and leaked in response. But the old lady had already turned away to begin rummaging around in an open chest at the side of her chair. Her pipe worked furiously up and down as she clawed through a jumble of fabrics: old-fashioned waistcoats and pelisses of yellowed brocade, petticoats and skirts dangling torn flounces.

"There we are," she said, hooking something dull brown to deposit it onto Elizabeth's lap. "And these. Make good use of them."

There were breeches and a loose-cut shirt. "This is very kind of you," Elizabeth said, resisting the urge to examine them for lice in front of the old lady.

Annie Stoker waved a hand dismissively. She pointed with her cane to another chest. "In that box there you'll find linen for binding. You wrap your chest up tight as ever you can stand it, that will help some. You can do it now. But if the pain gets to be too much anyway, you have that man of yours give you some ease."

"Ease," Elizabeth echoed. *What right do I have to ease?* And she saw with some distant surprise how her own tears fell to darken the rough homespun of the breeches. Her bodice was full wet now, but she did not have the strength to hide this from the old woman.

She said, "Why did they take your daughter from you?"

A shrug of the bony shoulders. "I was headed for the gallows at the time. You may not credit it to see me now, respectable old lady that I am, but I was a terror back

then, and I near swung for it. Until Paddy Stoker got a better idea and took me away to Ireland. We left the girl behind. I never knew what became of her." The old woman leaned forward to grasp Elizabeth by the wrist. Her skin was dry and warm, and her grip was unforgiving. "A bellyful of anger ain't the worst thing, right now," she said.

The last of the evening light shifted from the window to lay its warmth on Anne Stoker's face. Tears were swelling in Elizabeth's throat and she blinked hard as the old woman doubled in her vision. The blur of color around her neck glimmered and took on sudden clarity: a blue-tinted diamond the size of a woman's thumbnail. A string of square-cut sapphires, and a pendant of amber and worked silver. Coins of all sizes and lands. And half hidden in the folds of the faded calico shirt another coin, larger and heavier, on a chain of its own. A five-guinea gold piece, with old King George in profile.

Elizabeth touched the spot between her own breasts where that very coin had rested for almost a year, and then her gaze traveled up the length of the chain to Anne Stoker's face.

The old lady showed her empty red gums and two dimples carved new grooves on the lined cheeks. Then she reached into a crewel-worked pocket tied to her waist over a pair of leather breeches and drew out a pendant: a single pearl in a clutch of silver petals and curling leaves. She held it up so that the pearl twisted in the scattered light, and then she tossed it.

"Lookin' for that, are you?"

Elizabeth caught it with one hand. The metal was cold against her palm, but there was a warmth in the pearl that she had first noted when Nathaniel had put the chain around her neck as a wedding present. How it had hurt her pride to have this taken from her. Now it seemed a very small thing, and unimportant.

She sent Anne Stoker a sidelong glance. "I must have dropped it when I came on board at Sorel."

"Must have."

Her innocent tone was at odds with the satisfied expression in those bright eyes. A respectable old lady, indeed. Knowing that she flushed, and that her high color gave away something, Elizabeth said, "There was a panther's tooth, too."

"Was there now? And how did you come by such a thing as that?"

"It is a very long story."

"Aye, and what better way to pass the time than wit' a good, long story?"

Elizabeth considered for a moment. "I don't suppose you have a toothbrush in that trunk of yours? And a hairbrush?"

"I might do," said the old lady, her fingers winding through silver chains. "Why do you ask?"

"Stories do not come cheap," said Elizabeth.

The old woman's face lit up. "Oooh," she said. "Intend to haggle wit' me, do you?"

Whatever Elizabeth might have said to Anne Stoker was interrupted by the sound of running feet on deck and a call from the crow's nest: "Ship ahoy!" She started up from her seat, but the old woman never moved.

"Not the one you're looking for," she said evenly. "Not yet."

"Do you think we'll catch the *Isis* up, then?" It was the most important question, and Elizabeth feared the answer so much that she had not been able to ask the men outright.

Granny Stoker laughed, the tobacco-stained fingers threading through the lifetime's plunder hung around her neck. "Have you watched children playin' at tag, me dear?"

Elizabeth nodded. "I have." *Once I was a schoolteacher*, she might have said. But it seemed so long ago, and she would not think of home. Not now.

"Well, then, you'll recall as how little boys like the chase, but for little girls all fun is in the getting caught.

And she's no different at heart. Just a little girl running away to get caught."

"Who is no different?" asked Elizabeth, vaguely confused.

"Why," said Annie Stoker. "The Lass in Green, of course."

Though the *Jackdaw* was not a large ship, Mac Stoker managed to keep clear of Elizabeth. She supposed that his sudden deference had more to do with a healthy fear of the Bonner men than with some newfound consideration, but she did not mind the isolation from Stoker.

He sent her messages through his crew. It was Jacques, the boy who had lured her to the ship, who brought word that Granny Stoker was willing to have Elizabeth sleep in the captain's quarters with her. It was a kind offer, and Elizabeth was relieved to have recourse to the cabin throughout the day when she wanted privacy to see to her own needs, but she could not bear the idea of long hours without Nathaniel. Neither was she willing to share the crew's berth, as Hawkeye and Robbie were. This left only the open deck, and hammocks.

It was not the worst solution. Over the mizzenmast the stars turned in endless wheels, and Elizabeth could raise her head to look for the glimmer of sails on the horizon. It was something she did quite often, for even tightly bound the throbbing in her breasts was bad enough to keep her from a real sleep. Nathaniel was not better off; she could hear him constantly turning and shifting.

The hammocks were narrow and would never hold the both of them, but what she wanted, what she needed, was to sleep beside him, tucked into his side with his arm around her. With the sound of Nathaniel's heartbeat in her ear she might be able to find some peace for a few hours. But Elizabeth found that more

than her children had been taken from her: she no longer knew how to talk to her husband. How could she speak of her own discomfort when all of this was her fault? And if she said that to him, if she put the truth out in a line of words, one after the other, what would he do? She tasted salt on her skin and could not tell if it was sea spray, or her own tears.

"Boots," he called softly.

"Yes?"

His feet thumped on the deck, and then he was leaning over her. She could not make out his expression in the dark, but she could feel the sweet warmth of him.

"If you don't get some sleep you'll fall ill."

"You're not sleeping either, Nathaniel."

"I would if I could hold you."

What help was there for her then? She collapsed slowly inward, sorrow raking through the last of her self-control. The hammock shook with her sobs so that she could hardly breathe, aware only dimly of the milk that flowed from her breasts now, finally, as she wept. And then Nathaniel simply tipped the canvas sling toward him and she slid into the cradle of his arms.

He took the full force of her misery without protest, although there was a trembling in him. With her face pressed to his neck she wept herself into a quieter, duller place, and then Nathaniel turned and walked with her to the longboat that took up the center of the main deck. He set her on her feet to throw back the canvas cover and then he climbed in, and reached down to lift her over the side.

The cover made a cave of the boat once it was pulled back over their heads. Inside it was damp and close and it smelled of mildew and spilled ale, but it was quiet out of the wind and there was a tarpaulin to serve as a makeshift mattress and blanket both. There was just enough room between two benches to lie in a half-recline, side by side. Elizabeth settled against him carefully. Her whole body felt hollow and distant, a poor

quaking thing, but Nathaniel was solid and warm and immediately comforting. Last summer on the run in the endless forests they had slept like this sometimes, under an outcropping of cliff.

"A year ago," she said out loud.

"I been thinking about that too," Nathaniel said. "Solid ground under our feet and Richard Todd on our tails. And the day Joe died." His fingers traced the side of her face. "On the island, do you remember?"

Elizabeth rubbed her face on the rough linen of his shirt. "If I live to be a hundred I will remember that island."

"I suppose a woman likes to think of the day she gets with child for the first time."

Elizabeth jerked a little in surprise.

"You can't know that. It could have happened any time, we were . . . quite busy with each other."

Nathaniel pressed his mouth to the top of her head; she could feel him trying to smile.

"You've forgot your words," he said. "And I went to such trouble to teach them to you."

Elizabeth shook him lightly. "Don't change the subject, you know I can't be distracted so easily. Why are you so sure that I fell pregnant at that particular time?"

He shrugged. "Because I know. Because I felt it happen. And you did too, if you'll think about it and trust your gut."

"It is very strange how these conversations always come down to my inner workings," Elizabeth said, and she heard the tone of her voice, and regretted it. She wound her fingers in Nathaniel's shirt and squeezed his arm as hard as she could. "I trust you, that is enough. Right now, it's all that I have."

He whispered into her hair, his tone solemn now and nothing of teasing in him. "The world will be right again, Boots. Tomorrow or the day after we'll catch up with the *Isis*, but now we'll sleep. Sleep's the thing." He shifted her slightly against him and the pain in her over-

filled breasts flared hot, so that she had to stifle a cry against his chest.

Nathaniel jerked up, holding her so that he could peer into her face. "You're hurting," he said, his cool hands on her skin under the borrowed homespun shirt, full wet with tears and lost milk. "I didn't know it was that bad. Can I help you?"

"No," she said, trying to turn away in the narrow space, mortified and undone. "There are some hurts that even you cannot mend, Nathaniel."

"And some I can. Let me help you." His voice broke, and with it her resolve. And so she let him have his way, let him take what was meant for her children—their children—and tried not to imagine their sweet faces at a strange woman's breast as she wound her fingers in Nathaniel's hair hard enough to make him gasp. In time he brought her to a place where she could offer him some comfort in turn, and then she fell away shuddering still with his touch, and this newest burden of relief.

They woke to the sound of raised voices as the larboard watch came on deck, just as the first of the sun found its way through the seams on the canvas cover. Elizabeth blinked and rubbed her eyes, and then she heard the whisper she had missed at first: Robbie, standing at the side of the longboat.

"Are ye awake?"

Nathaniel stretched and reached out to toss back the cover. "We are."

Elizabeth stood, wobbling a little in her disorientation. Robbie sent her a sidelong glance, and she marveled that in all the time they had spent with this man, he still blushed furiously at the sight of her, whether she was in her finest gown or at her worst, as she was now. Her hair was a tangled mass and her face still swollen with weeping; Granny Stoker's borrowed shirt and

breeches were too large and hung awkwardly, cinched at the waist with a rope that served as a makeshift belt. And she itched, so that she could barely keep from scratching.

Robbie held out his arm and she took it, landing on deck with a thump. With both hands she swiped at herself in an attempt to dislodge the grit of the longboat, but her gaze moved out over the sea. It was a beautiful morning, and she had slept deeply. Nothing could lessen the ache and anger at the heart of this journey, and she was still in considerable—and renewed—discomfort, but she was heartened by the sun and the hum of the winds in the sails; her resolve was still firm, but despair had loosened its grip.

"Today," she said to Robbie. And saw what she had not thought to notice, that he was in need of a kind word, too.

He nodded. "It canna be too soon."

Nathaniel clapped Robbie on the back. "I'll bet you've already been down to the galley."

Robbie grimaced slightly. "Aye, that I have. But I wadna recommend it for Elizabeth—it's a wee rough. I'll bring ye what there is tae eat, but first there's word."

Elizabeth and Nathaniel turned to him in one movement.

"Hawkeye and Stoker are waitin' for the baith o' ye on the quarterdeck."

Elizabeth would have started off in that direction immediately, but Nathaniel caught her by the arm. "What's this about, Rab?"

"The Osiris."

"What of the Osiris?" asked Elizabeth, seeing how Nathaniel's expression darkened. He seemed as angry about Moncrieff's arrangements for them to be chaperoned to Scotland on the Osiris as he was about the kidnapping itself.

"She's been sighted, five miles off," said Robbie. He

looked toward the western horizon, where Elizabeth could see only a smudge of haze. She thought of climbing the rigging, and put the idea reluctantly aside, as light-headed as she was.

"The *Osiris* is following us?"

Nathaniel grunted softly. "Her captain can't much like the idea of explaining to Carryck why we aren't on board."

Her disquiet growing rapidly, Elizabeth said, "The *Osiris* must outgun us."

"Aye, that she does," said Robbie. "I saw her in Québec. Thirty-two guns, and near two hundred men. The equal o' the *Isis,* I'd say."

Elizabeth took in this information in silence. Throughout her girlhood she had been fed facts about the Royal Navy with her breakfast, for her uncle Merriweather had always wanted to go to sea, and lived the life vicariously and volubly—with the aid of newspaper reports. She knew very well what it meant for the *Osiris* to carry thirty-two guns. With four twelve-pounder carronades to a side, the *Jackdaw* was better armed than most schooners of her size, but she was undercrewed and in a battle she would never prevail. She wasn't made to fight, but to run: that's what smugglers did.

She squared her shoulders and met Nathaniel's eyes. "Moncrieff wants you and Hawkeye, after all. The *Osiris* wouldn't take the risk of firing on us."

"I suppose that's true enough, Boots," said Nathaniel quietly.

"What is it that you fear, then? Do you think she might try to board us?"

The men exchanged glances over her head.

"It wadna be easy for her tae get alangside a schooner," said Rob. "But I expect she'll try, and then she'll see us come on board, at the end of a muzzle, if necessary."

With a glance around them to make sure that they could not be overheard, Elizabeth said, "Does it not

strike you as odd that the Earl of Carryck should risk two valuable merchantmen in this pursuit? To have them cross the Atlantic without the protection of a convoy—it is remarkable to the extreme. I think we are missing something in all of this, and it may be quite important."

In a disgusted tone, Robbie said, "Carryck's naucht but a bluidy stubborn man, wha' will ha' his way, and gin it means he must strangle the heavens for it."

"No," said Elizabeth, her gaze still focused on Nathaniel. "It is more than tenacity. It is desperation."

All day they ran before the wind, with the *Osiris* behind them like a knot in the tail of a kite. Elizabeth borrowed a spyglass to have a look at her now and then, but she could make out nothing but the fact that the ship seemed to have a great many sails unfurled. Too many, according to Connor, Stoker's first mate, who stood at the wheel muttering loudly. "And they call us reckless. She'll snap a mast and then we'll laugh, won't we."

"Not if they catch us up first," Elizabeth said. It was a mistake, for he refused to lend her the spyglass again.

With each passing hour the tension on deck grew. Stoker alternated between climbing the rigging to hang there for long periods, conferring with Connor about speed and sails, and pacing the deck. He would not be drawn into conversation with his passengers, although Robbie tried more than once.

Finally Robbie gave up and settled down near the longboat where the Bonners had claimed a spot for themselves out of the crew's way. For a while they watched a pod of whales that was running along with them in great leaping dives, as sleek and fast and mysterious as lightning in a darkening sky. But none of them could concentrate on the sight for long, as beautiful as it was.

The Bonners had too little experience on board a ship the size of the *Jackdaw* to be of any real help, and so they found other things to occupy themselves. Nathaniel cleaned the muskets and the rifle while Hawkeye sharpened their knives with a whetstone borrowed from the galley. Robbie had found the sailmaker's kit and set himself to mending a rent in his shirt, while Elizabeth sorted through the few belongings that the men had had with them when they came so unexpectedly on board.

She was put in mind of her aunt Merriweather, who never traveled with less than six trunks, no matter how short the journey. They were four and they had among them a single carry sack with the gown and cape she had been wearing yesterday, two extra shirts and one pair of breeches, a half-horn of powder, some shot and a patch box, the bag of silver coin they had taken away from the *Isis* (Hawkeye wore both sacks of gold on leather thongs slung across his chest), a straight razor, and more curiously, a deck of cards and a few thick tallow candles wrapped in a piece of homespun.

She held one up, surprised at its weight although she knew very well that it held a blade at its center.

"From your friend the pig farmer in Moutréal?"

Hawkeye inclined his head. "You never know when you'll have need of a little light." His gaze scanned the horizon; Elizabeth knew what he was looking for.

"Hawkeye," she said. "Do you intend to kill Moncrieff?"

She felt Nathaniel's eyes on her, but she kept her gaze on her father-in-law. She had not often seen Hawkeye openly angry, and even now she could not call the expression she saw in his face so much anger as resolve.

"I intend to get my grandchildren back safe and sound," he said. "If no harm has come to them, and if nobody stands in my way, why then, nobody will get hurt. Unless you're wanting to see the man dead, that is. I could find my way to oblige you without too much trouble."

Elizabeth pulled her folded legs up and pressed her forehead to her knees, rocking slightly. She did not like this razor-sharp edge of herself: all emotion, and no reason at all. For she would gladly see Moncrieff dead; even to think his name filled her mouth with a bitterness she could barely swallow. And these three good men would take a life to appease the burning inside her. They were capable of that, for all their kindness and care; and so was she, now. *A man that studieth revenge keeps his own wounds green.* She might have said it aloud; she feared she had, for she felt Nathaniel's hand on her back.

"I want my children back," she said, able now to raise her head and meet his gaze. "Whatever the cost."

"Christ on the cross, ye useless bilge rat!" Stoker's voice carried the length of the ship, so that they turned just in time to see young Jacques scoot out of the way of his captain's swinging arm. Elizabeth drew in a sharp breath, but Stoker had already given up the chase, and the boy was safe.

"There's a mannie in a black mood," said Robbie.

Hawkeye nodded. "His reputation has caught up with him. He never thought they'd give chase, and now he's got to show us what he's worth." He looked at Elizabeth, his gaze narrowed and thoughtful. "The *Osiris* is gaining on us, anybody can see that plain. If push comes to shove, then you go belowdecks and sit tight."

"But we cannot take on a ship the size of the *Osiris*. That would be madness." Elizabeth looked at each of them, and got only dark expressions in return.

"It ain't up to us," said Nathaniel, wiping down the barrel of the musket. "It's Stoker's ship."

"Maybe not," said Hawkeye, and he pointed with his chin.

The first mate had appeared on deck carrying Granny Stoker in his arms. In the bright afternoon sunlight the old lady's complexion was a papery yellow and

she seemed as frail as dried grass, but her voice could still carry.

"You useless sons o' whores," she screeched. "Standin' about wit' your thumbs up your sorry arses! Connor, you damn idiot, put me down or I'll skin your ugly back meself, and wit' a dull knife."

The first mate did as she asked with a stony face, settling her into a sling chair hung from an arm low on the foremast.

Stoker came marching down the deck, his expression enough to make Elizabeth draw back into the circle of her menfolk.

"Mac, have you gone blind as well as daft?" His grandmother waved her cane in Stoker's direction as if she would gladly box his ears with it. "More sail, boyo, more sail! Put some muscle in it!"

Stoker bent his dark head down to hers and bellowed, "I'm the captain of this ship, you stinkin' old trout, and I'll sail her as I see fit!"

"Old trout, is it? And have ye had a sniff at your high-and-mighty self lately?" She swiped at him with the cane and he sidestepped.

"Go back to your hidey-hole, Granny. I've no need of you here."

"Is that so? And did I sign over this beauty of a ship to you to see her mishandled? She needs more sail to do her work, unless you're after havin' a great bloody merchantman slide up your skinny arse."

Elizabeth drew in a hiccup of surprise, but the men grinned into their hands.

"If I was a betting man, I'd put some coin on the old woman," said Hawkeye.

"I havena heard sic language since I left the army," said Robbie, his color rising a shade with every exchange between Stoker and his grandmother.

Elizabeth knew that she should be shocked, but at the moment she was more interested in what the argument revealed about their fate.

"Anne Bonney," said Hawkeye, studying the old woman with one eye squeezed shut against the sun. "I wouldn't have believed it."

Elizabeth said, "I wonder that I have never heard of her before, as she is known to all of you."

Robbie threw her a sidelong glance. "I expect the tales canna be tolt in polite company. Most folks believe she hung long ago, doon Jamaica way. A bonnie lass, wi' the heart o' a lion and the habits o' a crow—she'd snatch up any shiny bauble tha' took her eye. And in a battle, when things turned tae the worse and men began tae flee for their lives, she cursed them aa for cowards, and foucht on. So goes the tale o' the pirate Anne Bonney."

"*Pirate?*" Elizabeth's head came up in surprise.

"Och, aye," said Robbie. "A marauder o' the first rank, was Anne Bonney. Ye'll nivver see anither like her."

"Let's hope not," grunted Hawkeye.

Around them the sailors were spreading more sail in response to Stoker's shouted commands.

"Ye see," said Robbie. "She's no' the kind tae give in."

As if she had heard them talking about her, the kerchiefed head swiveled and the old lady fixed Elizabeth with a stare. The mass of jewels and coins hung around her neck sparkled in the sunlight.

With a reluctant glance at Nathaniel, Elizabeth left the men to go forward.

"There you are," said Granny Stoker. "I thought you and me had some trading to do."

Elizabeth was keenly aware of the captain standing there. He seemed to be watching the sails of the *Osiris* on the horizon, but she knew that he was listening. She answered, "I would like to talk to you about that toothbrush"—and saw him snort to himself in disgust.

Annie's cane came flashing out to poke him in the ribs, so that he jumped and turned on her, wild-eyed.

"Sweet bleedin' Jesus, Granny! And what was that for?"

"Gawping. Connor needs talking to and there you stand, sniffin' about a skirt."

Stoker scowled. "And why would I be botherin' wit' the likes of her? Don't grouse, old woman. I'll leave youse to your bloody hen party." And he leaped, with dexterity born of practice, out of the reach of the cane.

"You just see to your own business, boyo," called Anne Stoker, waving it after him. "And let us see to ours."

Elizabeth said, "You remind me of someone I know. She enjoys goading the people she loves best, too."

"Oh, so you think you've seen through me right to my soft heart, eh?" The old lady thumped her chest with a knotty fist. "Let me tell you, dearie, that if I ever had one it ran down long ago. Now, there's a story or two you've to tell me, is there not?"

"Tell me first about the ship that's following us," said Elizabeth.

The old lady narrowed an eye. "What is it you want to know?"

"I assume she can outgun us, but can she outrun us? She can't be more than a few miles off at this point."

"She's trying her damnedest, but it ain't time to break out the powder yet." The old lady's gaze wandered along the deck to where Nathaniel stood with Hawkeye, examining a carronade. "That must be your man, there." She pointed with her chin, a faint smile turning up one corner of her mouth. "No trouble on the eyes, that one. You get on well?"

"Yes," said Elizabeth. "We get on very well."

"Does he raise a hand to you when you're surly?"

Elizabeth fairly jumped with indignation, but she managed to keep her tone in check. "If I were surly, he would not."

This earned her a burst of those incongruous dimples. "Looks the lively type, he does. The kind to keep a

woman warm at night. Long of bone, big hands, muscled hard. Reminds me of a sweetheart I had once, in Monterey Bay. Soon as we docked he'd come striding up the gangplank bellowing so's the whole world could hear him: 'Anne Bonney! Take a hard look at the floorboards, lass, for ye'll be seein' naught but the ceiling ower ma bed for a guid while!' Aye, those were grand days. He was a Scot, like that man of yours."

"Nathaniel is American born and raised."

The old woman shrugged. "He ain't red-skinned, is he? His folks come from somewhere else, and he's a Scot if I ever saw one. The full-grown kind, up to trouble and with a keen eye for women. Now, about that man of yours, tell me this—"

Elizabeth held her breath.

"—has he taught you how to use a gun?"

It took some effort to bite back her smile, but Elizabeth managed to nod. "Yes. A musket and a rifle, as well."

"And have you ever shot a man?"

She slipped in that question so easily, as if it meant nothing more than idle talk of lovers long gone. Elizabeth looked out over the water. "I don't think the *Osiris* will attack."

A hoarse laugh. "Don't you, now? But that's not what I asked."

With a sigh, Elizabeth said: "I didn't shoot Jack Lingo, if that's what you're wondering about. Did you think you could get the story out of me so cheaply?" But she felt her color rising, and she knew that this fact did not escape Anne Stoker.

"There's more than one story, then. How you dealt with that bastard Lingo. And who it was you shot."

Elizabeth said, "For the first story at least I'll need that toothbrush, among other things. You said something of a hairbrush and a comb."

The old lady fumbled in her shirt and pulled out her pipe. "Did I?"

"Yes, I am sure you did," said Elizabeth firmly. "And I should think some soap, as well. If there is any to be had on board."

The soft white hair on Anne Stoker's chin was working up and down furiously as she sucked at her cold pipe, but her eyes never left Elizabeth.

"Is Jack Lingo worth all that?"

"You'll have to hear the story and decide for yourself," said Elizabeth.

From overhead came a cry as loud and harsh as any gull's. "Frigate on the starboard bow! Flying French colors!"

The old lady's head came around with a jerk. "Oh now, there's some good luck!"

Stoker shouted up into the rigging: "Can you make her out, Tommy?"

"Aye, Capting! I believe that's the *Avignon*."

"Has she seen us?"

"That she has! And she's running out her guns!"

"Guns?" asked Elizabeth, more mystified than frightened. "But France is not at war with the United States. We are flying American colors."

"Not for us, Boots," said Nathaniel, coming up behind her. "She'll have her eye on the *Osiris*. Ain't that so?" This question was directed to Granny Stoker.

"Oh, aye," agreed the old lady, pulling a telescope from her pocket. "The French fleet's been prowling the main shipping lanes ever since the Tory blockade shut 'em out of their home ports. That frigate will be in a foul mood. The *Osiris* will suit her just fine about now."

In a few blasts of Connor's whistle the other half of the crew had been called up from their berths, and all hands fell into a routine as practiced as a quadrille at a country ball.

"Helm's a-lee!" boomed Stoker from the forecastle.

"Look at the grin on him," said Nathaniel. "You'd think he was going to take the prize himself."

Robbie and Hawkeye came up the deck, dodging sailors until they stood in a circle around Granny Stoker, whose sling chair was rocking hard with the motion of the ship. She pointed her cane at Robbie. "You, Scotsman! Hold me steady!"

When he had caught up the sling, she fixed her glass on the horizon. And then: "Aye, there she is! God's bones, ain't she a pretty sight!"

"Mainsail haul!" bellowed Stoker. "Cheerly now, boys!"

The *Jackdaw* began to tack toward the *Avignon,* the beat of the waves on the bow picking up in time with Elizabeth's heartbeat. Nathaniel must have felt it, for he slipped an arm around her waist, as firm and steady an anchor as she could ask for on a deck pitched like a houseroof.

"We're headed for that frigate like a cat with a mad dog on her tail," said Hawkeye, looking hard.

"Aye," agreed Granny Stoker. "No better place to run than into the arms of a Frenchman when you've got a great fat East Indiaman tweakin' your arse."

And indeed it seemed as if the *Jackdaw* were of no interest at all to the *Avignon.* She swept forward at an angle that could be read without quadrant or compass: a confrontation with the *Osiris* seemed certain, and quick, unless the East Indiaman could change course immediately.

Elizabeth turned to Nathaniel. "But surely the *Osiris* will run?"

A warning shot echoed over the sea, and with it Elizabeth's stomach rose to her throat.

"Too late," breathed Nathaniel. "They're in for it now."

One of the crew was calling down from the rigging again.

"Capting! The *'Siris* is signaling! Hold a minute!"

Elizabeth crossed her arms across her chest and bowed her head, waiting.

"What is it, Tommy?" shouted Stoker.

"It's one of them bible signals, sir! Hold a minute!"

"A bible signal!" Granny Stoker's disgust was plain. "Bloody hell. Plain English ain't good enough for them."

"Here it is, Capting! Revelation, chapter three, verse eleven, it says."

Hawkeye and Nathaniel turned to Elizabeth together.

"I don't have the whole bible memorized, you know," she said with considerable irritation.

"Dinna fash yersel', lass," said Robbie. He raised his voice so that Stoker could hear him. "'Behold, I come quickly: hold that fast which thou hast, that no man take thy crown.'"

There was a whoop of dry laughter from Anne Stoker, "Now, that's rich. The *Osiris* warning *us* away from the Frenchman when every one of her own men is saying his prayers this very minute. Poor sods."

Elizabeth blanched and Hawkeye put his hand on her shoulder. "The frigate ain't about to sink the *Osiris*."

"Sink a merchantman?" Granny Stoker's kerchiefed head bobbed as she laughed. "She may be French and waspish, but she ain't mad. Sink a prize like that! D'you hear those warning shots? If she wanted to sink the 'Siris she'd yaw and let heave wit' her broadside."

"The *Osiris* is well armed," Elizabeth said hoarsely.

The old lady fixed her with a stare. "Mark my words—they'll rake each other bloody but in the end the *Avignon* will board her in the smoke."

"Then may God have mercy," whispered Elizabeth.

Granny Stoker's head swung away suddenly, the beetle-black eyes darting from the sails to her grandson. "Mac!" The thin high voice rose and cracked like a whip. "She's falling off too fast!"

Stoker jumped, the black hair lashing around his shoulders.

" 'Vast bracing!" he bellowed, running down the deck, passing close enough to spray them with his sweat. "Goddamn it! Helm's a-lee! Move sharp, now!"

There were a few minutes of tense silence as the *Jackdaw*'s speed picked up again, and then Granny Stoker turned back to Elizabeth.

"Still a Tory at heart, eh? Don't suit you to see the Frenchies with the upper hand. Damn the toothbrush, dearie—do you care to put a hundred pound on your countrymen?"

"I need not be English to regret the loss of life," snapped Elizabeth. The deck pitched, and her stomach rose again like a fist in her throat. She pulled suddenly away from Nathaniel and pushed past Hawkeye and Robbie to lurch toward the rail. Bracing herself with both hands, she leaned forward to get the full force of the spray in her face, wanting the sting of it and the cold. She heard Nathaniel behind her, but louder still was the memory of old Tim Card, and his talk of privateers.

"Most is just merchants, missus. Interested in the profit, is all. What ain't profitable goes over the side."

Before her eyes the *Avignon* was headed for a rare prize, but all Elizabeth could see was the *Isis*. What would a French privateer make of a cargo of three children? All they had between them and whatever might come was *Curiosity*. Elizabeth's stomach turned and heaved.

"Steady on, Boots." Nathaniel's hands were cool, bracing her neck and forehead while she retched and retched, until she brought up only bile. When she could breathe again, she pressed her face against his chest, and said aloud those words that came to her unbidden:

What though the sea be calm? Trust to the shore;
Ships have been drown'd, where late they danced before.

• • •

Before them the *Osiris* was in mortal danger, and the same could be true of the *Isis*. Now, or tomorrow, or the day after.

The frigate took that moment to fire another shot, stealing whatever calm words Nathaniel might have been thinking to offer.

17

Hannah slept badly, rising up from ragged dreams again and again to listen for a scratching at the door that might mean word of an approaching ship, or Mr. MacKay come to save them from his Christian hell. She woke for good at dawn, cocooned in a shift damp with sweat and the scent of her own fear. She woke overwhelmed and undone with wanting her grandmother's voice, her father's smile, the pine tree with the crooked top that stood outside her window at Lake in the Clouds. Hannah woke and wished she hadn't. She feared what the day would bring, and what it might not.

She rose quietly so as not to disturb the babies, dragged her spotted calico dress over her head and stumbled out into the other cabin.

Curiosity had fallen asleep at the workbench, her lap full of sewing and her breath rattling faintly with the last of the cold in her chest. Her head wrap had come undone and a thick braid fell to her shoulder, the colors of tarnished silver and rich loam. In his own cabin the Hakim was singing his prayers again. The ship rolled gently, a bird with clipped wings pinned to this patch of water between familiar worlds and strange ones.

With a small murmuring, Curiosity woke and rubbed at an eye with one knuckle. Then she looked at Hannah and closed her eyes again. "Squirrel," she said, smiling. "Ain't you a pretty sight to wake to. Do you think you could fetch me some of that spruce beer? Then we better see to those babies, I hear them stirring now."

Hannah might have cried in her frustration and disappointment. Instead she said, "I thought there would be word of the *Osiris*."

Curiosity held out a long hand, and curled her fingers upward. "Nothing yet."

"I think we should go with Miss Somerville," Hannah blurted out. "I think we should get away from this ship."

Curiosity gave her a sharp look, and then pulled her closer to smooth a hand over her hair. "I know, child. I surely do. And maybe we will. But we got to wait and see. But you hold tight, now. You'll need all your wits about you soon enough."

But she could not hold tight; at every creak of the boards she jumped, and when Charlie came with tea and goat's milk she could barely speak a civil word. His shy smile cut her because she could find none in herself to return to him. Things leaped out of her hands to roll across the floor and escape into dark corners; she slipped and knocked her hip on the writing desk, upsetting papers and quills. Curiosity saw how it was with her and let her be.

The Hakim came to share his breakfast of bread and fruit and cheese with them and he watched her just as quietly, until Lily began to fuss in Hannah's arms.

"Permit me," he said gently. "It is so seldom I have the chance to hold such a small child. May I feed her?"

Hannah flushed in embarrassment and clutched Lily tighter to her. The baby squeaked, the round blue eyes widening in surprise and distress. Then she thumped a small fist on Hannah's cheekbone and the tears did come in a hot rush. She handed the baby to the Hakim

and dashed them away furiously with the back of her hand.

Without looking up from Daniel, Curiosity said, "Don' you want to try on these things? The sewin's all done save the beadwork. Finished the moccasins, too."

That brought Hannah up short. Curiosity must have sewn all night while she slept, unaware. Hannah hid her face in the bundle and went into the privacy of the little sleeping cabin, and in a few minutes she came back, more slowly and feeling very ashamed of herself.

"That's better," said Curiosity with a smile. "You look like our Squirrel again."

It was all she could do to keep from wailing, and so Hannah nodded, fingering the fringe on her sleeve. The soft doeskin whispered as she bent over to touch her cheek to Curiosity's.

"Go on up on deck," said the older woman gently, patting her back. "Get some fresh air."

"No," Hannah said firmly. "No."

Curiosity cocked her head in surprise. "You don' like it up on deck in the fresh air?"

"Let me stay here," Hannah said, near tears again.

The Hakim said, "Has something frightened you on deck?"

She met his gaze. "No," she said, and did not know why she lied. "Nothing. Sir, I am grateful for your kindness." It was less than she wanted to say, and he seemed to see this.

"And if I should ask you to join me? I am going to tend to the ti-nain trees, and I would enjoy your company."

Hannah hesitated, feeling Curiosity's gaze on her, and the Hakim waiting.

"Yes," she said finally. "I will go with you on deck."

He smiled. "Very kind of you, Miss Hannah. I am reminded of something a good man once said to me. ''Tis not too late to-morrow to be brave.'"

"Now that's the right advice for Squirrel," said

Curiosity with a grin. "Bound and determined to save us and the world all at once. Did that come from your holy book?"

The Hakim shook his head. "No. It was written by a surgeon I knew once. He was only an average poet, but a good doctor and a wise man."

"From India, then," said Hannah.

"From Scotland," said the Hakim. "Does that surprise you? It should not. Our prophet teaches that we should seek knowledge wherever it might be."

Curiosity snorted. "I suppose that's why you took up with Pickering, eh?"

It was a personal question that Hannah would not have dared ask, but the Hakim seemed not to mind the question or the criticism of his captain.

He inclined his head. "I wish I could claim that my reasons were so simple and so noble, but it was something else."

They waited while he murmured encouraging words to Lily, who took gruel from his spoon without ever removing her eyes from his face. When he raised his head, there was a smile there that turned him into a younger man, a little embarrassed perhaps at the confession he was about to make to them.

"Have you ever heard of a microscope, Miss Hannah?"

"My stepmother told me about it," she said. "A thing made of metal and glass, she said, that helps the eye see more clearly."

Curiosity sniffed. "Spectacles, you mean."

"No." Hannah shook her head. "Not worn on the face. An instrument, you look into it. Is that right?"

The Hakim wiped Lily's cheek with the flat of his thumb. "Yes. The lens of the microscope is a wondrous thing. It is the key to learning what we do not yet understand about illness."

"So you come all the way from India to get yourself one of these machines." Curiosity lifted Daniel to smell his bottom, and then wrinkled her nose.

"That is how my association with Captain Pickering began, fifteen years ago," he said. "The best instruments were to be had in Europe, you see. I would be happy to show you the microscope itself, if you like. I have some specimens that might interest you."

Taken by surprise, Hannah had a hard time controlling her expression. It was a generous offer, and one she thought the Hakim would not make to many. But Hannah thought too of the *Osiris*, perhaps within sight now, and of Giselle Somerville. They might be gone from this ship in just a few hours; she hoped that they would be, if it would mean she would never see Mr. MacKay again. But the microscope was a sore temptation.

Curiosity cleared her throat. "First the child needs some sun," she said. "Then there's time for your microscope machine."

But a fine misting rain met them, and skies the color of old pewter. Hannah helped Hakim Ibrahim with the trees, which were watered from the rain barrels on deck. And all the time she kept an eye out for Mr. MacKay, and studied the horizon.

There was no sign of another ship like the *Isis*. After this first disappointment a truth showed itself to her as she stood at the rail: she would like the sea if she had come to it of her own accord. In the sharp salt air something deep inside her fluttered open as surely as pennants and flags fluttered overhead. Hannah drew in all the air that she could hold, and felt her skin rise with the pleasure of it.

It was very still; the winds had come to rest to suit the *Isis* drifting so aimlessly in the smoky green-gray sea. The sky was full of birds: black-backed gulls, skuas calling to each other in scratchy voices, *ha! ha! ha!*, others that the Hakim did not recognize, all of them coasting broad-winged on the scant wind. She envied the

birds, who would see the topsails of the *Osiris* first,
even before the lookout high in his perch above
their heads. She thought of climbing the rigging herself.
It would not be very hard: the cliffs on the north face of
Hidden Wolf were higher, with less to hold on to.

But the captain was watching her from the quarterdeck, so Hannah turned her attention out over the sea
to the north where a small ship sat hove-to with dories
scattered around it in an arc.

"Cod fishermen," the Hakim explained.

There were four dories, narrowly built and sharply
pointed at either end, just big enough for two fishermen
and their catch between them. Over the water came
the faint sound of singing from the dory nearest the *Isis,*
in a language Hannah could not name by its rhythms.
She watched as the two men stood, one after the
other, the dory tipping up to flash its red-painted under-
side: They began to haul in a line, one of them flipping
cod onto the growing mound with a back-handed jerk
while the other coiled the emptied line into a
great round tub. Hannah thought of her home waters
where full-grown men wrestled with sturgeon and
sometimes lost, waters full of wily trout and catfish
with fins that could slice a finger to the bone. These
saltwater cod had no fight in them, lining up to take the
hook like schoolchildren waiting patiently to have their
palms caned.

A voice behind them, and Hannah jumped in alarm.
But it was Captain Pickering this time, and his expression was one of real concern.

"You would be more comfortable in the round-
house," he said. "Out of the rain." He stood in the posture of all the officers, with his hands clasped at his
back and his misshapen head tilted to one side, trying
not to look at her clothing, the fringed overdress and
close-fitting leggings, the new moccasins, all darkening
now in the rain. His own face was shadowed by his tricorn. The Hakim moved farther along the deck, check-

ing to make sure that each tree was still securely tied. Hannah wished he would come back.

"I like the rain," she said.

The captain was the strangest kind of O'seronni, one of those who pretended not to see what was plain to see, as if to look at her and know her for who she was might cause them both to disappear. Elizabeth had tried to explain it to her many times: it was how they kept distance from one another in a world that had become too crowded, this seeing but not seeing.

He cleared his throat, once and then again. She knew very well that he was looking for some way to apologize to her.

Hannah said, "How long do you think it will be before the *Osiris* catches us up?" And waited to see if he could lie to her when she looked him in the eye.

The captain drew in his huge lower lip and let it out again. "I would expect her anytime. Midday, at the latest."

Unless something has gone wrong. He did not say it, but she saw it in his expression. Hannah studied his ruined face. Of course it was hard for him to look at the world, because the world did not like to look at him. She wondered if he would be surprised when Giselle Somerville left him. Some of her anger slipped away, although she did not want to let it go.

"Miss Somerville thinks Moncrieff will not allow my people to come on board the *Isis*."

"What a strange thing to say." He blinked his surprise. "I am the captain of this vessel, after all."

He did have a spine, then. "So they are on the *Osiris*, and you will allow them on board?"

He shifted his weight back on his heels, and then rocked forward again. "That was the intention, yes. I believe that is still the plan."

Not much of a spine, Hannah corrected herself. "I wonder what Miss Somerville meant."

The captain flushed. "I am afraid you will have to

ask her yourself, but you must be patient. She does not rise before eleven and it is not even eight of the clock now."

Hannah might have pushed a little harder, but a ship had appeared in the distance. For a moment she watched it over the captain's shoulder as it bobbed in and out of sight on the gently heaving back of the horizon. A fisherman, perhaps; perhaps something more. She knew she should look away, but she could not, and the captain turned to follow her line of sight.

"Mr. Smythe, sir!" he called in a booming voice toward the quarterdeck. "What have we there off the stern quarter? A schooner, as I see it."

"Aye, Captain. Don't recognize her, but she's flying American colors, and coming on fast. Perhaps a packet out of Boston. She's just hoisted the white flag, sir!"

A small shiver ran up Hannah's back, traveled down her arms to blossom in her fingertips. She sent the captain a sidelong glance.

"Ah, then," he said lightly. "Nothing to be concerned about." And still there was a worry line etched faintly between his brows; Hannah saw it, and she saw more: behind the captain's back Giselle Somerville came up on deck in a blaze of green silk with a parasol tilted at a pretty angle over her dark blond head.

The drizzle picked up, enough to send Hannah back to the surgeon's cabin to fetch a shawl and to tell Curiosity the little she knew: a ship was approaching, but it was not the *Osiris*. Whether or not it was the ship Giselle was waiting for was another matter.

"Maybe I should come up on deck," Curiosity said.

Hannah shook her head. "There's a cold rain."

Curiosity flicked her fingers. "I ain't lived through forty winters in the great north woods for nothing. A little wet won' hurt me." And she shooed Hannah away.

In the few minutes that Hannah had been away the sky had lowered still further and now a steady rain washed over the yellow planks of the deck to soak her new moccasins. Other things had changed, too: Mr. MacKay and Moncrieff were on the bridge with the captain. Hannah's belly twisted at the sight of them, and for the first time she truly understood what she had heard her grandmother Falling-Day say many times, that true anger lives not in the mind or the heart, but in the gut. She wondered if Runs-from-Bears and Robbie would be with her father and grandfather. Hannah could imagine them around her, a circle of trees, a magic ring, a hoop of fire, and MacKay would have to pass through them.

He and the captain stood side by side, both with long glasses trained on the approaching schooner, just a few miles away now.

Hannah felt disdain, that they should have eyes so weak. She was proud of her own eyesight, as sharp as her father's or grandfather's. Even with the rain in her face she could see a lot about this schooner that had all their attention: it had triangular sails rather than square ones like the *Isis*, which turned out to be more than a matter of fashion.

Standing at the rail with her, Hakim Ibrahim explained it: men had to be sent up into the rigging to set or trim square sails, but those on the other schooner could be managed from the deck, and with fewer men. It had less of everything, it seemed to Hannah. Fewer sails, guns, decks, and none of the intricate paintwork and gilded decorations that sparkled on every surface of the *Isis*. It did not carry a figurehead before it, and the name on the hull was too faded for even Hannah's eyes to make out. The most obvious thing about the schooner was that she moved fast under full sail even in such quiet conditions. The *Jackdaw* came at them like a bullet at a target. Hannah shifted a little with the thought.

At the other end of the *Isis* a warm yellow lantern light radiated out of the round-house, the little room that stuck up from the quarterdeck like a silly hat. Through the window in the door Giselle's green cloak flashed peacock-bright. She stood watching. Maybe this schooner was the ship she was waiting for, after all.

Hannah pulled the shawl tighter over her head and around her shoulders, but it could not keep out the damp cold and she shivered.

"Perhaps you should go below," said Hakim Ibrahim.

But the hatch clattered, and Curiosity appeared, blinking in the rain. From the depths of her great cloak of boiled wool four round eyes peeked out, sea green and blue. Daniel let out a shout at the sight of her, and wiggled a hand free of his swaddling to flap in his excitement. He was glad to be on deck, too, while Lily scowled out at the world.

Curiosity did not look very happy, either. Her face was a knot of concentration as she stared out at the schooner. "What ship is it? Can you make out her name?"

"It's nothing, just a packet," Hannah said, knowing this was not the whole truth but wary of saying too much in front of the Hakim. "You might as well go back where it's dry."

A muffled *boom!* stepped in on her last word. And before she could say another, a stuttering of guns: *boom boom boom.*

"Nothing, all right," Curiosity said dryly. "A whole lot of it, too."

All around them the sleepy *Isis* came to life like an anthill carelessly kicked. But the sailors were not running to the gunports, as Hannah thought they would.

"Signal shots," said the Hakim. "She has some message for us."

"By God!" thundered Pickering suddenly. "That's Mac Stoker. The impudent puppy. I'll show him to come running at me!"

But Mr. Smythe's voice rose, cutting off his captain. "Sir! The *Jackdaw* signals that she brings news from the *Osiris*—and an injured survivor."

Hannah felt Curiosity jerk as that single word—*survivor*—echoed down the length of the ship. In her own belly a fist closed hard, and forced its way into her throat. She looked for Moncrieff, but he had turned his back to them.

"How shall I respond, sir?"

"Tell her to come alongside," said the captain. And then, raising his voice: "Mr. MacKay! Fenders, and be quick about it!"

Just then Giselle came out of the round-house, her hood up over her face so that Hannah could not see her expression. With one gloved hand she pushed her hood back and she turned, the line of her neck very long and white, to look at them. Her color was high, as if she had a fever.

Giselle met Hannah's gaze and inclined her head slightly as if to say, *You see how easily men are made to dance.* Hannah might have approached her, but the crew had erupted into a commotion of movement. Some of the men were heaving large bags of sand over the side, where they came to rest with a series of heavy thumps.

Curiosity frowned. "The fool won't run clean into us, will he?"

The Hakim narrowed his eyes at the schooner. "Not many would try it, and fewer would manage it. Let us hope this Mr. Stoker is the sailor he thinks he is. Hold fast."

Hannah's heart was galloping faster than she could think. She sidled closer to Curiosity as they watched the schooner come on. A tall man stood on the deck, straddle legged with his hands on his hips.

"Stoker!" roared the captain, leaning over the rail. "What is the meaning of this!"

The tall man touched his cap. "News of the *Osiris* and a wounded lad that belongs to you!"

"By God, man, that's why you want to heave-to alongside? This is an outrage!"

As if he had not heard the captain, Stoker turned and gave a quick series of orders. There was a great deal of shouting from the *Isis*—Mr. Smythe was very red in the face, and Mr. MacKay had leaned so far over the rail that Hannah thought he might fall—but the other ship simply came on, her crew stepping up to the rail with grappling hooks like long crooked fingers.

When the *Jackdaw* was so close that Hannah began to really fear a collision, all the sails dropped at once as if somewhere a thread had been cut. The schooner changed direction slightly and then bumped up smartly against them once, and then again. Hakim Ibrahim steadied Curiosity as the *Isis* rocked hard.

Stoker was running toward them with something slung over his shoulder—a boy, struggling a little. From this angle they could see his face, rough boned and blond. A dirty bandage wrapped around his head and trailed down Stoker's back.

Hakim Ibrahim's face went slack with surprise and he drew in a sharp breath.

"Now what's this?" Curiosity asked sharply. "Do you know that boy?"

"He is called Mungo," said the Hakim. "Charlie's brother."

Hannah started. "Our Charlie? What would Charlie's brother be doing on that ship?"

The Hakim wiped the rain from his eyes. "He is cabin boy to the captain of the *Osiris*," he said. "I fear something has gone far wrong."

Elizabeth crouched in the shadows below the open hatch and wondered to herself if a person could feel themselves go mad. If there would be any warning, some soft sound from the heart, a sigh as reason folded in on itself and went away, never to come back.

Perhaps she made this sound she imagined out loud, because Nathaniel squeezed her hand hard enough to grind the bones of her fingers; she could feel how every nerve in his body hummed. She forced herself to open her eyes.

"Soon," he whispered. He was hunched forward, balanced on the balls of his feet. His breath touched her face and his gun was not five inches from her face; it seemed to be staring at her with its single eye.

Just behind her, Elizabeth could sense Robbie just as calm and still, crouched down with muskets crossed casually on his chest. He had spent all morning cleaning and checking them, again and again. When she turned to him she saw that his face was raised to the misting rain that came through the hatch. In that gentle light Robbie suddenly seemed his age, and more. There were deep circles under his eyes and a slackness to the flesh of his jaw, and it hurt her to see this evidence of Robbie's fallibility and weariness.

Overhead men moved in the dance that would bring the ship to a standstill. Mac Stoker's voice roared like a cannon and she shuddered with the sound.

"News of the *Osiris* and a wounded lad that belongs to you!"

From far above their heads came men's voices in reply. Nathaniel blinked at her. Yes. This was right, this was good. If only Stoker could strike the right tone with the captain and put him at ease. Pickering might be weak and under Moncrieff's control, but neither was he a fool, and he would remember Stoker from the dock at Sorel.

Voices back and forth; she strained to make them out but could not; the sea and the wind whipped them away too quickly. Only Stoker had a voice big enough to be heard distinctly.

Sails snapped and fluttered and came to rest. They thumped up against the *Isis* once, and again, and Elizabeth steadied herself by stemming her hand against

the wall. The shouting above them was too confused to make out.

"The lad is in poor shape! Where is your surgeon?"

The boy. His name was Mungo; he had had a blow to the head and he was confused, still. Elizabeth had spent the morning with him and he didn't seem to understand what had happened to him or his ship. No matter how many times he was told he could not remember that the *Osiris* had gone down. It was hard to credit, although Elizabeth had seen it happen herself. Mac Stoker had called that last and miscalculated volley of cannonfire a lucky shot and meant just the opposite: the French were better marksmen than they meant to be, and had destroyed what they meant to steal. The whole event had put Granny in a foul mood; she did not like it when her predictions went wrong and she had retired to her cabin like a spider to a dusty web. She was there now, chewing on her pipe stem and scowling into the shadows over the waste of the *Osiris*.

But the *Isis* was untouched. Nathaniel had roused Elizabeth at first light and handed her the long glass, and there she was: unharmed and whole and idling in fishing waters as if it were the safest place in the world and not a busy shipping lane, home to mercenaries and pirates and the displaced French Navy. The sight of her had filled Elizabeth with a terrible joy and a new flush of anger. That Moncrieff should take such chances with the lives of her children—it was another sin to lay at his doorstep.

From the corner of her eye Elizabeth saw Nathaniel's hand curled tight around the musket, the line of tension running up his arm to his shoulder so that his whole frame hummed with it. She thought that if she touched him he might shatter. She knew that she was about to.

A long, unhappy cry from above them and Elizabeth clutched her arms to her throbbing breasts. Nathaniel

grabbed her with his free arm. "A gull," he whispered against her ear. "Just a gull."

As if she would not know that sound anywhere on earth, or in hell itself. Her children were on that deck, and crying for her.

Mac Stoker's dark head appeared over the rail as sleekly wet as a newborn's. Hannah watched this strange, upward birthing and held her breath. They all did: the sailors, Moncrieff, the captain, even Miss Somerville, who stood completely still, one hand held to her throat as if to keep herself from speaking. Giselle's expression might have been carved from stone, but the man who came up the rope net had the kind of face that told stories. His black eyes chased the length of the ship, skimmed over Hannah and Curiosity, and skidded back again to come to rest on Mr. Smythe, who stood next to the captain with a musket aimed and cocked.

"Not much of a welcome, Pickering."

He was a big man, more than a head taller than any of the men on the *Isis*. Over one broad shoulder he carried the boy like a sack. Stoker set him on his feet and he stood wobbling, looking about himself uncertainly.

"Your reputation precedes you, Mr. Stoker. What are you doing in these waters, and how come you to this lad?"

Stoker clucked his tongue. "And what should I be doin' in these waters, but pursuin' me line of work? Here I am out of the goodness of me heart with news you'll be needing. And the lad, of course, unless you're not wanting him. He calls himself Mungo."

Hannah could barely withstand the urge to rush forward to shake news out of the boy, who stood squinting in the rain, pulling on the shock of blond hair that fell over his brow. There was dried blood on his ear.

"Mungo," said Captain Pickering. "What hap-

pened?" The boy tugged harder on his hair. His mouth worked, but nothing came out.

Moncrieff thrust himself in front of the captain. "Give us your news, lad! What o' your ship?"

Mungo flinched away, holding an arm up to his face.

"Addled," said Stoker. "He won't be talking much this day."

Hakim Ibrahim said, "He has had a blow to the head. I need to examine him." And without waiting for the captain's approval he took Mungo by the arm and led him away.

"That's too bad, but never mind," said Stoker. "I can tell you what happened to the *Osiris*."

Moncrieff whirled around to him. "Speak up!"

Stoker sucked in a cheek as he considered the smaller man. "And who might you be?"

"Angus Moncrieff. Factor and secretary to Earl o' Carryck, the owner of the *Osiris*."

"Ah," said Stoker. He scratched the corner of his mouth thoughtfully. "Well, then, it's bad news, I'm afraid. The *Osiris* is at the bottom of the sea."

Hannah's stomach rose into her gullet, pushing all her breath before it. Vaguely she felt Curiosity's hand on her arm, holding her up and steering her to rest against the rail. There was a rushing in her ears so that she could hardly hear. She pressed her cheek to the cold, wet oak of the rail and closed her eyes, waiting for the world to right itself.

". . . the *Avignon*. The captain meant to board her and take the cargo, but the gun crews were too enthusiastic in their work. She went down quick."

"How quick?" Captain Pickering's voice was hoarse.

"Before they could get much of the cargo or crew, that's for certain."

Hannah opened her eyes. Below her was the *Jackdaw,* rising and falling on the waves, grinding and nudging up against them like a stray dog that wants petting. Peeling paint, and gobs of tar leaking like clotting blood

from the joints. A dirty porthole. She blinked the rain out of her eyes and looked hard: a face at the glass. A woman's face, very old, grinned up at her. Her great-grandmother Made-of-Bones had had a grin like this one.

"Sir." Giselle's voice. It was enough of a surprise to make Hannah turn. "It is the American passengers who are of interest. What of them?"

He smirked. "Are you talking to me, sweetings?"

"Watch yourself, Stoker," said the captain, frowning.

"Watch meself? The lady spoke to me first, did she not? Oh, but look, she's in a snit now."

One eyebrow lifted in a scornful arch. Giselle said, "This person wants to be paid for his information."

"And keen eyed, too. Sure, and I've gone to some trouble and I've earned a coin or two. But tell me, darlin', are the rumors about you true, then? You're off to be married, they say. The Montréal garrison will be in mournin' for a year to lose your custom of a Saturday night."

Hannah could barely follow what happened next, for it all seemed to happen at once. The captain had grabbed the musket from Mr. Smythe even while the others rushed forward. Stoker tossed Moncrieff aside with a casual flick of his arm and did the same for the two sailors who came to Moncrieff's aid. There was a wild scrambling and then a musket shot sounded. On the quarterdeck a sailor screamed and grabbed his leg.

In the sudden silence, both babies began to cry. Curiosity grabbed Hannah's shoulder in a pinching grip meant to keep her just where she was.

When the black powder cloud had cleared, Mac Stoker stood with his back to the rail with Giselle Somerville held tight against his chest, a long knife held to her throat. The huge fist looked very dark against the white skin of her jaw and neck. Hannah thought that Giselle had swooned, but then she saw the blue eyes blink.

Moncrieff and Captain Pickering stood empty-handed before them. The captain had lost his hat and his wig; his short gray stubble stood up in peaks on his head. His chest heaved convulsively.

"Don't be a fool, man." His voice cracked and broke in an effort to keep it in control. "We will pound you to dust."

"And let your lovely bride go to hell with only me for company?" Stoker ran his open hand up the front of Giselle's bodice to pull her in tighter. She said nothing, but her eyes were very wide.

All the blood drained from Pickering's face. "Unhand her immediately, do you hear me? Unhand her!"

Stoker pursed his lips. " 'Tis a sad thing for a man to be in the power of a woman, is it not? Now, if you'll pardon us, we'll be takin' our leave."

"Wait!" Moncrieff shouted. "What of the passengers on the *Osiris*? Did you see them board the *Avignon*?"

Pickering wheeled around to him. "What does that matter now?" he roared.

"It's all that matters!" Moncrieff tried to push past him. In that moment Stoker simply twisted his upper body over the rail and dragged Giselle with him, where she hung, feet swinging freely.

"Lord Jesus," whispered Curiosity.

"Do I have your attention again, boys?" Stoker asked in a conversational tone.

"Damn your liver and your eyes, Stoker! Let her go!"

"That's just what I've got in mind, Horace me lad." He laughed, and pulled Giselle up closer. "When I let you go, sweetings, I suggest you push hard for the deck below you. The water is damned cold."

"No!" Pickering lurched forward, but it was too late. Giselle was already flying through the air, a strange butterfly with wings of emerald-green silk. Stoker vaulted the rail in a single movement and followed her, the knife in his hand catching the light as he went. The

drop was no more than fifteen feet, but it seemed to take forever. The entire crew of the *Isis* rushed to the rail just as two solid thumps sounded, one after the other.

The babies were still wailing, and behind them the injured sailor groaned, but Hannah barely heard any of it. She stood looking at Mac Stoker, who had gathered Giselle Somerville to him again. He grinned up at them, his face streaming with rain. Giselle's eyes were closed and her body hung limp against him. No man on board the *Isis* would dare aim a musket at Stoker for fear of hitting her.

"Stoker!" Captain Pickering roared. "Stoker, I'll hound you to the ends of the world!"

"Och, never worry about that," Stoker called back. "I won't be goin' anywhere until we've got what we came for. And if you're eyeing me masts, then I'll remind you that I like me knives sharp." To prove his point he flicked his wrist and a bead of blood appeared on Giselle's jaw.

Pickering's voice broke. "Name your price!"

Stoker looked at Giselle with a thoughtful expression and then squinted up at Pickering. "Not so fast. I haven't sampled the merchandise yet, have I?"

The noises that came from the captain were not quite human, but Stoker only laughed. "All right, then, man. My price is very reasonable. This pretty morsel in me arms for them—" And he pivoted and pointed with his knife at Hannah and Curiosity.

Shocked, Hannah stepped back from the railing. Curiosity drew in her breath sharply through her teeth.

"Christ, Pickering. You look like you swallowed your tongue, man. It's simple enough. I want the black woman and the three children. Hand them over and you can have this one back."

Giselle moaned in his arms, twisting slightly.

Moncrieff let out a strangled laugh. "We will do no such thing!"

"No?" Stoker shrugged. "I'll be sure to let the lady's father know how well you protected and valued her."

"I can pay you!" Pickering shouted. "What good are these children to you, Stoker?"

"No use at all." From behind the longboat that took up a good portion of the main deck, a familiar voice. Hannah felt the jolt of it, even before she saw her grandfather's long form unfolding. Hawkeye stood tall and straight, his hair fluttering in the rain and his rifle fixed on Moncrieff. "To him, at least. But I'm right fond of them. Surprised to see me, Angus?"

Moncrieff, struck dumb, took two steps back from the rail. Then he laughed. "Hell, yes. But come now, man. Even you couldn't make that shot from a rolling deck."

"Maybe not," said Hawkeye. "But then I expect one of us might get lucky."

And the hatch opened, and gave Hannah another surprise: her father, and just behind him, Elizabeth.

Elizabeth was trembling, frozen to the spot, terrified and overjoyed. She stood on the deck of the *Jackdaw* and looked up. Hannah. Curiosity. And the babies, both of them. Curiosity pulled open her cape so she could see them, blinking in the misting rain, curls floating around faces flushed pink in the cool air. Her vision blurred; she dashed the rain and the tears from her face. With some part of her mind she was aware of the others: Giselle Somerville struggling weakly in Stoker's arms, Hawkeye with his rifle sights on Moncrieff, and Pickering beside him. They were arguing loudly.

Nathaniel shouted, "Send them down now and nothing will happen to Miss Somerville."

Pickering began to give the order, but Moncrieff cut him off with a chop of his hand. "No. The earl's instructions are clear."

"Angus, it's the daughter of the lieutenant governor he's got there! How will you explain it if we arrive in Scotland without her?"

Moncrieff stood with both arms stemmed against the rail. His voice carried on the wind, clear as the air itself. "Do ye think Carryck cares aught for her, or for any of us, for that matter? It's his heir that he wants. Think, man! If we sail on now, the *Jackdaw* will follow us anyway."

"Maybe so," interrupted Hawkeye. "But you won't see that shore again yourself, Moncrieff. I've got you in my sights, and I ain't about to let you make off with my grandchildren again."

Moncrieff's face was a mask, his tone as cold as the rain on their faces. "Go on and shoot me, if ye must. The *Isis* will still sail for Scotland wi' the bairns and you'll still follow. And that's all that matters."

"Oh, I don't know," said Hawkeye. "I'd wager that Pickering will hand them over for the woman. Once you're dead, o' course."

Moncrieff's mouth turned down at one corner. "A noble plan, Hawkeye. And it would work, no doubt, but you dinna ken Pickering's situation. He can ill afford the earl's wrath. Ask him yourself. Horace, and were I deid, would you hand over the bairns? Think carefully now, before you answer."

The captain's expression stilled suddenly. He looked at Giselle, at Curiosity where she stood with the babies, at Moncrieff. He began to speak, and then stopped.

"Do you see?" said Moncrieff. "Shoot me if you must, but the *Isis* sails for the Solway Firth, and your bairns wi' her."

Robbie had hung back belowdecks, but now he rose out of the hatch in a fury. "Angus Moncrieff, ye bluidy dog. Ye'll beg tae die should I get ma hands on ye, man!"

Elizabeth saw something flutter across Moncrieff's long face. Regret? Doubt? But it was gone as quickly as it came, and he only shrugged. "You o' all people should understand what's at stake, MacLachlan."

"I understand weel enough. I understand that we sat in that hole o' a gaol for weeks because ye arranged for it! Ye abused our trust and friendship, Moncrieff. Ye're naught bu' a bairn-snatcher, a common thief, and a damned liar." Robbie spat over the rail in disgust.

Elizabeth drew in as much air as she could hold, and let it go in a rush. "Give me back my children!"

Moncrieff's head swiveled toward her. "Mrs. Bonner, you may come to your children," he said. "You alone. Sail on with us, in comfort."

Nathaniel turned his head and met her eye, and in his expression was failure, and regret, and a deep, abiding fury. They had risked this, and lost. Giselle was not enough to move Moncrieff; his own life was not so important to him as this errand for Carryck.

He touched her face, and swallowed so that the column of muscles in his throat worked hard. "Go on."

She caught his hand. "I will not go without you!" And she turned her face back up to Moncrieff. "All of us! All four of us must board!"

But Moncrieff was shaking his head. "I'm no' so verra soft in the heid, Mrs. Bonner, as to invite three men on board who want nothing better than to slit my throat. Come and care for the bairns, and you'll see your menfolk in Scotland."

Hannah leaned into Curiosity, who rocked all three children against her.

"I give you my word that I won't raise a hand to you!" Nathaniel shouted.

Moncrieff stood there, stone-faced. Pickering was talking in a low voice into his ear, but Moncrieff's gaze was unfocused, set on something on the horizon that they could not see, or even imagine. Her children were nothing to him but a problem to be solved. Elizabeth flushed hot; she could feel the anger pushing at her, pushing her forward.

"Coward!" She screamed it, and the word spiraled

up to him and hit him full in the face; she saw him flinch as if she had slapped him. Somehow Elizabeth had found the right weapon: she had shamed him by calling his courage into question.

He blinked. "Your husband can come on board, if he comes unarmed."

"Done." Nathaniel's voice was hoarse with effort.

"The wind is picking up," shouted Pickering. "There's no time to lose!"

Elizabeth took leave of Robbie and Hawkeye, who stood grim faced, their weapons still at the ready. She touched her cheek to their bristled ones, but they spoke little. What was there to say, after all? They were bound for Scotland; Moncrieff would have his way. She might try to convince them to go home now, but she knew that it was no good: they would follow, and if Moncrieff led them to China. Hawkeye could no more turn away and leave his son and his son's family to their fate than he could put a gun to Nathaniel's head. And Moncrieff knew it. She could see that certainty on his face: he would keep Nathaniel and Daniel close by, and Hawkeye would follow.

Elizabeth left the *Jackdaw* without a backward glance. Nathaniel followed her up the rope net with the carry bag slung over his shoulder. Halfway between the two decks, she paused to look back at Hawkeye and Robbie.

Nathaniel read her mind, as he did so often. "We're not beat yet," he said quietly. "Don't give up hope."

She nodded, wiped her face against her sleeve, and went up to claim her children.

There was a knot in Nathaniel's belly, a twist of pure anger and relief. The sight of his children whole and unharmed was one part of it; Moncrieff was another. He had given his word and he would do his best to

keep it, but it wouldn't be easy unless the man kept his distance.

The babies were howling in confusion or joy; he could not tell which. Even Squirrel wept openly. "We can't leave Grandfather and Robbie," she wailed in Kahnyen'kehàka. And then she said it again, yelled it down over the rail. Hawkeye raised a hand and touched his fingers to his mouth.

Nathaniel did not wipe her tears away; she had earned them, after all. But he put an arm around her and held her, felt the tension in her that matched his own.

"We will get through this, all of us." It was the most he could offer her.

Elizabeth was caught in a tangle with Curiosity, the squirming babies held between them. Curiosity said, "We was expectin' you on the *Osiris*," she said, laughing and scowling all at once. "And here you show up on a pirate ship."

"The captain of the *Osiris* didn't like the idea, either," Nathaniel said, reaching for Daniel. "He must have had a spy on our tails, because they set out after the *Jackdaw* as soon as we weighed anchor."

Elizabeth shook her head in irritation. "This discussion must wait," she said, her voice hoarse and tears running freely. "I want to get these children out of the rain."

"Wait." Curiosity twisted to look down at the deck of the *Jackdaw*. "We ain't quite done yet."

"Miss Somerville interests me not at all," Elizabeth said sharply, her chin going up at that angle Nathaniel knew too well, when her anger had the better of her. "She may go to the devil, for all I care. I wish she would, if it meant she will no longer interfere in our affairs."

"That's one wish you may just get," Curiosity said dryly.

"Will you hurry with those manropes!" barked Pickering.

"Never mind your manropes," Stoker shouted, putting Giselle on her feet and patting her rear in a familiar way. "We're pushing off. Move smart, lads! Jib aft!"

"Stoker!" roared Pickering. "What is the meaning of this!"

But it was Giselle who answered him. She stood there with a strange half-smile on her face, but her voice carried strong. "I am so sorry, Horace! But I should have made a very poor wife. We are both better off this way!"

Pickering stood, swaying slightly, like a man who takes a bullet but doesn't have the sense to fall down. Below him, Giselle spread out her hands in a gesture that might have been regret.

Scattered around the deck, men stood frozen in place, their expressions divided between surprise and disgust. All except Moncrieff, who was watching the captain closely.

"Captain!" Mr. MacKay's voice cracked like a boy's. "Sir, give the order and we'll demast her with a single volley!"

Pickering looked confused, as if his first officer spoke a language he had never before heard. Then he ran a hand over his eyes and finally turned and walked away, disappearing into the round-house to shut the door behind him.

Hannah said, "She was telling the truth. It was the *Jackdaw* she was waiting for."

Elizabeth let out a little sound of surprise. "Miss Somerville is running off with Mac Stoker?" And she sought out Nathaniel's gaze as if he might know more about this than she could. But it was Curiosity who answered.

"She had it planned all along. She didn't reckon on you showing up with him, though. That took her by

surprise. Us, too." Curiosity's dark eyes followed the smaller ship as it inched away, but Nathaniel was more concerned with Moncrieff, who came striding down the deck.

"Mr. MacKay!" The deep voice carried from one end of the ship to the other. "Carry on so long as the captain is indisposed. And mark me—no action is to be taken now or at any time against the *Jackdaw*." He rubbed a hand over his face. "Make sail, man. It's time we were hame."

18

As a young woman Nathaniel's mother had sailed from Scotland to join her father in New-York. When Nathaniel asked her about the journey, she had looked up in her thoughtful way, her eyes scanning the mountains, taking in ash and beech, birch and maple, endless stretches of white and red pine, blue spruce and hemlock: too many kinds of green to count.

"Imagine a world wi'oot trees, or a single growin' thing," she had said. "And should ye climb tae the highest point on the highest mast, there's naught tae see but water and sky cleavin' taegither."

Even as a boy this idea of a world without trees had not interested him, as wild and curious as he had been. And now, more than three weeks out of Québec, it still took him by surprise. Waking at sunset, Nathaniel was first aware of the lingering light, the color of meat gone bad.

For a long time he kept completely still. The bosun's whistle blew and the first watch started up from the lower decks. The ship wouldn't settle down again until the men coming off the last dog watch had made their way below and hung their hammocks: she moaned and quaked, shuddered and whistled, groaned and mur-

mured as she always did, a woman who knew her work and did it well but would not be quiet about it. Nathaniel had come to recognize all her voices, in storm and calm, and just now there was nothing to alarm him.

The sounds from the next room were just as unremarkable; Elizabeth and Curiosity were talking, their voices low. The twins hummed and burbled and crowed. Lily yawned and Daniel laughed as if he had never seen such a thing. And no sign of Hannah, who would be with the doctor, as was her habit at this time of evening.

In the wardroom just below them officers' voices rose and ebbed, interrupted by the rattle of dice and an occasional curse or shout of laughter. Moncrieff was among them; Nathaniel had not seen the man since the day he left the *Jackdaw*, but he heard his voice every day.

Steps in the other room; he sat up just as Elizabeth opened the door.

She leaned against the frame, her hands busy at the nape of her neck as she plaited her hair. Nathaniel watched her wrists flex, supple and strong; her raised arms pulled the fabric of her gown tight against her breasts.

"You're awake." She came to sit on the edge of the bed. "Come to table, then. The food is here."

Nathaniel ran a thumb over the line of her jaw. "You've got shadows under your eyes. Maybe you should come back to bed, instead."

She took his hand and kissed his knuckles, and then she stood. "I will admit that I haven't adjusted very well to this daytime sleeping and nighttime waking, but I am looking forward to walking on deck. Do come eat, Nathaniel."

Curiosity had already dismantled the joint of beef when they sat down. Steam rose gently from bowls of cabbage and beets. It had taken a sharpish note from

Elizabeth to the captain to get them plain food instead of the jellied eggs and partridge stuffed with sausage, as he had first sent to them.

Nathaniel tucked Lily into his left side and sat down to pour ale from the pitcher, keeping to himself his longing for venison, red corn soup, and water from the spring at Lake in the Clouds.

"Hannah?"

"I sent Charlie for her," said Curiosity. "The child cain't keep track of time when she all wound up with that microscope machine." Her tone was a cross between irritation and something else Nathaniel couldn't quite put a name to, something close to insult.

He could see Elizabeth thinking the same thing. She said, "We are very fortunate to have the Hakim's support and friendship."

Curiosity thumped her knife down. "Did I say we wasn't?"

"No, of course—"

"Then don't be puttin' words in my mouth."

There was a sudden silence while Elizabeth flushed, her chin up at an angle. Both babies began craning their necks between Elizabeth and Curiosity, more alarmed at this silence than they would have been at raised voices. Nathaniel put his free hand on his wife's knee under the table.

Curiosity met his eye. "You got somethin' to say to me, Nathaniel?"

"I suppose I do," he said. "Maybe you should tell us what's on your mind about Hannah."

Elizabeth said, "I wish you would."

There was a tic in Curiosity's cheek. She tapped her spoon on the edge of her plate twice, and then she put it down.

"It don't set right, this whole business. Now you two do me a favor, and don' start tellin' me again what kind of mess we're in. I guess I know that well enough myself. It don' mean I got to like sendin' the child out to spy."

"That is a very strong word," said Elizabeth testily. "I should not call what Hannah does *spying*. She merely listens, and tells us what she hears."

Curiosity snorted softly. "You call it what you want, but I'll tell you this: I ain't so sure as you that she safe on this ship, runnin' around by herself. But it seem like you happy to look the other way. And I hope that child don' have to pay the price."

All the high color drained from Elizabeth's face, leaving behind only the dark circles under her eyes.

"Has someone been bothering her?" she asked. "Is there some threat?"

Curiosity frowned. "I cain't say there is, but I can say this: there's something wrong. She don't sleep well, and ain't you ever took note that she won't go up on deck without somebody go along? Charlie or Mungo or the Hakim, or one of us."

Nathaniel said, "She's never said anything to me about trouble."

"O' course she ain't said nothing. She's a child. It don' take much to set her mind to workin', somebody lookin' at her too hard, or sayin' something nasty about the color of her skin. That might give her bad dreams, but she ain't goin' to come runnin' to you to say so, Nathaniel Bonner. She's prideful."

Nathaniel said, "I'll talk to her."

"Here she is," said Curiosity as the door banged. "I'd like to hear you get someplace with her, I surely would."

Hannah came flying into the room, one plait hanging half undone over her shoulder and her arms full of books, a covered basket, and a squirming bird. As she came to a halt the bird got the better of her and flapped away through the room to come to a standstill near the open transom windows. It stood upright to show off a white breast, its dark wings folded into its body. There was a broad white mask on its face with eyes almost

human, and a large triangular beak banded in yellow, red, and blue.

"Lord above," muttered Curiosity. "Do that creature call itself a bird?"

"It's a puffin," said Elizabeth, holding up Daniel so he could see it better.

"Puffed up, more like." But Curiosity was grinning.

The bird gave them all an indignant stare, turned, and seeing the open windows in the transom, began to lift its wings.

"Oh, no!" Hannah cried, and lurched toward the bird, dropping her basket and going down in a tangle. Papers flew everywhere and the basket rolled, spitting out a collection of small corked bottles.

The twins broke out in deep belly laughs just as Curiosity got hold of the puffin. In the crook of Nathaniel's arm Lily wiggled helplessly, her mouth spread wide to show her toothless gums as she laughed.

"Hannah," Elizabeth said. "Where did you get a puffin, of all things?"

"Mr. Brown gave her to me to keep for a while," she explained, picking up her papers. "He raised her from a chick. Her name is Sally."

Daniel's laughter had taken on a familiar note, one that meant his mood was about to turn for the worse. Elizabeth got up with him. "I'll have to hear about Sally later," she said, taking Lily from Nathaniel. "I fear it may take some time to settle these two for the night."

"You ain't finished your plate yet," Curiosity called after her, but Elizabeth was already closing the door firmly behind her.

"Don' nobody eat enough these days," she said, eyeing the bird that sat placidly in her arms. "Maybe this Sally'll come in handy, roasted crisp."

Hannah frowned. "That would hurt Mr. Brown's feelings, I think."

Nathaniel picked a feather out of Hannah's hair.

"Who is this Mr. Brown? You haven't told us about him yet."

A wide smile broke across the girl's face. "He grew up in Carryck. His father ran the farm for the earl, and now his older brother is the head gardener."

"Ah," said Nathaniel. "Now, that is good news." Any source of information about Carryck was welcome.

Curiosity seemed less impressed. "At least he ain't another one of them 'mac' kind of folk. Don't these Scots got no imagination? MacIver, MacIntosh, MacLeish, MacKenzie, MacLachlan. Tell me, do he talk your ear off like that Mungo, or is he like old Jake MacGregor back home. The kind that cain't spare a word unless his hair on fire and you the only one with a bucket."

Nathaniel laughed, but Hannah seemed to consider carefully. "Once he found out I speak Scots, he got curious and he wanted to know all about Granny Cora. I think he'll be talkative."

Curiosity thrust the puffin toward Hannah. "Go tie it up out on the gallery, child. We don't need the stink. Appetites poor enough as it is."

The few hours after sunset were the best of the day, as far as Nathaniel was concerned. It was the time they all sat together before Hannah and Curiosity went off to bed and he and Elizabeth began their night watch.

Every day they were at sea they faced real dangers—storms, pirates, privateers, a hungry French Navy—but what worried him enough to keep him awake was Carryck. He had fought in more than one kind of war, but he had never walked into a battle blind, with women and children at his back. It wasn't so much the lack of weapons that sat wrong—the ship was full of them, and he could put his hands on what he wanted without a lot of trouble.

What he needed most, and what was hardest to come by, was information.

Nathaniel stood at the transom windows. Somewhere behind them was the *Jackdaw*, and he scanned the darkened waters for a glimpse of her.

Curiosity came up beside him. Nathaniel was surprised, as he always was, at how slight she seemed when she was nearby, as if the sea were drawing the marrow from her bones.

"I saw them three times today," she said. "A few miles off. No sign of trouble."

The truth was, the *Jackdaw* had stayed close so far, but she might disappear without warning or explanation and never show herself again. And what Moncrieff would do then—if they would turn back to find her, or push on—that was a question Nathaniel didn't want answered. But Curiosity knew this and so he kept his worries to himself.

"Three times?" Elizabeth opened the little journal she had sewn out of paper provided by the Hakim. It was divided into sections with colored threads, and she found the page headed "Jackdaw." There were paragraphs about the ship, her crew and weapons, and Nathaniel's drawings, as well as a column for sightings. She noted the date and Curiosity's report and then she turned to another chart. Nathaniel leaned over her shoulder and read the last three entries.

Fraser, Peter. 45–50 years of age. Of Dumfries.
    Navigator
His whole life in this service. Multiple times to the East and West Indies. A wife and two grown children at home. Fond of pippins. Called the best navigator in the company by his mates.

Hamilton, Alex. Of Dumfries. Captain's cabin boy. In service on this ship since age 10. His father a textile merchant.

Jones, Ron. Of Cardiff. Ordinary seaman.
Flogged for repeated drunkenness and an assault on
another seaman. His wounds treated by Hakim
Ibrahim.

"Now about Mr. Brown," Elizabeth said.

Hannah's brow creased in concentration. "I don't
know his first name. He is Curiosity's age, I think."

Curiosity said, "You cain't tell with these sailors.
Could be a hundred from the face on him."

Elizabeth entered Carryck as his place of birth. The
quill hesitated. "His work?"

"He keeps the chickens and such. They call him the
duck-fucker."

Nathaniel would have laughed out loud if it weren't
for Curiosity's strangled cough and the color that
flooded Elizabeth's face.

Hannah looked directly at Nathaniel, raising a shoulder in confusion. "That's what the men call him," she
insisted.

Elizabeth hiccuped. "I have never heard the term. I
expect that you were not meant to hear it, either."

"Oh," said Hannah with an easy shrug. "The sailors
talk freely around me."

"So it seems," said Curiosity. She gave Nathaniel a
pointed look.

He said, "Call him the fowlkeeper, then. What else
do you know of him?"

She knew quite a lot. Elizabeth's quill scratched as
Hannah told them what she had noticed of his work,
his character, his likes and dislikes, and most important,
the little she had learned about the brother who was
Carryck's head gardener.

"Let's hope Brown likes to talk about home," Nathaniel
said when Elizabeth had put down her quill.

Hannah yawned. "I'll go by and see him tomorrow.

He'll be butchering some capons and he said I could help."

Elizabeth caught Nathaniel's eye but she spoke to Hannah. "I haven't seen capons on deck."

"He keeps them below, in the pens." And then seeing the doubtful look on her father's face, she said: "The Hakim said Charlie could go with me."

Nathaniel put a hand on her shoulder. "Make sure you watch yourself. Don't get caught alone belowdecks with any of them, you hear me?"

She studied her thumbnail. "Except Hakim Ibrahim," she said. "And Charlie and Mungo."

"Even Charlie and Mungo," said Curiosity. "I ain't sure either of them could stand up to some of the rougher types I seen around here."

Hannah dropped her gaze, and flushed. It was not like her at all, and it made Nathaniel uneasy.

He said, "It's a dangerous game we're playing, and there's too many men on this ship to keep track of."

She raised her face and he saw that Curiosity had been right: she was frightened, and trying to hide it.

"Come up on deck with me," he said.

Hannah did not argue, did not even speak a word until they were at the rail. He waited, because he had no choice. If she was to tell him what was wrong, she would do it in her own way. There were times when he thought he could see some of his own mother in his daughter's face and it was there now: that same reluctance to bend, a holding back that would bring her close to breaking.

She said, "Do you know about hell?"

He hid his surprise as best he could. "I know what the O'seronni believe about that place they call hell. I've heard enough church talk in my time, and so have you."

She hesitated. "Granny Cora believed in the O'seronni hell."

He had imagined all kinds of trouble on the short walk up to the deck—men who put hands on her, or tried to make her ashamed of the color of her skin—and this talk of damnation put him off balance. He said, "Do you think you're headed for hell?"

She let out a great sigh. "Not for me. I am not true O'seronni."

"Is it me you're worried about, going to hell?"

That got a small smile. "Your skin is white, but you are not O'seronni, either. But some say—" She glanced around herself, and then stepped closer to him. "Some say that the babies might . . ."

Nathaniel drew in a breath, and waited.

She looked resolutely out over the water. "They might, if they are not baptized. Or if they are baptized papist."

A slow flush began in Nathaniel's belly and worked its way up to his chest. It was hard to draw a normal breath, but he fought to control his voice. He put a hand on her arm and turned her so he could look in her face.

"If there's a Christian hell, then it's for the kind who would fill your head with such lies. Do you hear me?"

Her face crumpled, and she collapsed forward to put her face against his chest. She was mumbling, and Nathaniel had to lean over to catch her meaning.

". . . I thought he might try to take them, to save them from hell. But then you came back, and I *thought* they were safe."

"They are safe. Squirrel, they are safe, and so are you. He will never come near any of you again, I swear it."

She rubbed her wet cheeks with the back of her hand, and he thought his heart would break, with sorrow for her and with a terrible blind fury at the man who had brought her to these tears. She drew in a wavering sigh.

"But she watches."

"Who watches?"

"His wife. Mrs. MacKay. She watches the babies whenever we bring them on deck, and there's something in her eyes, like a cat that's hurt bad and won't come near to have her wounds tended. Maybe she thinks having the babies will fix whatever's wrong inside her. I can almost see her thinking it. I think—I think her husband promised them to her."

"The first mate?" Nathaniel asked, his voice sounding high and far away. "Adam MacKay?"

She nodded. "Mrs. MacKay watches and watches, and I'm worried that he might try to take them to save their souls. And to save her."

Later, when Hannah had gone off to bed, Curiosity said what they had all been thinking.

"Strong willed, but she comes from a line of strong women, and it will serve her well, in the end." She said this with a tired smile, and with a steady gaze in Elizabeth's direction. "There's worse faults for a woman."

"Curiosity," said Nathaniel. "Don't back down now. You were right."

Elizabeth sat up very straight, and put down her book. "Right about what, Nathaniel? Has someone been bothering Hannah?"

He told them, and watched their faces transform from surprise to anger.

"That black-hearted bastard," said Curiosity. "Using God to scare a child. There ain't nothing worse."

Elizabeth was pale. "I should have paid more attention."

Curiosity waved a hand in dismissal. "Never mind about that now. Go on and figure out what needs to get done to put things right."

In the sky above the *Isis,* the constellations were as clear as Elizabeth had ever seen: Dragon and Plough, and to

the east Cygnus, Lyra, and the Scorpion were rising.
The very same stars they would sleep under on hot summer nights at Lake in the Clouds. How strange that
they could be so far from home and still watch the same
stars rise and set, night by night; how little comfort they
provided.

Nathaniel put an arm around her. "What're you
looking for up there?"

"Some sense of order, I suppose. Something to explain Adam MacKay."

The anger in him hummed; she could feel it in his
arm, in his whole body.

"Can you let me take care of it?"

The truth was, she did not especially care what
Adam MacKay's fate might turn out to be at
Nathaniel's hands.

"I'm afraid I'm not quite so enlightened and rational
as I once was," she said. "You will do what you must."

"And so will you."

"Of course."

She thought he would be angry at her refusal to
agree to stay out of this trouble, but he slipped his arms
around her from the back and kissed her jaw. His
breath was warm at her ear, and deep in her belly there
was a quick blossoming of nerves. She turned in his
arms, and he came up tight against her.

"What have I done to bring this on so suddenly?"

His lips at her ear, and a shudder of gooseflesh
rushed up along her spine.

"I like it when you bare your teeth and get ready to
fight," he said. "And then of course you're breathing.
That always does the trick, too."

Elizabeth laughed, and he cut her off with a rough
kiss, deep and immediate, his tongue touching hers.
When he broke away she put her hands on his shoulders.

"I'm sure the bosun will find this all very enlightening, but—"

He pulled her into the shadows and kissed her again. Elizabeth felt all her objections slipping away when his hand grazed her breast. Then he stopped, and his eyes seemed very large to her, and his expression suddenly guarded.

"The watch."

She hadn't heard the footsteps, but the marine was upon them already. He walked on as if they were invisible; enough time for Elizabeth to gather her wits. She went back to the rail, and Nathaniel followed.

"So much uncertainty and trouble, and still you can make me lose my head. It is most unprincipled of me, given the circumstances." She said it aloud—a confession of sorts, and one that sounded silly to her own ears.

Nathaniel laughed, a dry laugh without conviction. "Only you can feel guilty about not feeling miserable, Boots."

She was not miserable, it was true. She had her children and her husband and Curiosity nearby, all in good health. Now that they knew what was bothering Hannah, that could be made right. There was every reason to believe that Hawkeye and Robbie were also well, if not as comfortable on the *Jackdaw* in the company of Giselle Somerville and Granny Stoker.

She was not miserable, because she knew with complete certainty that there was some way for them to get home, and Nathaniel would find it. She knew too that there was no way to say this to him. She might find some peace in the here and now, but Nathaniel would not be satisfied until he could act.

She put her cheek against his shoulder. "Do you remember *The Tempest*? We read it aloud last winter. One line stays with me these days: 'Now would I give a thousand furlongs of sea for an acre of barren ground.'"

"Ah," he said. "I know you're feeling yourself when you start quoting."

She pushed him playfully. "You once appreciated my quotes."

"I still do, Boots." There was something of his old teasing tone in his voice, something keen edged and welcome and she knew that he wanted to pick up where they had left off just a few minutes ago, but the hatch opened and he stepped away.

A shaggy blond head appeared above bony shoulders.

"Mungo," said Elizabeth, letting out a small hiccup of relief. "Why are you up so late?"

The boy hesitated, looking around himself as if he expected the quartermaster to jump out and box his ears. When he was sure there was no danger he sought out Nathaniel's gaze, as if to ask permission to come closer.

"Did you want to talk?" Nathaniel asked.

The boy nodded and came toward them, studying his feet with great interest. Mungo would go to great lengths to be in Elizabeth's company—it was not the first time he had sought them out so late at night. He had attached himself to her when they took him aboard the *Jackdaw*.

"I've got a wee somethin' for ye," he said, and brought out his hand from behind his back. Elizabeth drew back in surprise, for he held some kind of blade there, dark of color, long and slender.

"The neb o' a swordfish," said Mungo, touching his own upturned nose to illustrate. "It's gey sharp, missus. They swish it aboot tae kill squid and the like."

Elizabeth glanced at Nathaniel and he lifted one brow at her, not quite concerned and a little intrigued.

"It is very kind of you, Mungo, to think of us." He had wrapped the broader end in a piece of rawhide and she took it gingerly between two fingers. From the tip to the base it was as long as her arm.

"Did you catch the fish yourself?"

"Och, ne. A gey great monster, is a swordfish. The meat is richt tasty, forbye, bu' they fight like the de'il."

Nathaniel bent over to examine it more closely. "Where did you come by it?"

"A marine harpooned him. He gave the neb tae ma brother Charlie, and Charlie gave it tae me."

Elizabeth handed the sword to Nathaniel and resisted the urge to wipe her hands on her handkerchief. "Are you sure you want to part with such a treasure?"

Even in the near dark the boy's blush was clear to see. He sent her a sidelong glance. "Ye were kind tae me when I was injured, missus. I willna forget it."

Nathaniel asked, "How's that bump on your head today?"

The boy touched his forehead. "No' sae bad." He inched a little closer, still examining his own feet. Elizabeth sensed that he would roll over like a puppy if she patted his head.

"What's that?" Nathaniel asked, turning sharply toward the west, where a rushing noise seemed to come from the darkened sea.

"Sweet Mary," breathed Mungo. "A falling star."

It arched across the sky, its tail undulating in a blaze of white and yellow. The whole of it sizzled as if the air around it were on fire, and it seemed to Elizabeth as wide as the sky itself and as bright as the sun.

"White panther in the sky," said Nathaniel, his voice hoarse with excitement.

"Aye," Mungo whispered. "He roars."

It did roar, but more faintly as the star spun to the east. They watched, the three of them focused on the sight of it until the ferocious light disappeared into the sea.

Elizabeth said, "Do you think anyone else saw it?"

"No," said Nathaniel, still staring at the spot where it had disappeared. "The sign was meant for us."

He looked down at her, and for the first time in so many weeks he smiled, really smiled, his teeth sparkling white in the dark.

"A sign," Elizabeth repeated. After more than a year with Nathaniel she was still sometimes taken by surprise by his faith in things she would have once dismissed summarily: unseen worlds; dreams that evoked truths beyond the ones that could be dissected by reason; a sky that opened itself to offer faith and speculation.

"Is it a good sign, then?"

"The best kind before battle," Nathaniel said. He covered her hand and squeezed it hard.

Mungo glanced between them. "Battle? Surely ye canna mean ye want tae fight Carryck."

Nathaniel nodded. "If that's what it takes to get home."

The boy licked his lips nervously, glanced up at the quiet sky and back to Nathaniel. He started to say something and then stopped.

"Mungo?" Elizabeth tried to catch his eye, but he would not look at her. "What is it?"

"I'm feart for ye." He frowned, and ground a knuckle hard into his eye. "I'm feart for ye if ye stay and I'm feart for ye should ye slip awa' and head for hame."

Nathaniel's expression hardened. "Say what you've got to say, Mungo."

The boy's face crumpled suddenly. "Carryck will come after ye, and he willna be alone. The earl wants ye alive, ye see, but John Campbell o' Breadalbane wants ye daid."

Nathaniel's expression was almost one of relief, to hear finally what he had suspected. "Tell me what you know of this business."

Mungo's face drained of color until it was so white that it seemed to have soaked up the moonlight itself.

Elizabeth could hardly breathe. "Mungo, please. Think of the children. Please help us."

"I owe ye my life, missus, I ken that weel enough." He let out a whistling sigh and met Nathaniel's gaze. "I

can tell ye only what every man on this ship kens already. Some years syne, the earl's dauchter Isabel ran off tae marry Walter Campbell o' Loudoun."

Nathaniel jerked back. "Carryck has a living daughter?"

Mungo's voice shook. "He disowned her when she eloped wi' a Campbell o' the Breadalbane line. Wi'oot a male heir all Carryck falls intae John Campbell's hands. That canna happen, ye mun understan', and it willna happen, sae lang as there's a man alive under Carryck tae fight."

Nathaniel pressed his fingers to the bridge of his nose. "Are you saying that all this—kidnapping women and children, the loss of a ship with two hundred men aboard, and devil knows what else—that it was all to keep his money away from his own daughter because she married into this Breadalbane clan?"

"No!" Mungo's voice wavered and broke. "It's got naethin' tae do wi' money. It's the land. Can ye no' understand? Carryck and every man who ever swore him an oath wad die tae keep the Scot territories free o' the Campbells."

Nathaniel's brow creased. "What does it matter to the men who sweat in Carryck's fields who owns the land?"

"Nathaniel," Elizabeth said, as calmly and firmly as she could. "Surely you understand the concept of a blood feud. You have told me similar stories of the Hodenosaunee."

"No," Nathaniel said, his jaw set hard. "There's something else going on here. I can smell it, and I'll wager Mungo can tell us what it is."

The boy's shoulders rolled forward, and his gaze darted away into the shadows. When he looked at them again, he was calm. "If I had anythin' tae tell ye that wad keep ye safe, I wadna keep it tae masel'. And that's aye true."

The bosun's voice came to them, raised in conversation with the marine on watch. Mungo sent them a pleading look and slipped away silently.

When the watch had passed and they were alone again, Nathaniel put his arm around Elizabeth and pulled her close. "Boots," he said, his voice ripe with satisfaction. "Our luck is turning."

"I trust you are right. At least things are starting to make some sense now."

He grunted, a low and comfortable sound. "You can't fool me. You might believe in me, but you can't believe in a sign out of the sky."

She tugged on his sleeve. "What do you mean, Nathaniel Bonner, with 'might.' Of course I believe in you. I have never doubted you for a moment."

With a little laugh, Nathaniel pulled her face up to his. "Slippery as ever. Listen, Boots. It's time for you to go below."

She ducked her head away. "For me to go below? And where will you be?"

"I've got business with MacKay," he said.

He kissed her, a hard stamp of his mouth. His stubble raked her cheek and then he put his lips to her ear, nipping there so that a ripple ran down her spine to the small of her back. "I'll be with you at sunrise. I swear it."

Elizabeth lit every candle in the cabin and then she sat down to drum her fingers on the table. Directly in front of her the rosewood clock sat in its wall niche, and it gave her sorry news: just one o'clock in the morning, hours until sunrise. Hours in which irritation and worry would battle for the upper hand.

In front of her there was a small pile of books, Hannah's basket with its bits and pieces, papers and notes, Mungo's sword, paper, quill and ink, and a half-eaten orange. In any other setting these things would have been more than enough to pass the time until sunrise, but this evening Nathaniel was roaming the ship in search of Adam MacKay.

It is between Hannah and her father, Elizabeth told herself resolutely. *And between Nathaniel and Adam MacKay.* She picked up the orange and peeled off a section. It was parched and sour, but she swallowed resolutely. She would leave this to Nathaniel, as she had once left Billy Kirby to him.

Hannah's journal lay before her, the page held open by a small bottle of pale yellow fluid. Tucked into the leaves were odd pieces of paper, some in the Hakim's handwriting, others she did not recognize. On one page Hannah had begun to copy a letter addressed to Hakim Ibrahim from a Dr. Jenner of Barkeley.

Most of the journal was filled with Hannah's drawings, circle after circle of what she had seen through the Hakim's microscope, each carefully labeled: skin of an onion, human eyelash, chicken feather, codfish scale. And pages devoted to blood, the blood of every animal on board, and human blood, too. Elizabeth studied them for a good while and could decipher little beyond the notes that Hannah had already made in her small, neat hand: a sea of small oval shapes, and with an occasional larger, rounder shape among them. How strange that this unwanted journey should bring to Hannah an opportunity she would otherwise never have had. It was something to be thankful for, in spite of Adam MacKay.

But it was not enough. Elizabeth stood and pushed the journal away. She could not sit here; she would not. If Nathaniel might move about the ship at night with impunity, so could she.

19

The Kahnyen'kehàka knew that the best time to attack an O'seronni village was at night. As a young man training under Sky-Wound-Round, Nathaniel had heard the stories of such raids, where rich merchants came under the knife with an open tinderbox clutched in a fist. The Kahnyen'kehàka warriors, feared throughout the Hodenosaunee Nation and far beyond for their ferocity and courage, shook their heads over men afraid of the dark.

Nathaniel, growing up between red and white worlds, understanding the strengths and weaknesses of both, knew that this much was true: white men did not all fear the dark, but most of them forgot how to use their ears when the sun set.

Now he made his way through the darkened ship, navigating by his memory, by his senses of smell and touch, and most of all by an ability to listen hard. In the endless forests he knew the size of a doe by the sound of her step in the undergrowth; on the *Isis* he had come to recognize the walk of a dozen different men and boys by the way the boards gave under their feet. Now, just above him on the middle deck, the first officer was on his way to his quarters, weaving down a corridor he had

walked a thousand times, making as much noise as a child at play. Nathaniel kept pace with Adam MacKay, moving soundlessly in the dark.

MacKay had been in the round-house earlier in the evening, his strange profile standing out like a flag. Nathaniel knew of the man only a few things: that he ignored his wife, or beat her when he could not; that the sailors respected MacKay's seamanship but disliked him for his poor humor, the tight fist he kept with rum rations, and his generosity with the whip; that he took pleasure in giving little girls nightmares.

Nathaniel ducked around the thick pillar of the fore capstan, tucked his arms in close, and spidered his way up the narrow ladder to the middle deck. MacKay was just behind now, but not by much. Nathaniel crouched down low in the deeper shadows of the capstan wheel, its long wooden spokes polished smooth by generations of calloused hands. The wood smelled of salt and sweat, and the great wheel muttered softly to itself like an old horse at pasture.

Not ten feet away, MacKay sang in a crusty monotone:

Heart of oak are our ships
Heart of oak are our men
We always are ready
Steady, boys, steady
We'll fight and we'll conquer
again and again.

Nathaniel pulled in a lungful of stale air tinged with gunpowder, axle grease, and salt. A calm came over him; he could feel the blood moving through his arms and legs, pooling in his hands. His fingers twitched slightly. It was the feeling a man got when he came across a bear. Bear meant meat for a month or more, fat to cook with, a good pelt. But a bear was always a gamble. Most would take a bullet to the brain and lie down

without an argument, but every once in a while you got one too dumb or too ornery to give in quick, and that was the bear to watch out for: she'd take all the lead you could offer and come roaring for more. The trick was to strike fast and hard.

In a single quick movement Nathaniel rose out of the shadows. With one hand he grabbed MacKay by the throat, winding his fist in the white linen to yank him forward. With his other hand he caught the lantern before it could fall. Then he lifted the man off his feet and flipped him onto his back, pinned him down and straddled him, one knee in his soft gut with his hands caught behind his back. The lantern he put down out of reach, and then he grinned.

"You're up late tonight, Coo MacKay." It was the name the sailors called him behind his back, for his shape and his stare, dull as a cow's. The insult did its work: MacKay's expression changed from confusion and surprise to outrage. Keeping him off balance was Nathaniel's best chance of getting the man to say more than he wanted to.

"I'll let go now, but I'll come down hard again if you make a row. Are we clear on that?"

MacKay nodded. "Aye."

Nathaniel wiped his hands on his breeches. "Do you know what I want?"

MacKay's face went white under the stubble of his beard. His expression said he didn't understand plain English, or didn't care to.

"For the love of the Almighty, man," he breathed heavily. "It's too late tae be playin' games."

Nathaniel settled his knee a bit harder. "Now, that surprises me. After all I've heard about how fond you are of games."

The long face twitched. "I dinna take yer meanin'."

MacKay grunted as Nathaniel drew a knife from his belt.

"Think hard," he said. "It'll come to you."

The narrow brown eyes darted from the knife to Nathaniel's face. "Moncrieff willna like it should ye cut me."

"What'll he do, send me to bed without my supper?"

"Why dinna ye ask him, and leave me be?"

Nathaniel contemplated the tip of the knife. A casual flick netted one bone button off MacKay's shirtfront. A twitching began at the corner of the broad mouth.

"Now there's the riddle," Nathaniel said, studying the man's heaving chest. "Why would you set out to hurt a child who's done you no harm?"

His eyes darted away. "I dinna take yer meanin'."

The knife flicked again, and MacKay's face went one shade paler. Nathaniel kept his own expression flat as he took another button.

"I nivver laid a hand on the little savage."

The knife was sharp, and it slit the corner of the pale mouth with no sound at all. MacKay let out a little sigh and his whole body seemed to fold in, as if Nathaniel had punctured something deep inside him.

"Cut me, then," MacKay whispered, his eyes eager and bright. "Go on and cut me. It won't change anything. Ye'll burn in hell for your sins, for livin' among the infidels and fatherin' more o' the same. And yer spawn will burn richt beside ye."

In the heat of battle it was dangerous to let rage or fear get the upper hand. A man made mistakes when he let himself slip like that, and Nathaniel intended to make no mistakes here. He breathed deep and let the calm flow through him, feeling the knife in his hand and knowing what it would be like to put it in this man's throat and watch him choke on his own blood. How right that would feel, at this moment.

MacKay took his calm for fear. He smiled with bloody teeth and began to hiss, sputtering spit and blood and venom: "'Because I have called, and ye refused. I also will laugh at your calamity; I will mock when your fear cometh; When your fear cometh as des-

olation, and your destruction cometh as a whirlwind; when distress and anguish cometh upon ye. Then shall ye call upon me, but I will not answer; ye shall seek me early, but ye shall not find me.'"

"Proverbs, chapter one. Mr. MacKay, I suggest you concentrate on the New Testament." Elizabeth's voice came cool and calm, just above them. Her head poked through the ladder hole, and then she came down in a rustle of skirts.

"Boots," Nathaniel said. "I should have figured you couldn't sit still. I was just having a discussion with Mr. MacKay."

"Yes, I heard. Now, Mr. MacKay, are you familiar with the gospel of Mark?"

Some of the madness had slipped away from MacKay's eyes, and he seemed suddenly embarrassed at this situation he found himself in.

"O' course. Let me up, man."

"And with chapter ten, verse fourteen?" Elizabeth went on.

He flushed, and set his bloody mouth in a hard line.

"Let me quote: 'But when Jesus saw it, he was much displeased, and said unto them, Suffer the little children to come unto me, and forbid them not: for of such is the kingdom of God.'"

MacKay made a coarse sound in his throat.

"I see," Elizabeth said. "You are one of those faithful who pick and choose those parts of the scripture that best suit your purpose. And your purpose is to cause a little girl as much agony as possible."

MacKay struggled a little, and Nathaniel pushed harder with his knee until he stopped. "You don't want to be rude, now," he said, wiping his knife on the man's shirt. "The lady spoke to you."

"'Let the woman learn in silence with all subjection,'" MacKay replied.

Nathaniel leaned in closer, but Elizabeth stopped him with a hand on his shoulder.

"Let me be blunt, Mr. MacKay." She came closer, and crouched down to look him directly in the face. "If you come anywhere near any of my children again, if you speak a word within my stepdaughter's hearing, if you even look at any of them, I will not bother to intercede when my husband next chooses to come looking for you. And more than that, I will see to it that you lose your commission on this ship and never get another. Do we understand each other?"

MacKay's mouth contorted. "I understand weel enough," he said. "Papist savages and whores. Ye'll fit right in at Carryck, the lot o' ye."

His nose broke with a crack that made Elizabeth jump. Nathaniel hauled MacKay forward by the collar, and let him struggle while the blood ran down his face.

When he stopped coughing, Nathaniel said, "Right now I'm wondering just how dull-witted you are. You'll either give your word that you'll leave me and mine alone, or you and me will finish this conversation face-to-face."

Elizabeth was very pale, but she said nothing. And neither did MacKay, who hung limp from Nathaniel's fist.

"I will go, then," she said. "And leave you to it."

MacKay's head came up, eyes rolling in pain.

"Ye have my word," he coughed, covering his face with his hands.

A coward, in the end. Nathaniel let him drop to the floor.

"I will send word to the Hakim that you need his attention," Elizabeth said, over her shoulder. "Or would you rather have your wife's help?"

"A fine choice ye've given me." MacKay's shoulders shook, in pain or laughter it was not clear. "Infidel or witch. I'd rather bleed tae death right here."

"Let's hope for her sake you do just that," Nathaniel said.

MacKay drew his sleeve across his mouth. "Ye re-

semble the earl in mair ways than one. Has anyone tolt ye that?"

"It's been mentioned," Nathaniel said. "It means nothing to me."

"It will." MacKay's mouth twisted. "Soon enough."

20

Robbie MacLachlan sat with his back to the *Jackdaw*'s longboat and stared unhappily into the bowl cupped in his hands. "Should I nivver eat salt beef agin, it will be far tae soon."

Hawkeye raised a shoulder in agreement. Over the brim of his own bowl he was watching Stoker and Giselle, who stood at the rail.

Quarreling voices rose from the stern, a shout of pain and then silence, but these days Stoker didn't seem to hear or care about fighting among his men. Giselle gave him enough trouble all on her own. Now he was grinding his teeth, the muscles in his cheeks as tight as fiddle strings.

"Young love," said Robbie, following the direction of Hawkeye's gaze.

"That's one name for it, I guess."

"She's a braw lassie tae stan' up tae Sweet Mac Stoker, ye must leave her that."

Hawkeye flexed his fingers one by one. "I ain't sure that I'd leave her much at all, Rab. But I'll tell you this, watching her wrangle with Mac gives a man a new appreciation for the easements of old age."

"Aye," Robbie sighed. "Better sore joints than stiff ones."

Neither of them laughed; not only was the truth of it bittersweet, it was as close as they would come to an agreement about Giselle Somerville.

Hawkeye studied her, as he did whenever he could be sure that her attention was elsewhere. The skin across her nose and cheeks was peeling and the long plait of hair lying over her shoulder had gone almost white in the sun; her shirt hung loose to show her throat and chest, pink and glistening with sweat. Giselle looked more like a girl these days, nothing like the fine lady who had flown off the *Isis*. The truth was, she looked like herself at seventeen, when he had first seen her.

It was hard to believe that it was so long ago. He had gone north because Cora missed Nathaniel and was full of hazy fears for him, so far away in a place she knew nothing about, in a tangle with the daughter of a titled Englishman and a mysterious French lady. Cora sent him to bring Nathaniel home to Lake in the Clouds, with a rich wife, if there was no other way to do it.

All these years later Hawkeye wasn't sure what exactly had happened, except that Nathaniel had agreed to leave Montréal without Giselle, and without much of a struggle. Had he grown tired of the girl, or did she just refuse to leave her father's fine home for a rough cabin in the endless forests? On the way south, glad to be shut of Montréal, Hawkeye hadn't asked Nathaniel for an explanation, hadn't known how to ask, and thought it best to leave the boy his privacy.

What Hawkeye did know for sure was that he hadn't understood Giselle Somerville then and he didn't understand her now. The strange, strong girl who had taken him by surprise in Montréal had grown into a formidable woman, one who was smart enough to hide her ironwood core behind smiles and lace fans, and driven enough to take Mac Stoker to her bed if it served her purposes.

Hawkeye scanned the horizon for the *Isis*, and was disappointed again. They lost sight of her now and

then, but it was more than twelve hours since he had last seen her sails. It made him uneasy in his bones.

"Here's auld Jemmy, wi' a belly fu' o' trouble," said Robbie, bringing Hawkeye out of his daydreams.

The little man who limped toward them swinging a bucket of tar was one of the few sailors willing to give them the time of day. Now he nodded to them briskly and stopped, scratching a mole on the end of his nose with a blackened fingernail.

"Wind's comin' up again," he volunteered, tipping his face up and sniffing at the breeze so that his whiskery cheeks twitched. "We'll be rollin' gunwale-under by sunset, if the Tories don't get us first. Tories or sharks, mates, that's our lot. Tories or sharks."

"Ye've been through muny a storm," said Robbie. "And there ye stand, hale and hearty."

"Aye, but mebbe not for long." Jemmy squinted in Stoker's direction, ready to bolt if the captain's attention should wander his way. He spat a high brown arc of tobacco juice that cleared the rail neatly.

He hunched his shoulders toward them as if he had a secret. "Two times I've run afoul of the Tories, in these very waters. Once on the *Little Bess* out of Plymouth— the *Casterbridge* sank us without so much as a by-your-leave and skimmed what men could still swim off the water like cream off a milk bucket."

Robbie glanced uneasily at Hawkeye. "Aye, in the days before the war. But we're flying American colors, man."

Jemmy coughed out a laugh. "As if that would stop 'em. It was eighty-two when the *Little Bess* went down. Every one of us was American born, and they pressed us, all the same. Didn't have enough of a navy of our own in those days to do anything about it. Still don't. Not yet, at any rate."

He worked his jaw thoughtfully. "It was more than a year until I could slip away from the *Casterbridge*. Bad grub, that's what's wrong with them Tories. Cost me

four pegs, so it did." He bared what was left of his teeth to show them he was not exaggerating.

"Jemmy, you lazy bastard!" Stoker's shout brought the little man up sharp. "Be on your way or I'll set Granny Stoker on you. You know she'd like nothing more than to peel yer spotty arse."

The old sailor shrugged. "Aye, Capting. On my way." He shambled off, wise enough not to make excuses.

Stoker came over to hunker down next to them, his hands dangling between his knees.

"You've got shadows under your eyes," Hawkeye said. "Not getting enough sleep?" There wasn't a body on board who didn't know how much he slept, and didn't sleep. When Stoker's voice wasn't raised in an argument he was bellowing like a stag in rut.

The scar around Stoker's neck flamed red. "It's a smart mouth you've got, Bonner."

"Captain!"

Stoker raised his head with a jerk. "For bloody Christ on the cross, what!"

It was Micah, one of the younger sailors, a hard worker and keen-eyed. He pointed astern. "Sails, sir!"

Stoker's expression shifted suddenly. He got up and took his long glass from its loop on his belt; when he lowered it again there was a thoughtful crease on either side of his mouth.

"Trouble?" asked Robbie.

He shrugged. "Don't know yet. Micah! Keep an eye on her, and let me know when she raises her colors."

The boy grinned. "Aye, Captain."

Giselle still stood alone at the rail, but Stoker hunkered down again.

Robbie shot him a sideways glance. "The course o' true luv nivver ran smooth, so goes the auld sayin'. Take heart, laddie."

"Sure and I've had more than me share of your old sayings," Stoker snapped.

Hawkeye squinted into the sails overhead. "We had a cat lost her tail in a door, once," he said. "She was mighty jumpy after that, but I think you're worse, Stoker."

"Jumpy, am I? And why should I be any different, with the Tory navy thick as flies in these waters and two old men wasting me time."

"You'll be well paid for your time," said Hawkeye evenly. "I guess you'll survive another week of our company to get the gold you've got coming to you."

"Gold." Stoker spat the word. "Sure and you like to talk about it, but your pockets look empty to me."

Robbie bristled, but Hawkeye laughed softly. "You're right there. Nathaniel's got the coin, and you'll keep up with the *Isis* if you want to claim it."

Stoker frowned. His gaze skittered over to the rail and jerked away again when he saw the way Giselle was watching him. With the simple weight of her stare she was willing him to do her bidding. Cora would have called her fey, a woman who understood men better than they understood themselves. Thinking of his wife, who had crossed these waters to find a better life on the other side, a thought came to Hawkeye.

"She don't much like the idea of Scotland, does she? I'll bet she ain't eager to head back to Canada, either. Where's it to be, then? Ireland? France?"

A random shot, but it found a target. Stoker jerked as if Hawkeye had laid hands on him.

"France!" Robbie's head came up sharp. "Why wad Giselle want tae go tae France?"

"I never said she did!" Stoker barked.

All three of them came to their feet to stand in a triangle.

"The *Isis* is bound for Scotland," said Hawkeye. "That was our agreement, and you'll see it through."

"Damn me if I'll stand on me own deck to be ordered about like a bloody tar!"

Robbie clucked his tongue. "Shame, man. Tae let the lass lead ye aroond by the pecker."

Stoker flushed red to the roots of his hair and reached out with both hands to grab Robbie by the shirt. Robbie sidestepped neatly and brought up an arm as hard as a war club to cut him off.

Behind them, Giselle said, "I hope this boyish behavior is simple high spirits, gentlemen."

Stoker's head snapped around to her. "There you are, sweetings. These two are asking why you'd want to go to France. What I want to know is, what you'll live on while you're there."

Giselle pressed her lips together, inclining her head toward Hawkeye.

Stoker laughed at her. "Do you think he hasn't figured out that you stand there without a penny to your name?"

She flushed so that her sunburned skin mottled. "And whose fault is *that*? Who let Nathaniel Bonner leave this ship with the gold and never raised a finger to stop him?"

Stoker leaned in toward her. "If that gold had been on my ship, do you think I wouldn't have known it? No, it's your doing, sweetings. You let an old black woman and a little girl come between you and the gold."

"You can't prove that!" Giselle spat.

"And what does it bloody matter?" roared Stoker. "There's no gold on this ship, and you're not going to France without it. So shut your bleedin' gob, woman, and get out of the way of men's work!"

Giselle pursed her mouth. "Oh, I'll keep out of your way, *Captain* Stoker. As long as we're bound for Scotland, I'll make it my concern to do just that. I give you my word on it."

"Is that so?" Stoker produced one of his terrible grins. "There are bloody few hiding places on the *Jackdaw*, me darlin', and I know every one of them. And I give you me word on *that*."

"Captain!" Micah called again, his tone urgent

enough to get Stoker's attention. "She's a Tory frigate, and she's comin' this way at speed!"

"Damn!" Stoker swung away, Giselle forgotten. "All hands! Jemmy, rouse Connor, and tell him to bring Granny up on deck!" He trotted away, shouting orders for more sail.

Robbie narrowed his eyes at Giselle. "Giselle, ma sweet. Ye ken weel enough why we're bound for Scotland."

Hawkeye watched Giselle's face and saw there what Stoker would never understand about her: she had a mind ten times sharper than his own, and she would always calculate her own gain first, and that down to a tin penny.

"That is none of my concern," she said. "I made arrangements with Captain Stoker for passage to France. I have no intention of going to Scotland."

She spoke directly to Hawkeye, staring him in the eye like a man who wants a fight. The last time they had had words of any kind he had been a reluctant guest at her table. Party games and sugared fruit, and now she wore a knife on her belt.

He looked away, but he answered her. "France, is it? A bloody place these days for the wellborn. And there's the blockade, I suppose you ain't forgot that."

All around them the sailors jumped to Stoker's commands, but Giselle took no note of any of this; she was still studying Hawkeye, one corner of her mouth turning down while the opposite brow went up. "Still trying to interfere in my affairs, I see."

Hawkeye laughed. "You're a fine one to talk, missy. Or are you going to tell me that you ain't had a part in Moncrieff's scheme, right from the start?"

A plain woman is always well served by a smile, but when Giselle bared her teeth there was nothing pretty about it.

"Of course I had a part in it," she said. "Did you think he could have managed it on his own? It was time

to see old debts settled. Moncrieff made sure you three went off to see the captain of the *Providence,* and then I saw to it that the governor knew where to find Elizabeth while you were gone. The only question was whether he would take her to the château to question her, but luck was with us."

"You're right proud of yourself," Hawkeye said dryly. "But tell me this, what would those old debts be?"

"That is between your son and myself," Giselle snapped.

Robbie swayed as if he would lose his footing.

"Ye canna mean that ye had a hand in this, lass. Wad ye take babes from their mither, tae suit your hurt pride?"

Giselle drew herself up. "If you are looking for some remorse or soft feelings, then you will strain your eyesight to no good end, sir."

Robbie's face fell as if she had spat at him. "I wadna ha' thoucht it."

"Come now," said Giselle, creasing her brow in irritation. "You have seen what Pink George is capable of, after all. Why should you expect anything else from his daughter?"

"Because," said Robbie hoarsely, his whole body shaking. "Because I ken yer mither, too. And it's a shame and a pity that ye're no' mair like her."

Hawkeye wondered if he had heard right. Robbie MacLachlan had not been off the North American continent for some fifty years—how could he know a Frenchwoman who had never been farther south than Montréal? But he saw by the man's expression that he had spoken a truth so long held secret that letting it go had torn a hole in him. Robbie was breathing as though he had just fought a battle and lost.

Giselle had not moved. There was nothing in her expression to show that she had even understood except a tremor at the corner of her mouth.

"You're lying." Her voice was steady. "You cannot know my mother."

Robbie ran a hand over his face. "If that's what ye want tae believe, lass, then it's just as well. I should ha' held ma tongue."

Granny Stoker let out a cry of alarm louder than any war whistle.

"Jack Twist, ye reeky kack-handed gudgeon, you'll bleed for that!" Stoker roared.

"Oh, Christ," muttered Robbie. "He's broke the turnbuckle."

Hawkeye didn't know what a turnbuckle was, but he could see well enough that the line that hoisted the sail had given way. The jib slid down the forestay, snapping wildly and spilling wind. All the aft sails were suffering for it and their speed was falling off fast. From her sling on the middle mast Granny Stoker keened as if noise might fill the faltering sails.

Giselle was pulling on Hawkeye's sleeve. "If you think such sorry lies will change my mind about France, you are wrong. You can swim to Scotland for all I care, Mr. Bonner."

"I wouldn't count on France right now if I was you." Hawkeye had to raise his voice to be heard over Connor's alarm rattle. He turned to Robbie: "What's to be done?"

"They'll take doon the jib tae try and fix the turnbuckle. I'll see if I can help." And he ran off without another glance at Giselle.

She reached out and grabbed Hawkeye's lower arm before he could follow Robbie.

He shrugged his arm out of her grasp. "Christ, woman! Can't you see we're in trouble here?"

"Tell me what he meant. You owe me that much!"

Her expression made him pause. "Old debts again, is it?" Hawkeye studied her pretty face, the fine lines around her mouth and eyes that deepened in anger and something else, something that smelled of fear that lives

deep in the gut. "Sometime you'll have to explain to me exactly what it is you think you're owed."

"*Tell me.*"

"I don't know what he meant."

"You're lying!" Her voice cracked and wavered

"Is that so? And what could you do about it if I was?"

The ship rolled hard, and Giselle was thrown up against him. Hawkeye put both hands on her shoulders and pushed her away, feeling the heat of her through the thin shirt, feeling too much, his gut lurching like the deck underfoot.

"Mac's not watching, little girl," he said harshly. "Rubbing up against me won't get you what you want from him."

She curled a hand into the fabric of his shirt, her knuckles pressing against his chest. "Did you think I wanted something from Mac Stoker?" She laughed. "Your famous eyesight is failing you."

Hawkeye pushed her away again, feeling his temper flash and slide, ready to break its bounds. "I don't know anything about your mother. But if I did, I wouldn't tell you. I ain't a boy to let himself be sucked dry and cast off."

All around them the ship was in a dead rage as the Tory frigate gained on them, Stoker ranting, Granny screeching, the whole crew shouting as they struggled with the jibsail. But Giselle stood there pure deaf to it all. The blood left her face, and Hawkeye saw that he had struck too hard, hard enough to put her back against the wall.

"Daniel Bonner." Her mouth worked silently for a moment. "All these years I've had something of your son's, and none of you ever knew it." Her voice had dropped, but he could hear every word, more clearly than he wanted to.

Here it is, now. Finally. The first shot in the battle, or the last?

"And what would that be?"

Her mouth worked again, trying to spit out what lay so long and heavy on her tongue. "Your firstborn grandson. He turned sixteen the same week that blue-stocking of an Englishwoman gave birth."

He kept his peace; anything he could say would serve her purpose better than his own.

"It is true. I see you do not believe me, but it is true."

Hawkeye braced one arm against the longboat and stared at the deck. Giselle might be lying; it came to her easy enough. He shook his head to clear it.

"You're on your way to find this boy of yours, is that right?"

She pushed out a sigh. "Yes. He was taken from me when he was born and sent to my mother."

"In France."

She nodded impatiently. "My mother is in France. Yes."

Hawkeye considered his own hands. Skin like over-worked leather, but the tattoos around his wrists were still the same deep indigo they had been when they were new, in those days when he hadn't yet learned to think of himself as white.

Giselle was watching him warily, things moving behind pale eyes that were beyond his understanding. She had borne Nathaniel a son, and kept the boy away from him all these years. One part of him wanted to laugh in her face; the other did not dare.

"Does he have a name?"

The muscles in her throat worked. "Luc," she said. "The woman who attended me baptized him Luc."

Baptized. Some small connection flickered far away, and Hawkeye reached for it. A midwife, a Catholic.

"That would have been Iona," Hawkeye said.

"You know her?"

He had made her uneasy. *Iona is Robbie's good friend,* he might have said. But he kept it to himself. *A grandson who had never set his foot on Hidden Wolf,*

who knew nothing of his forefathers. Hawkeye said, "Does the boy look like Nathaniel?"

She frowned, her suspicion digging a furrow between her brows. "He had my coloring when he was born, but he was long of bone."

"Fair and light eyed, about eighteen." He spoke these words out loud, and each of them seemed to draw her closer, until her raised face was no more than a few inches from his own. But Hawkeye was far away, remembering the night of the fire at the garrison gaol in Montréal, and the boy who had led them to the river. Luke, Robbie had called him. Iona's grandson, he had called himself. Hawkeye closed his eyes and tried to draw a picture of the boy in his mind.

"Well grown. Big boned, but he moves cleverly. Like Nathaniel at that age."

Giselle's mouth contorted. "What are you talking about? Who are you talking about?"

"I ain't sure," Hawkeye said. "But it looks to me as if Rab MacLachlan has some explaining to do."

She pointed to the men working so frantically on the jibsail. "There he is. Call him over."

"You, Bonner!" screamed Granny Stoker, waving her cane at him. Hawkeye didn't know how long she had been calling his name.

"Are you deaf, man! Come here!"

It displeased Giselle, and maybe that's why he did it, simply walked away from one angry woman to another one, and was whacked twice with her cane for his trouble.

"Wake up, man." She jabbed toward the stern with her chin. "Look!"

The Tory frigate was closing fast, no more than fifty yards off now and bearing slightly away to come up broadside. Overhead the *Jackdaw*'s sails still fluttered and snapped, snatching at the wind but getting no purchase.

She thumped Hawkeye's shoulder. "Lift me up so I can see!"

Hawkeye did as he was asked, lifting the lumpy bundle of fidgeting woman out of the sling, taking in her smells: the dry rot of oldest age, sour tobacco, sweat. Her baubles slid and slithered around her chest; her legs flopped like sticks.

"Capting!" Behind them Jemmy was shouting shrill as a whistle above all the confusion. "Hulls down the horizon!"

Granny pushed on Hawkeye's shoulder to bring him around, even as she raised her long glass. Her hand trembled, the skin blotched with the sun and yellowish.

"Jaysus Mary and Joseph," the old woman breathed.

A forest of masts had appeared to the northeast, a world of sails. A hundred ships or more, maybe five miles off: no distance at all in good winds. Hawkeye felt the skin on the back of his neck rise in a slow shimmer.

"Micah!" Stoker grabbed the young sailor and shoved him hard. "Up the mast, lad, and see what you can see. Be quick about it! Connor, raise that jib *now*."

"I can't pull a friggin' turnbuckle out of thin air!" the first mate bellowed, his whole body jerking as he rounded on his captain. Then his expression shifted, anger slipping away suddenly to be replaced by surprise. He raised an arm to point. "The frigate's rolling her guns out!"

Hawkeye swung around without any prodding from Granny.

The frigate was no more than thirty yards off, her broad black side looming with all gunports open. Three officers stood on the quarterdeck, their hands crossed casually at their backs: hunters sure of their prey, and in no hurry.

Giselle pushed in front of Hawkeye, her jaw set like a child's who will not be ignored, but Granny reached out and grabbed her by the shirt before she could say a word.

"To the guns!" Granny shouted. "Don't stand there with your gob hanging open, girl! To the guns!"

Giselle shook the old woman off, all her concentration on Hawkeye, and so the volley took her by surprise, threw her off her feet as the twenty-pounder plowed into the forward mast where young Micah perched, still counting ships on the horizon.

Oak cracked like bad bone and the mast came down, rope and sail shrieking, and through it all the boy screamed. He hit the rail and his back snapped in two; the look of surprise on his face was the last thing Hawkeye saw before the deck filled with smoke and the terrible clatter and fizzle of grapeshot.

Granny slung her arms tighter around Hawkeye's neck, shouting hoarsely in his ear. The ship rocked hard as Giselle grabbed his legs to haul herself upright, but a twelve-pounder hit the mast directly overhead and they went down in a tangle, the three of them, Hawkeye bent over the women as a hailstorm of shattered rigging began to fall. It went on for minutes, and then in the sudden silence Giselle coughed.

"Have they sunk us?" Her voice calm, even cold.

Granny croaked a kind of laugh and pushed at Hawkeye to move him off her. "You'd be treadin' water already if that's what they had in mind, the bloody bastards."

"What do they want?" That same tone, as if she were discussing the price of a new bonnet.

Hawkeye pulled himself to his feet, feeling the bruises rising already on his back and a cut on his shoulder. He said, "They must be after fresh crew. They'll be boarding us next."

Granny's eye blinked, as bright as a crow's. "Aye, and you'll arm yourself right quick, girl, or those marines will be mountin' more than the poor old *Jackdaw*."

Connor's voice came to them from the quarterdeck where he stood looking not at the frigate, which could end them with one more volley, but in the opposite direction. "Blow me if that ain't the whole Atlantic fleet. And they've got two sloops-of-war headed this way."

Stoker lifted himself off the deck, fought free of a mass of shredded sail, and picked his way across the rubble.

Beside Hawkeye, Giselle let out a half-sigh, but Granny Stoker grinned.

"There ye are, boyo. Prime me musket double quick. Anne Bonney won't go down without a fight."

"It's a gey lot o' trouble they're goin' tae for a handfu' o' sailors," Robbie said darkly as they watched the *Leopard*'s longboat row toward them. "It makes no sense."

"They look healthy enough," Hawkeye agreed. If disease had reduced the crew to the point where they were desperate for replacements, there was no telling that by the brawny marines who manned the longboat.

There was only one officer among them. He raised his speaking trumpet so that the brass bell caught the light.

"*Jackdaw!* I am Captain Fane of His Majesty's Royal Navy. You will put down your arms and allow us to board or my gunners will sink you." With his other hand he raised his short sword and in response the *Leopard* fired a shot across the *Jackdaw*'s bow.

The sailors were muttering among themselves, but Granny Stoker was not intimidated.

"Poxy sons of ha'penny whores!" she shouted, leaning out of Hawkeye's arms as if she would fling herself overboard and take on the Royal Marines bare-fisted.

"Captain?" Connor stood beside Mac Stoker, shifting from foot to foot.

Stoker kept his gaze on the *Leopard*, the rows of cannons and gunners. He had a look about him that came to a man when he knew himself to be outmaneuvered, and no longer able to protect his own: just enough anger to keep a stranglehold on the shame.

He gave the order, and the *Jackdaw* prepared to be boarded.

•   •   •

The captain of the Leopard kept Stoker with him while the marines searched the ship, took weapons, and herded the sullen crew to the quarterdeck.

"Bloody Tory arse-wipers! You can kiss me blind cheeks, fookin' cowards, the lot of youse!" Granny had lost her musket and her knife to a marine three times her size, but her mouth was her own.

She perched on a water cask now, as there was no intact mast left on which to hang her sling. "Give me back me musket. Do you bloody hear me, boyo? I want me musket so I can stick it up your captain's arse! At least he'll die with a smile on his ugly phiz!"

Hawkeye heard Giselle draw in a breath, in disgust or distraction he couldn't tell. It was true that the captain of the *Leopard* was young, but Hawkeye wasn't so quick as Granny to discount a man with so much firepower at his back.

The wind was high and there was no hope of catching anything of the conversation, at least not while Granny kept up her steady stream of curses, spattering the circle of marines with her spittle.

"Godforsook shite-brained maw-dickers!"

Giselle grabbed the old lady by the shoulder. "Annie," she said sternly. "Enough. We cannot hear when you carry on so."

Granny Stoker peered at Giselle anxiously, one hand clawing at her arm. "Ah, there you be, sweetings."

Robbie stiffened in surprise, but the crew covered their mouths with tarry hands, trying to hold back their uneasy smiles.

"Christ," Connor muttered, wiping his sweaty brow with his cap. "She's off again."

The old lady grinned sweetly as if she had not heard this. "You'll fetch me musket, won't you, Mary, me love?"

"Later," said Giselle evenly. "When the time is right."

The old lady slumped down in Robbie's arms. She hung there, staring glumly at the marines and at the crew gathered around, all of them nervous enough to jump ship and swim for France, if that would keep them off the *Leopard*. At least the cutters had been signaled back to the fleet, which seemed to take no more interest in them, now that the gunplay was over. The Royal Navy was bound for France; and so might this crew be, by nightfall.

"Cowards," Granny muttered thickly. "Not a real man in the lot of youse."

The captain of the *Leopard* turned and pointed in their direction.

"Here we are then, mates," said Jemmy with a sigh. "Tories or sharks."

He was a man of no more than average height but with a keen look about him, battle scarred and burned deeply by the sun. His gaze slid over the crew, hesitated at Giselle, and moved on to Hawkeye and Robbie. When he came to Granny she reared up and grinned at him.

"Hello, luvy. Come closer and give us a kiss."

"Connor," snapped Stoker. "Take her below."

She puckered up her toothless mouth. "Ooh, that's not very friendly. All these lovely big marines. Look at the doodle sack on that one, will ye? A yard like an iron pike."

"Connor!" Stoker barked.

"Go with them, Quint," said Fane. "We want no surprises."

Connor did as he was bid with the marine at his back while Fane examined the rest of the crew.

He lifted his short sword so that his sleeve pulled up. A scar crossed the back of his hand and snaked up underneath his cuff. With a little flourish he pointed at a man Hawkeye knew only as Penny Whistle.

"You, there. Have you ever served on board a ship of the Royal Navy?"

Penny scowled. "I'm Massachusetts born and raised. What would I be doin' on a friggin' Tory shitebucket?"

It was calculated to make Fane angry, but the man wasn't so easily riled. He smiled with half of his mouth, the one side drawn down by a curving scar.

"An opportunity missed, then, eh? Captain Stoker, who else is on board?"

Mac shrugged. "I run a tight ship. This is my whole crew."

"All Americans, I'm sure you'll claim."

"Every man of them," Stoker said calmly, the Irish heavy on his tongue. "There was a war fought, if you'll remember."

"Ah, yes," said Fane thoughtfully. "That little squabble." He turned and met Hawkeye's gaze. Something flickered there, some curiosity. He jabbed the sword twice, toward Robbie and then Hawkeye.

"These two."

There was a moment's silence, and then Stoker began to sputter like wet gunpowder.

"Those two! Those *two*? Are you mad, man?" He thrust a shoulder forward toward Fane. The marines brought up their weapons, and he pulled back.

"You shoot me ship half to pieces for two men?"

"I can take them all, if you prefer." Fane's tone was icy. "And burn your ship, for good measure."

Stoker's expression shifted from outrage to suspicion. "Why those two? They're no sailors and they're older than sin, the both of them."

Fane was studying Robbie. "Not sailors? I suppose that one there is the King of Siam."

Stoker swung around to Hawkeye.

"Say something! Tell the man you're American."

"I ain't American."

"Of all the— Of course you're American. Sure and you were born and raised on the New-York frontier!"

Hawkeye met Stoker's eye. "That don't make me American if I don't want it to. I was raised Mahican, and Mahican I'll be until I die."

Stoker drew in his breath with a hiss. "You're damned easygoing for a man about to be pressed onto a Tory frigate."

There's good reason for that, Hawkeye might have said. He made himself look away from the deck of the *Leopard,* where a familiar figure had appeared at the rail with a long glass in his hand. A man of no more than medium build. Not a sailor, or an officer.

Hawkeye said, "I been taken prisoner more than once in my lifetime, and by worse scoundrels than these. Rab here was held by the Mingo for a whole year."

Robbie grunted, his brow furled down low. He hadn't seen the man studying them from the *Leopard*'s quarterdeck and he didn't follow Hawkeye's purpose, but they had hunted and fought together for fifty years; Robbie could tell well enough when Dan'l Bonner had a scheme.

"We lived this far to tell the tale, I expect we'll survive a Tory frigate," Hawkeye finished.

"Captain." Giselle had been hovering at the back of the crowd of sailors, but now she pushed forward and spoke up in her best drawing-room voice. "I will join you, as well. I have no business on this ship."

Hawkeye forgotten, Stoker's head snapped toward her. "You greedy bitch!" He lunged; the marine next to Giselle lifted the butt of his musket in a lazy swing and tapped him above the eye. Groaning, Stoker went down on his knees, pressing a fist to his bloody forehead.

"Captain Stoker, contain yourself," said Fane. "I shan't be taking your . . . lady on the *Leopard.*"

"Sir," Giselle said, and pressed her lips hard together. "You would deny my request for assistance without knowing my name, or my father's?"

Fane shrugged. "You came on board of your own accord, did you not, madam?"

"I did. And now I would leave."

"But not on the *Leopard*," said Fane firmly.

Giselle gave the man an injured look. "Captain, perhaps you know my father, Lord Bainbridge. He is lieutenant governor of Lower Canada."

Fane bit back a smile. "Captain Stoker, I am impressed. The King of Siam, an Indian chief, and now the daughter of the lieutenant governor . . . Ayres! We're away. Fetch Quint, and take these two men into custody."

At the rail, Fane came up behind Hawkeye. "Your son and his family are not on board?" he asked quietly.

Hawkeye shook his head.

Fane grunted, clearly not surprised but displeased all the same.

"Rob MacLachlan!" shouted Giselle from the quarterdeck. "You and I have unfinished business!"

But Robbie went down the rope ladder to the longboat without even looking in her direction.

"Captain Stoker," said Fane, touching the rim of his tricorn. "Until we meet again."

"Aye," said Stoker with a bloody frown. "Sure and that day will come sooner than you think."

The marines pulled the longboat through rough waters toward the *Leopard*. Hawkeye sat shoulder to shoulder with Robbie; Fane was out of earshot at the other end of the boat.

On the *Jackdaw* the crew had already set about repairs, half of them heaving the spare mast into place while the others were at work on the rigging. There was no damage to the hull, and Hawkeye didn't doubt that they would be under sail again before morning.

Below them, turning gently on their wake, Micah's body floated amid the jetsam. Only Giselle stood at the rail to watch them go, her fists clenched like stones.

Hawkeye said, "I should have seen it long ago. She's got Iona's eyes."

The wind whipped the words from him, but Robbie had understood. He wiped the sea spray from his face.

"I gave ma word that I wad nivver speak o' it."

Hawkeye tried to remember Wee Iona as he had last seen her in the shadows of the pig farmer's barn on the outskirts of Montréal, but another picture came to mind. A young Highland Scotswoman he had first met after the battle of Québec; she had put aside the veil to live among the roughest sort of men. It made too much sense to be doubted.

"I suppose Pink George must be her father, or he wouldn't have taken her in. But why would Iona give her up to him?"

Robbie hunched his shoulders. "It's a complicated tale, Dan'l. One I canna tell in guid faith."

Hawkeye put the question out between them, because he could do nothing else.

"And the boy? Is it true?"

Robbie ran a hand over his face. "Aye," he said hoarsely. "It's aye true. But Dan'l, ye mun believe me when I tell ye, I didna ken aboot the lad until I broucht Moncrieff tae Montréal just after the New Year. I couldna think how tae tell ye."

A flock of tiny seabirds settled around the longboat. The men called them little peters, the souls of lost sailors who danced along the tops of the waves; bound to the sea in death as they had been in life. Beneath the water long sleek forms wove silver streams, moving faster than any horse. Headed somewhere else. Hawkeye took a deep breath, salt and storm, the endless sea. One grandchild unclaimed; the others equally out of reach, headed for an unknown shore. He wished that he had Cora beside him, for her quiet counsel and the simple sound of her voice.

"Dan'l, do ye think we shall ever see hame agin?"

They were close enough to the *Leopard* now to make

out the voices of the men peering over the rail at them.
More officers and curious sailors, the gun crews still
standing alert at their cannons; sharpshooters up in the
rigging. And someone else.

"Look, Rab, here's an old friend," Hawkeye said by
way of answer.

Robbie raised his head. "Christ Jesus," he said softly.
"Young Will Spencer. For the love o' Mary, what is he
doin' on the *Leopard*?"

"Come to Elizabeth's rescue, looks like," said Hawkeye.
"Now we'll just have to track her down."

21

Almost two years out of home port, the *Isis* was overflowing with the evidence of her industry and enterprise. The hold was as big as a longhouse but still it was filled to bursting with kegs of cinnamon and mace, cardamom and saffron; endless bales of India silk, cashmere and cotton and a hundred seroons of indigo. On the last leg of the journey up the eastern seaboard to Halifax, the *Isis* had taken on what seemed to Hannah to be more Virginia tobacco than the whole Hodenosaunee nation had ever produced, or needed. And still, the sailors told stories of the real treasures kept in a locked room on the lower deck. None of them had ever been inside, but Hannah went there with Hakim Ibrahim early one morning when Charlie's brother Mungo lay dying.

It was not the blow to his head, but a mysterious ache in his lower belly that was dragging him away against his will. The pain had come and gone for a week and for that whole time the Hakim had kept Mungo in a darkened room where he was forbidden any activity at all. He had been given only boiled water and a tea made of flaxseed and steeped wild yam. Curiosity and Elizabeth took turns sitting with Mungo

to keep the cold compresses on his belly fresh, and for a time it seemed to Hannah that he would get well.

Then, on the very day that the *Isis* first came within sight of Scotland, he began vomiting again, and the pain settled in for good. Curiosity called it an angry belly, for its heat and hardness and the fullness of misery it brought with it. The Hakim called it the vermiform appendix and showed them drawings of a little finger of gut that was spilling poison into the blood. Mungo wrestled with the pain, and did not care what name they gave it.

After a particularly difficult night, Charlie came to the Hakim, his eyes red with weeping, but his voice steady. "Can we no' give him laudanum to ease his passing?"

Hannah held her breath. She knew well enough that Hakim Ibrahim had no more laudanum. He had used the last of it when a sailor called Jonathan Pike had mangled his hand in a winch.

Hakim Ibrahim pressed Charlie's bony shoulder. "I will do what I can for him."

So he took Hannah with him to the locked storage room and opened the door with a key that hung on a cord around his neck. A sticky-sweet, warmish smell met them. He reached up to hang the lantern from the hook in the ceiling, and the room came into focus.

In the middle of it all sat a throne. It was carved of some dark wood Hannah did not recognize and so tall that the curved back touched the timbers overhead. The whole of it glinted with inlay work of pearl and silver and gold that told a hunting story. Men with eyes like the doctor's held long lances. A tiger ran through tall grass, its tail winding.

"You may sit in it," said the Hakim, and so Hannah climbed up.

It was very uncomfortable, but she stayed to study the room so she could tell the story. Forests of ivory tusks longer than a man sprouted in dark corners. A

whole army of statues of all sizes crowded together, wrapped and padded with sacking so that only faces peeked out: some of polished white stone, others so old that noses and ears had been softened away to almost nothing. Animals, dragons, warrior women with furious hard faces. Piles of furs such as she had never seen before spilled out of trunks: some striped, some spotted, some deep black and others glossy brown. Spread out over a humped chest Hannah recognized the pelt of a lion by its mane, and because the paws and tail and head were still attached. The mouth was propped open with an ivory box, so that the lantern light played on the heavy yellow teeth. Dusty glass eyes stared into the shadows where wooden spice casks lined the walls.

Hakim Ibrahim opened one, and the sweet smell rose into the room in a fresh wave. Hannah went to stand beside him. There was another chair here and a little table, its rumpled cloth sprinkled with tobacco. On it were a flint box with a pierced tin lid, a few pewter plates, a half-bottle of port, a carved ivory case, a scale, and a worn hornpipe, the stem almost bitten through. Hannah wondered how often the captain sat here alone, smoking.

The Hakim took a cake from the open cask and put it on a clean plate. It was flattish, a deep dark brown, with small bits of leaf stuck to it.

"Laudanum would be easier," he said. "But raw opium will serve too, if he can keep it down."

He opened the ivory case. Inside, a row of metal weights nestled in green velvet, the smallest no larger than Hannah's thumbnail, and cast in the shape of a spider. She saw a deer, a fish, a turtle, a horse, a cow, a tiger. The largest, the size of a hen's egg, was fashioned in the shape of an elephant with a trunk curled upward.

The Hakim took the turtle weight and placed it on the scale. The knife flashed bright as he cut into the brown cake. When he had three pieces of opium, each

equal to the weight of the little turtle, he quickly put the cake back in the cask and replaced the lid.

He said, "I will miss your assistance in the surgery. You have been a very good student."

Hannah was so surprised that she could say nothing in return, but only bobbed her head.

"I need not encourage you to continue to study. But I will caution you to be alert in Scotland. Your natural curiosity is a powerful thing, but it may put you in danger."

"My father will protect me."

Beneath the red turban the Hakim's brow creased thoughtfully. "Your father is a brave man of excellent understanding. But he is coming to a strange land, and he will need all the assistance you can give him. There are men in Scotland—" He paused, and then went on. "There are bad men in Scotland who would do you harm."

"There are bad men everywhere," said Hannah. The images came to mind without her bidding: Mr. MacKay and his ruined face; a man hung from a dead oak with his hands hacked off; the old Tory with his notched ears and moccasins of skin, hissing at her in her own language. And Liam as he had first come to them, beaten by his only brother until his bones had broken inside him. She had not thought of Liam in days, and a sudden swell of homesickness came over her. But when she opened her mouth to say this, to talk about home, something else came out.

Hannah said, "Are there many men like Mr. MacKay in Scotland?"

"And what kind of man is Mr. MacKay?" the Hakim asked. He was looking at her thoughtfully, and he waited while Hannah gathered her thoughts.

"The kind who thrives on the pain of others," she said finally. Thinking of Margreit MacKay, worn so thin by grief that she lost all connection to the world.

"There are men like Mr. MacKay everywhere," said

the Hakim. "But there are also men like your father, and women like Mrs. Freeman and your stepmother. Like the woman you will be one day."

He was trying to comfort her, but the truth was simple. She said, "I am afraid of Scotland."

Hakim Ibrahim picked up the plate of opium, covered it with a cloth, and they went back to the surgery, where Mungo waited.

Dearest Many-Doves,

I write this letter in the trust that we will encounter a packet bound for Boston or New-York in the next day or so. By my calculations it is now the second week of June. God grant that it may reach you by September. I would wish for nothing more than to deliver it to you myself, but I fear it will be many months before we are safely home again.

From Runs-from-Bears you will have learned that the children were taken from us in Québec. Let me reassure you first that we were reunited with them within days, and that they suffered no permanent harm. Nathaniel, Squirrel, Daniel, Lily, Curiosity, and I are together now on the *Isis,* and we remain all in good health. It is a matter of great concern to us that we cannot give you word of Hawkeye and Robbie, but they follow us on the *Jackdaw,* and we have not seen that ship in more than a week.

This evening we came within sight of the Isle of Man; I expect we shall be in Scotland tomorrow morning. We are unsure of what is to happen next, except that we shall soon see the Earl of Carryck, who has caused us to come so far against our will. I pray that the earl proves a more reasonable and honest man than his emissaries Mr. Moncrieff and Captain Pickering have been. Nathaniel still hopes that an

opportunity will present itself to turn about
immediately and sail for home, but how that
might be achieved is unclear.

Daniel and Lily thrive, as does Squirrel, who
has been kept busy by studying with the ship's
surgeon. Nathaniel rarely sleeps, now that we are
within sight of land; Curiosity seems to do little
else. We think of you every day and pray that
you are all in good health, and that Blue-Jay
continues to thrive. Nathaniel bids me tell you all
that he has seen the Panther in the Sky, and it
was running toward home. A good omen.

Please share this letter with my father and
those friends who inquire after us.

Elizabeth Middleton Bonner
10th day of June in the Year 1794
Aboard the Isis

My dearest husband Galileo Freeman,

This ship will come to rest soon. I ask the Lord
what he has got on his mind for us in a country
as homely and wet as this Scotland I see outside
the window, but he don't talk much to me these
days.

Think of this when you worry about me:
Nathaniel Bonner is the same good man he has always been, and if there is a way in this world to
get me home to you he will find it. Otherwise I go
to my reward thanking the Lord for the good husband he sent my way all those years ago, and for
the fine children he put into my care.

Your loving wife
Curiosity Freeman
writ by her own poor hand this 11th day of June,
    1794
on board the Isis

My grandmother Falling-Day,

Elizabeth says I might write to you in our own tongue but there is not enough time for us to puzzle out the sounds on paper. These letters must go to the packet *Marianne*. She is bound for New-York on the evening tide. A courier will bring them up the Great River to Paradise and Runs-from-Bears or Otter will carry them to Lake in the Clouds. Many-Doves will read these words out loud before the fire, and you will all be together when you hear them.

We are well in body. My brother and sister are strong and healthy. But I am worried for Curiosity, whose spirits are very low, and for my father, who walks the ship staring at the shore, and for Bone-in-Her-Back, who is so distracted that she forgets to eat, and most of all for my Grandfather Hawk-Eye and for Robbie, who are behind us on another ship that hides itself in the fog.

I have many stories to tell of this journey. I have learned much. Yesterday a boy called Mungo died of a swelling that turned his belly as hard and hot as a boiling stone. He passed into the shadowlands quietly. I have seen others cured of strange illnesses and wounds. With a thin metal stick the doctor called Hakim reached into a sailor's body and crushed a stone that was blocking his water. He screamed so loud that he broke his voice but he is alive and will mend, now. The Hakim has given me medicines from his homeland to bring to you.

Scotland is wet and brown and green and yellow, but there are no trees only hills covered with rough grass and brush called heather that the sailors laugh and weep to see. They have been longer from their homes than I have been from mine, but I know what is in their hearts. I

would be very glad to see the fir with the broken top that stands outside my window. Bone-in-Her-Back says that there are trees here, but not many. They burned most of them long ago, and now they burn black rock they dig out of the ground, or even the ground itself, cut into squares. I do not wonder that my father's mother left this place.

Last night a woman called Mrs. MacKay disappeared. The sailors have searched every corner of the ship many times but she is nowhere to be found among the living. She mourned a lost child, and I think she has gone to find it.

My father says that we will finish our business here and sail for home soon. I know he wishes this to be true, and so do I.

Your Granddaughter called Squirrel

Dear Liam,

This ship has come to rest in a wide water called a firth with England on one side and Scotland on the other. Scotland is where my Grandmother Cora was born, and perhaps my grandfather's people, but it is a very strange and lonely kind of place. We were brought here against our wishes, and will stay only until we can find another ship to bring us home.

In my Grandmother's cornfield the bean plants will be winding up the young stalks toward the sun. I think of this time a year ago when we came upon bears eating in the strawberry fields under a fat moon, do you recall? And they chased us away, and we ran until we fell and then we laughed.

Elizabeth bids me give you her best greetings and to say she hopes you are keeping up with

your schoolwork. My father says he knows you
will be strong, and patient. Curiosity asks you to
visit with Galileo when you might. She fears he
must be melancholy. She says too she hopes you
never get it in your head to go to sea.

We never meant to be so long away, but I will
bring many stories with me, and you will tell me
your stories, too.

Your true friend Hannah Bonner,
also called Squirrel by the Kahnyen'kehàka
of the Wolf Longhouse, her mother's people

Elizabeth shredded her handkerchief into strips as
she watched the packet *Marianne* slip out of the Solway
Firth on the first leg of her journey to New-York.

Now there was nothing to do but wait. They waited
for high tide, which would bring the excisemen. They
would come in the morning to examine the captain's papers and cargo and collect their duties, and while the tide
was high and the broad sand flats covered, barges would
move between ship and shore with agonizing slowness.
When the last bale of tobacco and last keg of spice were
discharged, it would be their turn to go to shore. And
once on shore they would find quarters and wait until
Hawkeye and Robbie arrived on the *Jackdaw*.

If the *Jackdaw* arrived at all.

She paced to the other side of the room, where the
babies sat propped up in their baskets. Lily looked up
from mouthing her fist and smiled broadly. A little of
the unhappiness went out of Elizabeth as she sat down
on the floor next to her children and pulled Lily into
her lap. The baby grabbed at her hair, and Daniel
waved his hands in the air wildly, shouting for his share
of the diversion.

"Those children will pull every hair out of your head
before they weaned," Curiosity said at the door.

"Hair will grow back." But Elizabeth untangled Lily's fingers and blew a bubble against her palm to distract her.

Curiosity sat down heavily on the window seat to stare out the transom. The vague light and deep shadows made her face seem almost unreal, carved from some dark and unyielding stone. Her shoulders looked thin even under the heavy shawl she had wrapped around herself.

"It don't look like much."

Elizabeth got up and put Lily on her hip. For a moment she was silent as she studied the vague shape of Southerness lighthouse, a smudge of light in the slanting rain. "It is rather bleak. But Scotland has its own charm, when the weather is fair."

Curiosity's expression was so faraway that Elizabeth wondered if she had even heard. Concerned, she crossed to the settee and sat down. Lily leaned toward Curiosity and put out her arms.

"We got to keep our spirits up, for the children." Curiosity took Lily and settled her on her lap. And then: "I cain't get that poor MacKay woman out of my head."

Daniel squawked loudly, and Elizabeth was glad of the excuse to get up again. She did not like to think of Margreit MacKay, who had gone into the sea so quietly that no one—not even her husband, who had been on watch—had noticed.

"She must have been very distraught," she said finally.

"Maybe if we wasn't all so worried about Mungo—" Curiosity cleared her throat. "It's sorry times when a woman got no safe place to go but the other side."

Elizabeth buried her face in Daniel's neck. When she could speak again she said, "You have told me to keep faith so often," she said. "Now I will say the same to you. I know in my heart that we will get home."

Curiosity gave her a vacant smile, but before she could answer, Nathaniel had come through the door.

There were shadows beneath his eyes, but there was something bright and alive in his expression.

He looked from Elizabeth to Curiosity and back again.

"What is it?" Elizabeth's voice wavered.

"There's a ship you should know about," he said, and closed the door behind himself.

They sat around the table and listened to Nathaniel's story. The whole coast was alive with smugglers, it seemed, and there was one in particular that a talkative sailor had spoken of, called the *Black Prince*. If they could slip away once on shore and keep themselves hidden for even a day, it might be possible to make contact with its captain. He looked Elizabeth directly in the eye.

"It's a long shot," he said. "We may not get very far."

Curiosity grunted, an impatient sound. "Ain't nothin' gained if we don't try. If they catch us—"

She broke off, her brow creased as she studied Lily. Her mouth settled hard. "I say we should try."

Elizabeth heard herself sigh. Nathaniel reached over and took Daniel from her to settle the baby on his own lap. "Tell me what's on your mind, Boots."

But she could not. Looking into his face, alive now with hope, she could not ask all the questions that came to mind, or lay out for him the fears that would not rest, no matter what kind of logic she brought to bear on them.

Curiosity rose suddenly. "Give me that boy. I believe these children could use a little fresh air. We'll just go and see how your big sister is gettin' on with that Hakim fellow."

"There is no need," said Elizabeth, but Curiosity gave her a hard look.

"You turnin' down a little privacy when it's offered to you? Seem to me you two got some talkin' to do."

Elizabeth felt Nathaniel waiting behind her. She nodded. "Thank you."

"Just talk," said Curiosity gruffly. "That's all the thanks I need."

When she had closed the door behind herself, Elizabeth got up from the table and went to the windows. The shifting storm let the last of the evening light seep through the cloud cover, rough bars of gold against the hard lines of the coast. A two-masted schooner hugged the shore, bobbing about like a toy. If she went up on deck and turned in the other direction she would see England again. The very thought made her tired.

"Here I am back where I began," she said. There was a tremor in her voice she could not help.

Nathaniel's arms came around her from the back, and he leaned down to rest his chin on her shoulder.

"Does it look like Oakmere?" His tone was calm and even, and she was thankful for it.

"No, this is nothing like the Devon countryside. But I can smell England in the air."

He smiled; she could feel it.

"You do not believe me."

"I believe you, Boots. I was just thinking about your Green Man."

Elizabeth turned in his arms until she was facing him. "The Green Man? What brings that old tale to mind?"

He pointed with his chin toward the shore. "My mother told me about Scotland, what it looked like, but I never had much of a picture in my mind. Now that I've seen it, I wonder if that Green Man that comes and scratches at windows is all that's left of the trees."

Elizabeth jerked a little in surprise. "The spirit of the lost forests, you mean?" She put her head against his shoulder. "Of course," she said softly. "That's exactly what he must be."

"Boots," said Nathaniel, tightening his grip on her. "Listen to me."

She waited.

"I know you hate the idea of going off on a smuggler—wait, let me finish. There's no denying that it scares you. But we've survived this far, haven't we?"

"We have."

"What is it, then?"

She pulled away from him gently to walk to the far wall. There she stopped in front of Carryck's intricately carved coat of arms. A white elk, a lion, shield and crown. *In tenebris lux:* light in the darkness.

"I fear you will be angry at me if I say what I am thinking."

She had startled him; she felt it in the hand he put on her shoulder. In sudden resolution she spoke.

"Nathaniel, if we should get away, all of us—do you think that they will leave us alone? The earl will not rest until he speaks to your father, or to you—" She wavered, seeing his expression darken.

"So I think we should see this out. You see, I knew you would be angry."

Nathaniel inclined his head. "I'm surprised, is all."

"But don't you see, if we just spoke to him—"

"Are you hoping he'll change his mind, or I'll change mine?"

She threw up both hands in a gesture of surrender. "I knew we could not talk about this."

Nathaniel let out a long sigh. "So you think we should spend another week or two weeks or however long it takes, go see the man and let him have his say. Is that it? And what makes you think he won't try to keep us?"

Elizabeth shrugged. "He cannot be completely blind to propriety, Nathaniel. To keep a whole family captive indefinitely—"

"I wouldn't put it past him."

She wrapped her arms around herself. "Even if you

are right, you mustn't forget my aunt Merriweather. She knows where we are by now—Will is certain to have told her about Carryck when she came to Québec. She may be at Oakmere already, waiting for word. If she does not soon hear from me, she will take things into her own hands. She has an army of solicitors and lawyers at her disposal, you must realize."

He grinned sourly. "I don't doubt it."

Elizabeth ran her finger over the coat of arms and traced the elaborate gilded curls on the lion's tail. "There is another reason to at least let the earl have his say."

Nathaniel tensed, but she pushed on.

"There's something else at play here, some kind of real trouble . . ."

His expression shifted to disbelief. "You ain't worried about the earl? Boots, listen to me. Whatever troubles the man has, there's one thing for sure: he won't take no for an answer. We'll listen to his story and then wish him well and go home. You think he'll be satisfied with that?"

Elizabeth shook her head. "No," she said. "Of course he will not be satisfied. But then neither will you, if you walk away and never hear what he has to say. Five or ten years from now when we still look at every stranger who comes to Paradise as a danger to the children, will you regret not seeing this through?"

The rain had picked up again and it lashed itself against the transom windows in great sheets. Nathaniel seemed to be counting the raindrops, so concentrated was his expression.

"Let me ask you this, Boots. If a ship was to come alongside this minute and offer to take us all back home, what would you want to do?"

Elizabeth studied her own hands. She could give him the easiest, the most logical answer: *I want to go home.* And it would be the truth. She wanted to take her children away from this place with such intensity that she

sometimes woke from a deep sleep to find herself out of bed and half-dressed, with no sense of where she might be going except *away*. Away from Moncrieff and Carryck, away from the faceless Campbells.

"When we go, Nathaniel, then I want to leave all of this behind us. Forever. For good. I am afraid if we go now, we will drag it all home with us, and we will never really be free of Carryck."

Nathaniel pulled back, his eyes narrowing into slits. He ran a hand through his hair as he turned away, his shoulders rising hard against the fabric of his shirt. With his back still turned to her he said, "I'm going up on deck for a while. I need to think some things through."

Hannah had a game she played with the twins when they were put down for the night. She would lean over their crib, and in turn she would put a hand on each baby's chest to croon to them in Kahnyen'kehàka.

"You are Two-Sparrows, daughter of Bone-in-Her-Back, who took Wolf-Running-Fast as her husband. Your sister Squirrel is daughter of Sings-from-Books, daughter of Falling-Day, daughter of Made-of-Bones, who is clan mother of the Wolf longhouse of the Kahnyen'kehàka people who live at Good Pasture. Sleep well, my little sister."

By the time she finished, Lily's eyelids had fluttered closed. Even Daniel, who fought sleep as a matter of course, quieted when Hannah began to sing to him. She called him Little-Fox, the infant name that Falling-Day had given him when she came to them through the winter storm. The baby listened with his brow furrowed in such a comical way that Elizabeth might have laughed out loud.

Elizabeth wondered where they would be when they put the children down tomorrow night. She glanced again over her shoulder into the main cabin where

Curiosity sat staring blankly at a book in her lap while Charlie cleared the last of their meal away. He was red-eyed still, and there was a vacant look about him. Elizabeth wanted to speak to him, to offer some comfort; she knew very well what it was to lose a brother. But in her current state of agitation she thought she would do him little good.

Nathaniel had still not returned from his walk on deck; the little rosewood clock ticked on resolutely toward morning.

She did not think she would be able to sleep, but Elizabeth slipped away immediately and dreamed of Margreit MacKay. Mrs. MacKay paced the cabin, rocking her lost child against her breast and murmuring to herself, the same words over and over again: *Sancte Michael Archangele, defende nos in praelio.*

What danger? Elizabeth asked her. *What battle?*

But there was no answer, only the prayer said over the silent form of the child: *Archangel Michael, defend us.*

Elizabeth snapped up out of sleep, sweat running down her face.

"Boots," Nathaniel said from the dark. "You were weeping in your sleep."

She touched her face, and found it wet.

"Just a dream," she said, wiping her cheeks with her fingers. "Just a dream. Why don't you come to bed?"

She could barely make out his shape as he came to sit beside her. He smelled of salt air, and of himself.

"You've got a neck cramp again."

Elizabeth had to smile. "I do not know if I like the fact that you can see so well in the dark."

His fingers were strong and cold on her shoulder, his breathing was even and steady at her ear. She shuddered a little as he sought out the coiled muscles and began to knead them.

He said, "I shouldn't have left angry. I'm sorry for it."

Elizabeth leaned back harder against him, dropping her head to one side so that he could work the knot of muscle behind her ear.

"We are all on edge," she said softly.

He was still angry. She felt it in his hands and heard it too in the way he pushed out what he had to say.

"I guess you're right about Carryck, but I wish to God you weren't."

She drew in a deep breath and let it out again. "So do I."

Nathaniel's fingers dug hard into her sore shoulder and she struggled a little against him.

"Easy, Boots," he said gruffly. "Let me work."

Her nightdress had slipped down over her shoulder and her skin rose to the cool night air, but a drop of sweat trickled down her hairline. Nathaniel's hands coaxed and prodded, and little by little the knotty muscles began to relax.

"You're wound up like a clock."

"Oh, am I? And there's the pot calling the kettle black."

He snorted softly through his nose and dug his thumbs deeper into the muscles at the juncture of neck and shoulder.

Elizabeth squeaked. "You might just beat me, and get it over with."

He laughed. She reached behind herself to swat him, only half in jest. Nathaniel caught her wrist and in one movement he turned so that she was caught beneath him. He was breathing heavily.

"It's not a beating I've got in mind, Boots."

He pressed his mouth against her neck just below her ear, his tongue flickering. Elizabeth drew in a hard breath and buried her fingers in his hair, held his head as his mouth moved down. He set his teeth in the curve of her shoulder and she cried out a little, in pain and something more.

Suddenly he stilled and pressed his face to her skin. "Oh, Christ," he whispered. "God help us."

Frightened now as she had not been before, Elizabeth clutched at his shoulders.

"Nathaniel—"

"They might as well put me in chains, for all the good I am to you."

There was a swelling in her throat, things she wanted to say and could not, should not. Instead she rocked him while his tears wet her nightdress, hot enough to scald skin and bone. Too tenderhearted, he had called her, and he was right.

When the worst was over, he let out a terrible sigh. "I swear I'll get us out of this."

"I know that, Nathaniel. I know that as well as I know how to breathe."

He nodded absently, rubbing his eyes. "There's still no sign of the *Jackdaw*."

"Perhaps tomorrow," she said. "I suppose Mr. Moncrieff must be very ill at ease."

Nathaniel grunted, sounding more himself. "He spends all his time in the round-house, watching the water. They've posted an armed guard on deck."

"Perhaps they are worried about thieves," Elizabeth murmured. *One more danger,* she thought, but kept it to herself.

Nathaniel pulled her closer. "Or the Campbells."

"Or the Campbells," she echoed. "But I must admit that right at this moment the Campbells are as real to me as the Green Man."

"Let's hope it stays that way." He tugged on her hair. "Tell me, Boots, don't you ever get tired of being logical?"

She laughed. "Now that you mention it, yes. Sometimes it is a relief to stop thinking."

"Ah," he said. "Now there's something I can help you with."

His tone had changed, not to anger or irritation or

even worry, but in another direction, one that she knew very well. The air was chill and she had lost both her blanket and most of her nightdress, but she flushed with a new heat.

His mouth was at her ear, and an old teasing rhythm: "It's late, Boots. The logical thing would be to sleep."

"I suppose it would," she agreed. "You must be very tired."

He smiled against her neck, his fingers tracing gently, rousing every nerve. "And if I was, it wouldn't matter. The smell of you would wake a dead man."

Elizabeth put her hands in his hair and brought his face to her own to kiss him. She whispered against his mouth.

I dreamt my lady came and found me dead . . .
And breathed such life with kisses in my lips
that I revived, and was an emperor.

He laughed, and stripped the rest of her nightdress away so that they could curl together, legs entwined and arms and mouths, belly to belly. His body was a map she could read in the dark: the tiny hooked scar under his left eye; the cleft in his chin; the puckered bullet wound on his shoulder and another low on his right chest; a raised ridge carved into the hard plane of thigh muscle, leading her curious fingers up and up.

He caught his breath and let it go again. Kisses soft and softer, until every pore was saturated and he came to her in a single heavy stroke: the deepest touch. His place inside of her, where no one else knew her; where she did not know herself.

Nathaniel hovered over her, joined completely yet completely still. She touched his face, wound around him and murmured, a question half asked.

He hushed her. "Wait," and then hoarsely, "listen." And then she heard what he meant her to hear: his

blood and her own, surging like the sea itself in an endless circle between them.

Margreit MacKay was uneasy in death, or perhaps she was just lonely; she came to Elizabeth again to pace the cabin. This time her arms were empty, and in her dream state Elizabeth began to search for the lost child in every corner.

Mrs. MacKay took no notice of her loss; all her attention was on Elizabeth. "Be wary o' the cold damp," she sang in her clear, deep contralto. "Be wary o' the mists. Be wary o' the nicht air. Be wary o' the roads, and the bridges and the burns. Be wary o' men, and women, and bairns. Be wary o' what ye can see." Her voice grew faint and fainter. "And what ye canna."

22

It was just after dawn and the rain had stopped when Elizabeth roused herself to see to the babies. Behind her, a clean summer light filtered into the cabin through the shutters: the last day they would spend on the Lass in Green.

She looked like a fairy, or one of the selkies that Nathaniel's mother had told stories about, with hair as deep and dark as sleep itself against the white skin of her shoulders. It floated in tangled curls to the small of her back, and he could barely contain the urge to put his hands in it, to wrap it around himself so that he could breathe in her smell. He wanted to sleep the day away like that with her head tucked under his chin. But in the next cabin Daniel babbled, and he would not be content for long.

She lifted her arms over her head and took up her hair to plait it, her elbows pointed to the ceiling.

"Let me," he said.

She glanced at him over her shoulder. Her eyes were the color of a sky set on rain. "You could sleep."

"Could I? Come then, let me do that for you."

In the soft early light her expression managed to be both severe and sleepy, but she held herself steady while he worked.

He finished and let the plait drop over her shoulder. "I kept you up too late."

"Don't be absurd," she said, her voice muffled as she pulled her nightdress over her head. Then she leaned over to kiss him, a quick stamp of her mouth with a wayward curl caught between them. "I did not need very much persuading. Or don't you recall?"

"Oh, I recall very well," he said solemnly. He reached out to trace a finger along her collarbone where the skin was still mottled. She blushed, new color flooding her chest and throat, and grabbed his hand to still it. "You take delight in embarrassing me."

"That I do," he said. And then, "Promise me you'll still blush like that when you're seventy."

She slipped out of bed before he could stop her. At the door she paused to smile at him over her shoulder.

"If you'll promise to give me reason, why then, sir, I'll promise to oblige you."

Charlie brought their breakfast with the puffin tucked under his arm like a tame chicken.

"Good morning from Mr. Brown to Hannah," he reported dutifully. "And would she be so kind as tae look after Sally, who doesna take kindly to the rushing about on deck."

"Hannah has gone to take her leave from the Hakim," Curiosity said, taking a platter of bread and meat from him to put it on the table. "But I suppose Sally can bide a while out on the gallery. Now, you got any news for us?"

Charlie was full of news, and eager to share it: four excisemen had come on board, the first barges had already been loaded, and there was a report of the war with France and America—a huge sea battle and another victory for the Royal Navy's Atlantic fleet.

"America?" Nathaniel spoke more harshly than he meant to, and the boy jumped.

"Surely not, Charlie." Elizabeth looked up from the baby in her arms. "England is not at war with America."

Charlie bobbed his head so hard that his hair flopped into his eyes. "The Americans were trying to run the British blockade, missus, on account of the great hunger. A whole convoy of them loaded wi' corn. But the English chased them off awa hame, and made short work o' the French Navy what meant to protect them."

"Not war, then," Elizabeth said.

"Not yet," said Curiosity. "But it don't sound good. The sooner we get home, the better."

Nathaniel caught Elizabeth's gaze and he shook his head slightly; he wasn't ready to discuss the situation, and certainly not in front of the boy.

But Charlie took no note, so wound up was he in the rest of his news: a Manx smuggler had gone aground just south of the Southerness lighthouse and could be seen there plainly, listing hard. "The crew is still trapped on board, and they're armed. The excisemen have called out the dragoons from Dumfries," he finished. "They'll drag the whole lot off to gaol, wait and see."

Curiosity raised her head from her food and slanted a grim look in Nathaniel's direction.

The morning wore on and Nathaniel paced the cabin until even Elizabeth's patience had been tried beyond endurance.

"For heaven's sake, go up on deck," she said finally. "Take your son with you. Perhaps it will improve both your moods." She thrust Daniel into his arms.

The baby had been fussing all morning, but he stopped in mid-grizzle and gave his father a wide-mouthed grin.

"You see?" she said.

"It's got nothing to do with a bad mood, Boots," Nathaniel protested. "I'm just on edge, and so is he."

Hannah looked up from the basket she was filling. "He's on edge because you are, Da. He takes his mood from you."

As if to prove his sister right, Daniel settled against Nathaniel's shoulder with a satisfied grunt, pleased to have finally landed where he wanted to be. Nathaniel was in the habit of studying the baby, trying to find some trace of himself in his eyes or jaw or the rise of his forehead, just as he looked for Elizabeth in Lily's face. Now he wondered if he had been concentrating on the wrong things.

"He'll settle down if you walk him," said Curiosity.

"In the fresh air," added Elizabeth.

He laughed. "There's no arguing with the three of you." What he didn't say was, he was glad to have the excuse to go up on deck. There was a lot to think through, and he thought best while he was walking.

Nathaniel opened the door to find two redcoats waiting on the other side, muskets crossed and at the ready. Solidly built men, professional soldiers who held their weapons with the same affectionate ease that he held his son.

"Sir," the larger one snapped. Beneath the brim of his hat his gaze was brittle, his mouth hard set. Swollen red fingers clenched tight on the barrel of the musket. The second man was a head shorter, but cut from the same mold—the kind who liked confrontation, and was always looking for an excuse to unsheath his bayonet. Daniel took his thumb out of his mouth to stare at them, not in fear but interest.

"Who is it, Nathaniel?" Elizabeth came to the door with Lily in her arms.

Nathaniel answered her without looking away from the soldiers. "Redcoats. Looks like Moncrieff don't want us up on deck. Ain't that right?"

"Our orders are to see that no one leaves this cabin." The smaller soldier had an egg-round head on a mas-

sive neck. Both men stood with legs stemmed against
the roll of the ship, and Nathaniel knew that even
armed he would have little chance of forcing his way
through. Certainly there was nothing he could do with
Daniel on his arm.

He said, "I want to see Pickering."

The bigger redcoat thrust out his chin thoughtfully.
"We'll send word, sir."

"I want to see him now."

"No doubt you do, sir. But the gentlemen are occupied."

Nathaniel shut the door in their smirking faces.

"I feared as much," said Curiosity.

Elizabeth said nothing, but her expression was
drawn and tense. He touched her shoulder.

"What are you going to do?" Hannah asked as she
took Daniel from him. The baby began to fuss in
protest, and she jiggled him on her hip.

"I'm going to see Pickering."

Nathaniel opened the door out to the gallery and the
sea air rolled in, cool even in June. He put his hands
on the carved balustrade and leaned out, craning his
head upward to measure the distance to the gallery
overhead, the one off the cabins Giselle Somerville had
occupied. Behind him, Elizabeth said, "You cannot be
serious."

"There's nothing to it, Boots. I was climbing bigger
trees when I was Hannah's age. And so were you, according to your aunt Merriweather."

She let out a harsh laugh. "Don't try to mollify me,
Nathaniel. Trees do not buck like a horse when you
climb them."

But he had already found a good handhold in the
carved work of the support beams, and he hoisted himself up.

The sun struck sparks off the water, alive with the
wind. To either side land rolled away from the shore,
covered with grass of a green he had never seen before

on any growing thing, bright enough to make a man squint. The wind got under his shirt and made it billow out like a sail and his hair whipped into his eyes. He wished he had taken the time to tie it back.

"Nathaniel Bonner," Elizabeth said, mustering every ounce of resolve and severity she had to her name. "You'll land in the drink."

He studied her upturned face for a minute, measuring just how anxious she was. There was that line between her brows, the one that she used with unruly schoolboys. He said, "And if I do, Boots, they'll haul me out and I'll end up in front of Pickering, which is the whole idea."

He drew in a breath, braced himself with foot and hand against the choppy roll of the ship, and prepared to leap.

"Have you took leave of your senses, Nathaniel?" Curiosity stood at the open door, her hands on her hips. Elizabeth might be exasperated and anxious, but Curiosity was plain mad.

"You know I can't let him get away with locking us up."

She marched up to him and yanked on his shirttail. "Of course you cain't. But there's more than one way to skin that old cat, now ain't there? Your blood in such a boil that it has cooked your brain to pure mush. Come down from there and let me show you how to do it. Now where did that bird get to?"

She peered into the narrow corner of the gallery, bending over at the waist and making a clucking sound. When she straightened again she had Mr. Brown's puffin in her arms.

"What are you doing?" Elizabeth called after her.

But Curiosity only jerked her head impatiently and headed into the cabin.

"What can she possibly mean to do with Sally?" Elizabeth asked him.

"Hell if I know," he said, and swung himself back onto the gallery.

Curiosity waited for them at the door to the hall with the puzzled bird in both hands.

Hannah looked from Curiosity to her father to Elizabeth. Daniel put back his head and let out a high-pitched wail, and Lily joined him in furious voice. Rankled by Curiosity's tight hold and the crying babies, Sally opened her striped beak and began a great squawking.

"Curiosity." Nathaniel raised his voice. "Those dragoons are armed."

She threw him an offended look and flung open the door so that it crashed against the wall. At the same time she let out a keen-edged trill that made Nathaniel's own skin rise all along his spine.

Curiosity rushed the dragoons with the outraged bird thrust before her, flapping and screeching.

Nathaniel's legs moved of their own accord, past Elizabeth and Hannah and the howling babies. He barreled through the door behind Curiosity, flashing past two astonished faces. The bigger redcoat made a grab for him but Curiosity still had the bird by the feet and she swung it in his face like a battle-axe, her Kahnyen'kehàka war cry even louder in the narrow hall.

Behind him there was a thump and a hoarse shout but Nathaniel pushed hard up the stairs and burst onto the deck, careening into a line of sailors humping kegs. The whole queue went crashing one into the next. A keg hit the deck hard on its rim, sprang its hoops, and a great gush of brandy spattered in a wide arc. From the corner of his eye Nathaniel saw two kegs roll into Adam MacKay. There was the audible snap of bone, a short scream, and then he flipped over the rail in a flash of flailing legs.

"What's this? What's this?" The boatswain raised a cudgel but Nathaniel knocked him out of the way and

ran straight for the round-house. Half the crew was behind him, and the other half leaned over the side, fishing for MacKay.

Nathaniel kicked open the door and stood there, dripping onto the captain's polished floor.

Pickering and Moncrieff shot to their feet.

"Really, Mr. Bonner!" Pickering sputtered. "What is the meaning of this?"

"I don't take kindly to being locked up," said Nathaniel, wiping his wet face on his sleeve and frowning at the smell. "As Moncrieff there knows all too well. That's the meaning of this."

"It was for your own protection," Moncrieff said wearily, rubbing a hand over his chin. "But now that ye're here, the damage is done. Mr. Bonner, Mr. Burns of the excise office."

The man still seated at the captain's table got up from behind the pile of papers, his nostrils flaring as he sniffed

"Mr. . . . Bonner?" He bowed from the shoulders, but his eyes never left Nathaniel's face.

"Nathaniel Bonner of New-York, aye. What of it?"

The man blinked in surprise. "Your servant, sir." And then to Pickering, his mouth turning up at one corner: "I take it that ye've got nineteen kegs o' double distilled Indian arrack rather than the twenty noted here?"

Pickering nodded impatiently.

There was a shouting on the deck. The two dragoons he had left behind pushed their way through the crowd, jostling him farther into the cabin. The bigger one had a bloody nose and a long scratch on his cheek; the smaller man's arm was bleeding. He had lost his hat but gained a number of bird feathers, one sticking out of his left eyebrow.

It was the little one who lunged for him. Nathaniel sidestepped, slipping the knife strapped to his wrist into

his palm, and jabbed the man neatly in the back of the hand. He howled and fell back, fumbling for his musket.

"Enough!" Pickering's voice cut hard and cold into the confusion.

"Captain," panted the bigger one, pointing a shaking finger at Nathaniel. "He set a lunatic Negress on us so as to slip awa' while we were fightin' her off! Sinclair here almost had the better o' her when a redskin come up and stabbed him wi' a candle."

"Negress? Redskin?" The exciseman looked around himself as if they might jump out from a shadowy corner. "Stabbed him with a *candle*?"

Nathaniel snorted. "An old woman and a little girl."

"Old or young, they were armed!"

"Aye, with a bird and a bit of beeswax. It's a miracle these two escaped with their lives."

The big dragoon flushed purple to the roots of his hair. The smaller one had gone pasty white. Burns turned his head away and let out a great coughing laugh, and for a moment both Moncrieff and the captain studied their shoes.

"Sir!"

"Never mind," barked Moncrieff. "Go report to your sergeant, and tell him what a bluidy cock-up ye've made o' guardin' women and bairns."

The little one glared at Nathaniel. "You haven't seen the end o' us."

"Come calling anytime," said Nathaniel lightly.

"Enough!" Pickering marched to the door. "The rest of you men get back to your duties!"

"Women and bairns?" echoed Burns thoughtfully as he watched the crowd leak reluctantly away. He raised a brow in Pickering's direction. "I take it ye have mair passengers on board than Mr. Bonner, Captain."

"That depends on what you mean by passengers," Nathaniel said, staring hard at Moncrieff.

"Mr. Bonner travels with his family," said Pickering, as if Nathaniel hadn't spoken.

"Then I'll need tae inspect his baggage."

The captain blew out his cheeks and sucked them in again. "Is that really necessary, sir? I can assure you, sir, they carry nothing of interest to the Crown."

Burns picked up his hat from the table and smiled politely. "I'll have tae make that determination for masel', Captain."

Moncrieff cleared his throat. "May I have a word wi' you first, Mr. Bonner?"

Nathaniel's first instinct was to walk away, but Moncrieff had struck a tone that surprised him, hesitant and deferential. No doubt it was more trickery, but Nathaniel was curious enough to step onto the quarterdeck with him.

Elizabeth managed to calm the babies by setting them to nurse, although she herself was far from settled. She only had to look at Curiosity or Hannah and she would begin to laugh again. It was that kind of laughter that defies all logic and reason, doubling back on itself until the stomach ached with the effort to breathe normally.

Hannah's face was flushed too as she bent over Sally, murmuring to the puffin in the same voice Elizabeth had last heard from Falling-Day as she tended an injured dog. She ran fingers along wings and leg, flexing joints and looking for wounds. Elizabeth would have sworn that the bird gave Hannah an indignant look as she set it on the floor.

"She lost a few feathers, but there's nothing else wrong that I can see," Hannah announced.

"Joshua had his horn," said Curiosity with a satisfied grin. "And we had our Sally. Lord, but she made a fine batterin' ram."

She put an arm around Hannah and hugged her.

"You looked mighty fierce yourself, missy. You put the fear of God into that little man. If I live to be a hundred I won't forget the look on his face when you poked him with that candle."

There was something of Curiosity's old tone in her voice, a hopefulness that had been missing for these last long weeks. Elizabeth did not comment on it, did not even look too hard at her, for fear that these good spirits might flee as quickly as they had come. Certainly she did not dare scold Hannah. The impulse to defend Curiosity could not be faulted, but she had thrust Daniel at Elizabeth and rushed to take on two armed soldiers with little concern for danger. It had been frightening, and now she could not stop laughing when she remembered it.

Hannah was still agitated and worried about the puffin. "Perhaps the Hakim should have a look at her."

Elizabeth shook her head. "There's no telling what's happening on deck. It would be better to wait for your father."

Curiosity straightened. "I hear him now. And he ain't alone."

At Elizabeth's breast, Daniel's suckling had slowed down to the gentle rhythm that meant he would soon follow Lily's example and fall into a sound sleep. She pulled her shawl over both of them for modesty's sake, corrected her posture and composed her face, ready for more redcoats or even for Angus Moncrieff.

Hannah came to stand behind her, but Curiosity held her ground. Sally disappeared into the shadows under the table, as if she sensed more trouble just ahead.

The man who came in with Nathaniel was neither sailor nor soldier, but a stranger to all of them. What struck Elizabeth about him first was the contrast of the way he bore himself—very much the gentleman—and his hands, work roughened and thick fingered, the hands of a laborer or farmer. His dark eyes moved

through the room from person to person, pausing at
Curiosity and coming to rest on Hannah. He seemed
delighted with what he found, his expression so open
and intelligent that Elizabeth felt some of her apprehension flowing away to be replaced by curiosity.

"Ah," he said. "Now I take your meaning, Mr.
Bonner. I'll see tae it that those men are reprimanded
for their behavior, insolent puppies that they are."

Nathaniel's gaze settled on Hannah. In Kahnyen'kehàka he said, "You all right, Squirrel?"

She nodded.

"Curiosity?"

"Nothing ailin' me," she said, sniffing the air. "But I
see you been up to mischief."

"There was a problem with some kegs," Nathaniel
said.

He crossed the room to put a hand on Elizabeth's
shoulder. The smell of liquor rose about him in such a
strong wave that tears came to her eyes, but she blinked
them away.

"This here's the excise officer. Come to see what
riches we're smuggling into Scotland."

Elizabeth pulled both babies closer to her underneath the shawl. "I fear you will be sore disappointed,
Mr. . . ."

The exciseman made a sweeping bow, his dark hair
falling forward. "Robert Burns. At your service,
madam." He paused, throwing a sideways glance toward Curiosity.

"This lady is Mrs. Freeman," Elizabeth said pointedly. It was as close as she could come to stating openly
that Curiosity should not be mistaken for a servant, or
a slave. "And my stepdaughter, Miss Bonner."

If Mr. Burns was surprised by these introductions,
there was nothing of it in his expression.

"Mrs. Freeman," he murmured, but his gaze fixed on
Hannah. He studied her as he might study a piece of
the moon, or a Chinese vase—with great interest,

and no maliciousness at all. "Miss Bonner. My great honor."

Elizabeth thought of speaking to him sharply for staring, but she knew too that Hannah would encounter this kind of interest wherever she went in Scotland. Perhaps it was best to let her deal with it herself.

Hannah looked him up and down and said, "Is an exciseman a kind of pirate?"

Mr. Burns had a deep laugh. Even Curiosity smiled at the sound of it.

"Daughter—" said Nathaniel.

"Ach, dinna scold the lass for her honesty, Mr. Bonner. Those who wad prefer no' tae pay the king for the privilege o' drinkin' tea call us pirates, and worse. There's no' a day passes that someone doesna wish me awa' tae the devil."

"Oh," said Hannah, disappointed. "A tax collector."

"In a manner o' speakin'," conceded Mr. Burns.

"We got no tea here," said Curiosity impatiently. "No brandy or tobacco, neither. Just children, as you can see for yourself. Nothing to interest you."

"I'll take your word on that, madam. But if I might ask . . ." He addressed Nathaniel directly. "What brings ye tae Scotland, sir? Are ye perhaps visitin' kin in the area?"

Elizabeth felt Nathaniel stiffen. He said, "We have no family here."

The dark eyes blinked in surprise. "Pardon my presumption, sir. I've offended ye and I'm verra sorry for it."

Elizabeth might have spoken, but Nathaniel's grip on her shoulder tightened. He said, "Just what's your interest in us?"

He flushed, but he spoke with dignity. "It's no' often we see visitors from America in our wee corner o' Scotland, ye ken. I'll bother ye no mair. Guid day tae ye, and Godspeed on your journey."

His hand was on the door when Nathaniel stopped him. "A question before you go."

"Sir?"

"Have you heard any word of a schooner called the *Jackdaw,* flying American colors?"

He turned to face them. "The captain asked me the verra same question, no' an hour ago."

Curiosity made a deep sound in her throat that said exactly what she thought of Pickering and his questions.

"And?"

Mr. Burns said, "I should be gey surprised if the *Jackdaw* sailed intae these waters."

"And why is that?" asked Elizabeth.

"Why, smugglers dinna usually come up and introduce themsel' tae the representatives o' the Crown," he said with a small smile. "Should Mac Stoker hae business in the firth, he'll find a wee cove tae hide the schooner and make his way by night."

"So he might be here?" Hannah spoke up, her interest in the exciseman revived.

"Aa things arc possible wi' the likes o' Mac Stoker," said Mr. Burns. "He's a wily one. As ye seem tae ken yersel'." Elizabeth watched him swallow down a question he would have liked to ask.

Nathaniel said, "Any idea where we might get word of him?"

The exciseman ran a hand over his chin. "Ye might weel inquire at Mump's Hall, on the Dumfries Road."

"That's a tavern, I take it?"

"Aye. A favorite o' smugglers and freebooters. No' a place tae be after dark, if ye take my meanin', sir."

"I do," said Nathaniel. "And I'm indebted to you."

Once more he paused at the door. "If ye'll allow me a single suggestion?"

Nathaniel nodded.

"Should ye gae lookin' for Mac Stoker, wear a hat."

"You mean for me to hide my face," Nathaniel said.

"Aye," said the exciseman. "It wad be in your best interest."

• • •

"What's wrong with your face that he wants you to hide it?" Hannah demanded as soon as they were alone again.

Nathaniel pulled the wet shirt away from his skin as he answered her. "Moncrieff has been claiming all along that there's a strong resemblance to Carryck. I guess that's one thing he wasn't lying about."

"He locked us in here so the exciseman wouldn't see your face?" Curiosity shook her head. "I don' know about that man. Is he plain stupid, or just jittery?"

"Both," said Nathaniel. "And stubborn, too."

"What does it matter if you look like that old earl?" Hannah grumbled. "Whose business is it?"

Elizabeth shifted the sleeping babies so that she could lift them. "I would guess that Mr. Moncrieff is worried that the Campbells will take an interest, once word gets out. Is that not so?"

Nathaniel grunted. "That's the way he tells it, Boots. It seems that half of the dragoons quartered in Dumfries are Campbells, and the other half are related to them by marriage. Moncrieff pulled me aside up on deck to warn me about keeping my head low."

Curiosity waved a hand before her face. "While you're keeping your head low you'd best go change. I ain't never smelled anything like you, not even when Axel Metzler gets his still goin'."

"I'm on my way," Nathaniel said.

Elizabeth followed him into the side cabin, where she put the sleeping twins in the middle of the bed while Nathaniel stripped the wet shirt over his head and peeled his breeches off.

"Christ, what I wouldn't give for a bath. She's right, I stink."

Elizabeth wrinkled her nose. "If you are looking to me for a denial, I'm afraid I must disappoint you."

He did not laugh; he barely seemed to hear her. Standing at the window he had turned his attention to the traffic on the water, and he studied it closely while he wiped his chest with a piece of toweling. The light moved on him, claiming the broad plane of his shoulder and the line of backbone, sliding over the small of his back and down his thigh. He was completely at ease in his nakedness, without self-consciousness or vanity and so beautiful that her breath caught and she wondered if the next would ever come.

His face was hidden from her, and she was glad of it, feeling more naked than he in this moment, and inexplicably happy. Elizabeth touched each of the children in turn, to feel the rise and fall of their breathing. *In small proportions we just beauty see.*

"I can hear you thinking, Boots," he said finally.

"I don't doubt it. Your ears are entirely too sharp."

He stilled suddenly.

"What is it?"

"The Hakim," he said. "On a barge, headed for shore."

"The Hakim?" Elizabeth echoed. "But where would he be going?"

Nathaniel grunted. "That's the question, all right."

"Perhaps he has friends to visit in the area," Elizabeth said, more to herself than to him.

"Or maybe Carryck sent for him," said Nathaniel. "Maybe he has need of a surgeon." He pulled his only clean shirt over his head and reached for his breeches. "I suppose we'll find out soon enough."

Elizabeth drew in a wavering breath and let it out again.

He came to sit beside her, and slipped his arms around her waist. "You're loath to leave the ship."

"You've heard the old saying, I'm sure. Better the devil you know."

"Enough devils to go around in Scotland, no question about it." He stood, and drew her up with him.

"And dragons and giants and fairies and Green Men, too. But you and me, we've been through the endless forests, Elizabeth."

"So we have," she said. "I expect that we can manage Scotland, too."

PART III

Carryckcastle

23

The long road to Dumfries was muck and misery. Horses floundered and babies wailed, and yet Hannah could conjure no scowl, or even show the disinterest she thought she must owe this place. By the time the wooden box they called a coach entered the town she had rubbed the skin on her elbows raw leaning out the little window.

Daniel fussed in Curiosity's arms, but she freed a hand long enough to pull back the leather curtain.

"Must be some kind of celebration goin' on, all these folks headed in the same direction."

"I should like to get out and walk with them," Elizabeth said, shifting uneasily. "I had forgotten how uncomfortable it is to travel by coach."

Lily turned her head against Elizabeth's shoulder and frowned in her sleep.

Nathaniel said nothing, but his jaw was hard-set. He had asked for a horse, but Moncrieff had refused without explanation. Hannah wondered how long it would be before her father and Moncrieff had serious words.

The lane was busy with stray dogs and children, tradesmen and servants and ladies in hats sprouting long feathers dyed pink and yellow and green. They

held their skirts up from the cobblestones to display layers of lace and ribboned shoes. In New-York a rich man was known by his tall beaver hat, and here they were too, bobbing along in a stream of soft caps and old tricorns.

"It is much like Albany," Hannah said, surprised and a little disappointed.

Curiosity made a sound in her throat. "Look harder, child. This town was tired when Albany wasn't nothing more than a widening in the trail along the big river."

It was true: even the stones that lined the doorways seemed to sag. Windows leaned together and timbers bowed. Under thatched roofs the tiny stone cottages that lined the lanes looked to Hannah like rows of knowing old faces with sunken eyes. In one spot the road narrowed so that she might have reached out to pet a cat sleeping on a windowsill in the early evening light.

Hannah craned her neck to study the chimneys. "Look how black the smoke is." She wrinkled her nose at the greasy smell of it.

"Coal," said Elizabeth. "The dust coats everything."

A young boy raced by carrying an unlit torch almost as long as he was. He cast a sidelong glance at the coach and pulled up short, his mouth hanging open as he stared at Hannah.

"Boy," she said, taking this opportunity. "Where is everyone going?"

He walked along beside them with his mouth still gaping to show an odd collection of brownish teeth. His torch bumped behind him over the cobblestones.

"He won't have any English," said her father. "Speak Scots to him."

She might have done it just to see the look on the boy's face, but Moncrieff's horse moved up between the coach and the crowd, and he was lost to her. Hannah sat back and crossed her arms, determined to ignore the man until he went away again. But he had heard her question, and he talked to them through the window.

"The town is getting ready tae celebrate the navy's victory over the French. There'll be speeches and a bonfire. You'll be able tae watch from the inn. Here it is now, ye see. The King's Arms."

No one responded to him, but he didn't seem to mind.

"A warm meal and a good night's rest before we travel on," Moncrieff continued.

"Bathwater," Curiosity said. "Lots of it. And hot."

Hannah thought it might be the first words she had said to Moncrieff since they left Québec.

He pursed his mouth. "Aye, o' course. Whatever ye require."

Nathaniel studied the hat that Moncrieff had given him: dusty black, with a broad round brim. The kind of hat you might see on a preacher, or one of the tinkers who roved the edge of the wilderness, selling hair ribbon and buttonhooks from canvas packs and reciting bible verses for their supper. Now he pulled it low over his brow as he climbed out of the coach, unsteady still on his sea legs and feeling foolish and irritated to be hiding his face.

The inn sat on a cobbled square, where the crowd was still gathering. Nathaniel shielded the women on the short walk to the door, hanging back until they were safely inside. The lack of his own weapons weighed heavier than it had on the *Isis*.

The innkeeper showed them to their rooms, a man as long and thin as a birch sapling with a fringe of hair around his ears and the habit of addressing his feet when he spoke. Elizabeth immediately shed her shoes and disappeared with the babies behind the bed curtains while Curiosity directed servants who came with trunks and baskets, trays of food and tea, and the first buckets of hot water. Squirrel went straight to the window to watch the crowd below them.

Nathaniel joined her. Although the old clock in the hall had showed it to be more than eight in the evening, it was full light still.

"We're coming into the longest days," he said.

She looked up at him and it took Nathaniel by surprise, as it often did, to see her for what she was: a pretty girl, tall and straight. Only five years younger than her mother had been when he set his sights on her.

"You're going out, aren't you. To that tavern the exciseman told you about. We passed it on the road here."

He nodded. "This far north it won't be dark for a good hour yet, but then I'll have to go. There's a livery over there where I can rent a horse, or buy one."

She looked back out over the square. "I know you have to ask about the *Jackdaw,* but it worries me." She said it in Kahnyen'kehàka, to make it more true, to make him listen.

Nathaniel answered her in the same language. "Maybe your grandfather is nearby. Maybe he's looking for us."

Below them five ladies had come into the square in the company of redcoat officers. The crowd parted for them, and Nathaniel got a better look. Young women richly dressed, each of them wore a broad band across the breast, blue in color with white script: God Save the King.

He was in Scotland, and he was not: Nathaniel felt himself sixteen again, in those first years of the war, when the Tories still had a grip on New-York. He had seen this kind of display before. Loyalists parading silk banners for old George, determined to make the world England, even if they should have to die to do it. He had never thought to see the like again, and certainly not in Scotland. Not his mother's Scotland, or the Scotland Robbie had fought for on the battlefield at Culloden. Or even the Scotland Angus Moncrieff had talked about hour after hour in the Montréal gaol. Yet here it was, proof that those stories had told only part of the tale.

It's none of our concern, he reminded himself. *Don't let yourself get caught up in their business.*

Hannah slipped her hand into his, and he squeezed it.

Just next to the growing pile of refuse that would become the bonfire, workmen had begun building something that looked to Nathaniel like a makeshift gallows.

"Look, Da," Hannah said. "That man in the tall hat, there by the well. He's got a great doll dressed like a man. What are they going to do with it?"

It was a doll, one made of bound straw and rags. A shaggy old wig had been tied to the head, and it was dressed in breeches and a loose shirt. A board had been hung around the neck, and on this "Th. Paine" had been painted in large letters. The man held the doll over his head like a trophy, and then he jumped up on the platform to show it to the crowd. With a flourish, he turned it around so that they could read the board on the back: "The Rights of Man." A shrill whistle of approval, laughter; the ladies put their gloved hands together.

"Da?" Hannah was looking at him.

"They can't put their hands on Tom Paine, so they'll hang him in effigy," Nathaniel said. "And then they'll burn him. To celebrate the English victory over the French."

"Boots," Nathaniel called. "The servants are all gone. You can come out."

Elizabeth threw back the curtains and climbed down from the feather bed. She left the twins where they were, fed and content to babble at each other for the time being. They were in need of clean swaddling and a bath, and so was she. But first she must eat.

She paused a moment to study the room. It was of a good size, well furnished with mahogany furniture and a fine carpet. Almost certainly these were the best lodg-

ings to be had in Dumfries, but Nathaniel still must bow his head or knock it on the door frame as he came and went.

"Where is Curiosity?"

Hannah pointed with her chin toward the closed door to the adjoining room. "Hot water."

"Of course." Elizabeth made diversions around trunks and baggage on her way to the table, where Nathaniel offered her a tankard. She wrapped her hands around the cool pewter and sniffed. Small beer, sharp and yeasty. The smell of it told her she was in Britain again, as nothing else could.

"Sit." Nathaniel pulled gently on her elbow.

"I've been sitting more than half the day," she said. "Let me stretch a bit. And tell me, what is all this?" There were six trunks she did not recognize, in addition to their own few things.

"Giselle Somerville's baggage," said Hannah. "Moncrieff said that Captain Pickering did not want them, so he gave them to us."

"How very strange. Without first asking if we cared to have them?"

Hannah shrugged, her eyes sliding over Elizabeth's gray travel dress. It was one of the three she had left Paradise with, and like all of them it showed the strain of the journey.

Elizabeth reached for the platter of cold beef. "I will not wear her finery. If we come to the earl in tatters, it is his own doing. I daresay he will receive us anyway."

"Otherwise we'll just turn around and head home," Nathaniel said dryly, peering suspiciously into a bowl of pickled onions.

A knock at the door, and the innkeeper appeared. He bowed hastily, his pate flashing as round and white as a clockface. "May I inquire, is everythin' in order? Do ye require aught else, sir?"

"Mr. Thornburn." Elizabeth addressed him directly,

in a tone she knew he could not mistake. "Please see to it that these trunks are removed. Take them to Mr. Moncrieff, for they do not belong to us."

The innkeeper's head bobbed. "Mr. Moncrieff is across the way at the Globe, ma'am, takin' a drink wi' the Poet. But I'll see tae it directly."

Hannah's brow creased. "The Poet? Does Dumfries have its own poet, then?"

"We do indeed, miss. We count Rab Burns as our own. Did ye no' make his acquaintance when he came aboard the *Isis*?"

"Robert Burns?" Nathaniel sat up straighter. "The exciseman?"

"Aye, the verra one," said Mr. Thornburn, stroking his chin whiskers thoughtfully. "An exciseman, and Scotland's greatest poet, forbye. Is his verse kennt sae far awa' as America, then?"

Hannah put her hands flat on the table and she sang without hesitation, her voice steady but a little rough with disuse:

> *Ye flowery banks o' bonnie Doon,*
> *How can ye blume sae fair;*
> *How can ye chant, ye little birds,*
> *And I sae fu' o' care!*

Mr. Thornburn's jaw sagged, and then snapped sharply closed. "A Red Indian wha' kens Rab Burns's verse. It's aye true, then, they can be civilized."

Before Hannah could respond, Nathaniel had stepped between her and the innkeeper. He said, "We'll thank you for moving the trunks. There's nothing else we need."

"Aye, sir, as ye wish." Mr. Thornburn bowed again. At the door he hesitated, casting one last inquisitive look at Hannah, who raised her chin at him and stared, all indignation.

For a moment they were quiet, listening to the crowd in the town square. Then Elizabeth reached over and put her hand on Hannah's.

"I'm afraid you will hear many such terribly ignorant and rude things while we are here," she said. "Those who think themselves to be civilized are not always particularly intelligent, or rational."

Hannah nodded, the muscles in her jaw working silently. "I should have listened to you," she said finally. "I should have stayed at Lake in the Clouds."

Elizabeth saw Nathaniel tense, as she herself tensed. "I cannot deny that you would be safer at home," she said. "But you belong with us, and I am glad that you are here, just the same."

What Elizabeth wanted most in the world was to bathe in privacy and then to climb into the feather bed to sleep tucked up against her husband. It had been so many months since they had shared such a large and comfortable bed, and this half-day journey from the firth had been more difficult than the last few weeks on the *Isis*.

But it was an idle wish. The twins needed bathing, and more desperately than she did; the servants came again to remove the trunks, clear the tables, lay fires, empty cold bathwater and bring in new. Curiosity insisted on sorting through all their clothing, separating out those things that needed immediate laundering, and Hannah determined that one of the maids had an inflamed eye that must be treated with a particular herb the Hakim had given her, which required a long search through all her parcels.

Nathaniel stayed clear of all of this by keeping watch at the window. Dumfries celebrated its delight with the Royal Navy by having every man of consequence climb up onto a platform and give a speech, and Nathaniel reported now and then on particularly absurd or witless turns of phrase, of which there were not a few. At one

point a very drunk old man leaped up into the group of men on the stage and began to sing so loudly that for a moment the crowd stilled to listen for a few wobbling notes.

"Mick Schiell! Ye can sing nane!" The shout was accompanied by a well-aimed apple, and the old man gave in to the crowd and climbed down again so that the speech-making could continue.

Hannah was listening closely. At one point she looked up from her basket of herbs with a confused expression. "How can a frog be papist?"

"'Frog' is a disrespectful term for the French," Elizabeth explained. "Most of France is Catholic."

Curiosity made her own disrespectful sound. "I don' know why it is folks are always stirrin' things up. Always lookin' for a way to get bloody."

Hannah pursed her mouth thoughtfully. "It's not much different from home."

"True enough. We got enough trouble of our own, don't need to go lookin' for any fresh foolery."

But she met Elizabeth's eye when she said this, and there was a ghost of a smile there, a kind of weary acceptance. She got up, and spread her skirt smooth with her hands. "I'm tired," she announced. "And I cain't deny, that bed looks mighty sweet. I'll wish you all a good rest."

But even with the twins settled and Curiosity and Hannah in the next room, Elizabeth did not have Nathaniel's full attention. And how could she, when he finally lowered himself into hot water laced with soap? And so she took a turn at the window, her own attention divided between Nathaniel and the scene below in the square. Thomas Paine, or what was left of him, twirled at the end of a rope while boys pelted him with rocks and dung.

"Dumfries doesn't suit you, Boots."

She laughed. "Did you think it might?"

Nathaniel slid down deeper into the tub in a futile at-

tempt to submerge his shoulders and knees at the same time. "I can't figure out if it's Scotland or that crowd in the square that has you out of sorts."

"Both," she said, leaning against the wall with her arms crossed. "And I am worried about this outing of yours."

He met her gaze directly. "If you don't want me to go, you'd best just say so."

Elizabeth considered. She could ask him to stay, and in such terms that he would give up this scheme of a nighttime ride to an unfamiliar tavern frequented by rough trade. But then she would have accomplished very little: her own poor mood exchanged for his sleeplessness, and this she could not justify to herself.

Nathaniel bent his head to pour a dipper of water over his soapy hair. The twilight was deepening now, and it gilded the wet skin at the back of his neck. A neck like any other. He was blood and bone; he was strong, and clever, and quick. He would go out into this curious Scottish dusk, a sky streaked the color of gilded roses and ash and ocher, and when he had done what he must do, he would find his way back to her again. She must trust him, as he had once trusted her to undertake a perilous journey.

She said, "They will light the bonfire soon, and that will be a great distraction. I suppose that will be the best time for you to go."

He blinked the water out of his eyes. "That's not what I asked you, Boots."

"I know what you asked me." She came to kneel beside the copper tub and take the dipper from him. While she rinsed his hair she said, "Last night you said something to me, I cannot quite get it out of my mind. You said you might as well be in chains for all the good you are to me."

He started to speak, and she hushed him.

"I will not have you in chains, not even of my own

making. But promise me you'll be careful, and that you'll be back by dawn."

Nathaniel caught her wrist and pressed his mouth to her palm, his beard stubble rough against her skin. "I promise. Maybe I'll scratch at your window like the Green Man, come dawn."

"More likely you will come to wake me with cold feet," she said, surprised and disquieted by the shudder that ran up her spine. Come dawn, come dusk. *Superstition,* she reminded herself. *Nothing more. Nothing less.*

The bonfire came to life against the darkening sky with a roar that drowned out the crowd. Nathaniel watched from the lane beside the King's Arms while he planned his route to the livery through the mass of people, young and old, faces shining with excitement and their voices hoarse with liquor. Mr. Thornburn capered around the fire with the rest of them, and Nathaniel wondered if he had any idea how much Dumfries looked like any Kahnyen'kehàka village after a battle well fought.

He pulled his preacher's hat down over his brow and skirted the edge of the open area, staying out of the fire's light. And here he found there was another Dumfries, one that watched silently from the shadows.

Just beyond the tiled roofs of the inn and the red-sandstone assembly hall was a sea of small cottages. On every one of those thatched roofs, a man or boy sat perched with a bucket between his knees and a broom soaking, at the ready, wary eyes following sparks up into the deepening night sky. In doorways mothers stood with babies on their hips and silent husbands at their backs. An old man with cropped gray hair, hard faced and remote, sat straight spined on a mule and the fire reflected red in his eyes. In the near dark he put Nathaniel in mind of Sky-Wound-Round, his first wife's

grandfather, the man who had first led him into battle. Homesickness rose in him, but he put it away.

> *I dreamt my lady came and found me dead . . .*
> *And breathed such life with kisses in my lips*
> *that I revived, and was an emperor.*

Nathaniel looked back over the square and saw a single candle flame at the window. Elizabeth was watching still, the pale heart shape of her face floating in the dusk. She was waiting for him already, though he was hardly gone.

There was a light in the livery, and the ringing of hammer on metal. He went in, a sack of thick five-guinea pieces in his fist. The Tory gold had been nothing but trouble since Chingachgook brought it out of the bush almost forty years ago, but now he would put it to good use.

He did not offer his name, but he did not need to: the sight of the coins in the light of the fire did their work. The blacksmith put down his hammer and went to get the best horse he had.

It was a smithy like any other; it smelled of hot metal and manure and sweat. A tankard sat on a rough table next to the remains of an oat cake and a bit of dry cheese. On a nail next to the door hung a woolen cloak with well-worn boots standing beneath it, from the size of them the blacksmith's own.

He brought the roan fully saddled. A fine animal, no longer young but with strong legs and an intelligent look about her. Nathaniel offered him twice what she would have fetched in New-York, and the blacksmith sold her without hesitation.

"The boots and cape. What do ye want for them?"

The blacksmith watched him from the corner of his eye. "I've had yon boots a guid ten year. Broke in just richt, they are."

Nathaniel put another gold piece down and the man grunted in surprise. The coin disappeared into his fist.

"Anythin' else, Dominie?"

Dominie. In an hour the whole town would hear about a preacher with a pocket full of gold coin, foolish enough to spend five guineas on old boots and a worn cloak. A stranger whose Scots had an odd feel to it, like a Hielander who had learned it secondhand. It would not take Moncrieff long to put it all together, and Nathaniel did not want Moncrieff with him on this errand.

"Aye," he said. He put five more coins on the barrel. "Guns. And your silence."

The dark head swung around and the blacksmith looked straight at him for the first time. Sweaty hair plastered his temples; the left side of his face smooth and slack, the mouth dragged down at the corner. The right eye squinted. Nathaniel was glad of the shadows and his hat's broad brim.

From the tavern next door came the sound of a man singing, a strong voice, clear and true.

> *Does haughty Gaul invasion threat?*
> *Then let the loons beware, sir,*
> *There's wooden walls upon our seas,*
> *And volunteers on shore, sir:*
> *The Nith shall rin to Corsincon,*
> *And Criffel sink in Solway,*
> *Ere we permit a foreign foe*
> *On British ground to rally.*
>
> *O! let us not, like snarling curs,*
> *In wrangling be divided,*
> *Till slap come in an unco loon*
> *And wi' a rung decide it.*
> *Be Britain still to Britain true,*
> *Amang ourselves united;*

But never but by British hands
Maun British wrangs be righted.

The blacksmith's mouth twisted as he looked at the gold. As much money as he would make in two years of pounding out horseshoes. Without a word he went to a cabinet in the corner and selected a ring from the clutch at his waist to turn the lock.

What Nathaniel wanted was a rifle; the best he expected was an old musket. But when the blacksmith put the bundle on the barreltop and unwrapped it, he got more than he had hoped for: a pair of holster pistols, well balanced and easy in the hand. Long brass barrels and walnut stocks, etched silver lockplates. Weapons made for a rich man and rarely fired.

Outside the noise of the crowd rose and fell like an ill wind.

"How'd you come by these?" He wanted the pistols, but he wouldn't spend even an hour in the Dumfries tollbooth for thievery.

The man shrugged. "They're no' stolen." He dropped a sack of powder and another of bullets onto the barrel and swept the coins away into the front pocket of his apron. Then he touched his temple with two fingers, a salute of kinds for Nathaniel or his coin, and turned back to the forge.

Nathaniel strapped the holster across his chest and wrapped the cloak around himself. It smelled of cheap tobacco and wet sheep, but it was thick and the wide collar stood to the brim of his hat. It would keep him warm, and with any luck it would give him some degree of anonymity.

He left Dumfries behind at a trot, glad of the night wind in his face. The road was empty and the roan was surefooted and eager. Nathaniel gave her her head, and she skirted mudholes he wouldn't have seen in the dark.

By his reckoning Mump's Hall was six miles south on the road that went down to the sea. He kept an eye out for the markers he had found during the long coach ride: a collapsed stone wall, a wooden footbridge arched like a cat's back. In the light of the moon crofters' cottages seemed to spring directly out of the ground: piles of stones stacked together without mortar, more like caves than a home a man would build for himself.

An acre of wheat, and one of oats. A hill to the west with cows as shaggy as dogs grazing by moonlight. Sheep in a huddle against a fence, hayricks, more oats. A few poor trees marked a stream running noisily into the sea, just to the east now. The smell of it was in his nose: salt and sand and marsh. He went over another bridge and at a turn in the road the tavern, finally, with a lantern burning at the door.

Nathaniel tied the horse to the hitching post and paused to take his bearings. The building itself smelled of spilled ale and roasting mutton, and with every step the boggy ground gave out a soft belch and the stench of rotting greenery.

He pushed open the door.

In the dim light of a smoky fire men bent their heads together over tankards. Some of them looked to be farmers, but most had tarry hands and a sea squint. A few played cards in the farthest corner, but he could make out nothing familiar about any of them.

A man who sat with his bare feet on the hearthstones let out a long stream of tobacco juice into the flames. "Mump!" he shouted over his shoulder. "Custom for ye, man!"

The tavernkeeper came sideways through a low door at the back of the room. He was no taller than a boy of ten, but as wide around as a keg—a cork of a man, bobbing along on feet too small to bear his weight. His hair was clubbed but his beard flowed and twisted, black and gray to his waist. Under his arm he carried a bottle.

He wiped his mouth on the sleeve of his jerkin. "What'll it be?"

Nathaniel raised his voice, although the room was dead quiet. "A word."

"Oh-ho," said the little man, the round cheeks flushed. "Did ye hear, lads? It's a word he's wantin'. A word." He drew himself up to his full height as he came toward Nathaniel. "At Mump's Ha' ye'll get barleybroo, sae lang as ye can pay for it. There's a subscription library doon the road in Dumfries, gin it's words ye want."

It wouldn't be wise to flash gold guineas in a room full of men who made their living smuggling, and he had only a few pounds in silver coin that he did not like to throw away. But there was no help for it: Nathaniel knew these men would not talk unless he drank with them.

"Whisky, then."

The little man's expression softened. "Aye, whisky. There's nae better road tae start a conversation."

He hopped up onto a stool and gestured with an open palm for Nathaniel to take the one next to him. When the long bottle under his arm had been uncorked and the whisky had been poured, Nathaniel tipped it in one blazing stream down his throat. Satisfied, the tavernkeeper climbed back down off his stool and stood there chewing thoughtfully on a twist of beard.

"Dandie Mump is ma name. And ye are?"

Nathaniel considered. He could not pass himself off as a Scot for long here, and still he was not foolish enough to forget Moncrieff's warnings about the Campbells. "I'm American. Came off the *Isis* this morning," he said.

"The *Isis*!"

He might have offered to slit their throats for the reaction he got. Stools screeched as men came to their feet.

Mump narrowed his eyes at him. "Ye came aff yon great merchantman sittin' there in the firth?"

Nathaniel did not like the way the room was closing around him, but he kept his expression even. He nodded. "I did."

From the back of the crowd a tall man with a lump of tobacco in his cheek said, "Is it true that there's typhoid on board?"

Nathaniel jerked in surprise. "It is not. When I left her this morning there wasn't a sick man on the *Isis*. Who speaks of typhoid?"

Mump poured more whisky in Nathaniel's cup, and then drank it himself. "The captain willna allow the crew on land because o' the typhoid, so we've heard."

"Ma Nan's brither Charlie is on the *Isis*," said a man at Nathaniel's elbow. He was of middle years, windburned and gaunt. He smelled of fish and tar and weariness and his hands trembled a little. "She's aye worrit for him. Do ye ken the lad?"

"A cabin boy?" Nathaniel asked. "About twelve, fair-haired?"

"Aye, that's oor Charlie Grieve. Did ye see him this morn?"

"I did," said Nathaniel. "And he was healthy and looking forward to seeing his folks."

There was a thick muttering among the men, questions asked that had no answers. And Nathaniel could not help them: on the face of it, it made no sense for Pickering to keep the crew on board. But then there was Moncrieff, who had proved himself capable of worse things. He looked at the sailors gathered round, and they looked back at him with faces closed or curious. All of them waiting for word of sons or brothers or nephews on the *Isis*, and fearing the worst.

"Sam Lun, ye'd best get ye hame tae Nancy," said Mump. "The puir lass could use same guid tidings. Ye've lost Mungo, but Charlie will be hame soon."

Nathaniel's head came up with a snap. "What do you know about Mungo?"

Mump threw back his head to look at Nathaniel down the long slope of his nose. "The *Osiris* gaed doon near the Grand Banks," he said gruffly. "Mungo Grieve was amang the crew."

But he didn't die with the rest of them, Nathaniel thought. *Why don't you know that as well?*

"How is it that ye ken Mungo?" asked Sam Lun, suspicion clear on his face.

"He was brought on board after the French sunk the *Osiris,*" Nathaniel said, and quickly, before hope could take root in the man's thin face: "Mungo died of a fever after he came on board. But his brother was with him, and he slipped away quiet."

Sam Lun blinked twice, his eyes suddenly red rimmed. "Is that true? It wad be a comfort tae ma Nan, tae ken that the lad died easy."

"It's true," Nathaniel said. "I swear it."

There was a little silence in the room, broken only by the sound of the fire in the hearth. Finally Mump let out a great sigh.

"Weel, then. And what brings ye tae ma door, besides sad tidings?"

"I'm looking for Mac Stoker or any man of his crew."

The friendly expression on Dandie Mump's round face melted away. "Mac Stoker, is it? And why do ye think ye'll find that auld whoremaster here?"

"Because only somebody who was on the *Jackdaw* could tell you what happened to the *Osiris.*" Nathaniel spoke to Mump, but he watched the room. All around him men were exchanging glances he did not like, and did not know how to read.

"I mean Stoker no harm," he said.

One of the cardplayers in the corner spoke up for the first time. "That's a pity," he said, pushing himself up

from the table. "I masel' wad like naethin' better than tae see the man deid."

Mump scowled. "Haud yer tongue, Jock Bleek."

"And why should I haud ma tongue, Dandie? Is it no' true that Stoker left his crew tae the dragoons so he could chase after a woman?"

Sam Lun shook his head so that his dewlaps trembled. "And his granny, too! Dinna forget his granny, Jock. Carted aff tae gaol like a sack o' oats."

Nathaniel's breath hitched. "All of them in gaol?"

"Aye, ever' one o' them sittin' in the Dumfries tollbooth," said Mump. "I canna understan' it. Mac Stoker nivver was a mannie tae lose his heid ower a woman."

"Did you see this happen?" Nathaniel asked, looking around the room. "Did anyone here see the crew taken away?"

"Georgie here saw it, did ye no', Georgie. Come and tell the American what passed."

A young man pushed through the crowd to stand near Mump. He had a shock of red hair on his head, more of it growing out of his ears, up his neck, and over the back of his hands. The sight of him made Nathaniel's own skin itch.

"Aye, I saw it," said Georgie. "Yestereen."

"Yesterday evening?" Nathaniel frowned. "Just this morning one of the excisemen told me he hadn't seen the *Jackdaw*."

Mump let out a great laugh, so that his beard danced on his chest. "And ye believed an exciseman? Are aa Americans sae simple?"

Sam Lun nudged Georgie. "Tell the rest o' it."

Georgie nodded and cleared his throat. "On the road fra Corbelly, it was, at dusk. A whole pack o' redcoats wi' baig'nets at the ready, marchin' the crew o' the *Jackdaw* up the road tae Dumfries. One o' the redcoats was carryin' Granny Stoker on his back, tied han' and fit like a calf. A mair crankit auld chuckie ye'll nivver

see, swearin' and skirlin' and screechin'. It was a wonder tae behold."

"Did you notice two strangers among them?"
Nathaniel asked Georgie. "Older men, tall and well
built, both of them?"

The boy's brow furled itself down low. "I couldna
say. Granny Stoker was makin' such a fuss cursin' Mac
tae the de'il that I hardly looked at the rest o' them."

"And aa for a wallydraigle!" Mump moaned, rocking back and forth on his heels and hugging his bottle
to himself.

"What of the woman? What do you know of her?"

Jock Bleek snorted. "What does it matter wha she is?
Stoker's run aff tae find her, and he'll pay dear for it in
the end."

That he will, Nathaniel thought. *But first Giselle will
lead him a fine chase.*

He stood and tossed the last of his silver coin on the
table. "A drink for every man here," he said. "And my
thanks."

"Where arc ye aff tae, man? Will ye find Stoker and
bring him back here?"

Nathaniel shook his head. "I'm on my way to
Dumfries," he said. "To pay a visit to the gaol."

When the bonfire was nothing more than a few dull em-
bers and Tom Paine's ashes had floated away on the
night breeze, Elizabeth could fight her weariness no
longer. She climbed into the great ship of a bed hung
about with curtains furled like sails, and for all her mis-
givings she fell away into a deep sleep without dreams.

When she woke suddenly the moon was close to setting and Lily was whimpering softly. Nathaniel had not
yet returned.

Elizabeth wrapped a shawl around herself and found
her way to the babies' baskets. Daniel slept soundly,
suckling his fist in an easy rhythm, but Lily looked up

at her round-eyed and held out her arms to be picked up.

She was glad of the distraction. Walking up and down the room with Lily's solid warmth under her shawl was much preferable to lying awake, listening for the sound of Nathaniel's step while she reckoned out for herself all the things that might have kept him so long: difficult roads, poor directions, lamed horses. Other things she would not put a name to.

The wind had risen. It whistled down the chimney and rattled the windows. "Like the night you were born," she whispered against her daughter's ear. Lily had already drifted off to sleep, but she made a humming sound in response to her mother's voice.

From the corner of her eye Elizabeth caught movement in the square below the window, but when she turned to look again, there was nothing but debris from the bonfire skittering aimlessly over the cobblestones. And still she watched, because if she had learned anything from her time in the endless forests, it was to trust her senses.

And there, a wolf.

The skin on the back of her neck rose in a shiver even as her rational mind corrected her in a prim tone: *There have been no wolves in Scotland for a hundred years or more.*

It trotted out of the shadows and into the middle of the square, silver-gray in the moonlight, long legged, with a tail curled upward. Elizabeth's breath came to her again. No wolf, but a wolfhound, and now a second one came louping out of the shadows.

Then a man stepped into the open square, and Elizabeth's breath caught in her throat again.

Hawkeye. She blinked, and there he was still, walking in a long, steady gait directly toward the inn. His head uncovered, his hair flowing, rising and falling white in the wind. He stopped and raised his face to the night sky and for one second Elizabeth thought that her father-in-law was going to howl at the moon.

He looked up at her in the window as if he knew exactly where to find her, and touched a hand to his brow.

Not Hawkeye, but the Earl of Carryck, come to claim his own.

And what choice did she have but to open the door to him when he knocked?

He brought in the smell of horses and the night air. Plainly dressed, tall and straight with a deeply lined face and an energy at odds with his age. In the light of a hastily lit candle his eyes were a deep, pure bronze in color, not the hazel that was Hawkeye's.

"Madam." He bowed from the shoulders.

Elizabeth drew her shawl more tightly around herself. Some part of her mind marveled at her own calm in these strange circumstances. She stood barefoot in her nightdress before Alasdair Scott, the fourth Earl of Carryck. This man had caused her children to be taken from her, and now she faced him while behind her the twins slept, at peace and unaware.

"Ye ken who I am?" His voice was familiar and strange all at once: deep and melodious and Scots, with a rough edge to it.

"I do."

Elizabeth studied the earl as he studied her. He was perhaps two inches shorter and a little broader in the shoulder than Hawkeye, and the line of his nose was slightly out of kilter, as if it had been broken more than once. Certainly the resemblance was very strong, but she would never mistake this man for her father-in-law again. This realization gave her new calm.

"My lord Earl. My husband is not in."

He inclined his head. "Aye, I can see that."

"Then perhaps you would care to call again in the morning."

The earl walked to the windows and looked down

into the square. "He's aff lookin' for his faither, I take it."

Elizabeth chose not to reply.

"How lang has he been awa'?"

She did not answer.

Carryck turned. She could no longer make out his face where he stood in shadow.

"Ye understan' Scots, d'ye no'?"

"I understand you well enough, my lord."

He made a deep sound in his throat; it might have been amusement, or derision.

"He willna find his faither, nor MacLachlan. The *Jackdaw* came intae the firth yestere'en, but they werena on board."

And still he studied her, as if he had set her a test and was curious how she would meet the challenge. In the coolest tone she could muster, she said, "The exciseman lied, then. I suppose I should not be surprised. I gather that Mr. Pickering and Mr. Moncrieff knew about the *Jackdaw,* but chose to keep that information from us."

"Aye. He's owercautious at times, is Angus."

She could not help but laugh: a short, sharp sound. "His cautiousness, as you put it, has sent my husband out on a futile search. Let us hope that Mr. Moncrieff has wasted only his time."

If Carryck was worried about Nathaniel's welfare, he hid it well.

Elizabeth's throat was tight with anger. "Do you know where my father-in-law and his friend are, if they are not with Mac Stoker?"

He nodded. "A navy frigate boarded the *Jackdaw* ten days syne."

She dug her nails into the palm of her hand and forced herself to focus on the candle flame. *Pressed into the service of the Royal Navy.* When she had control of her voice she said, "The entire crew?"

The Earl of Carryck glanced out the window again.

"Just Bonner and MacLachlan. The rest o' Stoker's crew sits in yon tollbooth for smugglin'."

Elizabeth's thoughts raced so frantically that she must turn her face away so that Carryck could not see her distress. Nathaniel had gone out to find word of Stoker and his ship. He had taken enough coin with him to buy that information, and more. If he had learned that the dragoons had arrested the whole crew of the *Jackdaw,* he might well believe Hawkeye and Robbie to be in gaol. Again.

In his current state of mind, he would risk everything to free them. A small sound escaped her, and she pressed her hand to her mouth.

The earl was watching her. Elizabeth raised her head and swallowed.

"And the frigate?" Her voice came hoarse.

"I've made inquiries, but there's nae word o' her as yet." Carryck stood with his arms crossed, at his ease.

If they are dead, it is your doing. She did not speak the words; could not say out loud what she feared most, even to make clear to this man what he must know and acknowledge.

She drew herself up as tall as she could. "Sir, I will ask you again to leave and return in the morning."

"That I canna do, and should ye ask a hundred times. We must awa' tae Carryckcastle, for ye're in danger here."

"There is nothing new in that," Elizabeth said. "We have been in one kind of danger or another these many weeks."

"For the bairns' sake, then."

Elizabeth closed her eyes to rein in her temper. "If you were truly worried about my children, my lord, then they would be safe at home in New-York."

He rubbed a thumb alongside his mouth as he considered. "Ye dinna trust me."

"And does that surprise you?"

"No' in the least," said Carryck. "A sensible woman wad nivver entrust hersel' and her bairns tae a stranger."

"I see. You intrude in the middle of the night to test not only my composure, but also my character."

"I came tae see ye safely hame," he corrected her. "Moncrieff has been celebratin' aa night and canna be trusted wi' the job. Ma men are waitin' on the green wi' fresh horses."

Elizabeth crossed her arms. "And if a thousand men waited with a thousand horses, it would make no difference to me. Once again I will tell you, my lord. I will not leave this place without my husband. Have I not made myself clear?"

"Och, aye, woman." Carryck came away from the window. "Ye talk weel enough in yer strange English way, but ye canna hear." And he pointed with his chin to the hall.

Elizabeth spun around. The sound of a familiar step and then the door flew open, and Nathaniel came through with a pistol cocked and aimed at the Earl of Carryck.

"Nathaniel!" Elizabeth stepped toward him, her hands raised. "I'm in no danger. This is Carryck."

There was a shimmer of sweat on his brow, and something in his expression, something that struck such fear in her that her voice broke as she tried to speak. "Nathaniel, did you not hear me? This is the earl."

He blinked at her. "I heard you. My father and Robbie were pressed onto a frigate, Boots. I'd say my lord earl here has caused enough trouble." He lurched toward her. "But you'll have to shoot the man yourself."

Nathaniel grabbed her arm, his grip so fierce that she cried out as he pressed the pistol into her hand. His breath was warm on her face.

"The dragoons," he whispered, and collapsed at her feet.

Carryck forgotten, Elizabeth fell to her knees next to her husband. In the candlelight he was milk white, and his breath came shallow and fast. She had seen him this

way before; God, yes, and on that day had hoped never to see him thus again.

"He's been shot." Carryck crouched down next to her, but all his attention was on Nathaniel's face.

"Yes. Here in the left leg." She peeled away the cloak to get a better look, ran her hands over him and then stopped when her fingers came away red-stained. "And in the shoulder, as well."

Rage swept through her so that her hands began to shake even as she pressed her palms to the wound and leaned in hard to stop the flow of blood. When she raised her head, the earl's face was only inches from her own, and a wariness came into his eyes.

"He's bleedin' tae death," he said gruffly. "Shootin' me will ha' tae wait."

"I hope not for long," Elizabeth snapped.

There was a startled cry at the door to the adjoining room. Hannah stood there with both fists clenched at her chest.

"He's alive." Elizabeth spoke as calmly and as clearly as she could. "Get Curiosity, right now. Can you do that?"

"No need." Curiosity appeared out of the shadows, her nightdress floating along behind her. "Now hold down your voices unless you want those babies wailin', too."

Blood was seeping up through Elizabeth's fingers. The muscles in her lower arms quivered and jumped as she put more of her weight on the wound. Nathaniel groaned, and his eyelids fluttered weakly.

"You see," Elizabeth said fiercely, seeking out Hannah's gaze. "He is alive."

"And spoutin' like a geyser." Curiosity sent a pointed look at Elizabeth's nightdress, already streaked with blood. She knelt on Nathaniel's other side and put a hand to his neck.

"How bad is it?" Hannah asked, stepping closer.

Curiosity made a sound deep in her throat. "The man got a heart like a wheel, it just roll right on."

Hannah's breath hissed out through her clenched teeth, and Curiosity looked up at her sharply. "We fixed your daddy up before, and we can do it again."

Carryck had been following all of this silently, but now Elizabeth felt him jerk in surprise. His gaze swung first toward Curiosity, and then up to Hannah. Against the stark white of her nightdress her hands and face shone bronze in the candlelight. Tears sparked in her eyes, as dark as obsidian. When he looked away again the truth was written on his face.

Moncrieff had not told him about Hannah. Elizabeth flushed with a bitter satisfaction. If the earl had not known that Hawkeye's oldest grandchild was half Mohawk, what else had been kept from him?

Curiosity ripped Nathaniel's breeches to the knee in order to get a better look at the wound in his leg.

"This ain't too bad," she said. "Missed the bone, and passed clean through. Let me see that shoulder, Elizabeth."

Hannah said, "We'll need linen for binding."

"He needs a surgeon," said the earl to Elizabeth. "Pickering's Hakim is still at Carryckcastle."

This brought Hannah up short, but Curiosity's mouth thinned. "I take it this here is the earl," she said without even looking at him. "Tellin' us how to look after our own."

"But Curiosity—" Hannah began, but the older woman shook her head sharply.

"I'd be mighty pleased to see the Hakim, but he ain't here, and this bleedin' has got to stop right now. Skip and get that medicine basket of yours, child. Elizabeth, I need more light, and most of all I need Nathaniel up on the bed where I can work on him. If the earl here care to make hisself useful he'll help with the liftin'. Now move aside, both of you, and let me do what I can for him."

Elizabeth wondered when Carryck had last been given a command by anyone, much less a woman. And yet he looked more preoccupied than aggrieved as he stepped away.

She said, "There is no time for civilities, sir. Will you not assist us?"

Carryck exhaled strongly through his nose. "It's no' the civilities that concern me. Do ye trust this woman?"

"I trust her with his life, and with my own."

He crossed the room in a few strides. In a single movement he threw open the casement and whistled, one high piercing note followed by a falling tone. The last of it was still in the air when quick steps sounded on the stairs.

Three men appeared at the open door, young and well built, and all heavily armed. The tallest of them was black-haired, the other two fair and balding and as like to each other as boiled eggs. One of the twins carried a lantern that filled the room with swaying light, and showed up the widening red circle under Nathaniel's shoulders.

"Dugald, Ewen." Carryck's tone was short. "See him ontae the bed."

"That's more like it," Curiosity said. "You, there. Come over here and take him by the legs."

"Christ," breathed the tallest of them, staring openly at Nathaniel as the twins went to work. "It's aye true. Look at him."

"Lucas," Carryck barked.

The young man's jaw snapped shut, and he came to attention. "Aye, my lord."

"Walter's men are behind this. Send Davie tae take five men and see tae it."

Lucas left reluctantly, with a long look over his shoulder.

Nathaniel groaned as the twins deposited him onto the bed and his eyelids cracked open. "I can sit a horse."

"And ride it straight to the pearly gates while you at it," Curiosity snorted, stanching blood with the corner of the bedsheet. "This shoulder is a sorry sight."

"Nathaniel." Elizabeth leaned over him. "You have lost a great deal of blood. Surely Carryckcastle can wait one more day."

His hand sought out hers, and he grasped it hard. "Bind me up good and tie me to the saddle, if that's what it takes. But let's get out of Dumfries."

"There, ye see," said Carryck, spreading out his arms toward the women, as if to welcome them to his point of view. "If ye willna take my word, then I trust ye'll take his."

"I see, all right," Curiosity said, her brow furled down low as she turned back to tending Nathaniel's shoulder. "I see torn-up flesh and shattered bone. I see a man stubborn as rock."

"Aye," said Carryck, and he smiled for the first time since he had come into the room. "Exactly."

24

It was not the idea of traveling on horseback that bothered Hannah so much as the fact that she had to share a saddle with one of the earl's men. His name was Thomas Ballentyne; he was as large and dark and hairy as a bear, and he had a pistol in one boot and a long knife in the other. He took her up on the saddle before him with a resigned shrug.

"This is Meg." He gestured to his mare with a very horselike toss of his own head. "She's no' verra talkative, and no mair am I."

At least there would be no questions she did not care to answer. And he was a good horseman, as were all of Carryck's men. Hannah counted some twenty of them as they moved along the winding road at a sharp pace with the rest of her family hidden inside their ranks.

Hannah was tired, but she would not let herself be lulled to sleep by Meg's easy gait or the fact that Thomas Ballentyne radiated warmth like a well-laid fire. She must be the one to remember their route along these unmarked roads: Curiosity was preoccupied with Lily, and Elizabeth with Daniel; her father had lost too much blood to stay alert for long. It would take all of his concentration to stay upright in the saddle.

They were barely out of Dumfries when the first shifting light of dawn came up, and she turned her attention to the Scottish countryside, severe but still alive with new light. There were some trees now. Here and there a birch or elm crowded with rooks; a clutch of pines at a turning of the river, and in long misty stretches between the swelling hills. If they could be called hills. They put Hannah more in mind of children sleeping under blankets worn thin with use, crowded close together for warmth, rounded shoulders and hips and elbows jutting up. Nothing like the mountains of the endless forests.

Hannah wished for some quick look at her father, but he was hidden from her. An hour passed, and then another.

As they came around a corner there was a scattering on a far hillside.

"Wild goats." She did not realize she had said it aloud until Thomas Ballentyne grunted.

"Aye." And then, grudgingly: "Ye're sharp-eyed."

After that he began to put names to things, speaking them out over her head for her to take or leave, as she pleased. The Threewater Foot was a tangle of streams where they paused to let the horses drink without dismounting. It was a pretty spot, where guelder roses grew among the elms and willows overhung the stream, full of mossy boulders.

The dark-haired young man who had come into the inn at the earl's whistle stared at her from the other side of the water. Hannah was surprised to find that while she could ignore him, Thomas Ballentyne could not.

"Lucas! Stop oglin' the lass or I'll tell Mary!"

There were shouts of laughter. The younger man turned his horse away, blushing furiously.

"You embarrassed him," Hannah said.

He shrugged. "I canna thole sic impertinent behavior in ma own son."

Hannah craned her neck for another look at Lucas

to see if he resembled his father. Instead she caught sight of Elizabeth and Curiosity, horses side by side, their heads together. They seemed preoccupied and worried but not desperate, and that put Hannah at ease, for the moment. Just beyond them her father was a vaguely upright shape. He was very pale, and even from here she could see how it was with him.

"It's a braw mannie wha' can ride shotgun wi'oot complaint," said Thomas Ballentyne, showing a talent for reading thoughts that made Hannah shift uneasily.

They started up the river valley on a narrow road, now in groups of three and four. Low mountains came into sight: Gateshaw Rig, Croft Head, Loch Fell, like a gathering of old men with hunched backs.

"We're on Carryck land now," said Thomas Ballentyne, pointing to a mountaintop. "That's Aidan Rig."

The name meant nothing to Hannah, so she turned her attention to the pastures along the river, full of sheep and cows with heavy thick coats; men working in a field of oats who straightened to raise a hand in greeting. Young women raking hay into ricks, smiling and calling out names. One flipped her skirt in their direction and the others laughed and scolded.

They passed through a small village, and then another, moving so fast that Hannah could make out nothing about them except thatched roofs and stone walls, a common well, a low church steeple, a mill on a stream. Crofters' cottages with children playing around them, a boy herding a great sow, a woman scrubbing clothes in a stream, her skirts tucked up to show round knees purplered with cold. The road began to work its way upward toward the summit of Aidan Rig, twisting with the curves of the hill. The soil was thin here and everywhere stone pushed up out of the ground as if the earth were set on shedding her bones. A young bullock grazing among the heather raised a heavy head to watch them pass.

Meg began to blow and snort, surging forward eagerly in spite of the steep climb.

"Aye, lass," said Thomas Ballentyne. "Soon. Ye've earned yer oats this night."

Hannah sat up straighter, as anxious as she had ever been.

"There," he said, raising a gloved hand to point. "Carryckcastle."

She had steeled herself for this, and still Hannah was taken by surprise. To her mother's people, to the Kahnyen'kehàka, a castle was nothing more than a fortified village, longhouses surrounded by a wall of logs lashed together and sharpened to a point at the top. Carryckcastle was something very different: a vast expanse of smooth walls, turrets and towers, a hundred glass windows catching the sunlight and casting it out again. The castle grew out of the rock where the mountain thrust out over the valley below. Above it was only timber and a treacherous rock face; no man could approach it from below without being seen from a mile away. The home of a man who did not trust his neighbors.

Behind them, the sound of her father coughing from deep in his chest.

"Ye'll be safe here," Thomas Ballentyne said.

Hannah shuddered in the warm sunlight, and was silent.

All through this long journey, Elizabeth had dreaded the moment when they would first see this place, but when that time came she could feel only relief. Nathaniel had been listing hard to one side for the last half-mile of the winding road up the mountainside. She focused all her energy on him, willing him to stay upright for these last few minutes, trying at the same time to comfort Daniel with soft words. He mewled and hiccuped his unhappiness, straining away and clutching hard at the same time.

As the party turned the corner and started through the gate into the courtyard, Lily raised her voice, crying

in earnest now, hungry and angry about it. Elizabeth turned her head for a moment in Curiosity's direction, just as Nathaniel began a slow slide from the saddle.

It had been many years since she had played at such games, but now she left her horse in a vault, one arm wrapped around Daniel and her skirts flying. And still the earl was there before her, leaning over from his own mount to grab Nathaniel by the collar before he fell to the cobblestones. A legion of servants, men in leather aprons, footmen in blue and gold livery, stableboys, all rushed in to help, and Elizabeth lost sight of him until she could push her way through.

He was barely upright, supported on either side by two burly servants so that his cape gaped open. Curiosity had immobilized his left arm against his chest, and then bound him tightly from shoulder to waist. Now the whole expanse of linen was bright red. He looked down at himself and up at her with a puzzled expression.

"Boots." His voice was raw, and she saw now clearly what this ride had cost him. "The children?"

"All well." Her knees were trembling, but her tone was firm and she managed a small smile.

"Good," he said. "Good," and slumped forward in a faint.

There was no help for it: she must leave Nathaniel to the care of others while she tended to the babies. As soon as he had been carried into a room on the ground floor where the Hakim waited—Elizabeth caught his eye in passing, and was calmed by his kind and earnest expression as he turned to greet Hannah—she let herself be led, squalling children firmly in arm, down halls and up staircases to a chamber the size of their entire cabin at Lake in the Clouds. When the footman closed the door behind her, she went straight to the bed and its little flight of carved stairs.

Elizabeth climbed them and settled herself against the mountain of bolsters and pillows. She did not look up again until the twins had begun to nurse, and then she found she was not alone.

Three lady's maids stood waiting on the far side of the room, watching her. They curtsied and bobbed as if she were the king's consort rather than the wife of an American backwoodsman, coming forward in a rustle of skirts to take her shoes, spread a rug over her legs, and adjust the pillows under the twins more comfortably. Through all this they said very little, but Elizabeth saw them taking in every detail, from the pitch-stained hem of her gown to the way Daniel played with a stray strand of her hair as he nursed. The two older maids kept all expression from their faces, but the youngest one stood for a moment smiling at the sight of Lily's feet, which stuck out from under Elizabeth's arm, toes wiggling madly.

Elizabeth bore it all patiently until they stood away again, eyes downcast. The earl must have a very strict housekeeper, one who inspired real fear in her staff. *Or perhaps it's me,* she thought. *Perhaps they are afraid of me.*

"Thank you," she said. "You may leave me now."

They bobbed again, hands folded over starched aprons, and slipped away without a word. But the youngest one paused at the door to throw a curious last glance at her.

Elizabeth returned her shy smile. "What is your name?"

"Mally, m'leddy."

She bit back a smile. "You bestow a rank on me that is not my own. I am Mrs. Bonner."

"Aye, mem. Pardon me, mem."

"If there is any tea to be had, a cup would be very welcome."

"Och, aye, mem. There's coffee and hot chocolate, as weel."

"Tea is all I require." *And Nathaniel,* she might have added. *In good health.*

"Is there aught else, mem?"

Elizabeth said, "Yes. Tell me, whose chamber is this?"

"It was the laird's mither's, Appalina she was, the auld Leddy Carryck. But it's stood empty these many years since she passed on. That's her likeness, hanging there." She pointed to the portrait that hung over the mantelpiece.

"The earl's mother?" Elizabeth asked.

"Aye, she came ower fra' Germany tae marry the auld laird."

"And the earl's wife, where is she?"

The girl's brow lifted in astonishment. "Leddy Carryck's been deid these fifteen years, mem. There's a bonnie likeness o' her hangin' in His Lairdship's own chamber, and anither in Elphinstone Tower. But those chambers are locked."

"Elphinstone Tower?"

Mally nodded so that her white cap slid sideways and had to be righted.

"Aye, mem. The northeast tower, called Elphinstone for her faither. She was Marietta, a French leddy. Dauchter tae Lord Balmerinoch wha lost his heid after the Rising. Ye'll ha' heard o' Lord Balmerinoch?"

But Elizabeth had not, and so Mally went away, no doubt to tell the entire staff how poorly informed these visitors were about their host, while Elizabeth leaned back to study Appalina, once of Germany. A dark-haired woman in yellow brocade with Valenciennes lace at her wrists. She wore no jewels at all, but her arms were filled with long-stemmed tulips of such rich deep colors that Elizabeth thought the artist must have taken some liberties. But he had done Appalina no favors, and perhaps she had wanted it that way, insisting that he paint her as she was, neither beautiful nor plain. The extravagance of flowers in her arms drew a strong con-

trast to the resolute expression in her eyes, a firm and unflinching gaze the color of good brandy.

The earl had inherited his eyes from his mother. But how was it that his father had taken a German bride?

Elizabeth had time now to look at her surroundings, and the answer was all around her. It was there in the fine molded plasterwork of the ceiling, in heavy mahogany furniture, in silver candle sconces and Turkish carpets, in Chinese vases and marble mantelpieces. This was not the home of a Scots earl impoverished by years of revolt and warfare. No doubt Appalina had brought her new husband a handsome fortune.

A breeze from the open windows made the embroidered silk of the bed hangings flutter, stirring the roses and lavender that stood in a vase on a small table and spreading their scent through the room. She wondered if Appalina had seen to the planting of the garden, and if it had been a comfort to her in those first years so far from her home. Sometime soon after she arrived as a new bride, the earl's twin brother—Hawkeye's father—had gone off to seek his own fortune. Leaving his home as she had left hers, to look for a new life, a farther shore.

"Your great-grandfather was most probably born in this very bed," she whispered to her children. "But you were born in the endless forests, and that is where you will grow up."

Lily yawned in agreement, and Daniel followed her example.

Mally brought her tea and a tray crowded with scones, jam and cream. And she brought a word from the housekeeper, Mrs. Hope.

"If it pleases ye, mem, she'll be by shortly. Tae show ye the nursery."

"Will she?" Elizabeth hid her face in her teacup while she considered. In a great house where the lord

had lost his lady and remained unmarried, a house-keeper's authority was likely to grow to formidable proportions; this one, Mrs. Hope by name, was testing her to see what she was made of. Aunt Merriweather would be gratified to know that all her training and counsel were finally to be put to good use.

She swallowed the last of her tea, and getting up from the little bow-backed chair, Elizabeth smoothed her rumpled skirt as best she could. She smelled of horse, but this was not the time to worry about such things.

"The children will sleep here with me, so I have no interest in the nursery. Right now I will go to see my husband, if you will stay and watch over the babies?"

Mally lowered her eyes and nodded her agreement, but not before Elizabeth saw something flash across her expression—pleasure, and perhaps a little apprehension.

"You need do nothing but make sure they do not roll from the bed in their sleep. I will return before they awake, or I will send my stepdaughter."

The cheerful round face bobbed up toward her. "The red Indian, mem?"

Another truth she had forgotten: news spread among servants at an unthinkable speed.

"My stepdaughter is Miss Bonner," Elizabeth said firmly. She thought for a moment, knowing that whatever information she passed on now would make its way to the entire household, and would influence Hannah's stay here for better or worse. "I trust you will do all in your power to make her welcome, Mally. If she is unhappy at Carryckcastle, so will the rest of us be. Do you understand me?"

Mally's cheeks, already ruddy, flushed even darker. "Oh, aye, mem. I meant no offense, mem."

"I'm sure you did not. Now I must go see how my husband is faring."

"And what shall I tell Mrs. Hope, mem?"

Elizabeth paused at the door. "Is there a chamber that connects to this one?"

Mally nodded eagerly. "Aye, mem." She pointed to a closed door. "Through the dressing room."

"Do you know who Mrs. Freeman is?"

"The Negress, mem? I saw her frae the window."

Elizabeth said, "Give Mrs. Hope this message from me: Mrs. Freeman and my stepdaughter require that chamber for their own as long as we are here."

The girl swallowed hard—Elizabeth could almost see the thoughts moving behind her eyes—but then she bobbed her head. "Aye, mem."

"Otherwise I leave no message for her at all."

Some of Carryck's men were still milling about when Elizabeth found her way back to the hallway off the courtyard. As soon as they caught sight of her, their conversation faded away and they fell to studying the flagstones under their feet with great concentration and interest. They put her in mind of schoolboys, in spite of all their size and bulk.

"May I?" Elizabeth addressed the oldest of them, the man who had taken Hannah before him on his saddle. He ushered her through the men and then opened the door for her with an odd little bow.

"Thank you, Mr. . . . ?"

"Thomas Ballentyne, mem." He was gruff, but his expression was intelligent, and not unkind. She would ask Hannah about him when there was an opportunity.

It was a small room, and by its smell one used primarily for the storing of coffee and spices and dried herbs, but given over now to the Hakim for his surgery. A long table stood beneath a bank of windows, and on this, Nathaniel lay stretched out, his wounded leg elevated on a bolster. Hakim Ibrahim was bent over his wounded shoulder; just opposite him, Hannah stood with her back to the door. Curiosity was at a workbench, grinding a pestle into a small stone bowl.

"Mrs. Bonner," said the Hakim, glancing up only

briefly. "Just a few more stitches, and then the leg must be attended to."

"Boots," Nathaniel said. His voice was very hoarse. "The babies?"

"Fed, and sleeping." She came closer, but Nathaniel kept his gaze on the ceiling overhead. The muscles in his jaw jumped with every movement of the Hakim's needle.

"How goes it here?"

"Very well," said Hakim Ibrahim. "The bullet broke the bone, but there is no damage to the larger blood vessels."

"He is not in danger," Hannah translated.

Curiosity made a disapproving noise. "Maybe the shoulder won't kill him, but it wouldn't be the first time I saw a man die of pure stubborn."

"There is another scar here, well healed." The Hakim's tone was very calm, in spite of the speed with which he worked. "A battle injury?"

Nathaniel sent a sidelong glance toward Elizabeth. "You could call it that. My father-in-law shot me."

"A hunting accident." Elizabeth wiped the sweat that ran down his brow to his temple. "Will you tease me even now?"

"Especially now," he said, and closed his eyes. His left arm twitched convulsively.

Behind her Curiosity said, "Don' bother askin', 'cause he won't take no laudanum."

She looked up in surprise. "He's had nothing at all?"

Nathaniel squeezed her fingers so hard that she jumped. "No laudanum."

"You see?" Curiosity raised an eyebrow at Elizabeth. "Stubborn." There was a swipe of dried blood on her headcloth, dark brown against the sprigged yellow calico.

Elizabeth saw Hannah's mouth settle in a strong line. There was an expression about her that she had not seen very often: defiance, and disdain. She was proud of

her father's ability to withstand this pain, and resentful of the idea that he might not be equal to it.

"He doesn't want to sleep," Hannah said.

"And why should he?" Curiosity snapped. "Up all night chasing around strange roads, gettin' shot. Why sleep? Maybe the man got a bridge to build, or a war to fight."

Nathaniel closed his eyes briefly and then opened them again. "Curiosity, if there's a war that needs fighting, you go on ahead without me. They won't stand a chance."

Hannah ducked her head to hide her smile, but Curiosity sucked in one cheek and let it out again as she worked the pestle. "You better hope I don't take up weapons while I'm so put out with you, Nathaniel Bonner. I'll put a bullet in that other shoulder, fix you up proper."

The Hakim put down his needle and took up a feather, which he dipped in a bowl filled with a liquid, exactly the same shade of red as his turban. It had a strange scent, sharp and green, the smell of marshes and growing things.

"This is the sap of a tree that is native to Brazil," he told Elizabeth.

"It's called dragon's blood," said Hannah.

"Brazil?" Elizabeth looked more closely at the bowl.

"The earl has a specimen in his conservatory," said the Hakim. "Which is very fortunate."

It was clear that this was not Nathaniel's first encounter today with this feather, for he grasped Elizabeth's hand hard even before it touched the skin. He jerked convulsively and hissed through his teeth but Hakim Ibrahim continued painting the wound with quick, even strokes. "It will prevent infection. It is not pleasant, however. Much like salt in a wound."

"Too much like it," Nathaniel said.

"The shoulder will swell but the break was clean. I expect that in two weeks you will be able to use your arm again."

Curiosity sniffed. "I'd like to see you keep the man in bed for two weeks."

"I don't think that will be necessary," said the Hakim. "A few days' rest to regain his strength at most. And you must wear a sling, to protect the arm."

Nathaniel opened his eyes and looked straight at the Hakim. "I'm indebted to you for your help, but I can't go to bed right now. Hannah, tell the men out in the hall I'm ready to see Carryck."

Elizabeth held up her hand. "Nathaniel, please be reasonable. When the Hakim is finished dressing your leg, you will eat, and then you will rest for an hour, and then if you are sufficiently restored, you may speak to whomever you like. But right now Carryck can wait."

He blinked at her. "Maybe the earl can wait, Boots, but I can't. Whatever he knows about Hawkeye and Robbie, I need to hear it."

Hannah's expression went very still as she looked from Nathaniel to Elizabeth. "Are they dead?"

He raised a hand to touch her cheek. "I don't know, Squirrel. Maybe."

She made a little clicking sound deep in her throat, and Nathaniel's grip tightened on her shoulder. "It's a possibility, I can't tell you that it ain't. I managed to get a few words with Stoker's first mate before the dragoons caught wind of me, and he told me that they were picked off the *Jackdaw* by a frigate headed for battle."

Curiosity put down her bowl with a thump. "That don't make much sense," she said thoughtfully, all of her irritation suddenly gone. "Why take the two oldest men on board and leave the young ones? Maybe the man was lyin' to protect his own skin."

Elizabeth said, "I might come to the same conclusion, if the earl hadn't told me the same story right before Nathaniel came back to the inn."

"But how would the earl know about what happened on the *Jackdaw*?" asked Hannah. And then her face brightened. "Unless he has had word of the frigate?"

The Hakim had been strangely quiet as he dressed the wound on Nathaniel's leg, but now Elizabeth felt his attention on her.

He said, "The earl knows of what happened on the *Jackdaw* because he has questioned her captain at some length."

Nathaniel sat up with such suddenness that Elizabeth stepped back in surprise.

"Mac Stoker was here?"

Hakim Ibrahim nodded. "He is here still, and he will be for some time. I have been kept busy treating gunshot wounds just recently."

Nathaniel lay down again.

"I want to see him before I see Carryck."

"Good," said Hannah. "Let's go see him, then."

There was a small silence, and then Nathaniel reached out a hand to Hannah. She came to stand just beside him.

"Squirrel," he said, speaking Kahnyen'kehàka now to spare her embarrassment before the Hakim. "We need you to look after the babies."

"But—"

"I don't want you anywhere near Mac Stoker." His jaw clenched and then relaxed again.

Hannah turned on her heel and held out her palms toward Elizabeth. A request, written in worry lines that were out of place on a young girl's face. And Curiosity watching, wondering if she would give in this time, or do what was best for the child and send her away.

"Your father is right, Squirrel. I will bring you the news myself, if there is any."

She held her head up straight, but her mouth trembled slightly. After a long pause, she nodded.

A servant showed Hannah the way. He wore a long-tailed coat of dark blue with gold facings, and he had a twitch in his left cheek that reminded her of a bird flut-

tering. She wondered if he had had it all his life, but she could not ask him about it: all the way through halls he watched her out of the corner of his eye as if he expected her to pull a tomahawk from beneath her skirt and take his scalp.

She had been sent away like a little child, and she was angry about it, and hurt. But even in her poor mood, Hannah could not ignore the castle. It was full of interesting things: bears and stags and dragons carved into wood paneling and even into the rafters. A stag's head mounted on the wall. Paintings of dogs and horses and sailing ships in heavy golden frames. At the foot of a great stair two vases big enough for a girl to hide in, decorated with colorful birds.

There was a little man on the landing, made entirely of polished metal, and she could no more walk past him without stopping than she could have ignored a live monkey. He was barely taller than she was and cleverly made, down to the hinged fingers and the face, constructed of many small plates somehow held together to make a nose and cheeks and a chin. Behind grillwork the eye sockets were blank, and she found herself a little relieved.

"What is this?" she asked the servant.

He cleared his throat. "A suit of armor, miss. As the gentlemen wore tae joust in days lang syne." And seeing her blank look, he added, "Twa men runnin' at each ither on horseback wi' lances, ye ken?"

Hannah did not quite understand why men would wrap themselves in metal to get on a horse, but she sensed that the servant's patience with her questions might not reach so far. She nodded.

The upstairs hall was lined with candle sconces and small carved tables, and on each of them stood a carving of an elephant, some bone white and others milky green. She would have paused to look, but the servant stopped in front of a door.

Hannah did not like to be impolite, so she waited with him. "What is your name?"

One eye blinked, and then the other; it was a good trick. "MacAdam, miss."

"And what is it that you do here?"

"I'm one o' the footmen, miss."

She considered his feet, and saw nothing unusual about them.

"What is it that a footman does?"

"We look after the keeping o' the house, miss. The fires and the lamps, and the rest o' it. And servin' at table, o' course."

"Then I'll see you at supper?"

One corner of his mouth jerked upward before he could stop it. "Aye, miss."

Hannah wondered if he was not allowed to smile, or if he did not like to smile. But he opened the door, and there was nothing to do but to leave him there in the hall and go in.

In the middle of the room was a canopied bed bigger than Hannah had ever seen before, and in the middle of the bed sat a little girl with Lily sleeping in her arms. Her eyes widened when she saw Hannah and she put Lily down, very gently. Then she leaped off the bed and landed with a soft thump.

Hannah had thought her to be young, but she saw now that the girl must be her own age. She was slight, and a full head shorter than Hannah, with a cap of short blond hair as curly as a goat's and sea-green eyes. Her skirt was muddy at the hem, and her feet were bare. There was a smudge of jam on her chin.

She said, "Babies smell sae sweet, dinna ye think? Mally was called awa', and she asked me tae bide wi' them. I'm called Jennet. Was your mither an Indian princess?"

Her tone was curious and forthright and friendly, and it made something small and warm and unexpected blossom in Hannah's chest, so that her throat closed and she had to swallow very hard. She said, "My mother was Sings-from-Books of the Kahnyen'kehàka

people, and her mother is Falling-Day, and her mother is Made-of-Bones who is clan mother of the Wolf long-house, and her mother Hawk-Woman was clan mother before her. She killed an English colonel and fed his heart to her sons." She drew a breath and let it out again.

"Guid for your granny. The English sojers hung my grandda for—" She paused, and scratched her pointed chin thoughtfully. "Nae guid cause. What do they call ye, then?"

"My girl-name is Squirrel, but most everybody calls me Hannah. When the time is right Falling-Day will give me my woman-name."

Jennet smiled so broadly that two deep dimples carved themselves into her cheeks. "I like Squirrel better than Hannah. I'll call ye that." She plucked an apple out of her apron pocket and tossed it in a quick flick of the wrist.

Hannah caught it, and in that moment she realized how very hungry she was.

"I'll tell ye what I think, Squirrel. Ye can tell me tales o' the Indians and the great wilderness, and I'll show ye aa the best bits o' Carryckcastle, aa the secret places."

Hannah went up to the bed to check the twins. They were both sleeping soundly, but it would not be long before they woke. Then they would need new swaddling, and they might be afraid of this strange place.

Behind her Jennet said, "We'll bide here a while, aye? Ye'll want tae eat, and see tae the wee ones. I'll help. Then we'll gae explorin'. Wad ye like tae see the pit?"

"Is that where Mac Stoker is?" She spoke around a mouthful of apple, sweet and tart all at once.

"Och, ne," said Jennet, helping herself to a spoonful of jam from the pot on the table. "They dinna want the pirate tae die, after aa. Wad ye like tae see him? He canna hurt ye—'Nezer Lun stands guard at the door, and he's aye fierce."

"I have seen Mac Stoker," Hannah said. "I saw him shoot a man and kidnap a lady from the *Isis*. But I would like to see him again."

The spoon paused on its way back toward the jam pot and Jennet turned to look at her. She produced a single dimple. "We'll be fast friends, the twa o' us. Wait and see."

25

In all her time on the *Jackdaw*, Elizabeth realized, she had never seen Mac Stoker off his feet, but now he was abed. Under a few days' growth of beard he had gone a peculiar ashen shade; even the scar around his neck had gone pale. His temple was swollen, the color of an over-ripe plum.

Then he opened his eyes—red rimmed and fever bright—and his mouth worked slowly, as if he didn't quite have control over his tongue.

"Bonner," he croaked. "Damn your eyes and liver, you're alive. Have you come to pay me what you owe?"

Nathaniel limped to the chair next to the bed and sat down, sticking his injured leg out in front of him. He said, "We can talk about who owes what later. Now I want to hear what happened to my father."

Stoker raised a hand and let it fall. "Sweet Jaysus, not that again. I'm wishin' I never set eyes on the man, nor on any of youse."

"You can't blame the mess you're in on him. You got that bullet in your gut on your own time," Nathaniel said.

"Did I now?" Stoker grimaced. "I don't recall you bein' there. If you were, you'd know that it was

Hawkeye the bastards were lookin' for. Brained me proper with a musket when my back was turned and dragged me away, and now me men are sittin' in gaol cursin' me for a coward and a cur. Granny will eat me heart raw."

"Hawkeye has never set foot on Scottish soil," Elizabeth said. "What can he have had to do with this?"

"Sure and that may be true," said Stoker, wheezing a little now. "But there's plenty what are waitin' for him when he does, and he better keep his wits about him." He turned his head to look harder at Nathaniel, taking in the heavily wrapped shoulder and leg. "But maybe you've learned that for yourself already. Dragoons?"

"Aye."

"A pair of them, I'll wager. The bigger one with gray chin whiskers and as bald as a babby's arse, the other with a scar down his right cheek, and missing two fingers on his left hand."

Nathaniel glanced at Elizabeth, and his expression was not hard to read. Worry and anger, in equal measures. He said, "I never got close enough to see his hand, but that sounds about right. Why do you think they were looking for Hawkeye?"

Stoker let out a noisy breath. "They asked for him by name. Wanted to know where he was, and what happened to him. And failin' that, they wanted to put their mitts on you. If you had told me how popular youse Bonners were in Scotland I would have drove a harder bargain."

"Where is my father?"

He grimaced. "Damn me if I know. Last I saw of him and MacLachlan was when we got boxed in between the whole bloody Atlantic fleet and a frigate set on poundin' us to kindling. They stopped just short of sinkin' us and then boarded."

His voice wavered and he paused to drink from the cup that the Hakim offered him.

"When they left again they took your father and MacLachlan wit' them, and that's the last I seen of their sorry mugs." He shook his head wearily. "And don't be askin' why they took your father and nobody else. I'm puzzled meself. Unless you've friends in the Royal Navy and you kept it a secret."

Nathaniel smiled grimly at the idea of it. "Aye, and tomorrow we're taking tea with the king."

Elizabeth said, "What was the frigate called?"

Both men turned to her, Nathaniel with a curious expression, and Stoker with a suspicious one.

"The *Leopard*. Tell me now, sweetings—does that name mean anything to you?"

"Nothing at all," she said firmly, not meeting Nathaniel's eye. "Was it because you couldn't take them to Hawkeye that the dragoons shot you, or for the simple pleasure of it?"

"'Od's bones, she's got a gob on her. I don't envy you, man."

Nathaniel said, "You haven't answered the question."

Stoker's mouth thinned. "Never did I say 'twas the dragoons that put the bullet in me. It'll be a dry day in Ireland when a couple of lobsterbacks get the best of Mac Stoker. I was runnin' goods under their noses when I was but thirteen."

"Then who was it got to you if it wasn't the dragoons?" asked Nathaniel. He glanced at the Hakim. "Carryck's men?"

Stoker waved a hand dismissively. "No. If that crew hadn't come along I'd be dead. It was Giselle what shot me, the ungrateful bitch. And me tryin' to rescue her." His fist opened and closed again. "But she hasn't seen the last of Mac Stoker." And he smiled.

By the time Nathaniel made his way to the top of the grand stair, he had forgotten all about the agony in his

shoulder, simply because his leg throbbed like a war drum with every step. At his back two servants crept along, ready to catch him if he should fall but trying to look disinterested. He ignored them to lean on Elizabeth.

"It's just ahead," she said quietly. "There on the left."

Another servant opened the door and then shut it behind them, and Nathaniel simply sat down on the carpet; it was that or land on his face. He wiped the sweat from his brow with what remained of his shirt, but it took a full minute for the thud of blood in his ears to subside.

"I can hear Lily laughing," he said. "And Curiosity talking to her."

"Yes." Elizabeth put out a hand to help him to his feet. "There's another bedchamber that connects to this one through the dressing room. I'll check on them in just a moment. Here is the bed, Nathaniel."

"Damn," he muttered, considering the little flight of steps. "More steps. I suppose there's a ladder to get to the pisspot."

"Mac Stoker has a decidedly adverse effect on your vocabulary," Elizabeth said. When he had fallen back against the pillows, she set out to undress him, but he caught her wrist to stop her.

"Boots."

"Hmm?"

"I'm not so done in that I can't get out of my own breeks."

She nodded. "Perhaps we should wait until they bring our things from Dumfries anyway. I hope it is soon. We look like beggars, all of us."

He ran a hand over her hair. "You look mighty fine to me, darlin'. Except for those dark circles under your eyes."

She gave him a testy half-smile. "It has been an eventful night."

"Come here to me for a minute."

"If I lay myself down now, Nathaniel, I will most likely fall asleep."

"I'll keep you awake."

She drew up, clutching a fist to her breast in surprise. "You cannot be serious, in your condition—"

"Relax, Boots. I ain't got anything like that in mind. Not right now, any road. I just want to talk to you."

She studied him with narrowed eyes for a moment, and then she climbed up to sit next to him. There was a look she got sometimes, her chin set hard and a line between her brows, when she was chewing on something that she couldn't quite spit out. She could no more hide how she felt than she could change the color of her eyes. Right now they were storm gray.

"I should go check on the children."

"They sound happy enough," he said.

"Yes, well. I imagine Curiosity is tired, too. And I wonder where Hannah has got to—"

"Boots."

"What?" Her eyes blazed at him, daring him on.

"You're strung so tight, I can almost hear you humming."

She frowned at him. "Am I? And I wonder why that might be. Do I need remind you that your father and Robbie have disappeared into the Royal Navy?"

He smoothed a curl away from her face. "I remember. On a ship called the *Leopard*."

They stared at each other for a long minute, and then she said, "It's not what you think."

"Are you in the habit of reading my mind these days, Boots? What is it that I think?"

"That I know something about the *Leopard* that I'm hiding from you."

"Do you?"

"That *is* what you're thinking!" She pulled away from him and rolled off the bed in a flurry, pausing just out of reach to smooth her skirt. When she looked

up at him again, she had regained some of her composure.

"I once knew the captain of the *Leopard*, but that was seven years ago. He must have been posted elsewhere by now." And then, more slowly: "He was a friend of Will's."

Nathaniel sat up a little straighter. "Your cousin Will?"

She nodded. "But this must be simple coincidence, Nathaniel. It must be."

"Maybe so. But if it ain't—if you know the captain, and he knows you, is that good news for Hawkeye and Robbie, or bad?"

She let out a great sigh. "That's why I was hesitant to say anything, because I knew you would ask me that very question. The truth is, I don't know, Nathaniel. I truly don't know." And then: "If it is him, his name is Christian Fane."

She was anxious and skittish, and it worried him. But before he could even think how to ask the right questions to get to the bottom of it, Curiosity appeared at the inside door with one baby balanced on each hip. "Any news?"

Elizabeth smiled in relief and took Lily from her while Nathaniel told Curiosity the little they had learned.

"And the earl ain't got nothin' to add to that pitiful story?"

"We haven't seen him yet."

"Hmpf." Curiosity shook her head. "Is that scoundrel Stoker fixed on dying?"

Nathaniel said, "The Hakim got the bullet out of him. I expect he's tough enough to live through it."

"Good. Maybe he's the man to sail us home again."

"I don't know what's become of the *Jackdaw*," Elizabeth said. "The excisemen may have burned it."

Curiosity said, "Hawkeye will show up soon enough. There never was such a man for finding his way, and

Robbie is cut from the same cloth. Don't you forget that, now."

Elizabeth sent her a thankful look. Curiosity might know of every tisane and poultice and healing tea, but she also understood that sometimes the right words were the most powerful medicine.

She stood over Nathaniel and touched a hand to his forehead. "Got to get some food into you," she said. "I hope they bring us something more than that little bit of jam and bread that Hannah left behind."

Elizabeth took some pillows from the bed to build a small fortress on the carpet. "I asked them to send up food," she said, propping Lily there and gesturing for Daniel so she could sit him opposite his sister. "Perhaps these two will amuse themselves while we eat."

"Where is Hannah?" Nathaniel asked.

"She went off with a little girl by the name of Jennet. Said they was goin' to do some exploring." Curiosity went to the windows and she stood there, leaning with one shoulder against the frame. "You see." She pointed. "There they go now, barefoot the both of them."

Elizabeth joined her at the window. Beyond the castle the mountains rose up, granite and heather against a smoke-blue sky. A beautiful day, but in the courtyard below, servants went about their business. Watermen at the well, a gardener with a muddy apron and a basket of greenery, a dairymaid arguing with a groom twice her size, jabbing her finger at him. And Hannah and the girl called Jennet were walking toward the stables just outside the gate, talking as they went.

"Who is she?"

"I don' know exactly, but she's a friendly little thing."

The two of them made a strange pair—one tall with long blue-black braids; the other quick and small and white-blond—and still they looked like little girls anywhere on a summer's day.

"Do you think it's safe to let her wander off?" Elizabeth asked.

"Yes I do," Curiosity said firmly. "Let her be a child for once."

There were men working young horses in the paddocks to the northwest corner of the castle, but what interested Hannah more was the woodland that began just beyond the stables and ran up to the top of the mountain called Aidan Rig. There were pines, juniper, birch and oak, and a stream winding through it all. Somewhere in the distance there was the sound of waterfalls. Hannah would have liked to see them, but Jennet had other ideas: she headed straight for a sprawling oak, threaded her skirt through the waistband of her apron to free her legs, and began to climb, talking to Hannah over her shoulder as she went.

"This is my favorite climbin' tree. I fell frae that branch"—she paused to point—"and broke my arm. But I was much younger then, and Simon was chasin' me at the time." She hopped from limb to limb until she arrived at the offending branch, where she settled herself with one arm slung companionably around the trunk.

"Are ye no' comin'?"

It had been many months since Hannah had climbed a tree and she wanted to follow Jennet very badly, but she cast a look back toward the gates.

"Ye needna fash yersel'," Jennet said. "We can see intae the courtyard frae here, should someone come lookin' for ye."

This was encouragement enough. She launched herself at the tree and in a minute she landed, a little winded, beside Jennet on a wide, flat branch. She wiggled her toes in the breeze and sniffed: pine sap and musk roses, woodbine and wild thyme, and no trace of salt water. The air

hummed with bees at work, and she had never heard anything so musical.

From here Carryckcastle loomed even larger: too many rooms to count, and servants at work everywhere. Around them the mountain valley seemed strangely empty and glowing with color—purple heathers touched with yellow, gorse, scrub evergreens clinging to rocky slopes. Shadows shifted with the wind.

"Why are there trees here and not on those other mountains?"

Jennet cocked her head to one side and shrugged. "Nae man, nae woman," she sang very softly. "Nae creature wad dare take an axe tae even a single tree o' the wood on Aidan Rig. The whole ben belongs tae the Guid Neighbors." And then putting her mouth even closer to Hannah's ear: "A fairy place, ye ken. They come at dusk, dancin' and singin'. Simon tolt me that the fairy queen hersel' comes at dawn, lookin' for bairns tae steal awa'."

Hannah considered. She had heard tales of the fairies from her grandmother, and she was curious, indeed. But Jennet's unwillingness to speak about them within their hearing was something to be taken seriously. She nodded.

"Who is Simon?"

Jennet rubbed her cheek against the tree trunk. "Simon was ma brither. He died o' the putrid sair throat." She pulled a leaf to fan herself, and it was exactly the same color as her eyes. Then she threw out her free arm as if to take in the whole world.

"Ye can see forever frae this spot."

"Is this your hiding place?"

Jennet fluttered her fingers. "Ach, nae. Every bairn in Carryck has been up this tree, and their mithers and faithers afore 'em. There's aye better places tae hide in the castle. Secret passages and hidey-holes and such." She looked over her shoulder as if she expected to find someone behind her, listening.

Hannah didn't doubt that the castle would be a good

place to explore—it was as big as a village, after all. But she was glad to be out-of-doors right now and in no hurry to go back. Jennet seemed to understand this without being told.

She pointed to the castle and in a prim tone she said: "There's a tower on each corner, do ye see? Closest tae us is Elphinstone Tower, there. Then comes Forbes Tower, then Campbell, and on the far corner is Johnstone. The pit is in Campbell Tower, but Elphinstone is my favorite."

"Why is that?"

Jennet grinned. "That would be tellin' when I'd much rather show ye. But no' straightawa'." She pointed with her chin to the northwest corner, where Hannah could just make out the beginnings of a kitchen garden, and a few women at work among the green. "They'll put me tae weedin', should I show my face." The small nose crinkled. "I dinna like weedin'."

"At home I would be in the cornfield," Hannah said. "I'm tall enough for the hoe now." And homesickness blossomed up hot and sour in her mouth. On their ride here she had seen not a single cornstalk, but at Lake in the Clouds it would already be standing as high as her brow, with beans winding up to provide shade for the squash growing below. This year her grandmother and aunt would celebrate the Three Sisters without her.

"Look," said Jennet, pointing.

A few horses had appeared around the southeast corner of the castle, moving at a leisurely pace toward the open gates. Dogs trotted alongside them.

"The earl's hounds," Hannah said. "I saw them in Dumfries."

"Aye," said Jennet, getting ready to swing herself down. "And the wagons will be close behind."

"Wagons?"

She paused and looked up so that the light coming through the leaves dappled her face. "Wi' mair treasure," she said. "Frae the *Isis*."

· · ·

"Your mother is a most irrational creature," Elizabeth said to Lily. "Thousands of miles from home against our will, with no idea of how we will get away from this place or find your grandfather, no sign of the earl nor any word of explanation from him, and I can think of nothing but clean clothes and food."

The baby was studying an ivory elephant, thumping the carpet with it to see what noise it would make, and then frowning in dissatisfaction. Her brother was more pleased with the bannock in his fist, which he was using to scrub his face. Neither of them seemed very concerned with her confession, or with their own grubbiness.

Curiosity had found a comfortable chair near the hearth. Without opening her eyes, she said, "Here they come now, a whole army of them, from the sound of it."

Elizabeth bounded up from the floor before they could knock and wake Nathaniel. She composed her face and opened the door.

"Mrs. Bonner. Guid day."

The woman before her was tiny, with the carriage and figure of a girl, though the lines at the corners of her eyes and mouth put her at far more than thirty. She was not so much beautiful as striking, with small, sharply defined features, eyes so light as to be almost colorless, and blond hair wound around her head in a thick braid. And at the waist of her simple gown— *black for mourning?*—she wore the ring of keys that were the mark of her role as housekeeper of Carryckcastle.

"Mrs. Hope." Elizabeth smiled, even while her thoughts raced away, recounting all the housekeepers of her acquaintance at large houses and small throughout England. Every one of those who came to mind were

women of more than fifty, having spent a lifetime growing into a position of responsibility and authority; few of them had any beauty left, if they had ever had it at all.

"I am sorry tae disturb you, Mrs. Bonner, but your things are come from Dumfries. If you would care tae take dinner in the dining room, the maids will see tae the unpacking."

She had the composed manner of a woman who did not need to use her voice to make her wishes known, or have them followed. Utterly polite and deferential, but Elizabeth could not read the expression in her eyes. *Because she does not wish me to.* Dislike? Disdain? In another lifetime she would have wondered why this woman should bear her so little goodwill, but it did not matter: they would not be here long enough for her to make Mrs. Hope a concern.

Elizabeth said, "Does the earl wait for us at table?"

"The laird sends his apologies."

Carryck had more important things to do than to speak to those people he had dragged across an ocean for his own pleasure. Irritation flooded through her, but Elizabeth smiled politely.

She said, "My husband is resting and must not be disturbed. We will take our dinner here."

"Very well, madam. I'll put the maids tae work in the dressing room."

"Mrs. Hope."

The housekeeper paused. "Madam?"

"Where exactly is the earl engaged?"

A discourteous question, but it did its work: some unchecked surprise flickered across her face.

"He is in the conservatory, madam."

Elizabeth folded her hands before herself. "Is he? And I was planning to walk in that direction this afternoon, as the weather is so very fine."

Mrs. Hope inclined her head. "As you wish, madam. Entirely as you wish."

· · ·

Fine damask and heavy silver, porcelain and crystal and solid, hearty food served by footmen who moved about the room in perfect symmetry. There was marrow broth thick with barley and peas, roast partridge, red cabbage, runner beans dressed with cream. Curiosity ladled broth into the babies, and Elizabeth filled Nathaniel's bowl twice before he fell back into an uneasy sleep.

When the footmen had been dismissed, Elizabeth and Curiosity ate together while the twins rolled across the carpet, determined to perfect this new trick.

"Go on then," said Curiosity when they had eaten as much as they could hold. "Go find the earl. You won't rest until you talk to the man, anyway. The little ones are due for a nap, and I'll just take my rest with them. I can keep an ear out for Nathaniel, 'case he needs anything."

As tired as she was, Elizabeth knew that Curiosity was right; she was too much on edge to sleep. "Very well, but I must change first."

"I'd say so," Curiosity said with something close to her old grin. "A bath wouldn't be the worst idea, neither."

But in the dressing room Elizabeth found that the maids had been too thorough in their duties: both of her other gowns had been spirited away for cleaning. This news she had from Mally, who had stayed behind to begin the mending.

Elizabeth looked down at herself. It should not matter to her if the earl found her dowdy and poorly groomed, as long as he listened to what she had to say to him. And still it was very hard to go out among strangers in such a sorry state.

Mally was watching her with a puzzled expression. "The other gowns have been hung, mem." She pointed with her sewing needle.

"Other gowns?" Even as Elizabeth turned she knew what she would find.

In the confusion of transporting their belongings here from the King's Arms, someone had included Giselle Somerville's trunks. The maids had unpacked them all, and now Giselle's many morning gowns and evening dresses, shawls and capes and redingotes, had been carefully hung to shimmer white and silver, gold and green.

Her perfume, musk and lilac and something else, something sharper, clung to a brocade shawl that had been draped across a velvet settee. Silver-backed brushes had been carefully arranged on the dressing table, and a heavy-bottomed crystal flask caught the light to spin it into rainbows. Elizabeth picked up a small hand mirror with an elaborately engraved motto in the ivory and pearl handle: *Sans Peur*.

A woman without fear. For a moment Elizabeth found herself thinking of Giselle with envy.

The shelves were filled, too, with her hats and bonnets and gloves, scarves and petticoats, corsets and pelisses—exactly the kind of elegant dress that Elizabeth had always shunned. She had favored the simple Quaker gray that her mother had worn, and told herself that she did so out of admiration and rationality. But the truth was that she had left the finery to her younger and prettier cousins out of pride and—she could admit it now—pure willfulness. Her uncle Merriweather had called her a drab behind her back but within her hearing, and she had taken a perverse pleasure in his disapprobation.

Elizabeth sat down on an elegant little chair upholstered in blue and yellow brocade and considered. She should have all of it sent away, given to someone who knew nothing of Giselle and would be glad of such pretty things. It was what she wanted to do. But to indulge one kind of pride would mean sacrificing another, and at the moment she was more concerned about the

earl than she was about Giselle Somerville, wherever she might be.

Mally took her hesitation for indecision, and clearing her throat gently she ventured to make a suggestion. "Shall I send for hot water, mem? Wad ye care tae bathe first?"

Elizabeth let out a soft sigh. "Yes," she said, reaching out to run Mantua silk between her fingers. "Please do."

The simplest of Giselle's gowns was a clear lawn with a sash, bodice scarf, and shawl embroidered in silver and green. The matching kid slippers were slightly too small, but Elizabeth was glad of the distraction as she made her way down the grand stair. She felt like an imposter, awkward and out of place, and furious with herself for her timidity.

A scullery maid hurried by, pausing to curtsy without meeting Elizabeth's gaze and then continuing on her way, a bucket of ashes thumping against her leg. Elizabeth followed at a safe distance, knowing that there would be some access to the gardens from the hall that led to the kitchen. It took a full five minutes to find it, but then she stepped into the warm summer afternoon.

The gardens were situated on the west side of the castle, protected from the winds that came up the mountain valley. Scotland was not known for its excessively fine weather, but the situation was one that would make the most of the sun. A large kitchen garden, flower beds in full bloom, apple trees and raspberry canes, and roses interplanted with lavender. An unusual and completely lovely effect, so different from the gardens of her childhood at Oakmere, where nature was subservient to geometry.

Someone had put a great deal of planning into the grounds; someone both sensible and with a keen eye for

natural beauty. Appalina perhaps, or Marietta, she of the mysterious portraits.

For the first time in months Elizabeth was physically comfortable, freshly bathed and well dressed, her stomach full and the sunlight gentle on her back and shoulders. But she felt a little dizzy suddenly, and fought with the urge to turn back into the deep shadows of the hall and retreat, back to Nathaniel and Curiosity and the children. And how silly that was: once she had traveled alone through the endless forests, and here she stood trembling in the rose gardens at Carryckcastle.

She could not let herself be drawn into such a simple trap as a pleasing garden; she would not forget how she had come to be here. With new concentration, she started toward the conservatory that stood on the far side of a little stand of pear trees, its glass walls and roof reflecting bright in the sun. The gardens were not empty—men were at work weeding the beds and spreading manure, and far off she saw the Hakim, pushing a man in a wheeled chair. She paused to watch him, curious about this patient of his, an old man hunched forward. A maid came up and curtsied before him; he raised his hand to trace something in the air over her head.

"Might I be o' any help, mem?" A gardener popped up before her so suddenly that she stepped back in alarm and pressed a hand to her heart.

"I didna mean tae startle ye, mem, please pardon me. I'm the head gardener, and I thocht perhaps ye had questions—" The rims of his eyelids and the tips of his ears and nose were tinged pink and this gardener reminded her of a plump little rabbit.

"Not at all." Hannah had once brought them information about the head gardener at Carryck, and Elizabeth searched her memory for the name. Whatever connections she could make to the staff might help later on, when the time came to leave.

"The earl is in the conservatory, Mr. Brown?"

His eyes widened in surprise. "Aye, mem. So he is. I expect he'll be there aa day." And apologetically: "He doesna like tae be disturbed when he's workin', mem."

Elizabeth studied the rose before her. "I believe your brother serves on the *Isis,* does he not? Have you had a happy reunion with him?"

The little man's look of surprise deepened. "I've no' yet seen him, mem, but I hope he'll be doon the village when I get hame. Do ye ken oor Michael, then?"

"A bit. My stepdaughter spent some time with him, and the bird he raised—"

"Sally," supplied the gardener, grinning now.

"Yes, Sally."

With a little flourish he held out a single rose between a thumb and forefinger stained green. "Gin it isna tae forward, mem . . ."

"Thank you," said Elizabeth, accepting the blossom. "How pretty."

"She's aye bonnie tae look at, mem, but her smell is still sweeter."

"Very sweet, indeed. Your roses thrive very well given the climate here, do they not?"

He nodded solemnly. "Aye, mem, so they do. But that's the laird's doin', ye ken."

"Is it?" Elizabeth could not help smiling. "Does His Lordship command the weather to his roses' liking, then?"

The smooth brow crinkled under the straw brim. "There nivver was sic a mannie for growin' things," he said very seriously, looking toward the greenhouse. "Perhaps His Lordship will show ye his orchids, some day."

"What a splendid idea, Mr. Brown. I'll go now and ask him. Oh, and can you tell me—who was that elderly man in the wheeled chair? He's gone now, but he was there just a minute ago, with Hakim Ibrahim."

A pained expression flitted across Mr. Brown's face, gone as soon as it came. "That must ha' been Mr. Duppy, mem. A guest o' the earl's. He's verra tender, ye see. In puir health."

"I am sorry to hear that," Elizabeth said. And then, still vaguely uneasy, she took her leave of Mr. Brown.

The conservatory was an enormous building made almost entirely of glass. It was cleverly designed, so that the panels that served as walls could be adjusted individually, pivoted and propped up to regulate temperature and air flow. Each was covered on the inside by a fine mesh, surely a convenience when the midges were biting.

And such a profusion of greenery: full-grown trees, flowering shrubbery, a long table of orchids—Elizabeth knew them only from books in her uncle's library—under bell jars. A small red butterfly such as she had never seen before flitted by, and then another. There was no sign of the earl, but when she opened the door she heard voices.

"It looks like a wee monkey," said a young girl's voice. "For aa it's got a purple neb."

"Aye, and it's near as much trouble as a monkey wad be," said the earl. His tone was very different from the one Elizabeth had heard from him late in the night; he sounded perfectly at ease conversing with little girls.

Along the wall was a row of the potted ti-nain trees that the Hakim had tended so carefully on the deck of the *Isis,* come now to the end of their long journey. Elizabeth walked along, following the sound of the voices until she arrived at the work area in the very middle of the conservatory.

The earl sat at a high table, with Hannah and Jennet standing to either side. Their heads were bent for-

ward in concentration, and none of them took any note of her.

"Good afternoon."

"Elizabeth!" Hannah turned to her, and held out a muddy hand. "Come see the earl's new orchid. The Duke of Dorchester sent it to him, imagine."

Carryck stood, and Elizabeth saw that she need not have worried about her gown—he was wearing a pair of old breeks and a loose linen shirt with a leather apron over all. His sleeves were rolled up to the elbow, and he looked like any other man in the middle of a day's labor.

He nodded to her. "Guid day, madam."

Elizabeth inclined her head and shoulders. "My lord Earl. And this must be Jennet?"

The child seemed to glow, all sun colored among the greenery. "Aye, mem," she said. "But ye canna be the stepmother?" And she peered more closely, as if she hoped to see horns peeking out of Elizabeth's hair.

"I am that," Elizabeth admitted. "We are not all wicked."

"How is my father?" Hannah asked, with a guilty expression that said she had not thought of him for a little while.

Elizabeth put a hand on her shoulder. "You needn't worry. He has eaten, and he is sleeping. The Hakim will look in on him this afternoon."

"Guid tidings," said the earl.

Hannah was not an awkward child, but now she seemed truly at a loss, caught in this strange situation. *I am ill at ease, too,* Elizabeth wanted to say to her, but it would not do, not in front of Carryck.

Jennet seemed unaware of all of this. She looked between Hannah and Elizabeth with undisguised curiosity. "Have ye come tae see the tulips?"

"Oh, the tulips," said Hannah, relieved at this

change in subject. "See, Elizabeth, how they look like the Hakim's turban."

Rare tulips were exquisitely expensive, but here were at least a dozen, each in a pot of its own and in differing stages of bloom—and that out of season. It seemed that Carryck did have a gift for growing things.

"It is your diversion to cultivate tulips, my lord?"

He wiped his hands on a piece of sacking as he studied her. "My mither brought the roots wi' her as a gift tae my faither when they married. They've been grown at Carryckcastle ever since."

"They have names," said Hannah. "Don Quevedo and Admiral Liefken and Henry Everdene and this one is Mistress Margret. Is that not odd? That a flower has a name but that a man might not." She paused, throwing a wary look at the earl.

He peered at her with his brows drawn into a tight vee. "Aa God's creatures have names, lass. My name is Carryck."

Hannah met his gaze evenly. "But, sir, most people have first names. My grandfather is called Hawkeye or Dan'l Bonner and my father Wolf-Running-Fast or Nathaniel Bonner, but you—"

She glanced at Elizabeth, and then went on resolutely. "You are called 'my lord' or 'sir,' or 'Carryck.' And Carryck is the name of this place. It is as if my grandfather were called Hidden Wolf for the mountain where he lives."

Jennet was very still, all her attention on the earl and what he might say. And since the earl seemed to have taken no offense at Hannah's bold questioning, Elizabeth was quite interested, too, and content to stay out of the conversation for the time being.

"The difference is this," said the earl. "Your grandfaither chose his place and made it his own while I was born tae Carryck. I belong tae the place as much as it belongs tae me." He held up a finger to keep Jennet

from interrupting, but the look he gave her was
kindly.

"Now a man wha has a twisted leg may be called
Cruikshank in our tongue, or one wha works the
smithy may be called Gow, which is guid Scots as weel,
and means 'smith.' Or a man called Donald may have a
son, and that son might be called Donaldson or
MacDonald or FitzDonald, all meanin' 'the son o'
Donald.' My surname is Scott. The earliest o' my ances-
tors that I ken was Uchtred FitzScott—Uchtred the son
o' Scott—and his son Richard took the surname Scott,
as did most o' the men wha descended from him."

"But some men take their mither's faither's names."
Jennet pushed this out in a great rush.

The earl smiled at her, as if this knowledge of the
complications of the family genealogy excused her interruption.

"That's aye true. In the male line I descend from
anither family, but one o' my line wed a Scott and took
her name along wi' her lands. What ye must ken, lass, is
this: in Scotland there's naucht mair important than the
land. Which is why so muny men left Scotland for the
New Werld after the Rising. They were looking for a
place where a man could settle his family, and claim
new land."

Hannah's whole posture changed, uneasiness wiped
away suddenly by anger. "Steal land," she said stiffly.
"From my mother's people. From my people."

"Hmpf." One brow shot up and the earl sent
Elizabeth a questioning glance.

She said, "The matter looks very different from the
other side, my lord."

"Aye, so it must."

"Tell the rest o' it!" Jennet said impatiently.

The earl cleared his throat. "And so in the Hielands
and in much o' the Lowlands the lairds are called after
their lands. Ma surname is Scott but I'm called Carryck

after the earldom I inherited frae my faither. The king calls me Carryck, my tenants call me Carryck, my wife called me Carryck. And you, my wee cousin, will call me Carryck, too."

Jennet's mouth fell open in surprise and then shut with an audible click. Elizabeth might have laughed at the sight, if she were not herself so surprised.

"Does Jennet call you Carryck?"

She laughed out loud at the idea. "Ma mither wad beat me for sic an impertinence," she said. "And I wadn't be allowed tae visit the greenhouse." Something occurred to her, and she turned to Elizabeth, flashing her dimples.

"Wad ye like tae see the smelly tree?" she asked. "It stinks for aa the werld like a dog twa days deid in the sun."

Elizabeth did not know what to make of this offer, but the earl resolved the dilemma for her.

"The lady dinna come here tae see the conservatory, lass. I expect she wants a word wi' me."

Elizabeth inclined her head. "If it is not too much of an imposition, my lord."

"Och, ye canna talk tae the laird when he's putterin' aboot the greenhouse," Jennet said, brushing a curl out of her eyes. "Ye might as weel try tae get a song oot of Admiral Liefken here." And she wrinkled her nose at a tulip just on the verge of opening.

"Wheest, Jennet." The earl's mouth jerked at one corner, but his tone was stern. "Dinna forget your manners. I can weel spare time for our guest."

"Ye'll no' want us here, then. Do ye care tae see the rest o' the castle, Squirrel?"

"Jennet," said Carryck, and the little girl drew up suddenly, as if she knew what he might say, and did not care to hear it.

"Ye'll no' be snoopin' where ye dinna belong."

She bobbed a quick curtsy. "Ne, my lord."

"Verra weel. Awa' wi' the baith o' ye."

Hannah hesitated, but Elizabeth waved her on with a smile and then stood watching until the girls had disappeared into the rose garden. When they were gone she waited still, unsure where to begin now that she had the earl's attention. Everything that she might say to him seemed suddenly too obvious for words.

He said, "I've had no word o' the *Leopard,* if that's what ye want tae hear."

Elizabeth composed her face before she turned to him. "I was hoping you had, yes."

"I've sent word tae Dundas, and tae the Admiralty, as weel. If there's aught tae learn o' the ship, it willna be lang."

"Then you do not know if the *Leopard* was involved in this recent battle with the French?" It was a fear she had not yet spoken aloud, one she had not even shared with Nathaniel.

The earl's expression was unreadable. "I canna say."

"Then perhaps I might ask another question, my lord."

He worked his thumbs against the edge of his leather apron. "Wad it no' be better tae wait wi' this conversation until your guidman is recovered?"

"I am quite capable of asking questions without my husband's assistance, my lord."

"O' that I ha' nae doubt," he said dryly.

She clasped her hands together before her to keep them from shaking. "Perhaps you could tell me why it is that you have gone to such trouble and expense to bring us here, against our will and inclination."

His eyes narrowed. "Ye ken full weel, madam." Something hard had come into his tone, and he looked now more like the man she had met last night, the one who had commanded his men with so few words. But if she let him intimidate her at the beginning of these negotiations for their freedom, they would be here a very long time.

She said, "My lord. Neither my husband nor his father have any interest in claiming Carryck. And even if
they were interested, why should they be given prece-
dence over your own daughter?"

His neck flushed a mottled red. "I have no daughter." The earl spoke unaccented English for the first
time, keen-edged and stark.

"Really? As I understand it, your daughter Lady
Isabel married one Walter Campbell." And even as she
said that name aloud, she recalled the confusion at
the inn while Nathaniel lay bleeding on the floor.
The earl had said the same name: *Walter's men are behind this.* And then he had sent his own men out to
find the dragoons who had come so close to killing
Nathaniel.

Walter's men are behind this. Surely there were many
men named Walter in Scotland; the earl could not have
been speaking of that Walter Campbell who was married to his only daughter. And yet she saw on his face
that this was exactly whom he meant.

All the warnings of the past few months came back
to her: the Campbells wanted Carryck, and they would
do anything to achieve that end. The dragoons who had
kidnapped Mac Stoker and shot Nathaniel were Walter
Campbell's men, and acting on his orders.

"My lord!"

The young man called Lucas was at the door, hesitat-
ing there as if the greenhouse were forbidden territory.

"My lord, Davie and the others are come, and
they've brung the men ye wanted wi' them." He sent
Elizabeth a nervous glance.

"The dragoons," Carryck said to Elizabeth, taking
off his apron.

Lucas swallowed hard to catch his breath. "Will ye
come, my lord?"

"Aye. Where's Moncrieff?"

"Still doon the village, my lord."

"Send for him."

Elizabeth said, "My lord, I would like to be there when you question the dragoons."

He glanced down at her. "That's no' possible, madam. Unless ye've got the gift o' communin' wi' the deid."

Coming out of the sun into the shadows of the Great Hall, Hannah shivered. It was the biggest room she had ever seen, as long and more than twice as wide as the longhouse of the Wolf clan where her mother had been born, a space where eighty and sometimes as many as a hundred people worked and ate and slept. This Great Hall was empty but for tables and chairs, and more surprising still, it had colored glass windows that threw great patches of deep red and blue and gold down on the flagstone floor.

"Come on!" Jennet hissed, taking Hannah by the hand to pull her along. They passed through an open door into a hall and stopped. Jennet went up on tiptoe to whisper in her ear.

"The door makes an awfu' creak."

Hannah wanted to ask why they had to be quiet if no one was near to hear them, but Jennet was already working the latch with complete concentration, the tip of her tongue caught between her teeth as she wiggled it ever so carefully back and forth. Finally the latch gave with a small squeak and the door opened just wide enough for them to slip through into Elphinstone Tower.

Stairs wound upward in a spiral, sunlight falling in dusty bars through a small window at the first turning. Their bare feet made no noise on the cool stone, but Hannah's heart beat so loud in her ears that she feared that the men in the courtyard might hear it, as she could hear their voices. She wondered if this was one of the places that the earl had been speaking of when he had fixed Jennet with his stern expression. But it could not be; she seemed so much at ease, and not at all afraid.

They came to a small landing with a single door, tall and rounded at the top with a candle sconce to either side, but they passed by and continued up the winding stairs. Another door just like the first, and then at the very top was a third and final door, and here Jennet stopped. She made a funny little bow as she worked the latch, and ushered Hannah in.

A large room, but almost empty. A few trunks and a lopsided chair, a rolled-up carpet. It was full of light, with windows on three sides.

"This is my secret place," Jennet said proudly. "Ye can see the whole valley frae here, and the courtyard and the dairy and the stables and everythin'."

It was a wonderful room, and Hannah told her so. "Does no one ever look for you here?"

A thoughtful look came over Jennet's face. "Did ye take note o' the first chamber we passed?"

Hannah nodded.

"It belonged tae the lady." Her voice dropped to a whisper. "When she died, he locked the door and put up the key."

"And since then you've never seen inside?" Hannah asked.

"She died afore I was born."

"And no one else has been inside since her death?"

"Naebodie drawin' breath," said Jennet, with a significant nod.

"Ghosts?"

"Aye," said Jennet. "They say the lady sits at the window at dusk, watchin', wi' her dog beside her."

"Who says this?" Hannah asked. She was perfectly willing to believe that the lady's ghost lived in the tower, but she was also very curious about the details.

"MacQuiddy."

MacQuiddy was the house steward, a crooked old man with a single tuft of white hair and a red nose. Jennet had pointed him out to Hannah when she

showed her the kitchens, but he had been too deep in an argument with the cook to take note of them.

"Does he know about the ghosts, then?"

"MacQuiddy is aulder than the laird," Jennet said, fluttering her fingers. "He kens everythin'. Exceptin' my secret place." She said this very firmly, as if she expected Hannah to argue the opposite.

"My grandmother says that only guilty people are afraid of ghosts." *And white people,* Hannah might have added.

"Och, it's no' the ghosts that keep people awa' frae Elphinstone Tower—it's the laird. He has a devilish sharp way when a temper's on him."

Hannah could well imagine this—she had seen his face last night, when it was not clear how serious her father's injuries really were. But in spite of the fact that Jennet knew this side of the earl, she did not really seem at all worried about his temper. It was hard to know if this was foolhardiness, or simple faith in her own ability to charm.

"Come, look," she said, drawing Hannah to the window.

Jennet drew in a sharp breath, but it took longer for Hannah to make out what was happening in the courtyard below.

A group of men were gathered in a rough circle, and at their feet two men lay sprawled on the cobblestones. One of them stared up blankly into the summer sky, and even from this distance Hannah could see that his eyes were mismatched: the left was normal, and the right a bloody starburst. His mouth was contorted in a surprised O.

"Walter's men, the ones wha' shot yer faither. Baith deid," said Jennet calmly.

Hannah jerked back from the window. "How do you know that those are the men who shot my father?"

Jennet wrinkled her brow at such a strange question.

"Because the laird ordered his men oot after the dragoons wha' kidnapped the pirate and shot yer da. Are ye no' glad they're deid?"

"Of course I'm glad," Hannah said. And wondered why she was not.

The earl came striding into the courtyard and into the circle around the bodies. He stood looking down while one of the men spoke for some time. He had a high voice for a man, and it carried to them in bursts. "The Moffat road," Hannah heard, and "Walter."

"Davie likes tae spin a tale," observed Jennet. "He took a wild boar the winter past and the tellin' o' it lasted longer than the hunt."

The earl seemed to have heard enough, for he walked away.

"What will they do with the bodies?"

Jennet shrugged. "Why, the men will drop them on Breadalbane's doorstep. A message, ye see, that yer faither and the rest o' ye are under the laird's protection."

Hannah thought of Thaddeus Glove, who had been hanged in Johnstown for shooting an exciseman in the back, and of the Kahnyen'kehàka woman called White-Hair who had suffered the same fate for stabbing a soldier, even though the man had survived. She thought of Runs-from-Bears, who might have gone to the gallows for putting the Tory with notched ears in his grave, where he could make no more moccasins. She wondered if no one would be arrested for the murder of the two dragoons, or if the feuding between clans was so common that others stood back and let them get on with it. It was an interesting idea, that the Scots might turn out to be like the Hodenosaunee when it came to blood vengeance, but somehow Hannah understood that this question should not be asked, at least not of Jennet.

From the courtyard below them came a voice Hannah recognized: Angus Moncrieff. A shudder ran up her spine at the sound, and she touched a finger lightly to Jennet's

sleeve. "I had better go back. I would like to be there when Hakim Ibrahim visits my father."

Jennet had stepped back from the window, her arms wound around herself. Her complexion had gone suddenly pale beneath her suntanned skin. "Aye," she said. "I'll come, too, gin ye dinna mind."

Nathaniel dreamed of Angus Moncrieff. They were in the Montréal gaol again, alone this time, and Moncrieff was singing in the strong, echoing beat of a Kahnyen'kehàka war song.

> Were I m'self sixteen years old,
> Were I as I would fain be,
> Were I m'self sixteen years old
> I'd gang m'self with Charlie.

Outside a human form hung heavy from the gallows on a rope that creaked in the wind. In the way of dreams the wall was no barrier at all, and Nathaniel watched as the body turned to show him his father's face: slack in death, familiar and strange at once. Moncrieff watched, too, the brown eyes quick and eager under heavy lids.

In his fist was his grandfather's war club and it seemed to move on its own, up and through the air to meet Moncrieff's skull just above the left eye, the shock of bone giving way shooting up his arm and into his own skull with a dull crack. And then Nathaniel saw that it wasn't Moncrieff at all but Adam MacKay, grinning at him with bloodied teeth.

He woke in a sweat. His head hurt, and the wounds in his shoulder and leg throbbed with the beat of his heart.

Hakim Ibrahim stood next to the bed, and beside him Elizabeth in a gown he had never seen, some strange fabric that seemed to float around her. Curiosity's hand was on his cheek, long and cool.

"Hannah?" His voice cracked and wobbled like an old man's.

"I just saw her in the courtyard. She should be here any moment."

"I dreamed of Moncrieff."

"He's just come from the village," said Elizabeth. "We could hear his voice below the window. Perhaps you heard him in your sleep."

"I dreamed of him," Nathaniel repeated dully.

"Fever dreams," said the Hakim. "It was to be expected." He closed his eyes against the light. "My father?"

"No word yet. I did speak with the earl."

Curiosity made a noise in her throat. "Drink this tea, now. The earl ain't goin' nowhere, and neither are you until this fever has settled."

He took the cup from her and swallowed the bitter tea, and then she filled it again and he emptied that too. His stomach roiled in protest and for a moment he thought he would bring it all up again. When it settled, he lay back against the pillows and reached out to touch Elizabeth.

"Tell me about Carryck."

"Yes, go on and tell him," said Curiosity. "Take his mind off what we got to do here."

What Elizabeth had to report was quickly told, and none of it good.

The Hakim's attentions to his shoulder made him break into a new sweat, but he kept his gaze focused on Elizabeth. "You think this Walter Campbell is the daughter's husband?"

"Yes. It makes sense, and explains quite a lot. Perhaps the Hakim can tell us for certain . . ."

The surgeon did not look up from his work, but he nodded. "Lady Isabel eloped to marry Walter Campbell, Curator to Lady Flora of Loudoun."

"And thus the earl decided to send Moncrieff to find Hawkeye." Elizabeth supplied the rest of it.

"Yes."

"Why didn't you tell us this before?" Nathaniel asked.

Hakim Ibrahim met his gaze. "Would it have made any difference?"

Nathaniel's tongue felt suddenly thick in his mouth, and it was hard to focus on Elizabeth's face although she was close enough to touch. Outside the window the murmur of voices rose and fell again.

"What's that noise?"

"The earl's men," said Elizabeth. "The dragoons who shot you are dead. Apparently he means to send a message to the Campbells."

"And to us," said Curiosity. "The man don't like to be crossed. As if we didn't know that ourselves."

Nathaniel was more tired now than he could ever remember being but he reached out and took Curiosity's wrist. It was cool to his touch and solid and when she looked at him he saw that she was pleased with herself.

"What was in that tea besides willow bark for fever?"

She lifted one brow. "What you need."

"I need to get us away from this place."

"That's true enough. I expect you to get me home, and right quick. But you cain't do it dead, Nathaniel Bonner. Now sleep."

"You haven't left me any say in it." His own voice was thick in his ears.

Elizabeth leaned over him and her smell—milky sweet and summer flowers—came to him. At this moment he could think of nothing else in the world that he wanted except to pull her down beside him and keep her there. He could think of it, but his arms were suddenly too heavy to lift.

"I'm here," she said. "I'll stay with you."

Hannah was disappointed to find her father asleep, and then immediately ashamed of herself when she stood

beside his bed. His color was bad, and the sheen of
sweat on his brow told her something she had not
wanted to contemplate.

"Fever."

"Yes. But he is very strong." The Hakim sat beside
the bed, and he gave her the kind of reassuring smile
she had seen him give before, when there were no
promises he could make.

"I should have been here."

From her spot near the door Jennet said, "I shouldna
ha' kept ye sae lang."

Hannah jerked in surprise as Elizabeth took her by
the elbow and steered her away from the bed.

"Hannah Bonner," she said in her primmest school-
mistress voice. There was a line between her brows that
Hannah had not often seen, and did not care to see
now. "What is this foolishness?"

In her surprise, Hannah glanced at Curiosity. But
there was no help to be had from her; she looked quite
in agreement with Elizabeth.

"But—"

"Do not interrupt me. Do you think that hand-
wringing will help your father? When he wakes he will
want to hear all about the castle. Will you be ready to
answer his questions?"

Hannah blinked hard, and then she nodded. "Yes."

"Yes?"

It was not like Elizabeth to be unfair, and Hannah
felt herself flush with frustration. "We've only been
here a few hours," she said. "By tomorrow I'll know
more."

"Aye," volunteered Jennet, coming to her aid. "I'll
show her whatever she cares tae see."

"Good," said Elizabeth, more calmly. "Your father
will be very glad of it." She pushed out a long breath
and Hannah saw suddenly how very worried Elizabeth
was. She saw too that nothing she could say would help.

"The two of you might take the twins out into the garden for an hour. I will manage here well enough."

Curiosity said, "That's a fine idea. I'll come along, too."

There was a bit of sloping lawn that ran from the gardens down toward the dairy, and they settled there in the shifting shadows of a rowan tree.

"A pretty place," Curiosity said, spreading her skirts out around herself. "Cain't deny that."

Jennet sat beside her with Daniel in her lap. She was studying Curiosity's hand where it lay on the grass, palm up and fingers slightly curved. Hannah wondered what Jennet found so interesting, and so did Curiosity.

"Ain't you ever seen an African before?"

Jennet leaned over to look more closely at Curiosity's palm. "The Marquis o' Montrose came tae call on the laird, last summer it was, and he had a Moor for a footman. But I dinna see him sae close," she said. "Why are ye broon on one side and pale on the ither?"

Curiosity shrugged, and examined her own hand. "I have wondered that myself. When I get to the other side I'll be sure to ask the Lord what He had in mind."

Jennet propped Daniel on the ground beside Lily, and steadied him with one hand to see if he might sit on his own. He would not, but he found it a good game, and chuckled with great satisfaction each time she caught him and brought him back upright. She said, "I like your idea o' heaven. Imagine, askin' any question."

"I guess you'd keep the Almighty busy talkin' for a good while," said Curiosity, but there was real affection in her tone. Then she looked over at Hannah.

"You mighty quiet, Squirrel. Worried about your daddy?"

"A little. And about Elizabeth."

"No need," Curiosity said, holding up her face to the sun. "She'll settle, soon as his fever breaks." And then, without turning her head, she said, "Jennet, child. Now tell me, ain't that Mrs. Hope your mama?"

Hannah pulled up in surprise. It was true that Jennet had never mentioned her own family beyond her brother, Simon, and now she wondered why she would have been silent on that subject. Curiosity had come to the same question, and she was after something—Hannah had seen her at work too many times to mistake her tone.

"Aye." Jennet was preoccupied with Daniel, and she did not seem to mind Curiosity's questions.

"And she's a widow woman?"

"Aye," said Jennet. "Widowed young."

"Now that's too bad," Curiosity said, ignoring Hannah's pointed frown and moving right ahead to what she wanted to know.

"So it's just you and your mama."

"Granny Laidlaw's doon the village," said Jennet. "She's like you."

Curiosity drew up in surprise. "How is that?"

"Canny," said Jennet.

"I thank you kindly for the compliment," Curiosity said. "Now I suppose as young as you are, you wouldn't remember nothing 'bout this Isabel I hear tell about."

Jennet turned to look at Curiosity, and something much older than her years was there in her eyes. "Ye want tae hear how it is she ran off wi' a Breadalbane?"

Hannah gave Curiosity a triumphant look. Jennet was too clever to be wheedled out of a story, and Curiosity had underestimated her. But she wasn't displeased to have been outmaneuvered, and she gave Jennet a wide smile.

"Why, yes. I would."

"They'd beat me for even sayin' her name. The earl

forbids it. Auld Nick was sent awa' oot o' service for talkin' aboot her in MacQuiddy's hearin'.' "

"Then we won't ask." Hannah met Curiosity's raised brow with a furrowed one of her own.

"Och, I'll tell ye what I ken," said Jennet with an easy shrug. "It's no' verra much. A summer's night, it was. He was waitin' for her below—" She pointed with her chin toward the village. "I dinna ken how it was that she ever came tae meet a Breadalbane. My mither could tell ye, but she willna speak o' it."

"Were they good friends, then?" Hannah asked, drawn into this story almost against her will.

"Aye," said Jennet. "As close as sisters ever were. The earl sent his men oot tae bring her hame, but it was too late. Nae sign o' the lady until the spring, when she sent word that she was wi' child. The marriage couldna be undone, then, ye see."

"And I suppose these Campbell-Breadalbane folk all got tails and horns," Curiosity said.

Jennet fixed her with a serious expression. "Horns and tails, aye. I wadna doubt it. They like tae cut men's throats and leave them for the corbies."

"Bad blood," said Hannah. "The kind that starts wars."

"O' course," said Jennet, with a little bit of a smile. "We're Scots, aye?"

There was the sound of cart wheels on the gravel path that came around the corner of the castle, and Jennet's whole face broke into a smile. She jumped up so that Daniel tumbled over with an insulted squawk. In a quick swoop she grabbed him up and handed him to Hannah.

"It's Monsieur Dupuis," Jennet said, turning to wave. "And the Hakim."

It was not a cart, as Hannah had thought, but a cross between a cushioned chair and a wheelbarrow. In it sat an old man hunched forward, his legs covered with a

rug. The Hakim had been pushing, but he stopped to return Jennet's greeting.

"He's come out tae take the fresh air. Come along, I must introduce ye." And she skipped off ahead.

By the time they had gathered up the babies and made their way to the little group, Jennet was deep in conversation. She broke off in mid-sentence to make the introductions.

Monsieur Dupuis was a friend of the earl's and—if Hannah understood Jennet correctly—a permanent houseguest. But Hannah found it hard to concentrate on what Jennet had to say, because she could not look away from the stranger. This must be the man Elizabeth had seen in the garden. She had spoken of him as a very old man, and Hannah had seen him that way, too, at first, but now she saw she had been mistaken. He was middle-aged, but worn thin by pain—a man bent close to breaking. He was the kind of pale O'seronni who suffered most in the sun, burning again and again. Now, between his eyes a nest of dark moles seethed like milling wasps. There was another cluster on his jaw, and a larger one wrapping around his neck and reaching down into his clothing. They were like nothing she had ever seen before: black as tar, ulcerated and ragged, and she understood somehow that they would be the death of him. A cancer, one that grew inward from the skin rather than beginning deep inside the body.

She saw the truth of it in Curiosity's face, and in the Hakim's; now Hannah understood why he had disappeared so quickly from the *Isis*—the earl had sent for him in the hope that he could do something for this friend. And Hakim Ibrahim had disappointed them, because Monsieur Dupuis was beyond helping. O'seronni did not sing death songs, but maybe they would listen to his stories from the shadowlands and give him comfort that way.

The Frenchman was holding out a hand toward her,

fingers twitching, to draw her closer. Hannah came, and bent her head to his.

In Kahnyen'kehàka he said, "Little sister, you are very far from home."

She jerked away as if he had snapped his teeth at her. "You speak my language," she said. "Why do you speak my language?" She said it in English, to deny him what he was trying to claim for himself.

"Monsieur Dupuis lived for many years among your people," said Jennet, her smile fading away into confusion.

Hannah sent Curiosity a pleading glance and saw the same unease and suspicion that she knew must be plain on her own face. "My people? Among my people?"

"I thought ye'd be pleased," said Jennet sadly.

Curiosity shifted Lily and put a hand on Jennet's shoulder, but she spoke to the Frenchman. "Now, that's right interesting, monsieur. How'd you come to spend time with the Mohawk?"

But his gaze stayed on Hannah. In an English that was more Scots than French he said, "I knew your mother, Sings-from-Books. You are very like her. Your great-grandmother, Made-of-Bones. Is she still living?"

Hannah stepped back farther, clutching Daniel so that he squirmed in protest. "Did you tell him, Jennet? Did you tell him about my mother's people?"

The Frenchman held up a pale hand, and it trembled slightly. "She told me nothing, child. There is no reason to fear. None at all. As soon as your father is well enough, he and I must talk."

"You know my father."

"Yes."

Hannah felt the first flush of relief. Her father would know this man, or he would not. In either case, things would be made clear, and it would not fall to her to decide if Monsieur Dupuis was friend or enemy.

The Frenchman was watching her, and Hannah had

the disturbing feeling that he read her thoughts. In Kahnyen'kehàka he said, "Tell Wolf-Running-Fast that I send my greetings. It has been many years, but he will remember me. As I remember him. Will you tell him?"

26

For a day and a night the mountain called Aidan Rig pulled a soft rain about itself. Carryckcastle was wrapped in mists, set apart from the rest of the world just as Elizabeth isolated herself in Lady Appalina's bedchamber while she watched over Nathaniel and waited for his fever to break.

They roused him to take broth or the Hakim's willow bark tea; he seemed disoriented but always asked about his father and the children. Then he fell away again into dreams that made him twitch and flail. Elizabeth did not know how to reassure or comfort him, for his worries were real ones and they occupied her own dreams, when she could sleep at all.

The Hakim came every few hours. He brought tisanes, compresses soaking in bowls of scented water, and leeches for Nathaniel's thigh, which was bruised from knee to hip. Together he and Curiosity cleaned and disinfected the shoulder wound once again and left it open to the air. Hannah watched, her dark eyes unreadable. Elizabeth held Nathaniel's hand, flinching at the heat of him, like a fire laid too well, one that threatened to overwhelm the hearth that contained it.

The maids brought a steady stream of hot food, tea,

and clean winding cloths for the babies. Elizabeth nursed them when they were hungry, handed them over to Curiosity or Hannah, and went back to Nathaniel's bedside.

The second night, and still his fever would not break. Elizabeth made no pretense of sleeping.

Sitting beside him, she read through the little journal they had written together on the *Isis,* but no amount of examination turned up any word about this Frenchman whom Hannah and Curiosity had met in the garden. From their description it sounded as if it must be the same man she had seen with the Hakim. In her mind's eye she watched him draw a cross in the air in front of the maid who had curtsied so deeply before him. The sign of the cross.

When the Hakim next came to see Nathaniel, she asked him about this Dupuis, and got little satisfaction.

"A business associate of the earl's—a permanent guest," he said. "Ill unto death."

It should have put her vague uneasiness to rest—the earl's business associates would be merchants like himself. But if the man was a permanent fixture, why had none of the sailors who came from Carryck or Carryckton ever mentioned him in Hannah's hearing?

Neither was there any mention of Mrs. Hope, Elizabeth reminded herself. And still she could not help thinking of a summer night just a year ago at Lake in the Clouds. A night so calm and hot that they could not sleep, a moth fluttering in the light of a single candle, its shadow dancing frantically on the timbered ceiling. Nathaniel, stretched out on the bed in nothing more than a breechclout, telling her stories of the Kahnyen'kehàka at Good Pasture: *There was a priest living in the village then, a Frenchman who went by the name Father Dupuis. We called him Iron-Dog.*

Dupuis was a common name. Nathaniel's Father Dupuis and the earl's Monsieur Dupuis need have nothing to do with one another. Canada was full of French trap-

pers who traded with the Kahnyen'kehàka. Nathaniel seemed to know every man who ever sold a fur from Québec to New-York, and this Monsieur Dupuis would be one of them. It made so much more sense than the idea of a French priest spending his last days at Carryckcastle.

When Nathaniel was himself again—tomorrow, she was sure of it—he would tell her exactly that, and she could put this Monsieur Dupuis away, another detail of the earl's life to be set aside with his tulips and Lady Isabel's unhappy alliance.

Somewhere in the depths of the house a clock chimed midnight. She checked on the babies, asleep in a cradle that had been put in the dressing room, and stood for a moment listening to them breathe before she wandered back through the bedchamber to the window.

The casement opened silently, and she wrapped her arms around herself in pleasure as the cool air touched her face. There was a waxing moon and a breeze that brought the scent of fresh hay with it. An imprudent whim, this fondness she had for the night air; she could hear Aunt Merriweather sniffing in disgust—but it was a comfort to her.

A lantern cast a puddle of light at the courtyard gate where a guard leaned up against the wall, supporting his weight with one hand. Elizabeth could not see the person in the shadows, but it must be a woman, to judge by the tilt of his head. A young woman, one he was hoping to bed, or perhaps they were both too much in a hurry to wait.

The earl was awake too. The windows of his chamber—Jennet had pointed them out to her—were still lit. It was almost a comfort, to know that he slept no more soundly than did his unwilling guests.

A figure passed the window, but one too small and finely made to be the earl. Elizabeth stilled her breath and watched. And again: a woman in white at the window, and there was something about her bearing that spoke of ease and familiarity.

And what does it matter if someone shares the earl's bed? she asked herself sternly, and had no answer.

"Boots. What are you looking at?"

She pressed a fist to her heart to calm it. "Just the courtyard."

"Come here."

His eyes were clear, and when he took her hand his skin was cool to the touch.

"Your fever has broken," she said, her knees buckling with relief.

"Did you think I was going to die on you?"

She climbed up to sit beside him. "Of course not."

"Liar." A drop of blood appeared on his lower lip, fever-cracked.

"You would not dare," she said indignantly, wiping it away with her thumb.

It won her a weak smile. "You're sounding more like yourself, Boots."

"Peevish? Impatient?"

"Now you're fishing for compliments."

"But of course," she said, making an effort to tidy the bedclothes. "For what else do I live and breathe?"

He squeezed her wrist. "I won't die on you. Not for another forty years or so."

She nodded, because she did not trust her voice.

Nathaniel flexed his arm gingerly, and made an attempt to bend his knee. "I feel like somebody took a war club to me. How long have I been out, anyway?" His fingers rasped over his beard stubble. "A while, I guess."

"Almost two days."

"That long. Any word?"

She shook her head. "None at all."

"Don't matter. They're nearby."

This brought her up short. "Who is nearby?"

"My father, and Robbie. The look on your face, Boots. You think I'm out of my head with the fever."

"Are you?" She reached for his brow and found it damp, but still cool to the touch. "I expect you've been dreaming."

He drew her hand down to press his mouth to her palm. "That I have."

"Go back to sleep," she said. "And dream us away from here."

He tugged her closer. "I sleep better with you next to me."

She did not argue, but leaned over to blow out the candle and then settled herself against the pillows.

"Nathaniel," she said. She resisted the question pushing upward from her gut; afraid to put it into words, afraid of what he might have to say.

"Hmmm?" He was already half asleep.

"Do you remember telling me about the Father Dupuis who lived at Good Pasture?"

If he found this question strange, he hid his surprise in a yawn. "Iron-Dog. What brings him to mind?"

A Catholic priest in Protestant Scotland, and what that might mean about Carryck. About all of this.

"What happened to him?"

She felt him trying to come awake enough to answer. "He got killed trying to convert the Seneca, I think it was. I suppose that's what he was looking for all along."

Elizabeth curled toward him on her side, as close as she could come without disturbing his wounds. She said, "Are you certain?"

But he had already slipped back into his dreams, and she was left to her own.

"Please come," Jennet said, hopping from one foot to the other and managing somehow to eat a handful of berries at the same time. "Ye havena seen the village, and there's a band o' players come, jugglers and aa. We'll be back afore dusk."

Hannah considered. She was curious about the village, and at the same time the thought was a little frightening, to be so far away from her people. What if her grandfather should come? What if her father should fall back into his fever?

"Yer da is ever sae much better. He's said it hissel'," Jennet reminded her. "Are ye no' curious tae see Gaw'n Hamilton ride the stang?"

It was a tempting thought. A man whose wife had caused trouble in the village was to be punished for his laxity, by the minister's decree. From Jennet's colorful descriptions, it sounded to Hannah as if he would have to run a gauntlet of sorts, but one where the townspeople used words rather than clubs to make their mark.

"I'll get my shoes," Hannah said, suddenly resolved.

"Ach, dinna fash yersel' aboot shoon," said Jennet, sticking out one dusty foot to wiggle her toes. "We'll gang doon the brae i' the cart and come back the same road. Come on then, or Geordie will be awa' wi'oot us."

"I should say good-bye—"

"Ye've done that already," Jennet said impatiently. "Come on!"

Geordie did not want them crowding him on the driver's box, so they had to share the cart with a pair of nanny goats that bleated so loud and long that there was little chance for conversation. But Hannah did not mind; she was glad of this little time to herself. She liked Jennet tremendously, but she had so many stories to tell and so much information to share that sometimes it was hard to keep track of it all. Now while the cart rocked and jolted down the mountainside Hannah stood with a goat nosing her skirts, and watched to see what news she could take back to her father.

A carriage passed them where the mountain road broadened at the outskirts of the village. The liverymen were in brown and gold, and one of them stared at her

as they went by. Jennet raised her voice. "Wha is that, Geordie?"

Geordie was a thick young man with a blank look about him, but he provided information willingly enough. He twisted a shoulder toward her. "A gentleman come tae see the laird, says MacQuiddy."

"English?"

He shook his great shaggy head. "French."

Hannah might have asked him more about the visitor, but they had come into the heart of the village. Saturday market had filled the lanes, and the cart slowed and then stopped in the thick of it. Jennet jumped down from the cart and Hannah followed.

"Be back afore the kirk clock strikes four," Geordie shouted after them. "Or ye'll walk hame, ye wee gilpies!"

Jennet spun on her heel to wrinkle her nose and stick her tongue out at him. "Dinna lose aa yer coin at the cockfight, Geordie, or MacQuiddy will box yer lugs." And they slipped into the crowd before he could seek revenge.

They wound their way along among the marketers while Hannah tried to take in all at once. It was not much different than market in Johnstown, the same haggling and laughter and clink of coin. Chickens and piglets, kale, carrots. A sullen young girl with a rash of pimples on her chin stood behind a table to brush the flies away from treacle tarts. A little boy was tied to the table's leg with a hang of dirty rope, crying piteously and rubbing his eyes with a dirty fist.

Jennet seemed to know every person by name, and everyone had something to say to her even while they studied Hannah—some shyly, some with open curiosity.

"How d'ye fend, wee Jennet?"

"Whit fettle, lass? And how fares the laird this day?"

"Will ye no' come an' see oor Harry, Jennet? He's hame frae the *Isis* wi' muny a tale tae tell."

She answered them all with a few words and a smile,

and it was clear to see that Jennet was a great favorite in Carryckton.

Near an alehouse two men were juggling eggs, sending them in endless circles in the air with flicks of the wrist. One was as tall as Robbie MacLachlan; the other barely came to his knees, although he was full bearded and the short fingers that worked the eggs were covered with dark hair. Bells jangled at their elbows and knees and they bantered with the crowd, hardly watching their work.

Just around the corner a rough stage had been put up, and the traveling players had drawn a good crowd.

"Let's bide a while," whispered Jennet. Hannah had never seen a play, and so she was happy to watch as a young man with his face painted to look like an old man held out a vial of cloudy yellow liquid. He threw his voice out in a reedy wobble over the audience:

> *Sir doctor, please be sae kind and examine this piss*
> *Wi' ma bonnie young dauchter there's somethin'*
>   *amiss*
> *She stays tae her bed aa the night, aa the day*
> *Turns awa fra' her food, an' does naethin' but lie*
> *aboot in a hoose which is naucht but a mess*
> *Can this be the plague; can ye hazard a guess?*

Hannah had learned something from the Hakim about examining urine to diagnose an illness, and she was very curious as to what this doctor would say. With the rest of the crowd she leaned forward. He rocked back and forth on his heels and stroked his beard thoughtfully with one hand while he patted a round belly with the other. With each pat a small puff of feathers escaped from the juncture of breeches and coat, but the audience seemed not to mind.

> *Your ailing wee dauchter is a servant, I see*
> *She takes her work verra seriously*
> *She swabs the floors and cooks the food*

But the hired man is the cause o' her mood
When she bent ower her work he pressed his point
Tae a well laid table he added a joint
Tae carve her meat he supplied the blade
For a bluidy gash just as she bade
Soon her belly will grow and swell
Nivver fear! in the spring aa will be well.
Your bonnie Kate is no' alone,
Young and limber, muny maidens moan.
They curse and vomit and wring their hands
'Tis a problem that's growing across the land!

The crowd laughed, but Jennet pulled Hannah away, sniffing loudly in her displeasure. "Kate o' Lauchine, agin! What a lither lot those players are, always tossin' aboot words instead o' swords. They'll lift naethin' heavier than a filled tankard."

Hannah was about to tell her that as far as she knew, you could not read pregnancy from the color of urine, but just then a boy with a cast in his eye shoved himself in front of them. "Bi crivens, Jennet Hope, look what ye dragged doon the lane the-day. A heathen. Does it ken oor tongue?"

"Better than you, Hugh Brown," she snapped, going up on tiptoe to put her face to his. "Ye'll wish that ye had nae tongue a'tall once the minister kens how ye're cursin', ye scunnerin wee nyaff." And she poked her elbow in his gut hard enough to make him turn white.

They darted off into the crowd while he was still trying to get back his breath. The shadowy lanes were cool even on this sunny day, the cobblestones smooth underfoot and the smell of bread baking and brewing ale in the air. They came around a corner to a large open area of trampled earth with a pillar in its center.

"Och, look," Jennet breathed. "Dame Sanderson. There's goin' tae be a bear-baitin'."

"Bear?" Hannah looked harder and saw no more

than a dusty hump of fur chained to the pillar. "Dame Sanderson?"

"Aye." Jennet gave her a curious look. "That bear, there. She's called Dame Sanderson. Have ye nivver seen a bear?"

It was such a strange question that Hannah didn't know at first how to answer. When she needed more than her mother's milk she had sucked bear fat from her fingers; she had learned to recognize bear tracks when she was hardly old enough to walk herself. Bears played on the boulders above the waterfalls at Lake in the Clouds, and napped in trees and fished in the marshes on Big Muddy. Once an eagle had dropped a she-cub—mangled and close to dead—into the cornfield while they had been planting squash. Hannah had rescued her from Hector and Blue and tended her wounds until she died, and then she had taken her pelt and cured it. That pelt was on her sleeping pallet at Lake in the Clouds right now.

"I have an uncle called Runs-from-Bears," Hannah said.

Jennet's eyebrows shot up high in delight and interest. "Is he afraid o' them, then?"

"No," Hannah said, smiling at the idea of Runs-from-Bears afraid of anything. "Not at all." She could see that she would have to tell this story, even though the web it would weave might tangle her thoughts for the rest of the day.

"When my uncle was a baby he was called Sitting-Boy. Wherever Two-Moons—his mother—put him down he would stay, and while the others played he watched, and when they ran, he smiled. Two-Moons and her husband, Stands-Tall, worried that the boy was weak-witted, but for the bright look in his eyes.

"In his third year, in the Strawberry Moon, Two-Moons went with all the women to pick fruit for the festival . . ." Hannah swallowed, feeling the flush of the sun on her face and a clench of homesickness so deep and hard that she swayed with it.

"The women were busy gathering strawberries when a bear came out of the forest with her cub. The other women hurried the children away but Two-Moons could find no trace of Sitting-Boy. She looked and called and the bear came closer and closer until she was so close that Two-Moons could smell the river water on her fur.

"Just then Sitting-Boy let out a great laugh and he came running out of the field. The bear cub was chasing him, and Sitting-Boy laughed and laughed as he ran. It was a laugh so strong and sweet that the siskins in the trees stopped to listen, and the beaver in the river came to see, and even mother bear turned her head to watch.

"Two-Moons was very afraid for Sitting-Boy and she said 'Mother bear, I am thankful to your little one for showing my son how to use his legs. See how well they play together.'

"And mother bear called her cub to her, and they turned and left the strawberry fields to the women. That's when they gave my uncle the name Runs-from-Bears."

Jennet said, "I would like to meet Two-Moons and Stands-Tall and Runs-from-Bears and your aunt Many-Doves and your grandmother and all the rest of your people."

"Stands-Tall was killed in battle," Hannah said. "But if you come to visit us in the endless forests, you will meet the others." She looked at the hump of fur in the middle of the pit. "I have known many bears, but I have never seen one such as this. Is she ill?"

"Ach, ne. The hounds wi' bring her tae her feet soon enough. Last summer I saw her break the back o' a dog as big as a sow wi' one swipe o' her paw."

"Where did she come from?"

"A tinker called Alf Whittle bought her aff a ship come frae America, when she was sma'. They say he's taken her sae far as the Aberdeen fair."

A little boy came louping by and began pelting the bear with pebbles. The mass of flesh rippled and the great head reared up and around.

Hannah felt herself go very cold, as if a new wind had come down off snowy mountains. The bear was rolling her head back and forth, her broad wet nose quivering. The eye sockets were empty.

"She smells somethin'." Jennet stepped back.

"Me," Hannah said. "She smells me." She raised her voice and spoke in her own language. "When a pine needle falls in the forest, eagle sees it, deer hears it, and bear smells it. Do you smell me, sister?"

The bear was struggling to her feet now, her head swinging back and forth as she mewled, the sound a child makes when she is looking for comfort. Hannah stepped into the pit, and Jennet grabbed her by the shoulder.

"Ye canna," she screeched. "She'll lay ye open like a ripe plum."

The bear had come as close as the chain would allow. She stood up on her hind legs and her paws hung down before her, claws long and curved and blackened with age and blood. From toe to the top of her head she was covered with scars, and her fur was matted and filthy.

"They put out her eyes," Hannah said. "To keep her in line."

"Aye," said Jennet uneasily. "But she's a grand fighter any road. Shall we stay and watch?"

"No," Hannah said. "I won't watch that."

Jennet had a few coins in her apron pocket and she bought ginger nuts from the sullen girl behind the table. "For Granny," she explained, tucking them away with one reluctant look. She led Hannah through the lanes until they came to a little cottage—it could be no larger than the smallest cabin in Paradise—surrounded by a garden closely planted with cabbage, leeks, potatoes,

and carrots. Beans spiraled up a fence overhung by an apple tree. Neat beds of herbs clustered around the path to the door: sage, costmary, gillyflowers and clary, sorrel, chamomile, mint and verbena, borage and feverfew. Very different from the gardens at Carryckcastle, and so much more like home that Hannah wanted to sit right down and stay there for the rest of the day. She paused to run her hand over a spreading savin bush, the flattish evergreen needles prickling lightly.

When a pine needle falls in the forest, eagle sees it, deer hears it, and bear smells it.

"Granny Laidlaw was hoosekeeper at Carryckcastle afore her sight began tae fade. She's fu' blind these five years, but naught else fails her," Jennet said. "And here's ma auntie Kate."

The woman who came through the door with a basket over her arm was a younger version of Mrs. Hope, with blond hair tucked up under a neat white cap.

"Ye've come, then, she'll be pleased. I'm awa' tae fetch butter—dinna gae until ye've had some tea."

The cottage had rushes underfoot and a ceiling so low that Hannah could reach it if she stretched up on tiptoe. A speckled dog was sleeping near the hearth, where a kettle hung over the fire.

In the corner two women were shelling beans, one of them so small and delicately built that Hannah first mistook her for a child. But the face that peered out from a ruffled cap was old, indeed, and the blue eyes had gone as cloudy as marbles. Her hearing was good, for she turned her head toward them at the first creak of the door.

"Jennet, hen. I was hopin' ye'd come the day. I smell ginger nuts, and ye've broucht a visitor, too. Is it the wee Indian lass, Gelleys?"

"Aye." The other woman peered at Hannah with her whole face screwed into a knot. And then, with voice raised to a screech: "What are ye called, lass?"

"Red skin doesna make her deef, Gelleys." Granny Laidlaw shook with laughter. "Come hen, come closer. Tell me, how are ye called?"

"Hannah Bonner, mum."

"But ye speak English!" Gelleys squinted even harder, as if something in Hannah's face might explain the language that came out of her mouth.

"She speaks Scots, too," Jennet said, quite fiercely. "And her mother's language, wait till ye hear."

"Dinna fash yersel', lassie." Gelleys put down her bowl of beans. "I meant nae harm. Ma grandson Charlie tolt me aboot ye when he came awa frae the *Isis*."

This was a surprise, but a welcome one. Hannah said, "How is Charlie? Is he well?"

"He's weel enouch," said the old woman. "Mournin' his brither, as are we aa. Ye were a comfort tae oor Mungo in his last days, and it willna be forgotten, lass."

"He was a good lad," said Hannah. "Is Charlie here?"

"I wish he were," said Gelleys. "But they called him awa' back tae his ship, and it will be muny a year afore we see him agin. But ye didna come tae talk o' sic waerifu' things, I'm sure."

"I broucht her tae see ye because she's got ever sae muny questions," volunteered Jennet.

"Does she noo?" Granny Laidlaw looked distinctly pleased. "Weel then, we'll settle doon tegither and tell a tale or twa."

Hannah could not look away from Gelleys's hands. She had never seen the like on a woman—as large as a man's, swollen and red but with fingers nimble enough to snap beans at an amazing rate. Under grizzled eyebrows she was watching Hannah, too.

"It's a guid thing ye found baith o' us here," said Granny Laidlaw. "What I dinna ken aboot Carryckcastle, Gelleys Smaill does."

"Ha!" Gelleys put back her head. "Listen tae her. Did ye no hear the minister preachin' on false modesty no' a week syne? There's naebodie wha' kens mair aboot Carryckcastle than Leezie Laidlaw, no' MacQuiddy—bless his creaky auld banes—nor the laird hissel'. Certainly no' Gelleys the washerwoman."

"Did you work at the castle, too?" Hannah asked.

"Fifty year," Gelleys said proudly, her great fingers stirring the shelled beans in their bowl. "Went intae service as a wee maid nae bigger than Jennet, and there I stayed until ma shanks wad carry me nae further." She thumped on her knee as if to reprimand it for its poor service. "Thirty year was I heid washerwoman, wi' three guid maids under me. Six days a week did we wash and press."

Jennet let out a resigned sigh, but Gelleys took no note.

"On Monanday table linen, on Tysday bed linen, on Wadensday and Fuirsday clacs, on Freday rags and the like, and on Scturday—" She leaned forward and raised a finger to the air. "On Seturday we set soap. Just as Fiona is settin' soap this verra minute, her and the lasses. Is it no' sae, Jennet?"

"Aye," said Jennet. "They were hard at it when we came doon the brae."

"Ye see. And nivver a day did I miss except when ma lads came intae the world, and when ma guidman left it."

"And sae was it," said Granny Laidlaw, reaching over to grasp Gelleys by the forearm.

The old lady laid her own hand over Granny's. "We've seen a thing or twa, ha' we no', Leezie?"

"That's aye true." Granny Laidlaw turned her face toward Hannah as if she could see her. "Ye've come tae ask aboot Lady Isabel, have ye no'?"

Hannah glanced at Jennet, who simply shrugged a shoulder in surprise.

"How did you know?"

"Why, it's Isabel wha broucht ye and yer family here,

when aa is said and done. Isabel, and ma own dauchter Jean. It's nae wunder ye're curious."

"Ye canna find a soul at Carryckcastle tae tell it," said Gelleys, scowling into her bowl. "But auld carlines like us ha' naucht tae fear frae the truth. Set ye doon, lassie, and hark."

"On the morn my Jean turned ten years old, Isabel came intae the world," began Granny Laidlaw. "It was Lady Marietta's fourth confinement, ye ken—three sons she gave the earl, and aa stillborn. Ye can weel imagine what celebratin' there was at Carryckcastle that day—a healthy bairn, with her mother's bonnie face and her faither's brawlie constitution. And frae the moment oor Jean saw the wean, there was a bond between them."

"As close as sisters ever were," said Gelleys.

"Aye, that close," agreed Granny Laidlaw. "As soon as Isabel could walk she took tae followin' Jean aboot. She spent so much time belowstairs that she was mair at hame in the kitchen than she was in the drawing room. I couldna bring mysel' tae send her awa', sic a bonnie lass she was and sae cheerfu'. But the day came—the summer she was four—that the laird decided that it wadna do for his lass tae be spendin' aa her time wi' the servants."

Jennet was following this story with as much interest and concentration as Hannah. "And that's when the lady made ma mither Isabel's nurse," she volunteered.

Granny Laidlaw's eyes seemed to be following some scene only she could see. "Sae it was. At fourteen, imagine. Nurse and nursery maid, too. It was a verra great honor, wi' Jean sae young. Some wad ca' it foolish tae give a lass sae much responsibility, but Isabel wad ha' nae other and it suited the laird as weel—he didna like the idea o' a strange nurse comin' intae Carryckcastle."

Hannah had been raised to respect the storyteller's rhythm and not to interrupt, but she was confused now

and she had to ask. "And her mother? Wasn't she there to raise Isabel?"

"She was," said Granny Laidlaw, quite firmly, but Gelleys wrinkled her nose in disagreement.

"She was there in bodie, aye, but she wasna there in spirit."

A fine tension rose between the two old women, both of them silent for a moment. Jennet pursed her mouth, impatient and curious and unable to hide either of those things.

"Will ye no' tell the whole story, Granny?"

Gelleys sighed, rubbing the side of her nose with one red knuckle. "It's no' easy tellin' the truth aboot the people ye love best. Come, Leezie," she said in a companionable tone. "Shall I tell it?"

The old lady shook herself out of her daydream. "I'm no' sae auld that I canna tell a tale, Gelleys. And though I dinna like tae admit it, Leddy Carryck was no' the mither she should ha' been."

She folded her hands in her lap. "Now, as young as the baith o' ye are, ye'll ken the truth o' it when I say this: no' every woman makes a mither. Most can bring a bairn intae the world, but wi' some it gaes nae further. And sae it was with Leddy Carryck. The sweetest and maist generous leddy wi' the servants and the tenants and wi' any puir soul wha micht come tae the door wi' an empty kyte—but she couldna take her own wean in her lap tae noozle her, or sing tae her, or tae blether and laugh as aa women do wi' their bairns. And they baith suffered for it."

"It was losin' the lads, aa three," said Gelleys. "Every time they buried a son, the guid leddy put a piece o' hersel' in the grave wi' him. And there was naucht left ower for wee Isabel."

Granny pushed out a great sigh. "And sae Leddy Carryck was glad tae gie the raisin' o' her tae Jean."

"Aye, and Jean had a way wi' the lassie," said Gelleys. "Isabel was willfu', but for Jean she'd do anythin'. And aa was weel until—"

"Gelleys Smaill," interrupted Granny, frowning. "Wha's got the tellin' o' this tale?"

The old washerwoman grimaced. "Then get on wi' it, Leezie. Ye're gettin' verra langsome in yer auld age."

Granny sniffed. "As I was sayin'. Aa was weel until Ian Hope took note o' Jean one summer morn, and she o' him." The small head in its white cap turned toward Jennet, and when she smiled this time a dimple made itself clear on a deeply lined cheek. "One day, hen, ye'll ken what it is tae ha' a barrie young man look at ye the way Ian Hope looked at yer mither. As if the mune hung in the sky just tae shine on her face."

"Yer worse than Rab Burns wi' yer poetry," said Gelleys impatiently. "Can ye no' say it simple? Ian Hope was the richt guidman for Jean, and she the richt guidwife for Ian, and aa could see the truth o' it."

"Ye say it as ye like, and sae will I," said Granny peacefully. "It was a guid match, that's aye true. Ma Roddy was muny years in his grave, but it wad ha' pleased him tae see his lass married tae the son o' Alasdair Hope, just as it pleased the laird and the leddy and me. Aa were seifu' but Isabel.

"The day o' the wedding she went intae the fairy wood and wadna come oot, no' when her faither spake sharp words, no' when her mither spake soft ones. And sae Jean and Ian were joined wi'oot Isabel's blessing or fellowship, and sae far as she was concerned, there had nivver been a wedding, and Ian Hope was naucht but a nuisance tae be ignored. It pained Jean at first tae see the lass sae unhappy, and wi' time it made her mad, and then, why then, Simon came alang—"

"My brither," supplied Jennet.

"When Jennet's brither Simon was born . . . noo, ye can weel imagine that Isabel was jealous, and I suppose the truth o' it was she had cause. For a guid while Jean had nae time for the lass at aa—that was the year ma ees started tae fail, ye ken, and between takin' ower for

me and caring for Simon she was runnin' aa the day lang.

"And in her anger and pyne Isabel marched aff tae her mither and announced that a young leddy o' fifteen doesna need a nurse, and perhaps Carryckcastle could do wi'oot Jean Hope aategither. But the leddy wad ha' nane o' that, and sae it was that Jean came tae me as underhoosekeeper, just when I needed her most. It was a hard year," she said with a sigh.

"A dark year, ava," said Gelleys.

Granny Laidlaw's hands were resting in her lap, fingers twitching slightly. The room had gone silent but for the sound of the dog's snuffled breathing, the whisper of the floor rushes, and the crisp snap of beans as Gelleys continued her way through the great bowl in her lap. This time she did not rush her friend's story, but she watched her closely, as a mother might watch a frail child.

Granny cleared her throat and began again.

"That Janwar Lady Carryck took a fever and slipped awa', so sudden that there was nae time tae—" She paused and closed her eyes. "Tae take leave o' her. And that was the start o' the sorrows."

"In the village ten died o' the same weid," said Gelleys. "And the rains came that spring and wadna stop. And meece got intae the corn, and—"

"And the Campbells," prompted Jennet.

"Aye, the Campbells." Granny's voice rasped with anger or sorrow, Hannah could not tell which. "Every spring the laird sends his men oot tae see that the tenants are gettin' on, and that spring he did the same. Ian Hope and his brither Magnus went west, but Ian nivver came hame again. I had ma guidman for thirty year, but Jean had Ian for less than three, and the losin' o' him stole her youth awa'."

Hannah had lost her own mother when she was very young; she had seen death come suddenly to Elizabeth's brother Julian and more slowly to her own great-

grandfather, all in the last year. She knew sorrow and she understood how loss cut deep and left traces that would never fade, but she knew too that something was not right about the story being pieced together for her. She thought suddenly of Curiosity, who had asked Jennet so many questions in the garden. And here was a question she had not thought to ask:

How was it Jennet's father had died three years before she was born?

Jennet was watching her closely, and the two old women listened and watched, too, willing to let this part of the story be told by someone else.

"Ian Hope was Simon's faither," said Jennet. "But he wasna mine. When ma mither had been widowed for mair than a year, she took anither."

"The earl," said Hannah, seeing now how it all fit together, seeing the way Carryck put his hand on Jennet's head as she bent over a tulip, and hearing his voice, patient and responsive and affectionate. *As my father talks to me,* she thought.

Granny Laidlaw was moving ahead with her story. "Ye're oweryoung tae understan' how sic a thing micht come tae pass," she said, as if Hannah had been thinking critical thoughts. "But Jean was a widow, strugglin' with a young son and bent low by sorrow. And the laird was in mourning for his guidwife, and baith o' them in need o' comfort. Even half-blind I saw it comin'."

"They didn't marry?" Hannah addressed this question to Jennet, but it was Gelleys who answered her.

"Carryck marry his hoosekeeper? It wadna do."

Jennet frowned into her lap, but Granny Laidlaw spoke up clearly. "Stranger things ha' passed, and worse matches ha' been made."

"Och," said the old washerwoman with a real look of distress. "I didna mean tae hurt yer feelings. I canna deny that Jean wad make a fine mistress. But if the truth be tolt—dinna make sic a face at me, we said we'd tell the whole tale—yer Jean was ever an independent

lass, and she likes bein' hoosekeeper better than she wad like bein' Leddy Carryck. Ye've nivver seen sic a bodie for hard work."

Granny inclined her head in grudging agreement. "Yer forgettin' the point o' the story. It was Isabel we were talkin' aboot. Noo." She turned her blank eyes toward Hannah again. "Ye mun understan' that young Isabel had lost her mither, and she turned back to Jean wi' aa the unhappiness aboot Ian Hope set aside. And sae she was nivver tolt aboot Jean and her faither." She paused, her mouth set in a grim line. "Lookin' back, it's clear that it was a mistake. It wad ha been far better tae tell her, and tae let her greet and screech tae the heavens. Better a few tears than what passed later when the truth was kennt."

"Did she find out when Jennet was born?" Hannah asked.

Granny Laidlaw seemed to be studying her hands where they lay on her lap. "Ne," she said thoughtfully. "Isabel nivver asked aboot Jennet's faither. I've thoucht it through ower the years and it's come tae me that she didna ask because she didna care tae see. And what Isabel didna care tae see, she couldna see, and was it richt before her face.

"And sae they went alang, and sae wad it ha' stayed, but for Lammas Fair five years syne, when Isabel met Walter Campbell o' Breadalbane."

The door opened suddenly, letting in a great rush of wind and Jennet's auntie Kate. Her face was flushed and she thumped down her basket so forcefully that they all jumped in their seats.

"The minister is comin'," she said, pulling her cap from her hair. "I couldna put him aff, and though I tried ma best."

Gelleys heaved herself up from the chair with a great groan, clutching the bowl of beans to her generous middle. "Ye ken I luve ye dearly, Leezie, but I canna take tea wi' the minister the-day. It wad put me aff ma parridge for a week."

"But what about the rest of the story?" Hannah asked, looking between them. "What about the Lammas Fair?"

Granny Laidlaw smiled. "That I canna tell ye, lass. Onlie Simon and Isabel were there that day, and Simon was deid a month later. Aa I can say is this: Isabel ran aff wi' a Breadalbane, and she's nivver been hame agin, nor wad she be welcome were she tae come. The Campbells ha' nae place at Carryck, nor will they ever."

"No word for her father?" Hannah asked. "No explanation?"

"She sent Jean a letter," said Granny Laidlaw. "It came a week after she disappeared. I recall it weel, for it was the last thing I ever read for masel' before the blindness came doon hard. She wrote 'As ye sow so shall ye reap. Betrayal begets betrayal.' "

"I canna bide, Guidwife Laidlaw," the minister announced repeatedly as he ate his way through the ginger nuts. "I've come tae make sure ye'll be at the kirk at four—promptly at four, mind—when Gaw'n Hamilton rides the stang."

The minister was as long and thin as a stickbug, with great red-rimmed pop-eyes and a mouth that twitched constantly at one corner. Although he looked very different, something in his expression reminded Hannah of Adam MacKay, and she sat very still in the corner near the hearth.

Jennet had come to sit beside her, and she whispered in Hannah's ear whenever the minister's attention was on the plate before him.

"He's called Holy Willie," she whispered. "For he likes tae pray as loud as ever he can whenever anybodie is near tae hear him."

Hannah gave her a pointed look but Jennet shrugged, unconcerned. "There's naucht tae worra aboot. He's aye deef."

There was a tight, irritated expression on Granny Laidlaw's face, but she listened without interruption as the minister lovingly detailed Mrs. Hamilton's sins: a loud voice, a forward manner, and an irritating and inappropriate interest in men's affairs. Mr. Hamilton's inability to exert the proper authority could not be tolerated; public humiliation was the only solution.

"'He that loveth his son causeth him oft tae feel the rod, that he may ha' joy of him in the end,'" he intoned, wiping crumbs from the corner of his mouth with his little finger. "And I depend on your presence, Guidwife Laidlaw—God-fearin' woman that ye are and aaways ha' been—tae show Guidwife Hamilton the error o' her ways. Jennet Hope!" He turned toward the corner with a sudden snapping motion of his head.

Jennet stiffened. "Aye, Mr. Fisher?"

"You were no' in kirk the Sunday past. Wheest! Excuses wi' do ye nae guid when ye stand at the gates tae have judgment passed upon ye. Woman is the weakest vessel, and ye must be ever vigilant."

Jennet bristled darkly at this, but she held her tongue, to Hannah's amazement.

". . . ye'll come tae the riding o' the stang this day, and ye'll bring the Indian, for we are aa God's creatures. It will do her guid." He drew in a deep breath, warming to his work. "Ye'll bring her alang tae kirk. The laird willna want her in his pew, but we'll find a spot." His great bulbous eyes were flat gray, and they fixed on Jennet, who looked back at him furiously.

"Aye, sir. But she's a guest o' the laird's, and she'll sit wi' him."

Hannah might have said that she had no intention of coming to his kirk at all, but the struggle was between Jennet and the minister, and she would not get in her friend's way.

Mr. Fisher's nostrils trembled and his mouth jerked

at the corner. "We shall see," he said finally. "I'll take it up wi' the laird."

"Aye," said Jennet, ignoring her auntie Kate's distressed look. "That wad be best."

As soon as the ginger nuts were gone, the minister put back his head and prayed loudly to the ceiling for a good five minutes. He was no sooner out the door than Auntie Kate's sober expression gave way to a grimace. "'And the locusts went up over all the land of Egypt,'" she quoted. " 'And rested in all the coasts of Egypt: very grievous were they; before them there were no such locusts as they, neither after them shall be such.' "

Granny Laidlaw snorted. "Why is it that the locusts always ramsh ma ginger nuts? Why canna they be content wi' guid Scots oat cakes? And Jennet, hen—tell me this, why mun ye always provoke the mannie? Does he no' glower and fuss enough?"

Jennet wrinkled her nose. "I canna help masel', Granny. He makes ma tongue gae aa kittlie, and oot comes what I shouldna say."

"One day that kittlie tongue o' yours wi' cause ye sair trouble," said Granny, but it seemed to Hannah that she was more proud than worried.

"Come on, then." Auntie Kate smiled, helping her mother up from her chair. "It'll soon be four."

"Aye, perhaps we can gie puir Marjorie some comfort. But the lasses needna bide, and should it give Holy Willie the watter brash. Awa' tae Carryckcastle wi' ye baith. Geordie will be waitin'."

Jennet went up to her grandmother—the two were 1exactly the same height—and kissed her on the cheek.

Granny Laidlaw put her hands on Jennet's shoulders. "Bless ye, ye're sae much like yer mither. As willfu' as the day is lang. Tell me this, hen—ha' ye shown wee Hannah the kitchen window?"

Hannah's ears pricked up at this, but Jennet's whole

attention was on her grandmother and she did not look
in her direction.

"Ne."

"Then do it, and nae delay."

The goats had found another home, and so Hannah
and Jennet sat shoulder to shoulder at the edge of the
cart with their feet trailing in the dust. They were out of
the village before Hannah could think of a way to ask
her question.

"Do you miss her? Isabel?"

Jennet shrugged. "Aye, at first I did miss her. She
used tae let me comb her hair—sic bonnie dark hair,
heavy and sae soft. Naethin' like mine." She shook her
curls to make her point. "I thoucht she looked like an
angel. I used tae dream that she'd come hame agin and
we'd sleep in the same room, the twa o' us, and talk aa
the nicht through, as true sisters."

Hannah thought of the nights she had shared with
Many-Doves, who was not her sister but her mother's
sister, and she felt sorry for Jennet.

"Perhaps one day you'll see Isabel again, when all
this trouble is over. Where do the Campbells live?"

"The Earl o' Breadalbane, ye mean?"

"Is that the one called Walter who is married to
Isabel?"

Jennet produced an amused grin. "Walter Campbell,
the chief o' the Glenorchy line? Aye, weel, he's slippery
enough tae do the job. Ne, Walter is one o' the earl's
bastards. Breadalbane made him curator o' Loudoun.
That was before Walter ran aff wi' Isabel."

Hannah had grown up hearing her mother and
grandmother and great-grandmother recite their family
history, but she had to admit that the complexities of
the Breadalbane clan were a challenge. She rubbed a
hand over her eyes.

"So Walter Campbell and Isabel live with the Countess of Loudoun?"

Jennet rewarded her with a smile. "Aye, Flora by name. At Loudoun Castle, near Galston. That way—" She pointed west. "But ye willna find Isabel there the noo."

"I wasn't planning on going to look for her," said Hannah, and discovered to her surprise that perhaps her mind had moved a little in that direction.

Jennet tossed her head. "It wad be a lang journey for naucht. The countess is dwaumie—bad lungs, ye ken, and they carry her tae the spa at Moffat for the summer. Isabel and Walter will be there wi' her."

They were silent for a time. "We passed Moffat on the way here from Dumfries."

"Aye. Sae ye did. But what guid wad it serve tae talk tae Isabel?"

Hannah shrugged. "I don't know. I was just wondering." And more quickly: "What was it your granny said about the kitchen window?"

Jennet had an elaborate frown that involved her whole face. She said, "I'll ha' naebodie tae play wi', should ye run aff."

The cart bumped and swayed over the rocky ground. From the village the faint sound of a crowd and howling dogs rose up on the breeze. Dame Sanderson was fighting for her life to please the man who fed her.

"I have a grandmother, too," Hannah said gently. "And she doesn't know what happened to me, or where I am, or even if I'm alive."

Jennet looked straight ahead. "The laird wants yer faither tae stay."

Hannah said nothing. The question was not what the laird wanted—that was clear—but whether Jennet was enough of a friend to put Carryck's wants and wishes aside. For five minutes or more she said nothing, and then Jennet straightened her shoulders resolutely.

"Come on, then." She gathered her skirts together to hop off the wagon.

"Where are we going?" Hannah asked.

"Hame by way o' the kitchen window," Jennet said irritably. "Ye'll see soon enough for yersel'."

They cut up over the brae on a faint path that snaked around and between high stands of gorse covered with tiny yellow flowers. There was a clean, sweet smell about the hillside in the sun and Hannah was so happy to be walking again—walking uphill—that she did not mind the hot prickle of the nettle when it brushed against her bare skin.

A startled grouse rose up out of the heather and Jennet stopped to watch it go, shielding her eyes against the sun. Then she pointed. "Ye see yon rowan tree?"

Hannah did, and said so.

"There's a path there that gaes doon tae the north side o' Aidan Rig. It's aye steep and rocky, and I wadna chance it in the wet."

They walked on in silence, Hannah working hard to remark the way: a boulder in the shape of a man's face with moss pushing up through cracks in his cheeks, a stand of three thistles taller than herself, and just beyond a grouping of young white pines.

In the meager shade of one of the trees Jennet set herself on a large rock and wiped her face on her sleeve. They were close enough to the falls to hear the rushing of water.

Hannah climbed up a boulder to get her bearings. Just over this rise must be the wood that ran down to Carryckcastle.

"No' that road," said Jennet, reading her thoughts.

They walked through the wood for a good ways, Hannah memorizing the trees as she went and marking the position of the sun. All the time the sound of the waterfalls was getting louder, and then the forest opened up.

They stood on the shoulder of the mountain, with the whole valley spread out before them. A hawk circled on the uplifting wind, a sign too obvious to be overlooked. The skin on Hannah's back rose in a shimmer of renewed hope, as sweet and cool as the mist of the waterfall rising up around them.

Jennet put her mouth to Hannah's ear to be heard over the waterfalls. "There's nae time tae show ye the way doon tae the vale but ye see there—" She pointed. "The path. Ye need a guid hour, in the daylight."

They followed a spring up from the rock face and back into the forest to where it disappeared into the ground. Jennet turned to look at her, and Hannah saw many things on her face: sadness and resignation, and through that still a sense of excitement.

"Have ye heard tell aboot the Rising of '15, and the troubles that came after for the Jacobites?"

"A little," Hannah said, trying to remember the stories her Granny Cora had told. "Did the Duke of Argyll defeat the Stewarts?"

Jennet bristled. "Campbell defeat the Jacobites? Och, and wha's been tellin' ye such falsehoods? Oor troops walloped the usurper's men soundly at Dunblane!" Then her face fell. "But it was aa for naucht. Bobbin' John lost his nerve, ye see, and he fled tae France and betrayed muny guid men tae the Crown. And in the years that followed those wha were loyal tae the Auld Pretender paid dearly, for the Hanoverians werena wont tae be forgivin'. And that's why the third earl built Forbes Tower."

She gave Hannah a very close look. "Have ye took note o' how thick the walls are inside the kitchen?"

Hannah had not, really, and she admitted this.

"Six feet thick, can ye imagine? Ye see, in those days the earl needed a safe place. A hidey-hole and a way oot o' the castle, should the usurper's men ever take it intae their heids tae come askin' questions. And sae he built a stair intae the kitchen wall that goes doon tae the tunnels."

And without further explanation Jennet pushed aside the bushes to reveal a dark opening.

They walked with hands stretched out, trailing fingers along the walls as they went through the dark. There was the rustle of dry leaves underfoot and the scent of trodden pine needles and mouse droppings. They walked for a good while, and Jennet stopped. Hannah could not see her, but she could feel her warmth, and when she spoke her breath touched Hannah's face.

"Here's the door," she said. "We're under the castle."

The door swung open with a creak. On the other side there was a narrow hall with a low ceiling, lit by a single hanging lantern. To the left was a small stone stair. MacQuiddy's voice drifted down to them.

"Arguin' wi' Cook," said Jennet with a sigh. "We'll wait until he's awa'."

"Where does this corridor go?" Hannah asked, peering into the shadows.

"Doon tae Campbell Tower."

"The pit?" Hannah stepped in that direction.

"The hidey-hole under the pit." Jennet sat herself on the stone step and started rummaging in her apron for food, coming up with an apple which she broke in half.

"There's naebodie there the noo," she said, biting into her half and offering Hannah the other.

"Nobody at all," said a man's voice from the shadows, and both girls leaped to their feet just as Mac Stoker came forward, limping under the weight of a sack over his shoulder.

"The pirate," breathed Jennet.

There was a sheen of sweat on his brow, but his color was much better. Hannah realized that it was many days since she had last seen him or asked the Hakim about his condition—a vague guilt washed over

her at that thought—but it was clear that he was much better.

"Ladies. Sneakin' in through the kitchen, is it?"

"Where are you going?" Hannah asked.

"Sure, and have you forgot your manners?" He shifted his sack and there was the muffled clank of metal on metal. "Lucky for youse I've no time to be giving you any lessons. I'm away, to find me ship and me crew and the sweet Giselle, o' course. To settle accounts." There was nothing cheerful about his smile.

"Does the laird ken ye're goin'?" asked Jennet. She had stepped back a bit, just behind Hannah.

"Sure, and why should he care? He has no further need of me. So I'll thank youse to step out o' me way."

"We'll need passage home," Hannah said. "Soon."

He laughed, putting back his head to show the scar around his neck.

"Ah, you're your father's daughter, I'll say that for you. Give him this message from Mac Stoker: next time he wants to put a foot on a ship of mine, he'll pay me first. In gold."

27

"Now look at this." Curiosity stood at the open door with her arms crossed. "A house so big you got to write a letter to send word from one end to the other. That from the earl?"

The footman extended the note on a small silver platter. "Aye, mem."

"Ain't for me, I'm sure."

"No, mem. For Mr. Bonner."

Nathaniel had been walking back and forth to exercise his leg, and he came to the door to take the letter. But Curiosity was not yet done with the footman.

"MacAdam, is that right?"

"Aye, mem."

"Mr. MacAdam, tell me now, what was all the fuss in the courtyard earlier?"

He blinked. "Visitors for the earl, mem."

"Is that so. Anybody interesting?"

MacAdam's face crumpled in surprise, and then straightened. Nathaniel wondered if Curiosity would keep him there until she made the man laugh out loud.

"Monsieur Contrecoeur, mem, an associate o' the earl's. And two French ladies wi' him."

"That's what I wanted to know. Thank you kindly, Mr. MacAdam."

He bowed from the waist. "Is there a reply, Mr. Bonner?"

"Not right yet," Nathaniel said.

Curiosity said, "Before you go, tell me—have you seen our Hannah anywhere?"

He stopped. "She's in the kitchens, mem, suppin' on bread and new milk wi' Jennet."

"Is she, now? Thank you kindly."

She closed the door behind him and came over to Nathaniel where he was unfolding the note in the light of the window.

"You've made a conquest of that footman, Curiosity. I expect he'd tell you anything you care to ask."

"All it takes is some common courtesy," she said. "Now, what the earl got to say that he cain't tell you to your face?"

"We are summoned to dine."

Curiosity took it from him and held the heavy paper away, squinting at it. "You and your lady. Elizabeth won't like it."

"Elizabeth won't like what?"

She stood at the door to the dressing room, fixing the buttons on her bodice. She was wearing her gray linen again, and she seemed much more at ease. Nathaniel held out an arm, and she came to him.

"The little ones sleeping?"

"They are, finally. Now, what is it I won't like?"

"The earl wants to see the two of you at his dinner table," said Curiosity. "I suppose he wants to show you off to his friends from France."

"We don't need to go, Boots."

There was a line between her brows as she thought it through, and then she surprised him. "I think we should accept," she said. "Perhaps there is something to be learned from them."

•   •   •

Elizabeth had no interest in the earl's dinner guests, but she did hope that Monsieur Dupuis would be there, to lay her hazy fears to rest. She had asked about him today in the expectation that she could bring him and Nathaniel face-to-face, but thus far there had been no response.

She went to dress for dinner in a poor mood, made worse by the sad state of her best gown.

"No' the gray, mem," Mally said, unable to hide her horror at the idea. "No' wi' the ladies frae France at the table, and them sae fine."

"I do not care a fig what they think of my gown," Elizabeth said, trying very hard to mean what she said. "They will talk to me nonetheless, I am sure."

"Gin ye'll pardon me, mem—" Mally broke off and then started again, very earnestly. "If ye take yer place at the table lookin' like a puir governess, it willna matter what ye ha' tae say. They canna see beyond the claes. It's the way o' rich folk."

Elizabeth did not doubt Mally's sincerity and good-will, nor could she deny the simple truth of what she said. Rich French merchants and their wives would dismiss her out of hand if she went to the earl's table in a much mended Quaker-gray dress. The question was, did she really care if they took no note of her? Why had she agreed to this dinner at all?

A voice kept whispering that these French had something to do with Dupuis, and more—that Dupuis held the key to the mystery that had brought them here in the first place. Perhaps she was being silly and superstitious; perhaps tonight's dinner would give them a way to getting home.

"Very well, Mally. But nothing too pretentious. Did Miss Somerville have no simple gowns?"

Mally considered. "There's this lovely silk gauze. See the silver shells sae delicate on the hem. Or the silk drugget, wi' the fine embroidery."

They were beautiful, and Elizabeth resented them greatly even while she admired their artistry: silk

pongee, sequins of gold and silver paper appliquéd with invisible stitches, chenille embroidery, tiny pleats.

"A thousand hours o' work," said Mally, reading her mind. "Yer Miss Somerville had a verra guid seamstress, mem, and ye dinna mind me sayin'. She should be richt proud o' this fine stitchery."

"Yes," Elizabeth said, taking some satisfaction in this idea of the seamstress, whose work deserved to be admired. "So she must. The silk drugget, I think, Mally. Subtlety is the thing."

"Lord above," said Curiosity, breaking out into a great smile. "Is that you, Elizabeth?"

"I don't feel much like myself, I must admit." Elizabeth drew in a long breath and let it go again. "But it is only for one evening and tomorrow I will be back in my own clothes. Aren't you going to say anything, Nathaniel?"

He grinned at her. "I like you better in deerskin, Boots, but I can't deny how pretty you look."

It was a great irritation to her that she could not accept a simple compliment from her husband without flushing, but he was kind enough to take no note. Elizabeth gathered her shawl around her. The bodice of the gown was very low, indeed, and motherhood had made sure that she filled it just short of overflowing.

Nathaniel had had an easier time dressing. She made a turn around him. The cut of the dark blue coat was out of fashion, but the materials and workmanship were impeccable. The breeches and stockings were severe in line but very elegant, and the cloak that lay over a chair was lined with silk the same color as the coat. Understated, and effective.

"The earl was no macaroni as a younger man."

Curiosity laughed out loud. "A *macaroni*? What is that?"

"A man who spends too much of his income on his

wardrobe, and too much time before the looking glass,"
said Elizabeth.

"Not our Nathaniel," said Curiosity with a certain
satisfaction. "He sent back the flowered waistcoat.
Posies just don' suit the man."

And it was true: no clothes could do him justice.
Suddenly Elizabeth was glad that she had worn Giselle's
fine gown. She knew he really would prefer her in doeskin or gray linen, but tonight at least she would not be
a moth to his butterfly.

She smiled at him, and he took her arm.

"Let's get this over with, Boots. Then you and me
can take a walk in the garden I've heard so much
about."

In the hall they ran into Hannah, who drew up short
at the sight of them, her mouth falling open.

"Is it such a shock to see us well groomed?" Elizabeth
asked, putting a finger under her jaw to close it gently.

"Yes. No." She shook herself. "Are you going to eat
with the earl?"

"We are."

Hannah clenched her hands together before herself.
"But I wanted to talk to you about the village—"

Nathaniel frowned down at her, and put a hand on
her shoulder. "Are you all right, Squirrel? Trouble?"

"No." She swallowed. "No trouble. Just a story I
heard in the village—"

"You wait up for us," said Nathaniel. "We'll want to
hear it as soon as we get back."

The Frenchwomen were not wives at all. Madame Marie
Vigée was a widow and distant cousin to Monsieur
Contrecoeur, a wine merchant who had taken up residence in London. She was chaperoning her niece,
Mademoiselle Julie LeBrun, on her first tour of England
and Scotland. They presented the whole undertaking as
a lark, a journey for her amusement alone, but Elizabeth

knew without being told that these ladies had escaped the Terror in France, although not in any huge rush— they had brought their finery with them, including the mass of purple feathers that trembled above Madame Vigée's elaborately piled hair. The question was, why were they abroad in Scotland when sentiments against the French were so much in evidence? There was a story here, one that might be worth hearing.

But neither of the Frenchwomen were the type to tell such stories, or any stories at all. Julie LeBrun was very young, and the company either bored or intimidated her, for she kept her eyes on her plate, ate almost nothing, never spoke unless addressed, and then in a hesitant and diffident tone. Madame Vigée seemed more interested in her wine glass than in conversation, although she turned a generous smile toward the earl at every opportunity.

But it was the men at the table who surprised her. The earl, because he studied his guests at length but spoke so little; and Monsieur Contrecoeur.

He was a man of medium height, solidly built and muscled, and no longer young. His beard was entirely gray, as was the mane of hair severely combed back and tied in a queue. His face was still beautiful—there was no other word for it—but even in such perfectly proportioned features, his eyes drew attention. They were wide set and intensely blue-green, a color Elizabeth had never before seen. Aunt Merriweather would have found them excessive, and for once Elizabeth would have to agree. But he had an easy air about him, and a keen intelligence and calm that were as obvious as the strange color of his eyes and his odd habit of wearing gloves throughout the meal.

Contrecoeur's English had only the hint of an accent. "Mrs. Bonner." He focused his unsettling gaze on Elizabeth.

"Sir?"

"I understand that you grew up in Devon?"

"I did, sir, at Oakmere. Lady Crofton is my aunt. Have your travels taken you to Devon, Madame Vigée?"

"Devon?" Madame Vigée's head reared back and she looked at Elizabeth down the long slope of her nose. "There is nothing worth seeing south of London. It is all cows and peasants."

"Ain't France south of London?" Nathaniel asked, and Elizabeth hid her smile in her wine glass.

Madame Vigée pursed her mouth at him, but addressed Elizabeth. "Despite all its beauties, you left Devon for the Colonies, madame. How very . . . enterprising of you." Her gaze flickered toward Nathaniel and away again. Elizabeth had spent too many hours in drawing rooms to mistake her: *You could not find a husband at home, and so you cast your net in other waters.*

"I went to New-York to start a school," Elizabeth said. "And that is what I did. I will return to it, as soon as I may."

"A school?" Madame Vigée's eyes narrowed. "What an astounding thing for a young woman of fortune and family to do. Did your father not stop you?"

"He tried," Nathaniel said dryly.

Madame Vigée's wine glass paused in its path to her mouth. "But who could there be to teach, in your wilderness?"

"The children of the village, of course," Elizabeth said. "Quite a number of them."

Madame Vigée drew herself up into a disdainful posture. "The poor?"

"I suppose poor is about all we've got in Paradise. By your standards, anyway." Nathaniel sent a sidelong glance toward the earl.

But he had nothing to contribute to the conversation, and Madame Vigée clearly took this for approbation. She set her sights more firmly on Elizabeth.

"Madame Bonner. Do you not realize that by teaching the lowest classes to read and write, you take them out of

the station assigned to them by Providence and nature? It is this kind of foolish egalitarianism that is destroying France, madame. Have you not heard of the guillotine?"

The earl cleared his throat, and she turned to him eagerly. "Do you not agree, my lord Earl?"

He considered her for a moment, and then he shook his head. "No, madame. I dinna. The guillotine has mair tae do wi' bread than books."

Madame Vigée gave him a very disappointed look. "So the rabble would have us believe."

One white brow shot up in amusement. "Are ye callin' me gullible, madame, or rabble?"

The older woman's complexion went very pale beneath her rouge. "Neither, my lord. You mistake me. My point was simply that Madame Bonner has taken on a task of dubious merit. She should have stayed at home in Devon, where she could do no damage."

Before Elizabeth could respond to this impertinence, Nathaniel laughed out loud.

Madame Vigée looked at him as if he had belched. "I amuse you, sir?"

"By Christ, you do. Here you sit in Scotland, tellin' my wife she should have stayed at home. I'm right glad she didn't. England's loss was New-York's gain. And mine, to be blunt about it." And he ran a hand down Elizabeth's arm. It was such an affectionate and intimate gesture that she blushed to the roots of her hair, but it pleased her inordinately.

Madame Vigée's own jaw dropped in amazement, but Monsieur Contrecoeur jumped in before she could comment.

"I have visited Devon on business. It is a beautiful place, but it cannot be compared to the great forests of New-York."

Nathaniel turned to him with real interest. "You know our forests?"

"My work has taken me many places," said Contrecoeur.

"Is that how you met Monsieur Dupuis?" Elizabeth asked in the same polite and disinterested tone she might have asked him the time of day.

The earl put down his wine glass with a thump. "The gentlemen are colleagues."

Elizabeth said, "It is unfortunate that Monsieur Dupuis is too ill to join us tonight. He expressed an interest in meeting my husband."

Carryck's head came up slowly, his displeasure clear to see. "I canna allow it. The cancer has unsettled his mind."

Elizabeth remembered with great clarity the many dinners like this one she had endured at Oakmere. In polite society—in this kind of polite society—older ladies might speak their mind, but the young ones were not to discuss anything of importance, to ask a substantive question, or to express a real opinion. If a young woman was so brash as to turn her attention to any thing but the affairs of the neighborhood, music, or needlework, it was taken as a sign of excessive reading, a naturally intractable disposition, or an indulgent upbringing. Clearly Carryck—and Madame Vigée—were convinced she was a product of all three.

The old rebellious spirit that had gotten her through so many years at her aunt's table rushed up through her.

"It is a very unsettling disease indeed, my lord, if it gifts him with the knowledge of the Mohawk tongue while it robs him of his life."

There was a moment's awkward silence.

Monsieur Contrecoeur said, "Merchants are by nature inquisitive, madame, and must develop an ear for languages. I myself learned Huron during my time in Canada. And I speak French, Polish, German, Italian, and Russian."

"Huron?" Nathaniel asked, rather sharply. "How do you come to learning Huron?"

"The fur trade in Canada," said Contrecoeur. "I spent a number of years there."

Mademoiselle LeBrun's expression had not changed through all the table conversation, but she suddenly woke up from her daydream.

"Maman is in Russia." She had a very pretty smile in spite of a crooked front tooth, and it occurred to Elizabeth that she might not be so much bored with her company as simply shy and homesick.

"I have always been curious about Russia," Elizabeth said. "Perhaps you can join your mother there one day?"

"I will. Monsieur Contrecoeur is taking me with him to Russia to see her. The Russian court is very civilized," the girl offered, as if Elizabeth had expressed concern. "They all speak French."

Madame Vigée gestured to the footman for more wine. "We shall see about Russia, my dear. We shall see."

Nathaniel took her arm as they walked through the night garden in a hush punctuated by the soft trill of crickets and the rustle of Elizabeth's skirts along the path. Even in the cool dark the scent of the roses and phlox hung heavy in the air. Behind them, light still burned in the windows of the dining room.

"You let that woman get to you," Nathaniel said, slipping an arm around her shoulders. "I thought any minute you'd start quoting your Mrs. Wollstonecraft at her."

Elizabeth was irritated still, but this made her smile. "I was tempted, I admit it."

"I wish you had," Nathaniel said. "I would have liked to see her face. Now, what do you suppose that visit's really about?"

She glanced back over her shoulder. "Monsieur Dupuis."

"You haven't even laid eyes on the man, but he's on your mind a lot. Is there something you ain't told me?"

"Nothing concrete," Elizabeth said. "Just a vague feeling. Which I might have discounted, if it weren't for Carryck's defensiveness when I raised the subject."

"Maybe it ain't about Dupuis at all," Nathaniel said. "Maybe it was the visitors who put him in a sour mood. I got the idea that maybe the aunt is trying to marry the young one off to Carryck."

Elizabeth pulled up in surprise. Such matches were not unknown, and in fact Julie LeBrun was typical of those young girls of good—but impoverished—family who were often married to rich old men. Men with lands and titles, in need of an heir. It made some sense, and she wondered why it had not occurred to her.

"I guess not," said Nathaniel, seeing her expression.

"No," Elizabeth said. "There may be something to what you say, Nathaniel. But a French woman? And why wait so long, if he is hoping to father another heir? It has been a few years since his daughter ran away."

"Because he had high hopes for my father," Nathaniel said. "Or me, or Daniel."

Elizabeth did not like to think of it, but it was true: Daniel alone would serve the earl's purpose. The question was, just how desperate was he?

Nathaniel said, "Maybe it's finally getting through to him that we don't want to be here. Maybe he's still thinking of his wife. Or maybe he didn't want the trouble of a girl that young. A man that age—they say with some the urge just goes away."

"Not in his case," Elizabeth said. "There was a woman in his chambers a few nights ago. I saw her at the window."

"Is that so? Did you recognize her?"

"It was Mrs. Hope," Elizabeth said. "At first I thought I must be mistaken, but as I look back on it I am more and more sure. You do not seem surprised."

"I ain't, especially. She's a widow woman, and he's

lost his wife. I wouldn't call it unusual if they take some comfort from one another now and then."

"Curiosity thinks that Jennet is the earl's daughter."

Nathaniel laughed. "What else have you two figured out between you when I wasn't listening?"

"I didn't say that I agreed with her, Nathaniel. It seems to me unlikely that the earl . . ." She paused. "There is a great difference in their ages, and in their stations."

"You sound like your aunt Merriweather," Nathaniel said. "You know as well as anybody that the rules don't count for much when things start to happen between two like-minded people."

Elizabeth paused. "It is not so simple as you would make it. Those rules, as you call them, are still very much in place here, Nathaniel. If they are truly attached to each other, why have they not married? No, I will tell you. Because it would be a scandal of the first order for the earl to marry his housekeeper, no matter how well suited they may be."

"I don't doubt what you say, Boots. You know this world better than I do. But I'll tell you this much—if Mrs. Hope bore him a son, he'd marry her right quick. And I'd wager quite a lot on that."

The truth of this could not be denied. "You do not know she is at fault, Nathaniel. It might be—" She stopped.

"That he's infertile? With a daughter he claims as his own?"

Elizabeth broke off a sprig of lavender and brushed it against her cheek as she thought. "You are right, it is unlikely that the fault is entirely his. It does give Mademoiselle LeBrun's visit a new angle. It would speak to the earl's desperation. If it is so, I feel some sympathy for Mrs. Hope."

"And for the earl," Nathaniel added. "It's a high price to pay, turning the woman you love away because

she cain't give you a son. I still don't understand what's at the bottom of all this, Boots. But I'll tell you this much. Tomorrow I'll get some straight answers, or we'll leave this place with or without my father."

They walked on for a moment in silence. An owl called from the woods that climbed the hill, once and then again.

Finally she said, "Where are we going?"

He smiled a little. "What makes you think we're going anywhere at all?"

She tugged at his arm. "I know you well enough to tell when you've got a plan, Nathaniel Bonner. And why else would you suddenly get an urge to see the grounds?"

He sent her a sidelong glance. "Maybe I just want to be out-of-doors."

"You can be outside whenever you please, after all."

His expression went very still, and his whole posture changed. He steered her toward a bench under an arbor draped with twisting wisteria.

"Nathaniel?"

"Let me rest my leg here for a minute."

The garden spread out around them, silver stippled in the moonlight. It was a pleasant spot to sit, but Nathaniel's unease made it hard to take any diversion in the fine night.

He said, "I wonder sometimes how Carryck breathes, with so many people around him all day long. Don't it bother you, Boots?"

His tone was easy, but there was a tautness in his hand where it rested on her leg. He was asking something important, and perhaps he did not even realize it himself.

She took up his hand—she wondered sometimes if he knew what an effect even the sight of his hands had on her—and held it between her own two. "Nathaniel. I would wish us home this moment, if I could. This place—" She gestured around them. "None of this means anything to me."

He pulled her closer, wrapped his arms around her to bury his face in the crook of her shoulder.

"Thank God," he muttered.

"You did not really think I might want to stay in Scotland? Surely you know me better."

He touched her hair, smoothing it back from her face. "I was getting worried. Seeing you like this—" His fingers plucked at her gown. "I don't know, Boots. Seems like you were born to this kind of life."

"Oh, Nathaniel." She pulled his face closer and kissed him. "I left this world of my own free will once before. I was never happy. Why would I want to stay now?"

He shrugged, and she could feel him searching for words. "It ain't an easy life, back in Paradise."

"Ease is highly overrated."

"Is it? I hope you'll still feel that way in ten years or so."

"Nathaniel Bonner, do you doubt me?"

He pulled her close. "Never in this world."

This kiss was nothing playful; it was rough and sure, as purposeful as the hand that cupped her breast. He tasted of red wine and spiced peaches; his cheeks were rough with new beard.

When he let her catch her breath she said, "You take delight in putting me in these awkward situations."

"Want me to stop?" Even while his hands slipped into her bodice.

"Oh, no," Elizabeth said, pulling his face back down to kiss him of her own accord. "Nothing so rash as that."

A whirlwind of a kiss. She let it pull her along, feeling the center of herself go liquid and soft, no matter what her rational mind was saying about this exposed place, the nearness of the castle, the many windows where light still burned.

He lifted her so that she knelt over his lap, her skirts flung out. The shoulder of her gown had slipped to ex-

pose one breast and he tipped her backward to nuzzle, licking and suckling until she gasped with it.

"Your leg?" She touched his thigh where it was bandaged beneath his breeches.

"Never mind my leg." He caught her hand and put it where he wanted it. And then his own hands worked their way under petticoats and up her thighs, thumbs seeking. He was short of breath, this man who could run a mile without a hitch or pause, and how that pleased her. To have him want her so much: it was a gift he gave to her. And still, the wind moved in the gnarled limbs of the fruit trees and called her out of herself.

She raised her head. "Nathaniel. Perhaps we should—"

But he cut her off. Used his mouth and tongue and the strength of his desire to distract her, drawing her so close that she could not have taken note of the rest of the world even if it were to burst into flame. His hands busied themselves with silk and gauze and the flies on his breeches. Knuckles rasped against her tenderest flesh and then he lifted her, spread fingered.

"Aye," his breath warm against her ear as he fit himself to her, seeking and finding, and losing himself in the process. "We should."

They started back by way of the north side of the castle, arm in arm.

"You're asleep on your feet, Boots. Maybe I should carry you."

It was a tempting idea, as each and every one of her bones felt twice its normal weight.

"I should make you carry me," she said. "Perhaps then you would begin to see the advantage of keeping this kind of activity in the bedchamber."

His thumb traveled down her spine. "What kind of activity is that?"

"Public fornication," she said.

He choked on a laugh, and she pinched him.

"You needn't be so very satisfied with yourself. Someday we will get caught out. And I will leave the explaining to you."

"But I am satisfied," he said, pulling her in close as his hand traced her backside. "And so are you, darlin'. Ain't that explanation enough?"

She batted his hand away. "I should like to see you make that argument to Mr. MacQuiddy," Elizabeth said. "I believe he would box your ears, though he should have to climb up on a ladder to do it."

Nathaniel's laughter died away suddenly.

Before them was Elphinstone Tower. Hannah called this the secret tower, but it looked anything but secret at this moment. Some kind of gathering was going on, and no one had bothered to close the draperies.

Nathaniel took her arm and pulled her away, around the corner and toward the gates into the courtyard. They did not speak until they were out of the guard's hearing.

"What did Hannah say about that tower?"

She lifted a shoulder. "Not so very much, Nathaniel. Apparently Lady Carryck's chambers were locked at her death, on the earl's orders. She did not admit to it, but I would not be surprised if Jennet took her there somehow."

He said, "Right now it don't look locked at all."

"Perhaps the earl likes to spend some time there in privacy," Elizabeth suggested. "Perhaps he took his guests to see his lady's portrait. Did you recognize anyone?"

Nathaniel nodded. "Carryck himself, and Contrecoeur."

"And Mrs. Hope," she added. "But it may well be completely innocent, Nathaniel."

"Maybe so. But there's something about the way they were standing there. Can't put my finger on it right now."

"Nathaniel." Elizabeth pulled his face around to her,

and looked hard into his eyes. "They might be playing whist, for all we know."

He frowned at her. "Do you really believe that, Boots?"

Elizabeth shifted uncomfortably. Her upbringing told her that it was wrong to be so inquisitive about something obviously meant to be private; her experience with Moncrieff and Carryck made it clear that propriety and good manners were a luxury she must do without. None of it quite fit together, and it would keep her awake tonight.

They were in the hall off the courtyard when Nathaniel said, "What I want to know is, what Contrecoeur has got to do with all this."

"So do I, Nathaniel. But it can wait until tomorrow, can it not?"

He didn't even hear her. His attention had shifted away suddenly, as if he had caught the scent of something he had been looking for.

"Moncrieff."

She heard only the sound of steps in the Great Hall, but she had no doubt that Nathaniel was right. She followed him.

The courtyard lantern cast enough light through the windows to show them that the room was empty. Then Elizabeth's eyes adjusted to the shadows and she saw Angus Moncrieff at the far end of the hall, near the door that must lead to Elphinstone Tower.

"Avoiding us, Angus?" Nathaniel's voice echoed slightly. "Where you off to in such a hurry?"

They had narrowed the distance between them considerably before Moncrieff spoke.

"I have business," he said stiffly.

"With the earl," Nathaniel supplied. "And so do we. Maybe we'll just come along."

"I canna allow it," said Moncrieff. In the vague light

Elizabeth could see the perspiration on his forehead, just as she could read the flush of anger that ran through Nathaniel by the way his back straightened. But there was nothing of it in his voice.

"Now, that's curious," Nathaniel said, stopping just in front of the man. "You thinkin' you can forbid me anything at all."

In a corner a mouse scratched and worried, and for a moment that was the only sound. Then in one quick movement Nathaniel reached out and neatly plucked a string that hung around Moncrieff's neck and disappeared into his shirt. The string broke and Moncrieff jerked in surprise, his voice spiking in outrage. "What's this? Have ye no decency, man?"

Nathaniel stepped back, examining his prize.

"That was ma faither's. Ye've no use for it."

"I ain't so sure."

Elizabeth came closer to look, and was surprised to see that it was not a pendant or medallion, but a simple square of soft dark material, half the length of Nathaniel's thumb. In its middle was another square, this one of white linen sewn down with a zigzag stitch. The whole was faded and frayed at the edges, and the image on the white linen was so faint that Elizabeth could not make it out in the poor light.

"I'll thank ye tae give it back," Moncrieff said sharply. "It's got nothing to do with you."

"You'll thank me. Now, that's a novelty, ain't it. The earl wears something just like this around his neck too."

Moncrieff's head snapped back. "How—" And then, his whole body shaking in anger: "Ye canna ha' seen what the earl wears or doesna wear around his neck!"

"Maybe not, but you just told me what I suspected. So what is this thing?"

"I'll say nae more."

Nathaniel held it out to Elizabeth. "Do you recognize this, Boots?"

Elizabeth took it and went to the window to study it by the courtyard light.

"I do not," she said. "And it is too faded to read. But perhaps there is someone we could ask. The earl?"

Moncrieff stilled suddenly. "Ye canna bother the laird wi' this."

"I don't see why not." Nathaniel reached for the door. "He's up there in the tower, entertaining his visitors. A few more won't hurt."

"Ye have no idea," Moncrieff said.

Elizabeth said, "Exactly. That is exactly why we must persevere."

Whatever he had been expecting, the tower room took Nathaniel by surprise. It smelled nothing of a battlefield surgery and wounds gone bad.

Most of the people who had been here just ten minutes ago were gone. The Hakim stood close by, and on a chair next to a narrow bed sat Monsieur Contrecoeur, still dressed as he had been for dinner, all in black from the fine coat and breeches to his gloves. He had come here in a hurry, and the reason was clear: the man in the bed was dying.

"I tried—" Moncrieff began, and the Frenchman cut him off with a raised hand.

"Never mind, Angus. It doesn't matter now."

"Where's the earl?" Nathaniel addressed Contrecoeur directly, in part to see if he would lie.

"In the chamber just above us. I asked for a few minutes alone with Georges," said Contrecoeur.

"This is Monsieur Dupuis?" Elizabeth directed her question to the Hakim, but Moncrieff answered.

"Aye." Moncrieff's tone was bitter. "He's dying, as ye can see for yesel'. Will you no' leave him in peace?"

Nathaniel crossed the room and looked down.

The man in the bed blinked up at him, his eyes hazy with pain. Around his neck was a cloth medallion like

the one Nathaniel had taken from Moncrieff. A crucifix hung over the bed. A dying man; a Catholic. A stranger.

Then he smiled, and Nathaniel recognized him.

He was clean shaven, where once he had worn his beard long and ragged. The beard had first earned him the name Dog-Face from the Kahnyen'kehàka—an honor they reserved for the hairiest and ugliest O'seronni. But the priest had proved himself stronger and braver than his countrymen, walking the gauntlet without a sound, falling under one blow to get up again and take the next, and all so that he might be allowed to tell them stories of his strange O'seronni heaven. They had renamed him Iron-Dog.

"Wolf-Running-Fast," he whispered in the language of Nathaniel's adopted people. "You are here at last."

Nathaniel fell without a struggle into the rhythms of the language, and the things it demanded of him. "Iron-Dog, my friend. On the Great River they tell stories of you. They say that the Seneca burned you and ate your heart. They tell stories of your bravery."

Dupuis hitched a breath and let it go in a long wheezing sigh. "God delivered me from that fate," he said, switching into English. "He had other work for me, here."

"What work?"

That saintly smile, the one that had set him apart. "You know as well as I do. To see you and your father reunited with your family."

"You're the one who told Carryck where to find us."

He swallowed, and the tumors on his neck writhed like living things. "I told Moncrieff where to start looking. It took a long time. Almost too long." He closed his eyes, and for a moment Nathaniel thought he had gone to sleep, but he spoke again, his voice as strong as before.

"Your lady wife."

"Aye," Nathaniel said. "This is Elizabeth."

"English?"

Elizabeth stepped forward. "Yes, sir. I am English."

He swallowed again and held out a long white hand, his palm crisscrossed with old scars.

Once Nathaniel had allowed this man to baptize him although he had not ever believed, not in his god or his devil. But Iron-Dog was one of the few white men who had earned his respect in those days. Nathaniel took the offered hand.

Dupuis pulled him forward. His breath was sweet with laudanum.

"I baptized you by my own hand," he whispered. "But I can direct you no further on your journey. Listen to Contrecoeur. He will be your guide."

"I do not want him as a guide," Nathaniel said, because he would not lie to this man, on his deathbed or anywhere else.

"But you need him," said Iron-Dog. "As he needs you."

28

Contrecoeur led the way up the circle of stairs, followed by Elizabeth and Nathaniel. Moncrieff came close behind, sucking in each breath and pushing it out step by step.

Another tower chamber, but no sickroom this time. Like the rest of the castle it was overfilled with fancy furniture, paintings and china figurines and ivory carvings. A dozen wax candles were all burning at once, so that shadows jumped on polished silver and brass.

"Lady Carryck's chambers," Elizabeth said. She pointed with her chin. "You see, there is her portrait over the mantel."

It meant nothing to Nathaniel—one more pretty picture, this time a woman with hair the color of amber. The earl's dead wife. Nathaniel took Elizabeth's elbow to keep her next to him.

Carryck waited for them at a table, his hand curled around a cup. Mrs. Hope was on the other side of the room with sewing in her lap. She stood and smoothed her skirt, spoke without looking at anybody.

"I'll bide below."

"Stay where ye are, Jean." Carryck's voice was steady; nothing especially affectionate in his tone, noth-

ing to indicate what they might be to each other except for the fact that he called her Jean, in this place where first names were such rare currency.

The housekeeper sat down again and folded her hands in her lap. When Nathaniel met her gaze she looked away.

Candlelight was kind to old faces, but even so the earl looked his age; the whisky, maybe. Or sorrow for Dupuis. Nathaniel could still not quite get his mind around the fact that Iron-Dog was here. What it meant, how he fit in to all of this.

"Come then and sit ye doon."

The earl poured whisky for all of them—Elizabeth, too—and the room was filled with the bright, sharp smell of it. Nathaniel had never much liked hard liquor but he drank what was put before him, just as he took his turn with the pipe when it went around the Kahnyen'kehàka council fire.

It was Carryck who broke the silence.

"Ye've been waitin' a guid while tae say what it is ye have tae say, Bonner. I'll listen now, and then I'll take my turn and tell ye what ye need tae understand."

Elizabeth put her hand lightly on Nathaniel's knee under the table, and he covered it with his own. Then he looked the earl directly in the eye.

"My mother used to say that if you can't show a man respect when you sit down at his table, then don't accept his invitation. Now we're sitting here at your table, but it wasn't an invitation that brought us to this place. So maybe that gives me leave to say what I'm thinking."

"By all means," said Carryck dryly.

Nathaniel went on. "It was your man here who put me and my father and our friend in a garrison gaol for weeks, and then when that didn't do the job, he stole our children and put them and us at the mercy of every French warship between here and home. Took a woman like Curiosity—in all her days she has never done any-

thing but good— away from her husband and children, and I don't doubt the worry and aggravation has stole ten years off her life. The *Osiris* went down with two hundred men on it—and if Moncrieff had had his way, it would have taken my father and me with it. All this, just so you could see me and mine onto Scottish soil. Maybe my father and Rab MacLachlan are dead now, and if they are, that's on your head too. So what I see when I look at you is a rich man used to getting his way, no matter what the cost. And I'm wondering why I should believe anything you have to say to me."

Contrecoeur leaned forward. "It's true that two hundred men and more have lost their lives, but they died for a good cause."

Elizabeth's head snapped toward him. "Since we are to speak plainly, may I ask why you are here, monsieur? I do not understand your interest in this affair."

Nathaniel drew Moncrieff's cloth medallion from his shirt and dropped it on the table. "It's got something to do with this, I'll wager."

"He took it from me," Moncrieff said to the earl, who never even looked in his direction.

The Frenchman smiled at the bit of cloth as another man might smile at his child. "The scapular. Yes, it has everything to do with this. You see, the earl's motives are not entirely selfish. He is a true friend and protector to the most persecuted people in Scotland."

Nathaniel grimaced. "Speak plain, man. 'Persecuted' could mean a lot of things."

"By your lady's expression I see she understands me very well."

"The Church of Rome, Nathaniel." Elizabeth's voice wavered a little. "The Catholic church. The earl has given sanctuary to a priest."

"To more than one," Nathaniel agreed. "I expect that Monsieur Contrecoeur here ain't just passing through on a whim. Came to read the last rites, is what I'd guess."

A shoulder lifted in agreement. "I had that honor when I arrived, yes."

Elizabeth was surprised, he could feel it in the way she looked at Contrecoeur.

"He's a priest all right, Boots. Ask him to take off his gloves."

"That's no' necessary," said the earl.

"But I don't mind," said Contrecoeur. He pulled off the gloves to show them strong hands, broad of palm and long fingered. Where his thumbs had once been two twists of flesh were tucked into masses of silver-white scar tissue.

Elizabeth let out a soft gasp.

"That's what I thought," Nathaniel said. "The Huron liked to take the missionaries' thumbs off with clam shells. There was one sachem who wore Jesuit thumbs and ears on a string around his neck."

Contrecoeur flexed his fingers. "His name was Calling-Crow. I knew him well."

Nathaniel said, "What else did they do to you?"

For the first time a shadow crossed Contrecoeur's handsome face.

"I left with my soul intact. More I could not ask."

"The Jesuits are no more," Elizabeth said, more to herself than the table. "The pope suppressed the order some years ago, and all Jesuits were banished from England and Scotland."

Moncrieff grunted. "The Scots were ever a loyal folk."

"That is true." Contrecoeur nodded. "Not all of our friends abandoned us. There are those who took it upon themselves to provide the Society of Jesus with a home, and safe shelter—at great risk to themselves. Much as the earl has done."

"And Catherine of Russia." Elizabeth's expression was growing darker by the moment. "I understand now why it is that you want to take Mademoiselle LeBrun to her mother."

Contrecoeur looked more surprised than pleased that Elizabeth had made this connection. "You are very quick, madame."

"Am I indeed?" Elizabeth said sharply. "I assume you travel in disguise where you are not welcome."

"The society has always been active in trade," he said. "Those of us who remain true to it carry on as merchants where we cannot live openly as priests."

Elizabeth touched the square of brown material that still sat in the middle of the table. "Do you wear one of these too, my lord Earl?"

"Aye," Carryck said gruffly. "I am Catholic. I wear the scapular as my faither wore it, and his faither and grandfaither afore him."

"That little scrap of cloth can't be all that's at the bottom of this," Nathaniel said.

Elizabeth touched his sleeve. "You are right, Nathaniel. It is more complex. Things might get very complicated for the earl if his loyalty to the Church of Rome became public knowledge. If I remember correctly, the restrictions on Catholics and the penalties for evading them are unbelievably severe. And there has been great resistance to any Bill of Relief—riots, and the like."

"A Bill o' Relief was signed last April," said Carryck, his calm leaving him suddenly.

Elizabeth's surprise must have shown on her face, but he would not let her respond, leaning forward to speak directly to her.

"Dinna talk tae me o' Bills o' Relief. I wad be a fool tae put my faith and risk everythin' on the whim o' the English parliament."

Nathaniel sat back to think it through. "So let me see if I got this straight. All this trouble, men dead and missing, children stole—all this 'cause he's one kind of Christ worshiper, and those Campbells his daughter married into—the ones who tried to put a bullet in my head—are another."

"In essence," Elizabeth said.

Moncrieff was sputtering in anger and frustration, but Carryck silenced him with a sharp look. His calm restored, he said, "There's a wee bit mair tae it. It's many years now that I canna openly welcome my priest tae Carryckcastle wi'oot puttin' him in danger o' his life. The hearin' o' the Holy Mass or refusin' tae attend kirk instead could cost me everything I hold dear. Should the presbytery suspect me o' practicing my own faith, they can summon me—*me*—before them, and if I canna satisfy them that I'm no' papist, they will denounce me tae the Privy Council, and aa my property will be consigned tae my nearest Protestant relative—the Campbells o' Breadalbane—or revert tae the Crown. As a Catholic I canna buy real property, inherit an estate, or leave my property tae a Catholic son. And that same son couldna serve as a governor, factor, or even a schoolmaster. That's what it means tae be Catholic—and faithful—in Scotland."

Nathaniel said, "So your daughter ran off and married into the one family that would put you in the worst spot. What drove her to do something like that?"

The room was so quiet, it might have been empty.

"I did," said Jean Hope. "I wasna truthfu' wi' her when she needed it most, and she married intae the Campbell line tae strike a blow at me."

"Wheest, Jean." Carryck's voice came gentle. "We'll no' speak o' it."

"Won't we?" Nathaniel leaned back in his chair. "Seems to me we've got a right to know all of it. The truth is, all of this puts me in mind of that story—" He reached for Elizabeth's hand under the table. "Remember, Boots, the one you read out loud last winter? About that place with the little people who went to war because half of them liked to start with the big end of a boiled egg and the other half favored the small end. What was that book?"

"Mr. Swift's *Gulliver's Travels*," she said. "Thousands

of the Lilliputians died rather than be compelled to begin their eggs at the small end."

Moncrieff pushed back his chair so violently that it screeched and then crashed over. "How dare ye." He spoke softly, and with such venom that Nathaniel reached for a weapon that wasn't there and then rose to block Moncrieff's path to Elizabeth. "How dare ye insult Carryck in such a way."

"Angus," barked the earl. "Enough! Sit ye doon, man."

"I willna!" Moncrieff was pale with rage. "I willna sit here and listen tae this English bitch make light o' our travails."

Nathaniel grabbed him by the shirt and hauled him forward, bending over to meet his eye. "You're a foul-mouthed bastard," he said easily. "And a coward, to attack a woman when I'm standing right here in front of you."

Moncrieff spat in his face.

Contrecoeur and Carryck both sprang forward, but Nathaniel's fist had already buried itself in Moncrieff's gut. He sank to his knees, grunting and gasping for breath.

Nathaniel wiped the spittle from his face with his sleeve. His wounded shoulder was screaming, and he had broken into a sweat.

"Angus," said Carryck. "Ye disappoint me, man."

Contrecoeur said nothing, but merely helped Moncrieff to his feet. He hung there for a moment, sputtering and coughing, and when he looked up there was nothing of contrition in his expression.

"Aye, I lost my temper," he wheezed. "But I'll take no' a word back. I willna stand by and smile while they sneer at us."

"You are mistaken, Mr. Moncrieff," Elizabeth said. "I do not sneer, nor would I make light of these outrageous penalties and the deprivation of basic human rights. But I do—I *must*—challenge your interference in

our lives. We are not politicians, and we cannot be held accountable for these wrongs done to you."

Moncrieff coughed. "It has nothing tae do wi' politics. Should Breadalbane come tae Carryck it will have tae do wi' blood. They'll drive us out wi' whips and canes, the way they drove my grandfaither out o' Dumfries in the riots. He died in the mud, watching his roof burn. His guidwife would ha' froze tae death beside him and my faither wi' her, but for the auld laird. But he gave them work, and a croft and a place tae make their confessions, and tae hear the Mass without fear. Ye wi' yer superiority and yer weeping for the Africans, ye care nothing for what we've suffered under your countrymen. You stand there and speak tae us of eggs."

Elizabeth drew herself up to her full height. "You have suffered great injustice, but we are no part of that, sir."

Moncrieff's mouth twisted with disgust. "She doesna understand," he said to the earl. "I told ye how it would be."

"She understands well enough, and so do I," Nathaniel said. "You want to hold on to what's yours—there's nothing unusual in that. You're Catholics, and I'd guess you're Jacobites, too."

There was a sudden silence as Carryck and Contrecoeur looked at each other.

Contrecoeur said, "Our political aspirations are modest. We are interested only in surviving in these ungodly times."

Elizabeth let out a hoarse laugh. "You must think us very dense indeed, sir. You are asking us to join a lost cause. To allow ourselves to be used as pawns in your holy war."

"No," said Contrecoeur, leaning forward, his fervor so bright that it changed his face into a martyr's mask. "It is exactly that which we hope to avoid. The best

way to keep the peace is to keep Carryck free of Campbell influence."

Nathaniel studied the priest's face. "Your name ain't Contrecoeur, is it? You're no more French than I am."

Carryck looked up in surprise. "Can ye no see the resemblance tae Angus? Before he took his vows he was called John Moncrieff."

"Brothers," said Nathaniel. And saw it then, in the line of the jaw and the set of the eyes.

"Half brothers," said Contrecoeur.

Elizabeth said, "They sent you to France to be educated by the Jesuits."

Contrecoeur looked at his half brother. "You were wrong about her, Angus. About both of them. They are not so witless after all."

Nathaniel swallowed down the bile that rose in his throat, and he looked at Contrecoeur.

The man was nothing more than a priest. A priest like all the other priests he had ever known, steadfast in his conviction that his heaven was the only worthy goal and that every creature on the earth was in the world to serve his church, and his needs. He had known anger deep and cold enough to sear, and it all pushed up now from deep in his gut. He swallowed it back down, but it took everything in him.

He said, "So what happens to an exiled priest returned in secret to his homeland, if he's found out?"

Contrecoeur inclined his head. "You wish me ill, Mr. Bonner. Your life in the endless forests has hardened your heart."

Elizabeth said, "If we are hard, sir, it is because you have put our children in danger."

He put out a mangled hand, palm up, as if to offer her something worth taking. "As are the children of the church, Mrs. Bonner. As are we all."

Nathaniel took Elizabeth's arm. "There's nothing

else to be said here. You'll have to find another way out."

"You were baptized in the church," Contrecoeur said. "You are tied to this place by blood and faith."

Nathaniel laughed out loud. "I will never belong to this place. Do you hear me, Carryck? Marry the French girl and get yourself a son, or make peace with your daughter. I'm taking my family home."

The earl stared, his expression stony.

"I am sorry for your troubles," Elizabeth said to Mrs. Hope. "But we cannot help you."

Moncrieff put himself in front of Nathaniel, swaying slightly on his feet. "Ye'd turn yer back on yer blood kin?"

"Get out of my way," Nathaniel said softly.

Moncrieff did not move. "I should ha' taken the boy and killed ye when I had the chance."

Nathaniel studied him for a moment: the long face and sunken cheeks, the dark eyes bloodshot and still bright with anger.

"I was just thinking the same thing about you," he said. "I still am."

"Stand aside, Angus." Carryck's voice was hoarse, but steady. "Let them go."

"Aye, Angus," Nathaniel echoed. "Stand aside."

Hannah meant to read while she waited for her father and Elizabeth to come back from dining with Carryck, but the afternoon in Carryckton had been more tiring than she realized. She fell asleep after just a few pages, and dreamed of the bear wandering blind through the fairy wood, trailing a chain behind herself, and calling out for help.

The sound of her father's voice, hushed and urgent, woke her. Hannah righted herself so suddenly that the book in her lap slid to the floor with a muffled thump.

"What?" she asked, frightened by the expression on his face. "What's wrong?" She looked to Elizabeth and Curiosity, who stood behind him. "Is something wrong? My grandfather?"

And then she saw what her father held in his hands: the buckskin sacks, double sewn, that he had worn against his skin for so much of this journey. Empty.

She unfolded her legs and tried to stand up, suddenly as unsteady as a new colt. Her father steadied her with his free hand.

"Did you hear anything?" he asked. "Did anybody come in here while we were gone?"

Hannah shook her head. "No. Nobody."

"You see," said Curiosity. "I told you, I would have heard it if somebody came in. I don' sleep that deep, not here."

"All the coin?" Hannah asked. "All of it gone?"

"Yes," said Elizabeth. "All of it. One hundred and three gold guineas, and four pounds sixpence in silver. The sacks were undisturbed when I fetched a shawl in the late afternoon."

Hannah rubbed her eyes and tried to collect her thoughts. "I saw Mac Stoker," she said. "He was leaving."

Her father's back went very straight. "Where? When did you see him?"

"In the tunnels," said Hannah, and she saw how the grown-ups all looked at each other.

"Speak up, child," said Curiosity. "And tell us what you know about Mac Stoker."

It was quickly told—the tunnels under the castle, the staircase built into the thick wall of Forbes Tower that came out in the kitchen window casement. And Mac Stoker with a sack over his shoulder on his way to find his crew and his ship.

"I thought maybe he had stolen a teakettle, or a silver platter," she finished.

"I don't think it could have been Stoker," Nathaniel said. "He couldn't come up here without being seen. And the timing is off—that was before we left for dinner."

Curiosity's mouth was set in a hard line. "But who else knew about the coin?"

"Moncrieff," said Elizabeth. "Moncrieff knew, and he wasn't at dinner."

"Angus Moncrieff has not been in these rooms," said Curiosity firmly. "I could smell the man a mile off, rat that he is."

"The maids," Hannah suggested hesitantly. "The maids might have known. Maybe he sent one of them—"

"Or maybe Stoker did," said Elizabeth. "He is good at getting women to do his bidding."

Hannah watched her father's face, seeing the anger there just below the surface, and the frustration. He turned to Elizabeth.

"How much will it cost to buy passage home for all of us?"

Elizabeth spread her hands out on her lap. "About six pounds per person, if we want cabins. Perhaps half that for the twins. Another three pounds for provisions for each of us. Counting your father and Robbie that would be—"

"More than fifty pound," said Curiosity. "Might as well be a thousand."

"If only there were some way to contact my aunt Merriweather," Elizabeth said. "But I have no idea where she is."

Nathaniel turned away without a word. He took a candle from the mantelpiece and disappeared into the dressing room.

"Now what?" muttered Curiosity.

Elizabeth put her arm around Hannah. "I don't know."

A few moments later Nathaniel was back. He held out his hands, full now: a silver comb embedded with pearls and a set of brushes to match. A pair of shoe buckles encrusted with square-cut stones that caught the candlelight and cast it out again in a rainbow. A hand mirror, inlaid with ivory and pearl, and deeply carved: *Sans Peur*. He let them fall on the table and the sound of it was very loud in the room.

"Would these bring in enough money?"

"In London, yes," Elizabeth said. "But I doubt there are any jewelers in Carryckton. Perhaps in Moffat."

"Jennet told me about Moffat," said Hannah. "It's a place where rich people go to take baths."

A smile flickered at the corner of Elizabeth's mouth. "A spa, yes, and quite a fashionable one with the aristocracy. There would almost certainly be a way to dispose of these things."

"Lady Isabel is there, too," said Hannah. "And some of the Campbells."

Three heads came up suddenly to look at her. She said, "You made me start at the end, or I would have told you already."

Curiosity said, "Sounds like a long story, indeed. Let's set down."

It took almost an hour for Hannah to tell it. As she recounted what she had learned at the Laidlaw cottage, Nathaniel filled in the background that Contrecoeur—*John Moncrieff*, Elizabeth reminded herself—and Carryck had given them during their visit to Lady Carryck's chamber.

"A fine mess," Curiosity concluded when they had finished. "Priests and hidey-holes and runaway daughters. There ain't nothing like religion to bring out the worst in folks."

Elizabeth gestured toward the empty buckskin sacks. "And then this—"

"It don' much matter who took it," said Curiosity. "Not as far as I can see. Either way it's gone."

Nathaniel leaned forward to study a shoe buckle. "I don't know, Curiosity. If it was Moncrieff, or Carryck even, then that means they'll go to some lengths to keep us here. What we need is an ally, somebody to help us get away."

"I have rarely heard a master or landlord so universally praised," said Elizabeth. "It is hard to imagine that any one of his servants or tenants would be of any assistance. I think we must depend on ourselves alone."

Hannah said, "There's the Campbells. They want us gone, anyway. Maybe they'd help, once they know we've got no interest in Carryck."

"Maybe they would," said Nathaniel slowly. "But just because we don't want to claim this place don't mean we got to hook up with Carryck's enemies."

Curiosity put her chin down to her chest and gave Nathaniel a piercing look. "I don' wish the man ill, either. But tell me, what choice do we have? Cain't you talk to this Isabel, if not her menfolk? See if she's willing to send us on our way?"

Elizabeth watched Nathaniel struggle with this idea. She put a hand on his, and he looked at her.

"We must go to Moffat anyway to sell these things." She picked up the mirror and it flashed in the candlelight. "It might do some good to call on Lady Isabel. For us and perhaps for Carryck, as well."

Nathaniel ran a hand through his hair. He had discarded his coat, and the white linen of the shirt strained against his shoulders, all the tension in him rising up.

"I don't know, Boots."

She said, "Let me go. I could make the trip in one day, with a good horse."

Curiosity laughed. "Now, there's a rare idea. Send

you off with a load of jewels in your pocket—on your own, of course—through strange countryside to find the Campbells, after they put two bullets in your husband."

Elizabeth tried to keep her composure. "The Campbells do not know me," she said. "I am just another lady come to Moffat to take the waters."

Hannah cleared her throat and Nathaniel turned toward her.

"Say what you got on your mind, Squirrel."

After a moment she said, "It's when you two split up that there's trouble. I think you should both go."

Nathaniel's face went very still, and then he reached out a hand to put on her shoulder. "You're right. Sometimes it takes a child to point out the truth of a thing. What do you say, Boots?"

"I'd like to hear what Curiosity thinks of the idea," Elizabeth said.

Curiosity tapped the table with one long finger, her jaw working thoughtfully. "I suppose I can keep people out of here for a day, and there's goat's milk enough. We managed that way once before, after all. But how you going to get horses, without letting Carryck know what you up to?"

Hannah said, "The mailcoach leaves Carryckton for Moffat at half past five in the morning." And then, in response to Elizabeth's surprised look and Curiosity's suspicious one: "I saw it posted on the board outside the tavern. The Barley Mow, it was called."

"Is that so," Curiosity said grimly. "I'll tell you what I think, missy. I think you got this whole thing set in your head as soon as you heard that sorry story about Lady Isabel running off. Ain't that so?"

Hannah had an almost petulant expression, and she said nothing.

"The only problem is that we don't have the fare," said Elizabeth.

Curiosity's brow furled down low as she considered. Then she reached into her headwrap with two long fingers and drew out a single coin. A five-guinea gold piece sparked the light.

"In case of trouble." She let out a great sigh, and many things passed across her face in quick succession—desperation, anger, and a simple weariness that Elizabeth understood very well, and for which there was no immediate cure.

"Hannah," she said quietly. "Go fetch me my satchel, please."

"Curiosity—" Elizabeth began.

"Hush now, just wait." Curiosity held up a hand. And so they sat in silence until Hannah came back and put the small satchel on the table.

Curiosity opened it, and reaching down into the bottom, she pulled out the pistols and holster Nathaniel had been wearing when he came back from his nighttime ride in Dumfries. She rummaged a little longer and came up with a bag of bullets and one of powder.

"Nobody was paying any attention while you were bleeding half to death," she said to Nathaniel. "But I thought these might come in handy. I expect you paid a good deal for them."

"I did," Nathaniel said. "And I'm glad to see them again."

Curiosity surprised Elizabeth by leaning across the table and taking both of Nathaniel's hands in her own.

"You watch yourselves. I want to go home, and I won't take kindly to any more delays. Do you hear me, Nathaniel Bonner?"

Nathaniel nodded. "I do."

"One more thing," she said. "And then you need to get some sleep before you start off. I think you should take Daniel with you. I never did care for the way Moncrieff look at that boy, and I don' trust him now most especially."

At the nape of Elizabeth's neck the hair rose, and

she saw Moncrieff's face contorted with outrage. *I should have taken the boy and killed ye when I had the chance.*

"We'll take Daniel," Nathaniel said. "But I'm leaving you one of the pistols."

29

Moffat looked like any other town in a Sunday morning drizzle, the lanes almost empty under a lowering sky. Elizabeth took note of a theatre, an assembly hall, and along the High Street any number of discreet signs for the services of doctors and surgeons.

"Ye see, Mr. Speedwell's shingle just there," said the lady who sat across from her. She was a small, round woman by the name of Mrs. Eleanor Rae, and she had just spent a fortnight in Carryckton visiting her sister. "He's just the mannie tae see yer guidman weel agin, mark ma words." And she clucked her tongue in compassion, studying Nathaniel's silent form. "It's a pity, that's what it is. But nivver fear, ma dear, Mr. Speedwell will put him richt again."

Elizabeth resisted the urge to turn and look at Nathaniel. Curiosity really had done a fine job of transforming him into an invalid—his throat and jaw had been wrapped elaborately in flannel and dressings—but it was his mournful expression that engendered Mrs. Rae's compassion. Elizabeth had had no idea he would take so well to this charade, and she could not look at him for very long without fear of laughing.

The mailcoach jerked to a stop before a tidy inn.

"The Black Bull," Mrs. Rae announced. "As respectable a place as ever was. Guid food and clean rooms. Do tell MacDonald it was Eleanor Rae wha sent ye, mind." She leaned forward to peer at Daniel, who was mouthing his fist. He stared back at her with perfect equanimity, and she seemed to take this as a further sign of Elizabeth's sad state.

"Sic a pity," she hummed, and she gathered her parcels to herself.

In a moment the woman would be gone, and Elizabeth knew she was the best chance they had of making the necessary connections in the short amount of time available to them. She had been contemplating how to formulate her question for the last hour, and now there was no more time to waste.

"Mrs. Rae, if I might ask—"

"Anythin', ma dear." Her eyes went very wide and round. "Ask awa'."

"It is a rather delicate matter, you understand—"

Another bobbing nod, curiosity and goodwill wound together like the plump hands she clasped before herself.

"We find it necessary to dispose of some personal items to pay for my husband's treatment and our stay here. Could you direct me to a reputable . . . agent?"

"Plate, or jewels?" Her tone all business now, and a new light in her eye.

"The latter," Elizabeth said. Beside her Nathaniel shifted uneasily, but Mrs. Rae focused her smile on Elizabeth.

"Ah." She produced a small smile. "It's fate that's broucht us tegither the-day. Ye mun come alang wi' me, ma dears, and I will introduce ye tae ma neighbor, Mr. Babby-Sang-Way. An Italian gentleman, ye ken, but canny aa the same."

• • •

Elizabeth carried the boy with his face peeking out between two open buttons of her cape. He was curious about the world and had not yet learned fear or caution, and he would not be hidden away like an infant. His eyes—so green in this light—missed nothing, and his expression was very serious as they moved along the lanes.

Nathaniel had Curiosity's satchel—filled now with Giselle's fine things, but his injured arm he kept under his cloak, his hand resting on the butt of the pistol. At first he had liked this masquerade that permitted him to listen without ever talking—he owed Elizabeth a debt for coping with Mrs. Rae all the way from Carryckton without any assistance from him—but now the dressings on his face had begun to itch, and he had had enough of silence. The plain truth was that their options were few and their time was short—the mailcoach that returned to Carryckton would leave in just five hours. He had no choice but to carry on with this game.

They followed Mrs. Rae down a lane lined with small shops—a gunmaker, a saddlemaker, a cobbler, all shuttered. A redcoat passed, scratching his chest and yawning loudly. Nathaniel pulled his hat down tighter over his brow.

"Here we are, ma dears."

They had stopped before a tiny shop with a door painted bright yellow. Above it a shingle moved fitfully in the wind. G. Bevesangue, Importer.

Elizabeth thanked Mrs. Rae for her help, shook her hand, and then the older lady had pointed out her husband's shop down the lane—"the best milliner in aa o' Moffat, and do I say sae masel'"— and left them.

At Elizabeth's firm knock, the door flew open as if he had been waiting for them. The man who stood there was no more than thirty, with wild hair that stood straight up all over his head and a dark complexion. He had a thin, dry twist of a face and the darkest eyes Nathaniel had ever seen in a white man. He did not

seem surprised to find two strangers on his doorstep, but he did peer cautiously down the lane in both directions before he stepped back to usher them in with a bow and a sweep of his arm.

"Entrez, si vous plais." He smiled, and a gold tooth flashed beneath the neatly trimmed mustache. *"Guido Bevesangue, madame, monsieur."*

Elizabeth hesitated, glanced over her shoulder at Nathaniel, and stepped over the threshold.

It was a small room, furnished simply: in the corner a bed, a long table, a cabinet, two chairs, and a lamp. Clothing hung from pegs, and on the table were the remnants of a modest meal of bread and cheese and some kind of green paste. There was nothing here to indicate why this man might be interested in paying hard cash for what they had to sell but the far wall, which was crowded with clocks.

Elizabeth began to speak, but Bevesangue held up a hand to stop her just as all the timepieces came to life at once with a low whirring sound. Daniel's head popped out of Elizabeth's cloak and he let out a caw of pleasure and began to wiggle with excitement, flapping his arms.

When the last of the clocks had finished striking the hour and Elizabeth had quieted Daniel, Bevesangue bowed so that his hair flopped forward and then back again.

"Est-ce que je puis vous aider, madame, monsieur?"

"Sir," Elizabeth began. "Do you speak English?"

"But of course, madame." He put a hand to his heart, as if he were ready to swear to this. "Pardon me, I thought that you must be French. Most of my . . . visitors are French gentlepersons in unfortunate circumstances." His eyes trailed over them, taking note of the expensive cut of their cloaks, muddy at the hems. "I myself am Italian, of Genoa."

There was the sound of raised voices in the lane outside the window, and the pleasant expression on the man's face disappeared. It came flickering back very

slowly as the voices moved farther away. Nathaniel touched the pistol again, glad of the heft of it against his ribs.

"How may I be of assistance, madame . . . ?" He paused expectantly.

"Freeman," Elizabeth supplied. And then: "Mrs. Rae suggested that you might be interested in buying some items from us."

"Personal items, madame?"

"Yes. Personal items of some value," she finished firmly.

Bevesangue studied Nathaniel from the corner of his eye.

"Your husband is ill?"

Elizabeth's expression hardened a bit. "My husband is here to take the waters for a throat condition, sir. Nothing else fails him."

"But you have traveled far," he said. "You must be very tired. Please, won't you take a seat?"

Nathaniel put a hand on Elizabeth's arm to stop her. Then he stepped up closer to Bevesangue to look at him hard. Something about this Italian made the balls of his thumbs itch, but whatever it was he hid away cleverly behind those black eyes. After a minute, Bevesangue blinked.

"Your husband is a cautious man," he said, without looking away from Nathaniel. "And a dangerous one, I think."

Elizabeth smiled. "How very observant you are, Mr. Bevesangue," she said. "Perhaps we will be able to do business together after all."

A half hour later they paid for a room at the Black Bull with coin, and a maid showed them to their room.

"Sixty pounds," Elizabeth said, dropping the purse onto the bed. "It is more than I imagined we might get. You must have truly frightened him, Nathaniel."

"I don't know about that." He went to the window as he loosened the dressings on his jaw.

"But why else would he have given us so much, with so little bartering?" Elizabeth unbuttoned her bodice for Daniel, who was chattering impatiently and thumping at her with a small fist. She stilled suddenly, and looked up.

"Unless—"

"He plans on getting it back again," Nathaniel finished for her.

"Lovely," Elizabeth said grimly. "Just what we needed. A larcenous Italian after us as well as the Campbells and the Carrycks."

"Never mind, Boots. We'll be on the mailcoach by four, and he won't think to come looking for us before dark. In the meantime we'll just set tight right here."

Elizabeth considered. They had been up well before dawn to walk hard over unfamiliar territory for more than an hour. There had been no chance to sleep on the mailcoach—Mrs. Rae and Daniel both had conspired against that—and she was very tired. She could do as Nathaniel suggested, and sleep here until it was time to go back to Carryckcastle and claim the rest of their family before they started out for home. That was exactly what she should do.

Daniel's steady suckling was the only sound in the room. Nathaniel was still at the window with his back turned to her, watching the lane below. He said, "Spit it out, Boots, before it chokes you."

"If Lady Isabel is here, I think I should try to talk to her," Elizabeth said. "If I do not, I shall always wonder—"

"If you could have solved Carryck's problems for him. Christ above, you are worse than any missionary I ever ran into. Do you realize what kind of trouble you're headed for with this?"

This stung. Elizabeth bent her head over Daniel to hide her burning face and to get hold of her temper. She

heard Nathaniel crossing the room, and then his weight pressed down on the edge of the bed.

"I shouldn't have snapped at you like that."

"No, you should not have."

"You're nothing like a missionary."

"I should hope not."

He shot her a sidelong glance. "Maybe she ain't even here. And if she is, how would you find out without setting the Campbells on our tails? I don't suppose they'd mind putting another bullet in me, and one in you, too, if they had the chance."

Elizabeth met his gaze. "I am very capable of finding out what I want to know without providing any useful information in return. Leave that to me."

A flicker of a grin passed over his face. "That's fine with me, Boots. I'll sit back and watch."

They put Daniel down for his nap and then Nathaniel watched with equal parts amusement and disquiet as Elizabeth spun her web. First she rang for the maid, a slow young woman who took her time getting to them to bob a halfhearted curtsy. In a cool and superior tone Nathaniel hardly recognized, Elizabeth ordered a meal that would have fed them for days: white soup, a fricando of veal, vegetable pudding, a basket of breads, raspberry syllabub, coffee, and an expensive bottle of claret. The maid, suddenly much more awake, ran off to the kitchens with a new flush in her cheeks.

"You mean to spend the whole sixty pounds before we ever get out of town, or did walking just give you a big appetite?"

"No," Elizabeth said calmly. "I am hardly hungry at all, but I shall eat nonetheless." And she had nothing more to say to him, because a serving man had appeared with linen to set the table for their meal.

In the next hour Nathaniel learned things about his wife that he had not guessed, or maybe never let himself

think about. This was not the Elizabeth he knew, the woman who had set herself so resolutely to the task of learning how to skin game and cure deerhides, who climbed trees and swam in mountain lakes. This was Elizabeth Middleton of Oakmere, Lady Crofton's niece, raised to believe that servants had no names worth remembering, a lady who did not even think to pick up her own napkin to put it in her lap. It was surprising to watch her send back the sauce for the veal as unfit to eat, and disturbing to see her point to her glass to have it filled without ever looking in the serving maid's direction. And all the time she talked to him in a voice and manner that he knew not at all, and liked even less, of assemblies and dance parties and intrigues at court.

It was when the syllabub was before them that Elizabeth's plan was finally clear to him.

"It is too bad Uncle does not care to go so far as Galston," she said in a vaguely distressed way. "The countess asked me so pointedly to call on her, after all. I suppose it cannot be helped, although I do so hate to disappoint. You know Mama is hoping that our Roderick will take an interest in her. It would be a fine thing to see our families thus joined."

From the corner of his eye, Nathaniel saw something flicker across the serving maid's face.

Elizabeth carried on with a sigh: "I would give a great deal to see dear Flora. I am very disappointed, indeed."

The serving maid made a low sound in her throat, not quite a cough. Elizabeth raised her brow in the young woman's direction. "Yes?"

A deep curtsy. "Beggin' yer pardon, mem, I dinnae care tae intrude . . ." She paused, and when Elizabeth did not stop her, she continued in a rush.

"If it's the Countess o' Loudoun ye're speakin' aboot—I thocht it must be, hearin' ye talk o' Galston—pardon me for bein' sae forward, mem, but

did ye nae ken that the lady is come tae Moffat tae take the waters?"

For one long moment Elizabeth's face betrayed nothing at all, and the maid grew very pale.

Then Elizabeth smiled. "Is she, indeed? How kind of you . . ."

"Annie, mem."

"How very kind of you, Annie, to put my mind at ease. Such thoughtfulness must be rewarded."

A flush crawled up the girl's neck and she bobbed again. "It's nae trouble at aa, mem. The countess walks by every mornin'—the Earl o' Breadalbane has a hoose in Elliot Place, just doon the lane."

"Does he? What very good luck," Elizabeth said, picking up her spoon and smiling thinly at Nathaniel. "Very good luck, indeed."

"You are cross with me," Elizabeth said calmly. She was studying her reflection in the window glass as she tucked a stray hair away. Her hand was trembling, and she stilled it by pressing it against her waist. When Nathaniel came up to wrap his arms around her from behind, she stiffened, and did not know why.

"Not cross, that's the wrong word."

"Do be honest, Nathaniel. I have never seen you look so stern. You quite frightened me."

"Then we're even, because you scared me, too, Boots." He rocked her back against him. "But I have to admit, you put my mind to rest."

She turned in his arms and stemmed her hands against his chest. There was a guarded expression about him, a reserve that she hadn't seen in him since the first few times they had ever spoken to each other, when she was still Miss Middleton and she had insisted on calling him Mr. Bonner. It hurt her to see that look in his face.

"That is a very mysterious statement. Whatever does it mean?"

He said, "That lady sitting across from me at that table wrinkling her nose at the sauce and complaining about the coffee ain't the woman I married. Here I been worried about what you gave up to stay in New-York with me, and it never crossed my mind—" He stopped.

"Go on," she said dully. "Say it. It never crossed your mind that I might become . . . that kind of lady, if I had stayed to live my life here." She pulled away, unable to touch him and keep her composure at the same time. "Did you think it was all a girlish whim, my wanting to get away? Did you not hear me when I told you about what it was like here for women born to ease and wealth? Do you not see how easy it is to become manipulative and imperious when every other avenue, every opportunity to think independently, is denied?"

She felt the flush of anger spreading up over her face, and it took all her willpower to meet his gaze. "I knew what I should become if I stayed. I felt it growing in me like a cancer, day by day. And now you've seen it. It is me, Nathaniel. Whether you like it or not, that woman is part of me, too, and always will be."

"Ah, Boots," he said, pulling her close to put his cheek against her hair. His voice was hoarse but his hands on her shoulders were gentle. "If that's the worst you've got to show me, then I'm a damn lucky man."

Something small and warm broke open deep inside her, and rose up to her throat. When she could speak again she said, "I want to go home."

"So do I. And we will."

Just what is it you expect? Elizabeth asked herself sternly as she made her way to Elliot Place. *What is it you want of Lady Isabel?*

The truth was, she did not know what she would say to the lady when—if—she were finally to meet her. *Your father has made our lives very difficult; please come and tell him to stop right away.*

She smiled outright at the idea. A man passing her on the road paused as if she had spoken to him; Elizabeth gave him a cold look, and he dropped his gaze and moved on.

It was madness, of course. She could not tell them who she was without putting herself in real danger, but if she did not, what connection could she possibly claim that would open the door? Giselle Somerville's gown and cloak and bonnet marked her for a woman of quality and means, but the appearance of good breeding alone would not get her very far.

The reluctant sun had come to dry the cobblestones and a crowd of children ran out to greet it. Above her a window opened and the sound of a pianoforte being very ill used drifted down, undercut by the voices of young men bickering in French. A barouche went by at a solemn pace, in it two gentlemen with a medical look about them. And then she had come to Elliot Place, and Elizabeth must stop to gather her thoughts.

A single house stood on the lane, three stories high and surrounded by a large park. Elizabeth stopped before the garden gate, overrun with honeysuckle intertwined with roses, heavy headed and dripping with the recent rain, their scent rising now on the warmer breeze. The gate stood partially open, and beyond it a flagstone path wound through tall spires of deep blue delphinium and masses of white lilies. The path ended at a small flight of stone steps and then ran away again into the dappled light of the garden beyond.

"Were you wondering about the roses?" said a young voice behind her. Elizabeth's heart raced, but she composed her expression and turned.

"Everybody does. Wonder about the roses, I mean."

She was a plain girl of perhaps thirteen, with intelligent, bright brown eyes and a friendly expression. Her accent was not quite Scots and not English, but something in between, almost certainly the result of careful training.

"They are beautiful," Elizabeth said. "I have never seen roses of this particular shade of apricot before. I could not help but stop and admire them."

The girl smiled. "Apricot. I've never heard anybody call it that, but you are right, they are exactly the color of a ripe apricot. Would you like to see the rest of the garden?"

She took Elizabeth's surprise for hesitancy. "It's really all right. They like to show it off," she said in a low and conspiratorial tone.

"Is the countess an avid gardener, then?" Elizabeth asked, and saw the young girl's face contort first in surprise and then amusement. "Or perhaps it is the Earl of Breadalbane . . ."

The girl said, "Breadalbane doesn't care anything for flowers. I do, but I can't claim any part of this—" She inclined her head toward the garden. And then, perhaps because Elizabeth was looking confused, she added: "I am the Countess of Loudoun."

"Oh," said Elizabeth, quite taken aback. "Pardon me, I did not realize."

The girl flushed. "You are surprised. You must have heard those silly stories about my lungs," she said with some irritation. "Everybody thinks I'm an invalid. Well, I am not."

"Yes, I can see that," Elizabeth said. And then, "It must be very vexing to have people think you unwell when you are in good health."

The countess narrowed her eyes. "Yes. It is indeed very vexing, that is just the right word. You are very good with words."

"Thank you," Elizabeth said, amused in spite of the seriousness of this situation. "Who is it that takes credit for the garden, if it is not you, Countess?"

"It is Lady Isabel's doing," said the girl. "The wife of my curator. She spends all her time here terrorizing the gardeners, even though—" She stopped, and bit her lower lip thoughtfully. "Would you care to see the pond?"

Elizabeth wondered at herself, that she should hesitate when this opportunity came so naturally. She
clasped her hands together to keep them from trembling, and she followed the girl down the flagstone
path.

Even in her anxiety Elizabeth could not overlook the
beauty of the gardens. Around every corner was a surprise, a bench surrounded by rose campion and clouds
of white phlox, a corner where tiny bluebells cascaded
over a deep green mat, an arbor thick with scarlet
clematis as big as her hand. There were no gardeners at
work now, on a Sunday afternoon—just the subtle hum
of bees and, somewhere near, the soft splash of water
on rocks. Her guide was content to let her look, and
Elizabeth was very glad of it, for she had no idea what
she might say if she should come upon Lady Isabel unexpectedly.

They came out onto a grassy slope that ran down to
a pond, fed by a thin stream that erupted from an outcropping of rock. Three slender white birch stood at
one end, sending their shadows dancing over the water.
A dragonfly hovered above a clutch of cream and pink
water lilies.

"How lovely." Elizabeth only breathed it, but in the
shadows on the far side of the pond there was a rustle
of skirts. A woman sat up from a chair. She was
wrapped in a shawl, and veiling hung from the brim of
her hat.

"Flora?"

"There's a lady here to see the garden," called the
young countess. "An English lady. She stopped to look
at your roses."

Elizabeth's breath came short and fast, but she managed to control her voice. "Pardon me, please. I did not
intend to intrude—"

"You are not intruding," said the girl, with some irritation. "I brought you. Lady Isabel likes to take people
around her garden, don't you, Isabel?"

"I do." She pushed herself out of her chair with some effort—Elizabeth thought she must have been very deeply asleep—and started toward them around the pond. She moved like a woman of seventy rather than one of thirty, and for a moment Elizabeth wondered if she had come to the wrong place, stumbled upon some other Isabel. So complete was her confusion that when the woman stopped before her, she did not hesitate or think, but gave her own name to the anonymous face behind the veil.

"How do you do," she said. "I am Mrs. Elizabeth Bonner, of New-York State."

There was a small silence, which a jay interrupted with a harsh cry.

"Flora," said Lady Isabel softly. "Please tell Cook I will take tea here wi' my guest. And tell Mrs. Fitzwilliam that I dinna want tae be disturbed."

Elizabeth wished very much to see Lady Isabel's face, but she must be content with her voice, which gave no hint of surprise or displeasure.

"But—"

"It is verra rude tae stare, Flora," she said gently.

The girl nodded.

"Ye may come back tae sit wi' us after ye've talked tae Cook."

This seemed to reassure the girl, and she ran off.

Lady Isabel said, "I prefer tae sit in the shade, if that will suit?"

Elizabeth found her voice again. "Yes, thank you. That will suit very well." She touched her handkerchief to her brow, perspiring suddenly in the cool of the garden.

Flora was back very quickly, out of breath and flushed. She sat on the ground next to Lady Isabel's lawn chair and tucked her legs beneath herself.

"Ye came alone," said Lady Isabel. "Are ye verra brave, or just headstrong?"

"Perhaps I am both," Elizabeth said.

They sat for a moment listening to birds calling back and forth in the trees, and then Flora—it was hard to think of her as the Countess of Loudoun—surprised Elizabeth and Isabel both.

"Did Carryck send you, or was it Jean Hope?"

The girl knew the whole story, then—certainly she knew more than Elizabeth did of Lady Isabel's flight from Carryckcastle.

"No," Elizabeth said. "Nobody sent me. Nobody knows that I am here." *Except Nathaniel,* she might have added, but stopped herself.

"O' course they didna send ye," said Lady Isabel evenly. "Ma faither wadna take sic a risk. Ye do realize the danger?"

Elizabeth thought the time for polite conversation was past. She said, "My husband was shot twice. Yes, I realize the danger very well. But the fact is, Lady Isabel, that we did not want to be here, and were brought against our will—"

"Moncrieff," she interrupted.

"Yes." Elizabeth nodded. "And that is why I took the chance of coming to see you."

"Ye want my help tae get awa'. But what o' yer guid-man's faither and his friends?"

Elizabeth paused to think. Lady Isabel was much better informed than she might have guessed.

"We do not know where they are, but we can wait no longer. We must start for home."

"I can help ye, but no' in the way ye'd expect," said Lady Isabel. "They were here yesterday tae consult wi' my husband and wi' Breadalbane."

Elizabeth thought at first she must have misunderstood, but she saw by the girl's face that she had not. "My father-in-law was here?"

"And Robert MacLachlan and yer cousin Viscount Durbeyfield, as weel."

Elizabeth let out a sound of surprise. "My cousin Will, here?"

"Aye. Did ye no' ken they were travelin' tegither?"

"I did not," Elizabeth said, pressing two fingers to the bridge of her nose to stem the sudden ache there. "The last I saw of my cousin was in Canada. I assumed he was still there."

"He was here yesterday," said Flora quite firmly. "I shook his hand."

Elizabeth struggled with this unexpected news. What if it were a lie, nothing more than a subterfuge meant to put her off her guard?

Lady Isabel read her thoughts without any effort at all. She said, "You doubt my report, and wi' guid cause. Flora, describe the gentlemen wha came tae see the earl yesterday."

This was a task that suited the girl, and she sat up straight, and thoughtfully described all three men exactly, down to Robbie's florid complexion and the scar on Hawkeye's left cheekbone. They had been here; yes, she could accept that. But under what circumstances?

"And where are they now?" Elizabeth asked.

Lady Isabel said, "They left early this morning for Carryckcastle. Ye must ha' crossed paths wi' them."

Elizabeth stood abruptly, and then sat again. "But—"

"Mrs. Bonner," said Lady Isabel very gently. "Calm yersel'. Nae harm has come tae them. The viscount made sure o' that."

"She's confused," said Flora, watching Elizabeth closely.

"Yes, I am," Elizabeth said. "Why would the Campbells—why would you make an alliance with my father-in-law and let him go on his way without interference, when my husband was attacked and almost killed?"

Lady Isabel spread out her hands on her lap. "Because they came here tae ask for safe passage, just as you have."

"Mr. Bonner swore an oath," supplied Flora, not

meeting Elizabeth's gaze. "Never to come back to Scotland."

"I see." Elizabeth's thoughts were moving very quickly. She wanted to get back to Nathaniel and give him this good news—his father and Robbie were alive and well, and they were all ready to go home, right away. But it was almost too sudden to comprehend, and too many matters remained unsettled. Will, in Scotland— when Aunt Merriweather had gone to such trouble to remove him from danger of transportation for sedition. And all of them on the way to Carryckcastle. What kind of reception would they get there, when they announced their intentions?

And what of Carryck? She looked up at Lady Isabel, trying to see something of her face, but failing. She had been expecting the intense young lady of the stories she had been told, impetuous and angry; instead she had found a frail woman much older than her thirty years, perfectly in control of her emotions. But then her inheritance was safe now; she would have her revenge on her father and Jean Hope. Elizabeth saw now how foolish she had been to have thought that the rift between Lady Isabel and her father might be so easily addressed, and still she could not go away without trying.

She said, "I am very thankful for this good news, of course. We will start back to Carryckcastle much relieved. Is there any message you would like me to take to your father?"

Lady Isabel's gloved hands moved fitfully over the lawn of her gown. "Aye," she said finally and she lifted her arms—it seemed a considerable effort—to raise her veil and drape it back over the crown of her hat.

Elizabeth drew in a sharp breath. Isabel looked a great deal like the portrait of her mother that hung in Elphinstone Tower, but at first glance it seemed she had painted her face for a masquerade. Her skin was mottled stark white and bronze and something close to black in large patches over her face and neck. As shock-

ing as the condition of her complexion was, the resigned expression in her eyes was far worse.

"Ye can tell my faither that I've been punished for my
sins. First I bore Walter two deid bairns, and then this—"
She raised a gloved hand toward her face. "This will
be the death o' me. Carryck will be aye satisfied tae hear
it."

"Oh, no," Elizabeth said, more shocked at this idea
than she was at Lady Isabel's poor ruined face. "Surely
not. Not to see a child of his suffer so."

"Ye dinna ken ma faither, Mrs. Bonner." She said
this with a bitterness that Elizabeth could not counter.

"Is there nothing to be done for you?" Elizabeth
asked. "Perhaps Hakim Ibrahim—"

"The best doctors and surgeons have all been to see
her," said Flora almost huffily, as if Elizabeth had accused her of not taking sufficient measures. "None of
them can say what is wrong with any certainty, and
none of them offer her any cure."

"Everythin' possible has been done," agreed Lady
Isabel. "But the surgeons do agree on one thing—the attacks are comin' closer tegither, and I willna survive
much longer."

"I am so sorry," Elizabeth said, and then her voice
faltered; what was there to say that would not sound insincere or even dishonest? "Is there nothing else I can
do for you?"

"There is one thing," said Lady Isabel, pulling down
her veil again. "Wad ye be sae kind as tae take a letter
tae Faither Dupuis?"

Elizabeth had not been expecting this—*a letter to the
priest?*—and she waited too long to answer.

Lady Isabel went very still, and her voice came
cooler. "I see it wad be an imposition—"

"No," said Elizabeth. "No imposition at all. But I
fear I may not be able to deliver it. Yesterday evening it
seemed that Monsieur Dupuis would not live out the
night. Perhaps he did not."

The crisis came on very quickly—first Lady Isabel was sitting and then she had fallen back in her chair, her whole body shaking. Flora leaped up from the ground to bend over her, and Elizabeth did the same.

Isabel had begun to perspire so heavily that the neck of her gown was already wet through. She moaned and rolled to her side, retching.

"A doctor," Elizabeth said. She was shaking, too. "We must summon her husband."

"Walter's left for Edinburgh, and she doesn't want a doctor," said Flora, her face ashen but her voice steady. "They can't do anything for her. Help me lift her, please, so I can hold her head in my lap." And then, raising her gaze to look Elizabeth directly in the eye: "This will pass in ten or fifteen minutes. She would want you to stay."

The convulsive trembling seemed to subside a little when they had settled her more comfortably, but her breathing was very fast and shallow. They had removed her hat and Elizabeth saw that her face with its unnatural coloration was swelling visibly. She shook her head and moaned again.

"Is she in great pain?"

"Just in her back," said the girl, in such a composed way that Elizabeth knew she must have seen these attacks many times before. "I believe the nausea is much more of a trial to her. But she has nothing on her stomach to bring up, you see."

Something of the girl's calm communicated itself to Elizabeth, and she watched silently for a moment as the shaking subsided and Lady Isabel's breathing began to return to normal. Flora stroked her brow gently, with the loving touch of a sister. *Or a daughter,* thought Elizabeth. She must have been quite young when Isabel came to take up residence with them. It was not surprising that they had formed a close bond, one of them an orphan by fate and the other by choice.

"What do you think brought this on?" she asked.

"She is very fond of Monsieur Dupuis," Flora said. "If she speaks of Carryckcastle at all, it is of him."

Elizabeth turned her face away, torn between distress—had her news of Dupuis's condition brought on this crisis?—and confusion. Did Flora know that Dupuis was a Catholic priest, and that Isabel had been raised in the Roman faith? Would she have shared such sensitive information with a child, even one as dear to her as this girl must be?

"It is passed," said Flora. "Isabel, come, you must change out of this damp gown."

Slowly Lady Isabel righted herself. She looked about with some confusion and then her gaze settled on Elizabeth.

"Mrs. Bonner," she said, her voice so weak that it was hard to make her out. "I must see Monsieur Dupuis afore he dies. Do ye think there's any chance o' that?"

"I suppose—" Elizabeth faltered. "I suppose there might be. But in your condition . . ."

"I must see him," said Lady Isabel. "Flora, call for the carriage straightawa'."

30

In a half hour of intense activity all was made ready. From a chair in the hall—she was too weak to walk or even stand—Lady Isabel directed the preparations. She would brook no discussion of doctors; she would not allow Flora to accompany her.

"Think," she said to the despairing girl. "Think what Breadalbane wad make o' it, should he hear ye're at Carryckcastle. Do ye want a war foucht ower ye?"

The housekeeper, weeping openly, brought a hastily packed bag to the footman.

"Dinna greet, Mrs. Fitzwilliam," Isabel comforted her. "It will aa be weel in the end." Then she turned to Elizabeth.

"Shall we send word ahead so that your guidman can make ready?"

"No," said Elizabeth. "I think it would be better if I told him of this . . . change of plan."

Lady Isabel simply assumed that they would travel with her, and Elizabeth did not even think of opposing her. She did not like to imagine what would happen if she were to have another crisis alone in the carriage. And the quicker they were to return to Carryckcastle—

she thought of Hawkeye and Robbie and Will coming face-to-face with Moncrieff—the better.

"We will come by the Black Bull in a quarter hour," said Lady Isabel.

Elizabeth was almost out the door before Flora caught up with her. The young girl wiped her face with the back of her hand and drew in a deep breath to steady herself.

"She will have her way no matter what I say, but she need not suffer." She pressed a bottle into Elizabeth's hand. "Laudanum. It would be better if she slept during the journey."

"I will do what I can for her." Elizabeth wanted to offer the girl some words of comfort, but it would be no use at all: she knew what was ahead, and she could not be consoled.

"Send her back as soon as she has seen Monsieur Dupuis," said Flora. "Will you promise me that?"

"I promise you to try," said Elizabeth, turning again to go.

Flora came running after her again, just as she was about to turn the corner.

"Mrs. Bonner!"

There was an expression on the girl's face that Elizabeth recognized as uncertainty and willfulness all at once.

"What is it, Countess?"

"The earl sent Walter to Edinburgh to arrange for your passage to New-York." The words came tumbling out. "You are to sail as quickly as can be arranged."

Elizabeth tried to speak, but Flora cut her off and came very close.

"Pretend that you are in agreement," she whispered, taking Elizabeth's free hand to press a bulging purse into it. "Let everyone believe that you have boarded whatever ship Walter has arranged for you. But *find other passage in secret*. Do you take my meaning?"

Stunned, Elizabeth nodded.

"A hundred pounds," said Flora. "It is all I have to hand, but it should be enough." Her eyes were bright with tears.

Elizabeth put her arms around the girl and she felt her trembling, as she herself trembled. "Thank you," she said softly.

Flora pulled away, and wiped her face. "Take care of Isabel," she said. "She's all I have." And she ran off, her heels kicking up the hem of her skirt.

Nathaniel paced the room while she talked, asking questions now and then but mostly listening. When Elizabeth had recounted her last remarkable conversation with the young Countess of Loudoun, he stopped in his tracks.

"Walter Campbell's not a complete idiot," he said grudgingly. "It would be easier to get rid of all of us at once if he got us on that ship."

"I am so glad you approve of his methods," said Elizabeth dryly.

He grunted as he slipped the pistol back into its holster. Elizabeth lifted Daniel, still napping, into the cradle of her arms. He stretched and turned toward her, nuzzling sleepily. The weight of him was an anchor that brought her back to herself; she was still shaking a little, and she could not get Isabel's face out of her mind.

There was the sound of a carriage pulling up at the door, and Elizabeth was overcome with dread. She said, "The last time I had this feeling was when I set off by myself to fetch Robbie and I didn't know if I'd find you alive when I came back."

"That took a good end, and so will this," said Nathaniel, meeting her gaze. He was perfectly calm, and that did her more good than any promises.

"This time we're together, Boots. That makes all the difference."

•　　•　　•

The coach was pulled by a double team of eight horses. It had been outfitted for an invalid, with one seat as broad as a bed and deeply upholstered for comfort. Lady Isabel sat partially upright, her back supported by cushions and her body wedged carefully in place with pillows. She held her hat with its veils in her lap, perhaps because she felt she had nothing more to hide from Elizabeth; perhaps because she wanted Nathaniel to see her for what she was.

He showed no surprise at the sight of her ruined face, but Isabel hadn't anticipated Daniel. She looked from the baby to Nathaniel and back again.

"It's nae wunder that ma faither doesna want tae let ye leave," she said. "For sae many years he's wanted a son, and got none. And there ye sit, the answer tae aa his woes."

"It ain't that easy," said Nathaniel.

"Oh, but it is," said Isabel, closing her eyes briefly. "Let me explain it tae ye, for I'm sure Moncrieff nivver did."

Nathaniel might have stopped her, but Elizabeth put a hand on his arm. Isabel saw this, and she dropped her gaze to study her gloves as she spoke.

"What ye must understan' is this: I go tae my grave childless, and that will leave my faither wi' nae legal issue. If Daniel Bonner will no' come forward as the son o' Jamie Scott and claim Carryck, the peerage title will be extinguished and the lands will go tae the Campbells of Breadalbane anyway, according tae the entail o' 1541."

"Carryck could claim Jennet as his own," said Nathaniel.

Something slid across Isabel's face—jealousy or perhaps simple disbelief—before she banished it. "He could try tae claim her. But Breadalbane will prevail in the courts, that's a certainty."

Elizabeth said, "And if he married again, and had a son?"

"It's that verra thing that Breadalbane fears above aa else," Isabel conceded. "But I dinna think my faither can bring himsel' tae leave Jean, and it's been ten years since she brought a livin' child intae the world."

Nathaniel had been watching Isabel with a blank expression, but now he leaned forward suddenly and said, "Why is it you want to see Dupuis?"

Isabel lifted her head to look hard at him, her eyes intelligent and calculating, so strangely human and familiar in a face stippled bronze and black. For a long moment she was silent, but then she pushed out a sigh and answered him with a question of her own.

"Why should I care if ye think the worst o' me? I'll soon be deid."

"You didn't answer my question," said Nathaniel.

"But I will," said Isabel with a weary smile. "If ye'll listen tae the whole story. And if I live through the tellin' o' it."

"I met Walter Campbell at the Lammas Fair five years syne," began Isabel. "I was twenty-five years old, and nae man called me his sweetheart. Pridefu', they said o' me. Bonnie Isabel, the laird's massie dauchter. It's true, I was proud o' my beauty—but it was my faither wha sent the suitors awa'. 'A dauchter o' Carryck canna marry where she chooses,' he said that tae me oft and oft. 'Ye owe Carryck fealty.' And I—" She smiled bitterly. "I believed him.

"But I was young, and it wasna easy. David Chisholm—perhaps ye've seen him in the village. He's marrit these six years. David wanted me, and I wad ha' taken him. But he didna suit my faither, and sae I did as I was tolt, and turned my face awa' fra him. And there were others." She looked up at Elizabeth. "Ye wadna believe it tae see me now, but the lads liked tae see me weel enough.

"But it was aa for naught. My faither let it be kennt

that nane o' them wad do. They aa thoucht he wanted a title for me, or a rich man, anither fortune tae add tae his own. They didna ken the truth o' it, that he wad see me married tae a Catholic, or no' at aa. Wi' time I tired o' waitin' and said that I wanted tae be wed, but he wad tell me tae bide a while longer. 'Soon ye'll ken him, yer guidman.' He said it sae oft, and I trusted him. Fool that I was.

"And then came Lammas Fair. I went doon tae the village wi' Simon, for he luved naethin' better than a fair in summer. I begged Jean tae come, too, but she couldna get awa'. She gave aa the servants leave tae go, but she must stay behind wi' wee Jennet, for the bairn was puirly.

"And a fine evenin' it was, warm and bright and the smell o' fresh hay sae heavy in the air, and there was music. Mick Lun played the fiddle and there was a pennywhistle and a bodhrán, too. That was when the auld minister was still in Carryckton, and he didna mind a bit o' dancin'. That's how I met Walter, ye see. He fetched me tae the dance."

She paused, her breath coming a little faster now. Elizabeth leaned forward, but she held up a hand. "Let me rest for a moment," she said. "And then I must tell the rest."

For a while Elizabeth watched the cloud shadows chase each other across the rippling barley, waiting for Isabel to find the strength to tell them this story she did not really want to hear. She felt the need to reach out and touch Nathaniel, but she held back for fear of making Isabel feel all the more isolated.

"Perhaps ye willna believe me, but he didna tell me his whole name, and I didna ask," she continued after a while. "It was naethin' tae me but a flirtation. The others were afraid o' my faither, but this stranger wi' a clever tongue and a quick foot didna seem tae care that I was the laird's dauchter, and that pleased me.

"When it was time tae be awa' hame, he tolt me he

wad spend the nicht in the hayrigs were I tae promise tae come the next evening and dance wi' him agin. And I gave him that promise, but naethin' else. No' even a kiss.

"Simon and I, we walked up the brae singin' and laughin'. It had come tae rain, but we were in high spirits and didna mind. Do ye ken where the road turns sudden like and dips around a great outcroppin' o' stone?"

Nathaniel nodded.

"Aye, weel. He was there, waitin' for us."

"Walter?" Elizabeth asked.

"Moncrieff," said Isabel. "Angus Moncrieff, stinkin' o' whisky. I can see him still by the light o' his lantern, though I've tried my best these five years tae forget. And he stops us, Simon and me, and he says 'The whore and the whoreson, what a lovely pair.' "

Isabel had been watching the countryside pass by the window as she spoke, but she turned now to look at Elizabeth, her patchwork face drawn tight in remembered anger. "He called me a whore, untouched as I was."

Nathaniel's look of skepticism had been replaced by one of unease. "You don't have to tell the rest of this if you don't want to."

"But I do," said Isabel dully. "If Faither Dupuis is already gone, then ye must be my confessors." Her voice was very weak, but she smiled. "Why are ye surprised? Did ye think that marrying a Campbell makes me less o' a Catholic? I thoucht at first I could leave the church behind, but then I fell ill and ever since I've had a yearnin'— Ye wadna understand." She stopped herself.

Daniel squirmed and fussed on Elizabeth's lap, and she was glad of the distraction. Isabel did not know about Contrecoeur, but should they tell her? She cast a glance at Nathaniel and he shook his head very slightly.

Isabel took no note, wound up again in her story.

"Angus Moncrieff called me a whore tae my face.

But I was innocent, and that gave me the strength tae stand up and call him a liar. It was a mistake, drunk as he was. His face went aa still and white, and he stepped closer tae us baith. I remember that Simon was shakin' and sae was I, I suppose. And Moncrieff says in a voice sae soft and fine: 'I saw ye wi' Breadalbane's bastard, pressin' yersel' against him, lettin' him put his hands on ye. Did ye spread yer legs for him under the corn rigs, or did he cover yer back like the bitch in heat ye are?'"

Elizabeth rocked Daniel closer to her and made herself listen.

"He was fu' drunk, but I wasna afraid—foolish lass that I was. I wad ha' laughed in his face at the idea o' a Breadalbane come tae the Lammas Fair in Carryckton, if he hadna called me a whore. I raised my hand tae him, and he struck me doon, and Simon too when he came tae help me. And I shouted at him: 'Wha gives ye the richt tae raise yer hand tae me, Angus Moncrieff? Wha are ye but my faither's factor, and perhaps no' much longer that?'

"He smiled at me then and in perfect calm he said, 'I'll marry ye yet, and then I'll teach ye richt and proper wha yer faither canna be bothered tae teach ye.' He looked at Simon then, cowerin' on the road, and he said 'Ask the whoreson's mither what a guid teacher the laird is when he's got a willin' lass as pupil.'"

Isabel's hands had begun to twitch in her lap, and her voice seemed to fail her completely. She closed her eyes.

"Is that how you learned about your father's attachment to Jean Hope?" Elizabeth asked.

Isabel nodded. "But I dinna believe him. I couldna believe him." She had begun to perspire very heavily.

Nathaniel glanced uneasily at Elizabeth, and she leaned forward. "Flora gave me laudanum," she said. "To make you more comfortable."

"Comfort is for the grave," said Isabel shortly. "I will finish this tale, and should it be the end o' me.

Unless yer afeart tae hear it?" She looked at Nathaniel as she said this, and there was a flash there of the young woman who had challenged Angus Moncrieff on the mountain road.

"Go on," said Nathaniel. "We're listening."

"Ye'll think me aye donnert tae hear me admit it, but I nivver thoucht o' Jean wi' my faither. When Jennet came intae the world I believed— Ach, what does it matter now? I thoucht Jean was layin' wi' one o' the earl's men but that she wadna marry for my sake. What an eijit I was."

The anger was still there, in the way she raised her head as she talked, in the set of her jaw while she gathered her thoughts. Elizabeth remembered Hannah's story of her: *a headstrong young woman who did not see what she did not care to see.* It was hard to believe this was the same lady.

Her voice rough now with the effort, Isabel took up the story again. "I couldna think o' Jean wi' my faither, and no more could I think o' mysel' wi' Moncrieff. There he stood in the rain, sae proud o' himsel'. Mair than fifty, narrow o' shoulder and slack o' gut, a mean-spirited, cankert auld man wi' naethin' tae recommend him as a husband but the scapular he wore aroond his neck. I didna believe that my faither wad wed me tae sic a man, Catholic or no, and I laughed in his face. I said, 'I'll take every Campbell in Scotland tae my bed afore I'll marry ye, Angus Moncrieff.' And I saw too late what I had done."

Moncrieff's face rose before Elizabeth, contorted in rage about the Campbells. A sick knot rose in her throat. Nathaniel put his hand on hers, and she clasped it with all her strength.

"Ye can guess the rest. He threw me tae the ground. Simon screamed and screamed, but he wadna stop. I foucht him—" She paused. "I foucht him until he hit me in the heid sae hard that I saw stars. And then he finished what he had started."

She reached over and touched Elizabeth gently.

"Dinna greet for me, Mrs. Bonner. It's lang syne, and tears enough ha' been shed on account o' Angus Moncrieff. And look, the bairn is teary eyed, too. May I hold him?"

Nathaniel took Daniel and settled him on Isabel's lap. The baby looked up at her soulfully, and she ran her fingers through his curls. "What a braw laddie ye are, Daniel Bonner. Come, lay yer heid."

The baby seemed to understand her needs as well as his own, for he put his face against her thin chest, content to let her pet him. "Baith o' mine were laddies," she said, almost to herself. "But neither lived mair than a day. Walter wanted a son tae inherit my faither's title, but I wanted tae raise up a lad tae bring me Moncrieff's heart, still beatin'. The hardest thing aboot dyin' is that he goes unpunished. And perhaps that's why I'm tellin' you this tale." She met Nathaniel's gaze, and then looked away again before he could say anything.

"When I came tae masel' agin, I was alone on the road. My heid hurt and my knees were wabblin', but I feared Moncrieff had killt Simon, and sae I set aff hame as fast as I could, unsteady as I was. And I found him, too, just where I thoucht he micht be if he had got awa' frae Moncrieff. He was hidin' in the fairy wood. Feverish already, and shakin' wi' it.

"I luved Simon like a brither, though he was nane o' my bluid. And we sat taegither in the rain, shiverin' and greetin', and holdin' on tae one anither. And then I said tae him, 'Come, Simon, come. We must rouse the laird and tell him that Moncrieff has lost his mind. He'll send the men oot tae find him, and they'll kill him where he stands.' But the lad wadna leave aff wailin', and sae I rocked him and sang tae him quiet, there in the darkened fairy wood wi' the summer rain comin' doon. By and by he settled, and then he put his arms aroond my neck—I can feel him still, shiverin'—and he said, 'Moncrieff is aye mad, but he's no' a liar.'

"And that's how I came tae learn the truth aboot my

faither. 'Ye owe Carryck fealty,' he said tae me sae many times. And the while he was preachin' at me aboot my duty tae Carryck, he was wi' Jean. He sent David Chisholm awa'—a finer man ye'll nivver ken, for aa he's a Protestant—and promised his only dauchter and heir tae *Angus Moncrieff*.

"And sae I left. I left Simon there feverish in the rain, and I ran back doon tae the village tae find Walter. And I asked him was it true, was he truly a Campbell o' Breadalbane? And when he said it was, I asked him tae take me awa'. Even a day earlier I wad ha' cut my own throat rather than take up wi' a Campbell, but not then. Not then. I turned my back on Carryck, and Simon.

"It didna take lang for me tae learn the truth aboot Walter. I was naethin' mair tae him than a way tae win Carryck for his faither, and gain his favor. And then word came o' Simon, deid o' the fever he took that nicht in the fairy wood, and I saw then that I had nae choice. I marrit Walter Campbell, and went tae live at Loudoun Castle when his faither made him curator. Flora was my only joy in those years, orphaned as she was and needin' me.

"Perhaps now ye'll understand," she said softly. "It's my fault that Simon died. If I die unshriven, I'll burn for aa eternity. And now I'll take the laudanum, if ye'd be sae kind."

She slept so deeply that they might have talked, but Elizabeth had drawn deep inside herself and Nathaniel knew that there would be no comfort for her now; no words would wash away those pictures Isabel had drawn for them. It would take blood to do that.

There were reasons enough to kill Angus Moncrieff: weeks spent in the Montréal gaol, Hawkeye and Robbie lost, sailors drowned, children stolen, the new tremble in Curiosity's hands, Elizabeth convulsed in agony, her eyes blank with fear. Reason enough, but he might have

walked away and left the man standing, until today. Now when Angus Moncrieff died it would be for all those things, but most of all it would be for Isabel Scott Campbell, once of Carryckcastle. *My cousin.* Nathaniel thought it to himself for the first time, and knew that it was so. And it would be for Simon Hope.

No matter how he went back over the stories they had heard about Simon from Jennet and Isabel, it just didn't add up. That a boy as strong as Simon was said to be taking a fever in a summer rain and dying of it four weeks later made no sense. On the other hand, Simon had been the only witness when Moncrieff raped the laird's daughter, and that put him in a situation more dangerous than a summer cold.

Elizabeth put Daniel to the breast, leaning against Nathaniel for support. He put his arm around her and when his wife and son had fallen asleep he stayed awake to keep watch, his free hand on the butt of his pistol, his thumb moving slowly back and forth over the polished wooden stock.

They were traveling alongside the Moffat Water, no more than an hour away from Carryckcastle, when a sharp high whistle followed by rough shouting caused the horses to break their stride. The driver bellowed oaths as the coach jerked to a halt.

Nathaniel held Elizabeth steady with one arm while he leaned forward to stop Isabel from rolling off the makeshift bed. The laudanum had done its work and she hardly stirred, but Elizabeth came awake immediately as did the boy, stretching and fussing in her arms.

"What is it?" She clutched Daniel to her and he cried louder. "Nathaniel? Are we being attacked?"

"Highwaymen, it looks like," he said, trying to get a look at the horsemen who had come up on the coach without making a target of himself.

"Highwaymen in broad daylight?" Elizabeth was angry enough to march out there and confront them—he

had seen her do things like that before—so Nathaniel got hold of her.

"Easy," he said. "Let me take care of this." He drew his pistol.

"Walter Campbell!" called a man's voice, harsh and imperious. "Show yourself!"

Elizabeth's head snapped sharply in that direction. "Highwaymen, indeed," she said, incensed and relieved all at once. "Do you not recognize Will Spencer's voice? What can this mean?"

Nathaniel threw open the door with a grin. "It means the Campbells were dead wrong to think they had us fooled."

Elizabeth was still struggling with her open bodice when Nathaniel stepped out of the coach, but she heard the reunion well enough. A moment of silence and then voices raised, all of them talking at once, and through it all Robbie's roar, so loud that the horses reared and the coach jerked again. "Christ save me, Nathaniel!"

Isabel stirred slowly. Her face contorted, confusion and pain both. Elizabeth's surprise and elation at this unexpected reunion was replaced by concern for her.

"What is it?"

Elizabeth put a hand to her brow—her fever was high again, and her hair damp with perspiration. There was a jug of water, and she quickly poured some, her hands trembling so terribly that she almost dropped both jug and cup. Daniel fussed on the bench, furious at being abandoned.

"Drink this," she said. "And sleep. There is nothing to fear, it is just my father-in-law, come to intercept us."

Isabel struggled up, turning toward the men's voices. Then she closed her eyes and laid her head back again. "Waiting on the road to Edinburgh. Breadalbane underestimated them." And then: "How much farther?"

"Perhaps an hour," said Elizabeth. "We will not delay."

"Elizabeth?" Nathaniel calling for her.

Isabel put a hand on Elizabeth's wrist.

"Did Flora tell ye aboot the passage Walter is arrangin' for you?"

"Yes."

"Aye, I thoucht she wad tell ye. She has a guid heart," said Isabel. "When the time comes, will ye send word tae her, and tell her . . . tell her tae be strong. Will ye do that?"

Elizabeth nodded. "I will."

Elizabeth delivered Daniel—still howling his indignation—into his grandfather's arms. Eyes pooling with tears, the boy blinked, sniffed, and then smiled broadly.

"Ain't you a sight for sore eyes." Hawkeye lifted him up at arm's length and the two of them studied each other intently.

Hawkeye was sun-browned and leaner, but the serene self-assuredness that was his hallmark was still there. When he put his hand on her shoulder some of that quiet energy seemed to flow into Elizabeth, and for a moment her knees went soft with gratitude and elation and simple comfort to have these men near again.

She patted Robbie's arm compulsively and he patted her back, blushing and smiling in his pleasure.

"Mrs. Bonner!" The driver called to her. He held his whip raised over the horses and a desperate expression on his face, ready to bolt.

"MacArthur," she said, in a calm tone she knew he would recognize. "There is no cause for alarm. Lady Isabel is in no danger. These are friends, although I realize they gave you a shock. We will continue on our way in just a few moments."

The large jaw worked convulsively as he tried to take this in. Then he sat again, his whip across his lap.

"And here we thoucht we'd have tae storm Carryckcastle tae see ye again," Robbie repeated for the third time. "What are ye doin' here, and how come ye doon the road in a coach bearing the arms o' the Countess o' Loudoun?"

"What are *we* doing here?" Nathaniel laughed.

"Indeed," said Elizabeth. "We might ask you the same thing. You most especially, William Spencer."

"He came to rescue you from the *Jackdaw,* but he had to be satisfied with two old men instead," said Hawkeye, tucking Daniel into the crook of his arm just as Daniel tucked his thumb into his own mouth.

"Is that so?" Elizabeth slipped an arm through his. "This is a William Spencer I am unfamiliar with."

Will was not to be ruffled. "Elizabeth," he said calmly. "You did not really believe that once Runs-from-Bears told me of the kidnapping, I'd sit in Québec and wait for word of your fate?"

It was Will's voice and manner of expression, but otherwise Elizabeth hardly recognized her cousin. Gone were the elegant coats and silk stockings; he stood before her in a rough linen shirt and homespun breeches with a dark cape flung back over his shoulders, his hair shorn close to the scalp. He too was leaner, almost wiry now, and when he smiled he revealed the loss of an eye-tooth, giving him a decidedly disreputable look.

"I didn't think you'd come racing after me," she said.

An oxcart piled with manure and buzzing with flies came around the corner and slowed as the farmer gaped, openmouthed, at the strangers gathered in the road.

"This ain't the right place for a discussion," said Hawkeye.

"True enough," said Nathaniel. "But there's things to clear up before we get to Carryckcastle."

"And Lady Isabel is in great distress," Elizabeth added. "We can delay no longer."

The men exchanged glances, and then Will Spencer

spoke to Nathaniel. "You take my horse, and I will ride
in the coach with the ladies. That way we can exchange
news as we go along. Do you think that will be acceptable to Lady Isabel, Elizabeth?"

"I think she is insensible of most everything at the
moment," Elizabeth said. "But give me a moment to
make her ready."

"So it *was* Christian Fane," Elizabeth said later, when
her cousin had related the events of the last month: how
Will had crossed paths with his old friend in Halifax
when he had been desperately seeking a ship and captain willing to pursue the *Jackdaw.* The way they had
come upon Mac Stoker just as they had caught sight of
the fleet on its way to engage the French. The damage
done to the *Jackdaw,* and Stoker's pride. Will's disappointment to find that Elizabeth and Nathaniel were
not on board at all, but on the *Isis,* a much more formidable foe.

"Fane was eager to be of help," said Will. "As always, very glad of a chance to be of service to you.
Once we learned from Hawkeye and Robbie that you
were on the *Isis,* he wanted to set off in pursuit—" He
paused, and glanced at Lady Isabel.

Elizabeth had arranged her veils around her face to
spare her embarrassment, and her breathing—still shallow—caused the fine white netting to flutter fitfully. She
seemed still undisturbed by their conversation, and Will
continued.

"But the admiral got sight of us and there was no
help for it, we were ordered straight into battle," Will
concluded. "It was a most ill-timed and unfortunate diversion."

"A diversion," Elizabeth said dryly. "To have put
yourself in such danger—"

"You run the risk of offending me, cousin. Do you
think I was not equal to the challenge? I admit I did not

acquit myself in battle as well as your father-in-law and Robbie did. Fane would have liked to commission them on the spot. I myself caught a piece of shell—"

He turned his head to show her a healing wound on the back of his scalp. "It cost me my hair, as you see, but I find I quite like being shorn like a sheep. Amanda does not mind terribly."

"Amanda," said Elizabeth. "Where is she?"

"With her mother in Edinburgh," said Will. "Waiting for you, and very impatiently, I must say. They are greatly worried. Can you tell me what lies ahead for us at Carryckcastle? How difficult will it be?"

Daniel was sitting on Will's lap, examining the ties on his shirt with great interest and gumming them when he managed to get one into his mouth. Elizabeth watched for a moment while she gathered her thoughts.

"I suppose I must begin the story in Canada, with Monsieur Dupuis," she said, checking once again on Lady Isabel. "It begins with him, and I think it may end with him, as well."

Hannah and Jennet climbed the oak in the fairy wood with their pockets full of bread and cheese and pears from the conservatory, blush-pink and still warm from the sun.

"Ye're verra quiet the-day," Jennet said, contemplating Hannah's profile. "Can ye no' tell me what's the matter? Is it the story my granny tolt ye, or are ye still thinkin' aboot Dame Sanderson?"

Hannah bit into her pear and wiped the juice from her chin with her palm. "I dreamed about her last night."

It was not the whole truth, but it would have to suffice for now.

"This morning when I went doon tae kirk I heard that she killed three dogs yesterday at the baitin', wi' nary a scratch on her."

This was no comfort at all, but Hannah did not like

to distress Jennet about something she could not help, and so she changed the subject. "The French ladies left while you were gone," she said.

"Awa' tae find the young one a husband," agreed Jennet. "Perhaps she'll ha' better luck in Edinburgh."

"Monsieur Contrecoeur stayed behind." It was not a question, but Jennet understood it as one. She tucked a bit of bread into her cheek like a squirrel, chewing thoughtfully.

"He'll stay until Faither Dupuis passes ower," she said. "Perhaps longer—the earl doesna like tae be wi'oot a priest."

Now that they could talk openly about this—Hannah was relieved to be able to ask the questions that most bothered her—she hardly knew where to start. She said, "How many of you are there? Catholics, I mean."

"No' sae many. The Hopes, Laidlaws—my mither's folk, ye ken—alang wi' the MacQuiddys, the Ballentynes, and the rest o' the earl's men. And Gelleys, o' course."

"But you go to kirk anyway with the Protestants?"

Jennet looked at her as if she were soft in the head. "O' course. We must live in the world as Presbyterians, for there's nae place in Scotland for Catholics these days. We aa attend kirk, even the earl. Granny says it taxes the brain but it does the soul nae harm tae listen tae Holy Willie. Do ye miss goin' tae Mass since ye're here?"

"To Mass?"

Her confusion seemed to irritate Jennet. "Ye're baptized Catholic, and that by a *Jesuit*, were ye no'?"

Hannah had been baptized, it was true, as were many of the Kahnyen'kehàka at Good Pasture. Some had let the priests have their way out of curiosity, some because they did not want to offend them. But Jennet seemed to think that the baptism brought some kind of change with it, when Hannah knew that just the opposite was true among her mother's people. They might listen with interest to the stories of Jesus, but that did not stop them from praying to Ha-wen-ne'-yu or performing the six

thanksgiving rites that divided the seasons. The two had nothing to do with one another.

"I am baptized, but I am not Catholic," Hannah said firmly.

Jennet snorted through her nose. "The Protestants wadna agree wi' ye."

And of course this was true. Mr. MacKay rose before her mind's eye, sputtering his disgust and delighted with the proposition of her burning in hell for all eternity. *Papists among the savages.* She did not like to think of him, especially now with her father and Elizabeth secretly away in Moffat.

"A rider," said Jennet, her face transforming instantly into high curiosity. She stood, one arm slung around the trunk of the tree, to get a better view.

"'Nezer Lun," she said, looking troubled now. "I've nivver seen the man move sae fast."

The horse and rider had already disappeared into the courtyard by the time the girls had managed to scramble down the oak, and now they could hear more horses coming at a gallop. Inside the courtyard men were shouting for the earl.

The riders appeared, three of them, and drew up their mounts just outside the gate.

"An attack," whispered Jennet, suddenly very pale. And then, to Hannah's back as she ran off: "Wait! Ye canna!"

Hannah whirled, and threw out her arms. "But I can, I must. It's my grandfather and Robbie, and my father, too—" And she was away, with Jennet close behind.

Nathaniel watched the earl stride down the courtyard toward the gate, his men a solid wall at his back. He wondered what was in his father's head right now, to see Carryck for the first time. To see the line of his own brow, the set of his jaw, the very shape of his own

shoulders in a stranger, and to know now what he had been told was true: this man was his first cousin, and his own father had been born to this land.

When the earl stood before them, Hawkeye raised his voice, hard and sure. "Dan'l Bonner of New-York State. I'm here to claim the rest of my family. My two granddaughters, and Curiosity Freeman. Send them out to me here."

In the full force of the late afternoon sun Carryck looked drawn and older than his years, a yellowish cast to his skin. But his voice was strong and unwavering.

"You are welcome tae Carryckcastle, Daniel Bonner. I would like tae speak wi' ye, in private. Will ye no' come in and drink wi' me?"

For a long moment they watched each other, two old lions each in his full power and strength, neither willing to concede to the other.

"I will," said Hawkeye finally. "If you agree to call your man Moncrieff to account for the wrongs he has committed against me and mine. If you agree to let us pass when we decide it's time to go."

Beside Nathaniel, Robbie shifted in his saddle, still scanning the crowd of men in the courtyard for some sign of Moncrieff, and finding none. Then Hannah came up to him, and he leaned down to put a hand on her head.

The earl spoke over his shoulder. "Dagleish," he said. "Fetch Moncrieff here. Dinna tell him why. And take twa men wi' ye in case he should resist."

He raised his voice again. "My men will fetch Moncrieff fra' the village, and ye can call him tae account in front o' this company. Ye are free tae leave whenever ye like. Now, will ye accept my hospitality?"

"If it's meant for all of us, aye. Us and the others, who come after."

Carryck's eyes scanned their faces, and came to rest on Nathaniel, calculating how he had come to be there,

weighing his options. "I see ye've been awa'," he said dryly.

"I have," Nathaniel agreed. "Away and back again, to claim what is mine."

"Ye're mair Scott than ye'll ever ken," said Carryck. And then to Hawkeye: "Aa o' yer party are welcome. I will hear your complaints against my factor, and should punishment be warranted, punishment will be dispensed."

The sound of the carriage was louder now. The men behind Carryck began to look at each other, touching their weapons in that way that soldiers have, as automatically as they breathed.

One approached Carryck, and he spoke to them all. "Leave me."

They went unwillingly, murmuring among themselves. Now Nathaniel caught sight of Jean Hope and old MacQuiddy at the rear of the courtyard and in the window above them, Curiosity with Lily on her hip. Robbie had dismounted, and he crouched down next to Hannah, the two of them deep in conversation.

Later Nathaniel would tell Elizabeth that he had heard the story of Lot's wife more than once, but it wasn't until Carryck caught sight of the Loudoun coat of arms on the coach that he knew what it meant to see a living being turn to stone. His face went as glassy smooth as rock salt, and when he looked up at Hawkeye his eyes were dead.

"My daughter-in-law," Hawkeye said. "And your daughter, come home to die. But first she has her own charges against Moncrieff."

Jean Hope came forward, her hands pressed to her heart and on her face an expression Nathaniel had seen once before, the morning Sarah had gained a daughter and lost a son: a woman torn in half between joy and sorrow. He spoke to her gently.

"She's asked for the priest. Will you take her to him?"

This unexpected appearance of his daughter had

turned Carryck to stone, but all the bones seemed to
flow out of Jean Hope, her body curving forward. She
started toward the coach and then stopped, looked to
Carryck for something, some sign, but got none.

Robbie went to the coach as the door opened. Ever
since he had heard the story of Moncrieff's crimes
against Carryck's daughter he had been unusually still
and closed within himself; it was as if this final evidence
of Moncrieff's malice had broken some last faith in
him, and now he took it on as his own duty to offer
Lady Isabel whatever comfort he could.

When he turned around again, he held her in his
arms as carefully and lovingly as he would hold an infant. She had lost a shoe and one small foot swung free
in its white stocking, as fine and frail as a child's. Her
hands lay among the netting that covered her face and
fell down to her waist, discolored and swollen as a
man's fists after a hard fight.

For a moment Robbie stood there looking at
Carryck over Isabel's still form—Nathaniel could not
even be sure she was breathing—and then he walked
past the man without a word.

He stopped before Jean Hope and she placed her
hands on Isabel, touching her lightly here and there. And
then she turned and led Robbie toward Elphinstone
Tower. MacQuiddy fell in behind them, and from a
shadowy corner Jennet came running, too, with one
backward glance toward Carryck.

They gathered in the Great Hall: the earl at the head of
a long table under the carved and gilded coat of arms,
Nathaniel and Hawkeye to either side of him, and next
to them Elizabeth and Curiosity, each with a baby in
her lap. Will sat beside Elizabeth. Hannah would not
stay in her chair, but flitted between the men as if she
was afraid they might disappear again if she were to sit
down or look away.

Hawkeye asked her a question in Mahican and she answered it in Kahnyen'kehàka, and asked him a question in turn. Nathaniel was listening too but he did not interrupt, and Elizabeth had the sense that he had heard what he needed to know on the journey here. From the look on Robbie's face when he had taken Isabel in his arms, Nathaniel had told them her story, too.

Carryck poured whisky. Whatever he had wanted to say to Hawkeye, whatever arguments about family and duty and blood ties and the land—all seemed to have deserted him. He stared in turn at the door that led to Elphinstone Tower and the window into the courtyard.

Elizabeth rocked Lily to her, smoothing the skin of her face and thinking of Isabel who was someplace over their heads in the tower, seeking some consolation, some of the sense of herself that she had lost the night she ran away from this place. In the last few minutes of the journey she had had another crisis, this one much worse than the earlier one in the garden. It had come upon her there where the road to the castle turned suddenly and dipped around a great outcropping of stones. Will had spoken gentle words to her even in her extremity, and Elizabeth had sent her own prayers to whatever God was looking over Isabel. *Give her just one more hour. Let her face Moncrieff and go easy to her grave.*

Contrecoeur came in, his expression unreadable. He walked the length of the hall, his heels ticking against the flagstones like an overwound clock, to stop before Carryck.

"Dupuis has heard her confession and absolved her of her sins, but it took the last of his strength. She is asking for you, my lord Earl. The doctor says she is very close to death."

All faces turned to Carryck, but he studied the bottom of his cup with unflinching concentration. Curiosity hummed low in her throat, a mournful sound.

It wasn't until the horses came into the courtyard that Carryck raised his head. Contrecoeur still waited

for his answer, but he looked past the priest as if he were invisible.

Moncrieff's voice came to them, hoarse and angry, and then louder, an oath and a challenge to the armed men who had brought him. There was a scuffling as he was dragged down from his horse. Elizabeth's heart raced and Lily, nursing greedily as if to make up for the hours away from her mother, coughed on the quickened flow of milk.

He strode into the Great Hall alone. At the sight of Hawkeye he came to a sudden stop. For a moment he stared, and then he turned to Carryck, his head up at a proud angle.

"My lord Earl," he said, his voice ringing through the hall, unflinching. "Why have ye sent for me in sic a manner?"

Carryck closed his eyes and then opened them again slowly. "We have a visitor."

"I see that, my lord." Moncrieff pushed his chest forward. Bravado or courage, it was hard to tell what moved him. "I tolt ye he wad come, in the end."

"We have a visitor fra' Loudoun," said Carryck evenly. "Lady Isabel is come hame."

For a moment Moncrieff's expression did not change. Then a small tic began at the corner of his eye and spread by degrees over his face until it reached his mouth, which opened and then shut before he turned, eyes blazing, to Hawkeye.

"This is your doing," he said. "Ye've taken up wi' Breadalbane."

"Monsieur Contrecoeur," Elizabeth said before Hawkeye could respond to Moncrieff. "Would you kindly ask Robbie MacLachlan to bring Lady Isabel here? She will want to speak directly to this man in her father's presence."

Moncrieff flung out both arms in a frustrated appeal. "My lord Earl. This is a devious plot tae discredit me for doin' naethin' mair than what ye bade me tae do—

bring that man, yer bluid cousin, tae Carryckcastle. Can ye let a Breadalbane stan afore ye and believe even a word o' what she has tae say?"

Carryck poured more whisky into his own cup. When he had drunk, he wiped his mouth.

He said, "I gave Daniel Bonner my word that I wad listen tae the charges against ye His charges, and . . . hers, as weel. Ye'll stand there and listen wi' me, Angus. Unless ye have somethin' tae fear fra' her?"

Moncrieff held his gaze for a long moment, and then he nodded.

Carryck spoke to Contrecoeur without looking at him.

"Bring her," he said.

Elizabeth watched Contrecoeur walk back to the tower, willing him to move faster, to run. And then he opened the door and the hall filled with the sound of Jean Hope's weeping, a sound hardly human that washed over them like a fitful breeze. Robbie came down the tower stairs and through the door, his normally florid complexion ashen.

"She's gone."

"God have mercy on her soul," said Will quietly.

"Amen," added Curiosity.

Moncrieff started, turning first to Carryck and then back toward Contrecoeur, who stood still with his hand on the tower door.

He passed a hand over his face, and then he smiled. Isabel was dead, and Moncrieff could hardly contain his joy. Elizabeth shuddered in sorrow and a deep and absolute loathing for the man who stood there, smiling at them, blinking in confusion and relief so profound he could not hide it: a condemned man with a last-minute reprieve from the gallows.

Nathaniel pushed back his chair as he came to his feet. "Counting your blessings right about now, ain't

you, Angus? That she died before she could tell her father what you are."

Moncrieff's back straightened and he inclined his head, that artful tilt that Elizabeth had seen him use so many times when he was constructing a lie.

"Whatever complaints ye've got aboot me have naethin' tae do wi' Lady Isabel. May she rest in peace," he added solemnly.

Carryck drew in a breath through his teeth and then let it out again. Slowly he leaned forward to rest his head on his hands. His shoulders heaved once, and then again—a terrible dry retching that Elizabeth could not bear to see. She bent her head over her daughter and drew in Lily's smell, clean and sweet. Perhaps Carryck was thinking of Isabel when she was just as small, before she grew away from him; before he lost track of the woman she had become. Elizabeth had the power to give him back that daughter.

She stood, holding Lily to her breast. "My lord Earl, may I speak?"

Moncrieff made a small sound in his throat, but Carryck held up a hand to stop him. "Aye."

"On the journey here, your daughter Isabel told us the story of the day she eloped. Will you hear what she had to say?"

The room was so quiet that Elizabeth thought she could hear the beat of her own heart. She waited, and finally Carryck nodded. Moncrieff's face was vacant, waiting. Disbelieving.

"This is what Lady Isabel told us. After Lammas Fair five years ago, Angus Moncrieff confronted her on the road to the castle late in the night. Simon Hope was with her. He called Isabel a whore and Simon Hope a whoreson, and when she laughed at him for claiming that she had been promised to him in marriage, he told her of your alliance with Mrs. Hope. Then Angus Moncrieff assaulted and raped her there in the rain and dirt."

Nothing changed on Carryck's face, no acknowledgment or surprise. He said, "Angus. What say ye tae these charges?"

Flecks of color appeared high on Moncrieff's cheeks, just below the tic at the corner of his eye, as frantic as a heartbeat.

"Lies. Ye ken verra weel, my lord, that yer dauchter was promised tae John Munro o' Foulis on the verra day she ran aff."

From the back of the hall Jean Hope stepped forward from the shadows. Her face was red and swollen with weeping, and she wound her hands in her apron. "But Isabel nivver was told about John Munro!"

Moncrieff was untouched by Jean's sorrow and her logic. He shrugged. "Whether she knew or no', the oath was given and I witnessed it. Why wad I ha' tolt her anythin' else, or claimed her for my own?" More sure of himself now, he cast a glance toward Elizabeth. "Ye've got only the word o' a desperate woman. Elizabeth Bonner wad do anythin' in her power tae get her revenge on me, for takin' her bairns frae her in Canada. The bairns that ye see before ye, hale and hearty."

How perfectly calm he was, Elizabeth thought. And why not? Isabel and Simon were dead, and unable to call him to account.

Carryck looked so very tired. "Is there any evidence for yer charges, Mrs. Bonner? Witnesses?"

"No doubt she'll call Walter Campbell here tae swear the truth o' it," Moncrieff said angrily.

A voice rose up, high and clear. "Simon tolt me what happened. Does that make me a witness?" Jennet seemed as tiny and unsubstantial as a fairy as she came down the hall with Robbie MacLachlan, but her voice carried true.

"Come here, Jennet," said Carryck. His tone still weary, but there was something warm in it now. "Come here, lass, and tell me what ye heard."

Jennet stopped at the end of the table, and she

looked at each of them in turn. When she reached Hannah, she smiled.

"Ye've got them aa taegither finally, yer kin."

"Yes," said Hannah.

"I'm glad for ye."

Hannah left Hawkeye's side and went to stand between Jennet and Robbie.

"What did Simon tell ye, lass?" Carryck asked.

She kept her eyes fixed on the earl, as if the sight of him alone could bring this story out of her. "Simon tolt me that the factor was fou' drunk, and he foucht wi' Lady Isabel on the road tae the village, and threw her doon and hurt her. He said, 'She doesna want tae marry Moncrieff.' He said that muny times."

"The lad was fevered," said Moncrieff, almost dully. "In a delirium."

"He wasna fevered," Jennet replied indignantly. "He wasna, no' when he tolt me. And he swore me tae secrecy and made me put my hand on the Holy Bible, and noo I'm forsworn and must burn in hell, but I canna keep still no langer." Her voice wavered, but she pushed on, her anger rising hot now as she turned to face Moncrieff. "Simon thoucht it was his fault for no' protectin' her, and my mither thoucht it was her Isabel was runnin' from, but it was you. Ye couldna ha' the laird's dauchter and sae ye hurt her, and noo she's deid and ye'll burn in hell, too, for what ye did tae her and tae my brither."

"My lord Earl," Moncrieff said stiffly. "Can ye take the word o' a hysterical child ower my own?"

Carryck rose up to his full height. "She's my own flesh and bluid, Angus."

"She's your bastard, my lord."

Carryck said, "I've lost one dauchter. I willna lose anither. I'll marry Jean and make Jennet my heir."

Perspiration was beading on Moncrieff's upper lip and brow as he struggled for his composure. "Breadalbane will challenge ye in the courts."

"Aye. What of it?"

"My lord," said Moncrieff, his voice cracking. "Will ye gamble everythin' for a whore?"

The word seemed to echo down the hall. The color drained from Carryck's face to be replaced by a cold fury, the kind of rage that drives men to murder. Moncrieff saw it, too, and he drew in a hitching breath and let it go again as Carryck began to speak.

He said, "I find ye guilty o' rape on my dauchter. I find mysel' guilty o' puttin' my trust in a coward and a traitor. It is my punishment tae live knowin' tha' I let ye drive my dauchter awa', but ye'll hang on the morrow."

Moncrieff moved so fast that later Elizabeth would never be clear on exactly how it had all come to pass. His arm came up from his side with a glint of flashing metal and Elizabeth bent over in her chair to cover Lily, seeing Curiosity do the same with Daniel and taking with her a single glimpse of Jennet's blond head in the line of fire, with Hannah beside her. *Oh, God, Hannah beside her.* The men were scrambling, Nathaniel throwing himself across the table at Moncrieff but too late: the shot rang through the room and somebody screamed. *Me,* thought Elizabeth, *I screamed.* A second shot from the other end of the hall and a soft sound of surprise, a rush of breath followed by ringing silence. Elizabeth looked up from where she cowered on the floor, and she watched Angus Moncrieff fall, his throat opening like a flower, bright red petals cascading all around him.

Hannah was keening, a high, sorrowful sound. Curiosity grabbed Elizabeth's arm and pulled her to her feet to thrust Daniel at her. "Take your son," she said firmly. "Take him, now." And she climbed over Moncrieff's body—still twitching, Elizabeth saw, and drew away—in her rush toward the girls.

"Elizabeth." Nathaniel and Will together at her side, trying to lead her away. Both the babies wailing, but

Nathaniel whispered to them, *wheest*, and *wheest*, and then he was leading her to a chair near the door. "Come, come. Sit here. Sit down."

"Is she dead? Is Jennet dead? Is Hannah—"

He put his hands on her face. She had rarely seen him so pale, except when he was gun-shot himself.

"No," he said. "Neither of them hurt, not Jennet, not Hannah."

"But listen to her." She said this calmly, to make him hear what she could hear: Hannah's heart breaking and Hawkeye singing, very softly. A melody she knew; one she did not want to hear.

"Who?" she asked. "Whose death song?"

"Robbie's," Nathaniel said. "He stepped in front of the girls and the bullet caught him in the chest."

"But—" She looked over her shoulder at Moncrieff, curled like a newborn in his own blood. His brother had come to pray over him. He made the sign of the cross.

"Jean Hope," said Will. "It was Jean Hope who shot him."

Nathaniel said, "She took her revenge, and Isabel's. And ours, too."

"Good," said Elizabeth, more calmly than she felt. And then: "Let me go to Robbie. Let me say good-bye. Please."

He lay on the bloody flagstones, his head in Hannah's lap. The Hakim and Curiosity were bent over him, talking quietly together, no urgency now at all. Will had taken the babies out into the courtyard, where the maids fussed over them, bore them away to a safer place. And now Jennet wept in her mother's arms while behind them Contrecoeur murmured to his brother in Latin.

In the new quiet, Hawkeye sang a death song, telling the story of Robbie's life as he made his way through the shadowlands.

Elizabeth knelt in the blood and put her hands on

him. Smoothed his hair. "Robbie," Elizabeth called to him, and then again, louder. "Robbie?"

Hannah's eyes were bright with tears. "We must let him go," she said to Elizabeth in Kahnyen'kehàka. "It is his time."

31

They buried Robbie MacLachlan and Lady Isabel the next day, and that evening Nathaniel went looking for his father. He found him in the wood behind the paddocks, perched high in an oak, deep in conversation with Jennet and Hannah.

"When Simon died," Jennet was saying, "I thoucht perhaps it was just the fairies had stolen him awa', and that he wad come back one day. Did you feel like that when your brother Uncas died?"

Hawkeye said, "I still do." And then: "Here's your father, Squirrel, come to call us to table. Why don't you girls go along now. I've been trying to have a word with him all day."

When they had run off ahead, Nathaniel said, "I suppose I shouldn't be surprised to find you climbing trees."

"You can see a good ways from up here," said Hawkeye, dropping down as easy as a man half his age. "And that Jennet has got a story or two worth taking home."

"Squirrel will be sorry to leave her behind tomorrow."

Hawkeye nodded. His thoughts were someplace else, and Nathaniel waited for him to gather them together.

"I don't think Robbie ever expected to get back to New-York," he said finally. "Long ago some wise woman told him that he would be buried on Scottish soil. He said that to me the day we set foot on land. Said that he felt the truth of it in his gut."

Hawkeye looked around himself, at the sunset against the hills, deep gold and tawny, and he sighed. "This was the right place for him to come to die, but it ain't my place, no matter how I look at it. Ain't yours, either, from what I can tell."

In his surprise, Nathaniel stopped. "Did you think it might be?"

His father shrugged. "Don't know what I thought. I was sure before I got here how I'd feel about Carryck, but now I've seen him and it's not that simple. I don't think I've ever seen a man so tore up inside."

"It's a hard price he's paying for his mistakes," Nathaniel admitted. "But I don't see there's anything we can do for him. The Catholics and the Protestants have been at each other's throats for almost two hundred years. Even if we wanted to stay here there's nothing we could do to fix that."

Hawkeye was silent, and Nathaniel had an unsettled feeling, as if something was coming his way he couldn't predict or control. He said, "You're putting a fright into me."

"I know I am," said Hawkeye. "And with some cause. I thought about just letting what I know go to the grave with Robbie, but I couldn't live with it. I got no choice but to lay it out for you and let you make your own decisions. You and Elizabeth."

"What's this about?" Nathaniel asked.

His father put a hand on his shoulder. "Giselle Somerville," he said. "And the son she bore you the winter after you left her in Montréal those many years ago."

While his father talked, Nathaniel stood in the shadows of the forest and felt the truth of what he was saying crawl up through him and settle in his bones, word by word.

He said, "She never told me. Never said a word when I took leave from her, never sent for me."

Hawkeye pushed out a heavy breath. "I know that."

"But you believed her?"

"Not at first. Not until Robbie told me what he knew."

"Iona could have let me know." The first anger pushing up now, to be swallowed down again.

"She could have," Hawkeye said. "But then she would have had another child taken away from her. Do you think she gave Giselle up to Somerville of her own accord?"

Somerville. All the time he had been sitting in the Montréal gaol, the boy had been nearby and Somerville had kept it from him.

"All these years, Giselle thought he was in France, being raised by her mother."

"It looks that way."

"Christ," Nathaniel muttered. "Now what? Do I go looking for him, or do I leave him be? Maybe he won't want anything to do with me, or with his mother. I wish I had had more of a look at him that night in Montréal."

An ache swelled up deep inside him, like discovering a slowly seeping battle wound hours after the last shot had been fired.

Hawkeye rubbed a thumb over his chin. "You'll have to work that out with Elizabeth, son. And I expect Giselle will have something to say about it—she won't give up until she finds the boy."

"Unless Stoker finds her first."

Hawkeye inclined his head. "She's made an enemy of him, that's true."

From the courtyard gate came the sound of Squirrel's voice, calling for them. They started in that direction in silence, and then Nathaniel stopped cold.

"You were thinking of sending the boy— What did she call him?"

"Luke."

"You want to send Luke here, to Carryck."

Hawkeye nodded. "The thought crossed my mind, but it ain't my decision to make. You need to think that through."

"Do you think he'd take an interest in this place?" Nathaniel asked.

"Most men would," said Hawkeye. "Especially a young man with no land and no prospects. A young man raised Catholic."

"I'd never see him," Nathaniel said, feeling the loss already before he had even come to know the boy.

Hawkeye said, "I'd have to lay claim to Jamie Scott's place here. I couldn't do that without talking to Jean Hope and to Jennet first. Making sure they wanted it that way. Then you'd have to claim Luke as your firstborn."

They were just twenty yards from the gates now. From the courtyard came the sound of children's laughter, and Curiosity calling out after them. Elizabeth stood in the window with a baby on her arm. She had circles under her eyes, but there was a settled and peaceful look about her that he had last seen at home in Lake in the Clouds, before they had any idea of what lay ahead. She smiled when she saw him and raised her hand.

"She's a good woman," Hawkeye said. "It might hit her hard at first, but she don't have an unfair bone in her body. She'll come around to the idea."

"Maybe before I do," Nathaniel agreed, and he went in to tell Elizabeth about his son.

· · · ·

Hannah was waiting for her grandfather just inside the gate, and she pulled him aside. Something of the brightness in her had gone away with Robbie's death, some of her trust in the world. And he remembered now the morning he had walked out of Montréal with Nathaniel. How he had watched him change as they walked, leaving not just Giselle Somerville but some of himself behind, too.

"What is it, Squirrel?"

She said, "I need your help. I can't do it by myself."

He put a hand on her shoulder, felt the strength of her and the determination. People looked at the color of her skin and thought of her mother, but there was so much of his Cora in her, a fiery heart and a will of iron.

"Tell me."

In Mahican she said, "Will you come down to the village with me, Grandfather?" It was strange hearing that language of his boyhood in this place, and it did what she wanted it to: it shut out the rest of the world and drew them closer together.

"When?"

"After dark."

He kept his face impassive. To smile would be to make light of this errand of hers, and he would not insult her. "What is it that takes us to the village after dark?"

"Before I leave this place I must kill a bear," she said. And then, more quickly: "They blinded her and chained her to a post. She asked me to set her free of this place, and I gave her my promise."

A fine tension was in her now, her whole body shaking. She said, "I cannot go home and leave her."

"Then we'll go down to the village after dark," Hawkeye said calmly. "And we'll do what needs to be done. Let's go in to eat now."

She shook her head. "I have to go see the Hakim, first. Will you tell them?"

He nodded, and then waited and watched her run off, fleet as a deer.

Hannah found Hakim Ibrahim packing his instruments into their cases. He had seen three people he tried to save buried within two days, but when she hesitated at the door he looked up at her with his usual kindly and helpful smile.

"Ah," he said, wiping his hands on a bit of muslin. "I was hoping to see you this evening. I have something for you before you leave this place tomorrow."

Hannah drew in a deep breath and let it out again. She had feared he might be angry with her—it had been many days since she had come to work with him or even to speak to him—and found instead that nothing had changed. She said, "Are you leaving, too?"

"Yes. Tomorrow I must return to Southerness. The *Isis* is bound for Bombay."

"You are going home, too, then."

From the worktable he took a leather case the size of a large book and he put it down before her. Then he stood back, bowing from the shoulders. "Yes. And I have a parting gift for you."

Hannah was so surprised that she did not trust herself to speak. She ran a finger lightly over the leather and then, with unsteady hands, untied the lacings. Four scalpels, two with curved blades, forceps, probes, and suture needles, each secured by a leather strap in a bed of dark blue velvet. The instrument handles were made of ivory, slightly yellow with age.

He said, "It will be some time before you are skilled enough to use these, but I have no doubt that you will put them to good use one day."

She blinked the tears back, and nodded. "Thank you."

"You are welcome. Now, I believe you came to talk

to me about something else. Lady Isabel, or Rob MacLachlan?"

"I know what killed Robbie. The bullet must have hit the artery, here—" She touched her own chest at the midline. "The aorta. But no one can tell me what Lady Isabel's illness is called."

He folded his hands in front of himself. "There is no name for the affliction that I know. I have seen it only rarely, and each time it ends in death. In the *Al-Qanun fi'l-Tibb,* Ibn Sina writes of tubercles that settle in the kidneys. The condition of her skin would make that likely. The only way to know would be to perform an autopsy, but given the circumstances . . ." He paused. "I thought it best not to impose on the earl's grief."

Hannah thought for a moment. "But maybe it would be a comfort to him, to know why she died."

Hakim Ibrahim closed his eyes briefly and opened them again. "He believes that his lack of faith in her was what brought about her death, and even if I were to find her body full of tumors, I could not convince him otherwise."

Hannah said, "Then he is in need of your help, too."

The Hakim had a very sad smile. "You have a generous and compassionate spirit, Hannah. But if you are to be a good physician one day you must learn to recognize when your skills are not what is needed."

"'First do no harm,'" Hannah said, and now she understood this concept as she had not been able to understand it before. "But if you cannot help him, who can?"

"His God," said the Hakim. "And perhaps his priest. Now I have a question for you. Will you write to me, and tell me of your studies in medicine?"

"Yes," said Hannah. "I would like to do that."

"Then we will not say good-bye." The Hakim smiled. "For our discussions do not have to end."

She hesitated at the door, testing the weight of the surgical kit in her hands. "Do you really think I can be a physician one day?"

He bowed from the shoulders. "Of this, my friend, I am very sure."

32

The smell of the sea met them at Edinburgh, coming up suddenly as the coach started down a hill toward the city. Elizabeth sat up straighter, and even Hannah roused herself out of her daydreams.

"Headed home." Elizabeth said it aloud now and then, perhaps just to convince herself that it was really true. They would spend this evening with Aunt Merriweather and tomorrow they would board a ship. When they next stepped onto land it would be in New-York harbor.

Curiosity's thoughts were taking her in the same direction. She said, "Lord willing, we'll be in Paradise before summer's done. In time for the corn harvest, Hannah. Did you think of that?"

Hannah nodded. "In time for the festival at Trees-Standing-in-Water."

"Ain't even home yet and she ready to run off again," Curiosity said with a sigh. "Me, I ain't goin' any farther than Lake in the Clouds. Don' care if I never see another city. Or smell one, for that matter." And she sniffed at Edinburgh, ripe with waste in the summer sun.

· · ·

They came into the High Street, the women and children in the coach while Hawkeye, Nathaniel, and Will rode, surrounded by Carryck's men. The earl would take no chances with their safety; it would soon be common knowledge that Daniel Bonner of New-York State had signed a document declaring himself the son of James Scott, and with that they would become targets of the Breadalbane Campbells. It did not matter that Hawkeye would keep his vow to leave Scotland and never come back again. It did not matter, because the grandson he had left behind in Canada had made no such vow.

Daniel played peacefully in Elizabeth's lap. Nathaniel's second-born son. She still had not come to a quiet place with this idea, but she would in time. Nathaniel had expected her to be angry, or hurt, or worried about her own children's claims, but thus far she had felt nothing but confusion and some vague curiosity. He was watching her now from horseback, looking for some sign of her discontent, waiting for her anger to swell up.

Someplace inside, Nathaniel still believed that she regretted the life she was leaving behind, and only time would convince him otherwise.

"I suppose that Merriweather aunt of yours will want us all to set down with her," Curiosity said, jerking Elizabeth out of her daydreams. "She'll want the whole story."

"I suppose she will," Elizabeth agreed.

"But the whole story hasn't happened, yet." Hannah looked up from the piece of ivory she had been studying.

"Then we will tell her as much as we know," said Elizabeth. "What is that in your hand, Squirrel?"

She held it up. Not ivory at all, but a tooth yellowed with age, long and curved.

"A bear fang," Curiosity said, leaning forward to get a better look at it, and catching Lily's hand away as she

grabbed. "I didn't know there were bears around Carryck."

"There aren't," said Hannah, closing her fist around it. "Not anymore."

Curiosity was looking more closely at Hannah's face now, with concern and some disquiet. As Elizabeth was looking, seeing something new there in her familiar and beloved face, some equanimity that she had left behind her somewhere on this long journey and now found again. Robbie's sudden passing had moved her in ways Elizabeth had not quite imagined.

"Did it come from Jennet?" asked Curiosity.

"Jennet has one just like it," said Hannah. "She will wear it on a string around her neck."

"Elizabeth, my dear, we must see a milliner before you sail. To go about with no protection from the sun, have you forgotten all your training? Something must be done, for you are already as brown as a—as a—"

"As an Indian," supplied Hannah easily, looking at them over the rim of her teacup. She sent her father a sidelong glance, but Nathaniel kept his face impassive. He knew better than to get in the middle of one of Aunt Merriweather's discussions about hats.

"I admit I have not been thinking of my complexion these last few months," Elizabeth agreed, wiping biscuit crumbs from Lily's mouth. "But I promise to wear a hat on the journey home."

Aunt Merriweather had a way of rearing back with her head to look down the slope of her nose that always put Nathaniel in mind of a cross-eyed bird. She was doing it now, her mouth pursed into a little beak.

"I will charge Amanda with making sure of it," she said. "If it were not for my lumbago, I would make the journey myself. Heaven knows what you young women will get up to, you are all so set on your independence. I

did so count on bringing Kitty home to Oakmere with me, and see how she changed her mind at the last minute. I am still most seriously displeased, but perhaps you can persuade her, Elizabeth, once you are home again. Certainly you must see to it that she doesn't fall under Dr. Todd's influence. Such a very flighty young woman; she requires your firm hand if she cannot have mine." She sniffed. "Of course, you might still get it into your head to turn privateer and sail off to China, children in tow. Certainly my son-in-law already looks the part." And she scowled as if she had Will Spencer before her.

Elizabeth got up to plant a kiss on her old aunt's cheek. "You are worried for us," she said. "But please be assured, we have no interest in going anywhere but home, and that as quickly as possible."

"Do not try to mollify me," said her aunt, swatting at her with a folded fan. "I shall worry if it pleases me to worry, every day until I have word of your safe arrival. Now your husband has been waiting for you these twenty minutes, and his patience is not eternal, I am sure of it. Go on, the two of you, but do not be long."

They went to see the ship that would take them home. Hawkeye and Will had been here before, as had Thomas Ballentyne in his new role as Carryck's agent and factor. Even now Carryck's men milled around the dock, and there they would remain until the Bonners were safe away.

And still, Nathaniel knew maybe better than Elizabeth did herself that she would not rest easy tonight unless she had examined the ship and met its captain and officers.

She was called *Good Tidings*, a small but comfortable packet on her way to New-York with the mails and a shipment of Scotch whisky for the governor and porcelain for his wife. A fast ship, and not so large that

she would attract the attention of privateers—but well armed enough to repel anyone who showed unwelcome interest. The captain and owner was a Yorker by the name of George Goodey, a small man with a stern expression and a taciturn way about him; he showed them their quarters, had his sailors run out the guns for Nathaniel's inspection, and then he bade them goodbye. He suited Elizabeth very well.

"Curiosity will lock horns with him," she noted as they walked back to her aunt Merriweather's lodgings. "And she will enjoy every minute of it."

"It'll be close quarters," Nathaniel said. "Your cousin may get a little itchy."

"Amanda is too pleased to have Will back again—even her mother cannot interfere with her happiness."

"And what about you, Boots?" he asked, tucking her arm tighter under his own.

"Me? I would paddle a canoe home if that's what it required," Elizabeth said. "We have been gone only a little more than four months, but it feels like so much longer."

They walked on in a comfortable silence for a while, and then she turned to him suddenly, and stretching up on tiptoe, she kissed him there on the High Street, with people all around.

"What was that for, Boots?"

"For keeping our children safe."

"You're thinking of Isabel."

She nodded. "I can hardly think of anything else but Robbie, and Isabel."

A flush was creeping up her cheeks, anger and grief pushing her to sudden tears. Nathaniel put his arm around her as they walked, willing to wait for her to put words to what she was feeling. Until she did that, she would have no peace.

It came in a low rush. "I cannot imagine what Carryck is suffering now, to have lost his daughter not because she was disloyal, but because he was too blind to see Moncrieff's true nature."

Neither did we see him for what he was, not at first.
Nathaniel thought of saying this, but held his tongue,
knowing full well that they would have to deal with it
soon enough.

She said, "The look on Carryck's face when we took
our leave—I don't think he will ever forgive himself for
refusing to go to Isabel when he had a chance, there at
the end. And perhaps he does not deserve forgiveness."
She was flushed with remembering, still full angry.

"You know I'm not likely to make excuses for the
man," Nathaniel said, as evenly as he could manage.
"But it seems to me he knows well where the blame lies
and he ain't shirking it. I don't know that he'd survive
all this, if it weren't for Jean Hope and Jennet. And
you'll forgive me, Boots, if I point out that the man
buried his priest and his daughter within a day of each
other. That's punishment enough."

She shook her head, quite forcefully. "He is getting
what he wanted, Nathaniel. A way to keep Carryck free
of the Breadalbanes, and an heir. Do you not worry
about sending . . . Luke to him, knowing now how he
dealt with his own daughter?"

"I don't know that Luke will want to come here,"
Nathaniel said slowly. "He's more of a stranger to me
than Carryck is. And the truth is, it don't feel real, yet,
the news about the boy. You're asking me if I trust
Carryck with a son I don't know, and might never see
again. I've been thinking about that all day long, and
I'll tell you what. He's a man already, as old as I was
when he came into the world. We'll tell him what he
needs to know about this place, give him the good and
the bad of it, and he'll make his own decision. And if he
wants to come here and if that solves Carryck's problems, well then, I'll be glad for both of them, Boots. But
I know one thing for sure, and maybe it's something I
can see and you can't. Carryck will be relieved to get
the boy if that puts an end to his problems, but there's

no joy left in this world for him. He buried that part of his life with his daughter. And Moncrieff."

They had stopped walking while he said this, and Elizabeth was looking up at him with an expression divided between surprise and acknowledgment. A look came over her, the one that meant she was casting back through her memory for some words she had read somewhere, something to help her make sense of what she was feeling. And then she had them, and she spoke them out loud, but more for her own benefit than his.

> "*His flawed heart,—*
> *Alack! too weak the conflict to support;*
> *'twixt two extremes of passion, joy and grief,*
> *Burst smilingly.*"

"That's about it, I'd say. Now where did that come from?"

"*King Lear*," said Elizabeth. "A man who misjudged his daughter and paid for that mistake very dearly."

"Maybe I should read that book," Nathaniel said, trying to strike a lighter tone. "The days ain't far off when Squirrel will be moving off on her own, and I suppose I should be ready."

"We'll read it together," Elizabeth said firmly. "I'll see if we can get a copy before we set sail."

There was a carriage in front of the door when they arrived back at Aunt Merriweather's lodgings, with gold trim and an elaborate crest upon the door. Elizabeth caught sight of a young man waiting inside, lolled back against the cushions.

"Someone has come to call," she said to Nathaniel, and seeing the reluctant look on his face, she said, "I

don't care to sit with them, either. Let us go in through the kitchen entrance and see if we can avoid the visit."

Curiosity was waiting for them in the upstairs parlor. When they came in she said, "A letter came while you were away."

"A letter?" Elizabeth drew off her bonnet and put it on the table.

"From my Galileo," said Curiosity. "He sent it to Oakmere and they sent it up here." She stood and breathed deep, put back her shoulders and then smiled. Elizabeth smiled, too, realizing now that she had been holding her breath for bad news.

"Go on," Curiosity said. "Read it out loud, Elizabeth."

To my dear Wife, Curiosity Freeman
   Our good daughter Polly writes this for me, with a quill I sharpened for her and the ink you made of dried blackberries last December. May the Almighty God hear our prayer and send you home to us healthy.
   Lung-Fever has come to plague us here in Paradise. The Lord spared our girls and their husbands and this tired old man. Manny fell ill but his sisters nursed him back to health. The Judge is took right hard with it, but Daisy is nursing him and it look like he has weathered the storm. For the Lord thy God is a merciful God.
   We ain't seen Kitty since she took Ethan away to Albany, nor did we have word of her till just yesterday. She and the boy are well. She writes that last week she was married to Dr. Richard Todd. They say they will come home to Paradise in the fall, when the Fever is run its course and the Lord sees fit to lift this yoke.
   Yesterday evening I went up Hidden Wolf to see how the folks there were faring and found the place deserted except for Runs-from-Bears. He is in good health. The women are gone to

stay with their people in Canada, and Otter with them. I am sorry to pass on the news that Liam Kirby ran off some weeks ago when the affliction came upon us and he ain't been seen since. I know Hannah will be sorry to hear it, too.

The girls want you to know that they have set plenty of beans and onions and pomkin. The spring grass is sweet and the livestock getting fat. God willing, Daisy will bring our first grandchild into this world in the late fall. The Lord moves in mysterious ways, his wonders to behold.

Now in the warm months the Miseries have left my back, but the Lord's truth is this: the house is mighty quiet these days, but there's no peace to be found here with you gone. Hurry home.

Your loving husband of these many years
Galileo Freeman
Paradise, New-York State
writ this sixth day of May in the Year of our
Merciful Lord 1794

"I don't know what I dread more," Curiosity said. "Telling your aunt about Kitty and Richard, or telling Hannah about Liam running off."

Elizabeth sat down and spread the letter out on her lap, ran her finger over the finely formed letters. She said, "What do you think it means, Nathaniel?"

He shrugged, his face impassive. "I don't know. Maybe Richard is hoping we won't come home at all, thinking he's still got a chance at getting Hidden Wolf."

They were silent for a moment, each of them thinking about that and what trouble it would mean.

"Poor Liam," said Elizabeth finally. "He lost faith in us, and I cannot say that I blame him very much. They have been a long time without word."

"Well, I admit it ain't the best news," said Curiosity,

getting up. "But my folks are alive and well, and so are yours. Up at Carryckcastle they got four new graves, you'll remember. I'd say the Lord has been generous."

Elizabeth turned to Nathaniel, who was lost in his own thoughts, and far away—perhaps in Canada, with the boy he had already claimed as a son before he had ever seen him by daylight.

"Don't you think so, Nathaniel?" Curiosity pushed him.

He nodded. "Generous, indeed."

A soft scratching at the door, and Aunt Merriweather's waiting-woman came in. Maria had been in service at Oakmere for twenty years and Elizabeth had rarely seen her flustered, but now she was very much ill at ease. "Lady Crofton begs your company in the lower parlor."

"Who has come to call, Maria?" Elizabeth asked.

"A Miss Somerville, mum," said Maria, as she might have said *the devil's bride.*

"Lordy," said Curiosity, getting up with new energy. "I don't much like the woman, but I got to give her credit for landing on her feet. And imagine that, Giselle and Merriweather together in the same room. The feathers must be flying a good mile high."

Maria gave a tight little nod. "If you could come straightaway—"

"Where's my father, do you know?" Nathaniel asked. "She'll want to talk to him, too."

"Yes, she has asked for him repeatedly," Maria said. The sound of raised voices came up the stairwell, and she jumped nervously. "But Mr. Bonner went out with the viscount, sir. Some time ago. Please—"

"We'll be right there," Nathaniel said. "You can go tell her that."

"Soon as we prime the pistols," muttered Curiosity.

Elizabeth said, "I'm wearing her gown." And heard for herself how odd this sounded: Giselle Somerville had sought them out—*the mother of Nathaniel's first-born son* had sought them out—and all she could think

of was the gown she was wearing. But Nathaniel seemed to dread this meeting as much as she did, and he slipped an arm around her shoulders.

"We knew she might be in Edinburgh, looking for some sign of us," he said. "Once she hears what we have to tell her, she won't care what you've got on your back. She'll be on a ship to Canada as fast as she can find one."

They heard the irritated thump of Aunt Merriweather's cane as they came down the stairs, three sharp taps that did not bode well. Elizabeth was reminded of the day her aunt had confronted Julian about the real extent of his gambling debt.

Nathaniel looked very serious, but Curiosity did not seem concerned. Her grin did not leave her until the moment that the footman opened the door for them.

"Obstinate woman." Another three taps of the cane. Her aunt's head swiveled around toward them on its long neck, and Elizabeth saw two things straight off: she was terribly irritated, and she was actually enjoying herself.

Before her stood Giselle Somerville, as finely dressed as she had ever been in a round gown of dark gold Indian ikat muslin. She wore a turban of silk gauze on her head, and a fiery expression. She took no note of Elizabeth at all, her attention focusing immediately on Nathaniel.

"This lady refuses to tell me where to find your father," she said. "My business is with him, if what she says is true and Rob MacLachlan is dead."

"It's true, all right," said Curiosity. "God rest his immortal soul."

Aunt Merriweather's eyes had narrowed. "If what I say is true? If? Let me warn you again, Miss Somerville, I will not tolerate such impudence, such incivility. How dare you come here with such scandalous falsehoods?"

"Aunt," Elizabeth interrupted gently. "I think it would be best if Miss Somerville and Nathaniel were to have a word together, alone."

"My business is with Dan'l Bonner," Giselle said imperiously. "I have nothing to discuss with his son."

Under Elizabeth's hand, all the muscles in Nathaniel's arm were tense but his voice came steady. He said, "I know about the boy."

Aunt Merriweather turned as red in the face as Giselle was pale, but for once she was silenced by her surprise.

Giselle went still. "Very well, your father told you about him. And?"

"He ain't in France."

Some color came back into her cheeks. "Is it true, then. He's in Montréal. And my mother?"

"Your mother, too. We need to talk."

"I will make no apologies." Giselle was struggling desperately, but her composure had been taken from her for once and Elizabeth was struck suddenly with a memory of that moment on the dock at Québec when she realized that her children were gone, and she could not call them back. It had torn a hole in her. Giselle had been living with that for eighteen years.

And maybe Nathaniel saw it, too, because his voice softened. "I don't want any apologies," he said. "I'm as much to blame for what happened. But I'll tell you what you need to know. And something else—there's a place at Carryck for the boy, and for you, too, if you want it."

"Nathaniel," said Aunt Merriweather, regaining her voice and the use of her cane, one thump for each word: "What does this mean?"

"Aunt," Elizabeth said. "Let them discuss this matter in private. I promise, I will make everything clear to you."

.   .   .

Late in the night, Elizabeth woke to the whisper of a misting rain. She had dreamed of Margreit MacKay and of Isabel, too. Women she had known for such a short time while they lived, and still they seemed determined to accompany her on the voyage home. Perhaps Robbie would come, too, if she thought of him hard enough. Perhaps all the dead were that close, and only waited to be summoned.

Nathaniel turned in his sleep. When he had come to her after his long talk with Giselle, the telling of what had passed between them had been slow and awkward, more questions raised than answered. Listening to him, Elizabeth realized that it was not their son who had forged an uneasy bond between Nathaniel and Giselle, but the uncertainty they shared. Luke was a stranger to them both, and might never be anything else.

"I wish I had spent more time talking to him, that night in Montréal."

It was the last thing Nathaniel said before he fell into a sleep so deep that he did not stir when she rose to go to the window to look over the streets of Edinburgh, glistening damp in the lantern light, and in the distance, someplace, the sea.

She had once made the trip to Paradise full of dreams and visions of herself as a teacher. Now she made it again, and some of those same dreams were still with her, and within her grasp. *The Lord has been generous*, she whispered to herself. A prayer of acknowledgment and thanksgiving, the only one that would come to her now in spite of the dangers that lay ahead.

It turned out that Nathaniel was awake after all, coming up silently behind her to put a hand on her shoulder. She was shivering, and he slipped his arms around her.

"Goodness," she said softly. "Tomorrow you must get us all onto a ship in spite of the Breadalbanes, and here you stand. You need your rest."

"Ah, Boots. The bed's no good to me without you in it."

He felt her smile as she rocked back against him.

"So what are you looking at?"

"The first light of dawn," she said, pointing. "I imagine I can see all the way home."

It was a rare gift she had, this ability to look ahead, through the loss and heartache, beyond the hardship, to see so clearly the possibilities that waited for them. If they could be strong, if they could persevere.

"Listen," she whispered. "Do you hear the sea? Tomorrow there will be a good strong wind to take us home."

Epilogue

Miss Hannah Bonner
Lake in the Clouds
Paradise, New-York State

Dear Squirrel,

Now that your half brother and his mother
have settled in at Carryckcastle, I suppose it's
time I keep my promise and write and tell what
there is to say. Truth be tolt, tis no an easy task.
Ye'll want to hear guid tidings, and there's little
comfort in the tale I've got to tell.

He's a slink mannie, is Luke. Tall and braw
and bonnie, and slee as a fox. Cook calls him
luvey, and bakes him tarts wi the last o the
pippins. The Earl bought him a mare the likes o
which ye'll no see in all Scotland, as black as the
devil and that smart, too. The lasses come up the
brae for no guid reason but to sneiter and bat
their eyelashes at him, and then run awa when
Giselle catches sight o them. Even my mother
smiles at Luke for all she looks daggers at me
and makes me wear shoes. And what does it
matter that I'm eleven years? I fear it has to do
wi marriage, for it is first since she stood up wi
the Earl that she's turned so unreasonable. My
only hope for a peaceful life is Luke's mother,
wha seems a reasonable woman (for all her lace

and silk, she doesna mind what others wear on their feet or heids, either, and she is generous wi her stories o how she outfoxed the Pirate). They've become great friends, his mother and mine, and they sit tegither in the evening. If I'm aye chancie, some o Giselle will rub off and my mother will leave me be.

I must be fair and report that Luke is a hard worker and there's naught mean-spirited in him, but he's an awfu tease and worse luck he's guid at it, in Scots and English both. I'll admit that he's no so donnert as he first seems, for all his quiet ways. It would suit me much better were he witless, for my father has decided that since my guid cousin kens French and Latin (taught to him by his grand-mother in Canada, he says, and what grandmother teaches Latin, I want to know?), I must learn them, too, never mind that I speak Scots and English and some of the old language, too, having learned it from Mairead the dairymaid. But the Earl would no listen and so I sit every afternoon wi Luke, no matter how fine the weather. And just this morn I heard some talk o mathematics and philosophy, to make my misery complete.

He's aye hard to please, is Luke, but when he's satisfied wi my progress, he'll talk o Lake in the Clouds, and then it seems to me that he misses the place, in spite o the fact that he spent so little time wi ye there. And he tells outrageous stories o trees as far as a man can see and hidden gold and wolves that guard the mountain and young Daniel catching a rabbit wi his bare hands, and then I ken that he's a true Scott o Carryck, for wha else could tell such tales and keep a straight face all the while? But my revenge is this: I wear a bear's tooth on a string around my neck, and he has nothing but the scapular my father gave him when first he came and took the name Scott.

I'm sorry to say that I canna like your brother near as much as I like you. But tell me this, as you're as much my cousin as is Luke, do ye no think it's time for me to visit ye in Paradise? Perhaps the Earl would let me come, if your grandfather were to ask him.

My mother sends her greetings, and bids me write that the pear tree she had planted ower Isabel's grave has borne its first fruit this summer.

Your cousin and true friend,
Jennet Scott of Carryckcastle
First day of September in the Year of Our Lord
1795

Author's Note

Carryckcastle, Carryckton, and Aidan Rig are fictional places, just as the Earl of Carryck and his family are fictional. Real characters pop up throughout the story, however, and they include General Major Phillip Schuyler and his wife, Catherine; Sir Guy Carleton, Lord Dorchester, and his wife, Maria, Lady Dorchester; Anne Bonney, pirate; Robert Burns, exciseman and poet; Willie Fisher; Flora, Countess of Loudoun; John Campbell, 4th Earl of Breadalbane, chief of the Glenorchy line, and Flora's guardian.

While Carryck is a fictional character, the religious and political conflicts which define his character and his relationship to the nonfictional Campbells were all too real. Also very real were the growing tensions between England, British Canada, and the young United States. In 1794, the United States did try to ship grain to France in an attempt to relieve the great hunger which resulted from the British blockade. The ensuing naval battle in which Hawkeye and Robbie were entangled— the Glorious First of June—was won by the British over the French. The tensions between Britain and the U.S. continued to escalate, leading to the War of 1812, sometimes called the Second Revolutionary War.

Medicine was advancing at a rapid pace at the end of the eighteenth century, but physicians had not yet put a name to the disease that ended Lady Isabel's life—the same disease that killed Jane Austen. Its primary symptoms were debilitating fatigue, weight loss, nausea, and

discoloration of the skin. It is now known as Addison's disease, and sometimes as tubercular kidney—a type of tuberculosis which settles in the adrenal glands, causing them to stop producing cortisol, a hormone necessary to sustain life. Today this is a rare, chronic but treatable condition.

Monsieur Dupuis suffered from end-stage melanoma of the skin, a disease that is still fatal unless it is caught early.

About the Author

SARA DONATI was born and raised in Chicago, but she has lived for longer periods in the Austrian Alps, on the East Coast (where she earned a Ph.D. in linguistics from Princeton), and Michigan. After twelve years as a tenured professor—getting up early and staying up late to write fiction—she took heart in hand and left academia. She now writes full-time from her home in the Pacific Northwest, where she lives with her husband, daughter, and three cats. These days she divides her time between her family, the next novel in the wilderness series, and a large, demanding but ever-rewarding garden.